REX·LIBRIS

BOOK OF MONSTERS

D0050337

BY JAMES TURNER

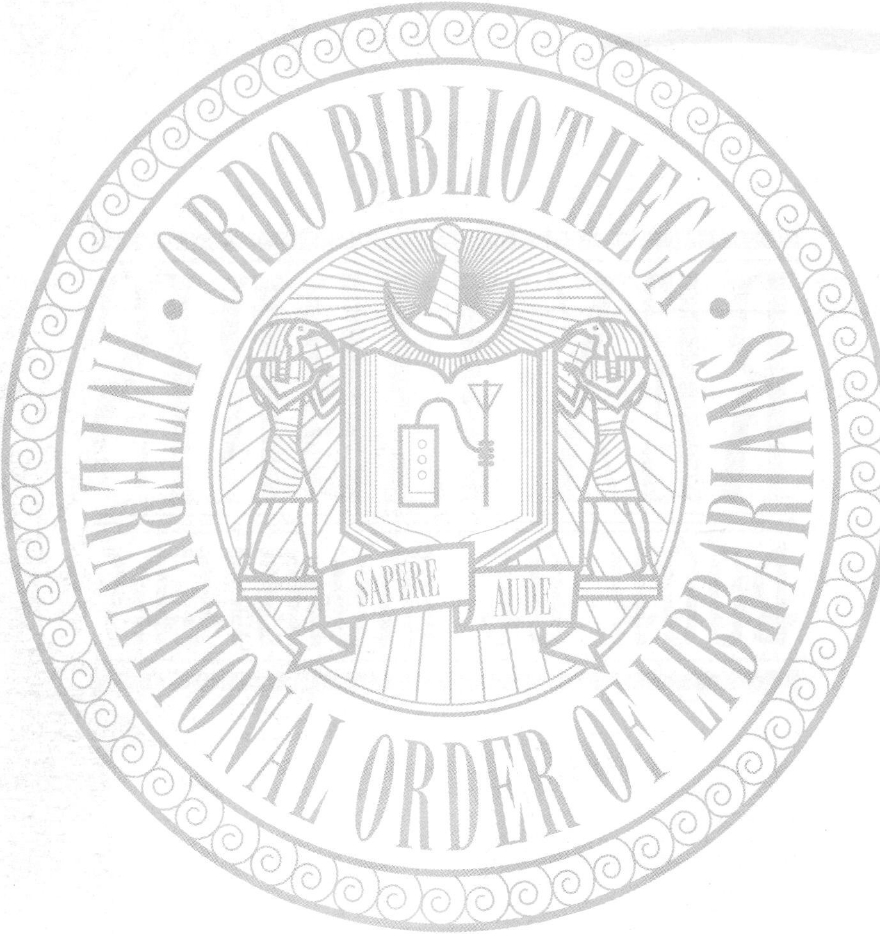
ORDO BIBLIOTHECA
INTERNATIONAL ORDER OF LIBRARIANS
SAPERE
AUDE

Written and Illustrated by
James Turner

Published by
SLG Publishing

P.O. Box 26427
San Jose, CA 95159

www.slgcomic.com

Rex Libris Volume Two: Book of Monsters collects issues #6-13 of the SLG series *Rex Libris.*

First Printing: April 2009
ISBN 978-1-59362-153-7

CHAPTER SIX

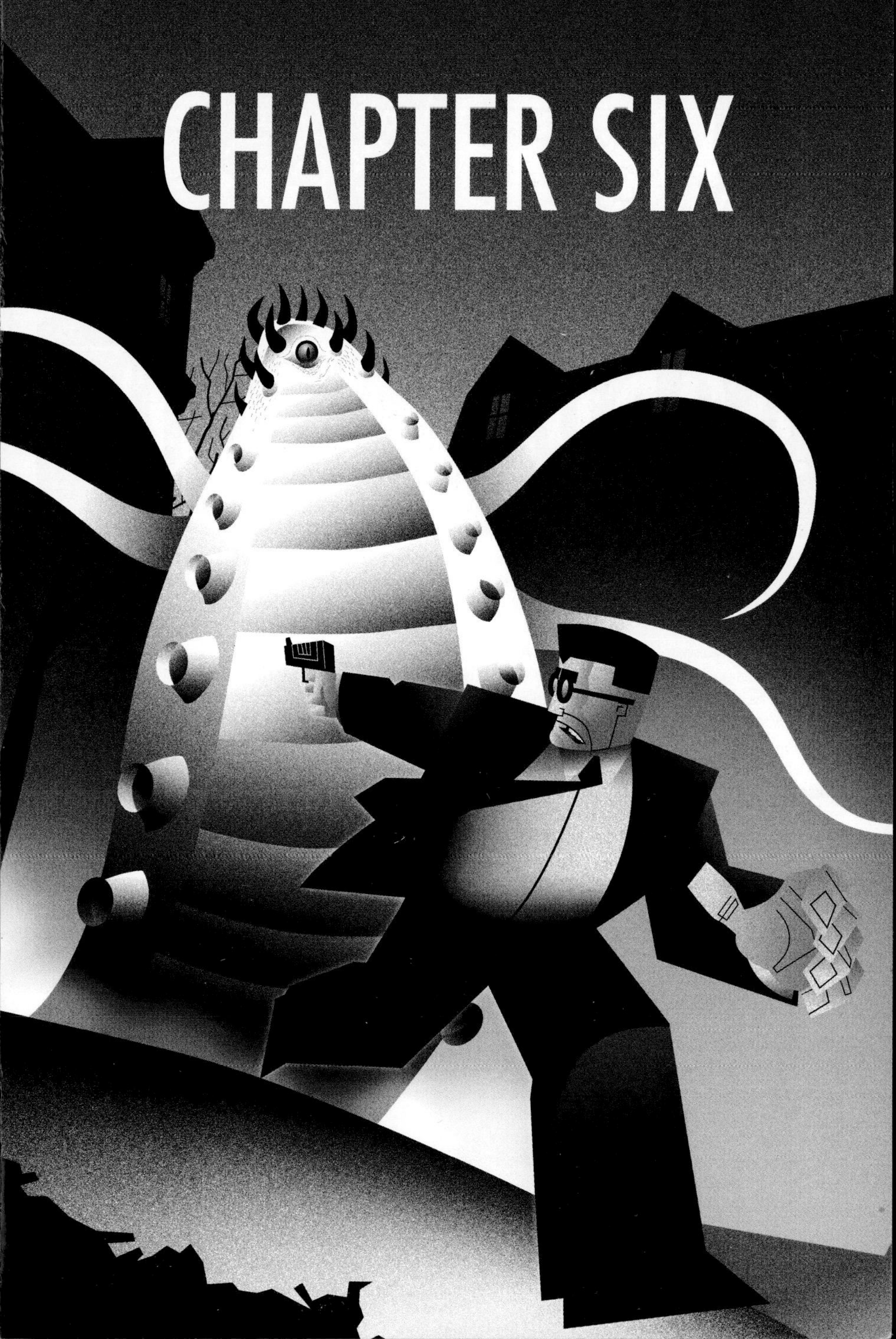

BARRY'S BRAIN

The ancient Spartans used to flog children for each use of an unnecessary word. Obviously, everyone here at Hermeneutic Press would be beaten to death if we were to live under their rigid rule. No matter! We'll leave that particular scenario to the fantasies of our detractors. Sparta was a proto-totalitarian hell hole anyway (Damn good enemies to be known by; Hermeneutic Press is proud to be at odds with their dead civilization). Let the words and the information flow freely, I say! Let prolixity run amok, rampage down the streets, and wax eloquent! Let the river of verbal diarrhea flow like the mighty Yangtze! Let it overflow the banks and spread out unto the floodplains! In this way we shall fertilize the world of comics and give rise to a new creative golden age of innovation, verbal inebriation, and turgidity! No other brand is so fearless in the face of huge hordes of words. Dictionaries brim with them, an almost endless stream of named memes which threaten to drown us in their great numbers. We shall co-opt them in the name of the comic book medium, like no other before us, and harness their eco-friendly powers for the good of all humanity! Remember, if anyone can bring hyperbole into reality, we're the ones to do it. It will be just one more great triumph for the pioneering medium of Visicomboics! Why do we do all this silliness? This insouciant madness? Why, to have fun, by God!

We have already taken steps in this direction with the employment of the greatly under-used word **floccinaucinihilipilification** in issue four. We have every reason to believe that this is the first time in the history of the comics that the word floccinaucinihilipilification has ever been employed. And who brought it to you first? **Hermeneutic Press!** Not only that, we have now included this fabulous word in our introduction, increasing its exposure by 100%! This is just the beginning. With a little effort, it is conceivable that we could replace every commonly used word in this

comic with a more obscure equivalent. We could resuscitate such words as **arenaceous**, **fissiparous**, **barbate**, **duopilomundopothic**, and **tramontane**. The elites will have no choice but to notice comics by the time we are done!

They say brevity is the soul of wit. Make no mistake: here at Hermeneutic we are doing **dirty things** to wit's soul. And as everyone knows, **dirt sells!**

Prolixity!

B. Barry Horst

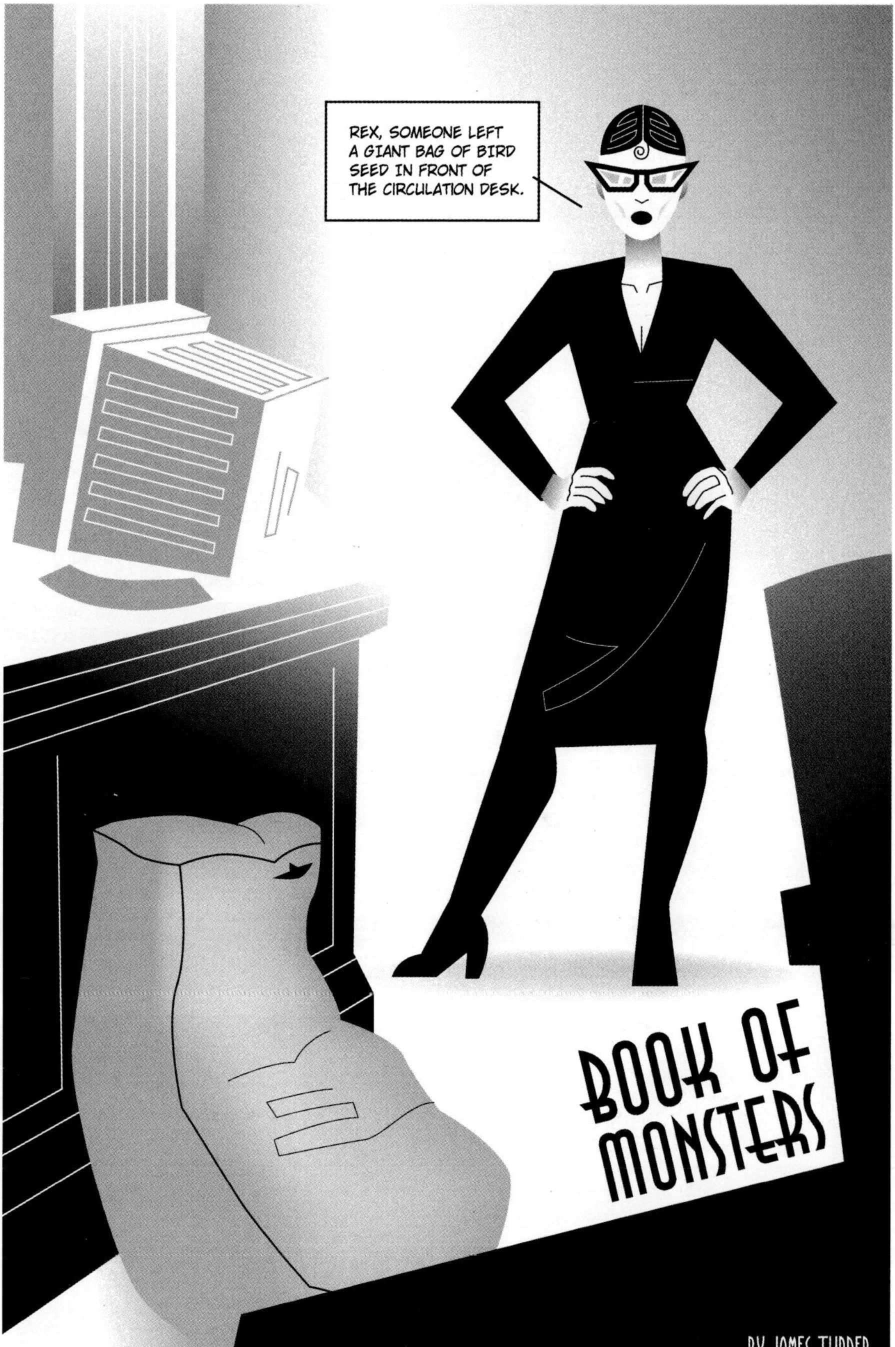

REX, SOMEONE LEFT A GIANT BAG OF BIRD SEED IN FRONT OF THE CIRCULATION DESK.
BOOK OF MONSTERS
BY JAMES TURNER

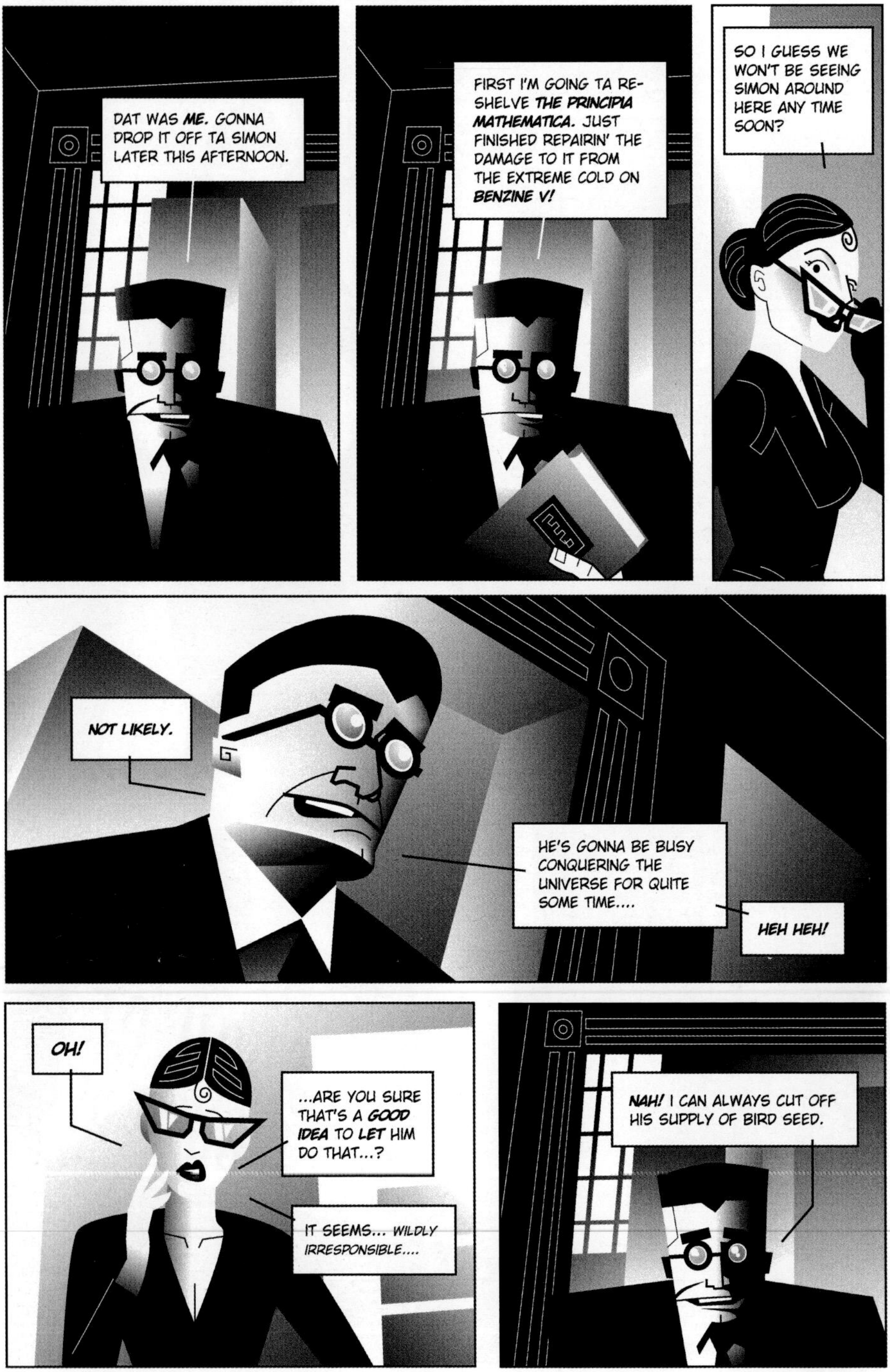
DAT WAS ME. GONNA DROP IT OFF TA SIMON LATER THIS AFTERNOON.
FIRST I'M GOING TA RE-SHELVE THE PRINCIPIA MATHEMATICA. JUST FINISHED REPAIRIN' THE DAMAGE TO IT FROM THE EXTREME COLD ON BENZINE V!
SO I GUESS WE WON'T BE SEEING SIMON AROUND HERE ANY TIME SOON?
NOT LIKELY.
HE'S GONNA BE BUSY CONQUERING THE UNIVERSE FOR QUITE SOME TIME....
HEH HEH!
OH!
...ARE YOU SURE THAT'S A GOOD IDEA TO LET HIM DO THAT...?
IT SEEMS... WILDLY IRRESPONSIBLE....
NAH! I CAN ALWAYS CUT OFF HIS SUPPLY OF BIRD SEED.

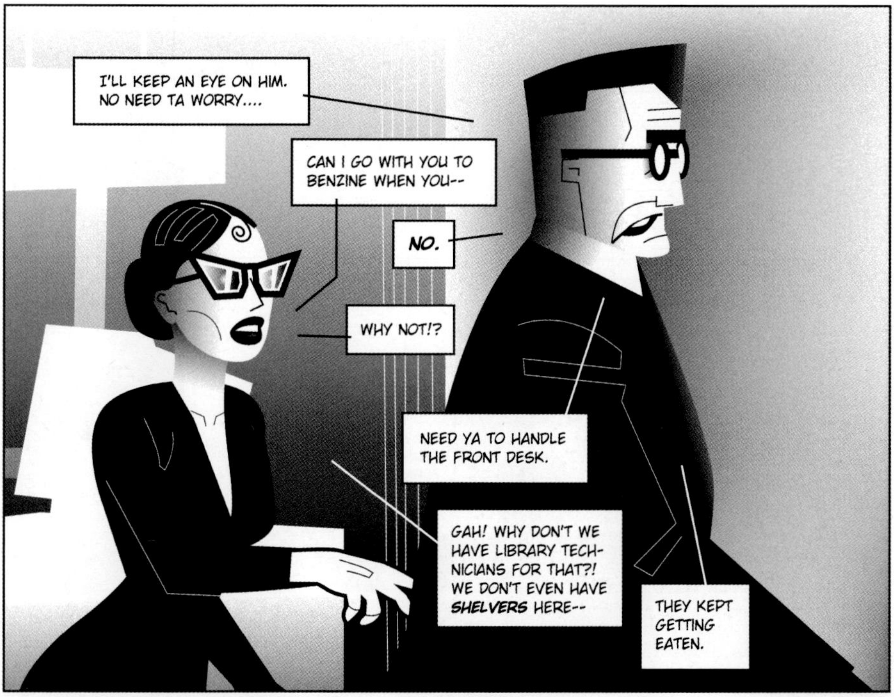
I'LL KEEP AN EYE ON HIM. NO NEED TA WORRY....
CAN I GO WITH YOU TO BENZINE WHEN YOU--
NO.
WHY NOT!?
NEED YA TO HANDLE THE FRONT DESK.
GAH! WHY DON'T WE HAVE LIBRARY TECH-NICIANS FOR THAT?! WE DON'T EVEN HAVE SHELVERS HERE--
THEY KEPT GETTING EATEN.

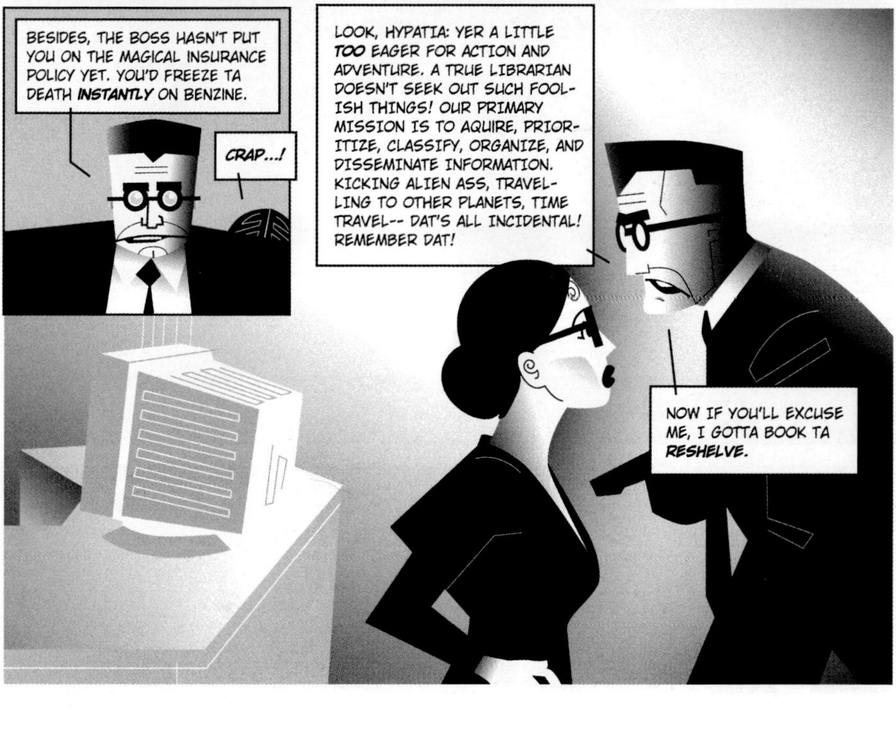
BESIDES, THE BOSS HASN'T PUT YOU ON THE MAGICAL INSURANCE POLICY YET. YOU'D FREEZE TA DEATH INSTANTLY ON BENZINE.
CRAP...!
LOOK, HYPATIA: YER A LITTLE TOO EAGER FOR ACTION AND ADVENTURE. A TRUE LIBRARIAN DOESN'T SEEK OUT SUCH FOOL-ISH THINGS! OUR PRIMARY MISSION IS TO AQUIRE, PRIOR-ITIZE, CLASSIFY, ORGANIZE, AND DISSEMINATE INFORMATION. KICKING ALIEN ASS, TRAVEL-LING TO OTHER PLANETS, TIME TRAVEL-- DAT'S ALL INCIDENTAL! REMEMBER DAT!
NOW IF YOU'LL EXCUSE ME, I GOTTA BOOK TA RESHELVE.

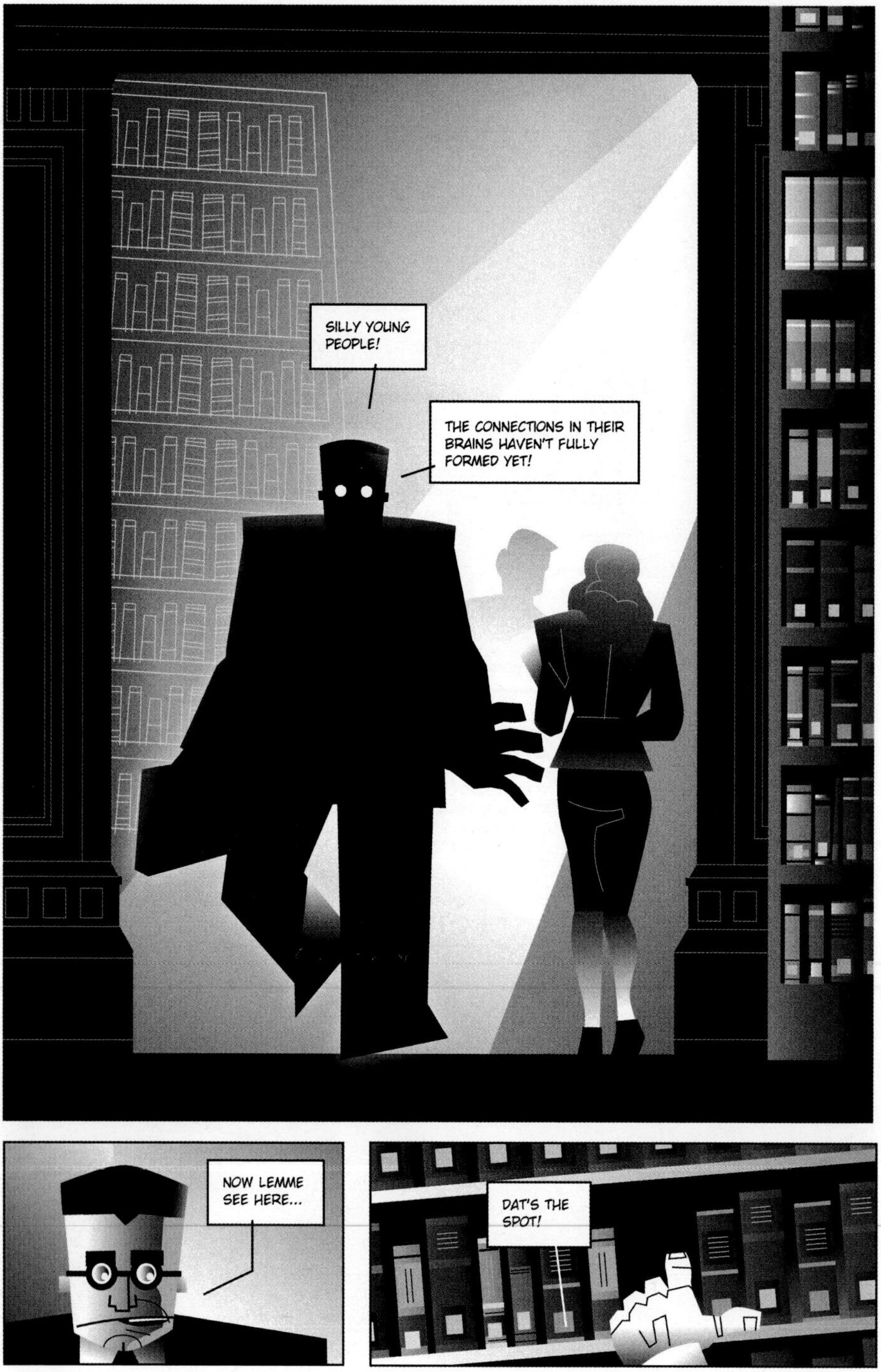
SILLY YOUNG PEOPLE!
THE CONNECTIONS IN THEIR BRAINS HAVEN'T FULLY FORMED YET!
NOW LEMME SEE HERE...
DAT'S THE SPOT!

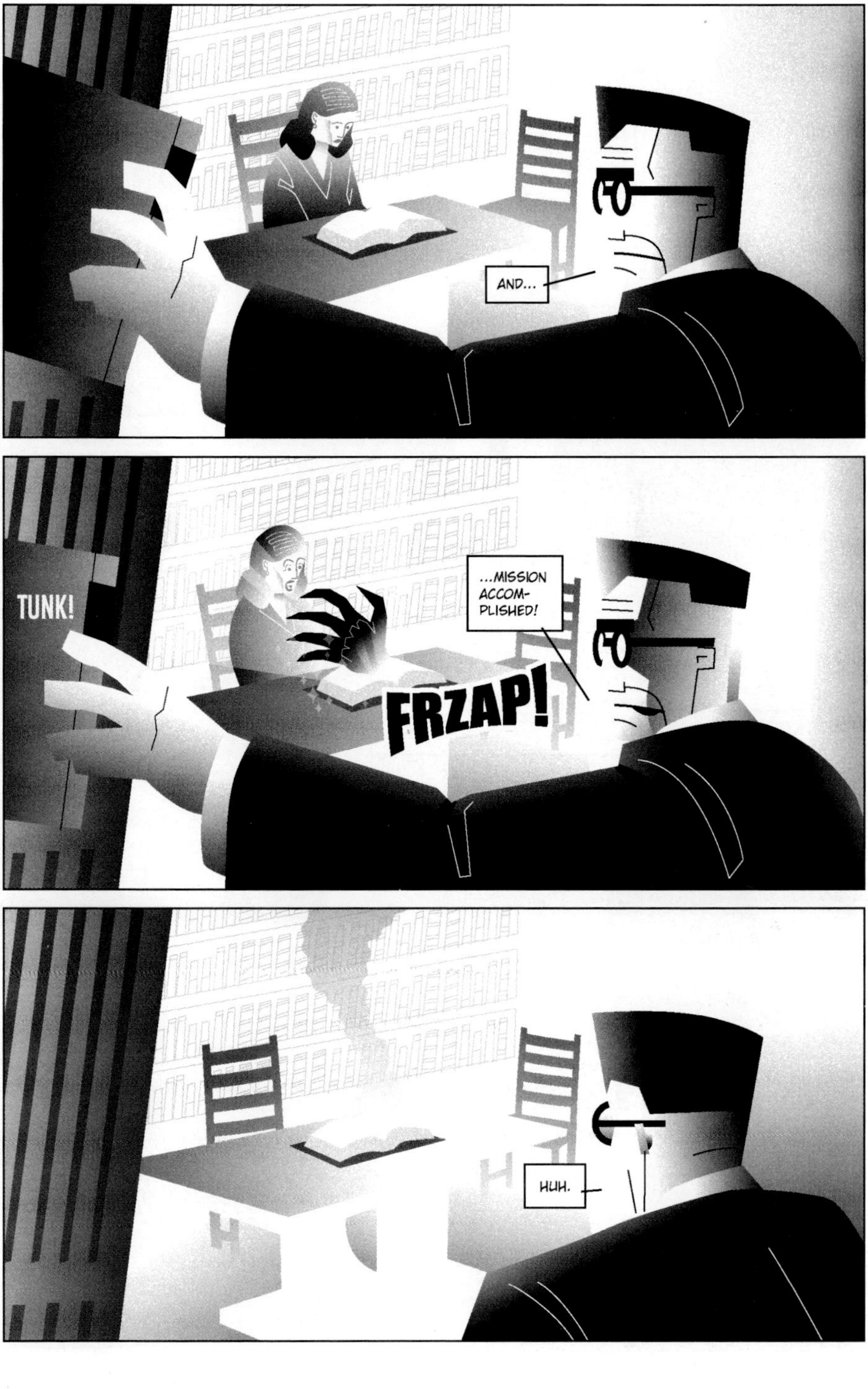

AND...
TUNK!
...MISSION ACCOM-PLISHED!
FRZAP!
HUH.

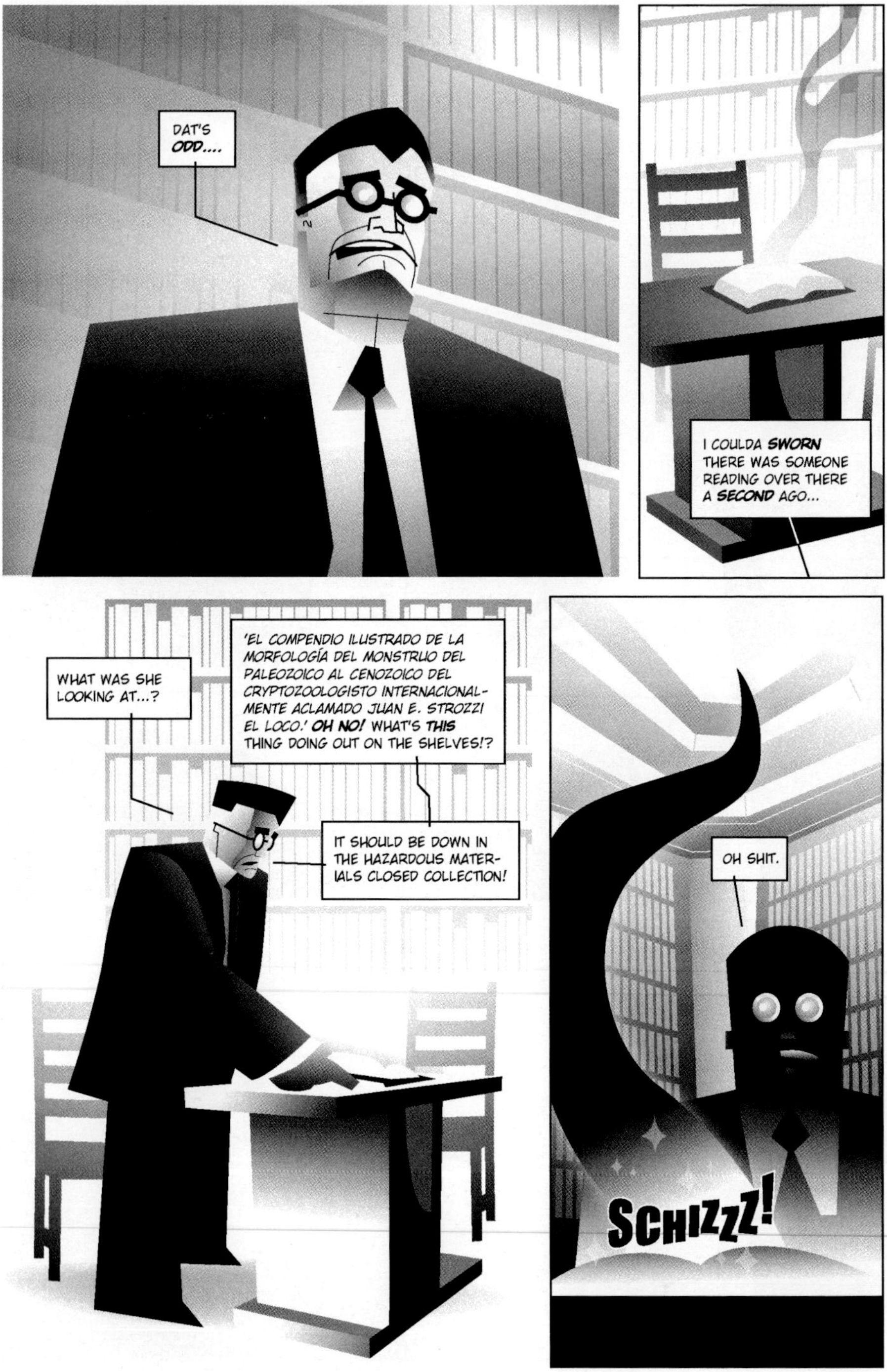
DAT'S ODD....
I COULDA SWORN THERE WAS SOMEONE READING OVER THERE A SECOND AGO...
WHAT WAS SHE LOOKING AT...?
'EL COMPENDIO ILUSTRADO DE LA MORFOLOGÍA DEL MONSTRUO DEL PALEOZOICO AL CENOZOICO DEL CRYPTOZOOLOGISTO INTERNACIONAL-MENTE ACLAMADO JUAN E. STROZZI EL LOCO.' OH NO! WHAT'S THIS THING DOING OUT ON THE SHELVES!?
IT SHOULD BE DOWN IN THE HAZARDOUS MATER-IALS CLOSED COLLECTION!
OH SHIT.
SCHIZZZ!

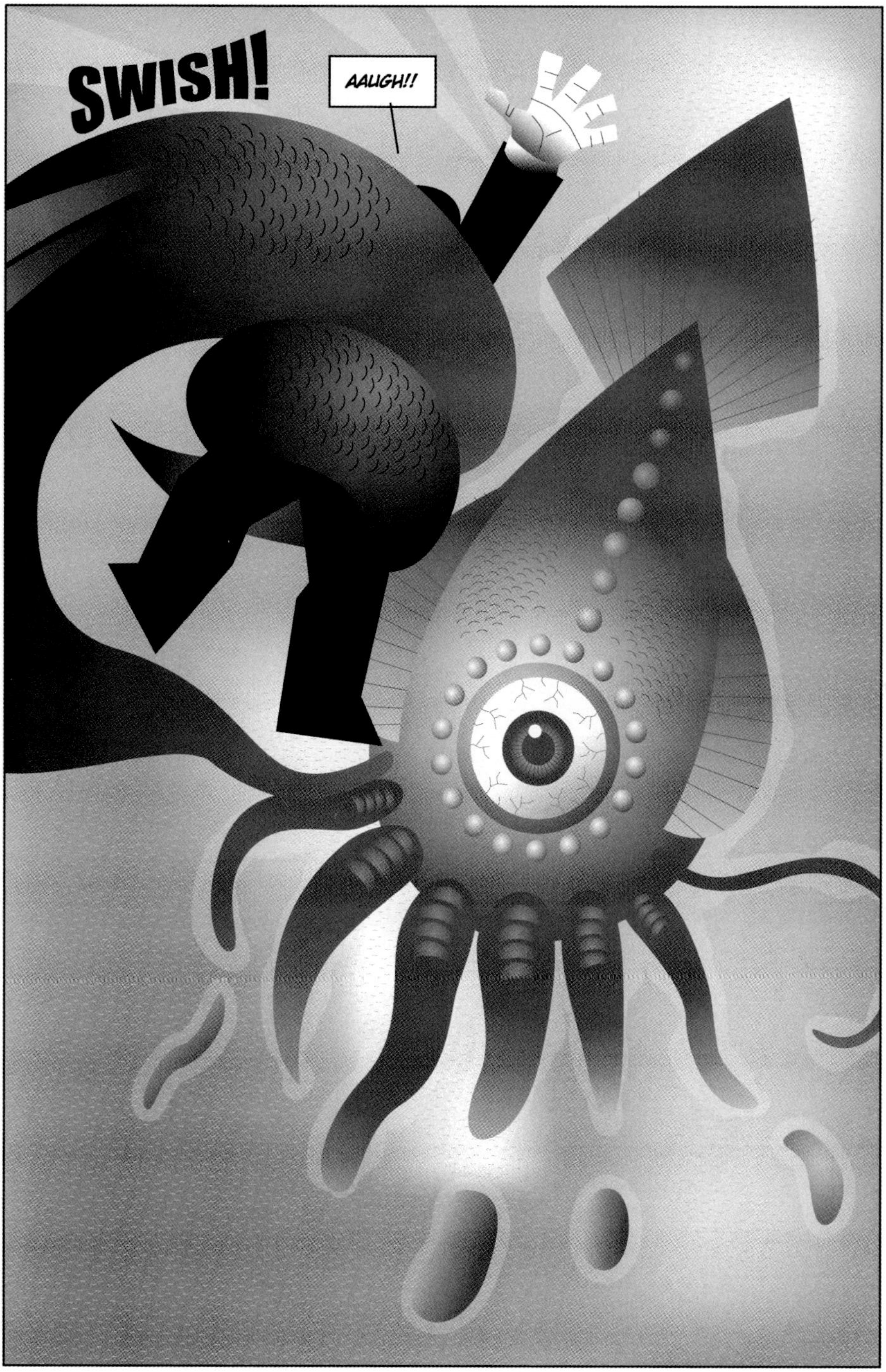
SWISH!
AAUGH!!

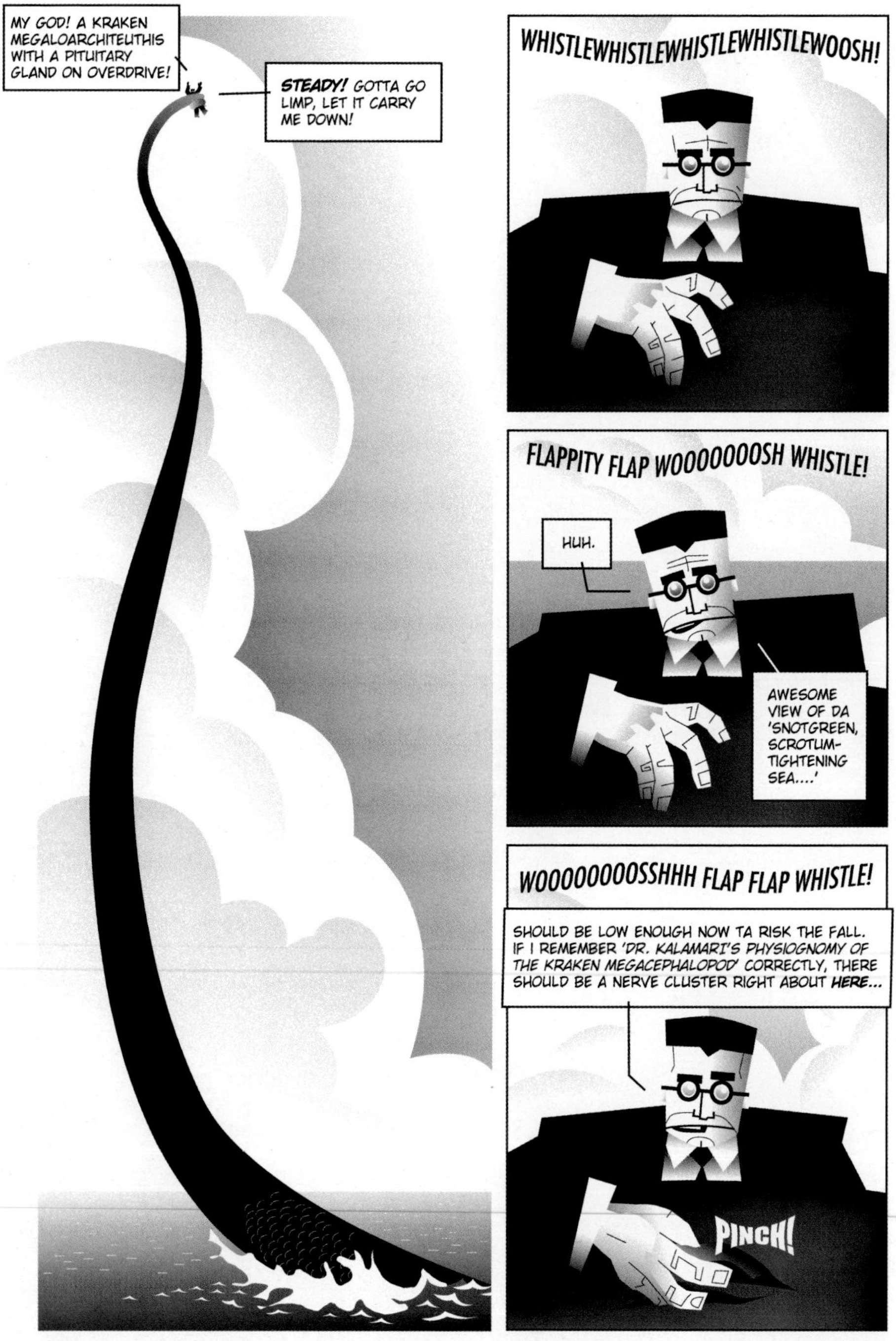

MY GOD! A KRAKEN MEGALOARCHITEUTHIS WITH A PITUITARY GLAND ON OVERDRIVE!
STEADY! GOTTA GO LIMP, LET IT CARRY ME DOWN!
WHISTLEWHISTLEWHISTLEWHISTLEWOOSH!
FLAPPITY FLAP WOOOOOOOSH WHISTLE!
HUH.
AWESOME VIEW OF DA 'SNOTGREEN, SCROTUM-TIGHTENING SEA....'
WOOOOOOOOSSHHH FLAP FLAP WHISTLE!
SHOULD BE LOW ENOUGH NOW TA RISK THE FALL. IF I REMEMBER 'DR. KALAMARI'S PHYSIOGNOMY OF THE KRAKEN MEGACEPHALOPOD' CORRECTLY, THERE SHOULD BE A NERVE CLUSTER RIGHT ABOUT HERE...
PINCH!

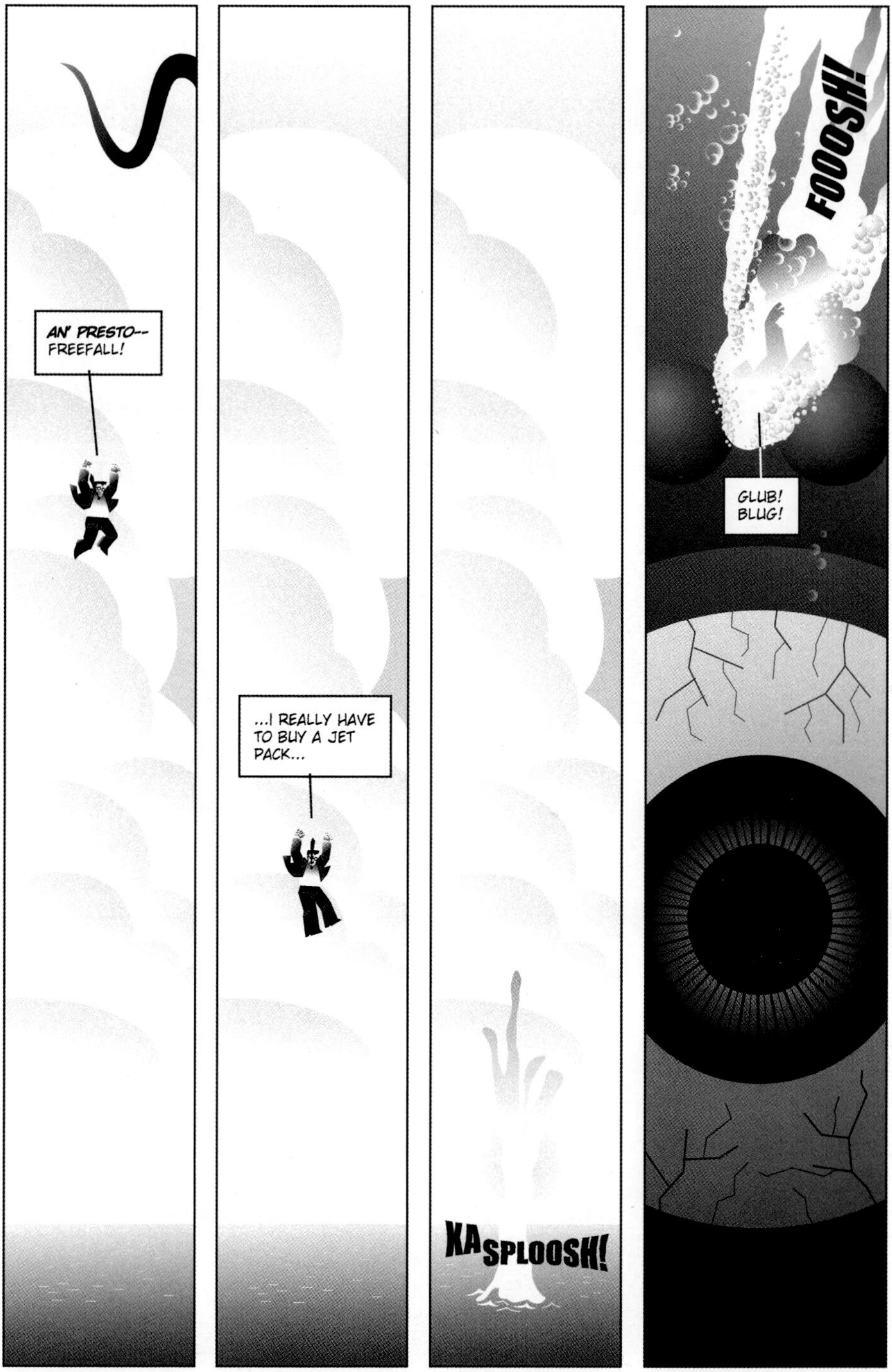
AN' PRESTO--
FREEFALL!
...I REALLY HAVE TO BUY A JET PACK...
KASPLOOSH!
FOOOSH!
GLUB! BLUG!

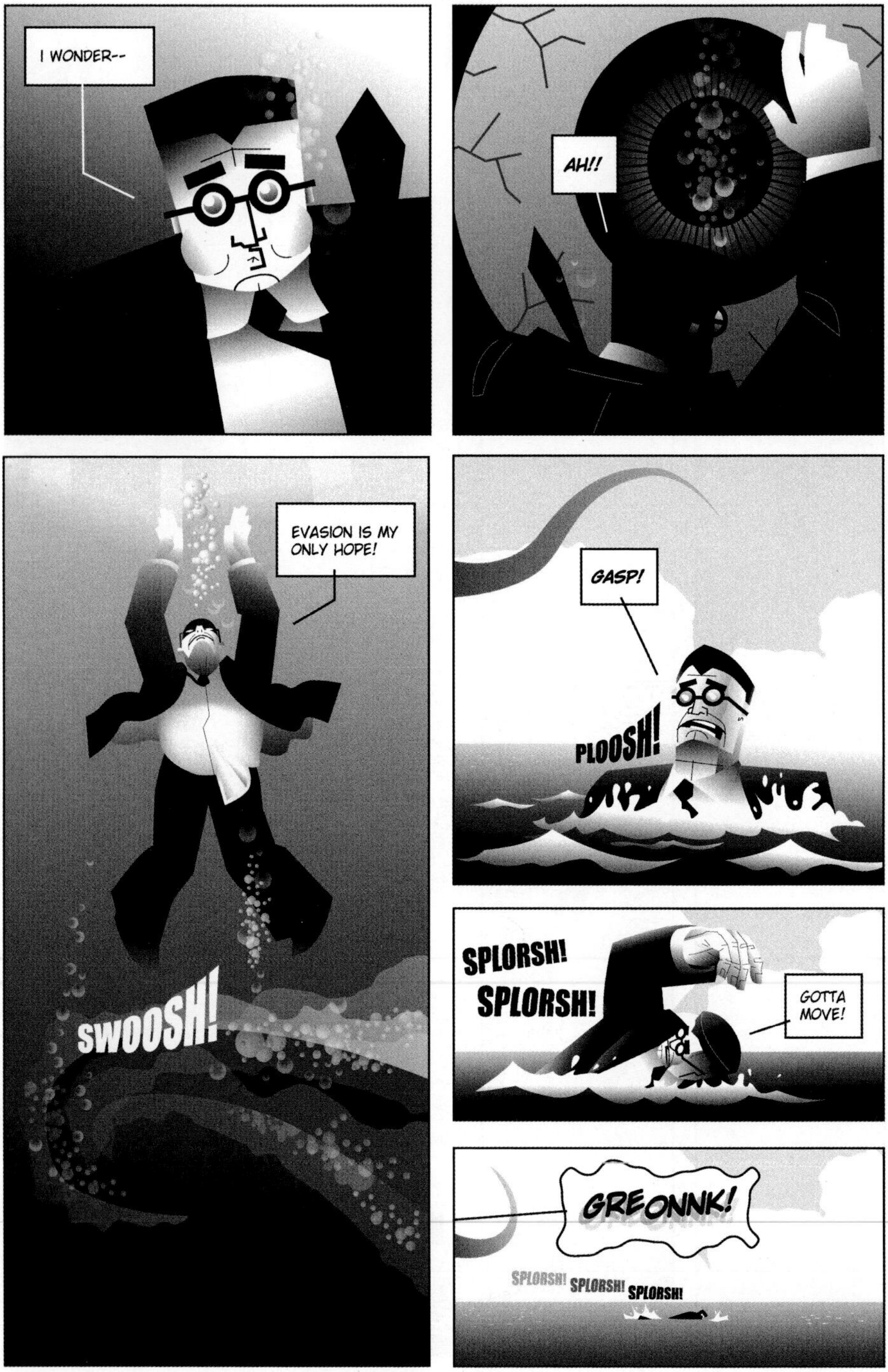

I WONDER--
AH!!
EVASION IS MY ONLY HOPE!
SWOOSH!
GASP!
PLOOSH!
SPLORSH!
SPLORSH!
GOTTA MOVE!
GREONNK!
SPLORSH! SPLORSH! SPLORSH!

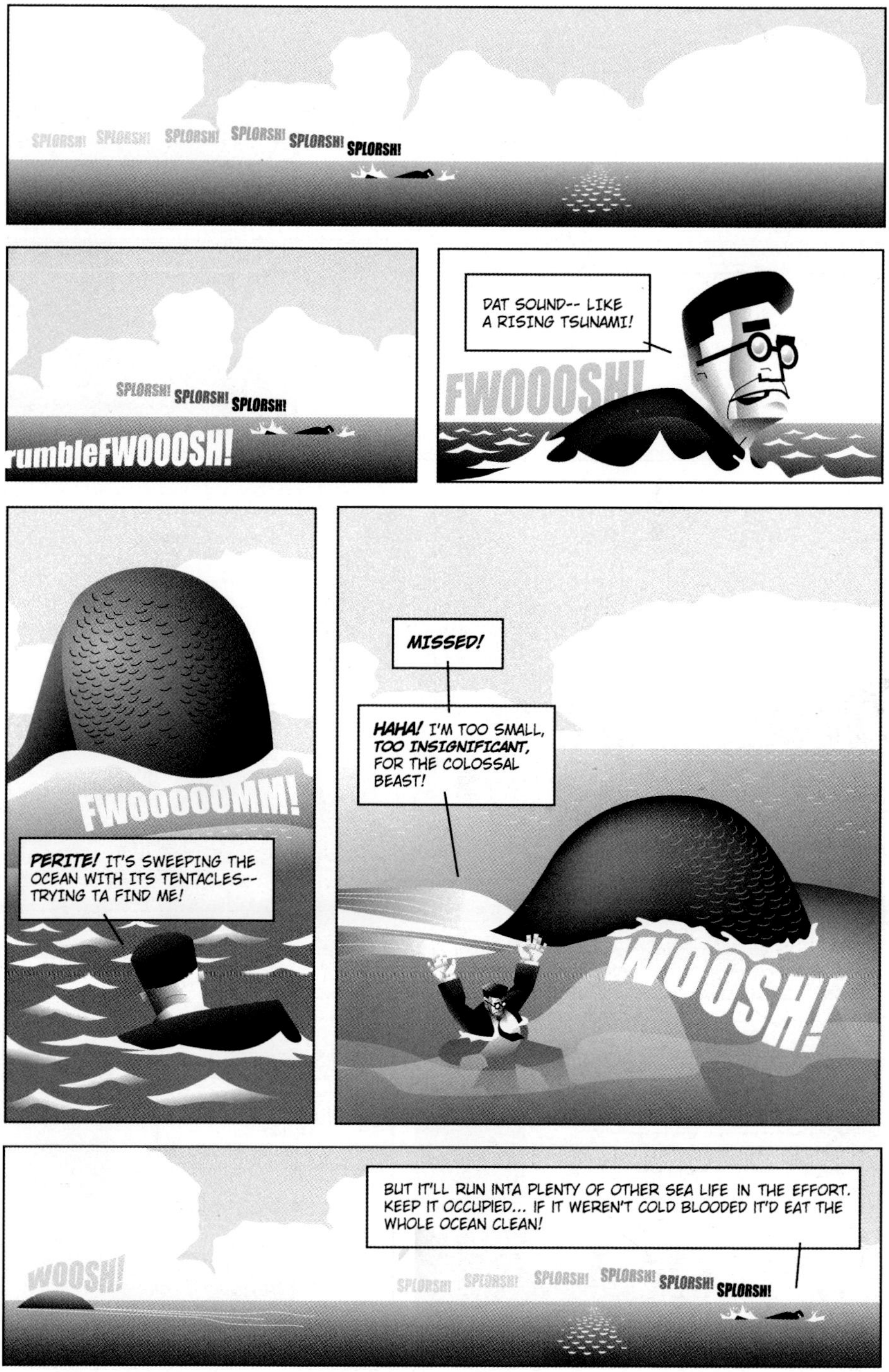
SPLORSH! SPLORSH! SPLORSH! SPLORSH! SPLORSH! SPLORSH!
SPLORSH! SPLORSH! SPLORSH!
rumbleFWOOOSH!
DAT SOUND-- LIKE A RISING TSUNAMI!
FWOOOSH!
FWOOOOOMM!
PERITE! IT'S SWEEPING THE OCEAN WITH ITS TENTACLES-- TRYING TA FIND ME!
MISSED!
HAHA! I'M TOO SMALL, TOO INSIGNIFICANT, FOR THE COLOSSAL BEAST!
WOOSH!
BUT IT'LL RUN INTA PLENTY OF OTHER SEA LIFE IN THE EFFORT. KEEP IT OCCUPIED... IF IT WEREN'T COLD BLOODED IT'D EAT THE WHOLE OCEAN CLEAN!
WOOSH!
SPLORSH! SPLORSH! SPLORSH! SPLORSH! SPLORSH! SPLORSH!

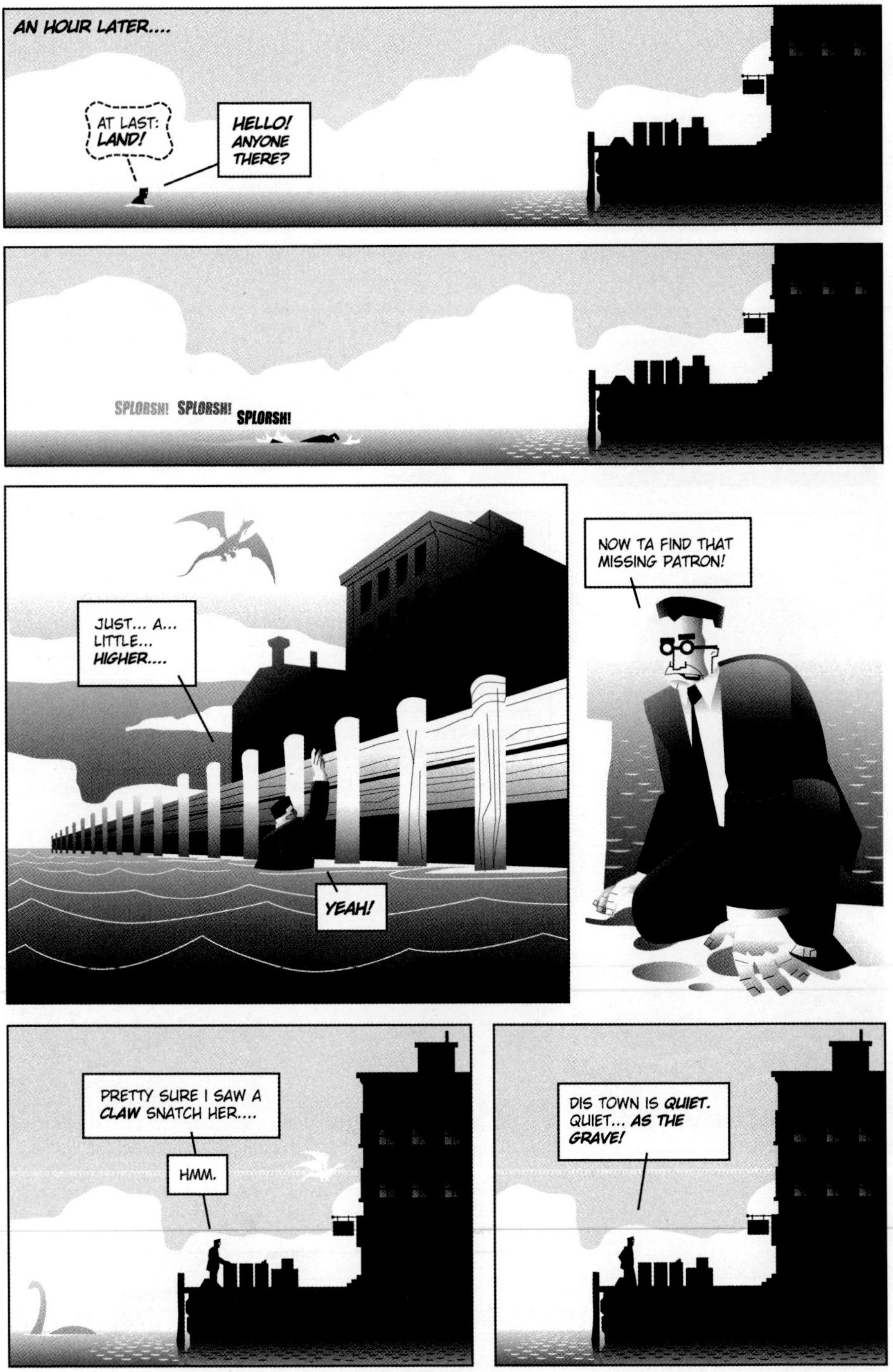
AN HOUR LATER....
AT LAST: LAND!
HELLO! ANYONE THERE?
SPLORSH! SPLORSH! SPLORSH!
JUST... A... LITTLE... HIGHER....
YEAH!
NOW TA FIND THAT MISSING PATRON!
PRETTY SURE I SAW A CLAW SNATCH HER....
HMM.
DIS TOWN IS QUIET. QUIET... AS THE GRAVE!

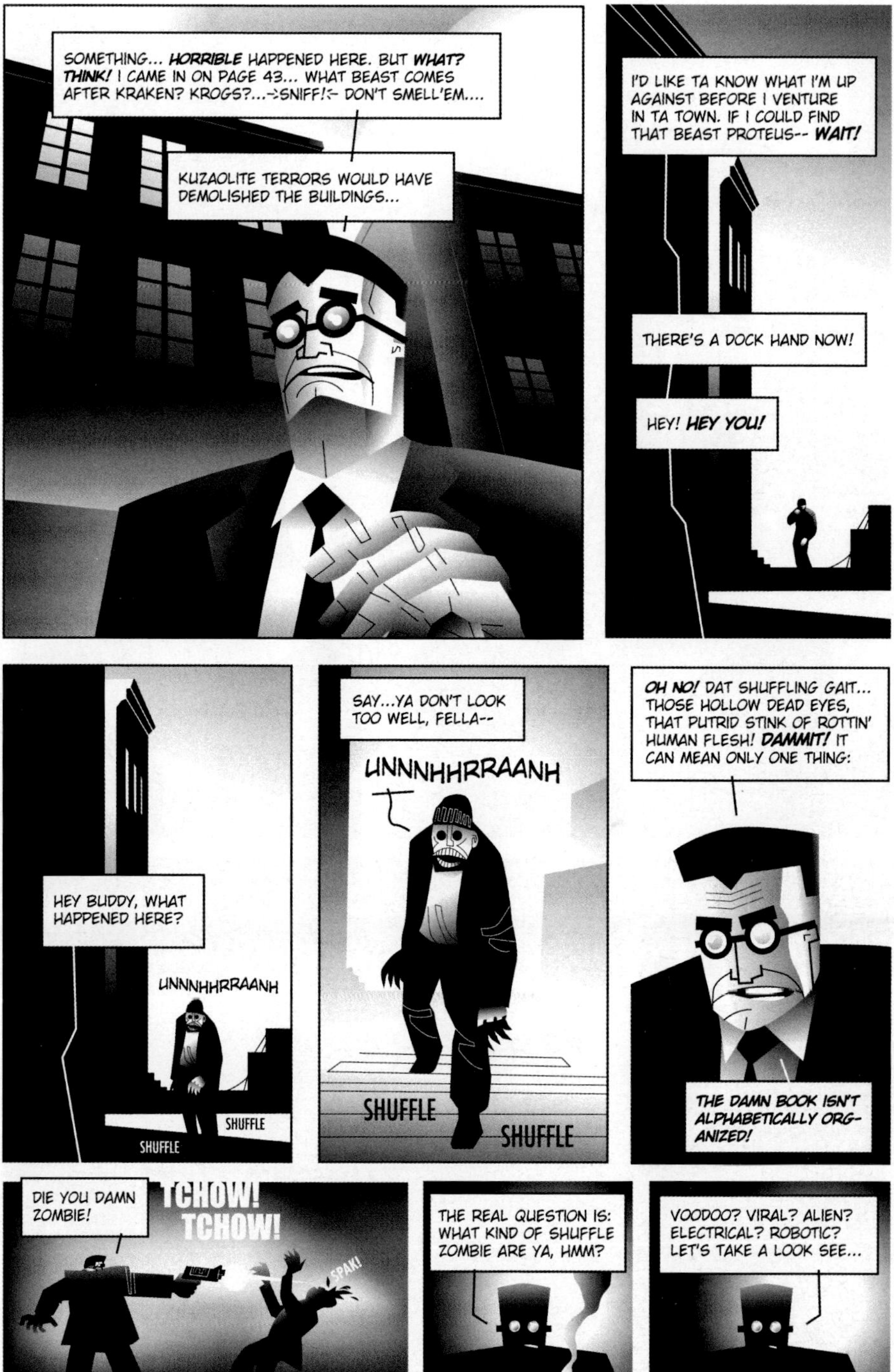

SOMETHING... HORRIBLE HAPPENED HERE. BUT WHAT? THINK! I CAME IN ON PAGE 43... WHAT BEAST COMES AFTER KRAKEN? KROGS?...->SNIFF!<- DON'T SMELL'EM....
KUZAOLITE TERRORS WOULD HAVE DEMOLISHED THE BUILDINGS...
I'D LIKE TA KNOW WHAT I'M UP AGAINST BEFORE I VENTURE IN TA TOWN. IF I COULD FIND THAT BEAST PROTEUS-- WAIT!
THERE'S A DOCK HAND NOW!
HEY! HEY YOU!
HEY BUDDY, WHAT HAPPENED HERE?
UNNNHHRRAANH
SHUFFLE
SHUFFLE
SAY...YA DON'T LOOK TOO WELL, FELLA--
UNNNHHRRAANH
SHUFFLE
SHUFFLE
OH NO! DAT SHUFFLING GAIT... THOSE HOLLOW DEAD EYES, THAT PUTRID STINK OF ROTTIN' HUMAN FLESH! DAMMIT! IT CAN MEAN ONLY ONE THING:
THE DAMN BOOK ISN'T ALPHABETICALLY ORG-ANIZED!
DIE YOU DAMN ZOMBIE!
TCHOW!
TCHOW!
SPAK!
THE REAL QUESTION IS: WHAT KIND OF SHUFFLE ZOMBIE ARE YA, HMM?
VOODOO? VIRAL? ALIEN? ELECTRICAL? ROBOTIC? LET'S TAKE A LOOK SEE...

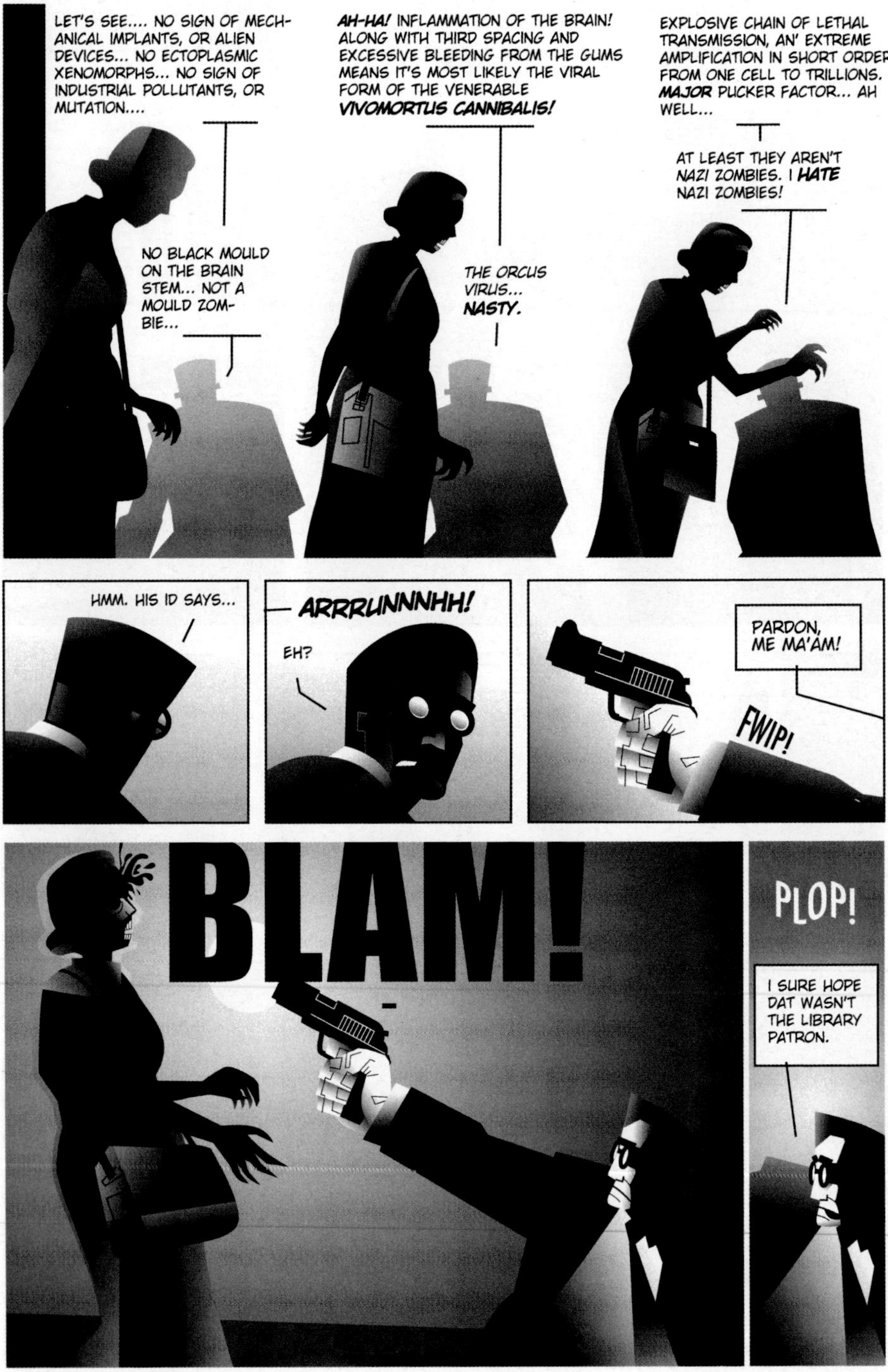
LET'S SEE.... NO SIGN OF MECH-ANICAL IMPLANTS, OR ALIEN DEVICES... NO ECTOPLASMIC XENOMORPHS... NO SIGN OF INDUSTRIAL POLLUTANTS, OR MUTATION....
NO BLACK MOULD ON THE BRAIN STEM... NOT A MOULD ZOM-BIE...
AH-HA! INFLAMMATION OF THE BRAIN! ALONG WITH THIRD SPACING AND EXCESSIVE BLEEDING FROM THE GUMS MEANS IT'S MOST LIKELY THE VIRAL FORM OF THE VENERABLE VIVOMORTUS CANNIBALIS!
THE ORCUS VIRUS... NASTY.
EXPLOSIVE CHAIN OF LETHAL TRANSMISSION, AN' EXTREME AMPLIFICATION IN SHORT ORDER. FROM ONE CELL TO TRILLIONS. MAJOR PUCKER FACTOR... AH WELL...
AT LEAST THEY AREN'T NAZI ZOMBIES. I HATE NAZI ZOMBIES!
HMM. HIS ID SAYS...
ARRRUNNNHH!
EH?
PARDON, ME MA'AM!
FWIP!
BLAM!
PLOP!
I SURE HOPE DAT WASN'T THE LIBRARY PATRON.

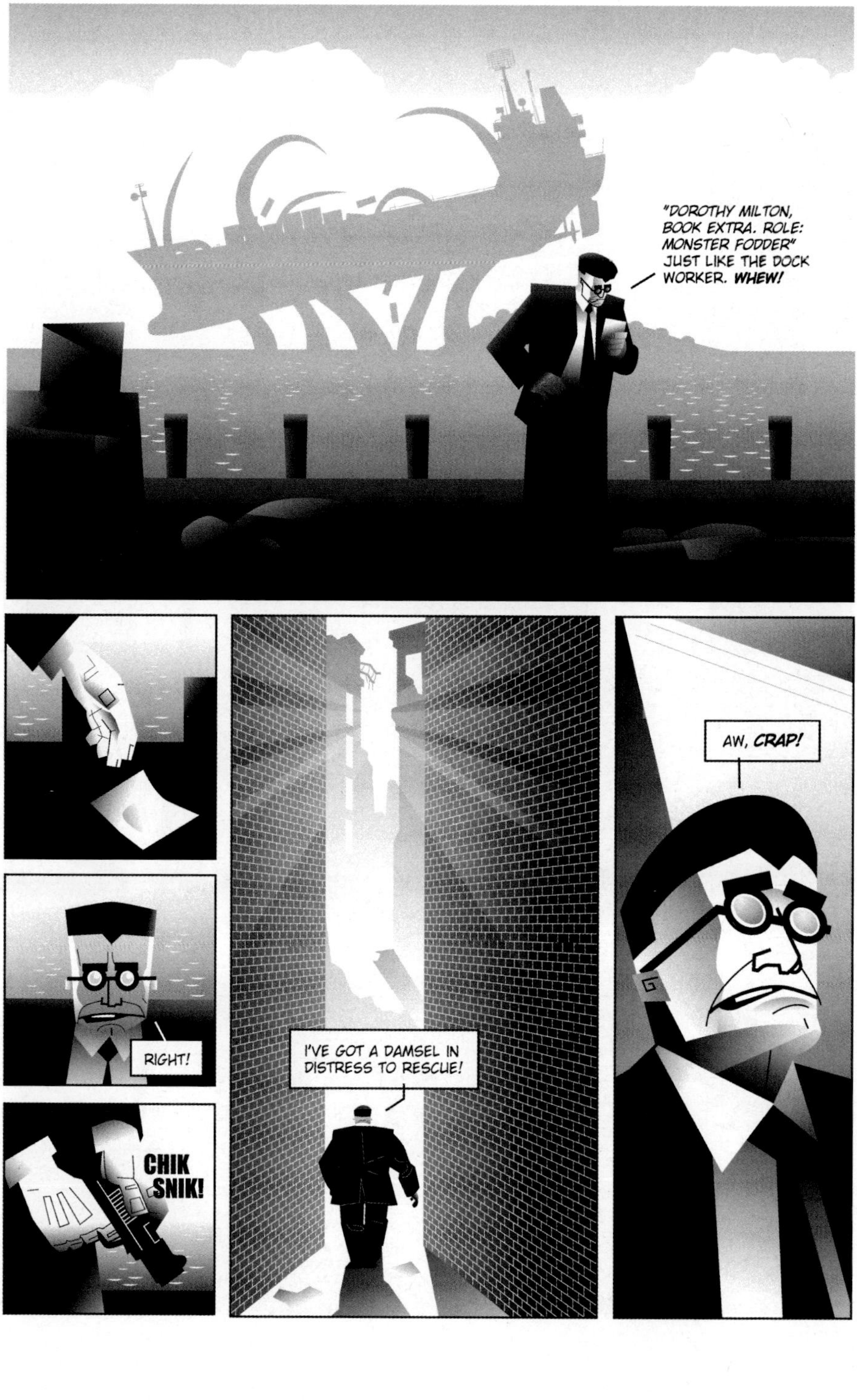
"DOROTHY MILTON,
BOOK EXTRA. ROLE:
MONSTER FODDER"
JUST LIKE THE DOCK
WORKER. WHEW!
RIGHT!
CHIK
SNIK!
I'VE GOT A DAMSEL IN
DISTRESS TO RESCUE!
AW, CRAP!

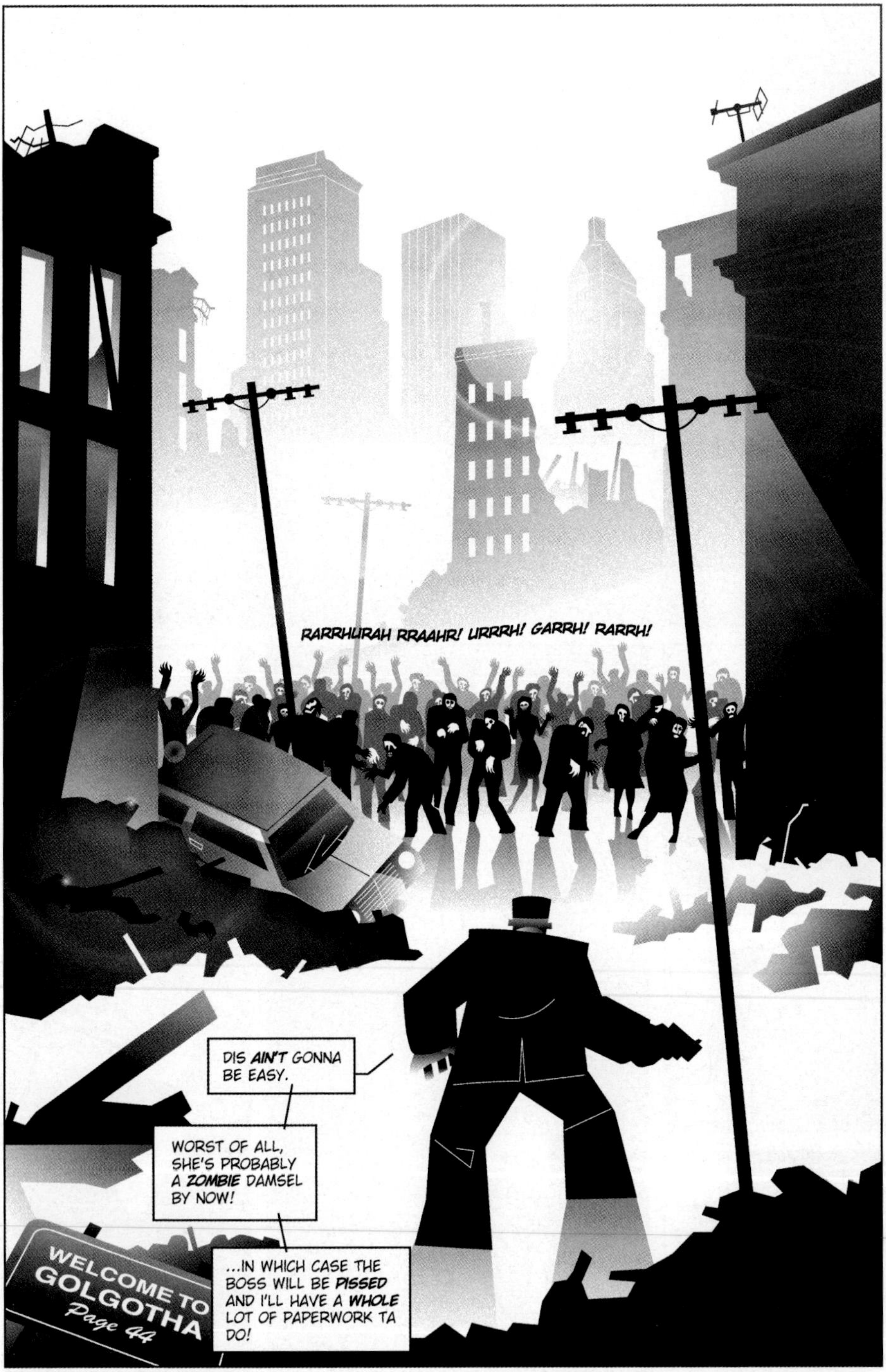
RARRHURAH RRAAHR! URRRH! GARRH! RARRH!
DIS AIN'T GONNA BE EASY.
WORST OF ALL, SHE'S PROBABLY A ZOMBIE DAMSEL BY NOW!
...IN WHICH CASE THE BOSS WILL BE PISSED AND I'LL HAVE A WHOLE LOT OF PAPERWORK TA DO!
WELCOME TO GOLGOTHA
Page 44

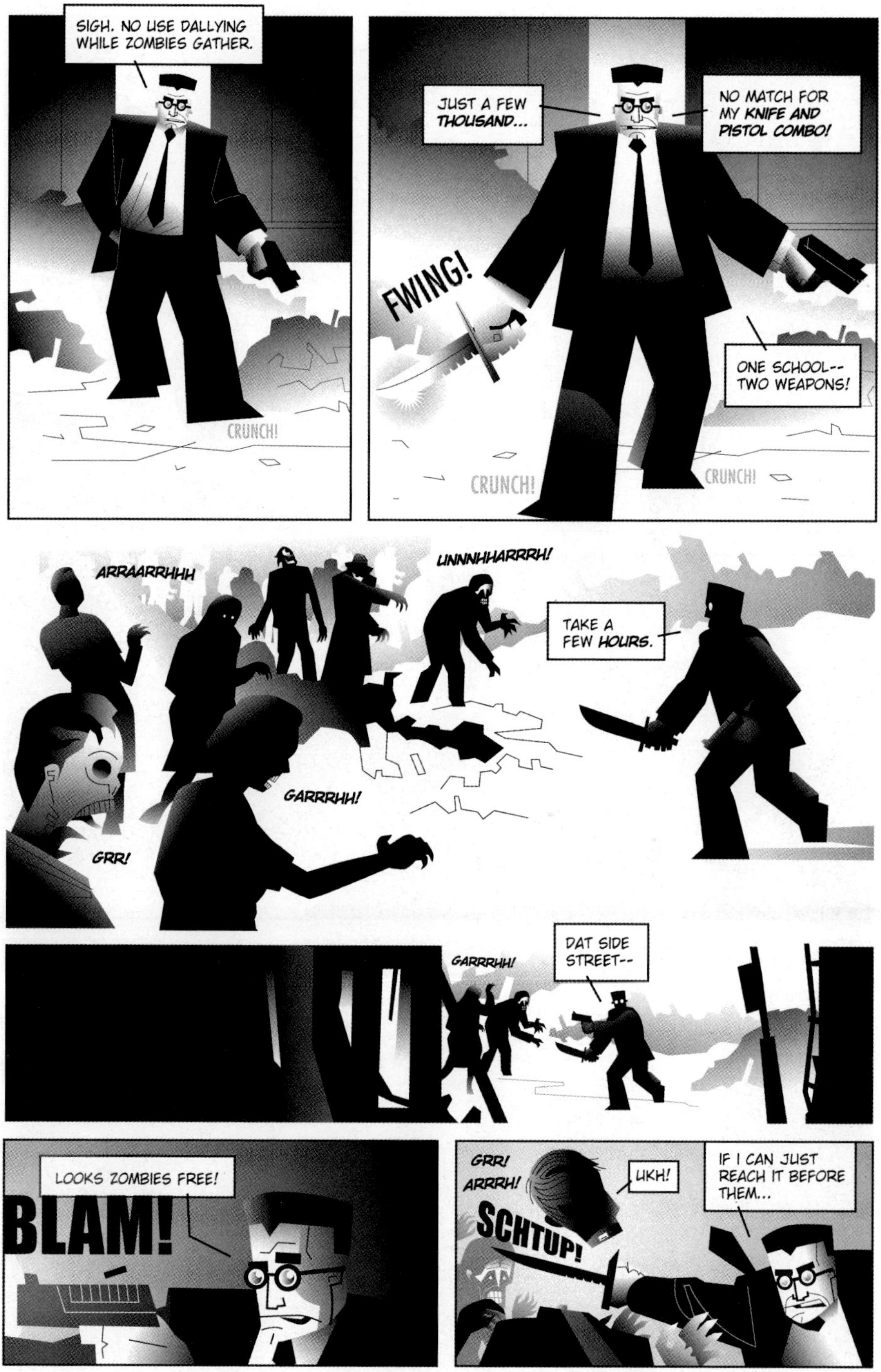
SIGH. NO USE DALLYING WHILE ZOMBIES GATHER.
CRUNCH!
JUST A FEW THOUSAND...
NO MATCH FOR MY KNIFE AND PISTOL COMBO!
FWING!
ONE SCHOOL-- TWO WEAPONS!
CRUNCH!
CRUNCH!
ARRAARRHHH
UNNNHHARRRH!
TAKE A FEW HOURS.
GARRRHH!
GRR!
GARRRHH!
DAT SIDE STREET--
LOOKS ZOMBIES FREE!
BLAM!
GRR!
ARRRH!
UKH!
IF I CAN JUST REACH IT BEFORE THEM...
SCHTUP!

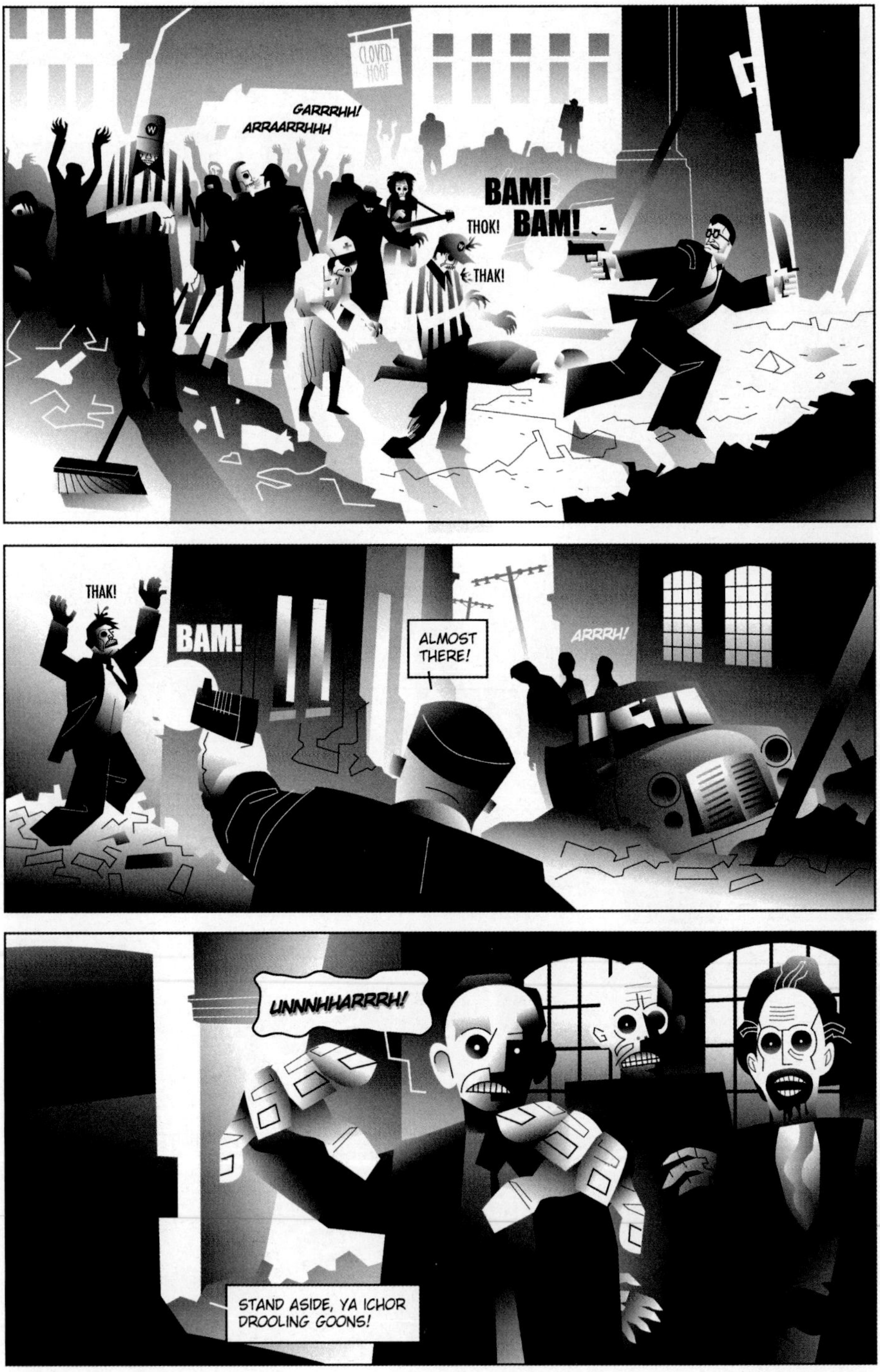
CLOVEN HOOF
GARRRHH!
ARRAARRHHH
BAM! BAM!
THOK!
THAK!
THAK!
BAM!
ALMOST THERE!
ARRRH!
UNNNHHARRRH!
STAND ASIDE, YA ICHOR DROOLING GOONS!

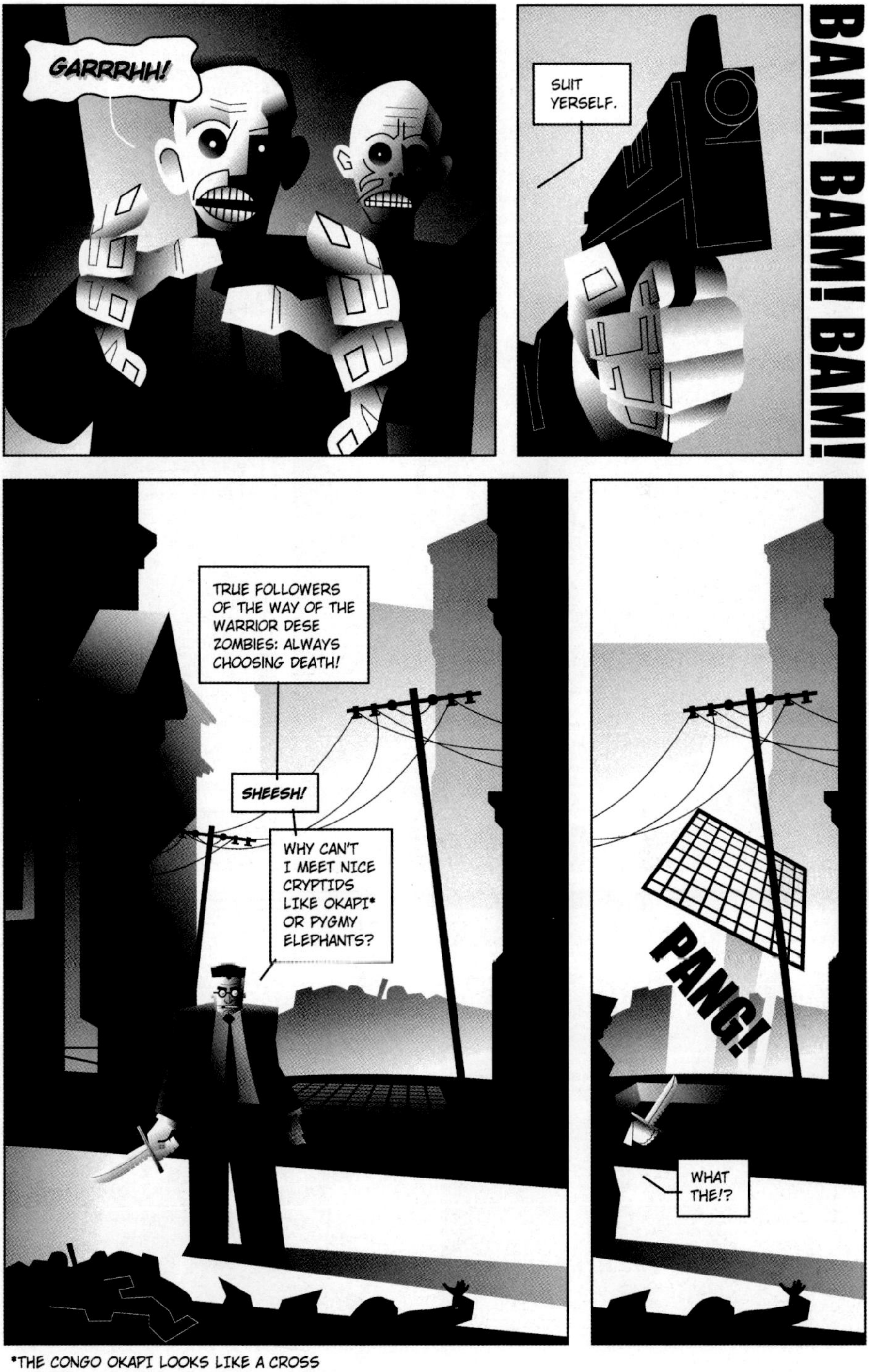
GARRRHH!
SUIT YERSELF.
BAM! BAM! BAM! BAM!
TRUE FOLLOWERS OF THE WAY OF THE WARRIOR DESE ZOMBIES: ALWAYS CHOOSING DEATH!
SHEESH!
WHY CAN'T I MEET NICE CRYPTIDS LIKE OKAPI* OR PYGMY ELEPHANTS?
PANG!
WHAT THE!?

*THE CONGO OKAPI LOOKS LIKE A CROSS BETWEEN A GIRAFFE AND A ZEBRA.-- BARRY

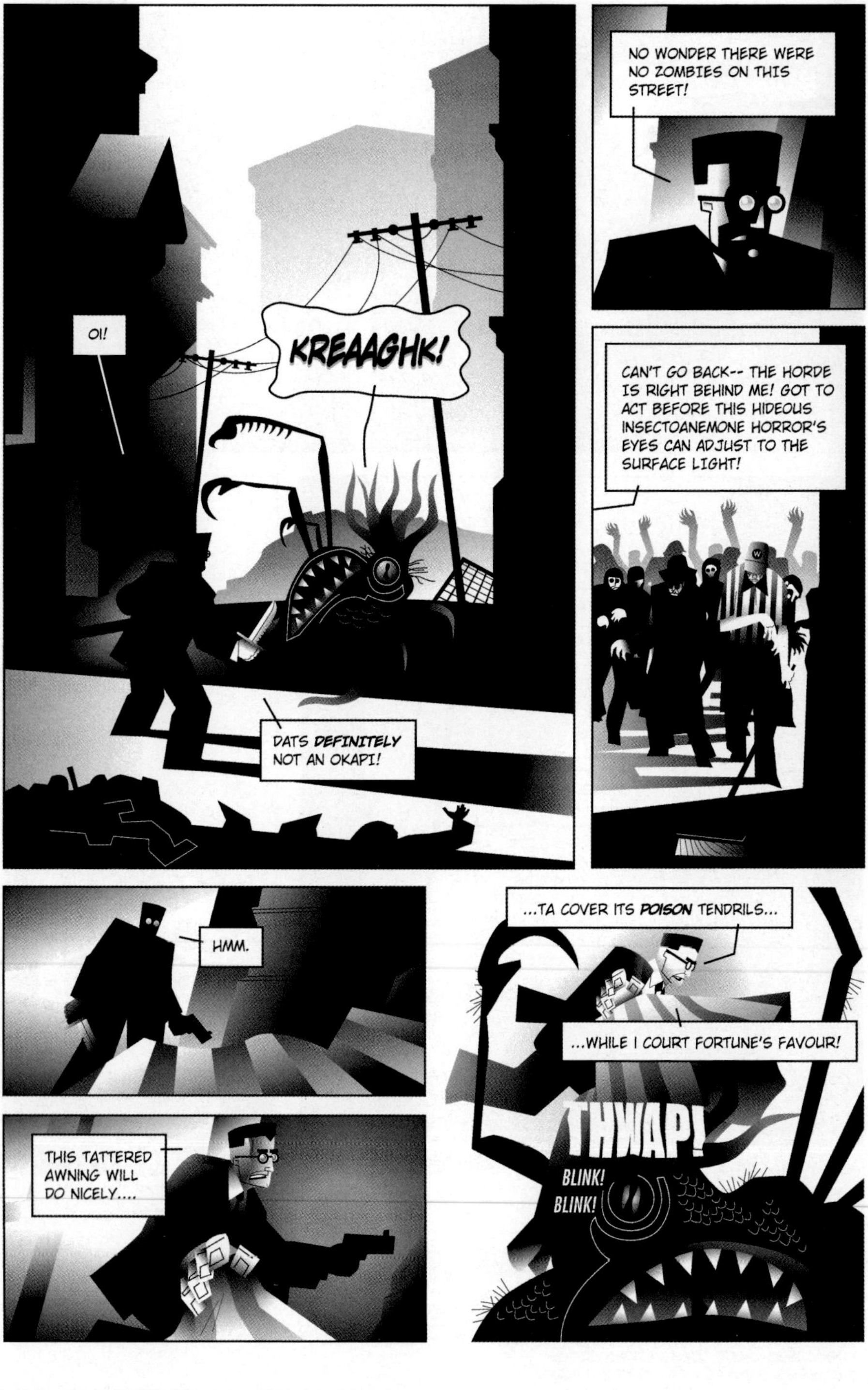
OI!
KREAAGHK!
DATS DEFINITELY NOT AN OKAPI!
NO WONDER THERE WERE NO ZOMBIES ON THIS STREET!
CAN'T GO BACK-- THE HORDE IS RIGHT BEHIND ME! GOT TO ACT BEFORE THIS HIDEOUS INSECTOANEMONE HORROR'S EYES CAN ADJUST TO THE SURFACE LIGHT!
HMM.
THIS TATTERED AWNING WILL DO NICELY....
...TA COVER ITS POISON TENDRILS...
...WHILE I COURT FORTUNE'S FAVOUR!
THWAP!
BLINK! BLINK!

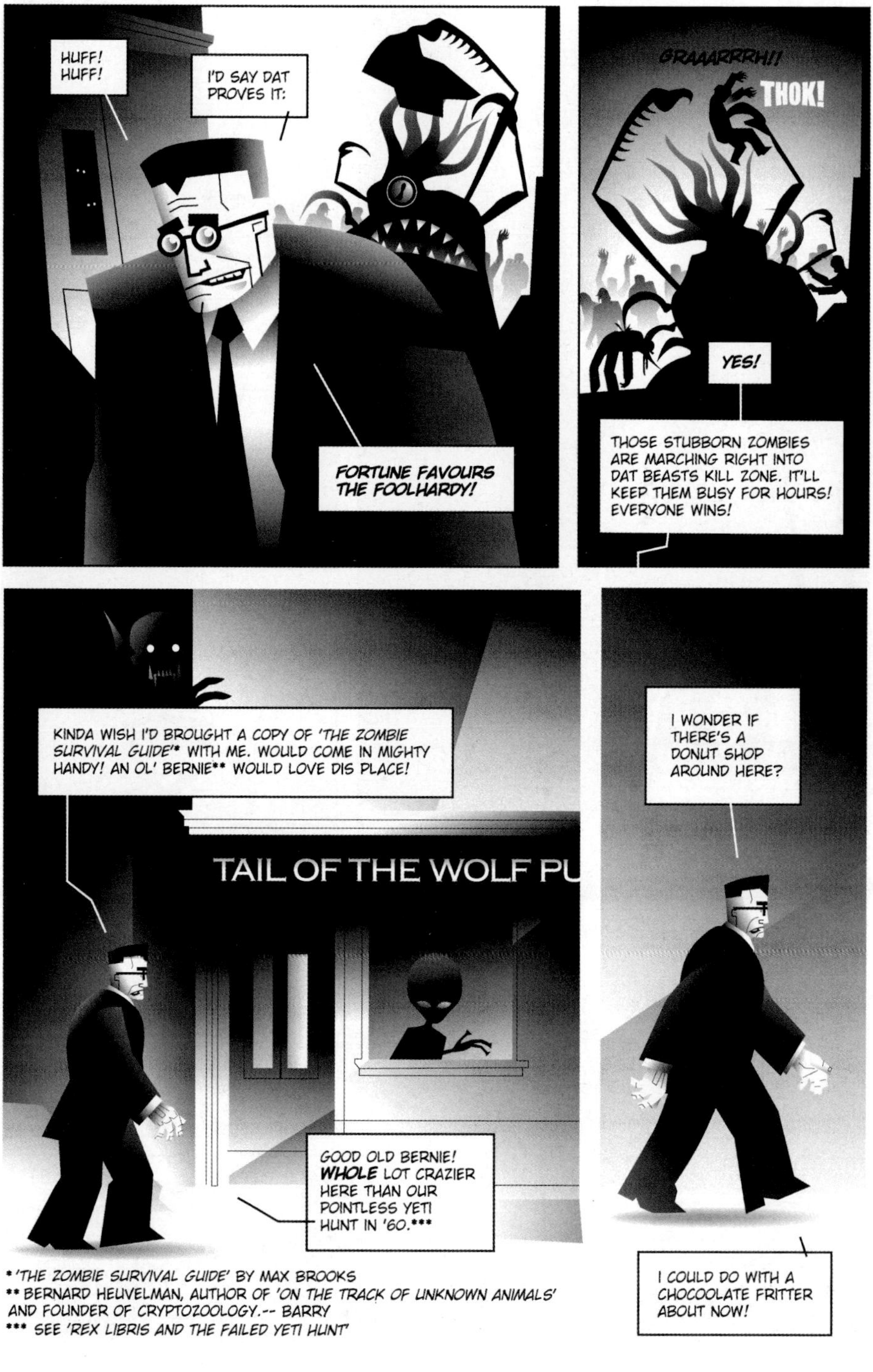
HUFF!
HUFF!
I'D SAY DAT PROVES IT:
FORTUNE FAVOURS THE FOOLHARDY!
GRAAARRRH!!
THOK!
YES!
THOSE STUBBORN ZOMBIES ARE MARCHING RIGHT INTO DAT BEASTS KILL ZONE. IT'LL KEEP THEM BUSY FOR HOURS! EVERYONE WINS!
KINDA WISH I'D BROUGHT A COPY OF 'THE ZOMBIE SURVIVAL GUIDE'* WITH ME. WOULD COME IN MIGHTY HANDY! AN OL' BERNIE** WOULD LOVE DIS PLACE!
TAIL OF THE WOLF PU
GOOD OLD BERNIE! WHOLE LOT CRAZIER HERE THAN OUR POINTLESS YETI HUNT IN '60.***
I WONDER IF THERE'S A DONUT SHOP AROUND HERE?
I COULD DO WITH A CHOCOOLATE FRITTER ABOUT NOW!

* 'THE ZOMBIE SURVIVAL GUIDE' BY MAX BROOKS
** BERNARD HEUVELMAN, AUTHOR OF 'ON THE TRACK OF UNKNOWN ANIMALS' AND FOUNDER OF CRYPTOZOOLOGY.-- BARRY
*** SEE 'REX LIBRIS AND THE FAILED YETI HUNT'

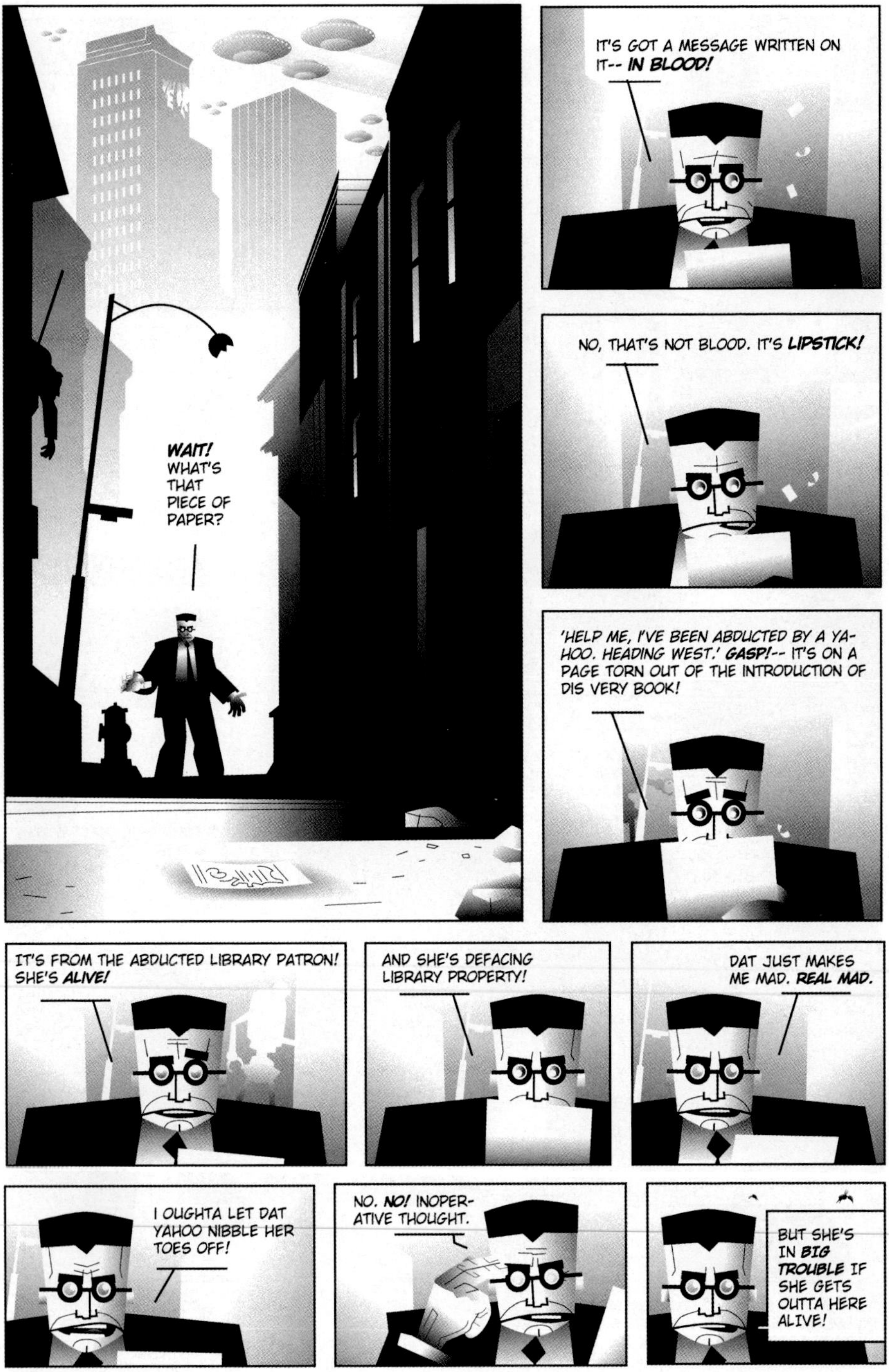
WAIT! WHAT'S THAT PIECE OF PAPER?
IT'S GOT A MESSAGE WRITTEN ON IT-- IN BLOOD!
NO, THAT'S NOT BLOOD. IT'S LIPSTICK!
'HELP ME, I'VE BEEN ABDUCTED BY A YAHOO. HEADING WEST.' GASP!-- IT'S ON A PAGE TORN OUT OF THE INTRODUCTION OF DIS VERY BOOK!
IT'S FROM THE ABDUCTED LIBRARY PATRON! SHE'S ALIVE!
AND SHE'S DEFACING LIBRARY PROPERTY!
DAT JUST MAKES ME MAD. REAL MAD.
I OUGHTA LET DAT YAHOO NIBBLE HER TOES OFF!
NO. NO! INOPERATIVE THOUGHT.
BUT SHE'S IN BIG TROUBLE IF SHE GETS OUTTA HERE ALIVE!

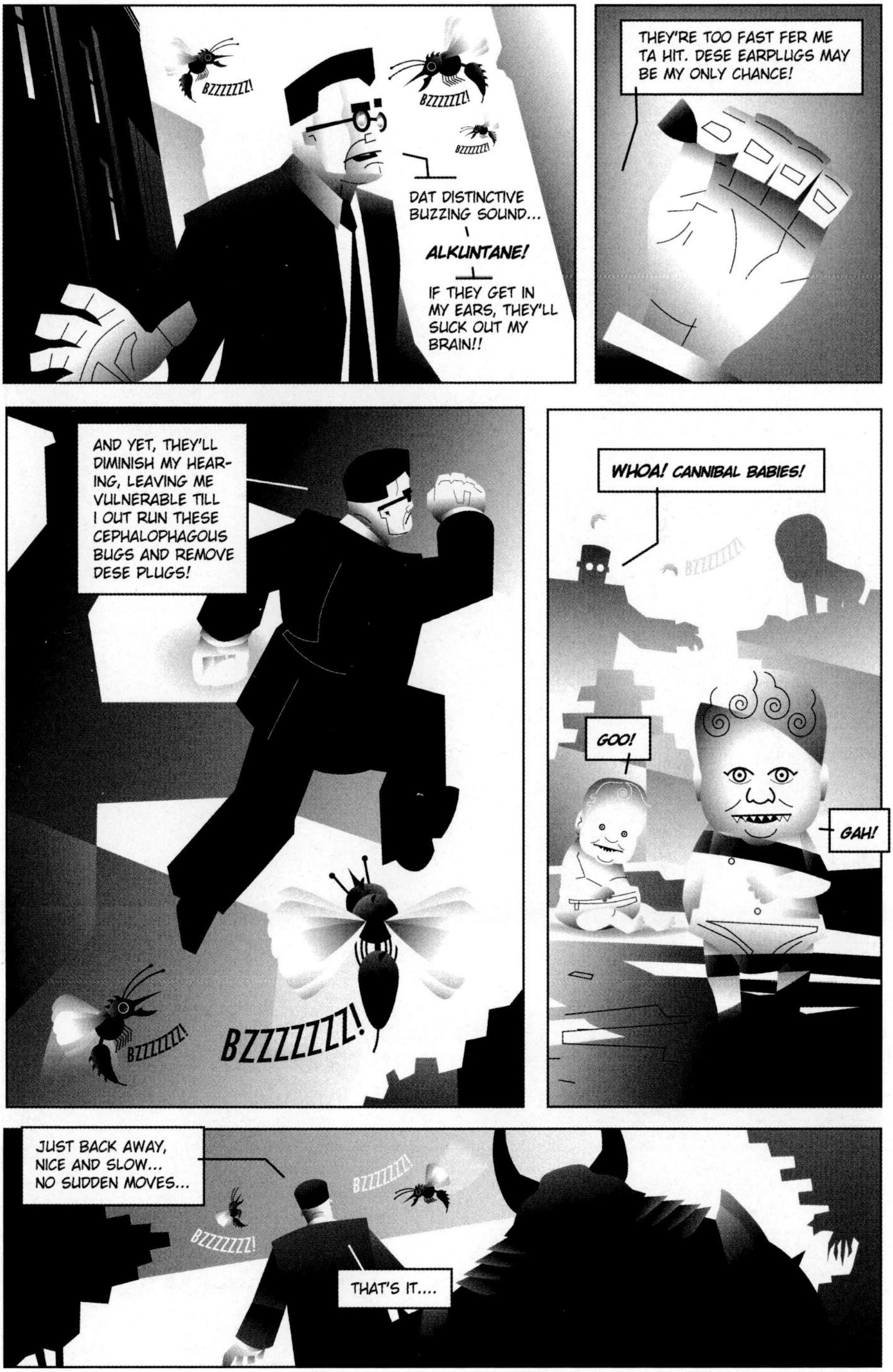
BZZZZZZ!
BZZZZZZ!
BZZZZZZ!
DAT DISTINCTIVE BUZZING SOUND...
ALKUNTANE!
IF THEY GET IN MY EARS, THEY'LL SUCK OUT MY BRAIN!!
THEY'RE TOO FAST FER ME TA HIT. DESE EARPLUGS MAY BE MY ONLY CHANCE!
AND YET, THEY'LL DIMINISH MY HEAR-ING, LEAVING ME VULNERABLE TILL I OUT RUN THESE CEPHALOPHAGOUS BUGS AND REMOVE DESE PLUGS!
BZZZZZZ!
BZZZZZZZ!
WHOA! CANNIBAL BABIES!
BZZZZZZ!
GOO!
GAH!
JUST BACK AWAY, NICE AND SLOW... NO SUDDEN MOVES...
BZZZZZZ!
BZZZZZZ!
THAT'S IT....

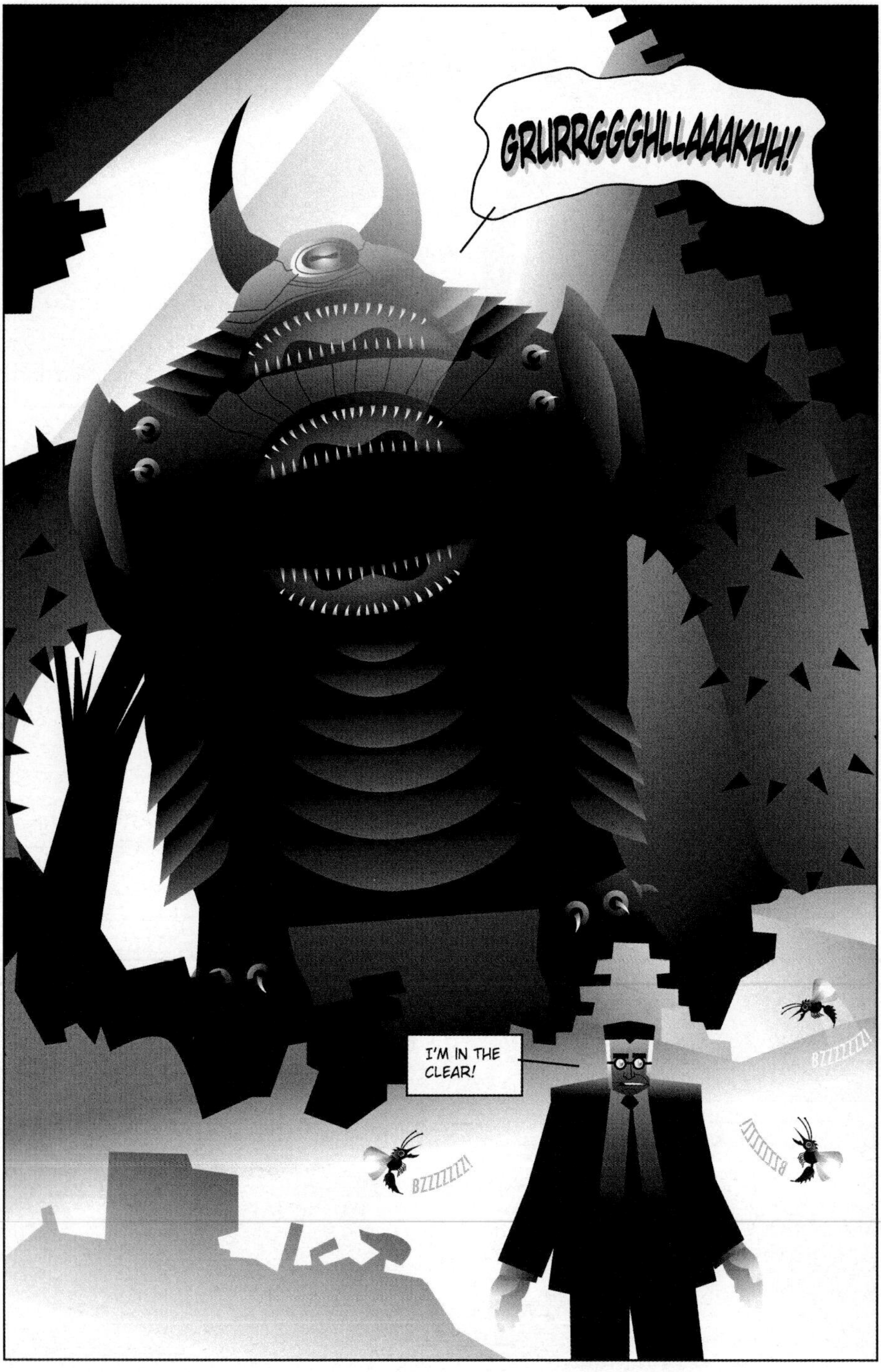
GRURRGGGHLLAAAKHH!
I'M IN THE CLEAR!
BZZZZZZZ!
BZZZZZZZ!
BZZZZZZZ!

CHAPTER SEVEN

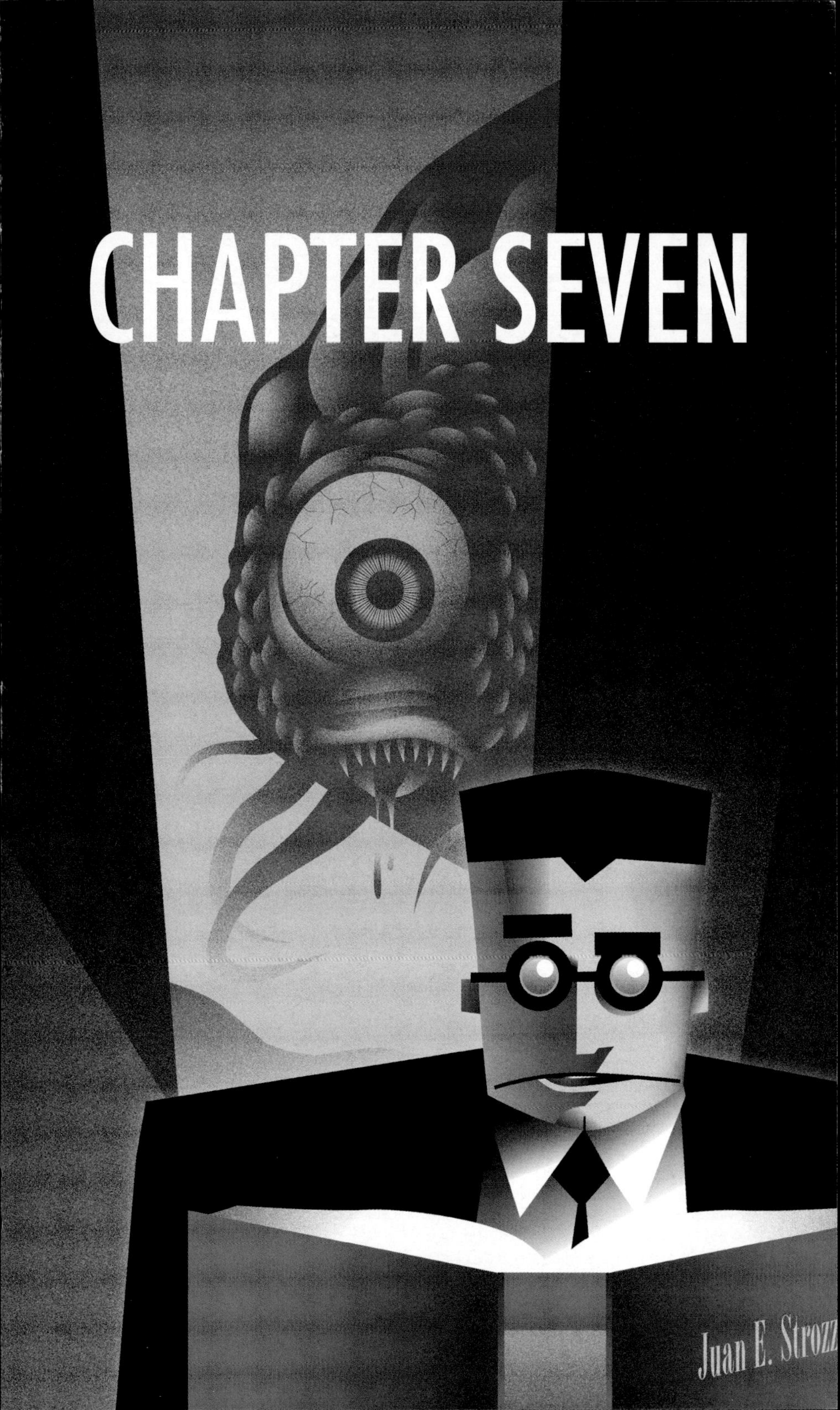
Juan E. Strozz

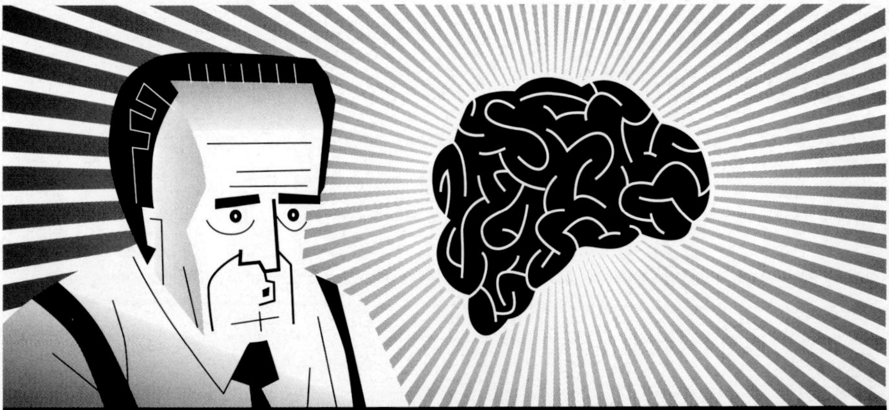

BARRY'S BRAIN

Monsters! Almost ***everyone*** loves them. Sure, there are those who prefer stories based on human relationships and all ***that*** stuff, without the goo and slime and the crypts of the undead. But to them I say: why not have ***both?*** Now with the miracle of visicomboics, you ***can!*** This issue is jam packed with ***both*** monsters ***and*** in-depth character studies! We go from intense action to introspective discussion of life and buttertarts with a deftness that will surely leave you stunned! Impossible, you say? Not for us! This leaves us space to include an excerpt from the famed *Compendio Ilustrado de la Morfología del Monstruo del Paleozoico al Cenozoico del Cryptozoologisto Internacionalmente Aclamado Juan E. Strozzi el Loco* (translated by Randolph A. Tenndleson, to whom I am deeply indebted).

From the monsters of ancient literature, such as Medusa (not to mention the Cyclops, Scylla, the Harpies, the Hydra, the Nemean Lion, the Minotaur, Grendel, and Cerebus), to modern day threats such as the pod people, we just can't seem to get enough of bizarre beasties. The selection of monster tales, both novels and short stories, is virtually endless; among the best are (in no particular order): Mary Shelley's *Frankenstein: The Modern Prometheus* (Haven't read it but I hear it's a classic), Bram Stoker's *Dracula* (Saw the movie), *Gulliver's Travels* by Jonathan Swift (Densely written but filled with the wild, weird, and satirical), *Voyage au Centre de la Terre* by Jules Verne, *The Strange Case of Dr. Jekyll and Mr. Hyde* by Robert Louis Stevenson, Homer's *The Odyssey,* H. P. Lovecraft's highly descriptive and disturbing *Call of Cthulhu, The Colour Out of Space, At the Mountains of Madness, The Dunwich Horror,* and *The Lurking Fear; Demon Seed* and *Phantoms* by Dean Koontz, *Relic* and *Reliquary* by Douglas Preston and Lincoln Child, *Beast* by Peter Benchley, *The Legacy of Heorot* and *The Mote In God's Eye* by Larry Niven, Edgar Rice Burrough's *Out of Time's Abyss, The People That Time Forgot, The Warlord of Mars, John Carter of Mars,* and *Land of Terror;* John Wyndham's *Day of the Triffids, The Midwich Cuckoos,* and *The Kraken Wakes; It, Christine,* and *Tommyknockers* by Stephen King, *The Year of the Angry Rabbit* by Russell Braddon, *The Lost World* by Sir Arthur Conan Doyle, Robert E. Howard's *Conan of Cimmeria, The Savage Tales of Solomon Kane, The Black Stone,* and *The Fire of Asshurbanipal,* L. Frank Baum's *Dorothy and the Wizard in Oz* and *Ozma of Oz;* the *Narnia* series by C. S. Lewis, *Lord of the Rings* by J. R. R. Tolkien, *The Tower of the Elephant* by Robert E. Howard, *The Time Machine, War of the Worlds, The Island of Doctor Moreau, The Empire of the Ants* (also see *Doomsday Deferred* by Will F. Jenkins), *The First Men in the Moon, The Flowering of the Strange Orchid,* and *In the Abyss,* all by H. G. Wells; Ray Bradbury's *The Fog Horn,* Arthur C. Clarke's *A Walk in the Dark,* Damon Knight's *To Serve Man,* Jack Finney's *Sleep No More* (aka *Invasion of the Body Snatchers*), John W. Campbell's *Who Goes There?*, *The Fly* by George Langelaan, and Richard Matheson's *I Am Legend.* This is just the tip of the iceberg, of course, as pulp magazines were filled—***filled*** I say!—with glorious monster stories. If you can think of any that I've missed, by gum, ***write in.*** We'll include the recommendations in the next issue. And I am more than out of space.

Until next time, *extirpate!*

B. Barry Horst

B. Barry Horst

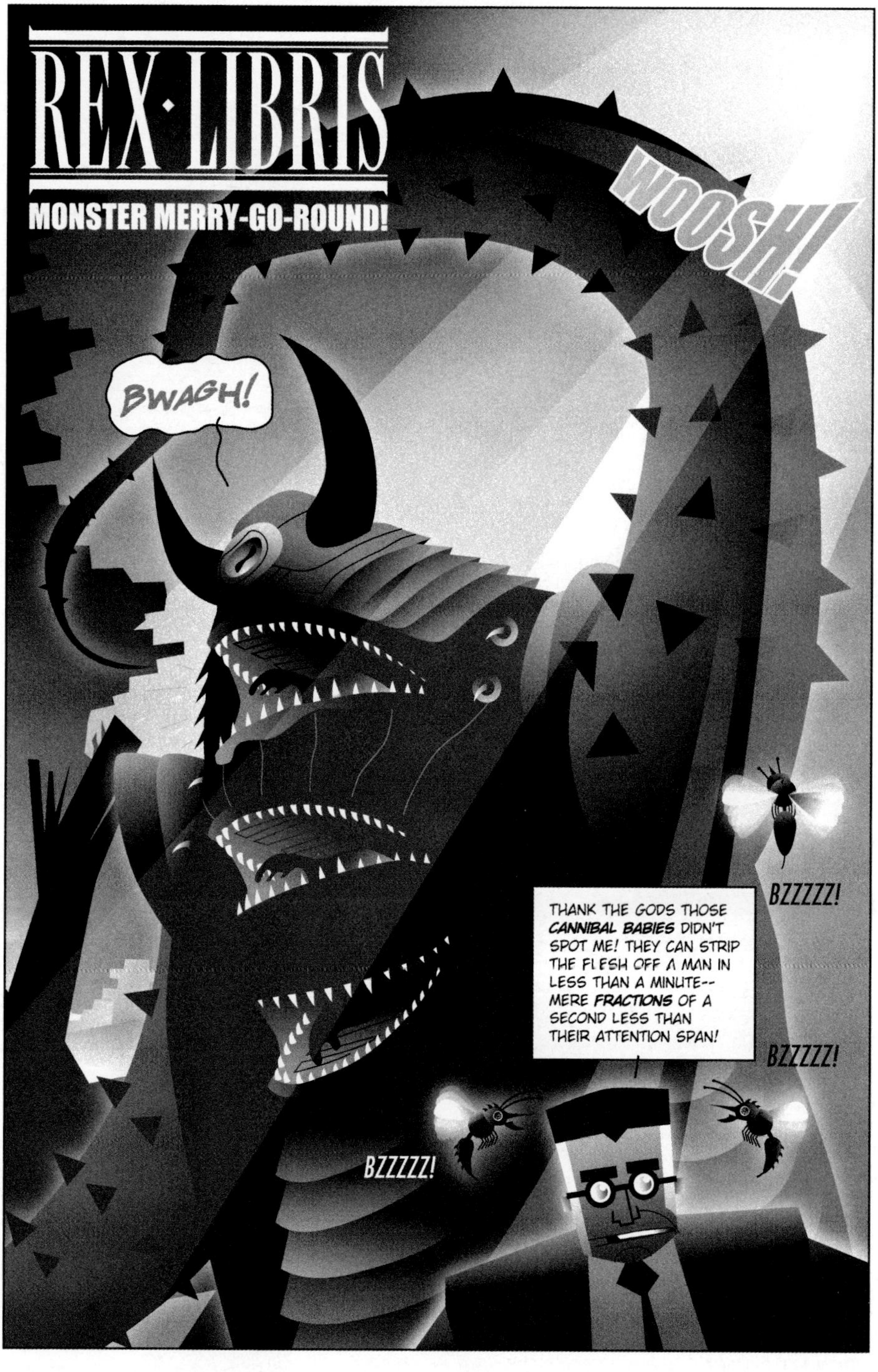

REX·LIBRIS
MONSTER MERRY-GO-ROUND!
WOOSH!
BWAGH!
BZZZZZ!
THANK THE GODS THOSE CANNIBAL BABIES DIDN'T SPOT ME! THEY CAN STRIP THE FLESH OFF A MAN IN LESS THAN A MINUTE-- MERE FRACTIONS OF A SECOND LESS THAN THEIR ATTENTION SPAN!
BZZZZZ!
BZZZZZ!

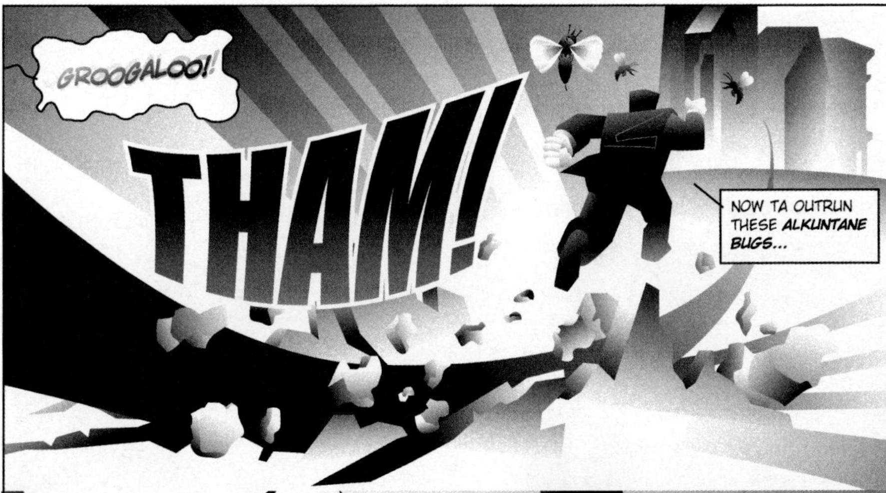
GROOGALOO!
THAM!
NOW TA OUTRUN THESE ALKUNTANE BUGS...

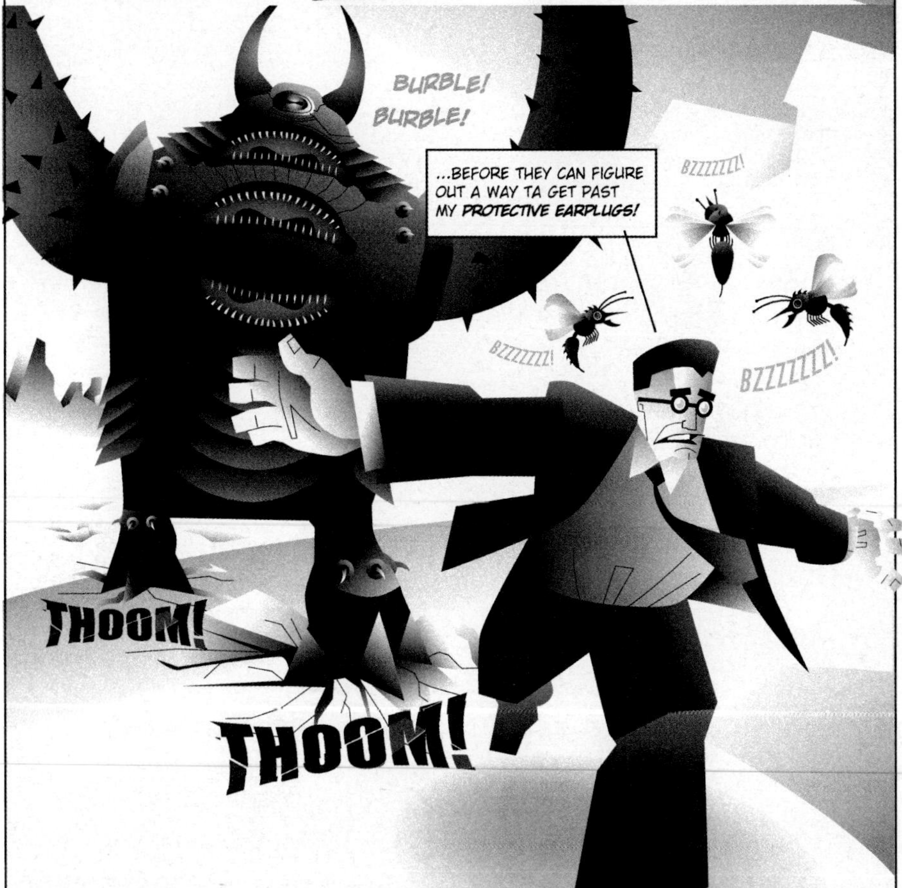
BURBLE! BURBLE!
...BEFORE THEY CAN FIGURE OUT A WAY TA GET PAST MY PROTECTIVE EARPLUGS!
BZZZZZZZ!
BZZZZZZZ!
BZZZZZZZ!
THOOM!
THOOM!

EDITORS NOTE: ALKUNTANE BUGS HAVE LIGHTNING FAST REFLEXES AND ARE THE MOST AGILE AND MANEUVERABLE BRAIN SUCKING INSECTS IN THE GALAXY. THEY CAN SENSE THE SLIGHT DISTURBANCE IN THE ATMOSPHERE THAT PRECEDES AN ATTACK -- ***BARRY***

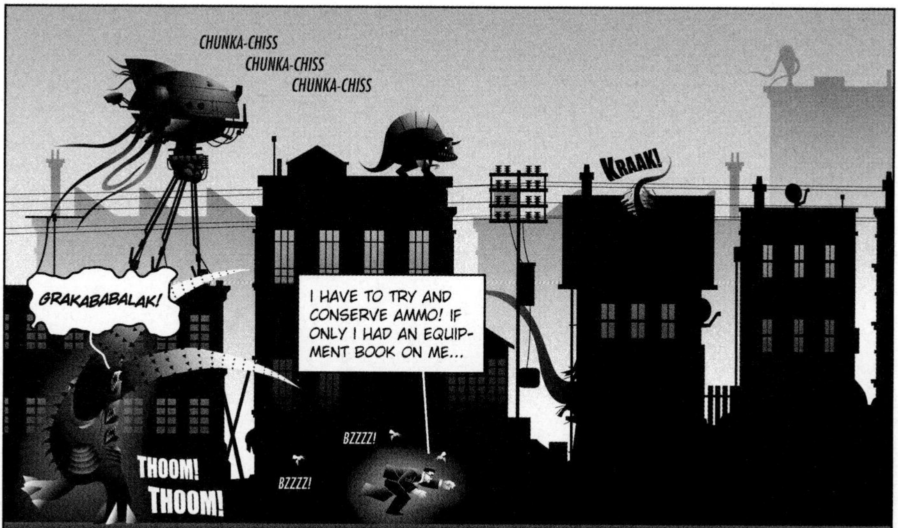
CHUNKA-CHISS
CHUNKA-CHISS
CHUNKA-CHISS
KRAAK!
GRAKABABALAK!
I HAVE TO TRY AND CONSERVE AMMO! IF ONLY I HAD AN EQUIPMENT BOOK ON ME...
BZZZZ!
BZZZZ!
THOOM!
THOOM!

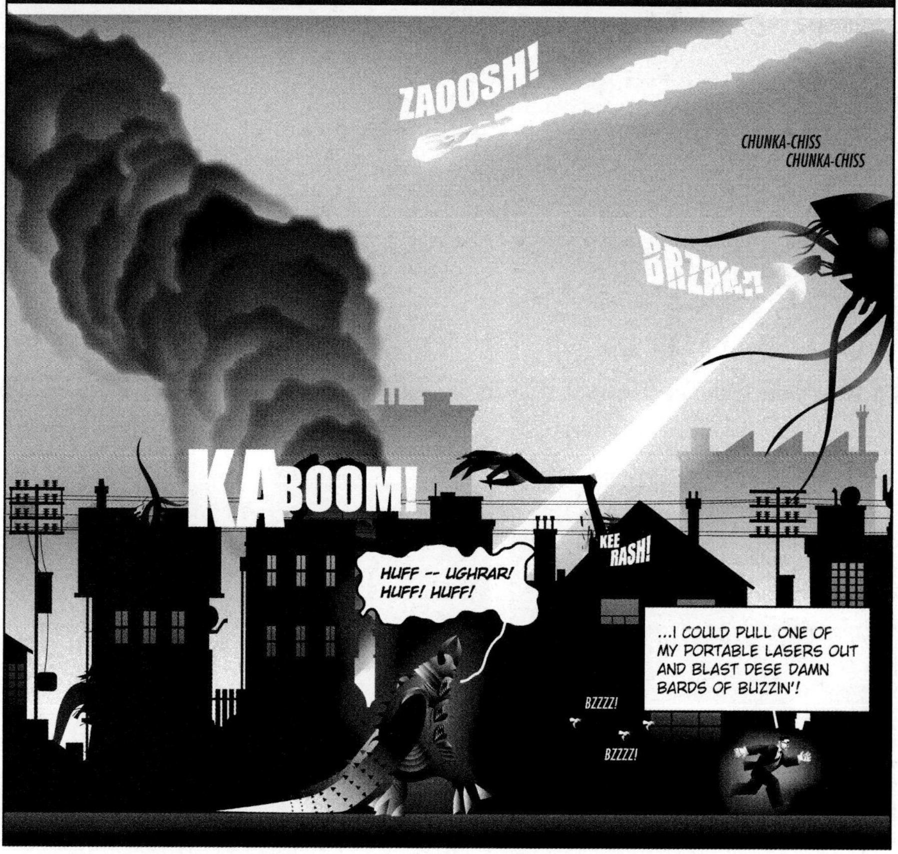
ZAOOSH!
CHUNKA-CHISS
CHUNKA-CHISS
KABOOM!
KEE RASH!
HUFF -- UGHRAR! HUFF! HUFF!
...I COULD PULL ONE OF MY PORTABLE LASERS OUT AND BLAST DESE DAMN BARDS OF BUZZIN'!
BZZZZ!
BZZZZ!

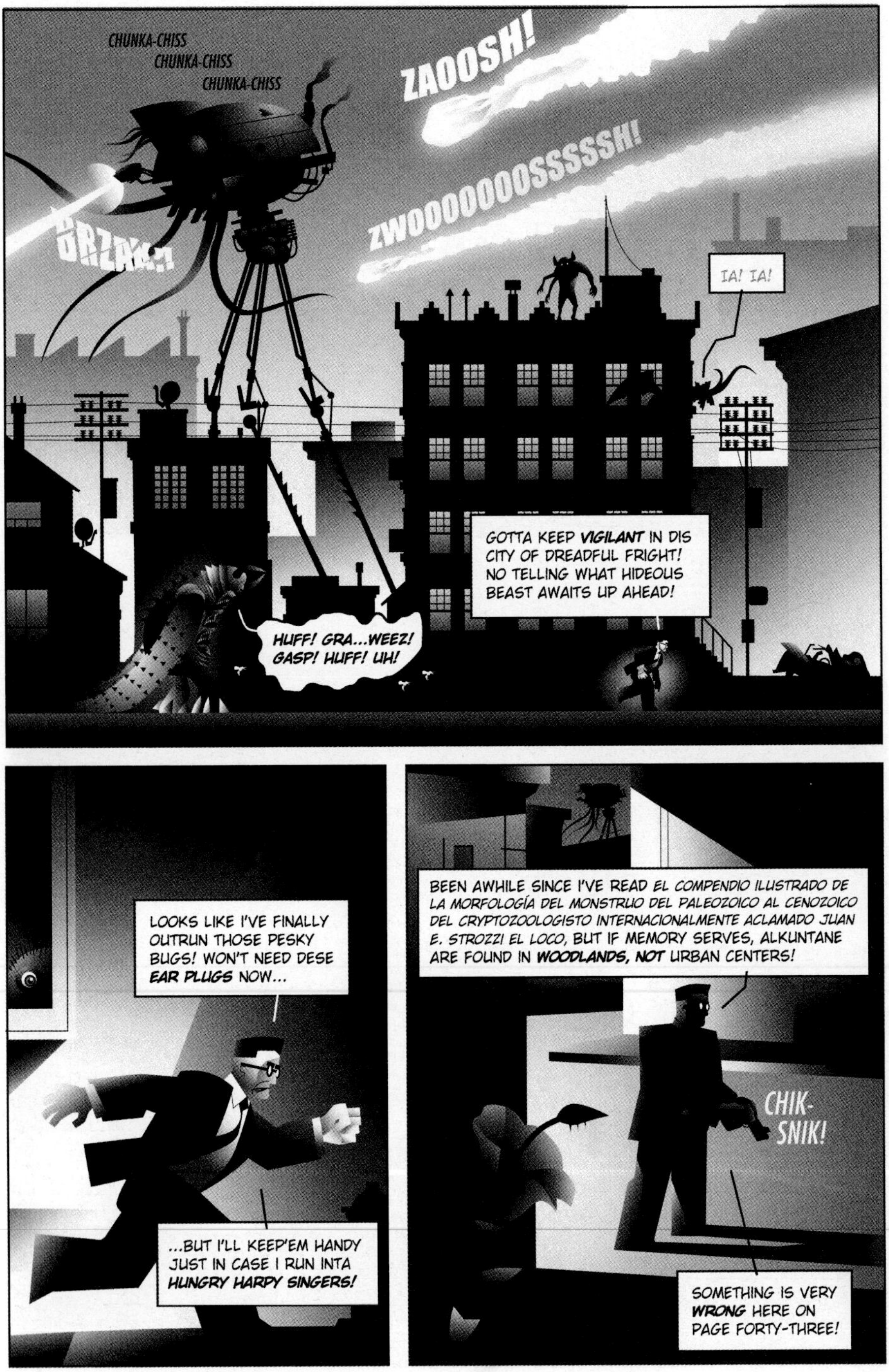
CHUNKA-CHISS
CHUNKA-CHISS
CHUNKA-CHISS
ZAOOSH!
ZWOOOOOOOOSSSSSH!
BRZAK!
IA! IA!
GOTTA KEEP **VIGILANT** IN DIS CITY OF DREADFUL FRIGHT! NO TELLING WHAT HIDEOUS BEAST AWAITS UP AHEAD!
HUFF! GRA...WEEZ! GASP! HUFF! UH!
LOOKS LIKE I'VE FINALLY OUTRUN THOSE PESKY BUGS! WON'T NEED DESE **EAR PLUGS** NOW...
...BUT I'LL KEEP'EM HANDY JUST IN CASE I RUN INTA **HUNGRY HARPY SINGERS!**
BEEN AWHILE SINCE I'VE READ *EL COMPENDIO ILUSTRADO DE LA MORFOLOGÍA DEL MONSTRUO DEL PALEOZOICO AL CENOZOICO DEL CRYPTOZOOLOGISTO INTERNACIONALMENTE ACLAMADO JUAN E. STROZZI EL LOCO*, BUT IF MEMORY SERVES, ALKUNTANE ARE FOUND IN **WOODLANDS, NOT** URBAN CENTERS!
CHIK-SNIK!
SOMETHING IS VERY **WRONG** HERE ON PAGE FORTY-THREE!

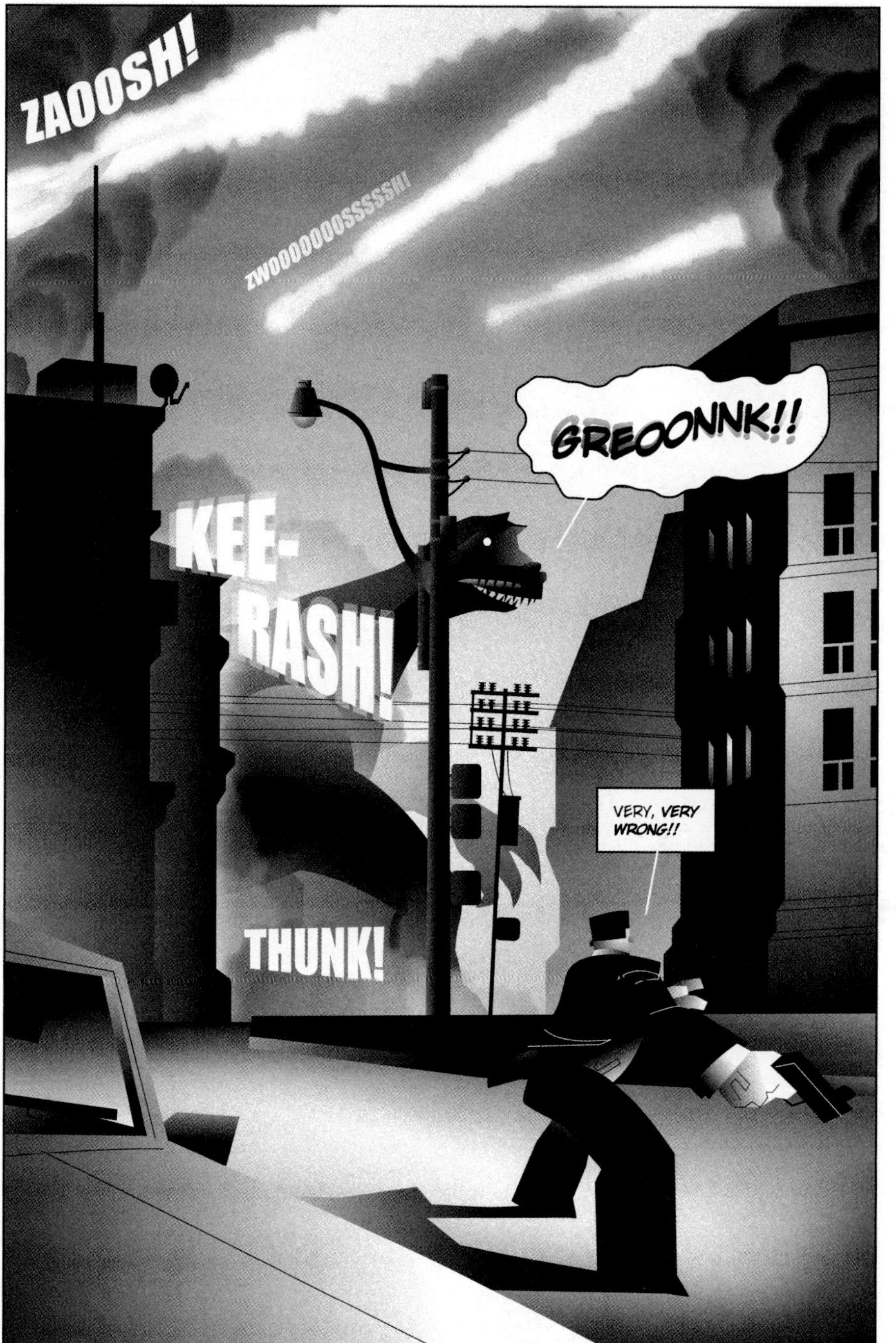
ZAOOSH!
ZWOOOOOOOSSSSSH!
GREOONNK!!
KEE-RASH!
VERY, VERY WRONG!!
THUNK!

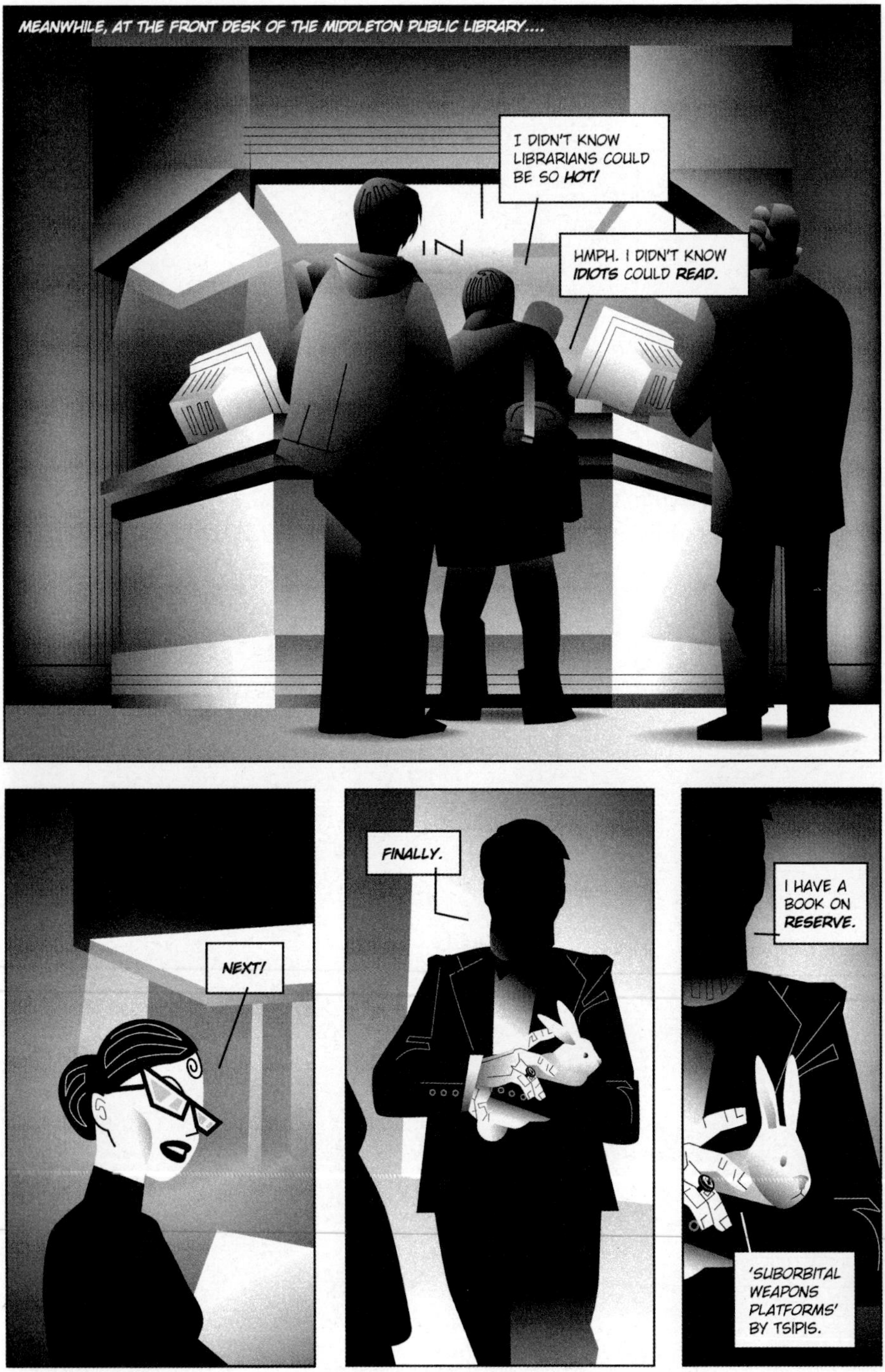
MEANWHILE, AT THE FRONT DESK OF THE MIDDLETON PUBLIC LIBRARY....
I DIDN'T KNOW LIBRARIANS COULD BE SO HOT!
HMPH. I DIDN'T KNOW IDIOTS COULD READ.
NEXT!
FINALLY.
I HAVE A BOOK ON RESERVE.
'SUBORBITAL WEAPONS PLATFORMS' BY TSIPIS.

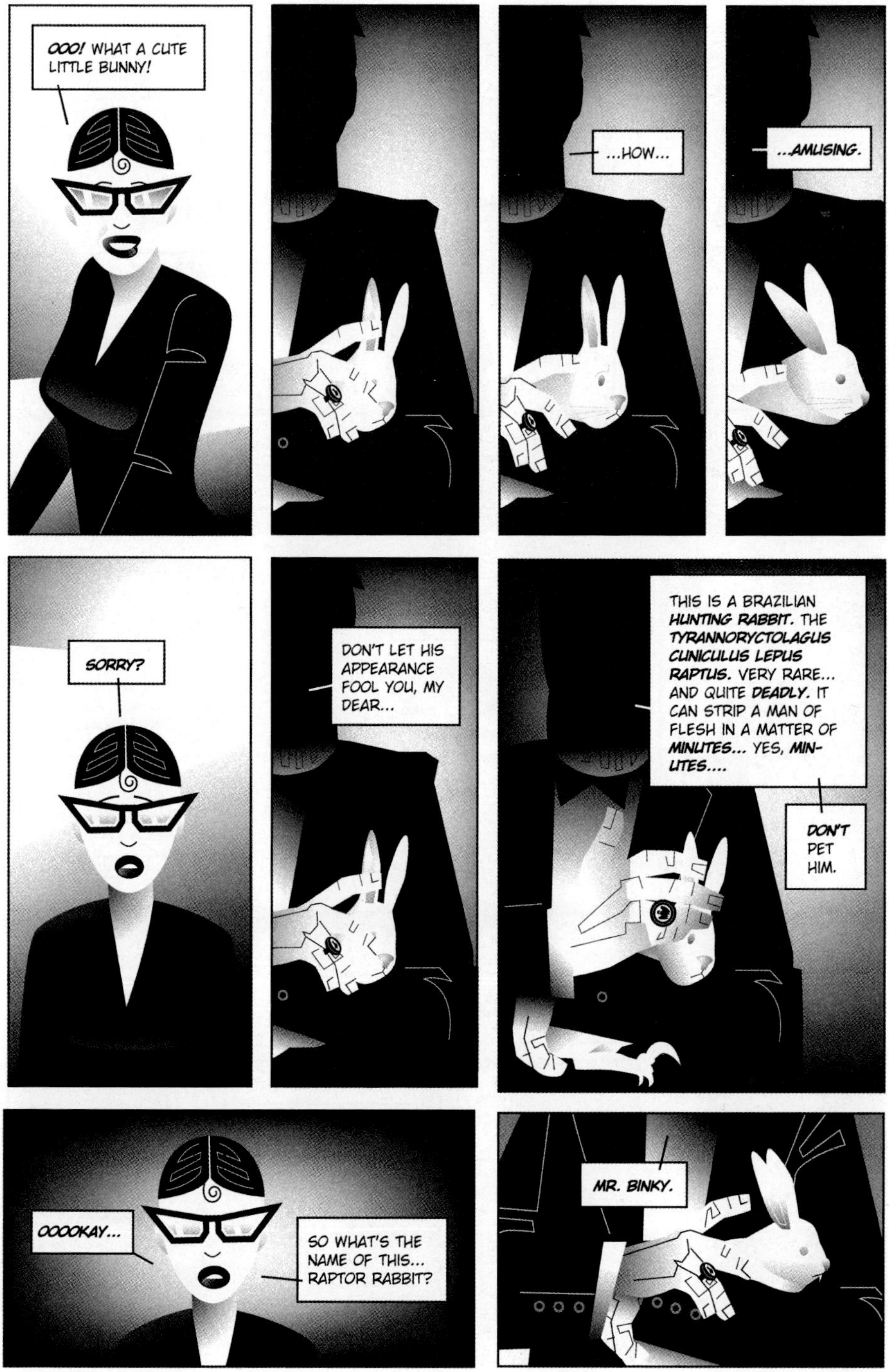
OOO! WHAT A CUTE LITTLE BUNNY!
...HOW...
...AMUSING.
SORRY?
DON'T LET HIS APPEARANCE FOOL YOU, MY DEAR...
THIS IS A BRAZILIAN HUNTING RABBIT. THE TYRANNORYCTOLAGUS CUNICULUS LEPUS RAPTUS. VERY RARE... AND QUITE DEADLY. IT CAN STRIP A MAN OF FLESH IN A MATTER OF MINUTES... YES, MIN-UTES....
DON'T PET HIM.
OOOOKAY...
SO WHAT'S THE NAME OF THIS... RAPTOR RABBIT?
MR. BINKY.

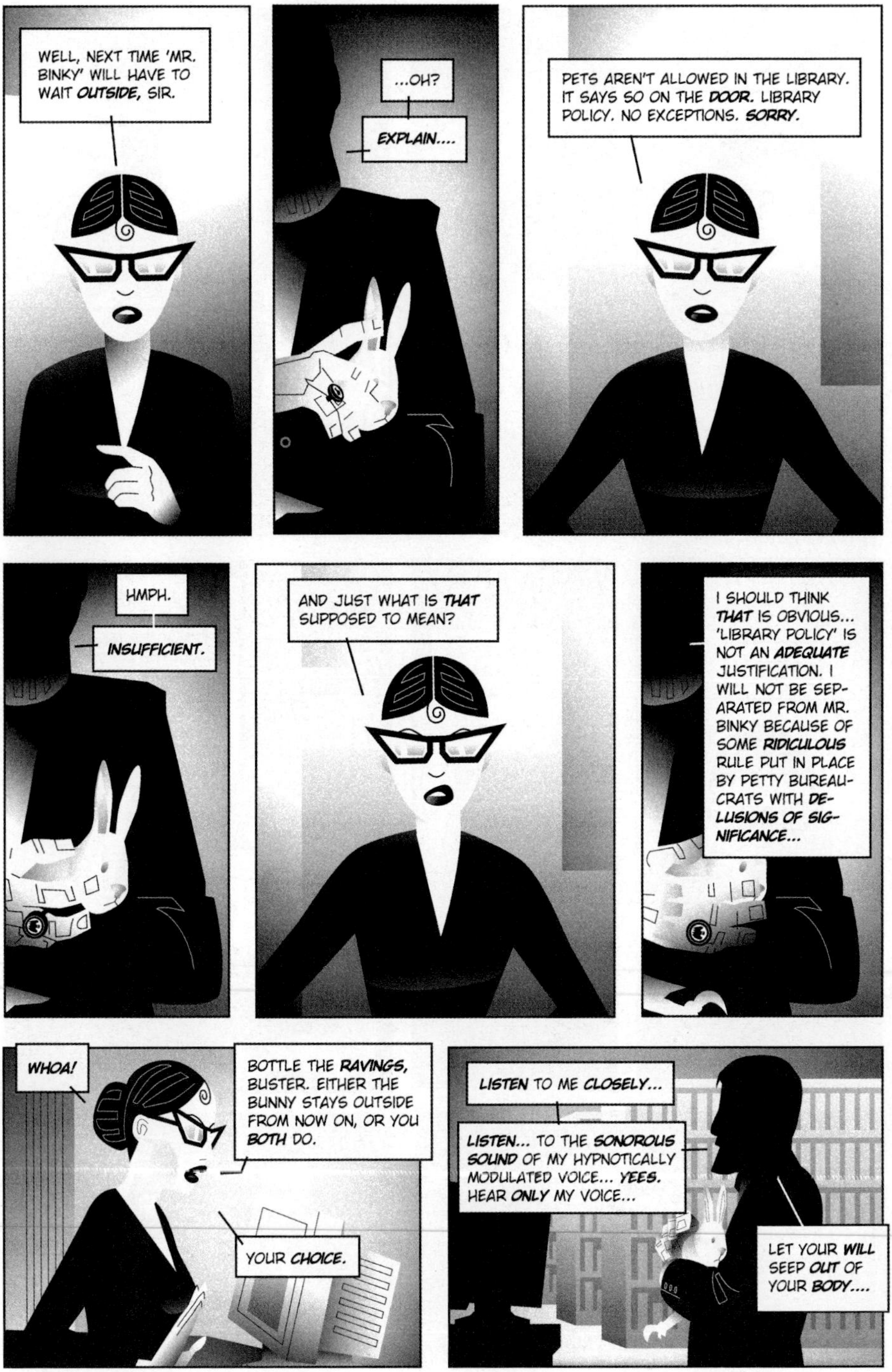
WELL, NEXT TIME 'MR. BINKY' WILL HAVE TO WAIT OUTSIDE, SIR.
...OH?
EXPLAIN....
PETS AREN'T ALLOWED IN THE LIBRARY. IT SAYS SO ON THE DOOR. LIBRARY POLICY. NO EXCEPTIONS. SORRY.
HMPH.
INSUFFICIENT.
AND JUST WHAT IS THAT SUPPOSED TO MEAN?
I SHOULD THINK THAT IS OBVIOUS... 'LIBRARY POLICY' IS NOT AN ADEQUATE JUSTIFICATION. I WILL NOT BE SEPARATED FROM MR. BINKY BECAUSE OF SOME RIDICULOUS RULE PUT IN PLACE BY PETTY BUREAUCRATS WITH DELUSIONS OF SIGNIFICANCE...
WHOA!
BOTTLE THE RAVINGS, BUSTER. EITHER THE BUNNY STAYS OUTSIDE FROM NOW ON, OR YOU BOTH DO.
YOUR CHOICE.
LISTEN TO ME CLOSELY...
LISTEN... TO THE SONOROUS SOUND OF MY HYPNOTICALLY MODULATED VOICE... YEES. HEAR ONLY MY VOICE...
LET YOUR WILL SEEP OUT OF YOUR BODY....

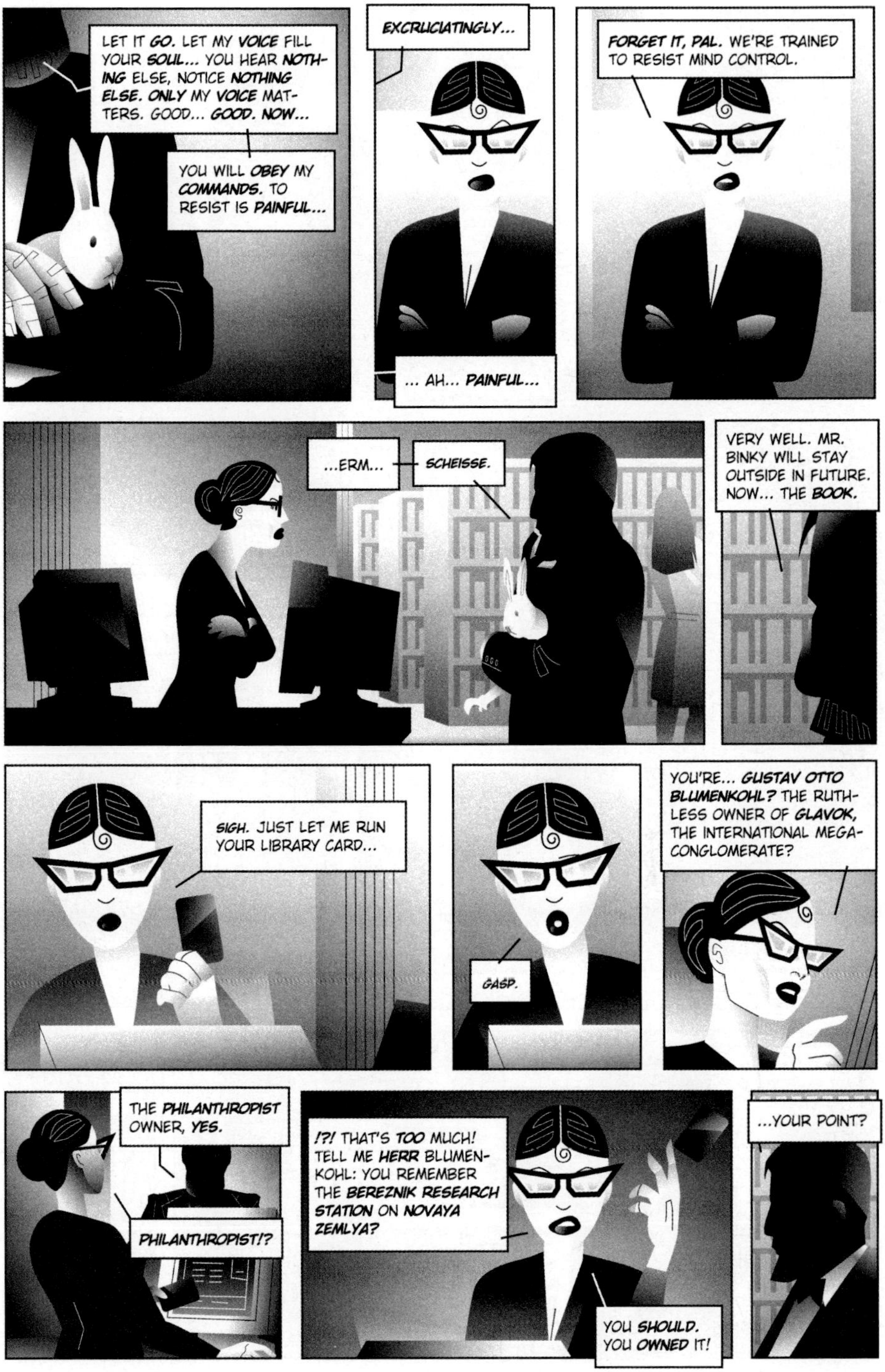
LET IT GO. LET MY VOICE FILL YOUR SOUL... YOU HEAR NOTHING ELSE, NOTICE NOTHING ELSE. ONLY MY VOICE MATTERS. GOOD... GOOD. NOW...
YOU WILL OBEY MY COMMANDS. TO RESIST IS PAINFUL...
EXCRUCIATINGLY...
... AH... PAINFUL...
FORGET IT, PAL. WE'RE TRAINED TO RESIST MIND CONTROL.
...ERM...
SCHEISSE.
VERY WELL. MR. BINKY WILL STAY OUTSIDE IN FUTURE. NOW... THE BOOK.
SIGH. JUST LET ME RUN YOUR LIBRARY CARD...
GASP.
YOU'RE... GUSTAV OTTO BLUMENKOHL? THE RUTHLESS OWNER OF GLAVOK, THE INTERNATIONAL MEGA-CONGLOMERATE?
THE PHILANTHROPIST OWNER, YES.
PHILANTHROPIST!?
!?! THAT'S TOO MUCH! TELL ME HERR BLUMENKOHL: YOU REMEMBER THE BEREZNIK RESEARCH STATION ON NOVAYA ZEMLYA?
YOU SHOULD. YOU OWNED IT!
...YOUR POINT?

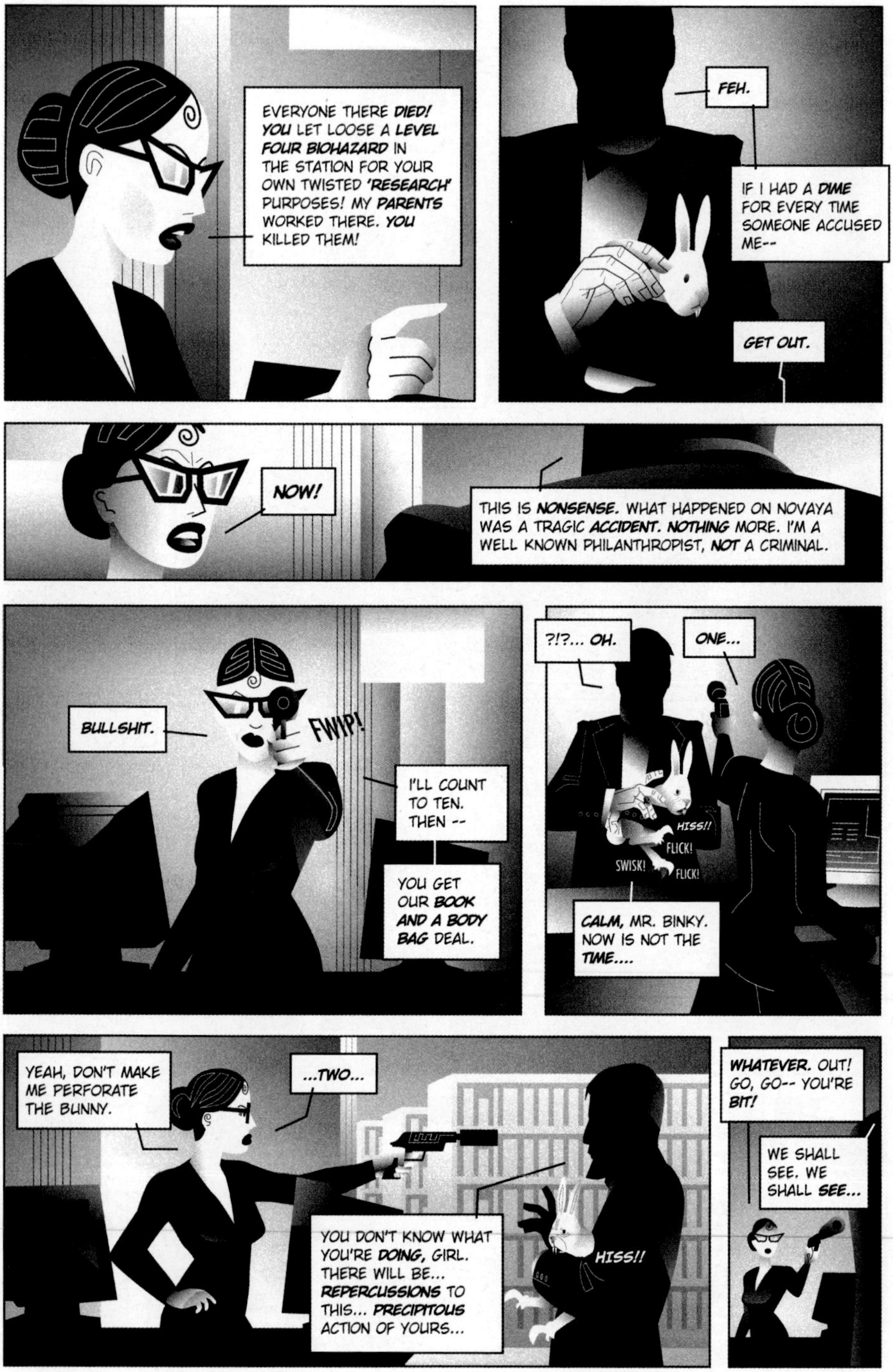
EVERYONE THERE DIED! YOU LET LOOSE A LEVEL FOUR BIOHAZARD IN THE STATION FOR YOUR OWN TWISTED 'RESEARCH' PURPOSES! MY PARENTS WORKED THERE. YOU KILLED THEM!
FEH.
IF I HAD A DIME FOR EVERY TIME SOMEONE ACCUSED ME--
GET OUT.
NOW!
THIS IS NONSENSE. WHAT HAPPENED ON NOVAYA WAS A TRAGIC ACCIDENT. NOTHING MORE. I'M A WELL KNOWN PHILANTHROPIST, NOT A CRIMINAL.
BULLSHIT.
FWIP!
I'LL COUNT TO TEN. THEN --
YOU GET OUR BOOK AND A BODY BAG DEAL.
?!?... OH.
ONE...
HISS!!
FLICK!
SWISK!
FLICK!
CALM, MR. BINKY. NOW IS NOT THE TIME....
YEAH, DON'T MAKE ME PERFORATE THE BUNNY.
...TWO...
YOU DON'T KNOW WHAT YOU'RE DOING, GIRL. THERE WILL BE... REPERCUSSIONS TO THIS... PRECIPITOUS ACTION OF YOURS...
HISS!!
WHATEVER. OUT! GO, GO-- YOU'RE BIT!
WE SHALL SEE. WE SHALL SEE...

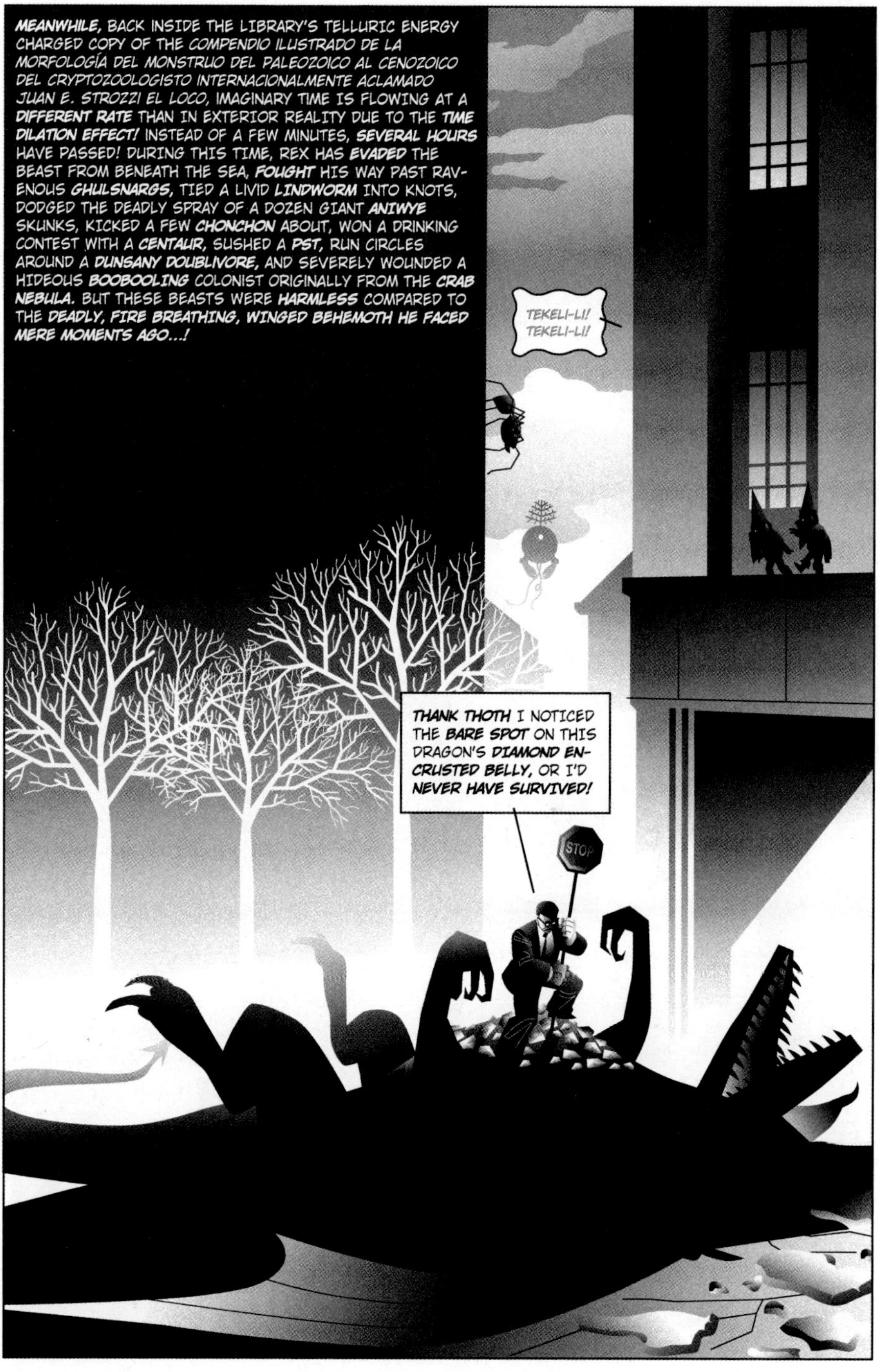
MEANWHILE, BACK INSIDE THE LIBRARY'S TELLURIC ENERGY CHARGED COPY OF THE COMPENDIO ILUSTRADO DE LA MORFOLOGÍA DEL MONSTRUO DEL PALEOZOICO AL CENOZOICO DEL CRYPTOZOOLOGISTO INTERNACIONALMENTE ACLAMADO JUAN E. STROZZI EL LOCO, IMAGINARY TIME IS FLOWING AT A DIFFERENT RATE THAN IN EXTERIOR REALITY DUE TO THE TIME DILATION EFFECT! INSTEAD OF A FEW MINUTES, SEVERAL HOURS HAVE PASSED! DURING THIS TIME, REX HAS EVADED THE BEAST FROM BENEATH THE SEA, FOUGHT HIS WAY PAST RAVENOUS GHULSNARGS, TIED A LIVID LINDWORM INTO KNOTS, DODGED THE DEADLY SPRAY OF A DOZEN GIANT ANIWYE SKUNKS, KICKED A FEW CHONCHON ABOUT, WON A DRINKING CONTEST WITH A CENTAUR, SUSHED A PST, RUN CIRCLES AROUND A DUNSANY DOUBLIVORE, AND SEVERELY WOUNDED A HIDEOUS BOOBOOLING COLONIST ORIGINALLY FROM THE CRAB NEBULA. BUT THESE BEASTS WERE HARMLESS COMPARED TO THE DEADLY, FIRE BREATHING, WINGED BEHEMOTH HE FACED MERE MOMENTS AGO...!
TEKELI-LI! TEKELI-LI!
THANK THOTH I NOTICED THE BARE SPOT ON THIS DRAGON'S DIAMOND ENCRUSTED BELLY, OR I'D NEVER HAVE SURVIVED!
STOP

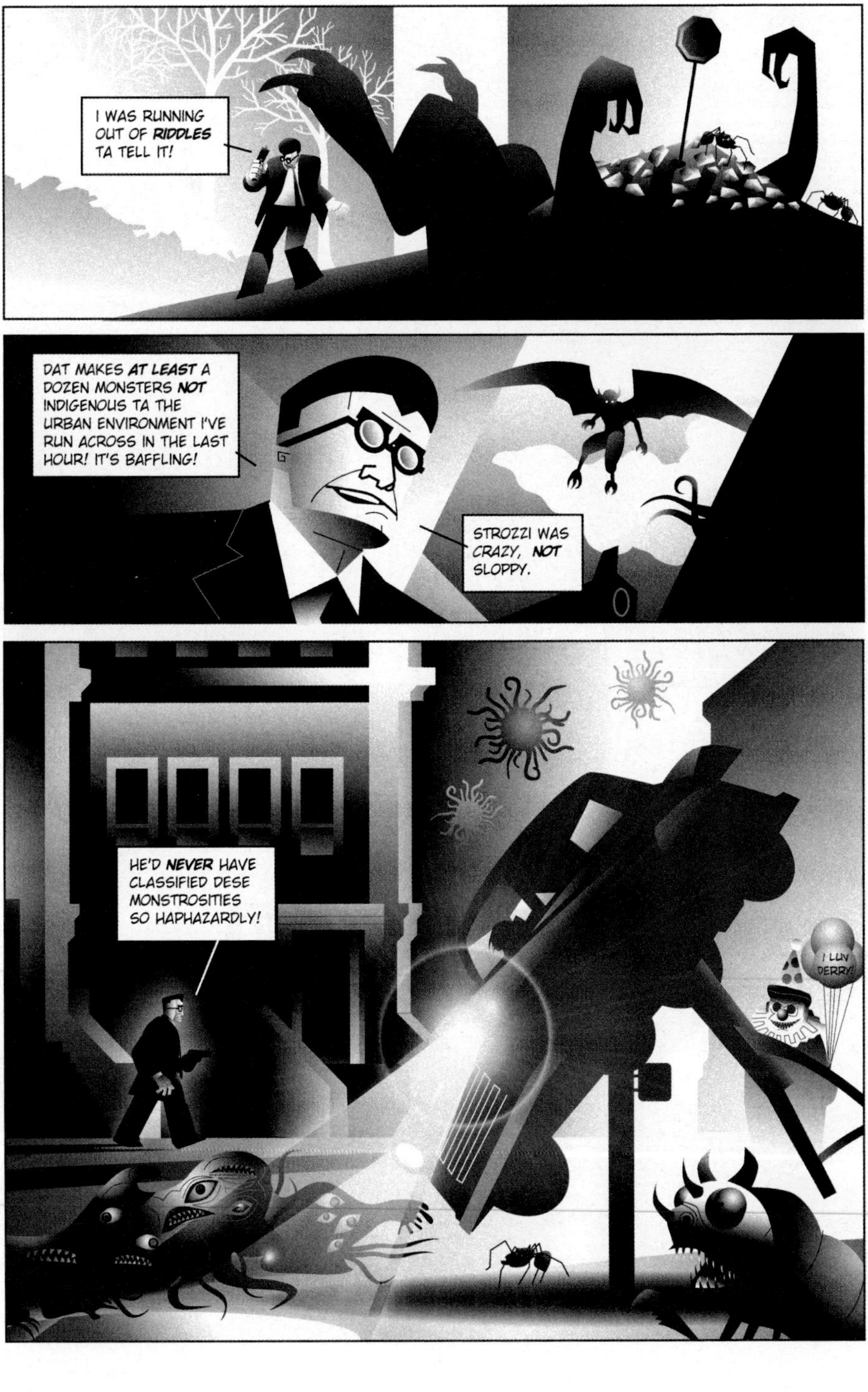
I WAS RUNNING OUT OF RIDDLES TA TELL IT!
DAT MAKES AT LEAST A DOZEN MONSTERS NOT INDIGENOUS TA THE URBAN ENVIRONMENT I'VE RUN ACROSS IN THE LAST HOUR! IT'S BAFFLING!
STROZZI WAS CRAZY, NOT SLOPPY.
HE'D NEVER HAVE CLASSIFIED DESE MONSTROSITIES SO HAPHAZARDLY!
I LUV DERRY!

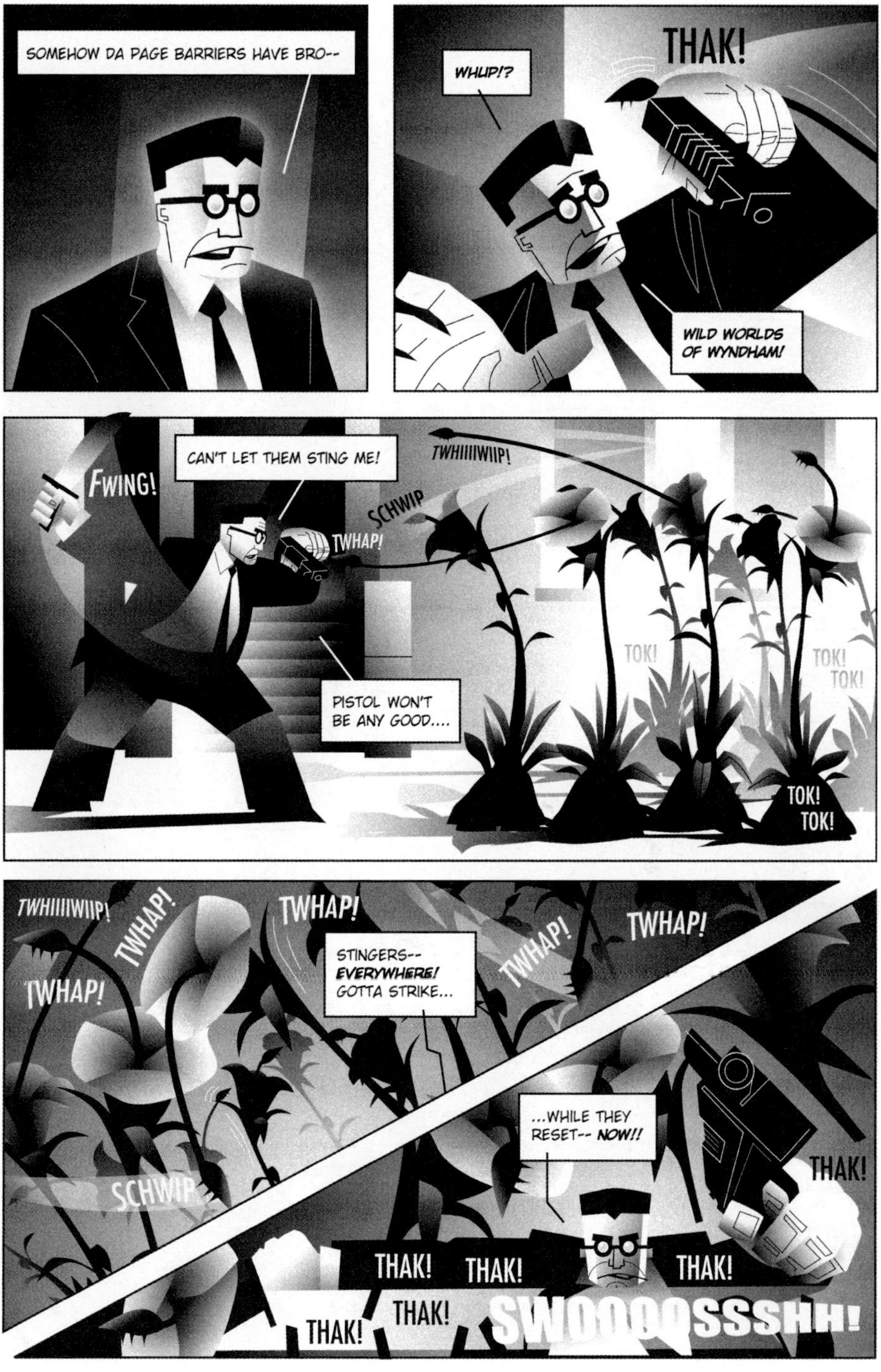
SOMEHOW DA PAGE BARRIERS HAVE BRO--
WHUP!?
THAK!
WILD WORLDS OF WYNDHAM!
CAN'T LET THEM STING ME!
FWING!
TWHIIIIWIIP!
SCHWIP
TWHAP!
PISTOL WON'T BE ANY GOOD....
TOK!
TOK! TOK!
TOK! TOK!
TWHIIIIWIIP!
TWHAP!
TWHAP!
TWHAP!
TWHAP!
TWHAP!
STINGERS-- EVERYWHERE! GOTTA STRIKE...
SCHWIP
...WHILE THEY RESET-- NOW!!
THAK!
THAK!
THAK!
THAK!
THAK!
THAK!
SWOOOOSSSHH!

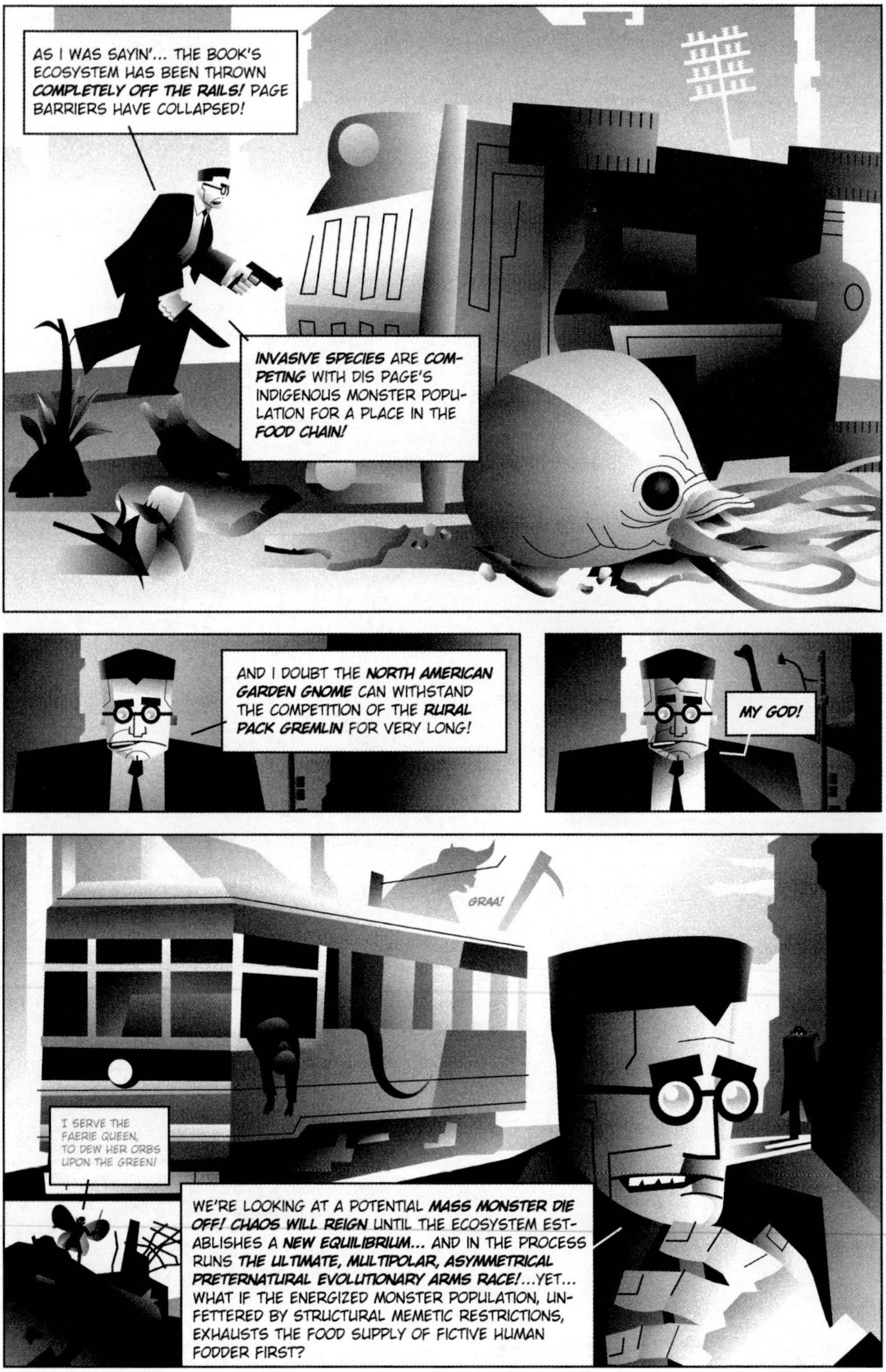
AS I WAS SAYIN'... THE BOOK'S ECOSYSTEM HAS BEEN THROWN COMPLETELY OFF THE RAILS! PAGE BARRIERS HAVE COLLAPSED!
INVASIVE SPECIES ARE COMPETING WITH DIS PAGE'S INDIGENOUS MONSTER POPULATION FOR A PLACE IN THE FOOD CHAIN!
AND I DOUBT THE NORTH AMERICAN GARDEN GNOME CAN WITHSTAND THE COMPETITION OF THE RURAL PACK GREMLIN FOR VERY LONG!
MY GOD!
GRAA!
I SERVE THE FAERIE QUEEN, TO DEW HER ORBS UPON THE GREEN!
WE'RE LOOKING AT A POTENTIAL MASS MONSTER DIE OFF! CHAOS WILL REIGN UNTIL THE ECOSYSTEM ESTABLISHES A NEW EQUILIBRIUM... AND IN THE PROCESS RUNS THE ULTIMATE, MULTIPOLAR, ASYMMETRICAL PRETERNATURAL EVOLUTIONARY ARMS RACE!...YET... WHAT IF THE ENERGIZED MONSTER POPULATION, UNFETTERED BY STRUCTURAL MEMETIC RESTRICTIONS, EXHAUSTS THE FOOD SUPPLY OF FICTIVE HUMAN FODDER FIRST?

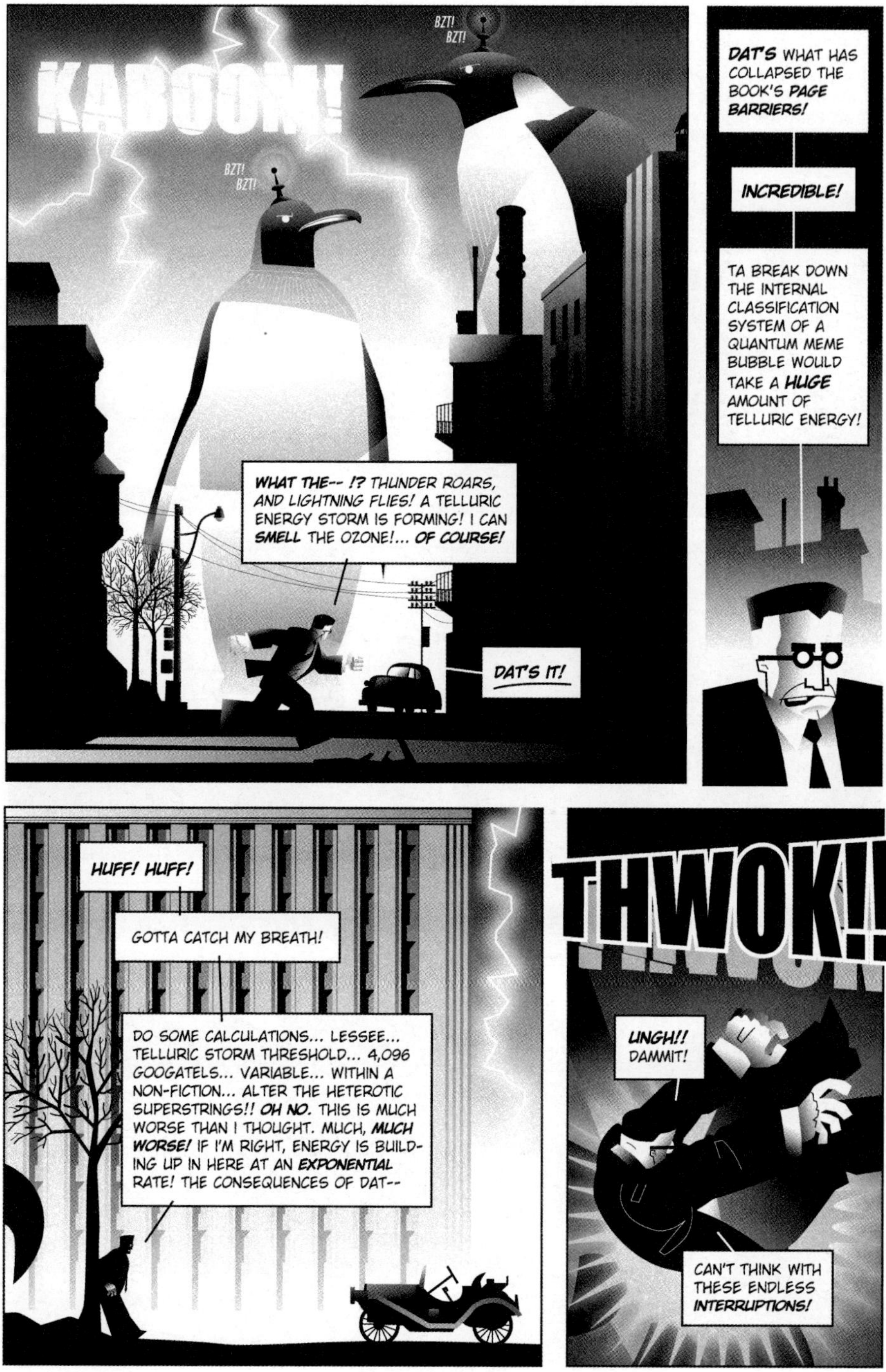
BZT! BZT!
KABOOM!
BZT! BZT!
WHAT THE-- !? THUNDER ROARS, AND LIGHTNING FLIES! A TELLURIC ENERGY STORM IS FORMING! I CAN SMELL THE OZONE!... OF COURSE!
DAT'S IT!
DAT'S WHAT HAS COLLAPSED THE BOOK'S PAGE BARRIERS!
INCREDIBLE!
TA BREAK DOWN THE INTERNAL CLASSIFICATION SYSTEM OF A QUANTUM MEME BUBBLE WOULD TAKE A HUGE AMOUNT OF TELLURIC ENERGY!
HUFF! HUFF!
GOTTA CATCH MY BREATH!
DO SOME CALCULATIONS... LESSEE... TELLURIC STORM THRESHOLD... 4,096 GOOGATELS... VARIABLE... WITHIN A NON-FICTION... ALTER THE HETEROTIC SUPERSTRINGS!! OH NO. THIS IS MUCH WORSE THAN I THOUGHT. MUCH, MUCH WORSE! IF I'M RIGHT, ENERGY IS BUILDING UP IN HERE AT AN EXPONENTIAL RATE! THE CONSEQUENCES OF DAT--
THWOK!!
UNGH!! DAMMIT!
CAN'T THINK WITH THESE ENDLESS INTERRUPTIONS!

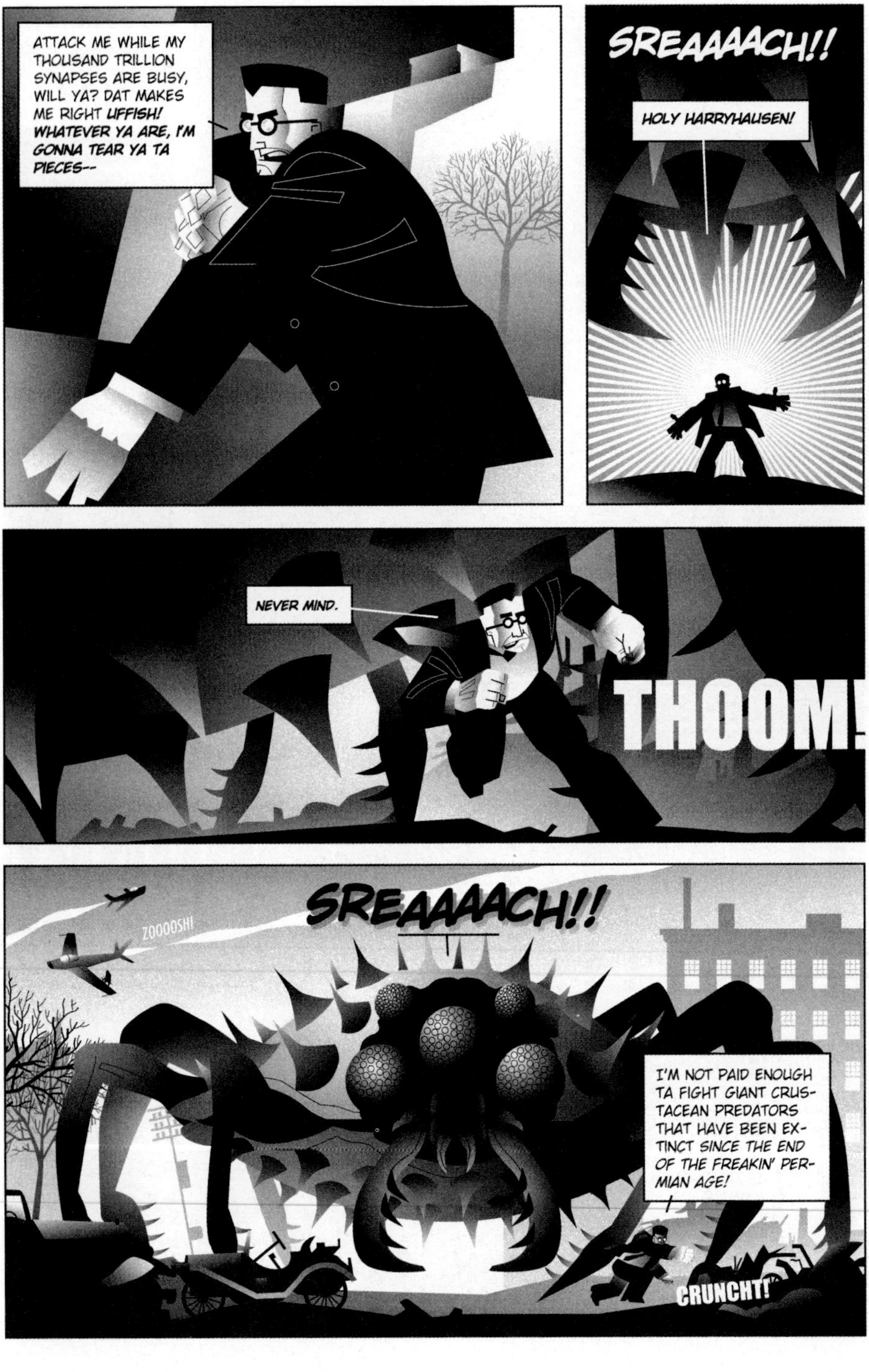
ATTACK ME WHILE MY THOUSAND TRILLION SYNAPSES ARE BUSY, WILL YA? DAT MAKES ME RIGHT UFFISH! WHATEVER YA ARE, I'M GONNA TEAR YA TA PIECES--
SREAAAACH!!
HOLY HARRYHAUSEN!
NEVER MIND.
THOOM!
SREAAAACH!!
ZOOOOSH!
I'M NOT PAID ENOUGH TA FIGHT GIANT CRUSTACEAN PREDATORS THAT HAVE BEEN EXTINCT SINCE THE END OF THE FREAKIN' PERMIAN AGE!
CRUNCHT!

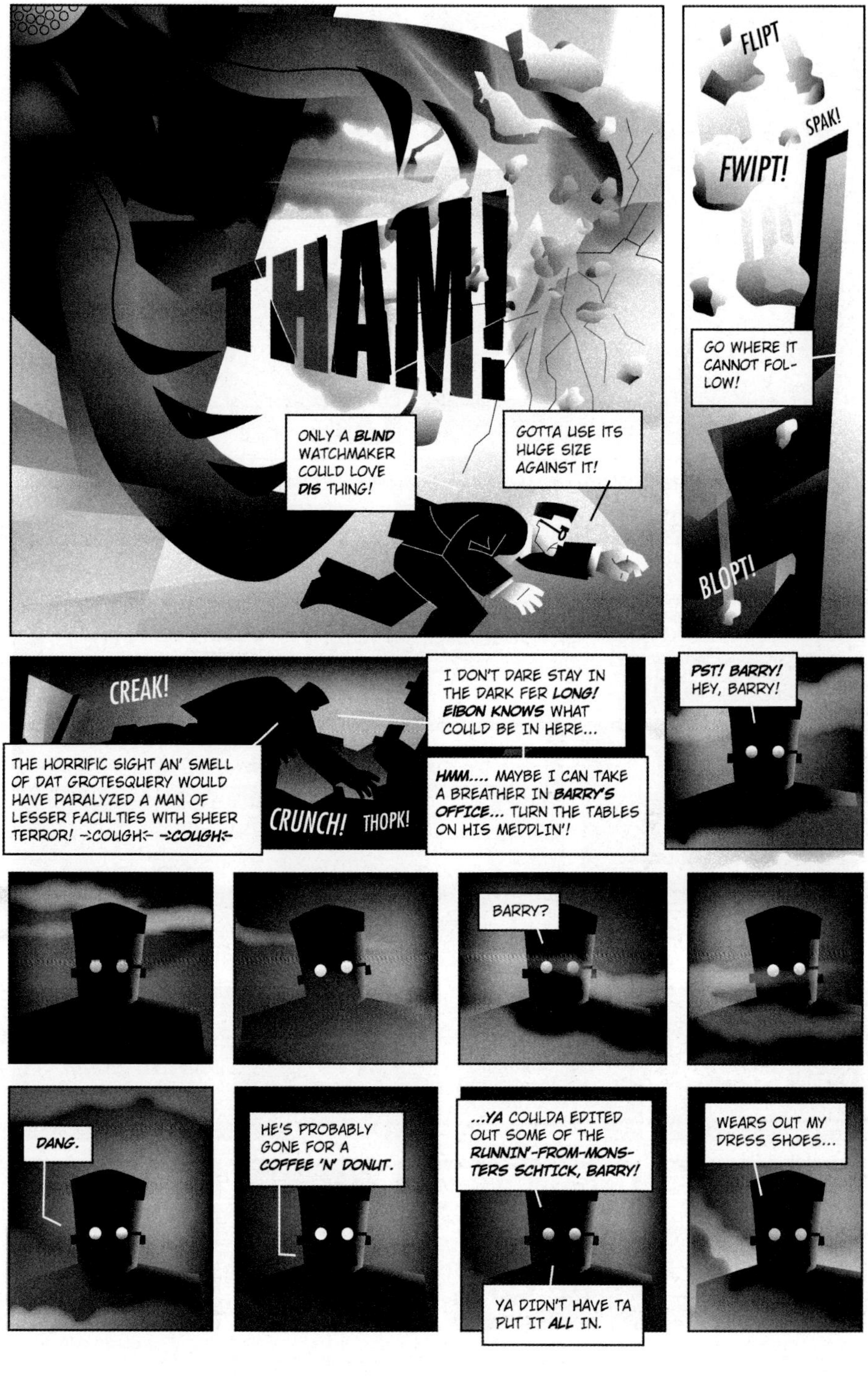
THAM!
ONLY A BLIND WATCHMAKER COULD LOVE DIS THING!
GOTTA USE ITS HUGE SIZE AGAINST IT!
FLIPT
SPAK!
FWIPT!
GO WHERE IT CANNOT FOL-LOW!
BLOPT!
CREAK!
THE HORRIFIC SIGHT AN' SMELL OF DAT GROTESQUERY WOULD HAVE PARALYZED A MAN OF LESSER FACULTIES WITH SHEER TERROR! →COUGH← →COUGH←
CRUNCH! THOPK!
I DON'T DARE STAY IN THE DARK FER LONG! EIBON KNOWS WHAT COULD BE IN HERE...
HMM.... MAYBE I CAN TAKE A BREATHER IN BARRY'S OFFICE... TURN THE TABLES ON HIS MEDDLIN'!
PST! BARRY! HEY, BARRY!
BARRY?
DANG.
HE'S PROBABLY GONE FOR A COFFEE 'N' DONUT.
...YA COULDA EDITED OUT SOME OF THE RUNNIN'-FROM-MONS-TERS SCHTICK, BARRY!
YA DIDN'T HAVE TA PUT IT ALL IN.
WEARS OUT MY DRESS SHOES...

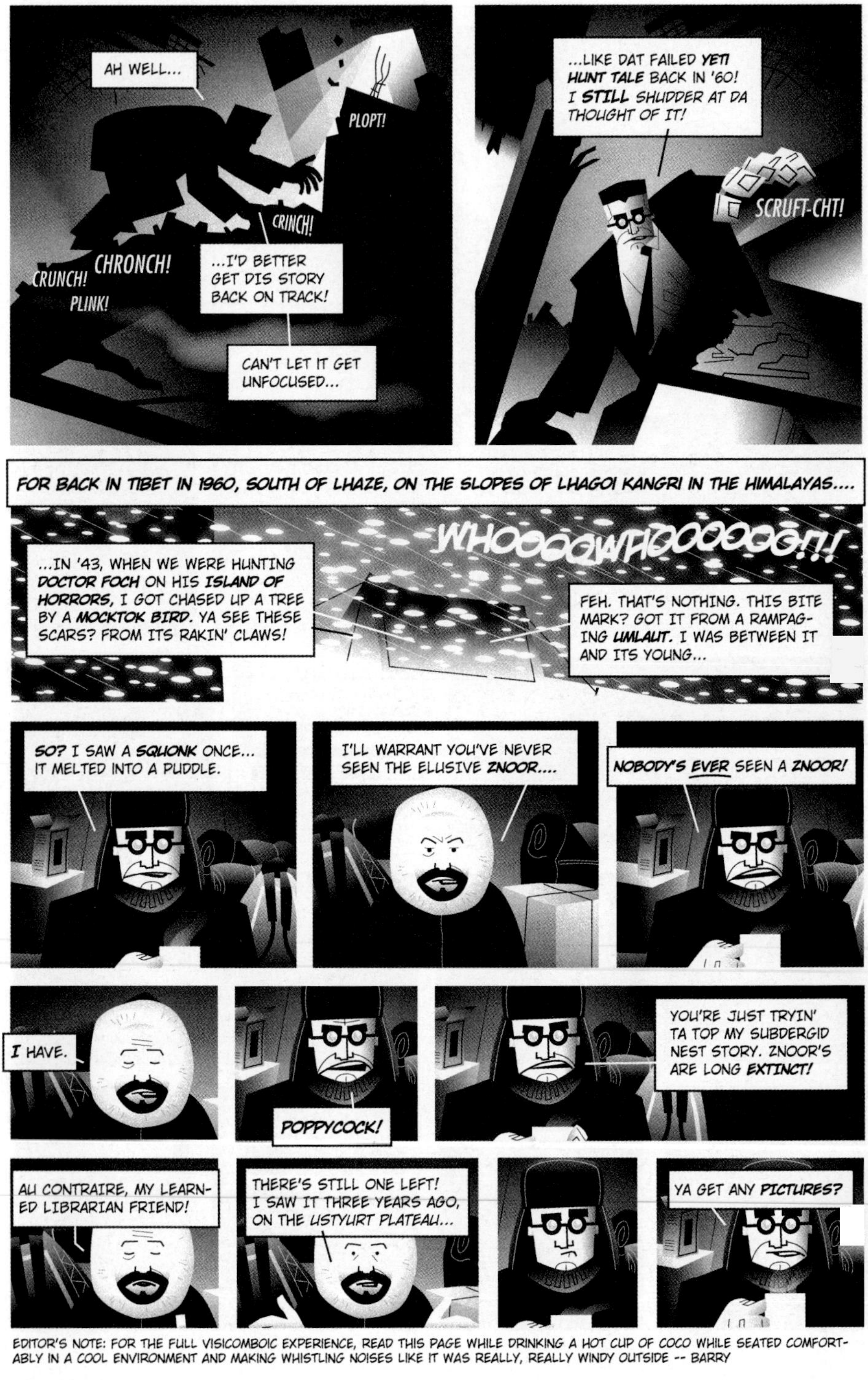

AH WELL...
PLOPT!
CRINCH!
CHRONCH!
CRUNCH!
PLINK!
...I'D BETTER GET DIS STORY BACK ON TRACK!
CAN'T LET IT GET UNFOCUSED...
...LIKE DAT FAILED YETI HUNT TALE BACK IN '60! I STILL SHUDDER AT DA THOUGHT OF IT!
SCRUFT-CHT!
FOR BACK IN TIBET IN 1960, SOUTH OF LHAZE, ON THE SLOPES OF LHAGOI KANGRI IN THE HIMALAYAS....
WHOOOOWHOOOOOOO!!!
...IN '43, WHEN WE WERE HUNTING DOCTOR FOCH ON HIS ISLAND OF HORRORS, I GOT CHASED UP A TREE BY A MOCKTOK BIRD. YA SEE THESE SCARS? FROM ITS RAKIN' CLAWS!
FEH. THAT'S NOTHING. THIS BITE MARK? GOT IT FROM A RAMPAGING UMLAUT. I WAS BETWEEN IT AND ITS YOUNG...
SO? I SAW A SQUONK ONCE... IT MELTED INTO A PUDDLE.
I'LL WARRANT YOU'VE NEVER SEEN THE ELUSIVE ZNOOR....
NOBODY'S EVER SEEN A ZNOOR!
I HAVE.
POPPYCOCK!
YOU'RE JUST TRYIN' TA TOP MY SUBDERGID NEST STORY. ZNOOR'S ARE LONG EXTINCT!
AU CONTRAIRE, MY LEARNED LIBRARIAN FRIEND!
THERE'S STILL ONE LEFT! I SAW IT THREE YEARS AGO, ON THE USTYURT PLATEAU...
YA GET ANY PICTURES?

EDITOR'S NOTE: FOR THE FULL VISICOMBOIC EXPERIENCE, READ THIS PAGE WHILE DRINKING A HOT CUP OF COCO WHILE SEATED COMFORTABLY IN A COOL ENVIRONMENT AND MAKING WHISTLING NOISES LIKE IT WAS REALLY, REALLY WINDY OUTSIDE -- BARRY

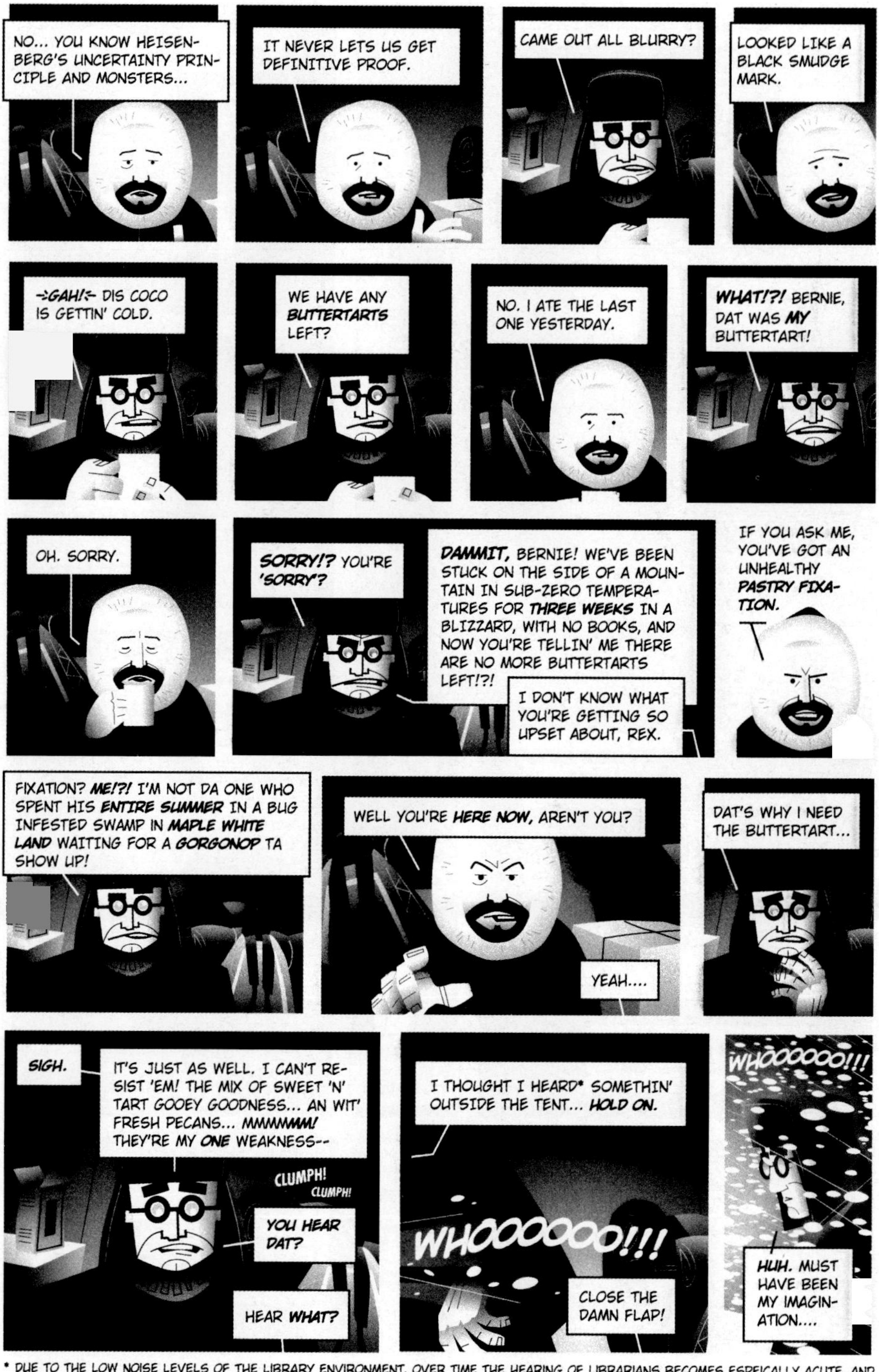
NO... YOU KNOW HEISEN-BERG'S UNCERTAINTY PRIN-CIPLE AND MONSTERS...
IT NEVER LETS US GET DEFINITIVE PROOF.
CAME OUT ALL BLURRY?
LOOKED LIKE A BLACK SMUDGE MARK.
-GAH!- DIS COCO IS GETTIN' COLD.
WE HAVE ANY BUTTERTARTS LEFT?
NO. I ATE THE LAST ONE YESTERDAY.
WHAT!?! BERNIE, DAT WAS MY BUTTERTART!
OH. SORRY.
SORRY!? YOU'RE 'SORRY'?
DAMMIT, BERNIE! WE'VE BEEN STUCK ON THE SIDE OF A MOUN-TAIN IN SUB-ZERO TEMPERA-TURES FOR THREE WEEKS IN A BLIZZARD, WITH NO BOOKS, AND NOW YOU'RE TELLIN' ME THERE ARE NO MORE BUTTERTARTS LEFT!?!
I DON'T KNOW WHAT YOU'RE GETTING SO UPSET ABOUT, REX.
IF YOU ASK ME, YOU'VE GOT AN UNHEALTHY PASTRY FIXA-TION.
FIXATION? ME!?! I'M NOT DA ONE WHO SPENT HIS ENTIRE SUMMER IN A BUG INFESTED SWAMP IN MAPLE WHITE LAND WAITING FOR A GORGONOP TA SHOW UP!
WELL YOU'RE HERE NOW, AREN'T YOU?
YEAH....
DAT'S WHY I NEED THE BUTTERTART...
SIGH.
IT'S JUST AS WELL. I CAN'T RE-SIST 'EM! THE MIX OF SWEET 'N' TART GOOEY GOODNESS... AN WIT' FRESH PECANS... MMMMMM! THEY'RE MY ONE WEAKNESS--
CLUMPH!
CLUMPH!
YOU HEAR DAT?
HEAR WHAT?
I THOUGHT I HEARD* SOMETHIN' OUTSIDE THE TENT... HOLD ON.
WHOOOOOOO!!!
CLOSE THE DAMN FLAP!
WHOOOOOO!!!
HUH. MUST HAVE BEEN MY IMAGIN-ATION....

* DUE TO THE LOW NOISE LEVELS OF THE LIBRARY ENVIRONMENT, OVER TIME THE HEARING OF LIBRARIANS BECOMES ESPEICALLY ACUTE, AND THEY ARE ABLE TO DETECT FAINT NOISES INAUDIBLE TO ORDINARY MORTALS. -- BARRY

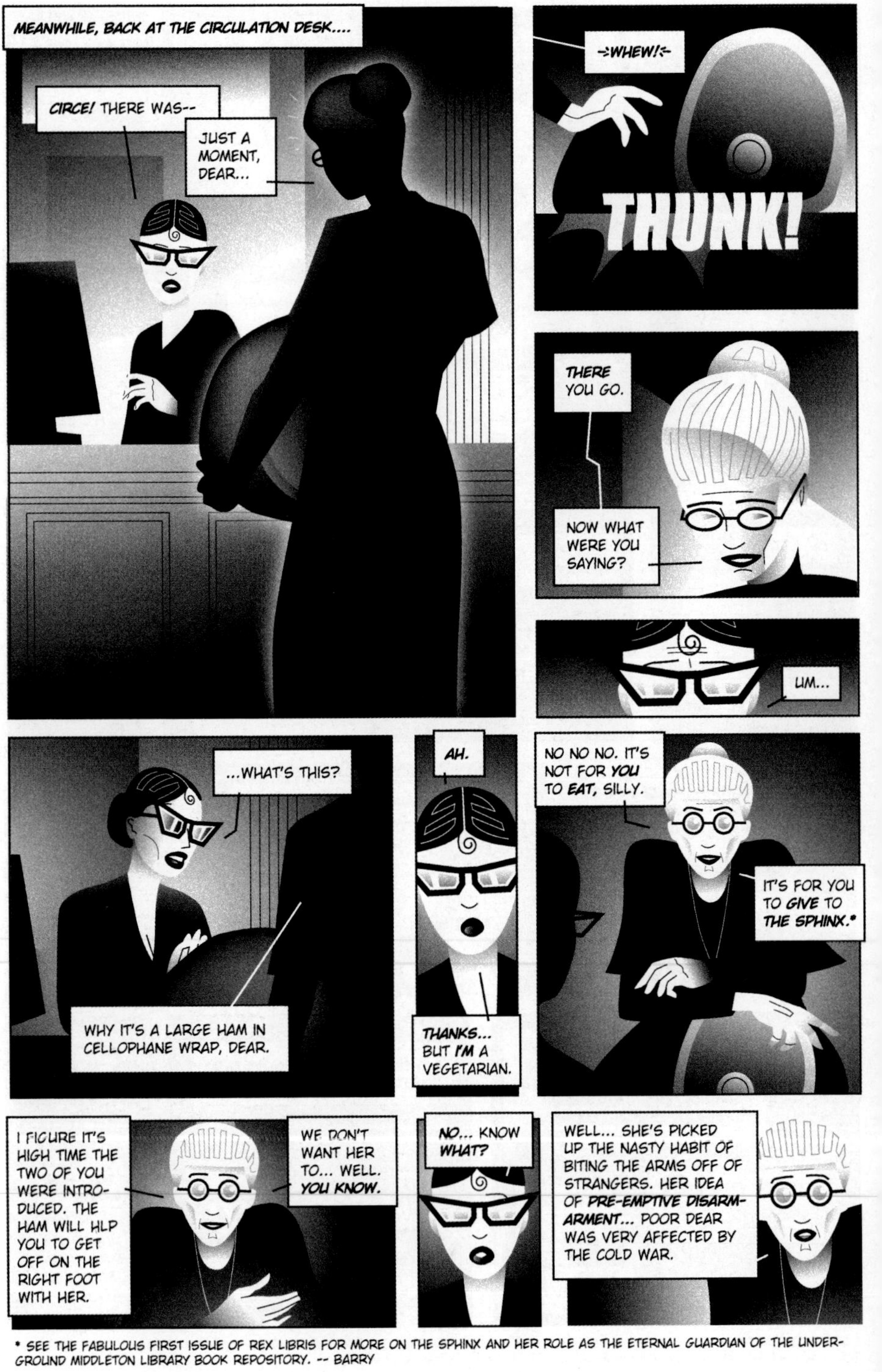
MEANWHILE, BACK AT THE CIRCULATION DESK....
CIRCE! THERE WAS--
JUST A MOMENT, DEAR...
-WHEW!-
THUNK!
THERE YOU GO.
NOW WHAT WERE YOU SAYING?
UM...
...WHAT'S THIS?
WHY IT'S A LARGE HAM IN CELLOPHANE WRAP, DEAR.
AH.
THANKS... BUT I'M A VEGETARIAN.
NO NO NO. IT'S NOT FOR YOU TO EAT, SILLY.
IT'S FOR YOU TO GIVE TO THE SPHINX.*
I FIGURE IT'S HIGH TIME THE TWO OF YOU WERE INTRO-DUCED. THE HAM WILL HLP YOU TO GET OFF ON THE RIGHT FOOT WITH HER.
WE DON'T WANT HER TO... WELL. YOU KNOW.
NO... KNOW WHAT?
WELL... SHE'S PICKED UP THE NASTY HABIT OF BITING THE ARMS OFF OF STRANGERS. HER IDEA OF PRE-EMPTIVE DISARM-ARMENT... POOR DEAR WAS VERY AFFECTED BY THE COLD WAR.

* SEE THE FABULOUS FIRST ISSUE OF REX LIBRIS FOR MORE ON THE SPHINX AND HER ROLE AS THE ETERNAL GUARDIAN OF THE UNDER-GROUND MIDDLETON LIBRARY BOOK REPOSITORY. -- BARRY

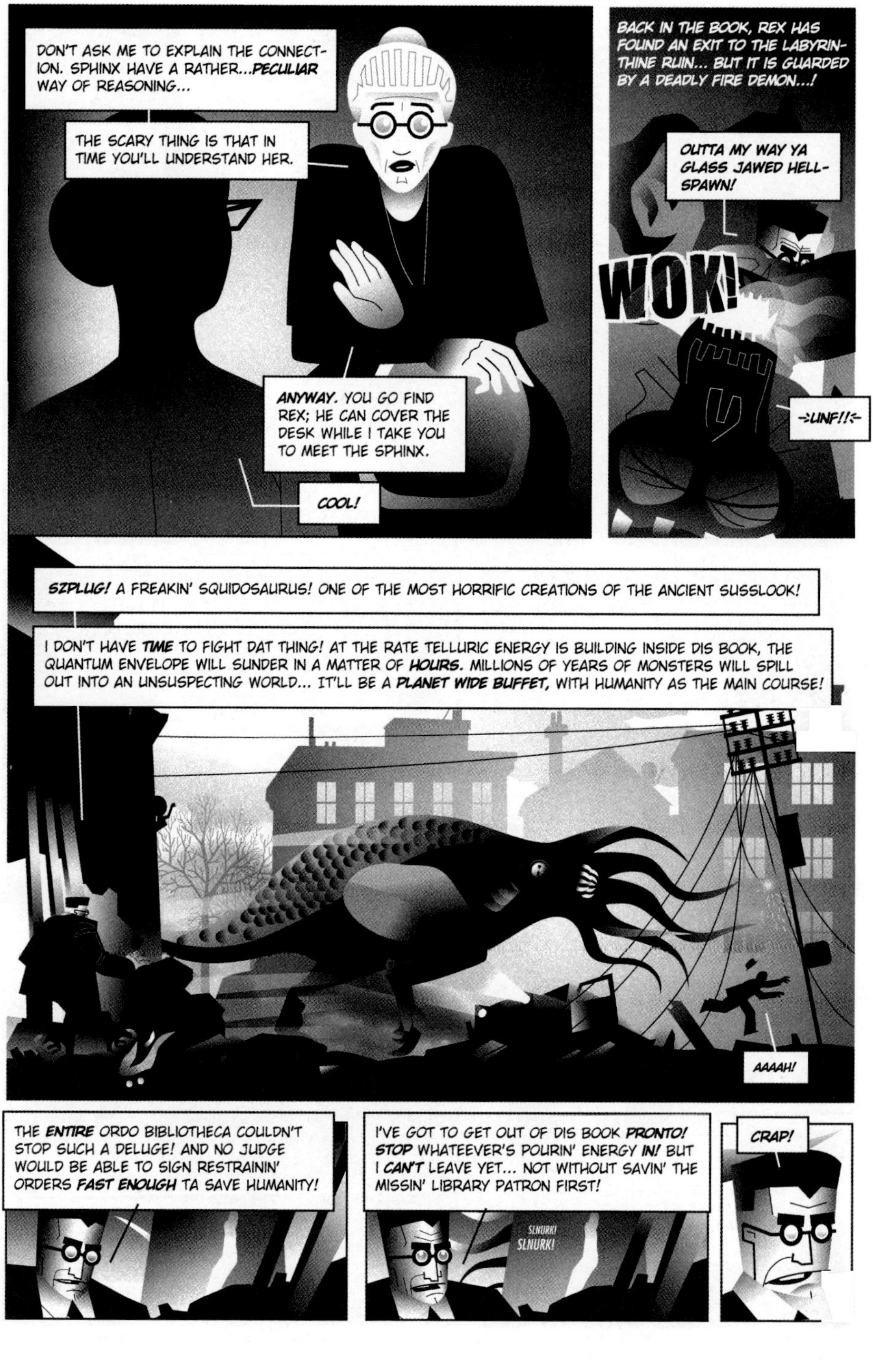
DON'T ASK ME TO EXPLAIN THE CONNECT-ION. SPHINX HAVE A RATHER...PECULIAR WAY OF REASONING...
THE SCARY THING IS THAT IN TIME YOU'LL UNDERSTAND HER.
ANYWAY. YOU GO FIND REX; HE CAN COVER THE DESK WHILE I TAKE YOU TO MEET THE SPHINX.
COOL!
BACK IN THE BOOK, REX HAS FOUND AN EXIT TO THE LABYRINTHINE RUIN... BUT IT IS GUARDED BY A DEADLY FIRE DEMON...!
OUTTA MY WAY YA GLASS JAWED HELL-SPAWN!
WOK!
UNF!!
SZPLUG! A FREAKIN' SQUIDOSAURUS! ONE OF THE MOST HORRIFIC CREATIONS OF THE ANCIENT SUSSLOOK!
I DON'T HAVE TIME TO FIGHT DAT THING! AT THE RATE TELLURIC ENERGY IS BUILDING INSIDE DIS BOOK, THE QUANTUM ENVELOPE WILL SUNDER IN A MATTER OF HOURS. MILLIONS OF YEARS OF MONSTERS WILL SPILL OUT INTO AN UNSUSPECTING WORLD... IT'LL BE A PLANET WIDE BUFFET, WITH HUMANITY AS THE MAIN COURSE!
AAAAH!
THE ENTIRE ORDO BIBLIOTHECA COULDN'T STOP SUCH A DELUGE! AND NO JUDGE WOULD BE ABLE TO SIGN RESTRAININ' ORDERS FAST ENOUGH TA SAVE HUMANITY!
I'VE GOT TO GET OUT OF DIS BOOK PRONTO! STOP WHATEEVER'S POURIN' ENERGY IN! BUT I CAN'T LEAVE YET... NOT WITHOUT SAVIN' THE MISSIN' LIBRARY PATRON FIRST!
SLNURK!
SLNURK!
CRAP!

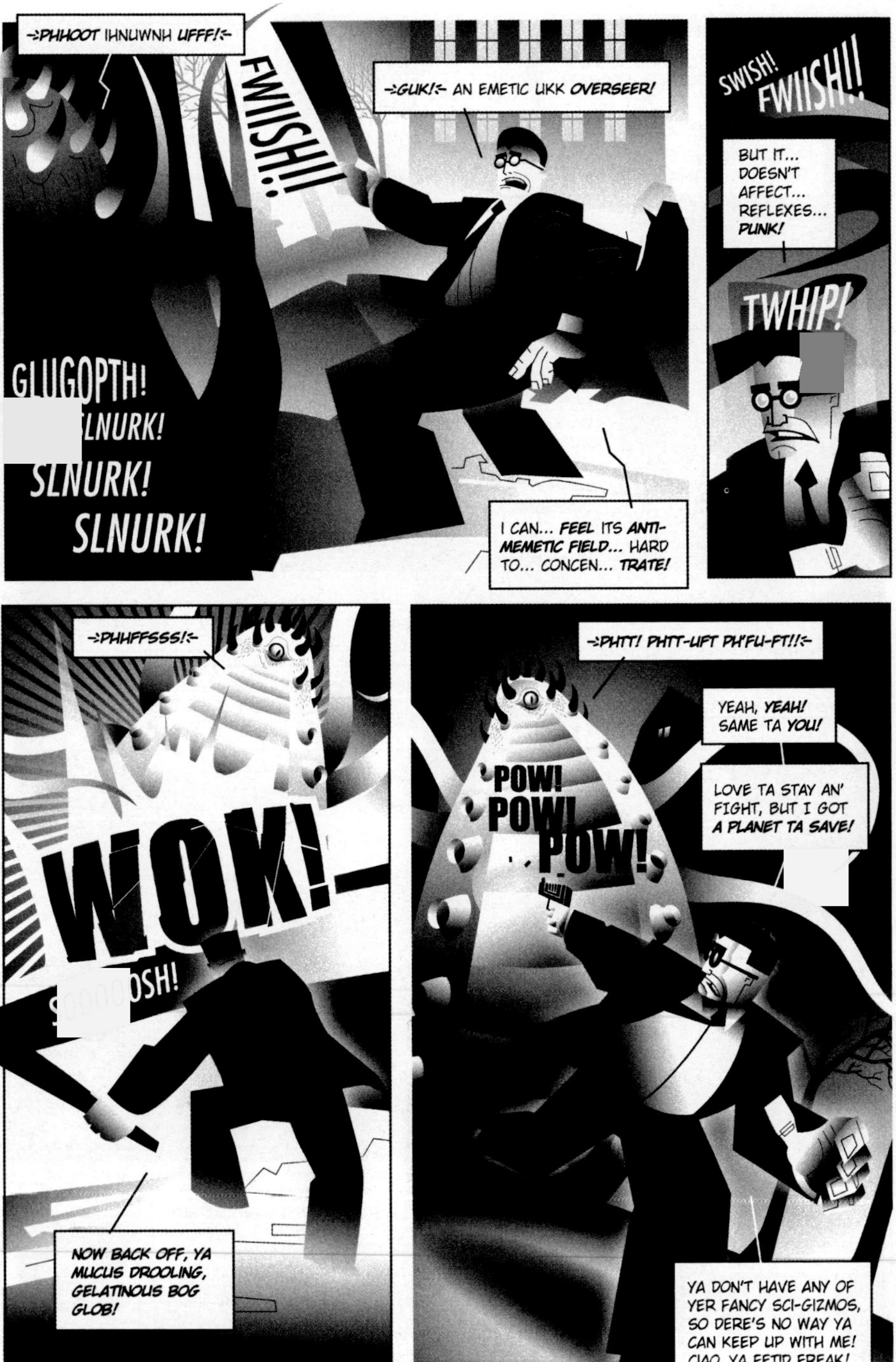

PHHOOT IHNUWNH UFFF!
FWIISH!!
GUK! AN EMETIC UKK OVERSEER!
GLUGOPTH!
SLNURK!
SLNURK!
I CAN... FEEL ITS ANTI-MEMETIC FIELD... HARD TO... CONCEN... TRATE!
SWISH! FWIISH!!
BUT IT... DOESN'T AFFECT... REFLEXES... PUNK!
TWHIP!
PHHFFSSS!
WOK!
NOW BACK OFF, YA MUCUS DROOLING, GELATINOUS BOG GLOB!
PHTT! PHTT-UFT PH'FU-FT!!
POW! POW! POW!
YEAH, YEAH! SAME TA YOU!
LOVE TA STAY AN' FIGHT, BUT I GOT A PLANET TA SAVE!
YA DON'T HAVE ANY OF YER FANCY SCI-GIZMOS, SO DERE'S NO WAY YA CAN KEEP UP WITH ME! CIAO, YA FETID FREAK!

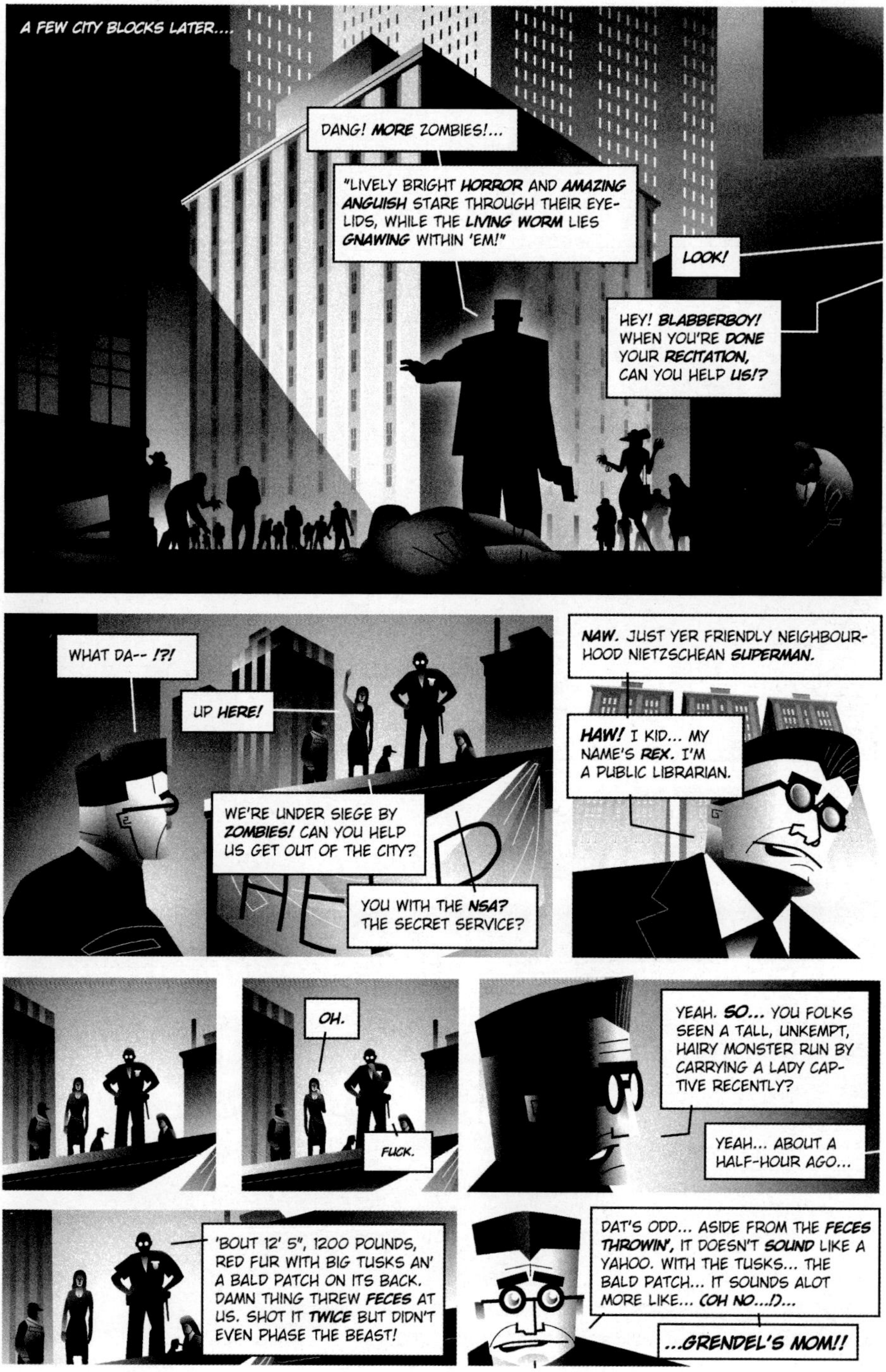
A FEW CITY BLOCKS LATER....
DANG! MORE ZOMBIES!...
"LIVELY BRIGHT HORROR AND AMAZING ANGUISH STARE THROUGH THEIR EYE-LIDS, WHILE THE LIVING WORM LIES GNAWING WITHIN 'EM!"
LOOK!
HEY! BLABBERBOY! WHEN YOU'RE DONE YOUR RECITATION, CAN YOU HELP US!?
WHAT DA-- !?!
UP HERE!
WE'RE UNDER SIEGE BY ZOMBIES! CAN YOU HELP US GET OUT OF THE CITY?
YOU WITH THE NSA? THE SECRET SERVICE?
NAW. JUST YER FRIENDLY NEIGHBOUR-HOOD NIETZSCHEAN SUPERMAN.
HAW! I KID... MY NAME'S REX. I'M A PUBLIC LIBRARIAN.
OH.
FUCK.
YEAH. SO... YOU FOLKS SEEN A TALL, UNKEMPT, HAIRY MONSTER RUN BY CARRYING A LADY CAP-TIVE RECENTLY?
YEAH... ABOUT A HALF-HOUR AGO...
'BOUT 12' 5", 1200 POUNDS, RED FUR WITH BIG TUSKS AN' A BALD PATCH ON ITS BACK. DAMN THING THREW FECES AT US. SHOT IT TWICE BUT DIDN'T EVEN PHASE THE BEAST!
DAT'S ODD... ASIDE FROM THE FECES THROWIN', IT DOESN'T SOUND LIKE A YAHOO. WITH THE TUSKS... THE BALD PATCH... IT SOUNDS ALOT MORE LIKE... (OH NO...!)...
...GRENDEL'S MOM!!

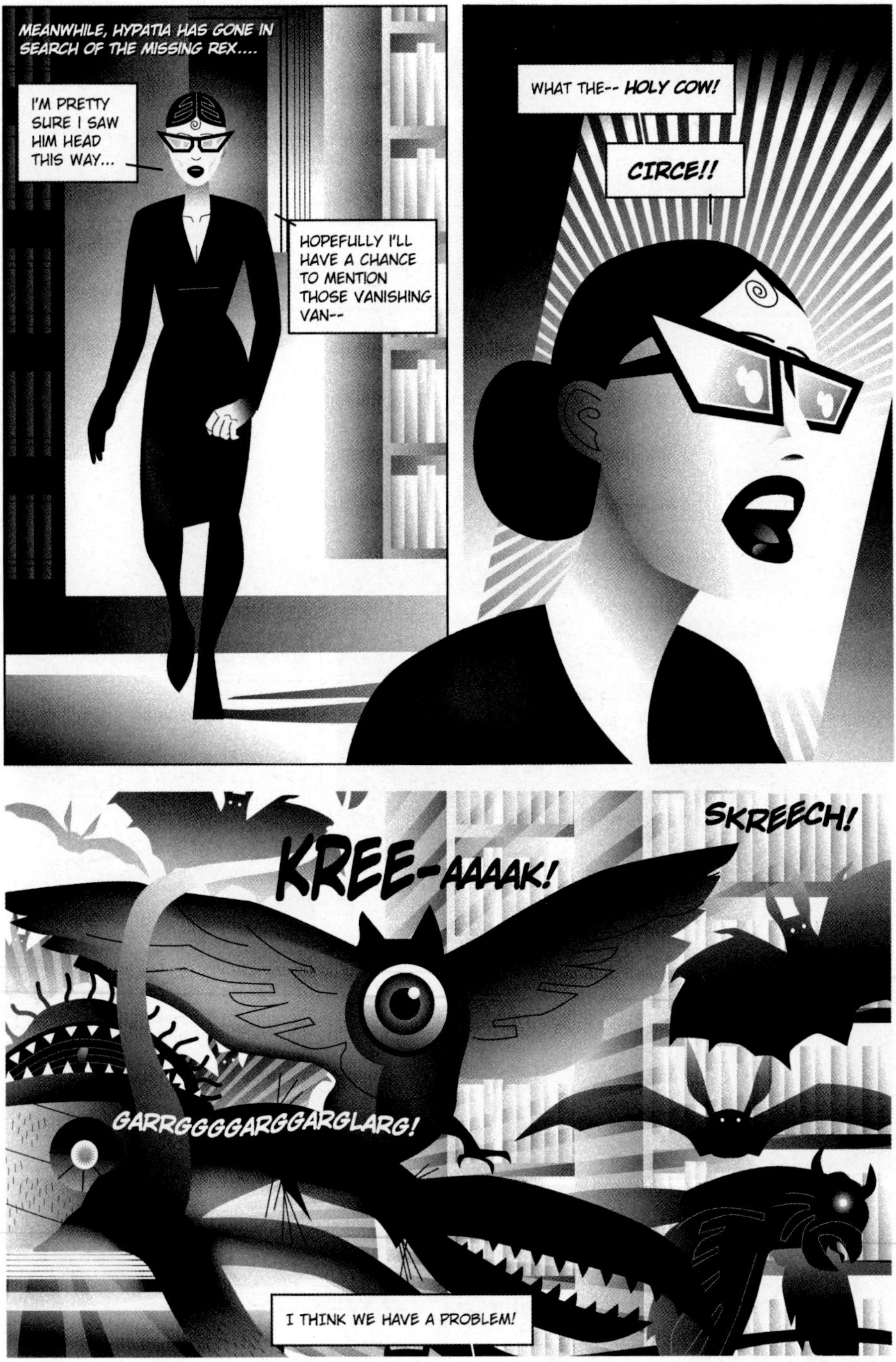
MEANWHILE, HYPATIA HAS GONE IN SEARCH OF THE MISSING REX....
I'M PRETTY SURE I SAW HIM HEAD THIS WAY...
HOPEFULLY I'LL HAVE A CHANCE TO MENTION THOSE VANISHING VAN--
WHAT THE-- HOLY COW!
CIRCE!!
KREE-AAAAK!
SKREECH!
GARRGGGGARGGARGLARG!
I THINK WE HAVE A PROBLEM!

CHAPTER EIGHT

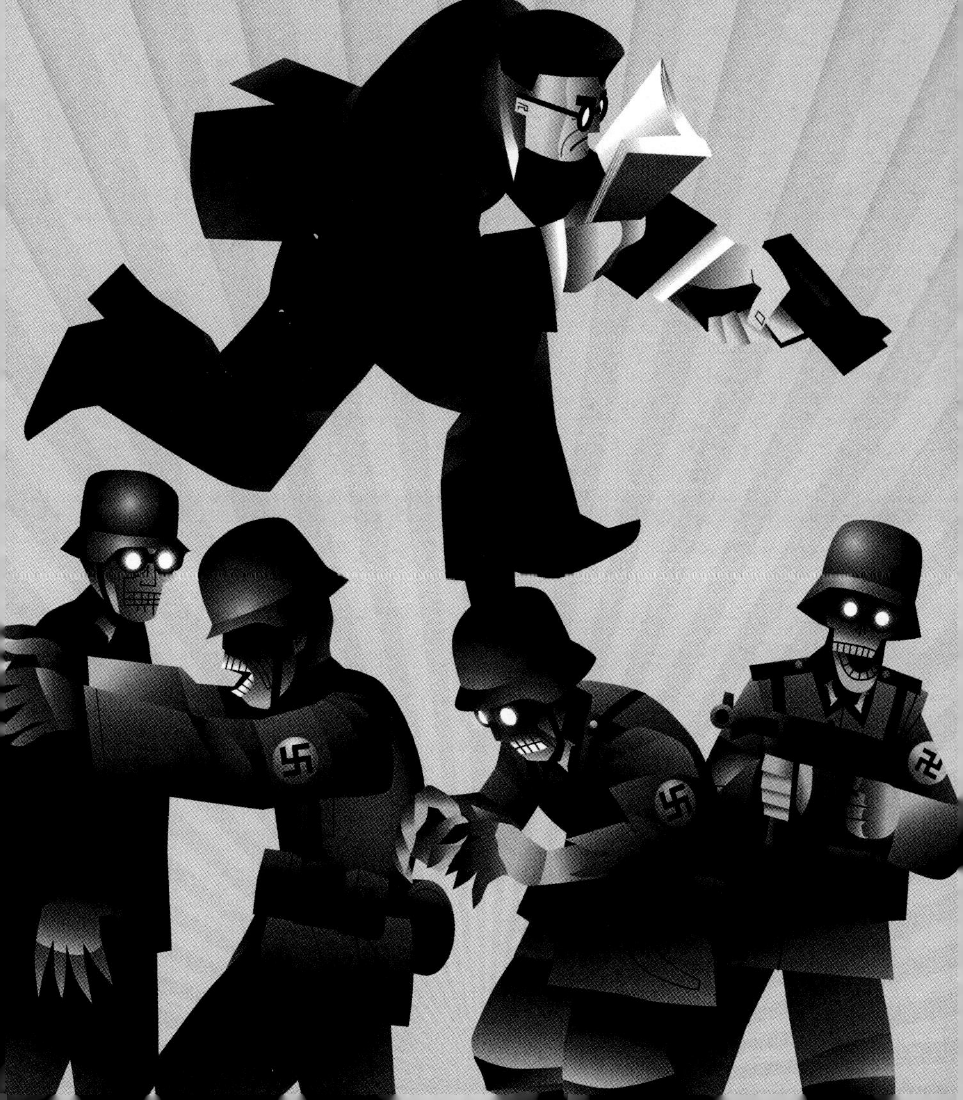

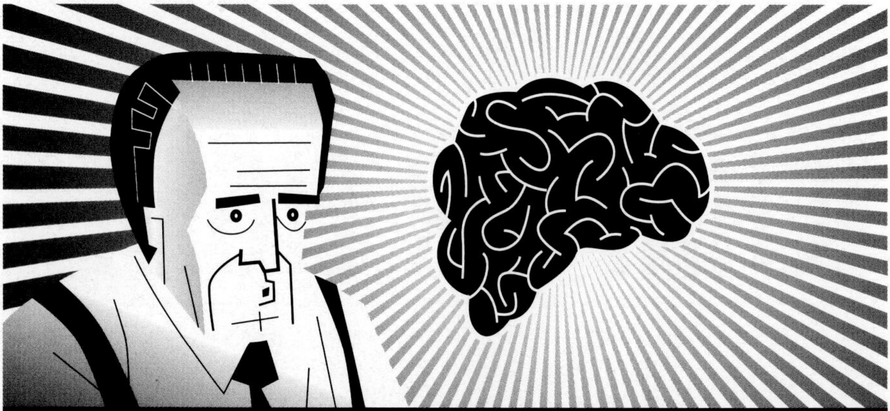

BARRY'S BRAIN

This is it, dear readers! The all-action beer and pretzel (or popcorn and pop) issue! Meaningless mayhem from cover to cover! It's so jam packed with thrilling fight scenes, we recommend that you don't read it if you have a weak heart, for the unrelenting pulse pounding excitement of crack librarians in action could be too much for your ticker!

Indeed, this issue almost did in our staff *artiste,* **Juame the Magnificient**, for he is not by nature a heroic action renderer. Yet we threw at him more action than we felt a comic could possibly contain (thanks to the miracle of Advanced Visicomboics, it can!), and he (albeit with the extensive employment of curses and thrown objects) survived! Incredible! Just don't look at the anatomy too closely. And we had to promise him that next issue would be a conversation between two talking heads to get him to finish, but such promises are easily broken, if not forgotten.

Now, on to the nuances of the peerless **Maximum Mayhem**™ issue. There are some who may say that the underlying logic of the issue is rather weak. Well. We all know the answer to that question, don't we my friends? Who needs plot when you're kicking the putrifying butt of blood-boltered, mindlessly anthropophaginian zombies? Plot is not by nature an element of **Maximum Mayhem**™. Besides, we had to eliminate *something* to fit so many monsters in. Blame Hollywood. We're just following in the wake of their success. I also feel compelled to point out that this comic is based upon Rex's autobiography, so if things don't necessarily make dramatic sense, blame him for failing to live his life in three acts and a climax.

Remember what so many people have said: if it works, use it. Pillage genius until genius can give no more. God knows we all want what we don't have, and by God do we want genius. Mass appeal genius preferably. *Harry Potter*-style-sales-figures genius if you know what I mean. In any case, we have tried to collect the greatest monsters from human history, myth, and imagination and place them all in one book. It's our tribute to the wonderful things that romped about inside our heads when we were kids. Of course, most of them really *are* real, but it's best to pretend they *aren't.* We don't want to get the kids upset after all. And the Floot Fleet of Doom is definitely upsetting if you're on the receiving end of their atomic gatling guns. No question! I have seen it with my own eyes, and it is not something I'd want to face again, unless there were a stalwart librarian at my side, dictionary and automatic at the ready.

Elucidate!

B. Barry Horst

B. Barry Horst

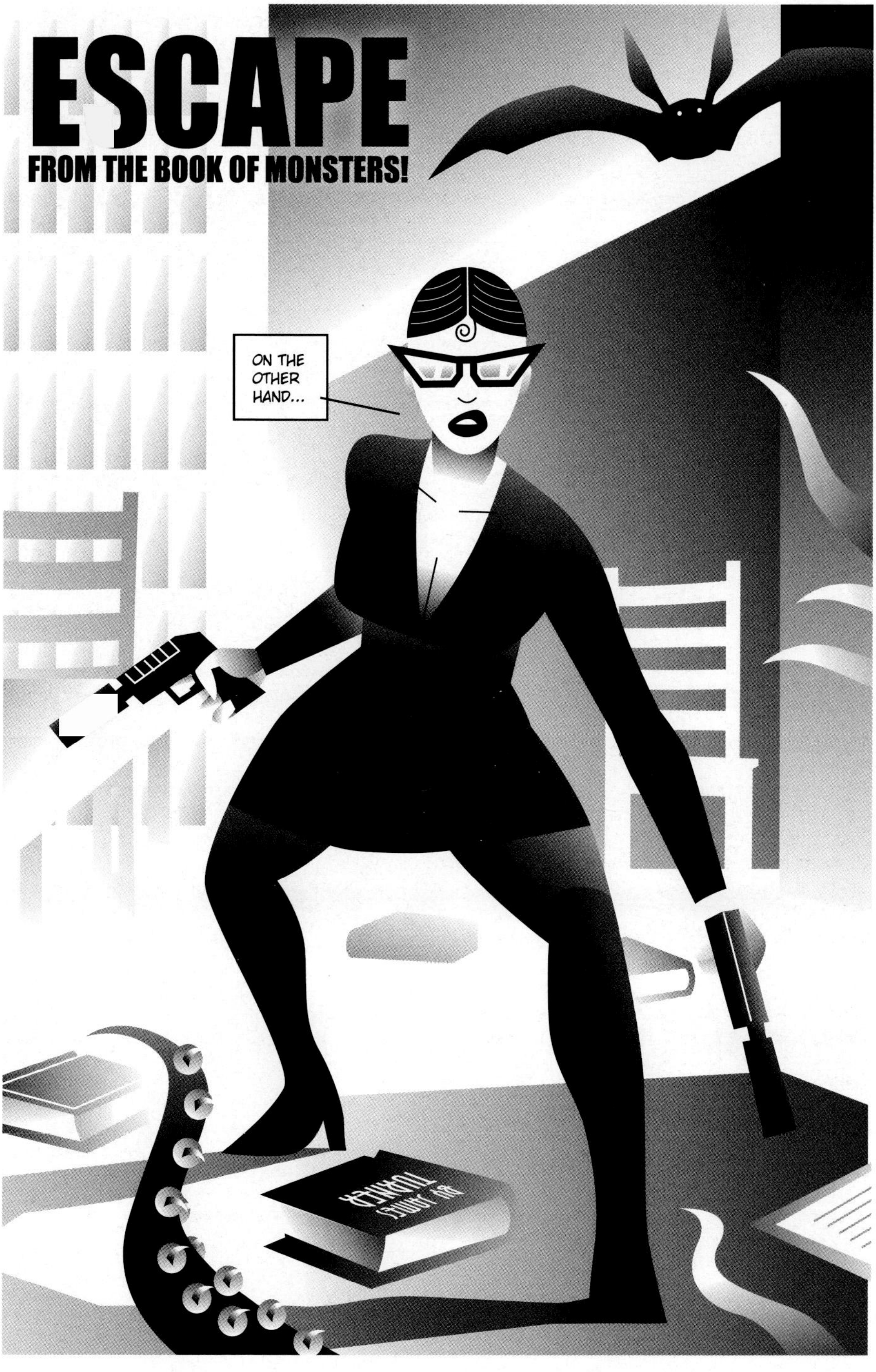
ESCAPE
FROM THE BOOK OF MONSTERS!
ON THE OTHER HAND...

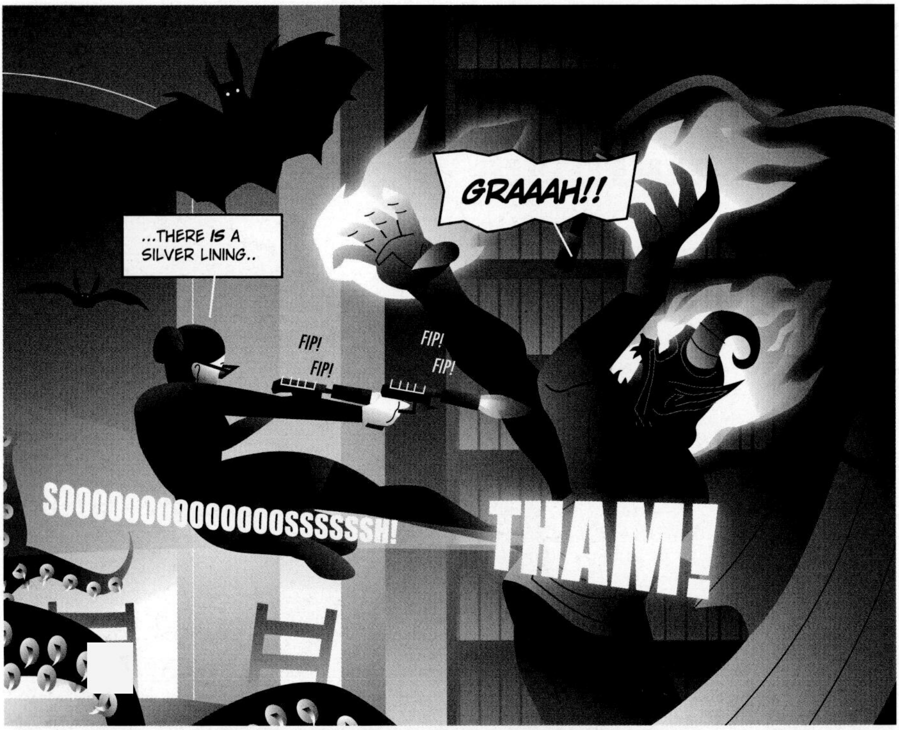
...THERE IS A SILVER LINING..
GRAAAH!!
FIP!
FIP!
FIP!
FIP!
SOOOOOOOOOOOOOOOSSSSSSH!
THAM!
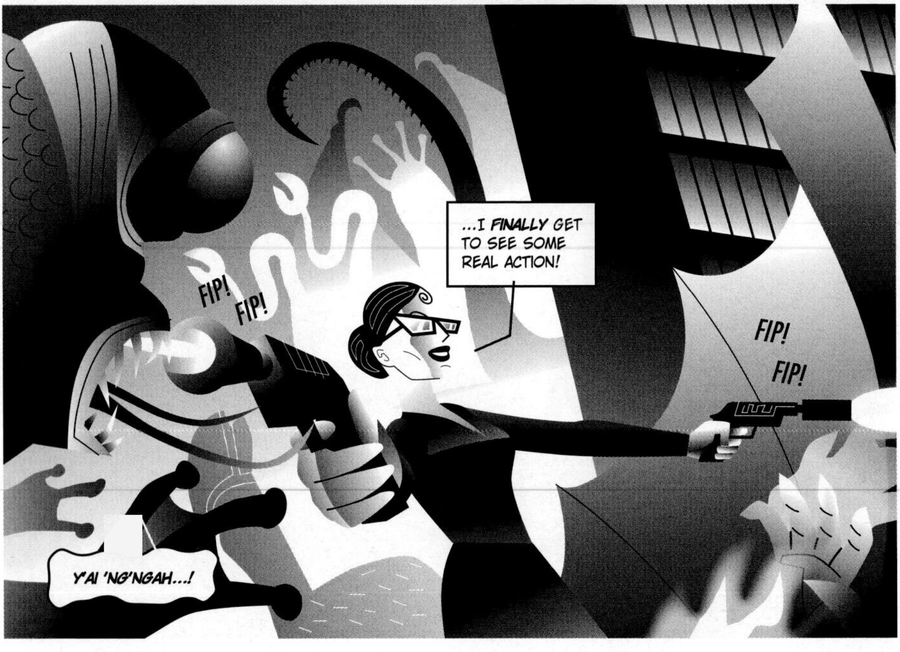
...I FINALLY GET TO SEE SOME REAL ACTION!
FIP!
FIP!
FIP!
FIP!
Y'AI 'NG'NGAH...!

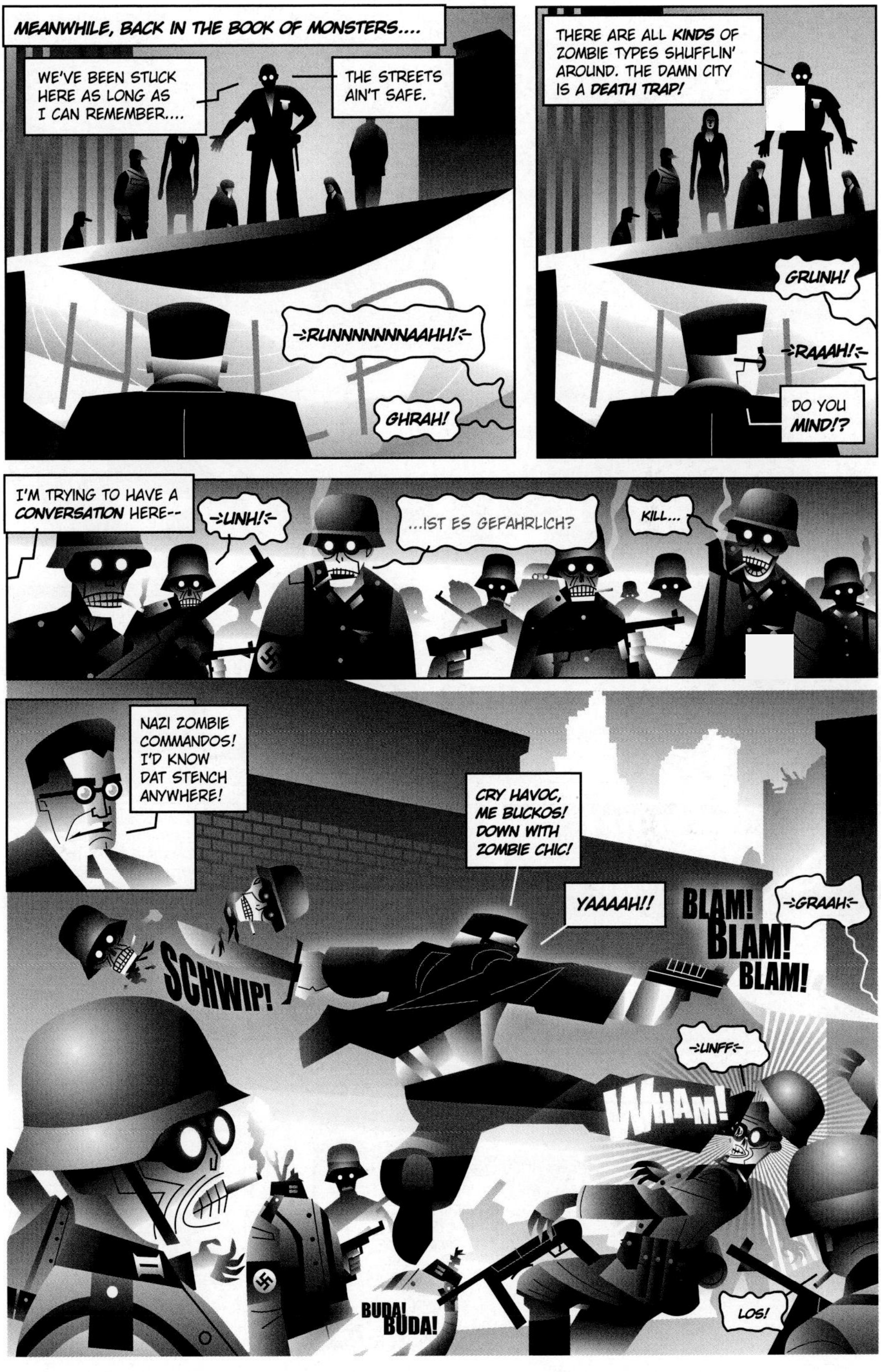
MEANWHILE, BACK IN THE BOOK OF MONSTERS....
WE'VE BEEN STUCK HERE AS LONG AS I CAN REMEMBER....
THE STREETS AIN'T SAFE.
RUNNNNNNNAAHH!
GHRAH!
THERE ARE ALL KINDS OF ZOMBIE TYPES SHUFFLIN' AROUND. THE DAMN CITY IS A DEATH TRAP!
GRUNH!
RAAAH!
DO YOU MIND!?
I'M TRYING TO HAVE A CONVERSATION HERE--
UNH!
...IST ES GEFAHRLICH?
KILL...
NAZI ZOMBIE COMMANDOS! I'D KNOW DAT STENCH ANYWHERE!
CRY HAVOC, ME BUCKOS! DOWN WITH ZOMBIE CHIC!
YAAAAH!!
BLAM! BLAM! BLAM!
GRAAH
SCHWIP!
UNFF
WHAM!
BUDA! BUDA!
LOS!

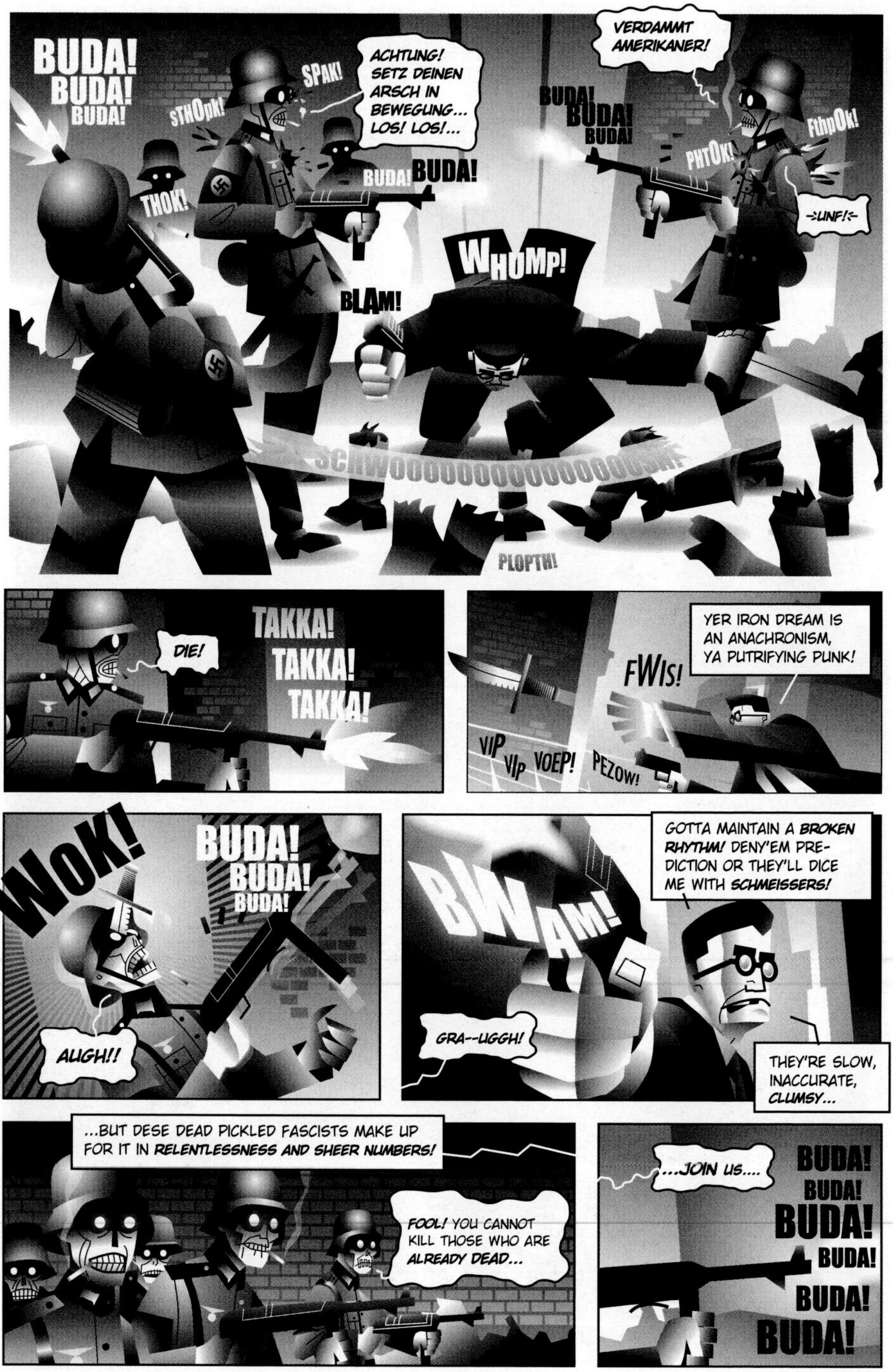
BUDA! BUDA! BUDA!
sTHOpk!
SPAK!
ACHTUNG! SETZ DEINEN ARSCH IN BEWEGUNG... LOS! LOS!...
THOK!
BUDA! BUDA!
VERDAMMT AMERIKANER!
BUDA! BUDA! BUDA!
PHTOK!
FthpOk!
-=UNF!=-
WHOMP!
BLAM!
SCHWOOOOOOOOOOOOOOOSH!
PLOPTH!
DIE!
TAKKA! TAKKA! TAKKA!
YER IRON DREAM IS AN ANACHRONISM, YA PUTRIFYING PUNK!
FWIS!
VIP VIP VOEP! PEZOW!
WOK!
BUDA! BUDA! BUDA!
AUGH!!
GOTTA MAINTAIN A BROKEN RHYTHM! DENY'EM PRE-DICTION OR THEY'LL DICE ME WITH SCHMEISSERS!
BWAM!
GRA--UGGH!
THEY'RE SLOW, INACCURATE, CLUMSY...
...BUT DESE DEAD PICKLED FASCISTS MAKE UP FOR IT IN RELENTLESSNESS AND SHEER NUMBERS!
FOOL! YOU CANNOT KILL THOSE WHO ARE ALREADY DEAD...
...JOIN US....
BUDA! BUDA! BUDA! BUDA! BUDA! BUDA!

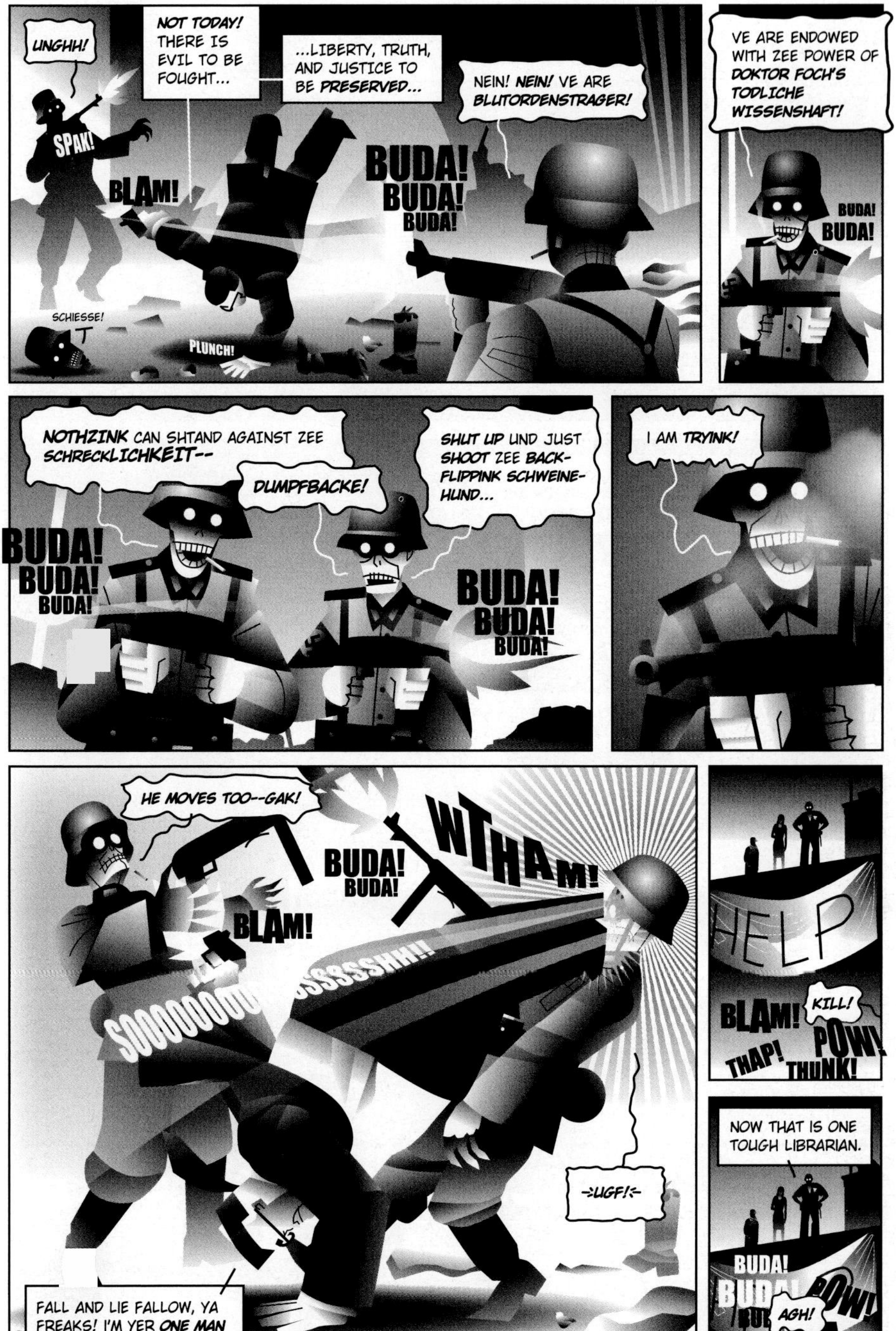
UNGHH!
SPAK!
BLAM!
NOT TODAY! THERE IS EVIL TO BE FOUGHT...
...LIBERTY, TRUTH, AND JUSTICE TO BE PRESERVED...
NEIN! NEIN! VE ARE BLUTORDENSTRAGER!
BUDA! BUDA! BUDA!
SCHIESSE!
PLUNCH!
VE ARE ENDOWED WITH ZEE POWER OF DOKTOR FOCH'S TODLICHE WISSENSHAFT!
BUDA! BUDA!
NOTHZINK CAN SHTAND AGAINST ZEE SCHRECKLICHKEIT--
DUMPFBACKE!
SHUT UP UND JUST SHOOT ZEE BACK-FLIPPINK SCHWEINE-HUND...
BUDA! BUDA! BUDA!
BUDA! BUDA! BUDA!
I AM TRYINK!
HE MOVES TOO--GAK!
BUDA! BUDA!
WTHAM!
BLAM!
SOOOOOOO...SSSSSHH!!
UGF!
FALL AND LIE FALLOW, YA FREAKS! I'M YER ONE MAN ARSENAL OF LIBERTY!
HELP
BLAM!
KILL!
POW!
THAP!
THUNK!
NOW THAT IS ONE TOUGH LIBRARIAN.
BUDA!
AGH!
WRAM!

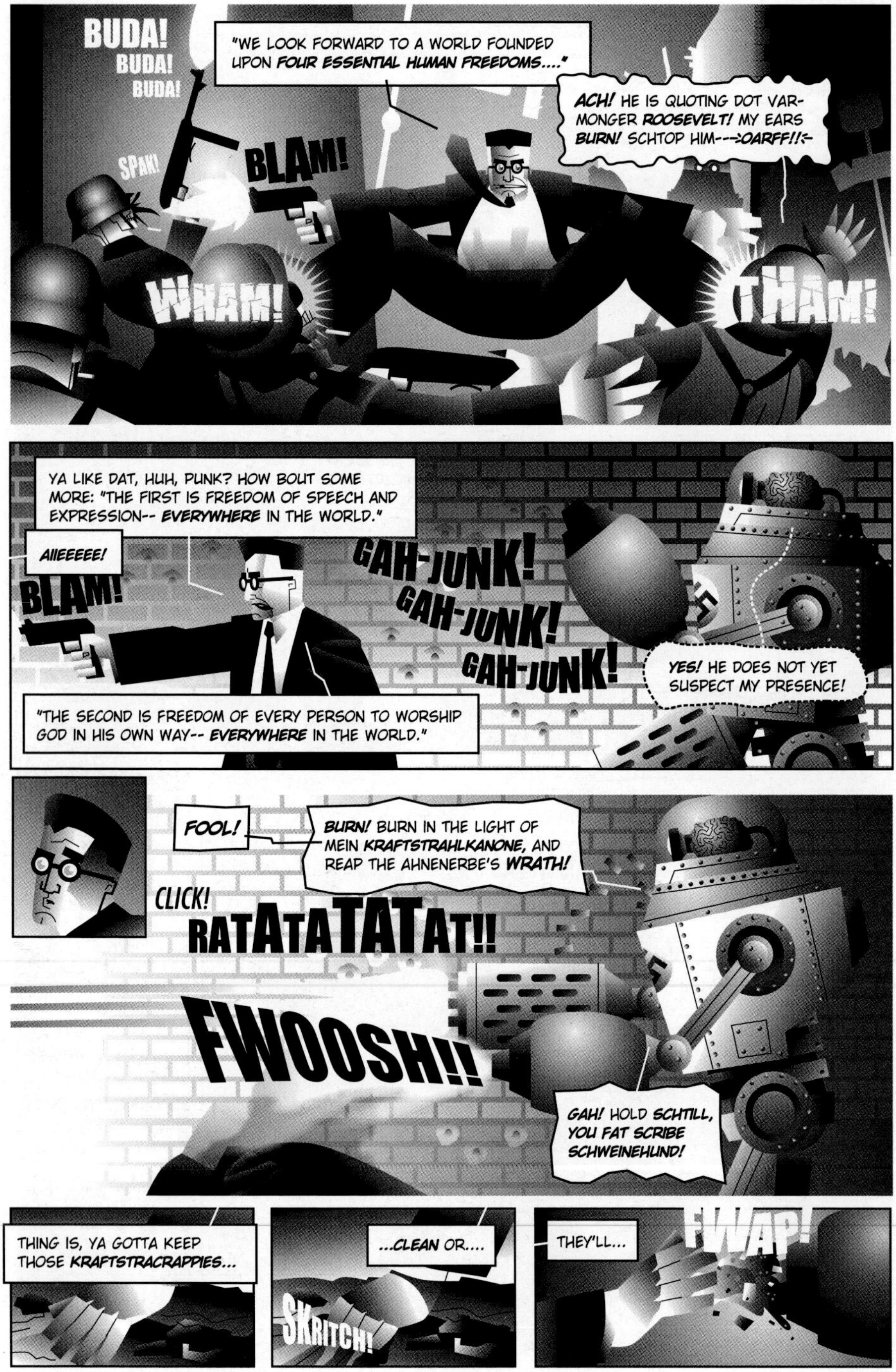
BUDA! BUDA! BUDA!
"WE LOOK FORWARD TO A WORLD FOUNDED UPON FOUR ESSENTIAL HUMAN FREEDOMS...."
ACH! HE IS QUOTING DOT VAR-MONGER ROOSEVELT! MY EARS BURN! SCHTOP HIM---OARFF!!
SPAK!
BLAM!
WHAM!
THAM!
YA LIKE DAT, HUH, PUNK? HOW BOUT SOME MORE: "THE FIRST IS FREEDOM OF SPEECH AND EXPRESSION-- EVERYWHERE IN THE WORLD."
AIIEEEEE!
BLAM!
GAH-JUNK! GAH-JUNK! GAH-JUNK!
YES! HE DOES NOT YET SUSPECT MY PRESENCE!
"THE SECOND IS FREEDOM OF EVERY PERSON TO WORSHIP GOD IN HIS OWN WAY-- EVERYWHERE IN THE WORLD."
FOOL!
BURN! BURN IN THE LIGHT OF MEIN KRAFTSTRAHLKANONE, AND REAP THE AHNENERBE'S WRATH!
CLICK!
RATATATATAT!!
FWOOSH!!
GAH! HOLD SCHTILL, YOU FAT SCRIBE SCHWEINEHUND!
THING IS, YA GOTTA KEEP THOSE KRAFTSTRACRAPPIES...
...CLEAN OR....
SKRITCH!
THEY'LL...
FWAP!

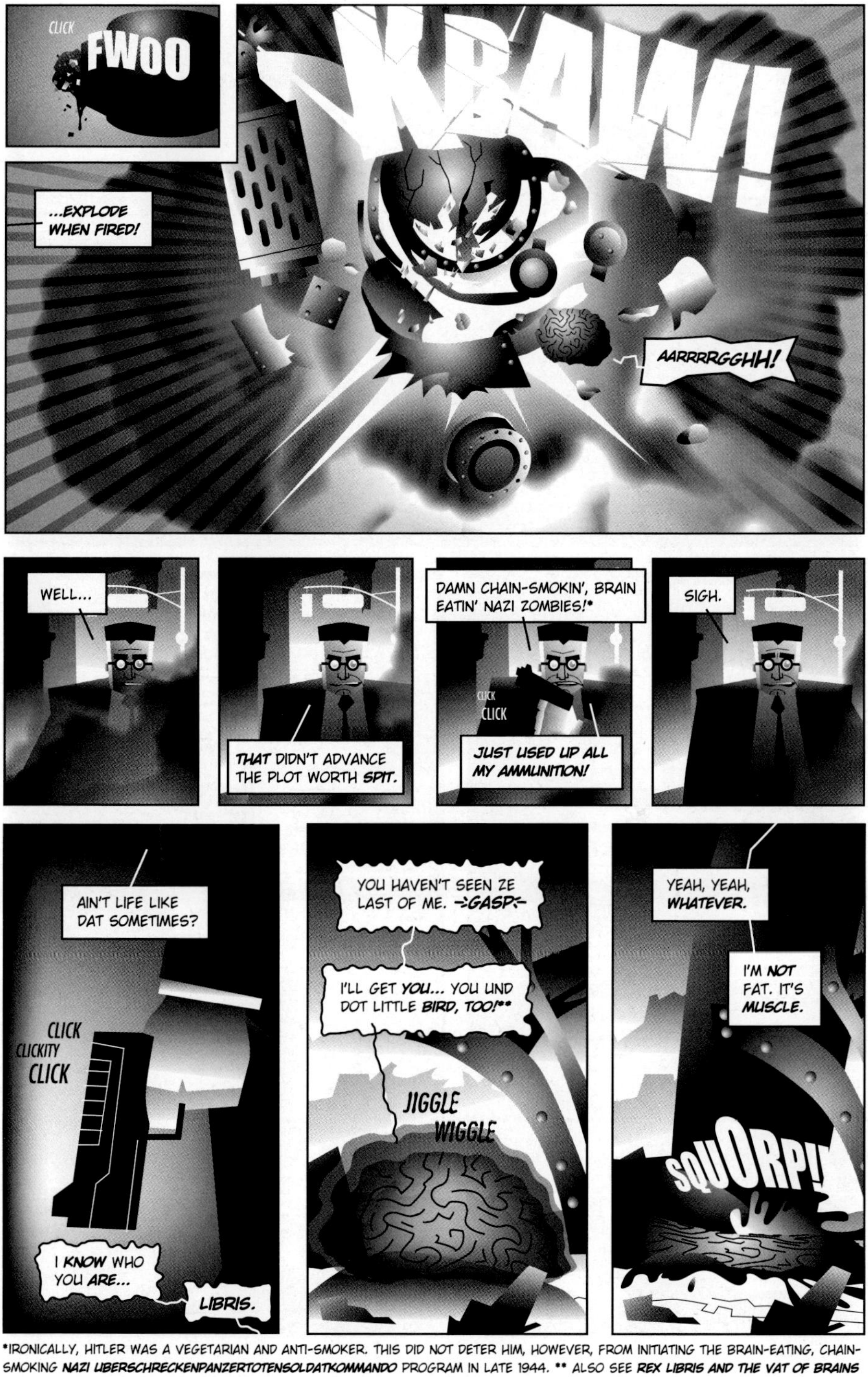
CLICK
FWOO
KRAW!
...EXPLODE WHEN FIRED!
AARRRRGGHH!
WELL...
THAT DIDN'T ADVANCE THE PLOT WORTH SPIT.
DAMN CHAIN-SMOKIN', BRAIN EATIN' NAZI ZOMBIES!*
CLICK
CLICK
JUST USED UP ALL MY AMMUNITION!
SIGH.
AIN'T LIFE LIKE DAT SOMETIMES?
CLICK
CLICKITY
CLICK
I KNOW WHO YOU ARE...
LIBRIS.
YOU HAVEN'T SEEN ZE LAST OF ME. -GASP-
I'LL GET YOU... YOU UND DOT LITTLE BIRD, TOO!**
JIGGLE
WIGGLE
YEAH, YEAH, WHATEVER.
I'M NOT FAT. IT'S MUSCLE.
SQUORP!

*IRONICALLY, HITLER WAS A VEGETARIAN AND ANTI-SMOKER. THIS DID NOT DETER HIM, HOWEVER, FROM INITIATING THE BRAIN-EATING, CHAIN-SMOKING ***NAZI UBERSCHRECKENPANZERTOTENSOLDATKOMMANDO*** PROGRAM IN LATE 1944. ** ALSO SEE ***REX LIBRIS AND THE VAT OF BRAINS***

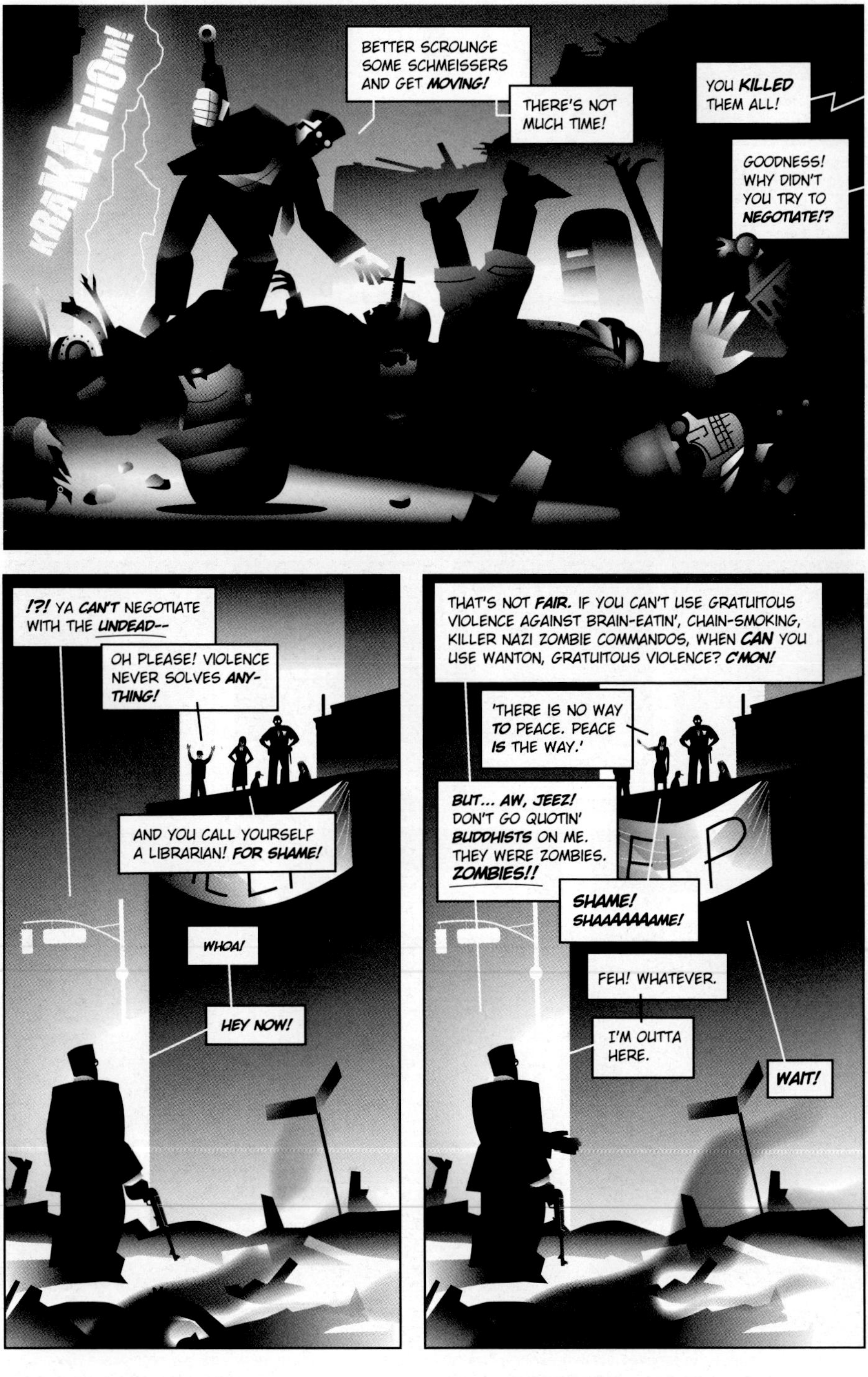
KRAKATHOM!
BETTER SCROUNGE SOME SCHMEISSERS AND GET *MOVING!*
THERE'S NOT MUCH TIME!
YOU **KILLED** THEM ALL!
GOODNESS! WHY DIDN'T YOU TRY TO ***NEGOTIATE!?***
!?! YA ***CAN'T*** NEGOTIATE WITH THE ***UNDEAD--***
OH PLEASE! VIOLENCE NEVER SOLVES ***ANY-THING!***
AND YOU CALL YOURSELF A LIBRARIAN! ***FOR SHAME!***
WHOA!
HEY NOW!
THAT'S NOT ***FAIR.*** IF YOU CAN'T USE GRATUITOUS VIOLENCE AGAINST BRAIN-EATIN', CHAIN-SMOKING, KILLER NAZI ZOMBIE COMMANDOS, WHEN ***CAN*** YOU USE WANTON, GRATUITOUS VIOLENCE? ***C'MON!***
'THERE IS NO WAY ***TO*** PEACE. PEACE ***IS*** THE WAY.'
BUT... AW, JEEZ! DON'T GO QUOTIN' ***BUDDHISTS*** ON ME. THEY WERE ZOMBIES. ***ZOMBIES!!***
SHAME! SHAAAAAAAME!
FEH! WHATEVER.
I'M OUTTA HERE.
WAIT!

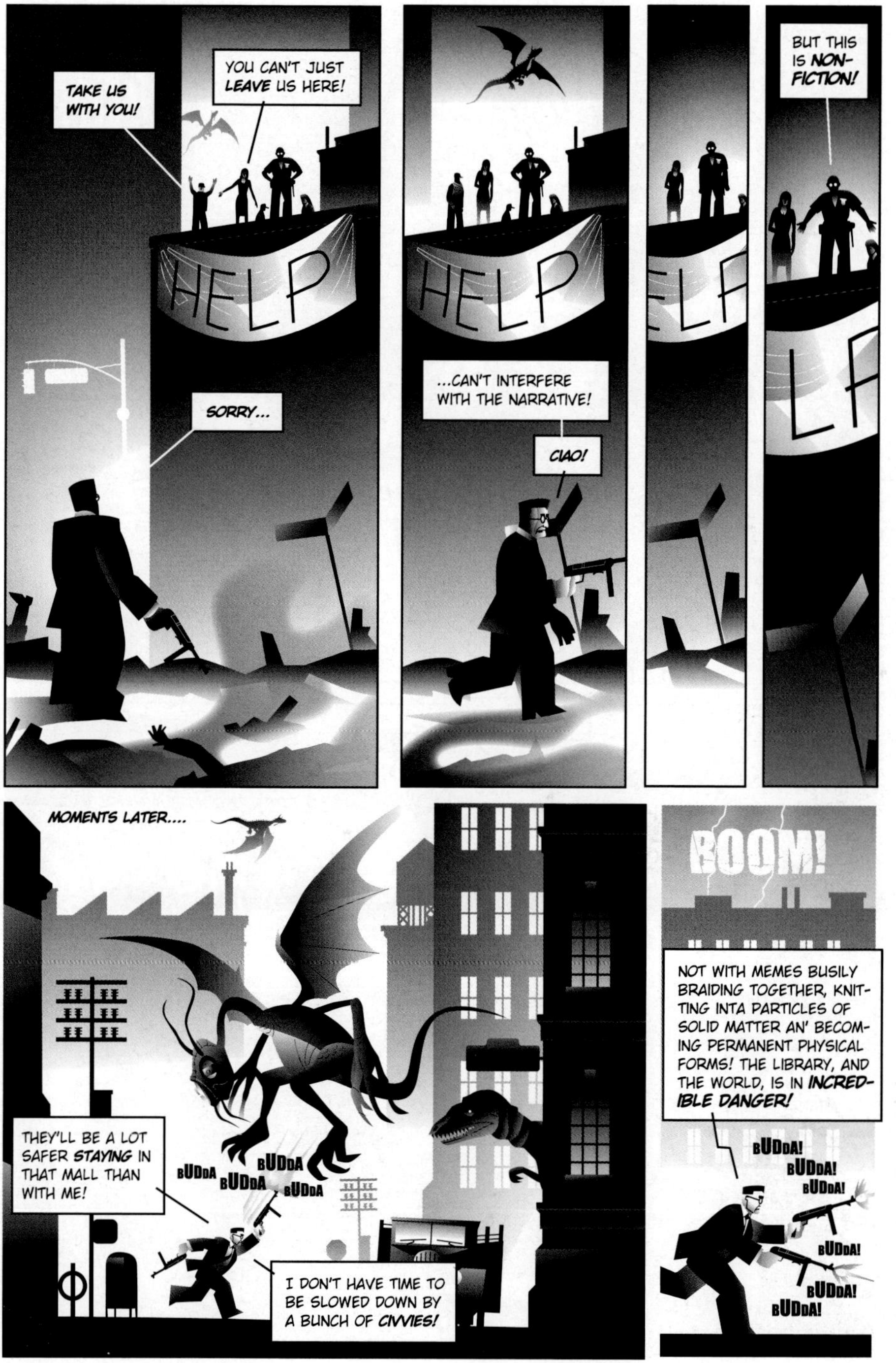
TAKE US WITH YOU!
YOU CAN'T JUST LEAVE US HERE!
SORRY...
...CAN'T INTERFERE WITH THE NARRATIVE!
CIAO!
BUT THIS IS NON-FICTION!
HELP
MOMENTS LATER....
BUDDA BUDDA BUDDA BUDDA
THEY'LL BE A LOT SAFER STAYING IN THAT MALL THAN WITH ME!
I DON'T HAVE TIME TO BE SLOWED DOWN BY A BUNCH OF CIVVIES!
BOOM!
NOT WITH MEMES BUSILY BRAIDING TOGETHER, KNITTING INTA PARTICLES OF SOLID MATTER AN' BECOMING PERMANENT PHYSICAL FORMS! THE LIBRARY, AND THE WORLD, IS IN INCREDIBLE DANGER!
BUDDA! BUDDA! BUDDA! BUDDA! BUDDA! BUDDA!

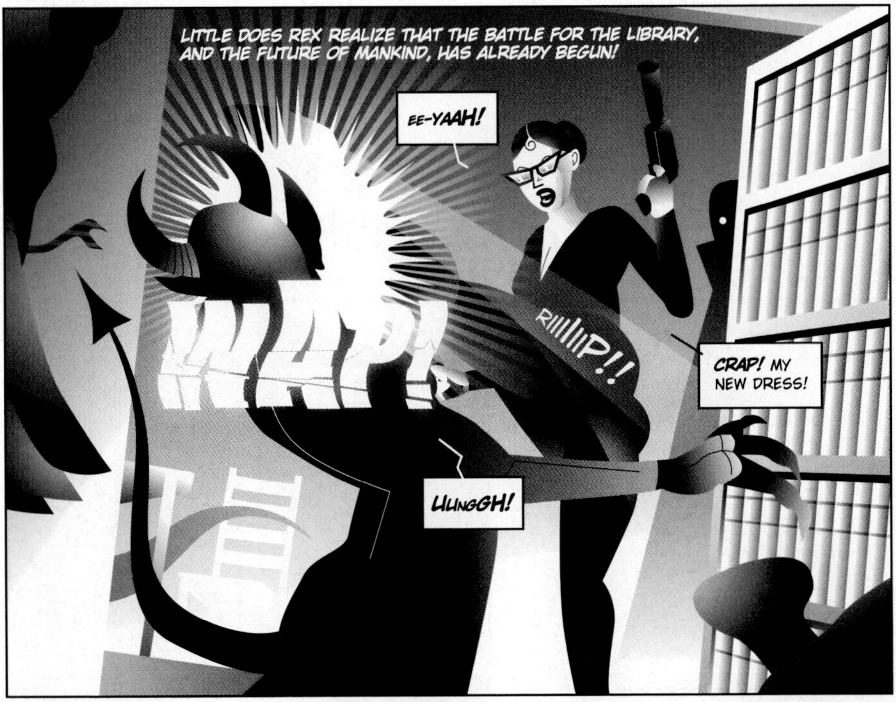
LITTLE DOES REX REALIZE THAT THE BATTLE FOR THE LIBRARY, AND THE FUTURE OF MANKIND, HAS ALREADY BEGUN!
EE-YAAH!
RIIIIIIP!!
CRAP! MY NEW DRESS!
UUNGGH!
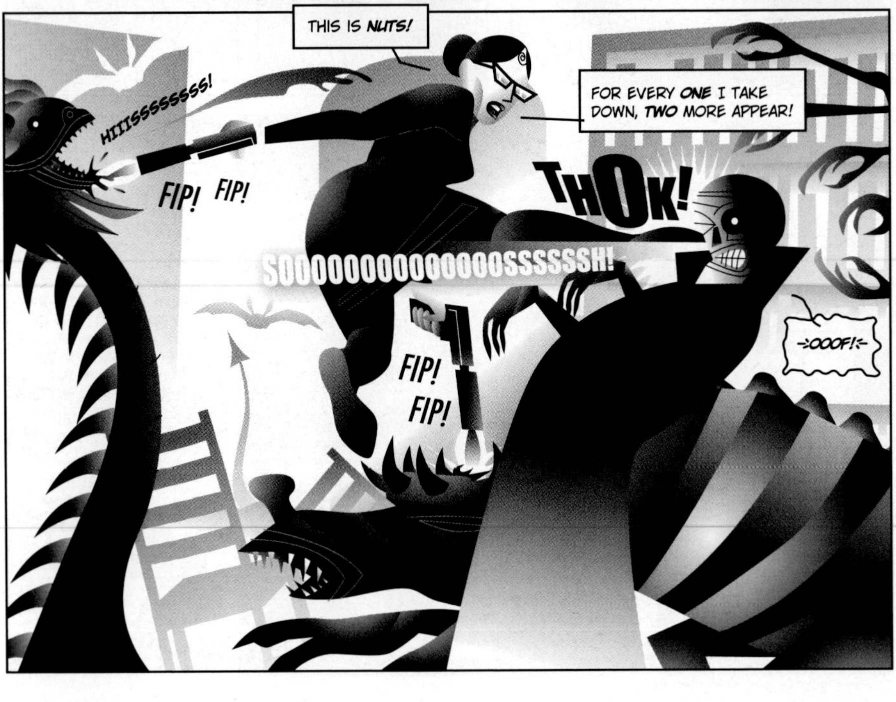
THIS IS NUTS!
FOR EVERY ONE I TAKE DOWN, TWO MORE APPEAR!
HIIISSSSSSSS!
FIP! FIP!
THOK!
SOOOOOOOOOOOOOOOSSSSSSH!
FIP! FIP!
-OOOF!-

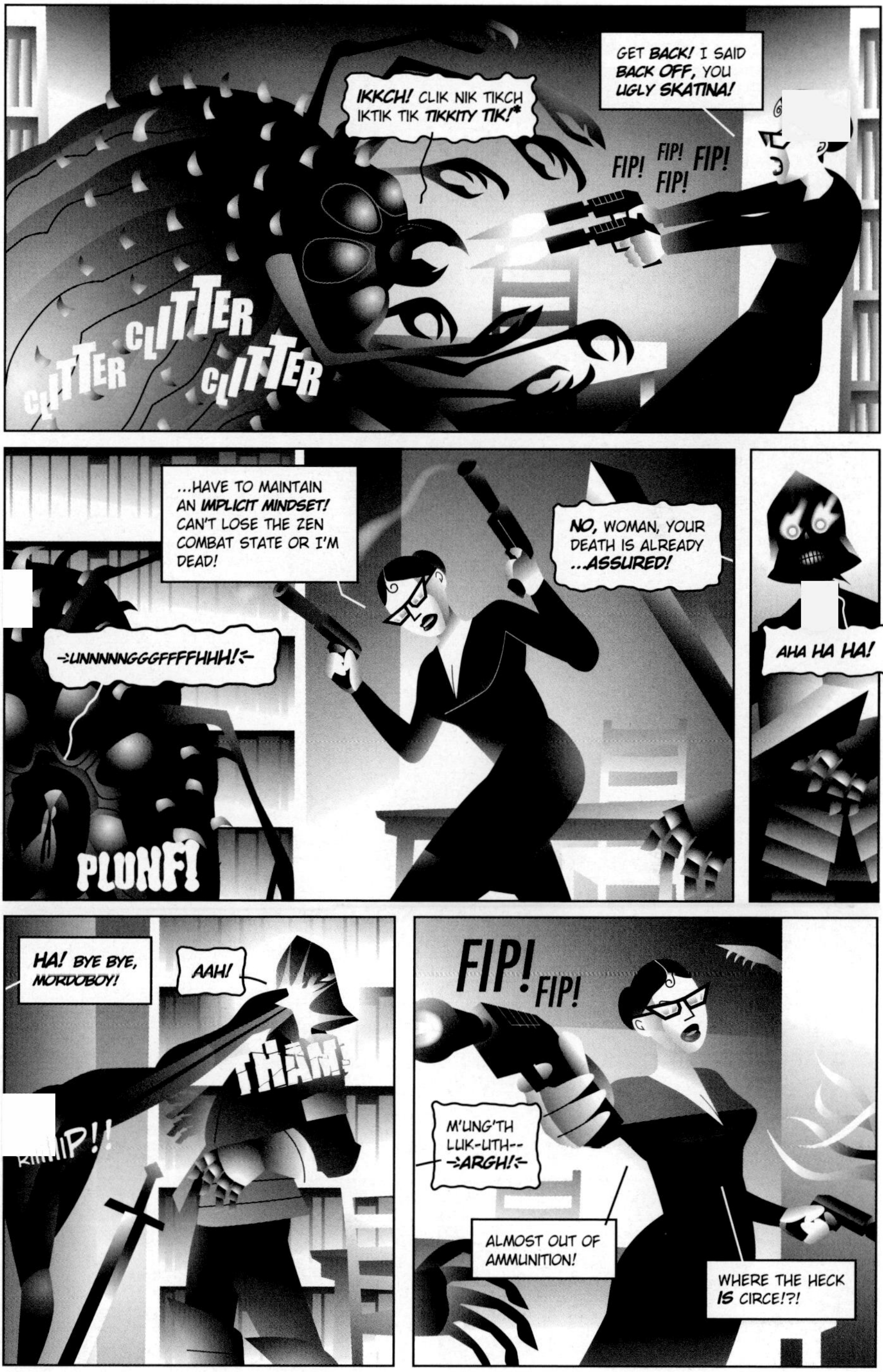
IKKCH! CLIK NIK TIKCH IKTIK TIK TIKKITY TIK!*
GET BACK! I SAID BACK OFF, YOU UGLY SKATINA!
FIP! FIP! FIP! FIP!
CLITTER CLITTER CLITTER
...HAVE TO MAINTAIN AN IMPLICIT MINDSET! CAN'T LOSE THE ZEN COMBAT STATE OR I'M DEAD!
UNNNNNGGGFFFFHHH!
PLUNF!
NO, WOMAN, YOUR DEATH IS ALREADY ...ASSURED!
AHA HA HA!
HA! BYE BYE, MORDOBOY!
AAH!
THAM!
FIP! FIP!
M'UNG'TH LUK-UTH-- ARGH!
ALMOST OUT OF AMMUNITION!
WHERE THE HECK IS CIRCE!?!

*'LOOK OUT! SHE'S GOT A GUN!

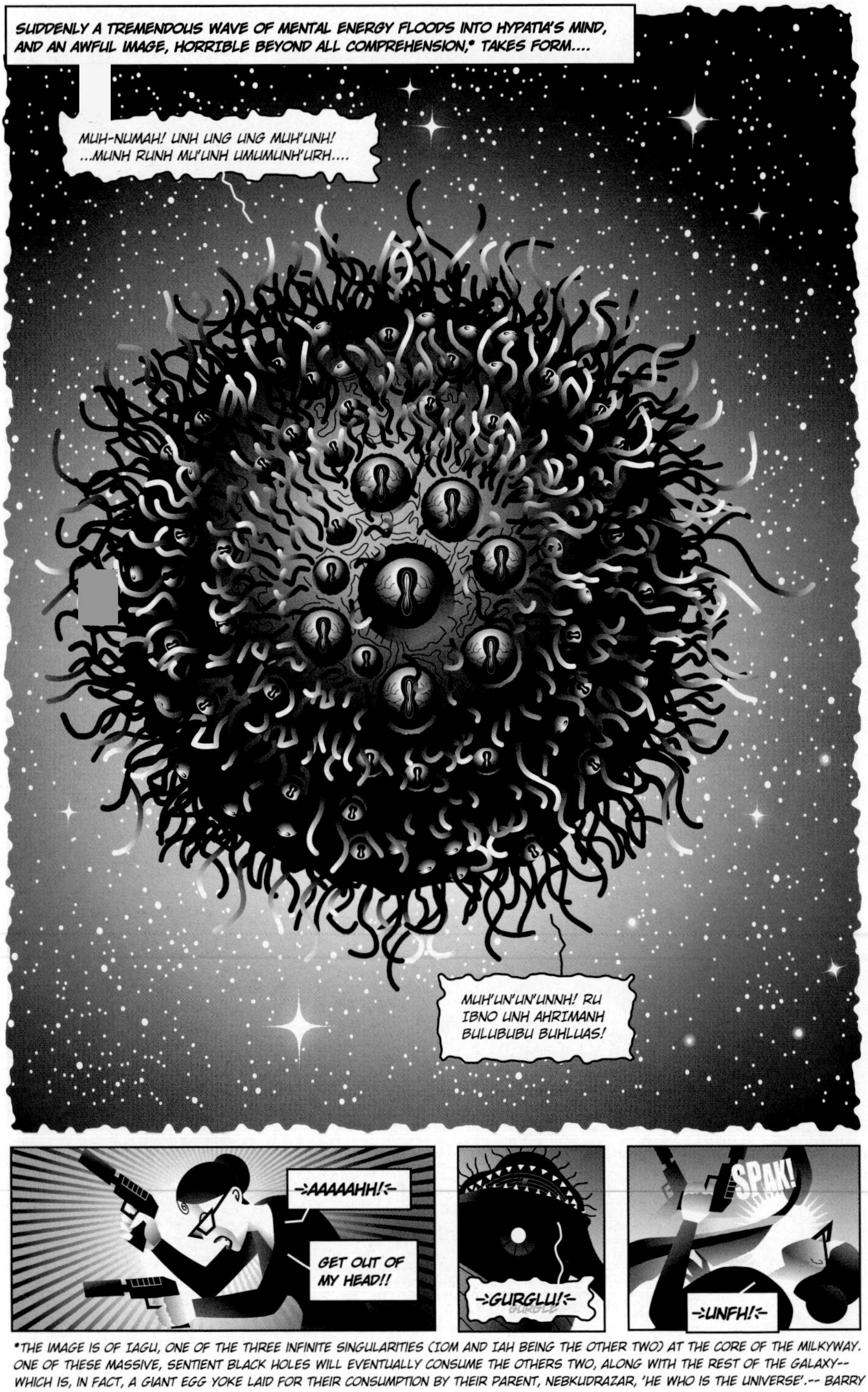
SUDDENLY A TREMENDOUS WAVE OF MENTAL ENERGY FLOODS INTO HYPATIA'S MIND, AND AN AWFUL IMAGE, HORRIBLE BEYOND ALL COMPREHENSION,* TAKES FORM....
MUH-NUMAH! UNH UNG UNG MUH'UNH! ...MUNH RUNH MU'UNH UMUMUNH'URH....
MUH'UN'UN'UNNH! RU IBNO UNH AHRIMANH BULUBUBU BUHLUAS!
-AAAAAHH!-
GET OUT OF MY HEAD!!
SPAK!
-GURGLU!-
-UNFH!-

*THE IMAGE IS OF IAGU, ONE OF THE THREE INFINITE SINGULARITIES (IOM AND IAH BEING THE OTHER TWO) AT THE CORE OF THE MILKYWAY. ONE OF THESE MASSIVE, SENTIENT BLACK HOLES WILL EVENTUALLY CONSUME THE OTHERS TWO, ALONG WITH THE REST OF THE GALAXY-- WHICH IS, IN FACT, A GIANT EGG YOKE LAID FOR THEIR CONSUMPTION BY THEIR PARENT, NEBKUDRAZAR, 'HE WHO IS THE UNIVERSE'.-- BARRY

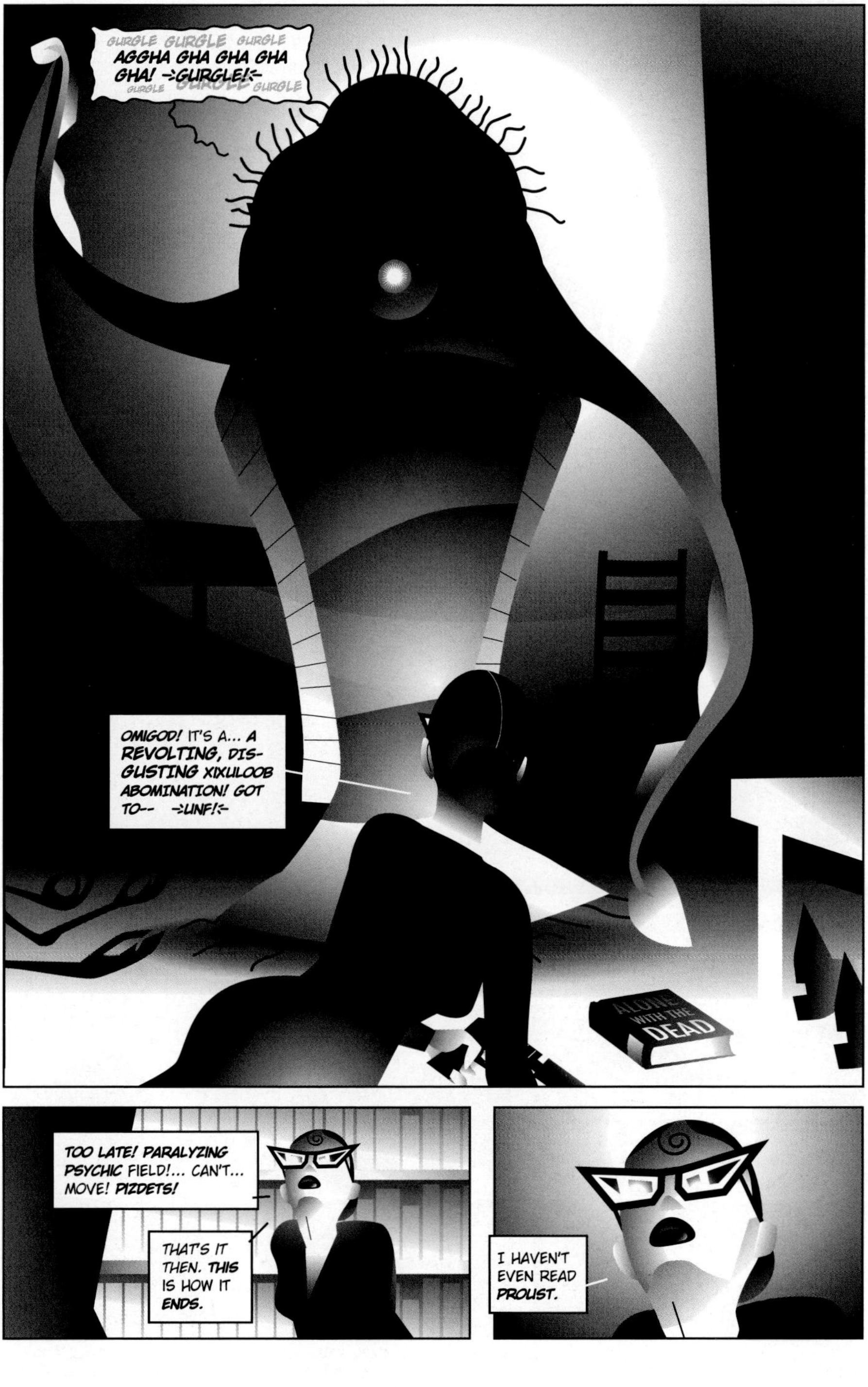
GURGLE GURGLE GURGLE
AGGHA GHA GHA GHA GHA! -GURGLE!- GURGLE GURGLE GURGLE
OMIGOD! IT'S A... A REVOLTING, DIS-GUSTING XIXULOOB ABOMINATION! GOT TO-- -UNF!-
ALONE WITH THE DEAD
TOO LATE! PARALYZING PSYCHIC FIELD!... CAN'T... MOVE! PIZDETS!
THAT'S IT THEN. THIS IS HOW IT ENDS.
I HAVEN'T EVEN READ PROUST.

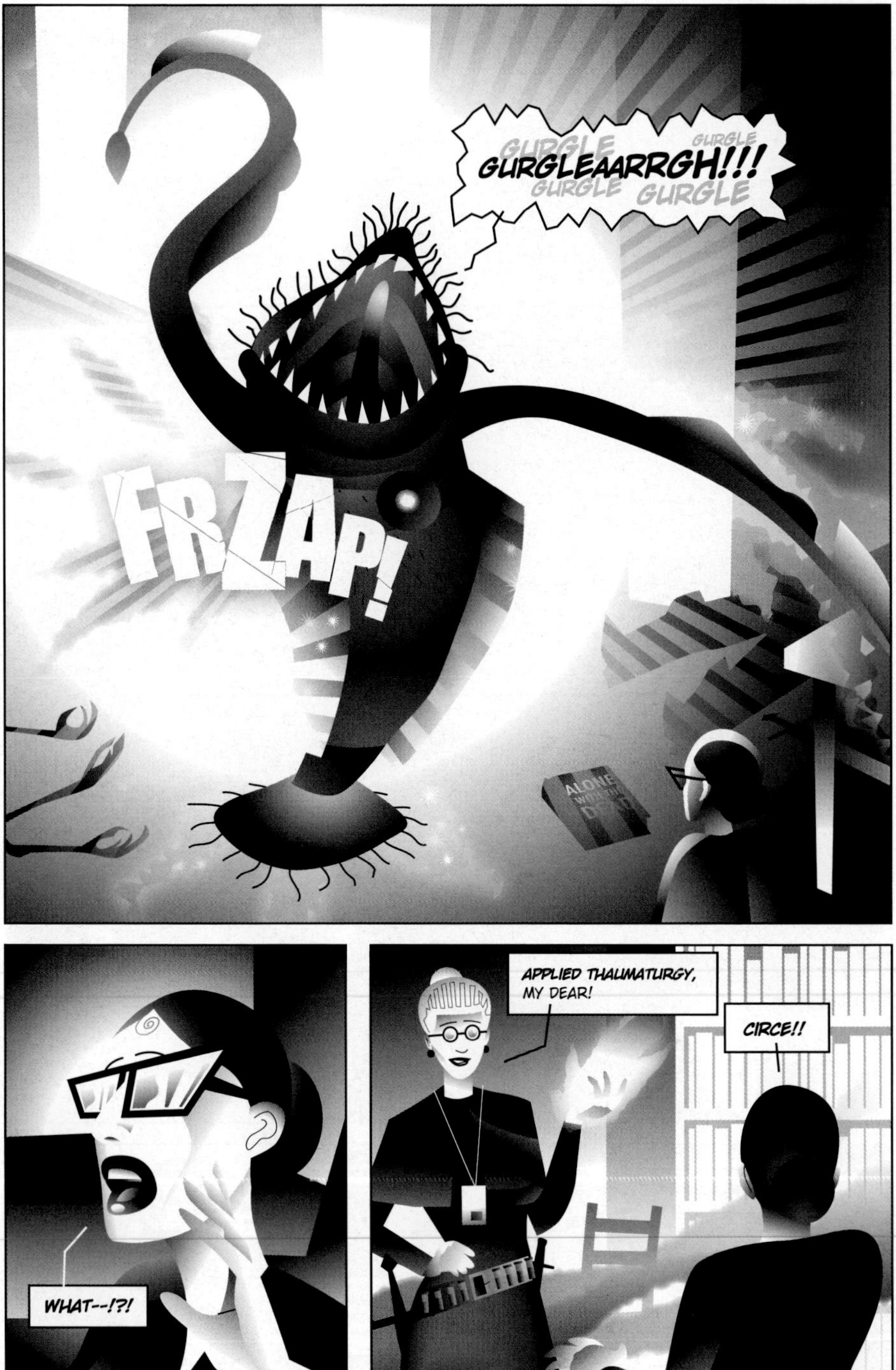
GURGLE GURGLE
GURGLEAARRGH!!!
GURGLE GURGLE
FRZAP!
ALONE
WHAT--!?!
APPLIED THAUMATURGY, MY DEAR!
CIRCE!!

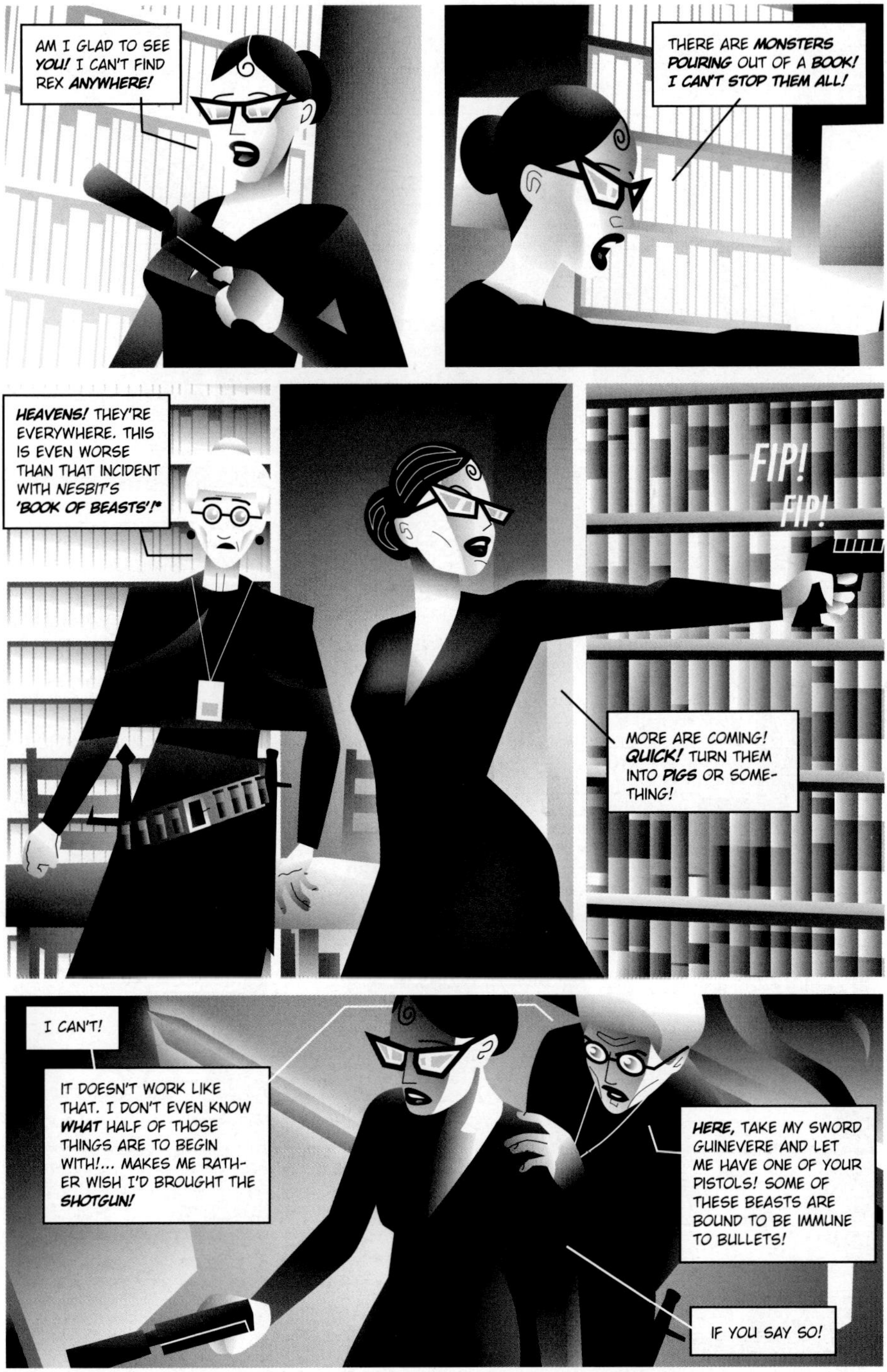
AM I GLAD TO SEE YOU! I CAN'T FIND REX ANYWHERE!
THERE ARE MONSTERS POURING OUT OF A BOOK! I CAN'T STOP THEM ALL!
HEAVENS! THEY'RE EVERYWHERE. THIS IS EVEN WORSE THAN THAT INCIDENT WITH NESBIT'S 'BOOK OF BEASTS'!*
FIP!
FIP!
MORE ARE COMING! QUICK! TURN THEM INTO PIGS OR SOME-THING!
I CAN'T!
IT DOESN'T WORK LIKE THAT. I DON'T EVEN KNOW WHAT HALF OF THOSE THINGS ARE TO BEGIN WITH!... MAKES ME RATH-ER WISH I'D BROUGHT THE SHOTGUN!
HERE, TAKE MY SWORD GUINEVERE AND LET ME HAVE ONE OF YOUR PISTOLS! SOME OF THESE BEASTS ARE BOUND TO BE IMMUNE TO BULLETS!
IF YOU SAY SO!

* THE INCIDENT OCCURRED IN 1901, SHORTLY AFTER THE SHORT STORY WAS PUBLISHED. THE BLUE BIRD OF PARADISE AND THE DRAGON OF PAGE THREE ESCAPED INTO THE MIDDLETON LIBRARY AND WREAKED HAVOC! -- BARRY

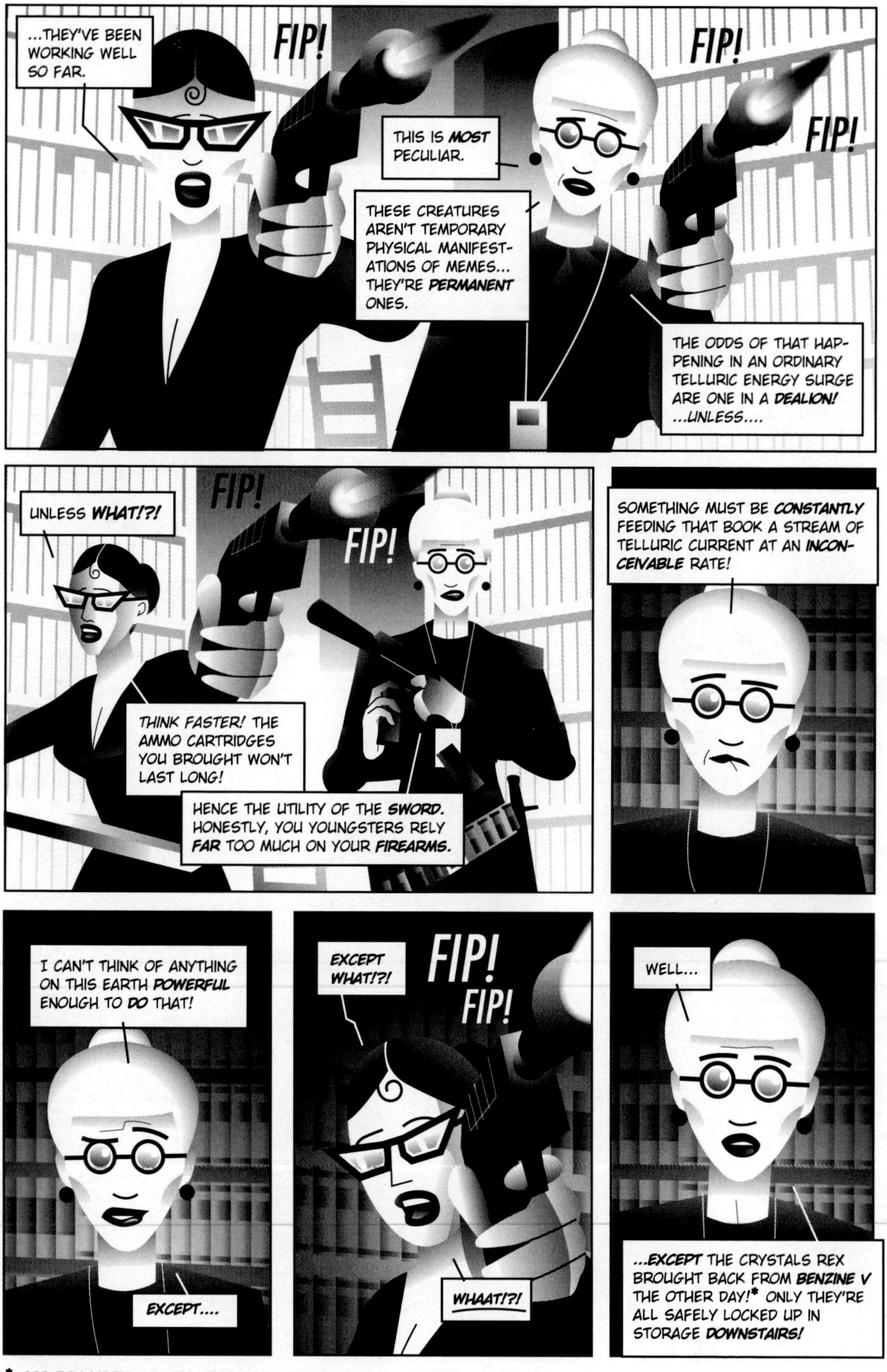
...THEY'VE BEEN WORKING WELL SO FAR.
FIP!
FIP!
FIP!
THIS IS MOST PECULIAR.
THESE CREATURES AREN'T TEMPORARY PHYSICAL MANIFEST-ATIONS OF MEMES... THEY'RE PERMANENT ONES.
THE ODDS OF THAT HAP-PENING IN AN ORDINARY TELLURIC ENERGY SURGE ARE ONE IN A DEALION! ...UNLESS....
UNLESS WHAT!?!
FIP!
FIP!
THINK FASTER! THE AMMO CARTRIDGES YOU BROUGHT WON'T LAST LONG!
HENCE THE UTILITY OF THE SWORD. HONESTLY, YOU YOUNGSTERS RELY FAR TOO MUCH ON YOUR FIREARMS.
SOMETHING MUST BE CONSTANTLY FEEDING THAT BOOK A STREAM OF TELLURIC CURRENT AT AN INCON-CEIVABLE RATE!
I CAN'T THINK OF ANYTHING ON THIS EARTH POWERFUL ENOUGH TO DO THAT!
EXCEPT....
EXCEPT WHAT!?!
FIP!
FIP!
WHAAT!?!
WELL...
...EXCEPT THE CRYSTALS REX BROUGHT BACK FROM BENZINE V THE OTHER DAY!* ONLY THEY'RE ALL SAFELY LOCKED UP IN STORAGE DOWNSTAIRS!

* SEE ***REX LIBRIS #5: TEA WITH VAGLOX*** FOR MORE! -- BARRY

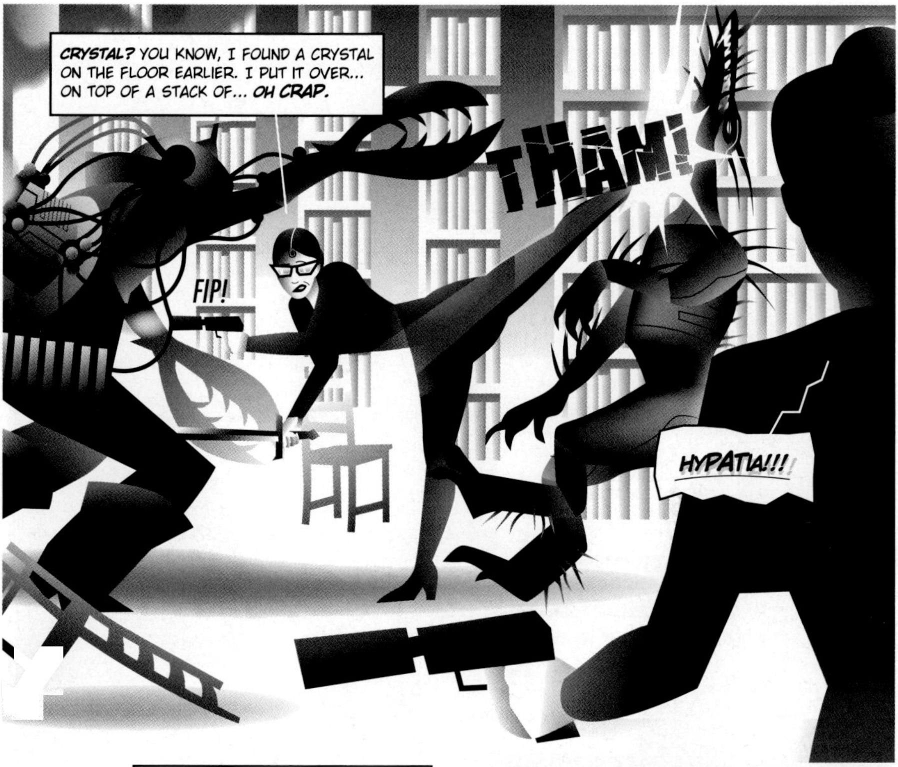
CRYSTAL? YOU KNOW, I FOUND A CRYSTAL ON THE FLOOR EARLIER. I PUT IT OVER... ON TOP OF A STACK OF... OH CRAP.
THAM!
FIP!
HYPATIA!!!

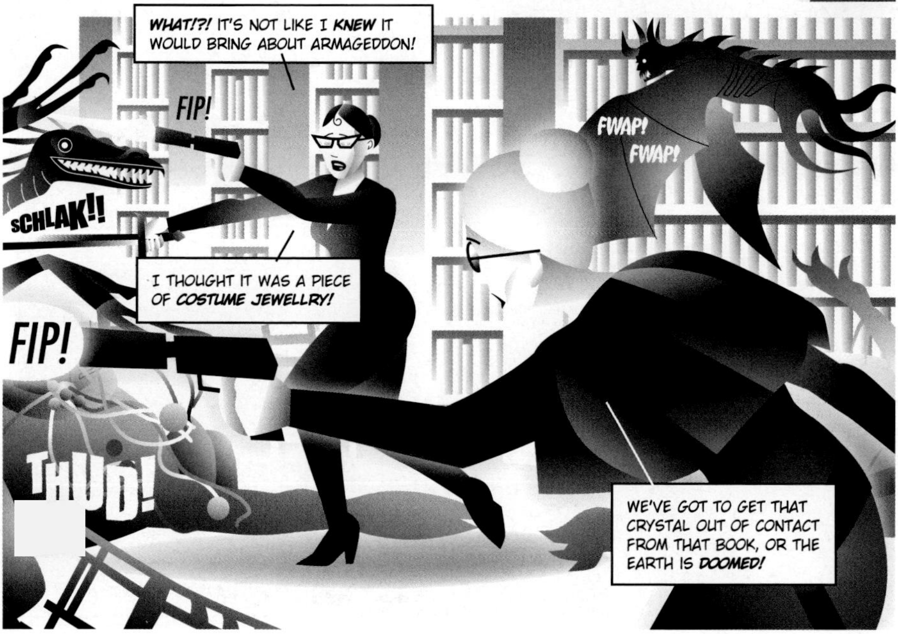
WHAT!?! IT'S NOT LIKE I KNEW IT WOULD BRING ABOUT ARMAGEDDON!
FIP!
FWAP!
FWAP!
SCHLAK!!
I THOUGHT IT WAS A PIECE OF COSTUME JEWELLRY!
FIP!
THUD!
WE'VE GOT TO GET THAT CRYSTAL OUT OF CONTACT FROM THAT BOOK, OR THE EARTH IS DOOMED!

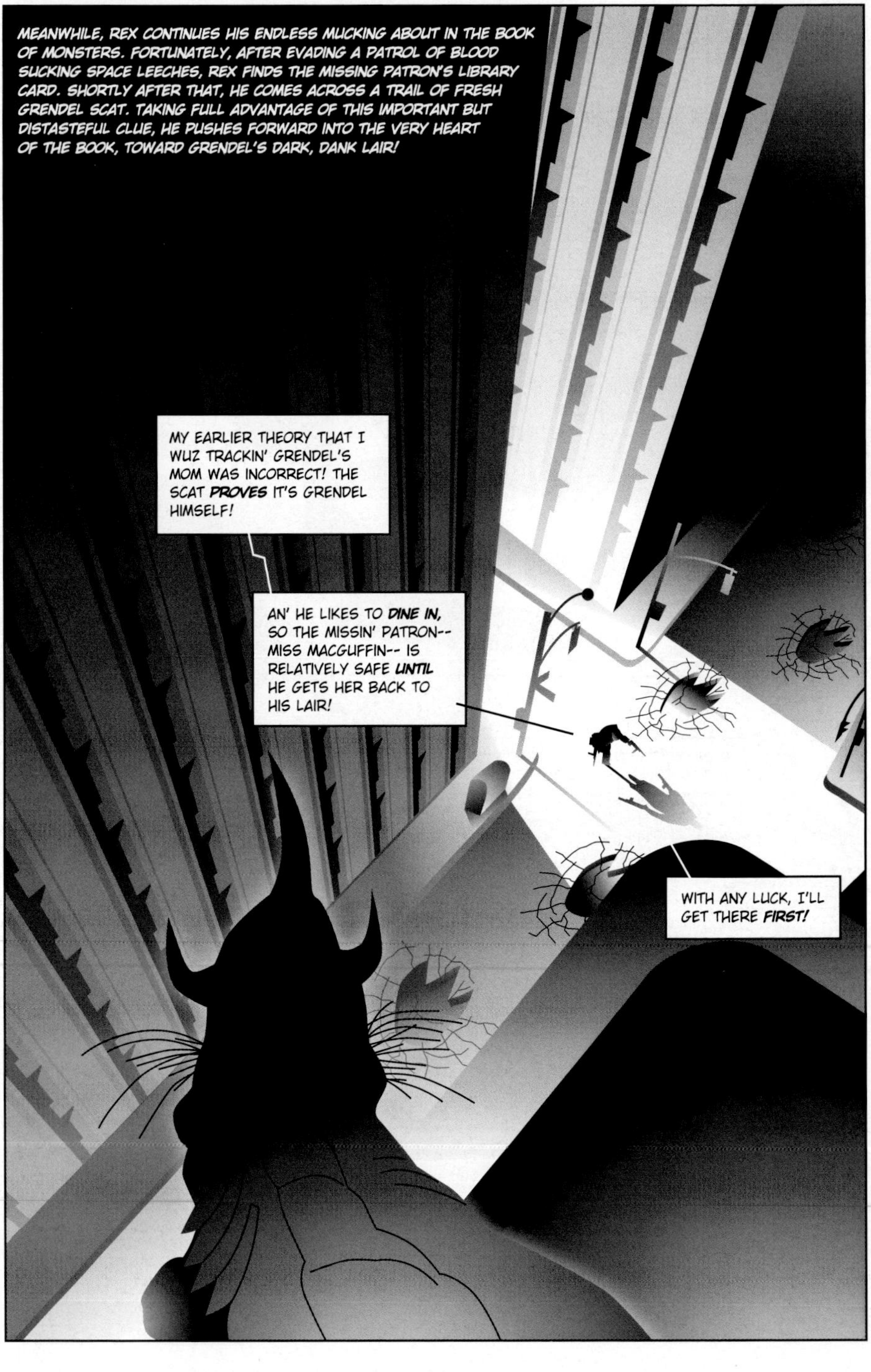
MEANWHILE, REX CONTINUES HIS ENDLESS MUCKING ABOUT IN THE BOOK OF MONSTERS. FORTUNATELY, AFTER EVADING A PATROL OF BLOOD SUCKING SPACE LEECHES, REX FINDS THE MISSING PATRON'S LIBRARY CARD. SHORTLY AFTER THAT, HE COMES ACROSS A TRAIL OF FRESH GRENDEL SCAT. TAKING FULL ADVANTAGE OF THIS IMPORTANT BUT DISTASTEFUL CLUE, HE PUSHES FORWARD INTO THE VERY HEART OF THE BOOK, TOWARD GRENDEL'S DARK, DANK LAIR!
MY EARLIER THEORY THAT I WUZ TRACKIN' GRENDEL'S MOM WAS INCORRECT! THE SCAT **PROVES** IT'S GRENDEL HIMSELF!
AN' HE LIKES TO **DINE IN**, SO THE MISSIN' PATRON-- MISS MACGUFFIN-- IS RELATIVELY SAFE **UNTIL** HE GETS HER BACK TO HIS LAIR!
WITH ANY LUCK, I'LL GET THERE **FIRST!**

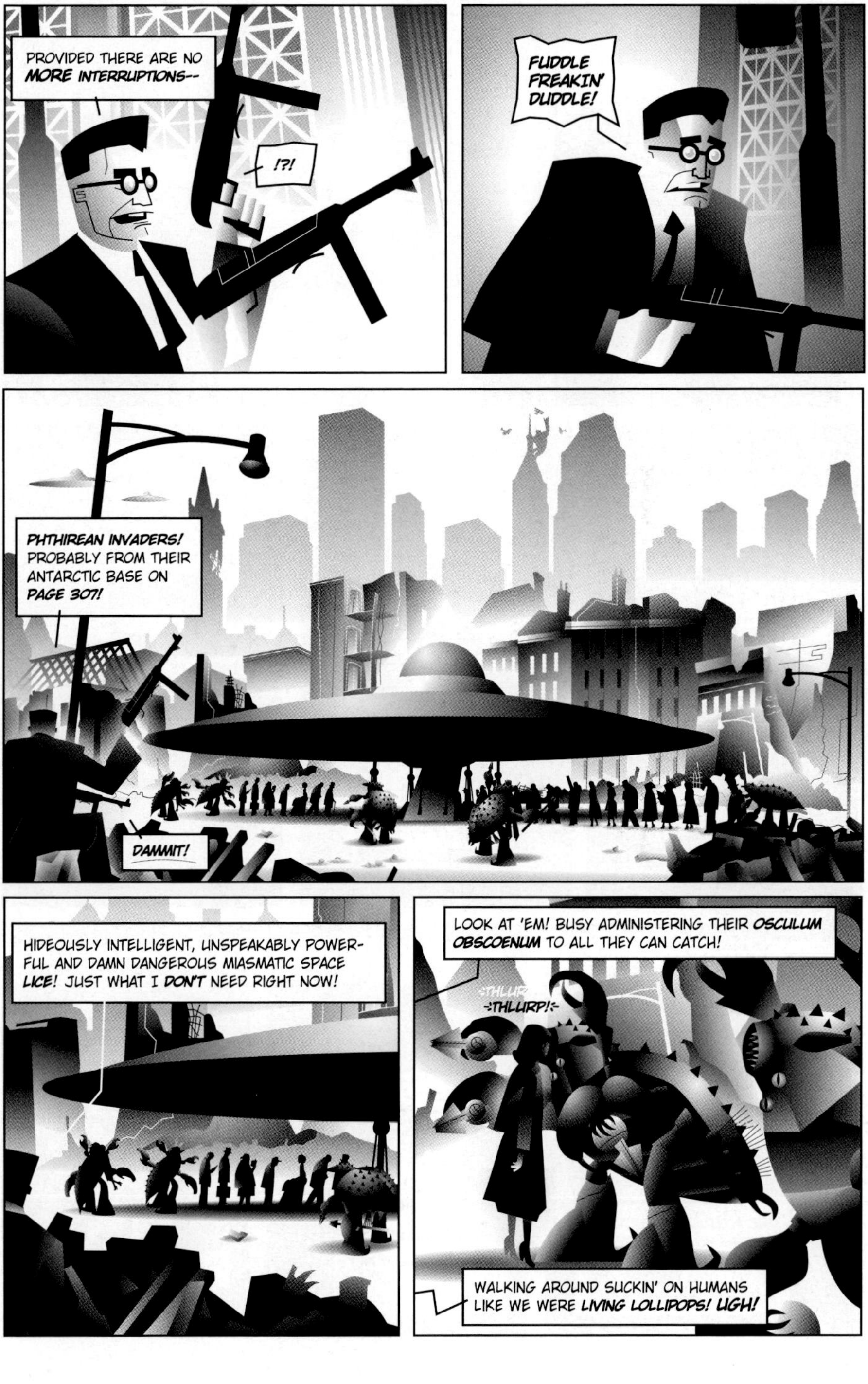

PROVIDED THERE ARE NO MORE INTERRUPTIONS--
!?!
FUDDLE FREAKIN' DUDDLE!
PHTHIREAN INVADERS! PROBABLY FROM THEIR ANTARCTIC BASE ON PAGE 307!
DAMMIT!
HIDEOUSLY INTELLIGENT, UNSPEAKABLY POWERFUL AND DAMN DANGEROUS MIASMATIC SPACE LICE! JUST WHAT I DON'T NEED RIGHT NOW!
LOOK AT 'EM! BUSY ADMINISTERING THEIR OSCULUM OBSCOENUM TO ALL THEY CAN CATCH!
THLURP!
WALKING AROUND SUCKIN' ON HUMANS LIKE WE WERE LIVING LOLLIPOPS! UGH!

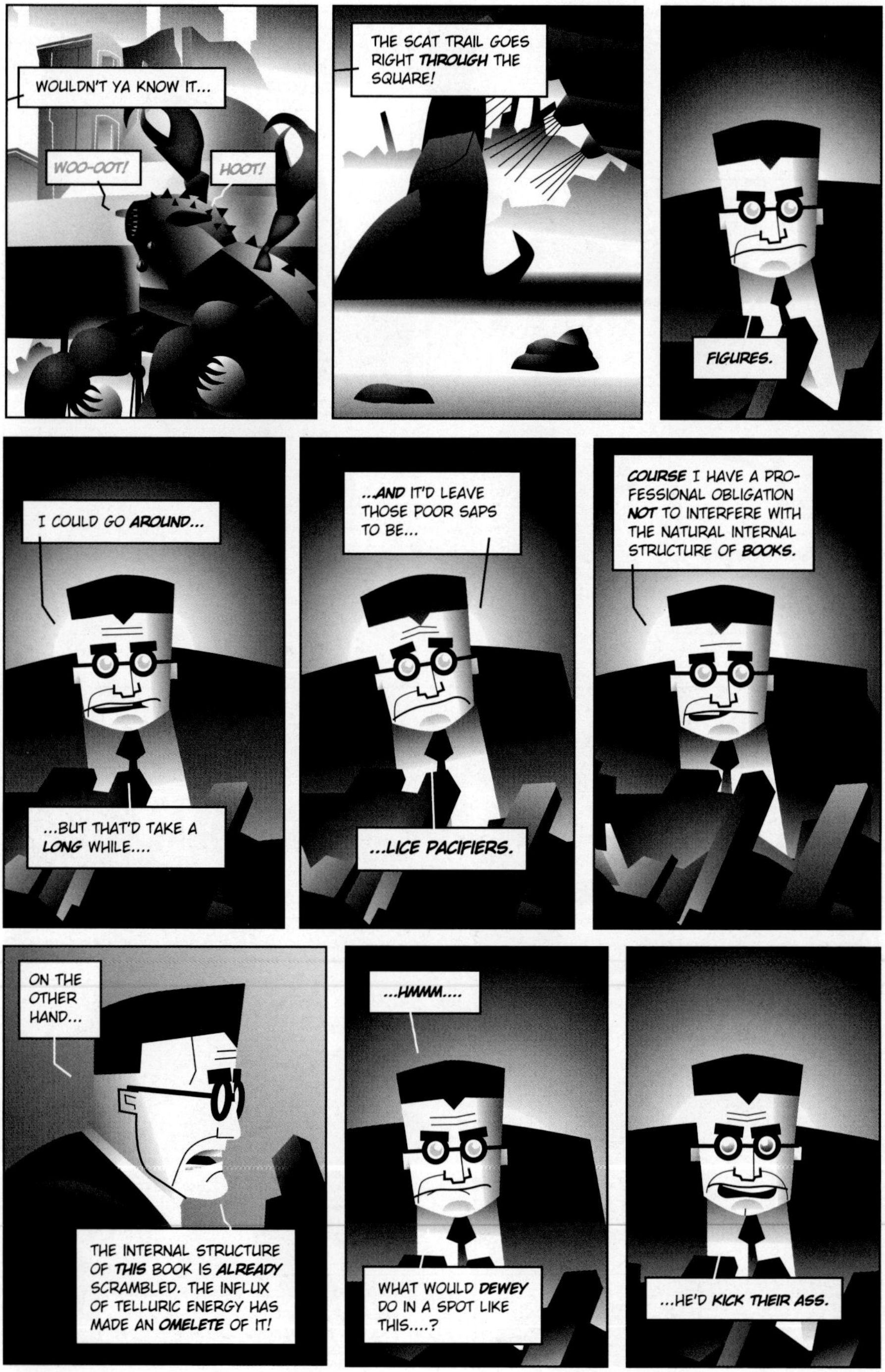
WOULDN'T YA KNOW IT...
WOO-OOT!
HOOT!
THE SCAT TRAIL GOES RIGHT THROUGH THE SQUARE!
FIGURES.
I COULD GO AROUND...
...BUT THAT'D TAKE A LONG WHILE....
...AND IT'D LEAVE THOSE POOR SAPS TO BE...
...LICE PACIFIERS.
COURSE I HAVE A PRO-FESSIONAL OBLIGATION NOT TO INTERFERE WITH THE NATURAL INTERNAL STRUCTURE OF BOOKS.
ON THE OTHER HAND...
THE INTERNAL STRUCTURE OF THIS BOOK IS ALREADY SCRAMBLED. THE INFLUX OF TELLURIC ENERGY HAS MADE AN OMELETE OF IT!
...HMMM....
WHAT WOULD DEWEY DO IN A SPOT LIKE THIS....?
...HE'D KICK THEIR ASS.

COUPLE OF **POP GUNS** WON'T BE ENOUGH TA TAKE'EM ON WITH. I LEARNED **THAT** IN '34 FIGHTING THEIR HARVESTING OPERATION IN THE MIDWEST! THEIR THICK CHITIN SHELL IS PRACTICALLY BULLET-PROOF! THEY'VE GOT THE STRENGTH OF **TEN MEN** AND THE CONSTITUTION OF AN OVERGROWN **COCKROACH,** WHICH, IF I REMEMBER CORRECTLY, THEY'RE DISTANTLY RELATED TO. AND THEY'VE GOT ENOUGH FIRE POWER TO **FLATTEN A PLANET** ON THAT ONE SLICK LITTLE SAUCER-SHIP...!

...BUT I EXPLICATE.

BLAISDELL'S
EXOTIC PET SHOP

OOOT! OOOT!

AH! THERE GOES ONE... OUT ON PATROL, OR TO FORM A PICKET LINE OR SOME-THING....

DAT GIVES ME AN IDEA.

IT WORKED IN '33, IT'LL WORK IN (INSERT CURRENT YEAR*)!

TIME TO RECRUIT SOME UNWITTING PROXIES!

AH!

THERE HE IS...

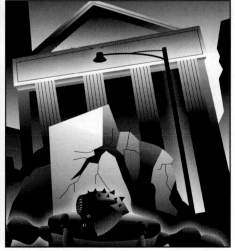

* ANOTHER SIGN OF OUR COMMITMENT TO BEING CURRENT!-- BENEVOLENT BARRY

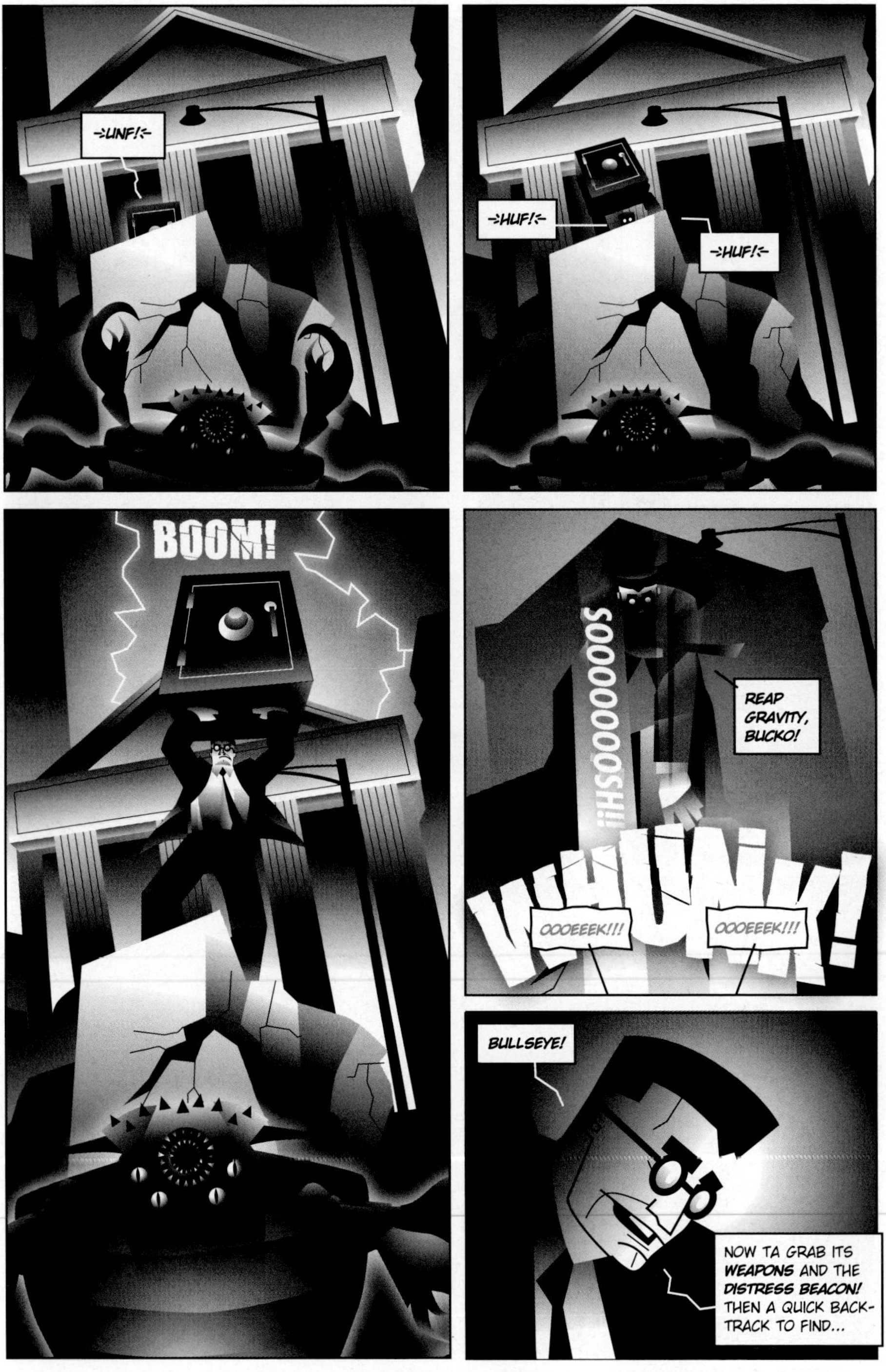
-UNF!-
-HUF!-
-HUF!-
BOOM!
SOOOOOOOOSH!!!
REAP GRAVITY, BUCKO!
WHUNK!
OOOEEEK!!!
OOOEEEK!!!
BULLSEYE!
NOW TA GRAB ITS **WEAPONS** AND THE **DISTRESS BEACON!** THEN A QUICK BACK-TRACK TO FIND...

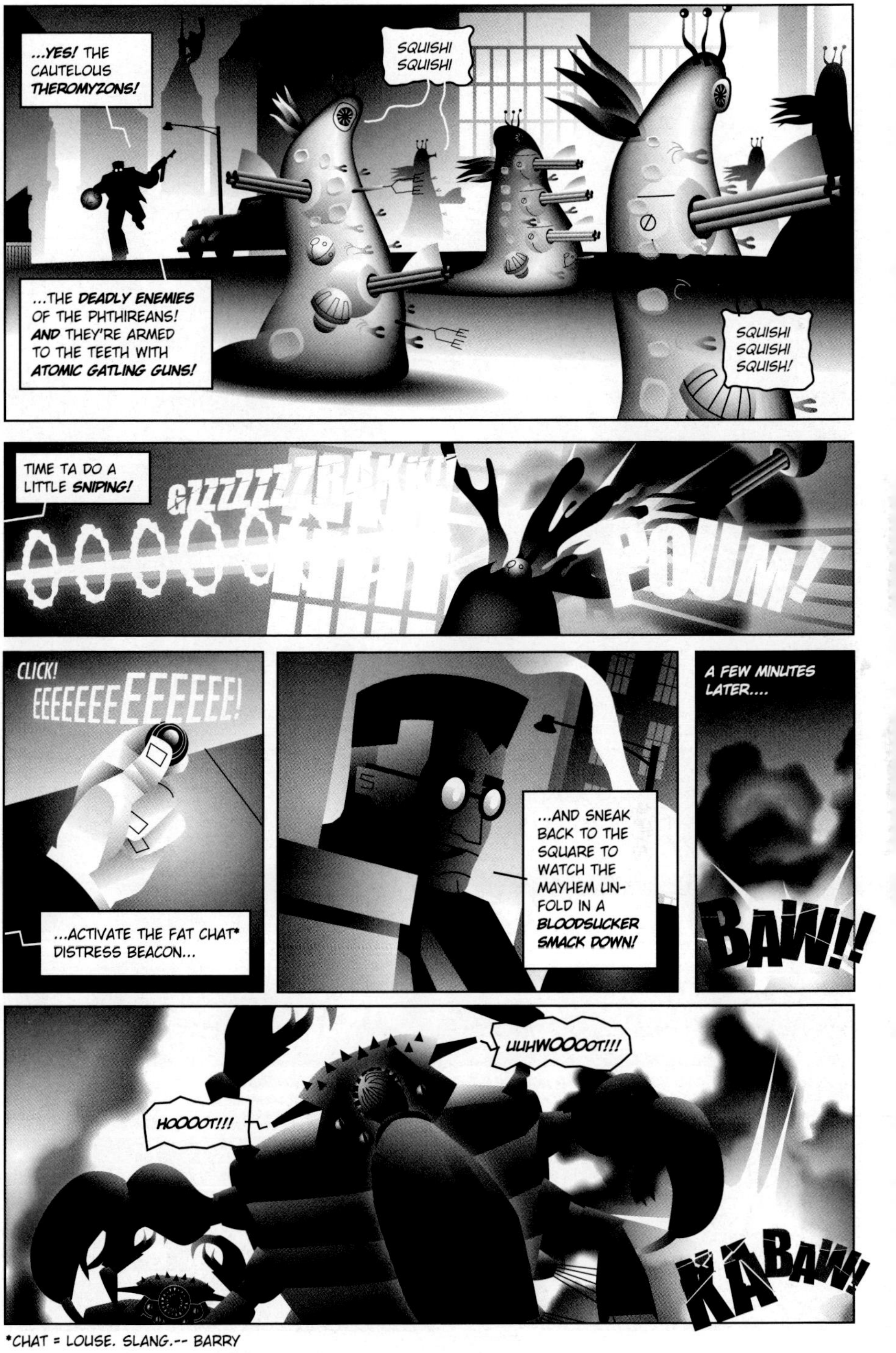
...YES! THE CAUTELOUS THEROMYZONS!
SQUISHI SQUISHI
...THE DEADLY ENEMIES OF THE PHTHIREANS! AND THEY'RE ARMED TO THE TEETH WITH ATOMIC GATLING GUNS!
SQUISHI SQUISHI SQUISH!
TIME TA DO A LITTLE SNIPING!
POUM!
CLICK!
EEEEEEEEEEEE!
...ACTIVATE THE FAT CHAT* DISTRESS BEACON...
...AND SNEAK BACK TO THE SQUARE TO WATCH THE MAYHEM UN-FOLD IN A BLOODSUCKER SMACK DOWN!
A FEW MINUTES LATER....
BAW!!
UUHWOOOOT!!!
HOOOOT!!!
KABAW!!

*CHAT = LOUSE. SLANG.-- BARRY

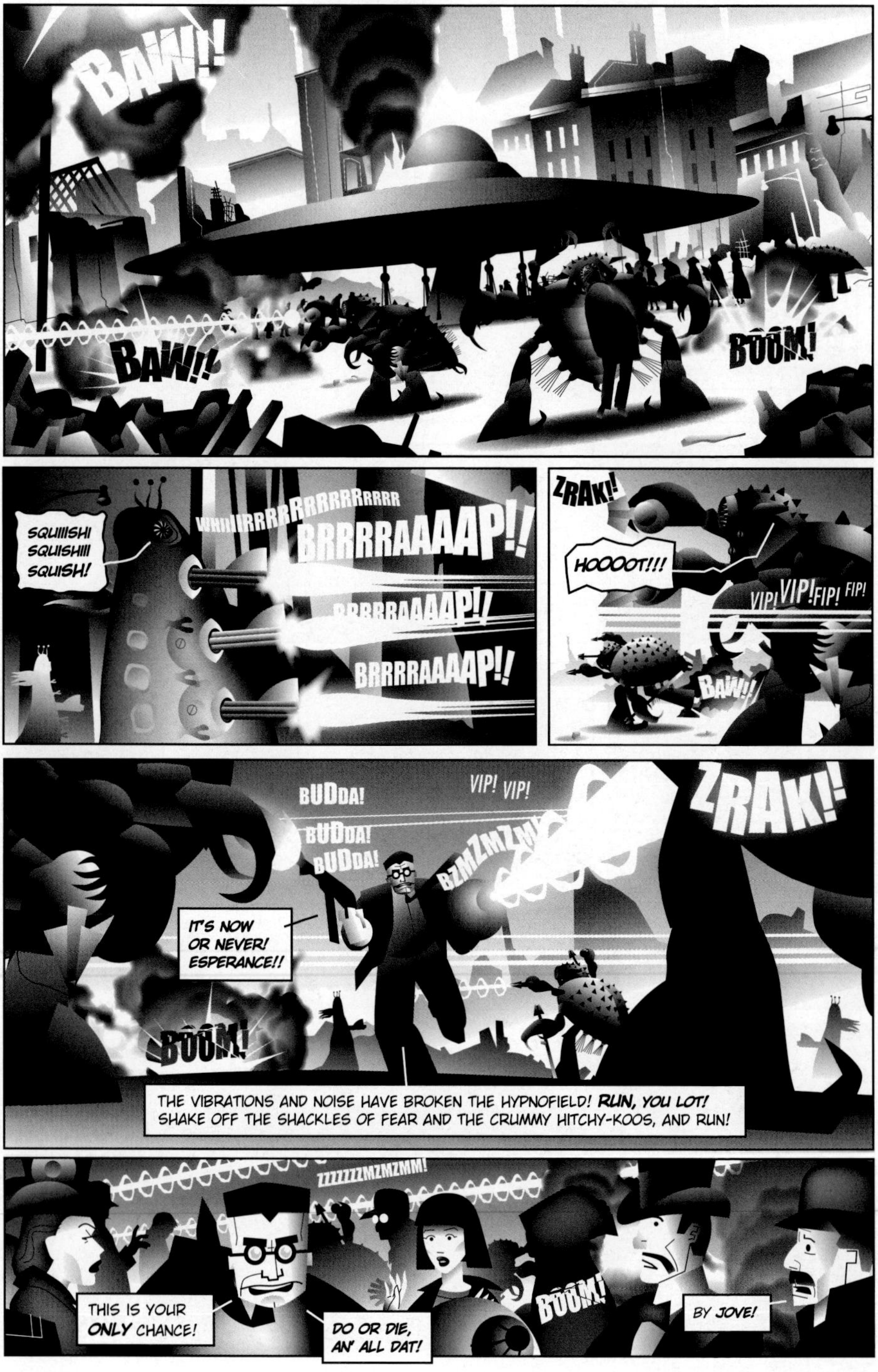
BAW!!
BAW!!
BOOM!
SQUIIISHI SQUISHIII SQUISH!
WHIIIIIRRRRRRRRRRrrrr
BRRRRAAAAP!!
BRRRRAAAAP!!
BRRRRAAAAP!!
ZRAK!!
HOOOOT!!!
VIP! VIP! FIP! FIP!
BAW!!
BUDDA!
BUDDA!
BUDDA!
VIP! VIP!
ZRAK!!
BZMZMZM
IT'S NOW OR NEVER! ESPERANCE!!
BOOM!
THE VIBRATIONS AND NOISE HAVE BROKEN THE HYPNOFIELD! RUN, YOU LOT! SHAKE OFF THE SHACKLES OF FEAR AND THE CRUMMY HITCHY-KOOS, AND RUN!
ZZZZZZZMZMZMM!
THIS IS YOUR ONLY CHANCE!
DO OR DIE, AN' ALL DAT!
BOOM!
BY JOVE!

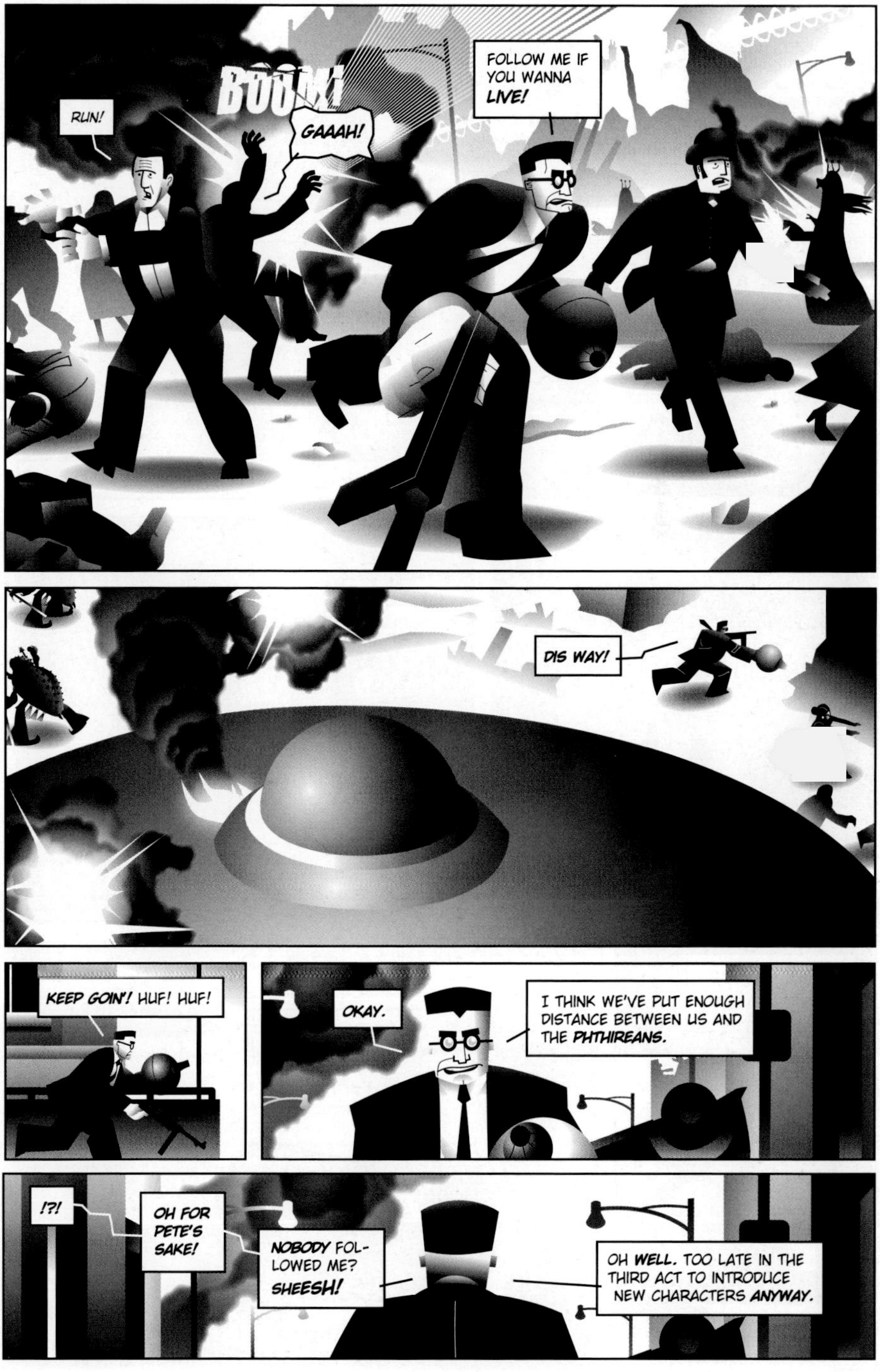
RUN!
BOOM!
GAAAH!
FOLLOW ME IF YOU WANNA LIVE!
DIS WAY!
KEEP GOIN'! HUF! HUF!
OKAY.
I THINK WE'VE PUT ENOUGH DISTANCE BETWEEN US AND THE PHTHIREANS.
!?!
OH FOR PETE'S SAKE!
NOBODY FOL-LOWED ME? SHEESH!
OH WELL. TOO LATE IN THE THIRD ACT TO INTRODUCE NEW CHARACTERS ANYWAY.

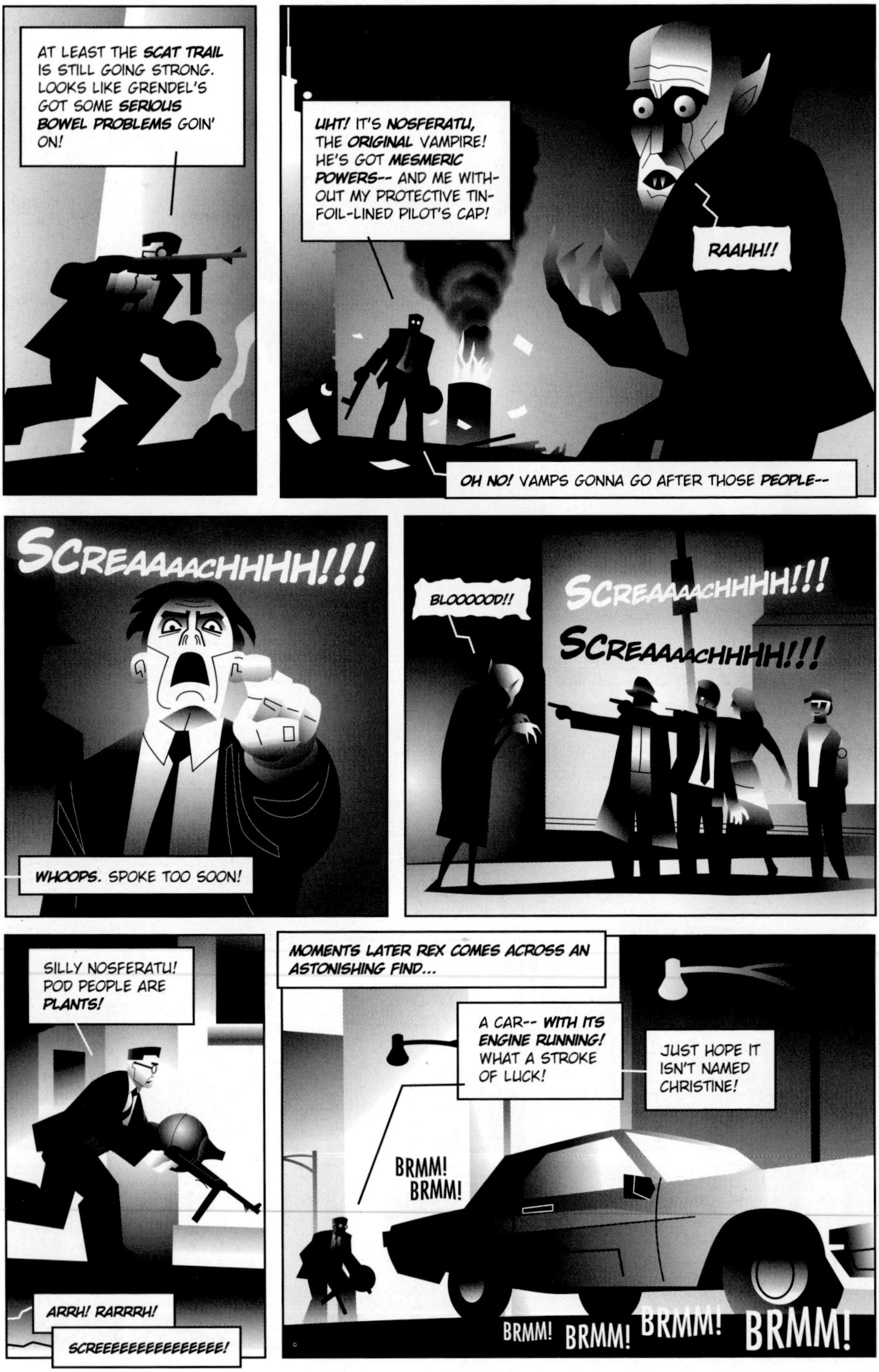
AT LEAST THE SCAT TRAIL IS STILL GOING STRONG. LOOKS LIKE GRENDEL'S GOT SOME SERIOUS BOWEL PROBLEMS GOIN' ON!
UHT! IT'S NOSFERATU, THE ORIGINAL VAMPIRE! HE'S GOT MESMERIC POWERS-- AND ME WITH-OUT MY PROTECTIVE TIN-FOIL-LINED PILOT'S CAP!
RAAHH!!
OH NO! VAMPS GONNA GO AFTER THOSE PEOPLE--
SCREAAAACHHHH!!!
WHOOPS. SPOKE TOO SOON!
BLOOOOOD!!
SCREAAAACHHHH!!!
SCREAAAACHHHH!!!
SILLY NOSFERATU! POD PEOPLE ARE PLANTS!
ARRH! RARRRH!
SCREEEEEEEEEEEEEEE!
MOMENTS LATER REX COMES ACROSS AN ASTONISHING FIND...
A CAR-- WITH ITS ENGINE RUNNING! WHAT A STROKE OF LUCK!
JUST HOPE IT ISN'T NAMED CHRISTINE!
BRMM! BRMM!
BRMM! BRMM! BRMM! BRMM!

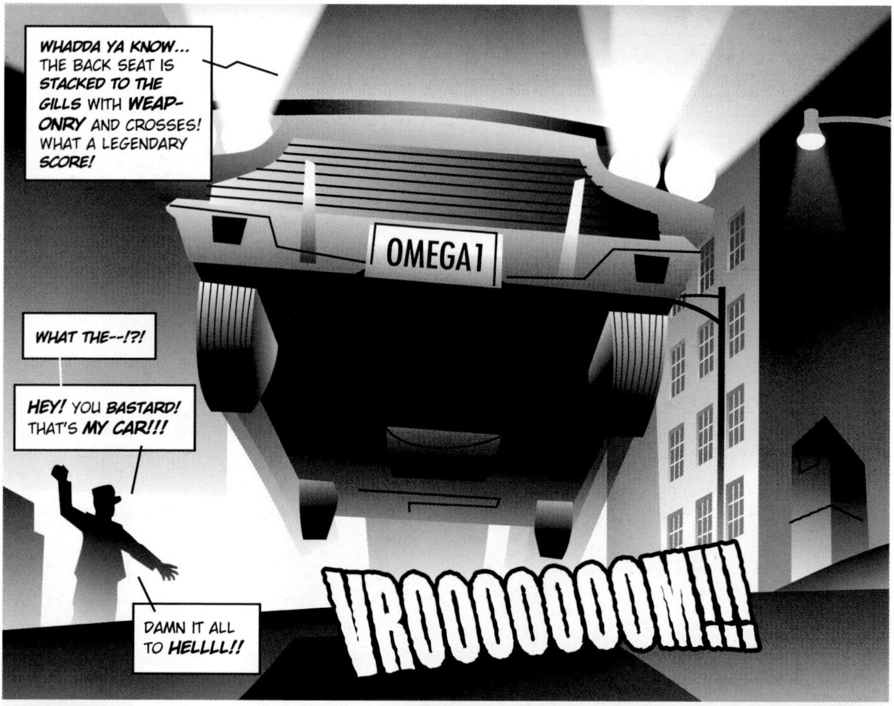
WHADDA YA KNOW... THE BACK SEAT IS STACKED TO THE GILLS WITH WEAP-ONRY AND CROSSES! WHAT A LEGENDARY SCORE!
OMEGA1
WHAT THE--!?!
HEY! YOU BASTARD! THAT'S MY CAR!!!
DAMN IT ALL TO HELLLL!!
VROOOOOOOOM!!!

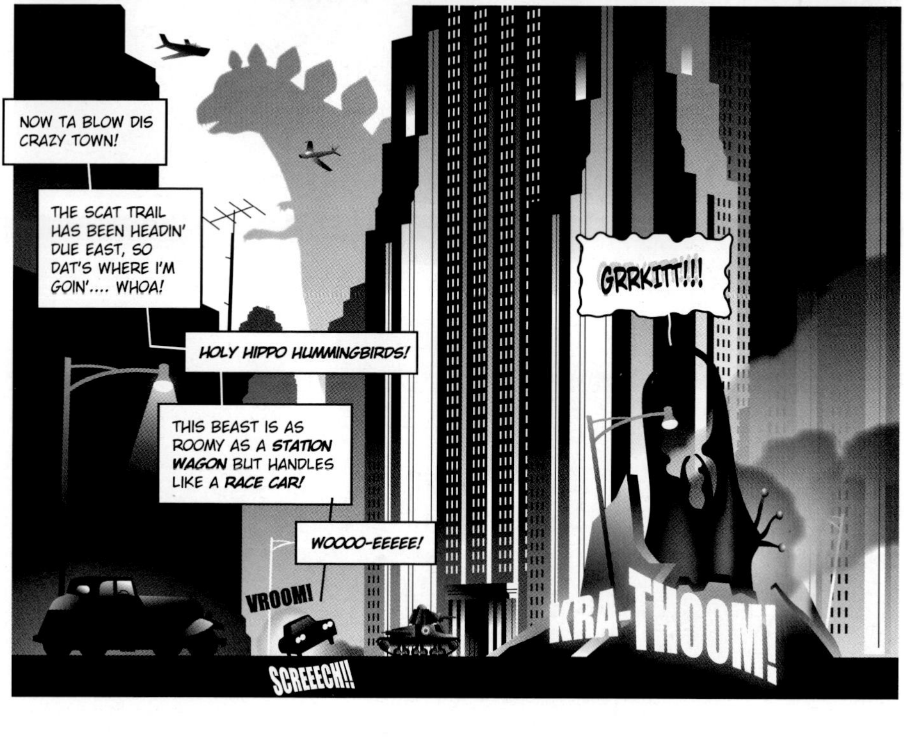
NOW TA BLOW DIS CRAZY TOWN!
THE SCAT TRAIL HAS BEEN HEADIN' DUE EAST, SO DAT'S WHERE I'M GOIN'.... WHOA!
HOLY HIPPO HUMMINGBIRDS!
THIS BEAST IS AS ROOMY AS A STATION WAGON BUT HANDLES LIKE A RACE CAR!
WOOOO-EEEEE!
GRRKITT!!!
VROOM!
KRA-THOOM!
SCREEECH!!

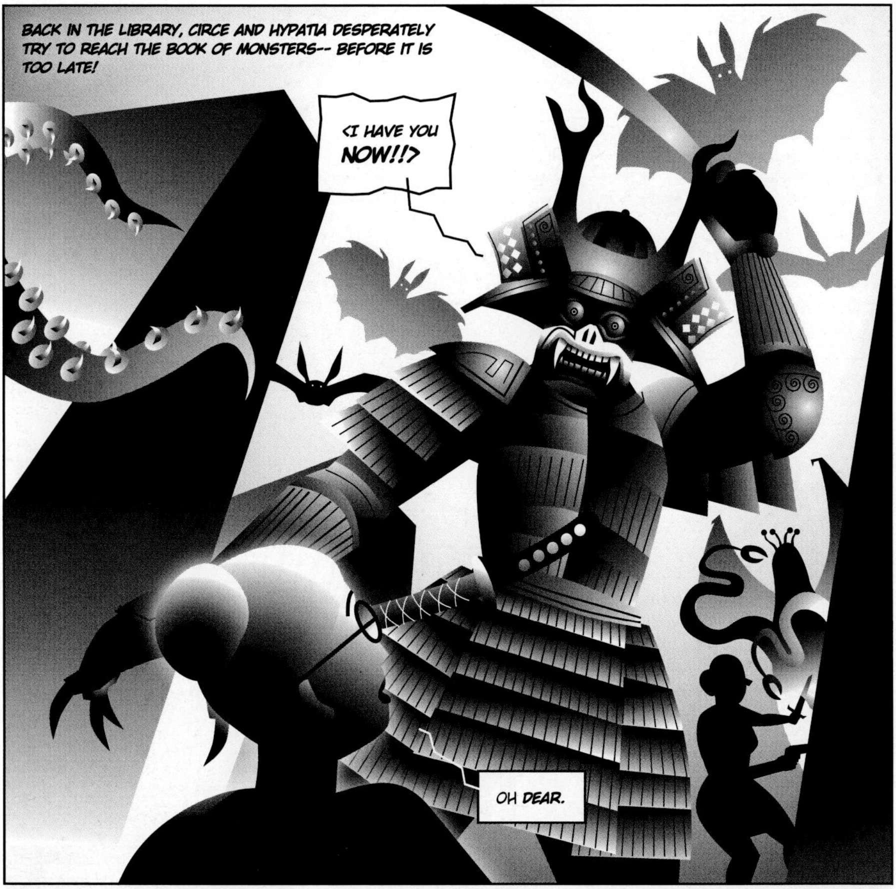
BACK IN THE LIBRARY, CIRCE AND HYPATIA DESPERATELY TRY TO REACH THE BOOK OF MONSTERS-- BEFORE IT IS TOO LATE!
<I HAVE YOU NOW!!>
OH DEAR.

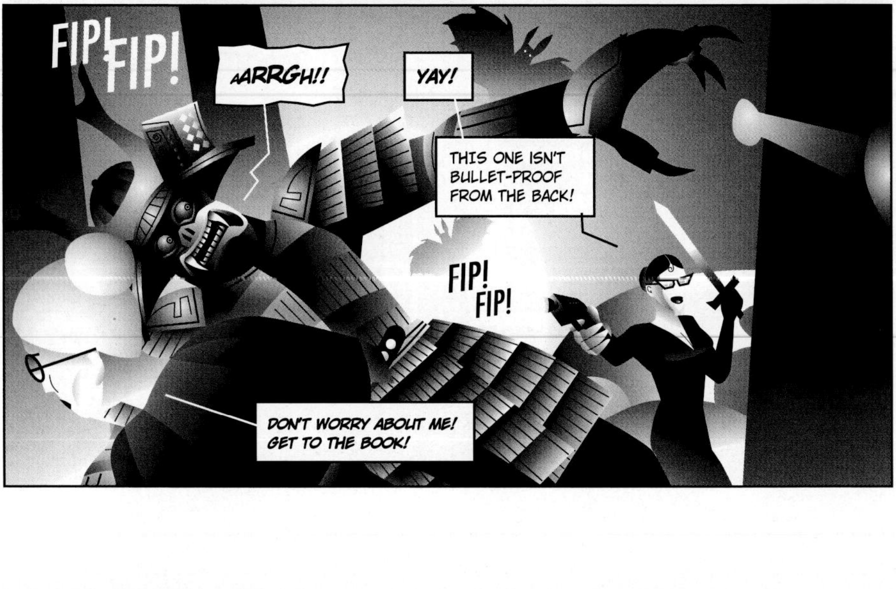
FIP! FIP!
AARRGH!!
YAY!
THIS ONE ISN'T BULLET-PROOF FROM THE BACK!
FIP! FIP!
DON'T WORRY ABOUT ME! GET TO THE BOOK!

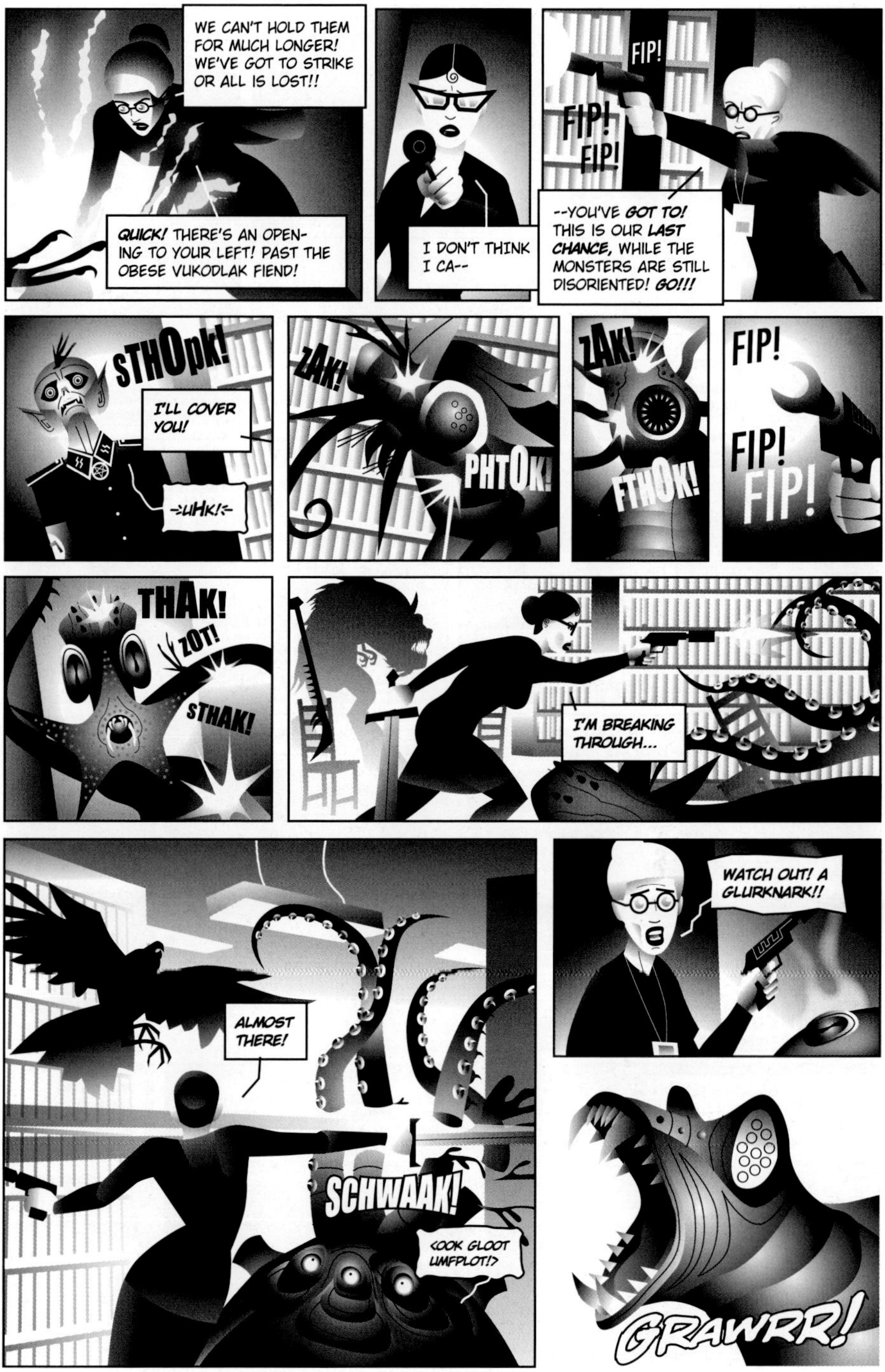
WE CAN'T HOLD THEM FOR MUCH LONGER! WE'VE GOT TO STRIKE OR ALL IS LOST!!
QUICK! THERE'S AN OPENING TO YOUR LEFT! PAST THE OBESE VUKODLAK FIEND!
I DON'T THINK I CA--
FIP!
FIP!
FIP!
--YOU'VE GOT TO! THIS IS OUR LAST CHANCE, WHILE THE MONSTERS ARE STILL DISORIENTED! GO!!!
sTHOpk!
I'LL COVER YOU!
-uHK!-
zAK!
PHTOK!
zAK!
FTHOK!
FIP!
FIP!
FIP!
THAK!
zOT!
STHAK!
I'M BREAKING THROUGH...
ALMOST THERE!
SCHWAAK!
<OOK GLOOT UMFPLOT!>
WATCH OUT! A GLURKNARK!!
GRAWRR!

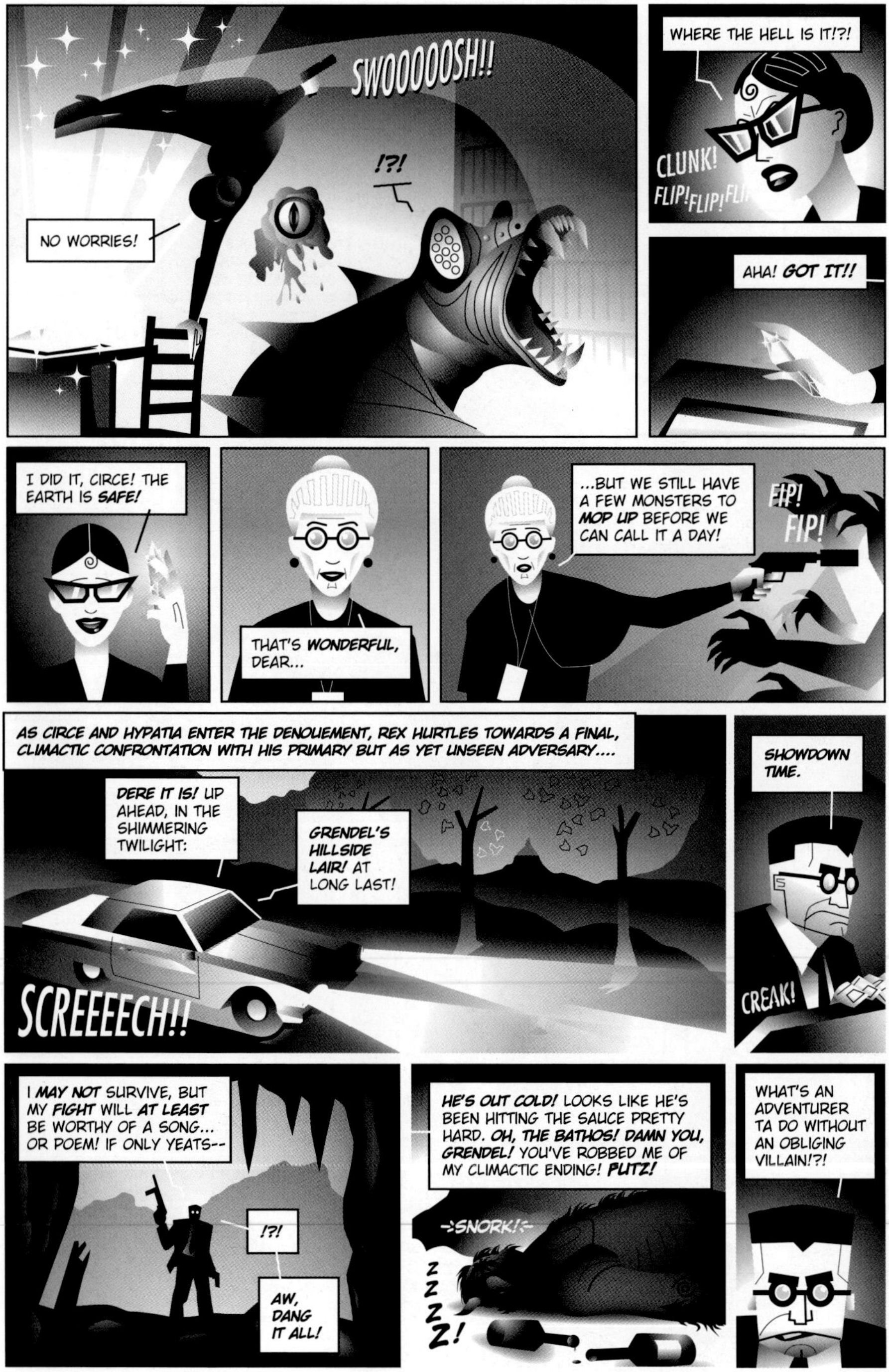
SWOOOOOOSH!!
!?!
NO WORRIES!
WHERE THE HELL IS IT!?!
CLUNK!
FLIP! FLIP! FLIP!
AHA! GOT IT!!
I DID IT, CIRCE! THE EARTH IS SAFE!
THAT'S WONDERFUL, DEAR...
...BUT WE STILL HAVE A FEW MONSTERS TO MOP UP BEFORE WE CAN CALL IT A DAY!
FIP! FIP!
AS CIRCE AND HYPATIA ENTER THE DENOUEMENT, REX HURTLES TOWARDS A FINAL, CLIMACTIC CONFRONTATION WITH HIS PRIMARY BUT AS YET UNSEEN ADVERSARY....
DERE IT IS! UP AHEAD, IN THE SHIMMERING TWILIGHT:
GRENDEL'S HILLSIDE LAIR! AT LONG LAST!
SCREEEECH!!
SHOWDOWN TIME.
CREAK!
I MAY NOT SURVIVE, BUT MY FIGHT WILL AT LEAST BE WORTHY OF A SONG... OR POEM! IF ONLY YEATS--
!?!
AW, DANG IT ALL!
HE'S OUT COLD! LOOKS LIKE HE'S BEEN HITTING THE SAUCE PRETTY HARD. OH, THE BATHOS! DAMN YOU, GRENDEL! YOU'VE ROBBED ME OF MY CLIMACTIC ENDING! PUTZ!
SNORK!
Z Z Z Z!
WHAT'S AN ADVENTURER TA DO WITHOUT AN OBLIGING VILLAIN!?!

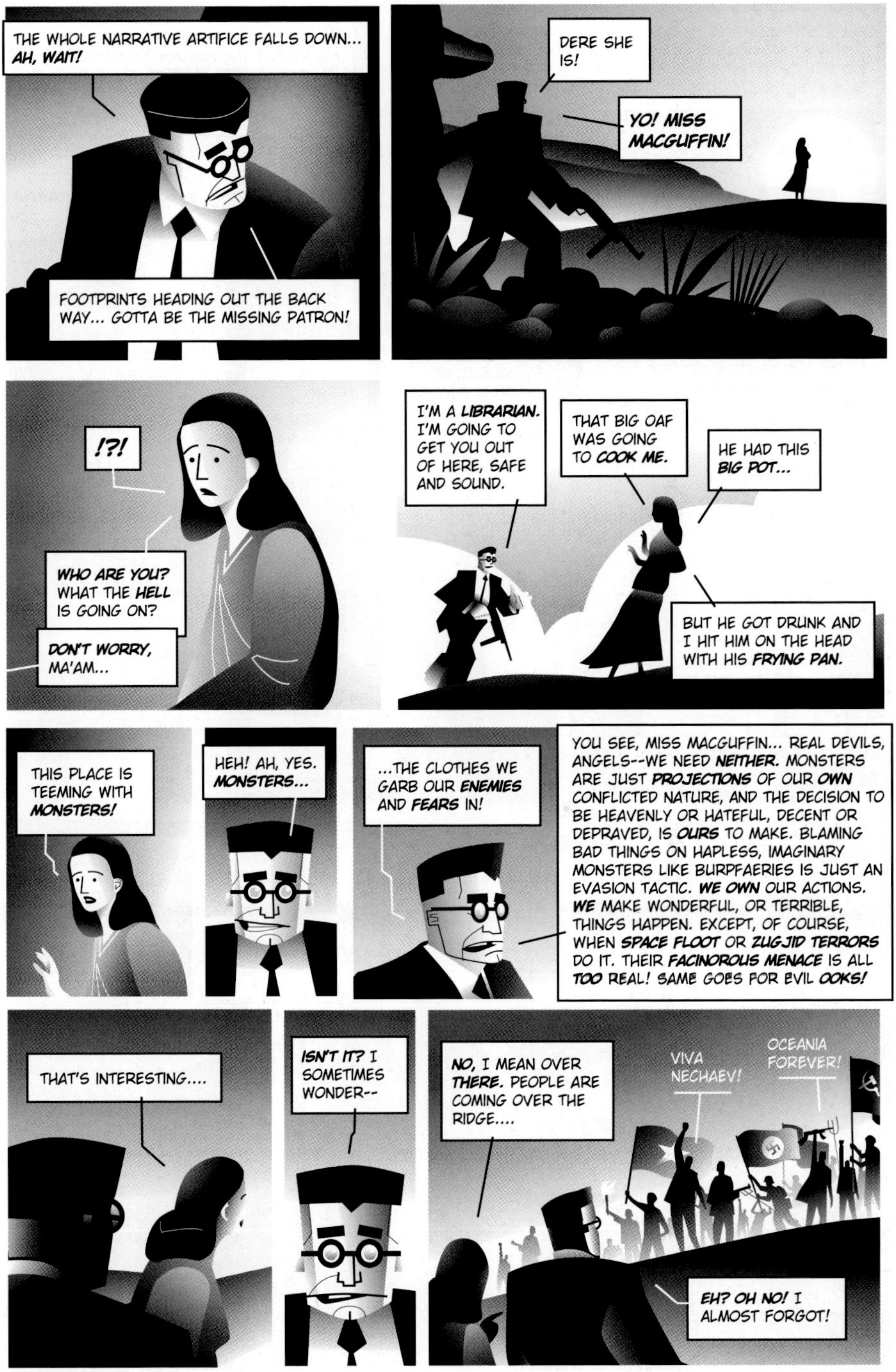
THE WHOLE NARRATIVE ARTIFICE FALLS DOWN... AH, WAIT!
FOOTPRINTS HEADING OUT THE BACK WAY... GOTTA BE THE MISSING PATRON!
DERE SHE IS!
YO! MISS MACGUFFIN!
!?!
WHO ARE YOU? WHAT THE HELL IS GOING ON?
DON'T WORRY, MA'AM...
I'M A LIBRARIAN. I'M GOING TO GET YOU OUT OF HERE, SAFE AND SOUND.
THAT BIG OAF WAS GOING TO COOK ME.
HE HAD THIS BIG POT...
BUT HE GOT DRUNK AND I HIT HIM ON THE HEAD WITH HIS FRYING PAN.
THIS PLACE IS TEEMING WITH MONSTERS!
HEH! AH, YES. MONSTERS...
...THE CLOTHES WE GARB OUR ENEMIES AND FEARS IN!
YOU SEE, MISS MACGUFFIN... REAL DEVILS, ANGELS--WE NEED NEITHER. MONSTERS ARE JUST PROJECTIONS OF OUR OWN CONFLICTED NATURE, AND THE DECISION TO BE HEAVENLY OR HATEFUL, DECENT OR DEPRAVED, IS OURS TO MAKE. BLAMING BAD THINGS ON HAPLESS, IMAGINARY MONSTERS LIKE BURPFAERIES IS JUST AN EVASION TACTIC. WE OWN OUR ACTIONS. WE MAKE WONDERFUL, OR TERRIBLE, THINGS HAPPEN. EXCEPT, OF COURSE, WHEN SPACE FLOOT OR ZUGJID TERRORS DO IT. THEIR FACINOROUS MENACE IS ALL TOO REAL! SAME GOES FOR EVIL OOKS!
THAT'S INTERESTING....
ISN'T IT? I SOMETIMES WONDER--
NO, I MEAN OVER THERE. PEOPLE ARE COMING OVER THE RIDGE....
VIVA NECHAEV!
OCEANIA FOREVER!
EH? OH NO! I ALMOST FORGOT!

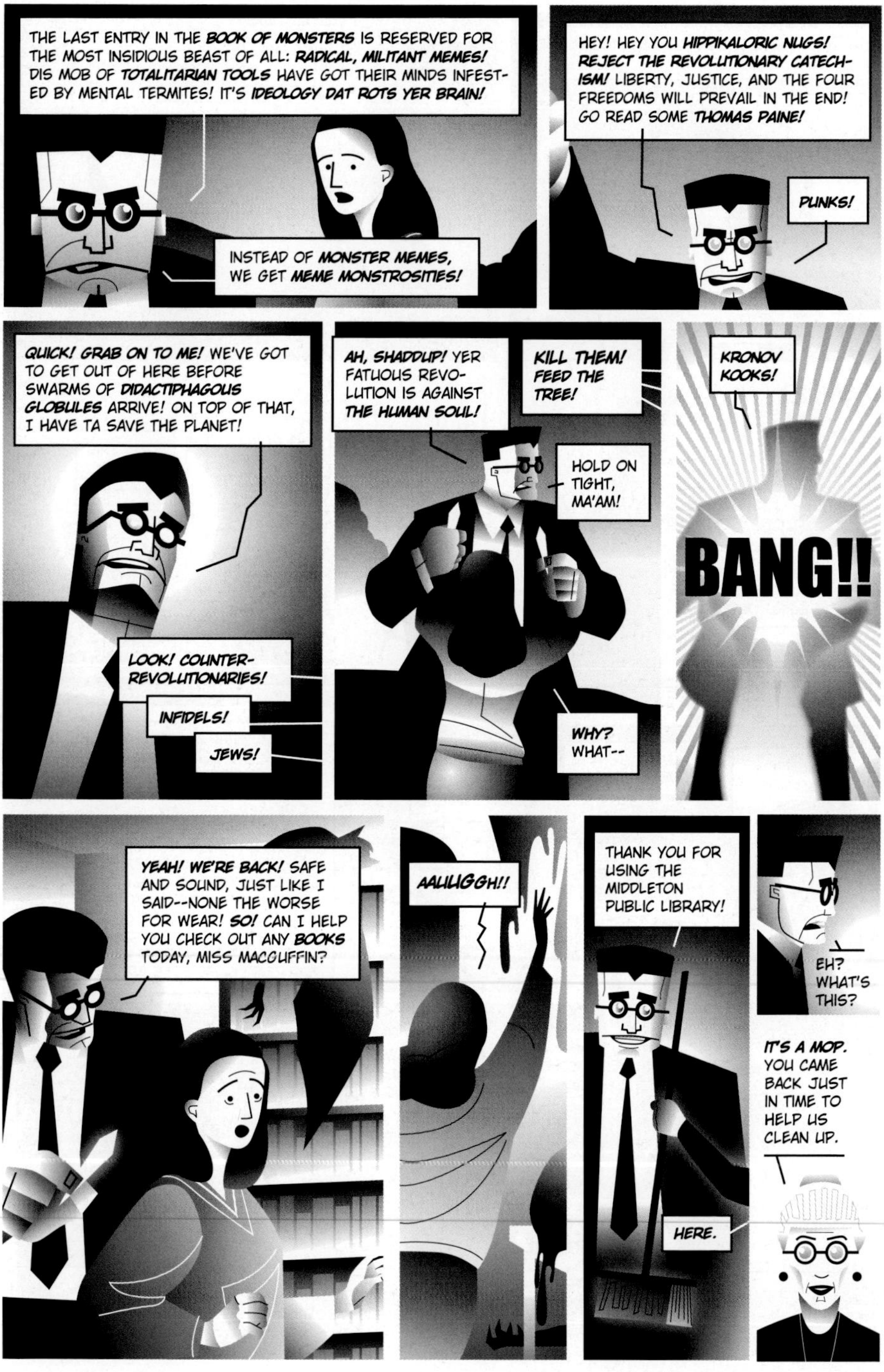
THE LAST ENTRY IN THE BOOK OF MONSTERS IS RESERVED FOR THE MOST INSIDIOUS BEAST OF ALL: RADICAL, MILITANT MEMES! DIS MOB OF TOTALITARIAN TOOLS HAVE GOT THEIR MINDS INFESTED BY MENTAL TERMITES! IT'S IDEOLOGY DAT ROTS YER BRAIN!
INSTEAD OF MONSTER MEMES, WE GET MEME MONSTROSITIES!
HEY! HEY YOU HIPPIKALORIC NUGS! REJECT THE REVOLUTIONARY CATECHISM! LIBERTY, JUSTICE, AND THE FOUR FREEDOMS WILL PREVAIL IN THE END! GO READ SOME THOMAS PAINE!
PUNKS!
QUICK! GRAB ON TO ME! WE'VE GOT TO GET OUT OF HERE BEFORE SWARMS OF DIDACTIPHAGOUS GLOBULES ARRIVE! ON TOP OF THAT, I HAVE TA SAVE THE PLANET!
LOOK! COUNTER-REVOLUTIONARIES!
INFIDELS!
JEWS!
AH, SHADDUP! YER FATUOUS REVOLUTION IS AGAINST THE HUMAN SOUL!
KILL THEM! FEED THE TREE!
HOLD ON TIGHT, MA'AM!
WHY? WHAT--
KRONOV KOOKS!
BANG!!
YEAH! WE'RE BACK! SAFE AND SOUND, JUST LIKE I SAID--NONE THE WORSE FOR WEAR! SO! CAN I HELP YOU CHECK OUT ANY BOOKS TODAY, MISS MACGUFFIN?
AAUUGGH!!
THANK YOU FOR USING THE MIDDLETON PUBLIC LIBRARY!
HERE.
EH? WHAT'S THIS?
IT'S A MOP. YOU CAME BACK JUST IN TIME TO HELP US CLEAN UP.

CHAPTER NINE

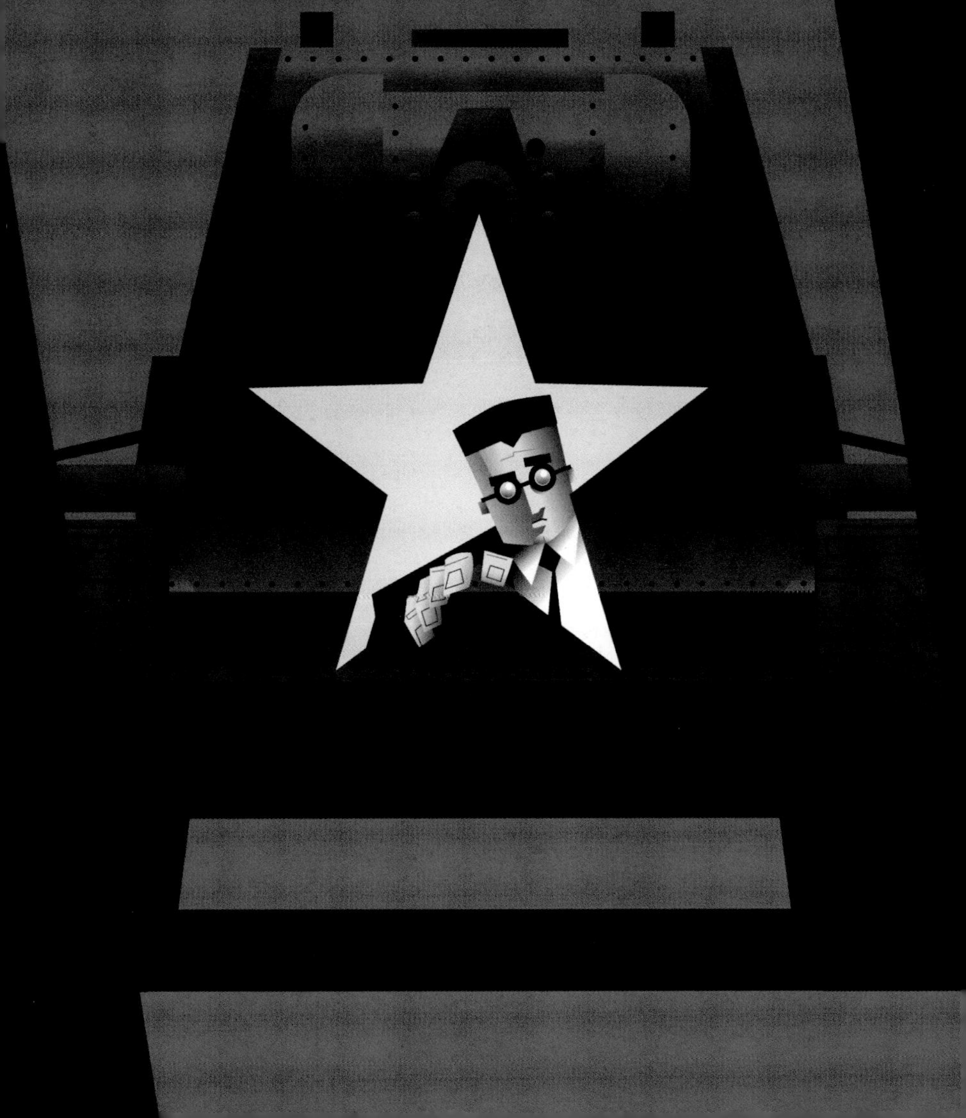

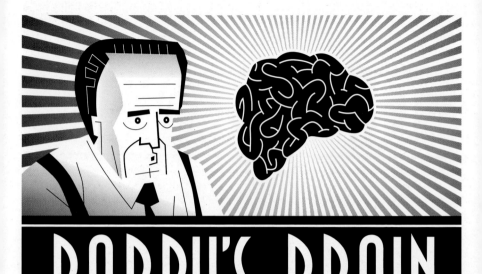

BARRY'S BRAIN

This fantastic issue marks the beginning of our third fabulous story line. Third *official* storyline I mean. I'm not counting the dozen or so unresolved plot threads. Rex leads a complicated and multi-layered life. Streamline, I say. Prioritize. Shave off the excess fat of real life and get down to the plump meat beneath. But no, Rex wants to keep it real. The journey is the thing, not the destination, he says. He sounds like Tristram Shandy if you ask me—not exactly in tune with the action hero genre. The dear boy has much to learn about the nature of the publishing beast. But that's why he's here with Heremeneutic! Why? Because this is what Hermeneutic is all about: breaking barriers, contravening conventions, and doing things differently until sales fall flat and we come to our senses.

There are those who say that the comic book market these days is not as profitable as it once was. True, over the last few years I could have made more money panhandling than publishing independent comics, but where would that leave the rest of the world? Without the wonder of Hermeneutic Press and the earth shattering innovation of Visicomboics! Can you imagine a world without them? Neither can I.

This issue Rex deals devastation upon the goons of OGPU, the secret police of the Soviet Union before they got a spiffier acronym. Surely 'NKVD' and 'KGB' conjure up more dread with their initials than the title 'OGPU' does. It's like a cross between Goops and poo, which is frightening only from a hygiene and taste point of view. It isn't as outright goofy as CRAP (the acronym of the Canadian Reform Alliance Party—before they quickly renamed themselves the Conservatives), for example, but it just isn't the kind of menacing acronym you want for a murderous organization of busy-body thugs.

Our other projects continue to toddle along. *The Immovable Man* is another series not to be missed: the latest issue sees him up against The Boggart Gang, who always rob banks with more than one exit—presenting the Immovable Man with a seemingly unsolvable dilemma! *My Breasts Came From Mars* is selling beyond all expectation in the direct market and is likely to become our new flagship title. A big screen adaptation is in the works! Casting directors are already amassing the necessary supply of silicone.

Speaking of which, we here at Hermeneutic Press are proud to present the first chapter of my debut novel: *A World FUBAR: Heironymous Snogg and the Sex Vixen Factory of the Post-Apocalypse.* It's sure to be a conversation starter. All the lessons I have learned from being in the comic publishing industry these many years I have applied to this piece. It's like some kind of sci-fi spaghetti sauce. Saucy!

Bloviate!

B. Barry Horst
Publisher

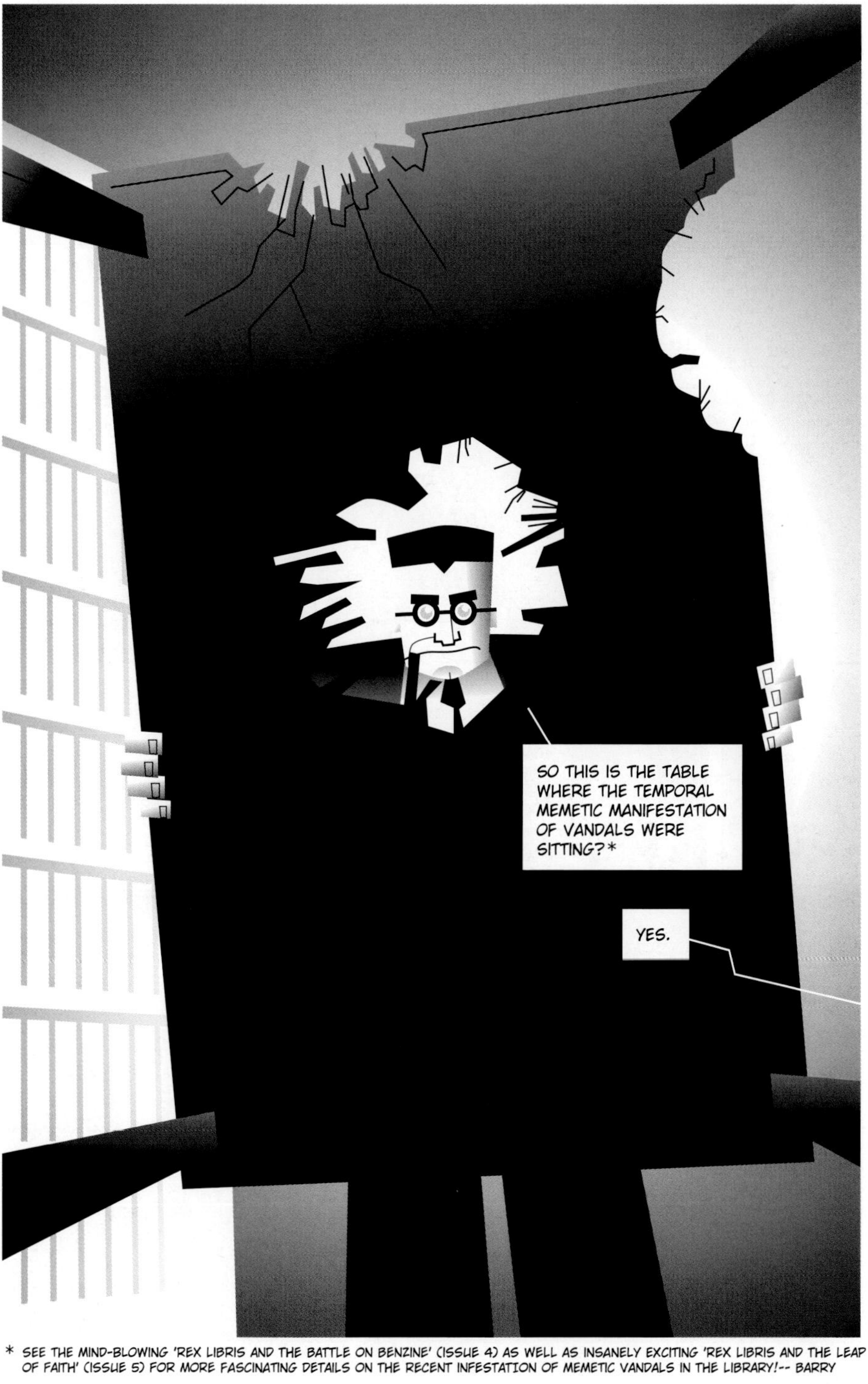
SO THIS IS THE TABLE WHERE THE TEMPORAL MEMETIC MANIFESTATION OF VANDALS WERE SITTING?*
YES.

* SEE THE MIND-BLOWING 'REX LIBRIS AND THE BATTLE ON BENZINE' (ISSUE 4) AS WELL AS INSANELY EXCITING 'REX LIBRIS AND THE LEAP OF FAITH' (ISSUE 5) FOR MORE FASCINATING DETAILS ON THE RECENT INFESTATION OF MEMETIC VANDALS IN THE LIBRARY!-- BARRY

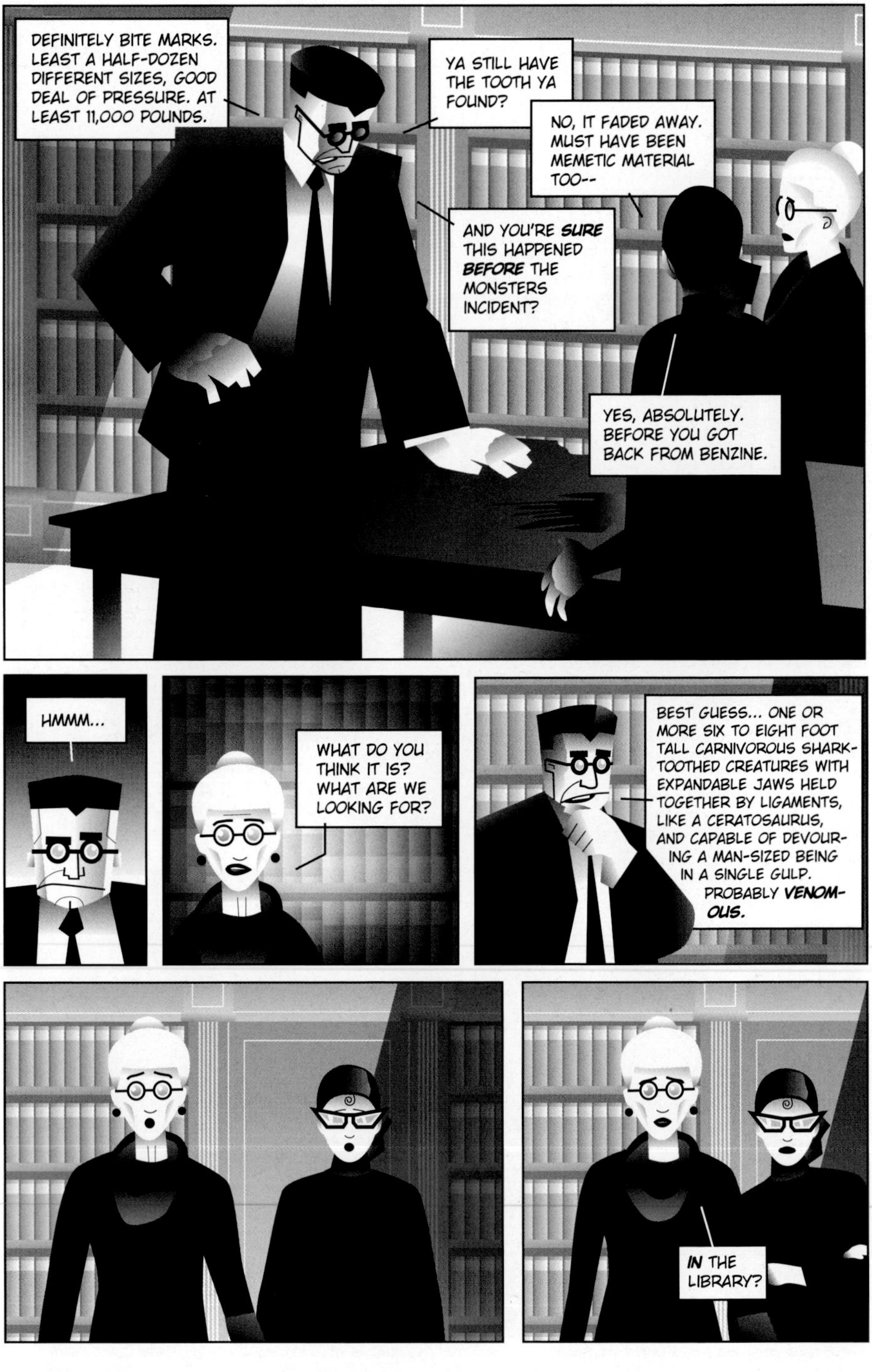
DEFINITELY BITE MARKS. LEAST A HALF-DOZEN DIFFERENT SIZES, GOOD DEAL OF PRESSURE. AT LEAST 11,000 POUNDS.
YA STILL HAVE THE TOOTH YA FOUND?
NO, IT FADED AWAY. MUST HAVE BEEN MEMETIC MATERIAL TOO--
AND YOU'RE **SURE** THIS HAPPENED **BEFORE** THE MONSTERS INCIDENT?
YES, ABSOLUTELY. BEFORE YOU GOT BACK FROM BENZINE.
HMMM...
WHAT DO YOU THINK IT IS? WHAT ARE WE LOOKING FOR?
BEST GUESS... ONE OR MORE SIX TO EIGHT FOOT TALL CARNIVOROUS SHARK-TOOTHED CREATURES WITH EXPANDABLE JAWS HELD TOGETHER BY LIGAMENTS, LIKE A CERATOSAURUS, AND CAPABLE OF DEVOURING A MAN-SIZED BEING IN A SINGLE GULP. PROBABLY **VENOMOUS.**
IN THE LIBRARY?

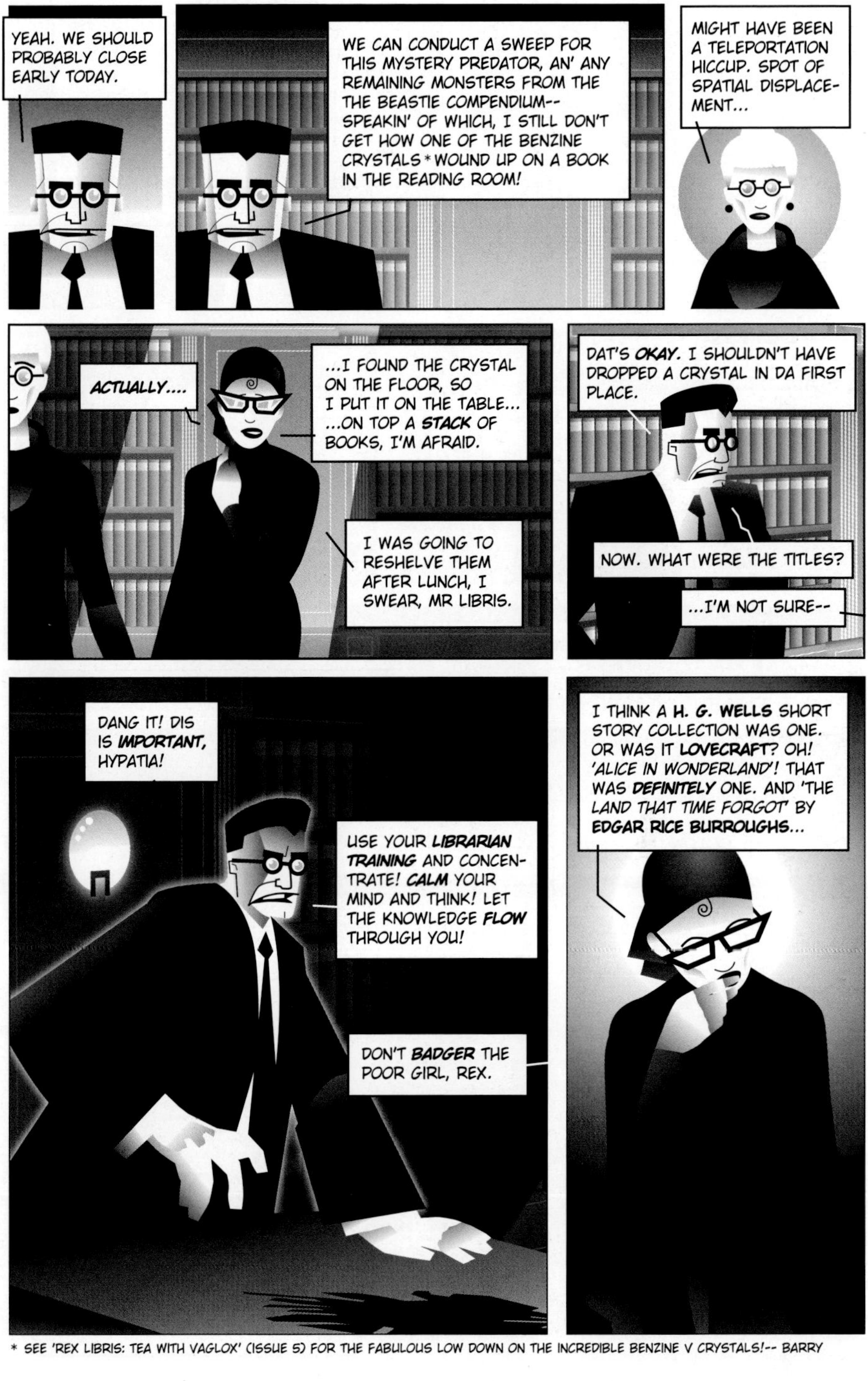
YEAH. WE SHOULD PROBABLY CLOSE EARLY TODAY.
WE CAN CONDUCT A SWEEP FOR THIS MYSTERY PREDATOR, AN' ANY REMAINING MONSTERS FROM THE THE BEASTIE COMPENDIUM-- SPEAKIN' OF WHICH, I STILL DON'T GET HOW ONE OF THE BENZINE CRYSTALS* WOUND UP ON A BOOK IN THE READING ROOM!
MIGHT HAVE BEEN A TELEPORTATION HICCUP. SPOT OF SPATIAL DISPLACEMENT...
ACTUALLY....
...I FOUND THE CRYSTAL ON THE FLOOR, SO I PUT IT ON THE TABLE... ...ON TOP A STACK OF BOOKS, I'M AFRAID.
I WAS GOING TO RESHELVE THEM AFTER LUNCH, I SWEAR, MR LIBRIS.
DAT'S OKAY. I SHOULDN'T HAVE DROPPED A CRYSTAL IN DA FIRST PLACE.
NOW. WHAT WERE THE TITLES?
...I'M NOT SURE--
DANG IT! DIS IS IMPORTANT, HYPATIA!
USE YOUR LIBRARIAN TRAINING AND CONCENTRATE! CALM YOUR MIND AND THINK! LET THE KNOWLEDGE FLOW THROUGH YOU!
DON'T BADGER THE POOR GIRL, REX.
I THINK A H. G. WELLS SHORT STORY COLLECTION WAS ONE. OR WAS IT LOVECRAFT? OH! 'ALICE IN WONDERLAND'! THAT WAS DEFINITELY ONE. AND 'THE LAND THAT TIME FORGOT' BY EDGAR RICE BURROUGHS...

* SEE 'REX LIBRIS: TEA WITH VAGLOX' (ISSUE 5) FOR THE FABULOUS LOW DOWN ON THE INCREDIBLE BENZINE V CRYSTALS!-- BARRY

...UM...

'THE WONDERFUL WIZARD OF OZ' WAS ANOTHER... AND... 'PARADISE LOST' AND... ONE OR TWO MORE. I REALLY **DON'T** REMEMBER.

IT'S NEVER A HOME RENOVATION BOOK!

BELGIUM, BELGIUM, BELGIUM!!

I DON'T GET IT. WHAT'S THE BIG DEAL?

THOSE BOOKS HAVE TO BE AROUND HERE **SOMEWHERE.**

I'M AFRAID **NOT.**

DON'T YOU SEE?

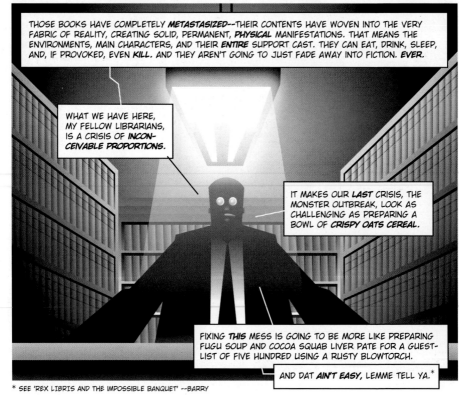

THOSE BOOKS HAVE COMPLETELY **METASTASIZED**--THEIR CONTENTS HAVE WOVEN INTO THE VERY FABRIC OF REALITY, CREATING SOLID, PERMANENT, **PHYSICAL** MANIFESTATIONS. THAT MEANS THE ENVIRONMENTS, MAIN CHARACTERS, AND THEIR **ENTIRE** SUPPORT CAST. THEY CAN EAT, DRINK, SLEEP, AND, IF PROVOKED, EVEN **KILL.** AND THEY AREN'T GOING TO JUST FADE AWAY INTO FICTION. **EVER.**

WHAT WE HAVE HERE, MY FELLOW LIBRARIANS, IS A CRISIS OF **INCON-CEIVABLE PROPORTIONS.**

IT MAKES OUR **LAST** CRISIS, THE MONSTER OUTBREAK, LOOK AS CHALLENGING AS PREPARING A BOWL OF **CRISPY OATS CEREAL.**

FIXING **THIS** MESS IS GOING TO BE MORE LIKE PREPARING FUGU SOUP AND COCOA SQUAB LIVER PATE FOR A GUEST-LIST OF FIVE HUNDRED USING A RUSTY BLOWTORCH.

AND DAT **AIN'T EASY,** LEMME TELL YA.*

* SEE 'REX LIBRIS AND THE IMPOSSIBLE BANQUET' --BARRY

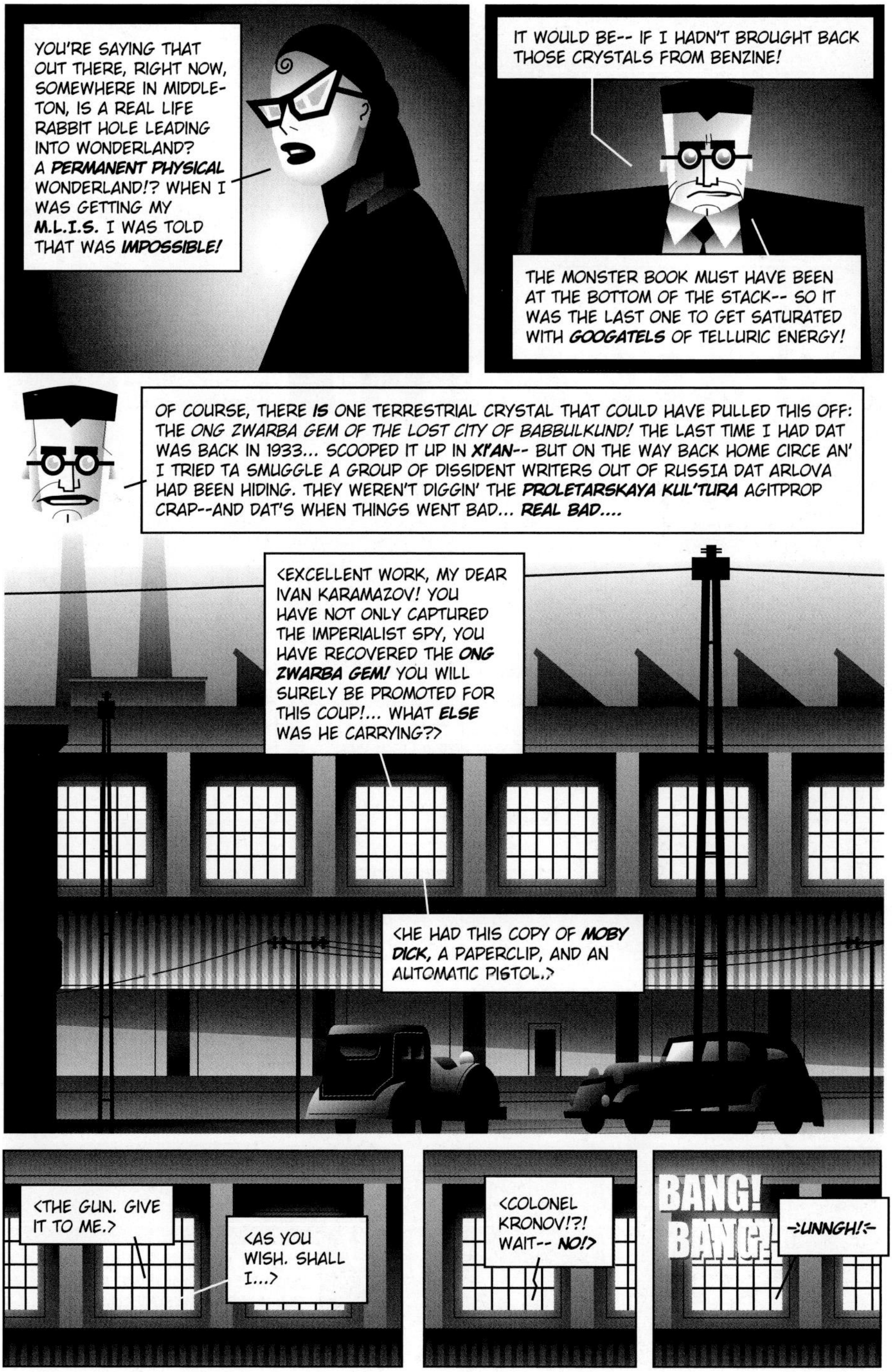
YOU'RE SAYING THAT OUT THERE, RIGHT NOW, SOMEWHERE IN MIDDLE-TON, IS A REAL LIFE RABBIT HOLE LEADING INTO WONDERLAND? A ***PERMANENT PHYSICAL*** WONDERLAND!? WHEN I WAS GETTING MY **M.L.I.S.** I WAS TOLD THAT WAS ***IMPOSSIBLE!***
IT WOULD BE-- IF I HADN'T BROUGHT BACK THOSE CRYSTALS FROM BENZINE!
THE MONSTER BOOK MUST HAVE BEEN AT THE BOTTOM OF THE STACK-- SO IT WAS THE LAST ONE TO GET SATURATED WITH ***GOOGATELS*** OF TELLURIC ENERGY!
*OF COURSE, THERE **IS** ONE TERRESTRIAL CRYSTAL THAT COULD HAVE PULLED THIS OFF: THE ONG ZWARBA GEM OF THE LOST CITY OF BABBULKUND! THE LAST TIME I HAD DAT WAS BACK IN 1933... SCOOPED IT UP IN **XI'AN**-- BUT ON THE WAY BACK HOME CIRCE AN' I TRIED TA SMUGGLE A GROUP OF DISSIDENT WRITERS OUT OF RUSSIA DAT ARLOVA HAD BEEN HIDING. THEY WEREN'T DIGGIN' THE **PROLETARSKAYA KUL'TURA** AGITPROP CRAP--AND DAT'S WHEN THINGS WENT BAD... **REAL BAD....***
<EXCELLENT WORK, MY DEAR IVAN KARAMAZOV! YOU HAVE NOT ONLY CAPTURED THE IMPERIALIST SPY, YOU HAVE RECOVERED THE ***ONG ZWARBA GEM!*** YOU WILL SURELY BE PROMOTED FOR THIS COUP!... WHAT ***ELSE*** WAS HE CARRYING?>
<HE HAD THIS COPY OF ***MOBY DICK,*** A PAPERCLIP, AND AN AUTOMATIC PISTOL.>
<THE GUN. GIVE IT TO ME.>
<AS YOU WISH. SHALL I...>
<COLONEL KRONOV!?! WAIT-- ***NO!***>
BANG! BANG!
UNNGH!

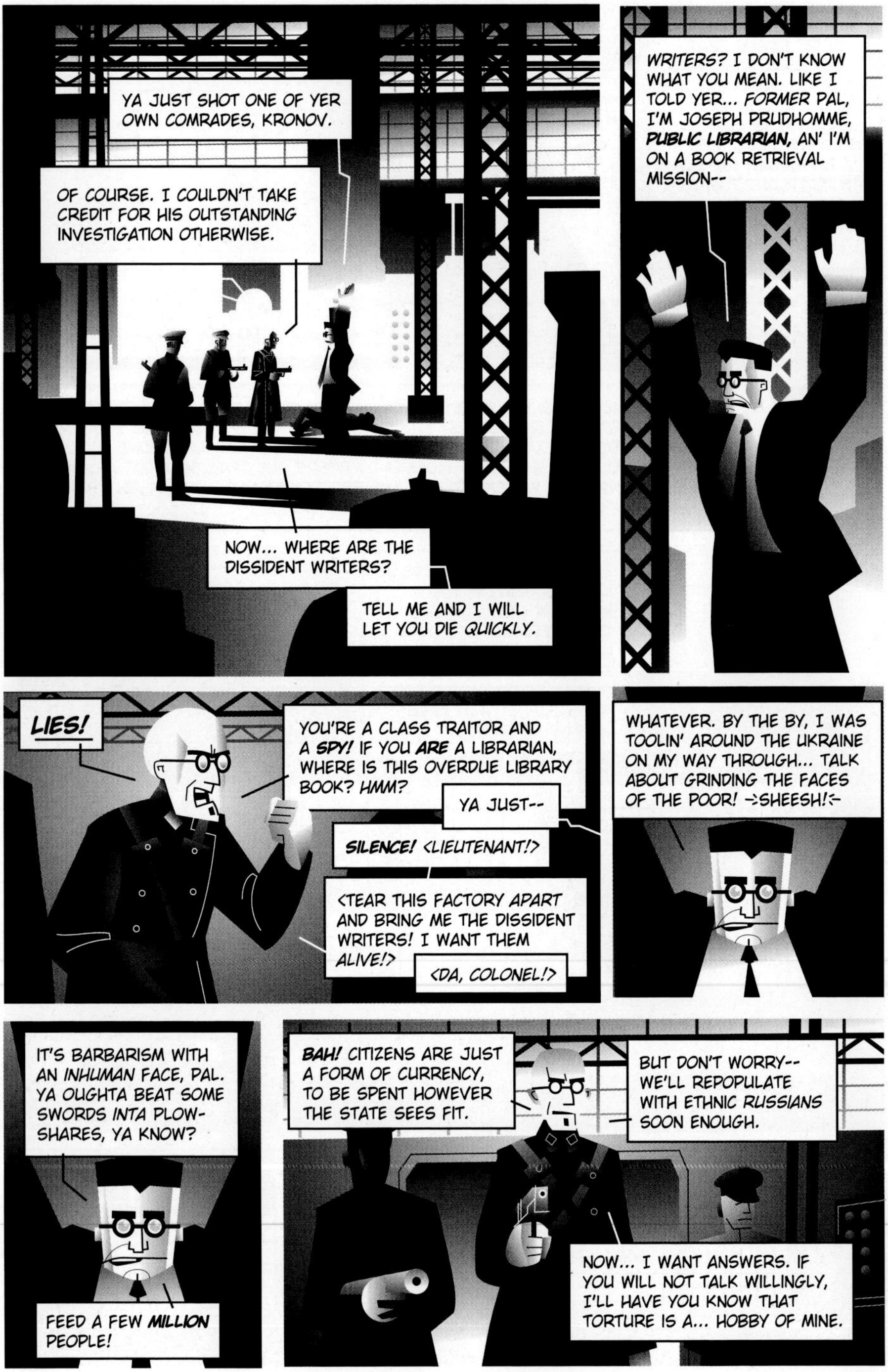
YA JUST SHOT ONE OF YER OWN COMRADES, KRONOV.
OF COURSE. I COULDN'T TAKE CREDIT FOR HIS OUTSTANDING INVESTIGATION OTHERWISE.
NOW... WHERE ARE THE DISSIDENT WRITERS?
TELL ME AND I WILL LET YOU DIE *QUICKLY.*
WRITERS? I DON'T KNOW WHAT YOU MEAN. LIKE I TOLD YER... *FORMER* PAL, I'M JOSEPH PRUDHOMME, ***PUBLIC LIBRARIAN,*** AN' I'M ON A BOOK RETRIEVAL MISSION--
LIES!
YOU'RE A CLASS TRAITOR AND A ***SPY!*** IF YOU ***ARE*** A LIBRARIAN, WHERE IS THIS OVERDUE LIBRARY BOOK? *HMM?*
YA JUST--
SILENCE! <LIEUTENANT!>
<TEAR THIS FACTORY APART AND BRING ME THE DISSIDENT WRITERS! I WANT THEM ALIVE!>
<DA, COLONEL!>
WHATEVER. BY THE BY, I WAS TOOLIN' AROUND THE UKRAINE ON MY WAY THROUGH... TALK ABOUT GRINDING THE FACES OF THE POOR! ->SHEESH!<-
IT'S BARBARISM WITH AN *INHUMAN* FACE, PAL. YA OUGHTA BEAT SOME SWORDS *INTA* PLOW-SHARES, YA KNOW?
FEED A FEW ***MILLION*** PEOPLE!
BAH! CITIZENS ARE JUST A FORM OF CURRENCY, TO BE SPENT HOWEVER THE STATE SEES FIT.
BUT DON'T WORRY-- WE'LL REPOPULATE WITH ETHNIC *RUSSIANS* SOON ENOUGH.
NOW... I WANT ANSWERS. IF YOU WILL NOT TALK WILLINGLY, I'LL HAVE YOU KNOW THAT TORTURE IS A... HOBBY OF MINE.

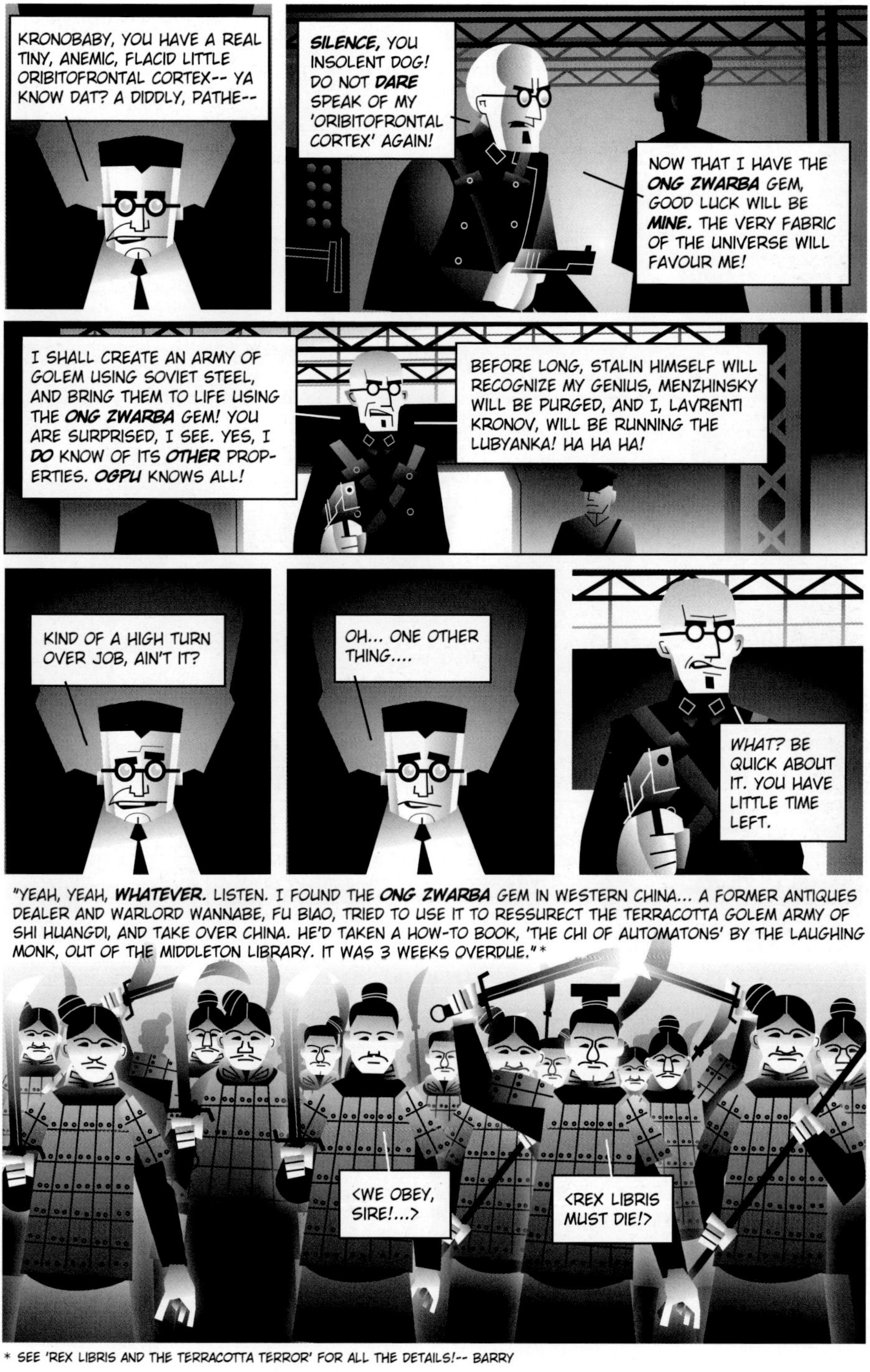

KRONOBABY, YOU HAVE A REAL TINY, ANEMIC, FLACID LITTLE ORIBITOFRONTAL CORTEX-- YA KNOW DAT? A DIDDLY, PATHE--
SILENCE, YOU INSOLENT DOG! DO NOT DARE SPEAK OF MY 'ORIBITOFRONTAL CORTEX' AGAIN!
NOW THAT I HAVE THE ONG ZWARBA GEM, GOOD LUCK WILL BE MINE. THE VERY FABRIC OF THE UNIVERSE WILL FAVOUR ME!
I SHALL CREATE AN ARMY OF GOLEM USING SOVIET STEEL, AND BRING THEM TO LIFE USING THE ONG ZWARBA GEM! YOU ARE SURPRISED, I SEE. YES, I DO KNOW OF ITS OTHER PROPERTIES. OGPU KNOWS ALL!
BEFORE LONG, STALIN HIMSELF WILL RECOGNIZE MY GENIUS, MENZHINSKY WILL BE PURGED, AND I, LAVRENTI KRONOV, WILL BE RUNNING THE LUBYANKA! HA HA HA!
KIND OF A HIGH TURN OVER JOB, AIN'T IT?
OH... ONE OTHER THING....
WHAT? BE QUICK ABOUT IT. YOU HAVE LITTLE TIME LEFT.
"YEAH, YEAH, WHATEVER. LISTEN. I FOUND THE ONG ZWARBA GEM IN WESTERN CHINA... A FORMER ANTIQUES DEALER AND WARLORD WANNABE, FU BIAO, TRIED TO USE IT TO RESSURECT THE TERRACOTTA GOLEM ARMY OF SHI HUANGDI, AND TAKE OVER CHINA. HE'D TAKEN A HOW-TO BOOK, 'THE CHI OF AUTOMATONS' BY THE LAUGHING MONK, OUT OF THE MIDDLETON LIBRARY. IT WAS 3 WEEKS OVERDUE."*
<WE OBEY, SIRE!...>
<REX LIBRIS MUST DIE!>

* SEE 'REX LIBRIS AND THE TERRACOTTA TERROR' FOR ALL THE DETAILS!-- BARRY

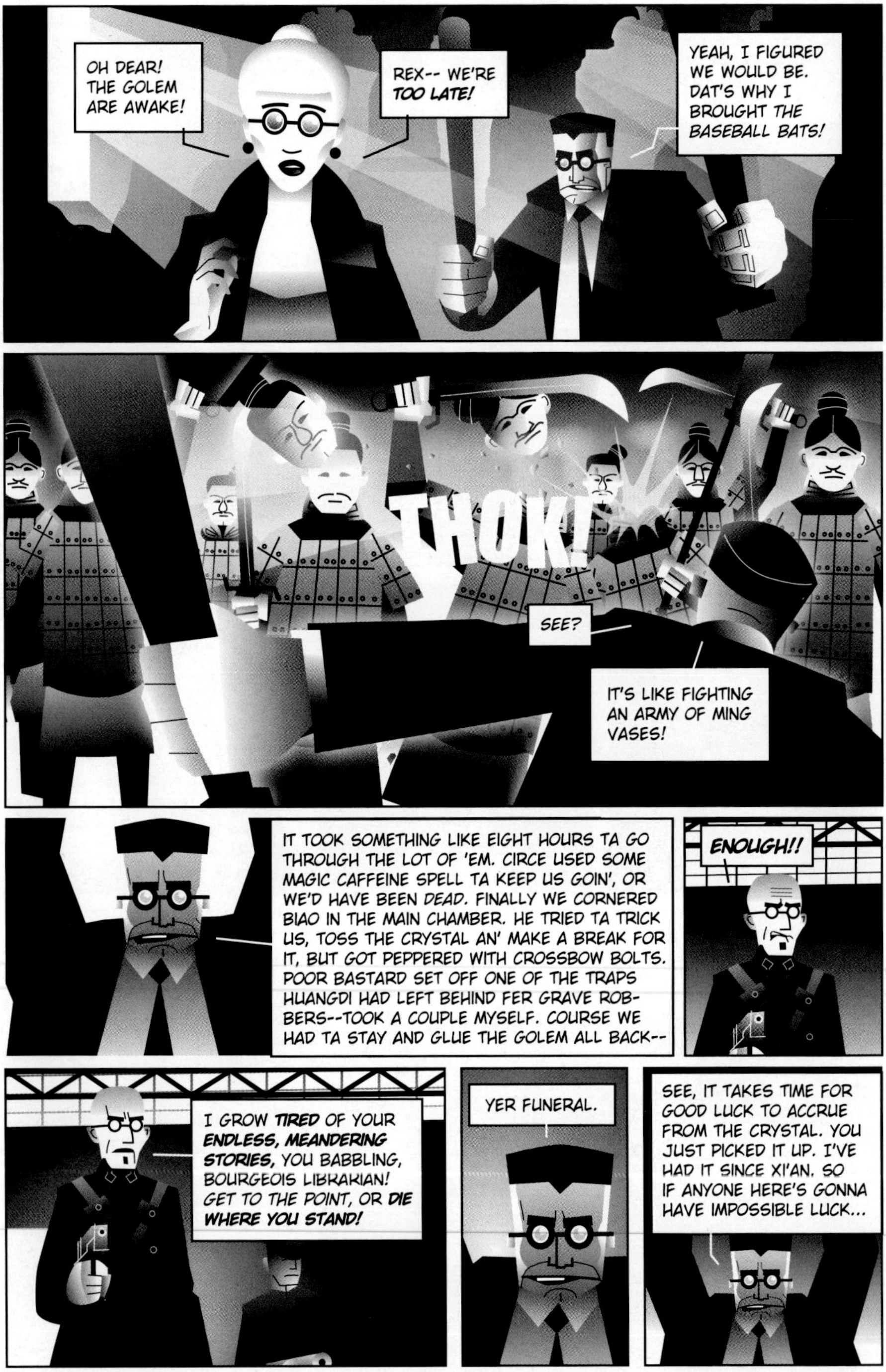
OH DEAR! THE GOLEM ARE AWAKE!
REX-- WE'RE *TOO LATE!*
YEAH, I FIGURED WE WOULD BE. DAT'S WHY I BROUGHT THE *BASEBALL BATS!*
THOK!
SEE?
IT'S LIKE FIGHTING AN ARMY OF MING VASES!
IT TOOK SOMETHING LIKE EIGHT HOURS TA GO THROUGH THE LOT OF 'EM. CIRCE USED SOME *MAGIC* CAFFEINE SPELL TA KEEP US GOIN', OR WE'D HAVE BEEN *DEAD*. FINALLY WE CORNERED BIAO IN THE MAIN CHAMBER. HE TRIED TA TRICK US, TOSS THE CRYSTAL AN' MAKE A BREAK FOR IT, BUT GOT PEPPERED WITH CROSSBOW BOLTS. POOR BASTARD SET OFF ONE OF THE TRAPS HUANGDI HAD LEFT BEHIND FER GRAVE ROB-BERS--TOOK A COUPLE MYSELF. COURSE WE HAD TA STAY AND GLUE THE GOLEM ALL BACK--
ENOUGH!!
I GROW **TIRED** OF YOUR **ENDLESS, MEANDERING STORIES,** YOU BABBLING, BOURGEOIS LIBRARIAN! GET TO THE POINT, OR **DIE WHERE YOU STAND!**
YER FUNERAL.
SEE, IT TAKES TIME FOR GOOD LUCK TO ACCRUE FROM THE CRYSTAL. YOU JUST PICKED IT UP. I'VE HAD IT SINCE XI'AN. SO IF ANYONE HERE'S GONNA HAVE IMPOSSIBLE LUCK...

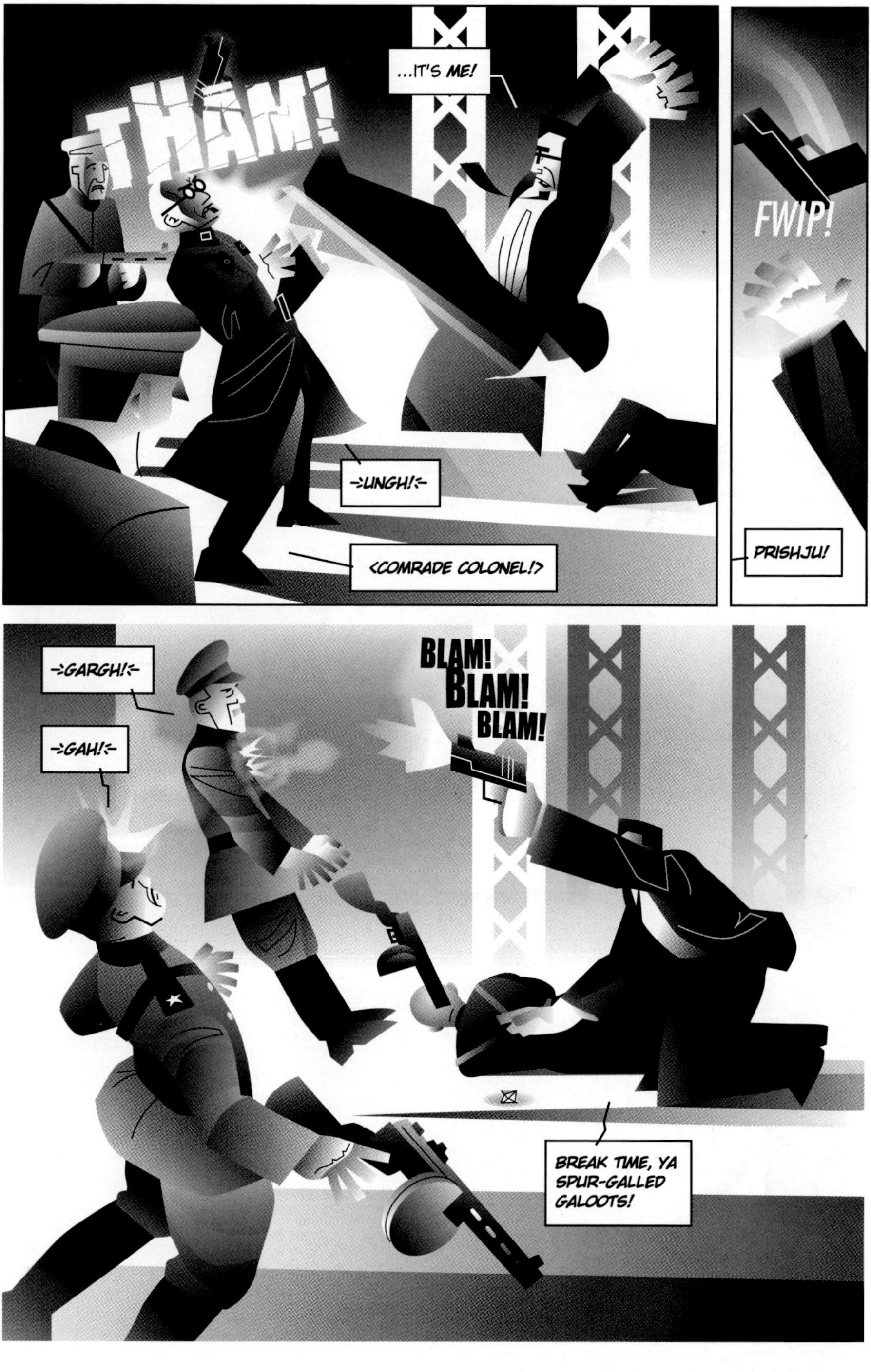
THAM!
...IT'S ME!
-=UNGH!=-
<COMRADE COLONEL!>
FWIP!
PRISHJU!
-=GARGH!=-
-=GAH!=-
BLAM!
BLAM!
BLAM!
BREAK TIME, YA SPUR-GALLED GALOOTS!

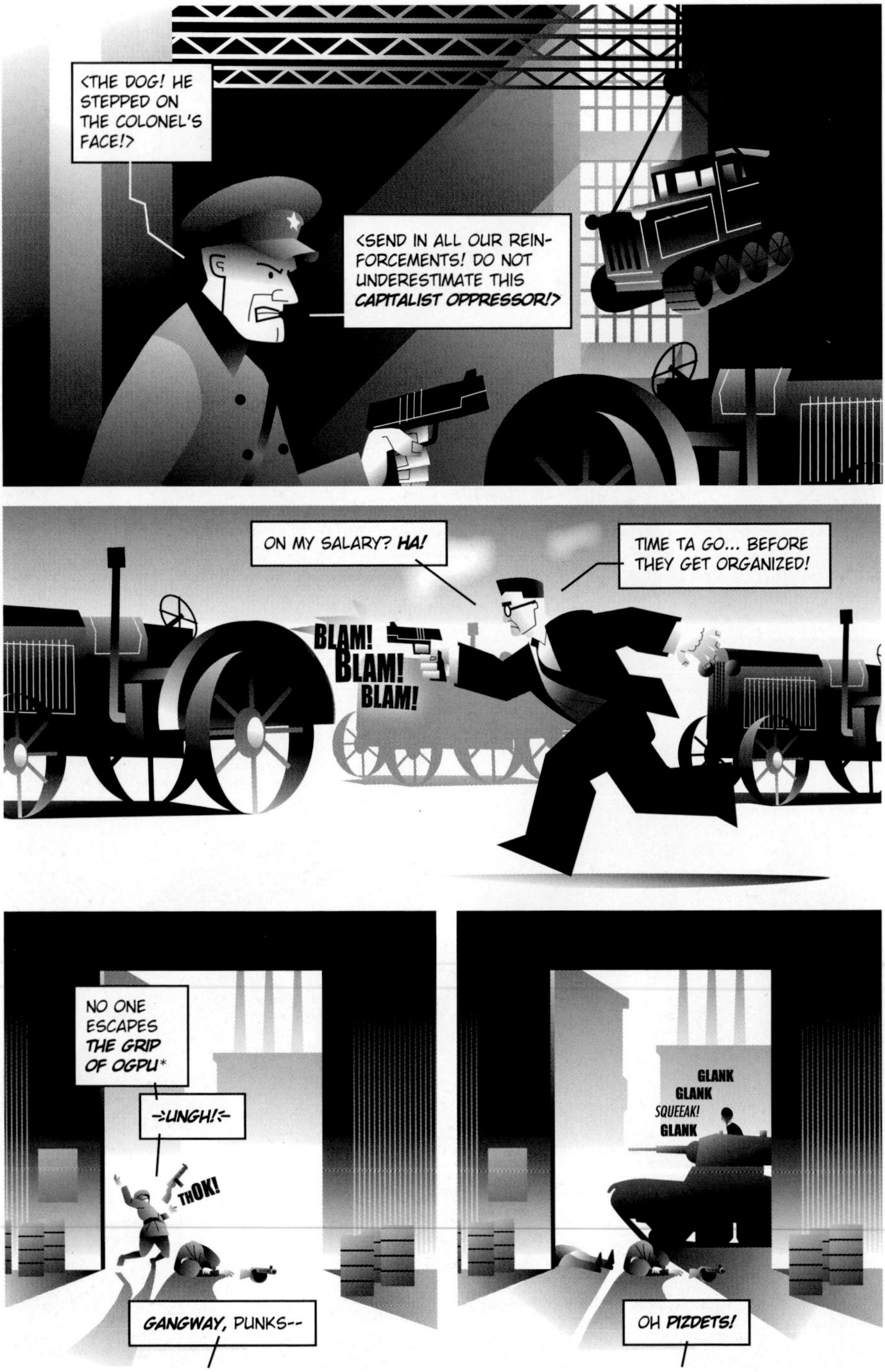
<THE DOG! HE STEPPED ON THE COLONEL'S FACE!>
<SEND IN ALL OUR REIN-FORCEMENTS! DO NOT UNDERESTIMATE THIS CAPITALIST OPPRESSOR!>
ON MY SALARY? HA!
TIME TA GO... BEFORE THEY GET ORGANIZED!
BLAM! BLAM! BLAM!
NO ONE ESCAPES THE GRIP OF OGPU*
UNGH!
THOK!
GANGWAY, PUNKS--
GLANK GLANK SQUEEAK! GLANK
OH PIZDETS!

* ***OGPU: O**'B'EDINENNOE **G**OSUDARSTVENNOE **P**OLITICHESKOE **U**PRAVLENIE, THE JOINT STATE POLITICAL DIRECTORATE. GIVEN A BETTER ACRONYM IN 1934. RUSSIAN SECRET POLICE. --BARRY

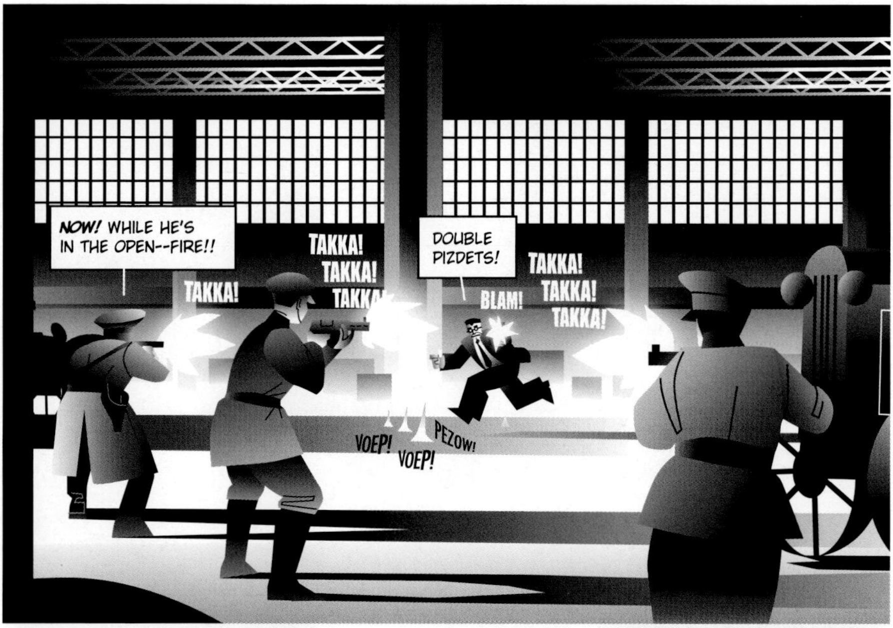
NOW! WHILE HE'S IN THE OPEN--FIRE!!
TAKKA!
TAKKA!
TAKKA!
TAKKA!
DOUBLE PIZDETS!
BLAM!
TAKKA!
TAKKA!
TAKKA!
VOEP!
VOEP!
PEZOW!

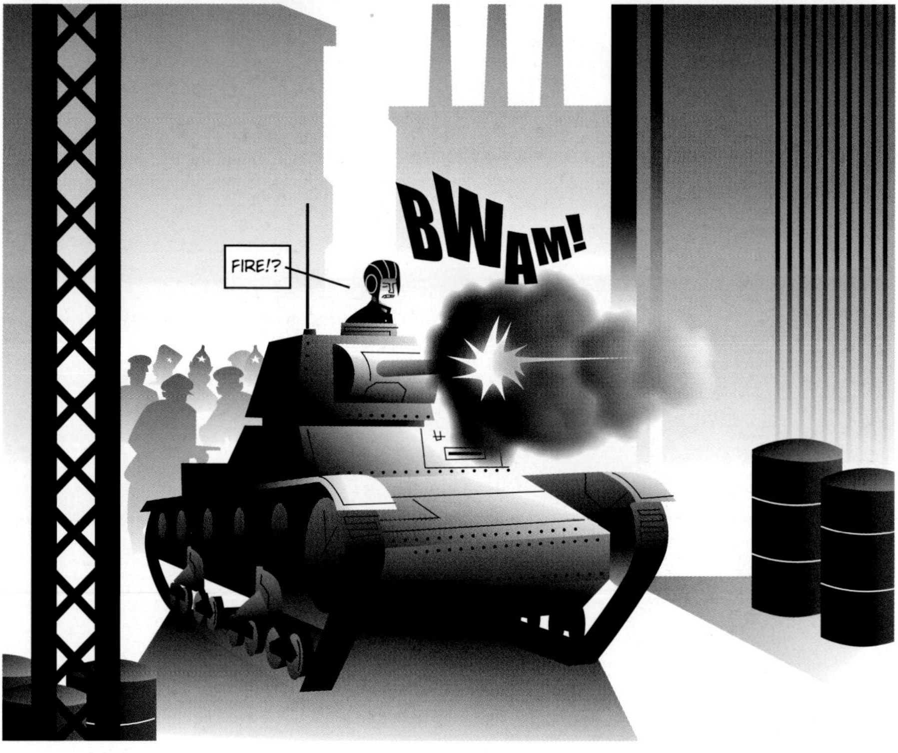
FIRE!?
BWAM!

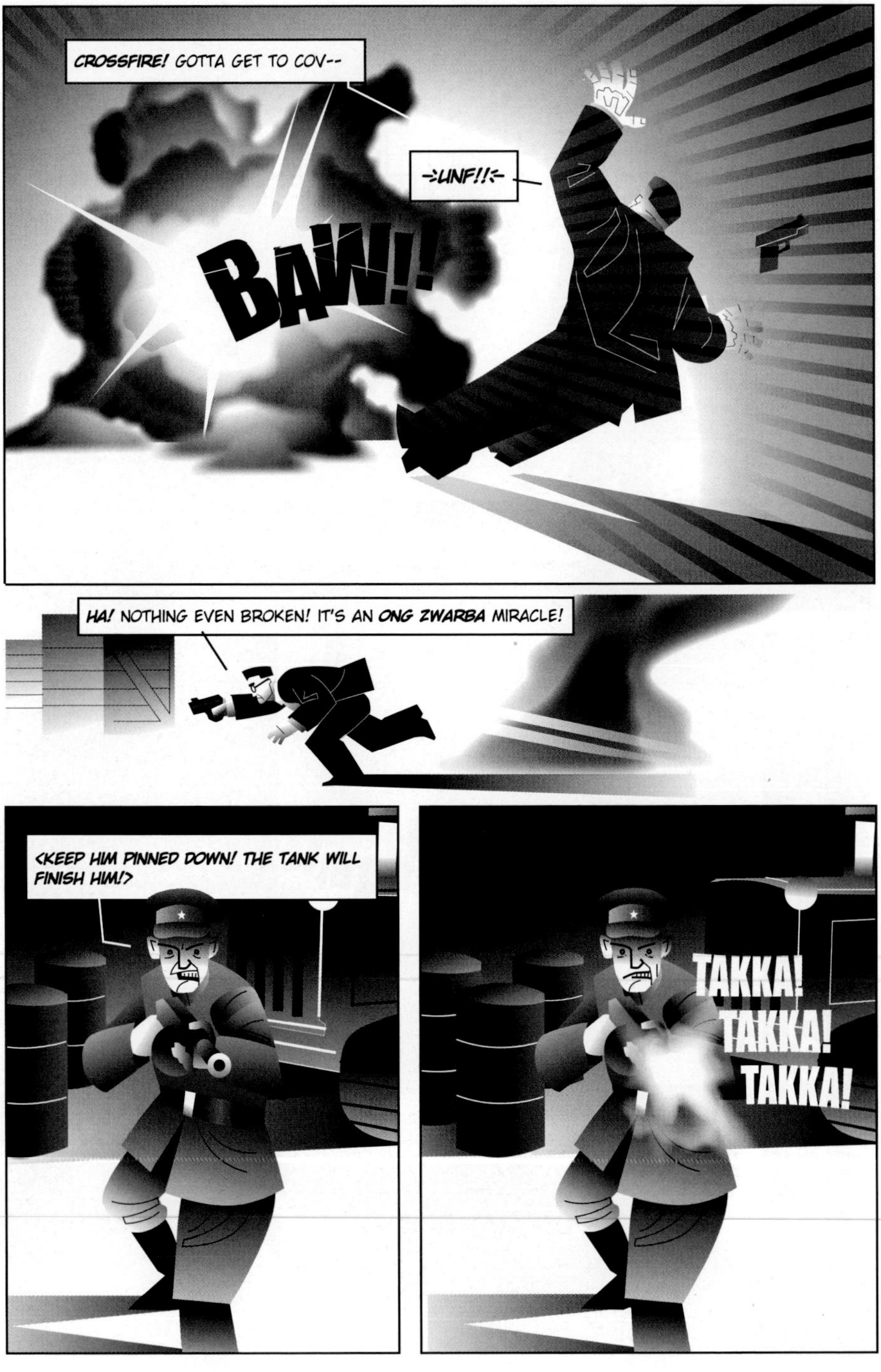
CROSSFIRE! GOTTA GET TO COV--
-:UNF!!:-
BAW!!
HA! NOTHING EVEN BROKEN! IT'S AN ONG ZWARBA MIRACLE!
<KEEP HIM PINNED DOWN! THE TANK WILL FINISH HIM!>
TAKKA! TAKKA! TAKKA!

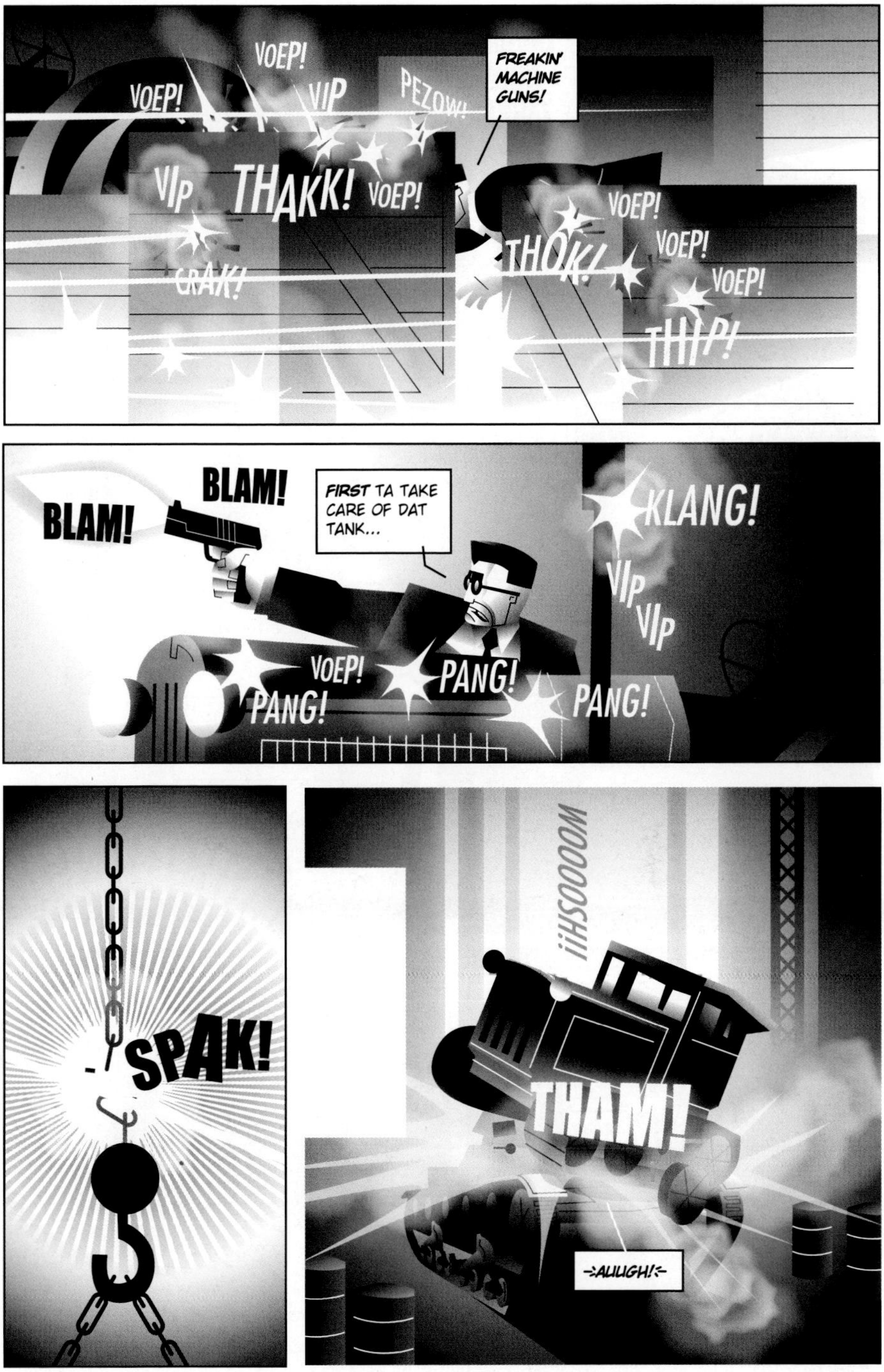
VOEP!
VOEP!
VIP
PEZOW!
FREAKIN' MACHINE GUNS!
VIP
THAKK!
VOEP!
CRAK!
THOK!
VOEP!
VOEP!
VOEP!
THIP!
BLAM!
BLAM!
FIRST TA TAKE CARE OF DAT TANK...
KLANG!
VIP
VIP
VOEP!
PANG!
PANG!
PANG!
SPAK!
WHOOOOSH!!
THAM!
-AUUGH!-

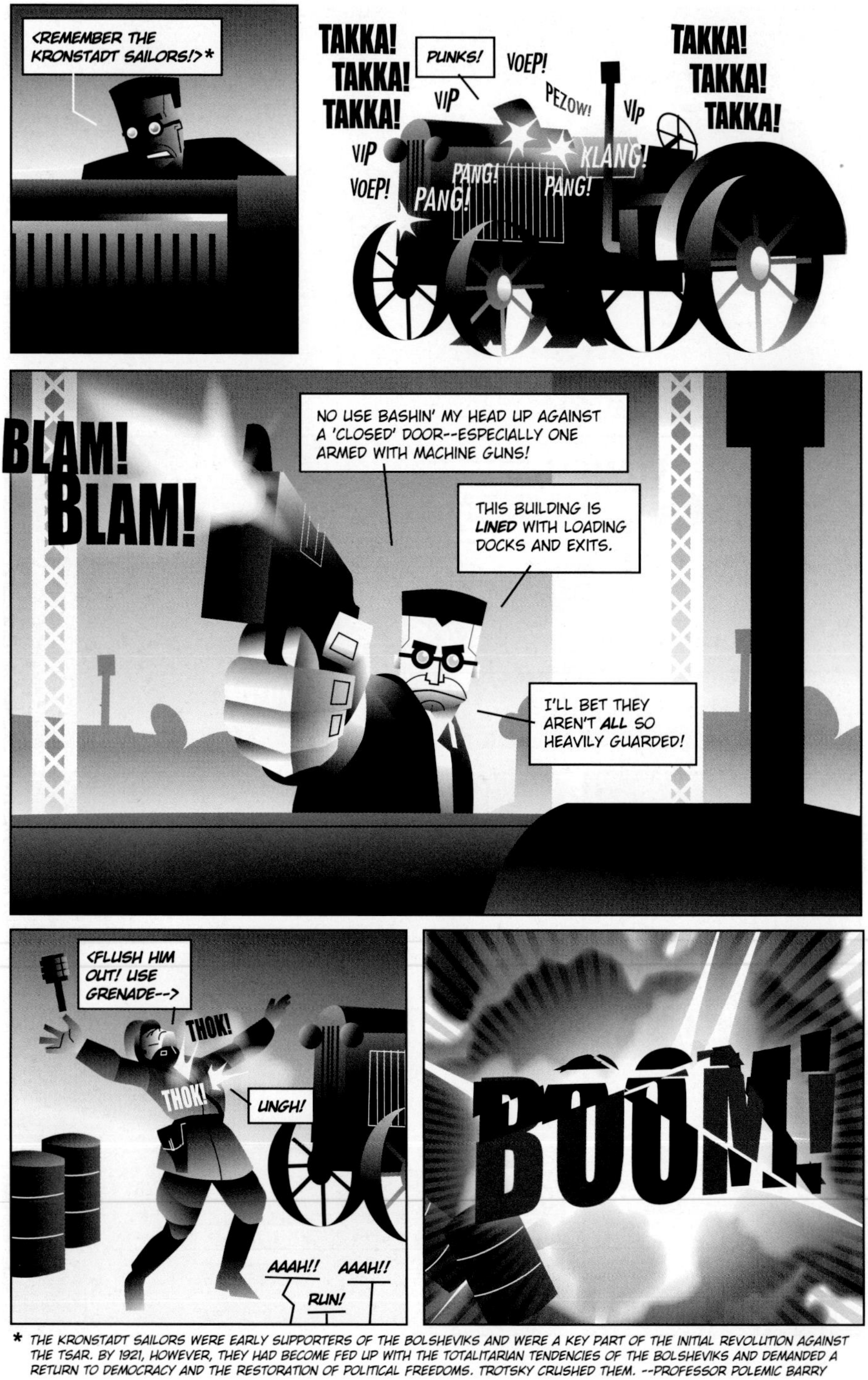
<REMEMBER THE KRONSTADT SAILORS!>*
TAKKA! TAKKA! TAKKA!
PUNKS!
VIP
VOEP!
PEZOW!
VIP
TAKKA! TAKKA! TAKKA!
VIP
VOEP!
PANG!
PANG!
KLANG!
PANG!
BLAM! BLAM!
NO USE BASHIN' MY HEAD UP AGAINST A 'CLOSED' DOOR--ESPECIALLY ONE ARMED WITH MACHINE GUNS!
THIS BUILDING IS LINED WITH LOADING DOCKS AND EXITS.
I'LL BET THEY AREN'T ALL SO HEAVILY GUARDED!
<FLUSH HIM OUT! USE GRENADE-->
THOK!
THOK!
UNGH!
AAAH!!
AAAH!!
RUN!
BOOM!

* THE KRONSTADT SAILORS WERE EARLY SUPPORTERS OF THE BOLSHEVIKS AND WERE A KEY PART OF THE INITIAL REVOLUTION AGAINST THE TSAR. BY 1921, HOWEVER, THEY HAD BECOME FED UP WITH THE TOTALITARIAN TENDENCIES OF THE BOLSHEVIKS AND DEMANDED A RETURN TO DEMOCRACY AND THE RESTORATION OF POLITICAL FREEDOMS. TROTSKY CRUSHED THEM. --PROFESSOR POLEMIC BARRY

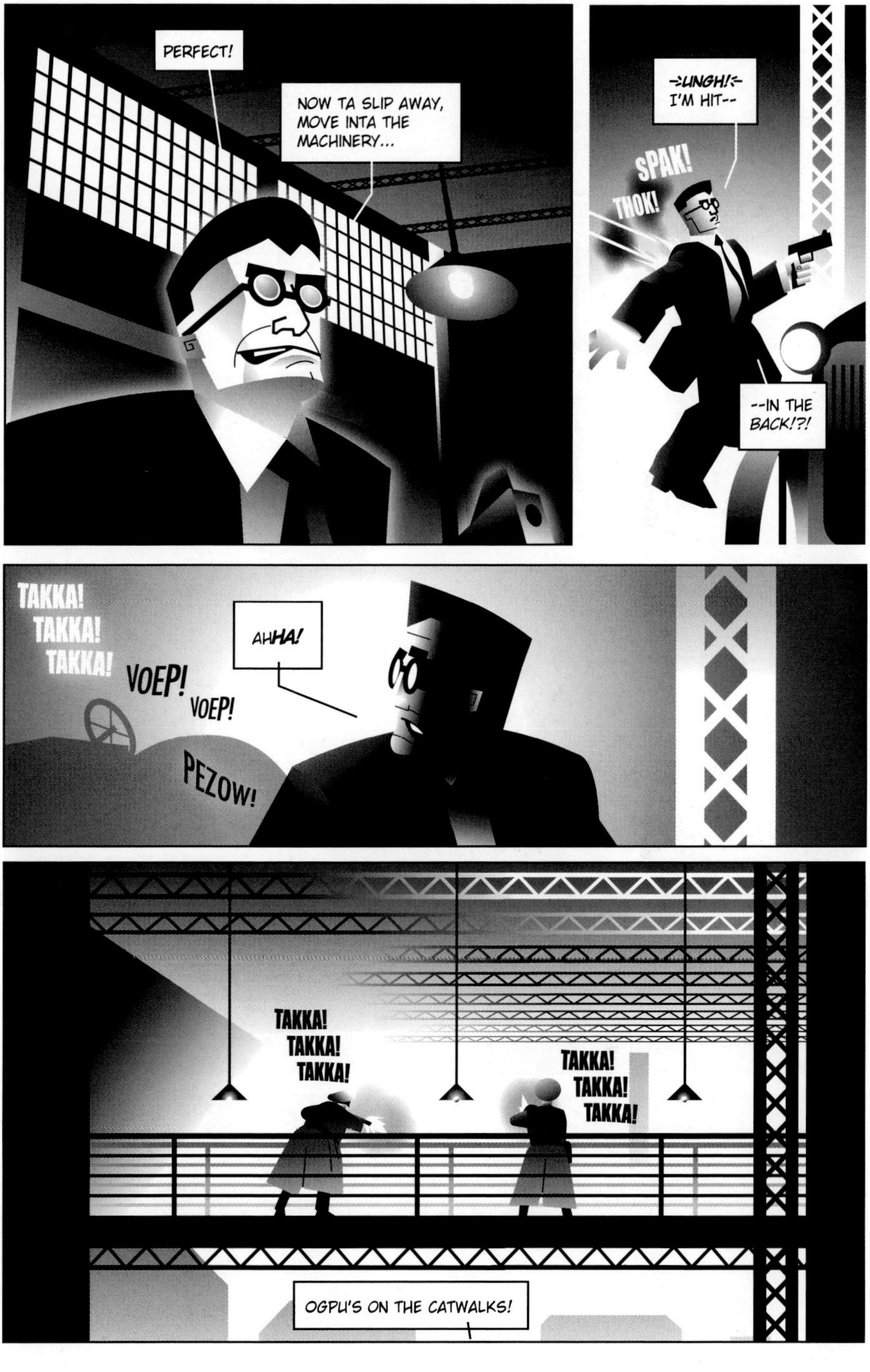
PERFECT!
NOW TA SLIP AWAY, MOVE INTA THE MACHINERY...
SPAK!
THOK!
-UNGH!- I'M HIT--
--IN THE BACK!?!
TAKKA! TAKKA! TAKKA!
VOEP! VOEP!
PEZOW!
AHHA!
TAKKA! TAKKA! TAKKA!
TAKKA! TAKKA! TAKKA!
OGPU'S ON THE CATWALKS!

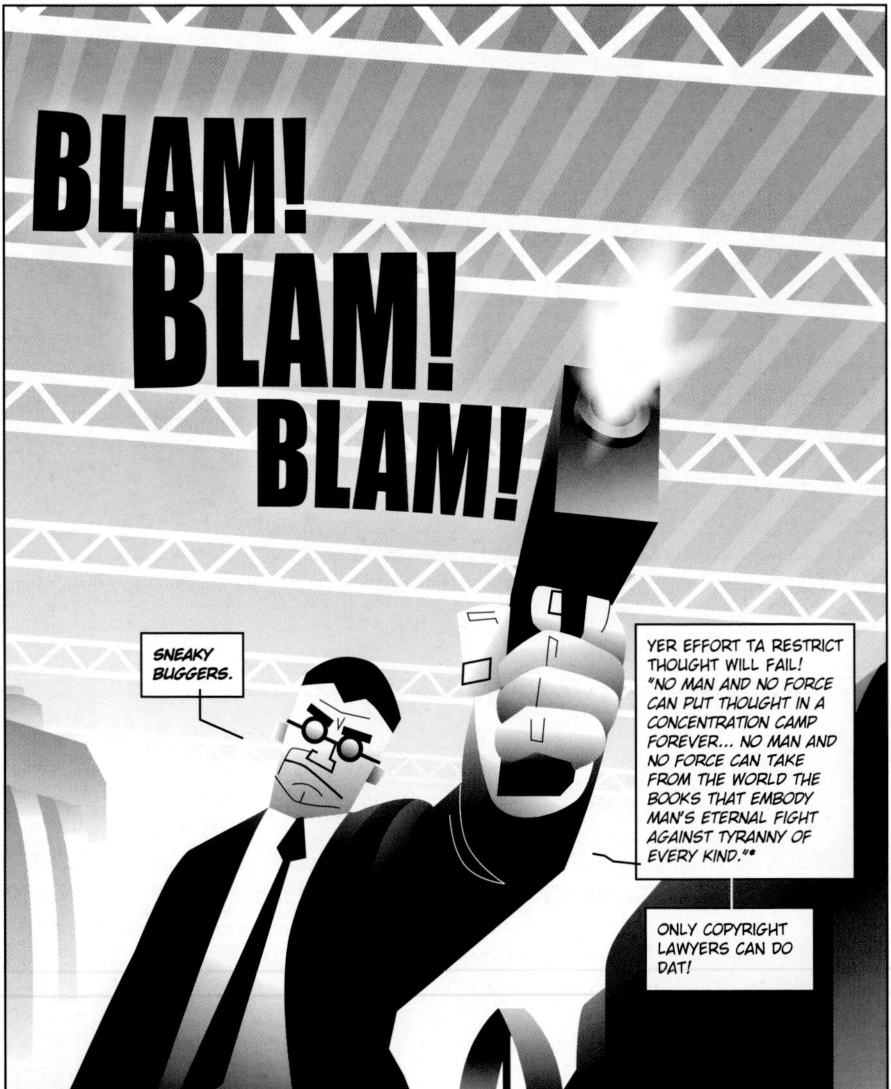
BLAM!
BLAM!
BLAM!
SNEAKY BUGGERS.
YER EFFORT TA RESTRICT THOUGHT WILL FAIL! "NO MAN AND NO FORCE CAN PUT THOUGHT IN A CONCENTRATION CAMP FOREVER... NO MAN AND NO FORCE CAN TAKE FROM THE WORLD THE BOOKS THAT EMBODY MAN'S ETERNAL FIGHT AGAINST TYRANNY OF EVERY KIND."*
ONLY COPYRIGHT LAWYERS CAN DO DAT!

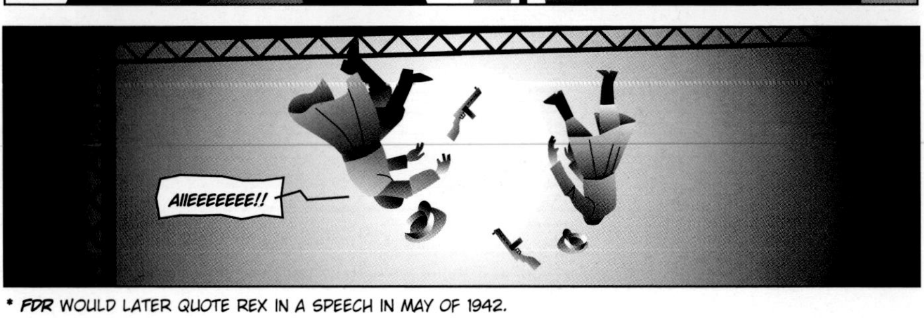
AIIEEEEEEE!!

* ***FDR*** WOULD LATER QUOTE REX IN A SPEECH IN MAY OF 1942.

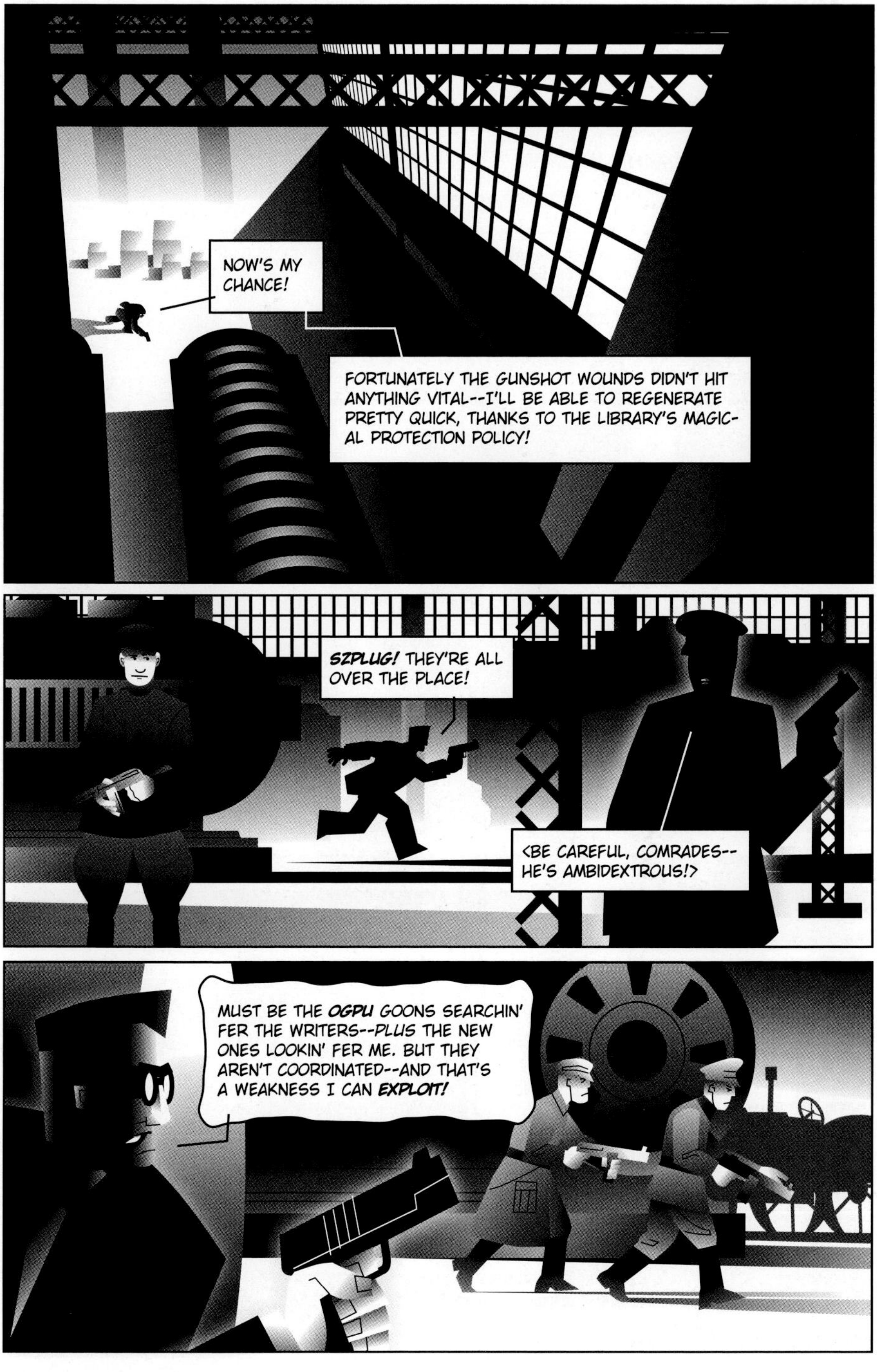
NOW'S MY CHANCE!
FORTUNATELY THE GUNSHOT WOUNDS DIDN'T HIT ANYTHING VITAL--I'LL BE ABLE TO REGENERATE PRETTY QUICK, THANKS TO THE LIBRARY'S MAGIC-AL PROTECTION POLICY!
SZPLUG! THEY'RE ALL OVER THE PLACE!
<BE CAREFUL, COMRADES--HE'S AMBIDEXTROUS!>
MUST BE THE *OGPU* GOONS SEARCHIN' FER THE WRITERS--*PLUS* THE NEW ONES LOOKIN' FER ME. BUT THEY AREN'T COORDINATED--AND THAT'S A WEAKNESS I CAN *EXPLOIT!*

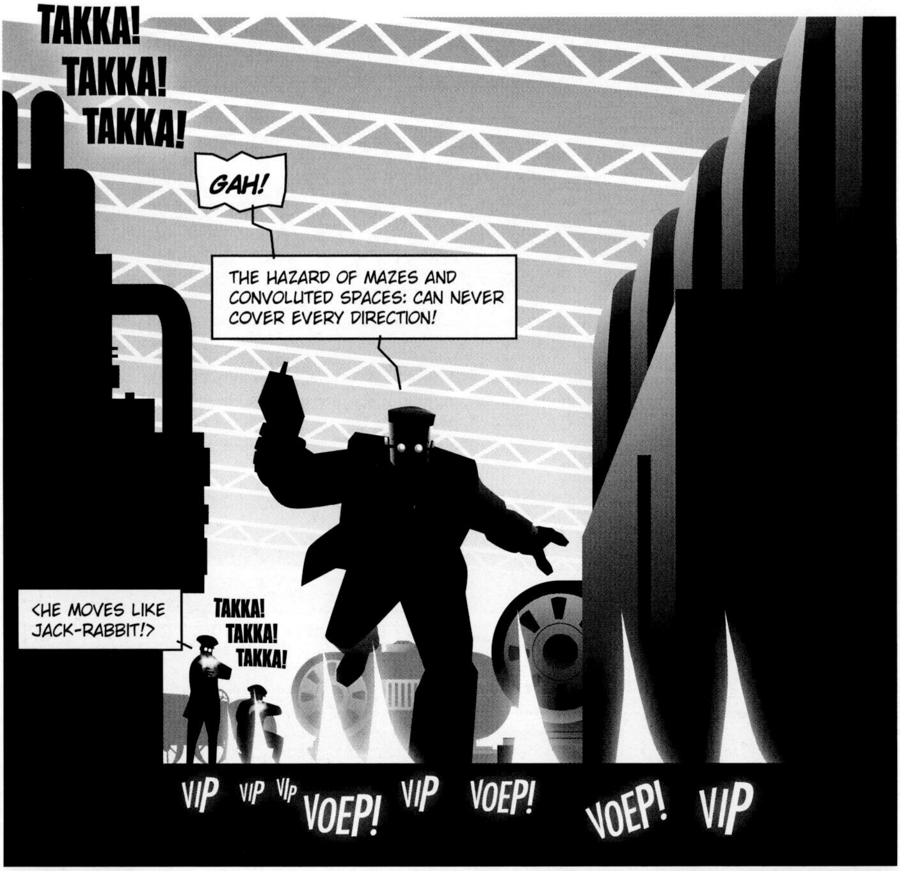
TAKKA! TAKKA! TAKKA!
GAH!
THE HAZARD OF MAZES AND CONVOLUTED SPACES: CAN NEVER COVER EVERY DIRECTION!
<HE MOVES LIKE JACK-RABBIT!>
TAKKA! TAKKA! TAKKA!
VIP VIP VIP VOEP! VIP VOEP! VOEP! VIP

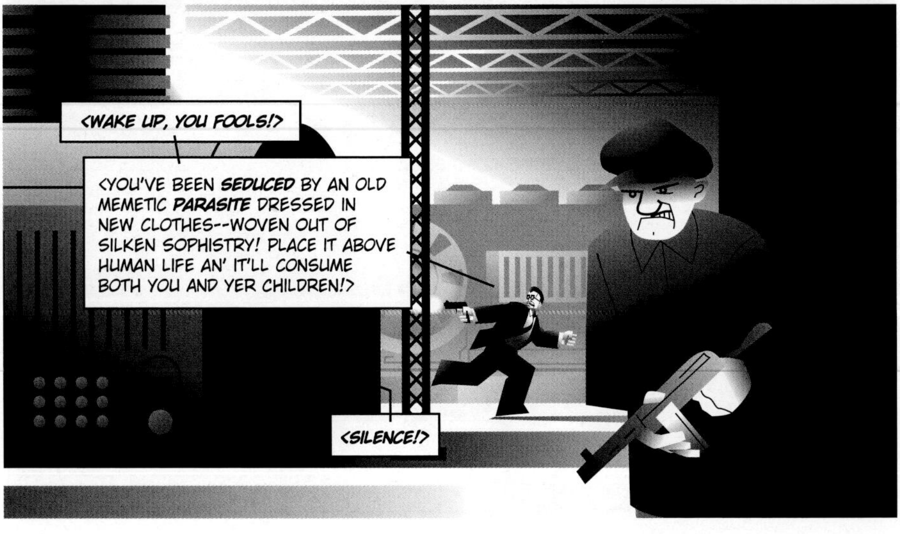
<WAKE UP, YOU FOOLS!>
<YOU'VE BEEN SEDUCED BY AN OLD MEMETIC PARASITE DRESSED IN NEW CLOTHES--WOVEN OUT OF SILKEN SOPHISTRY! PLACE IT ABOVE HUMAN LIFE AN' IT'LL CONSUME BOTH YOU AND YER CHILDREN!>
<SILENCE!>

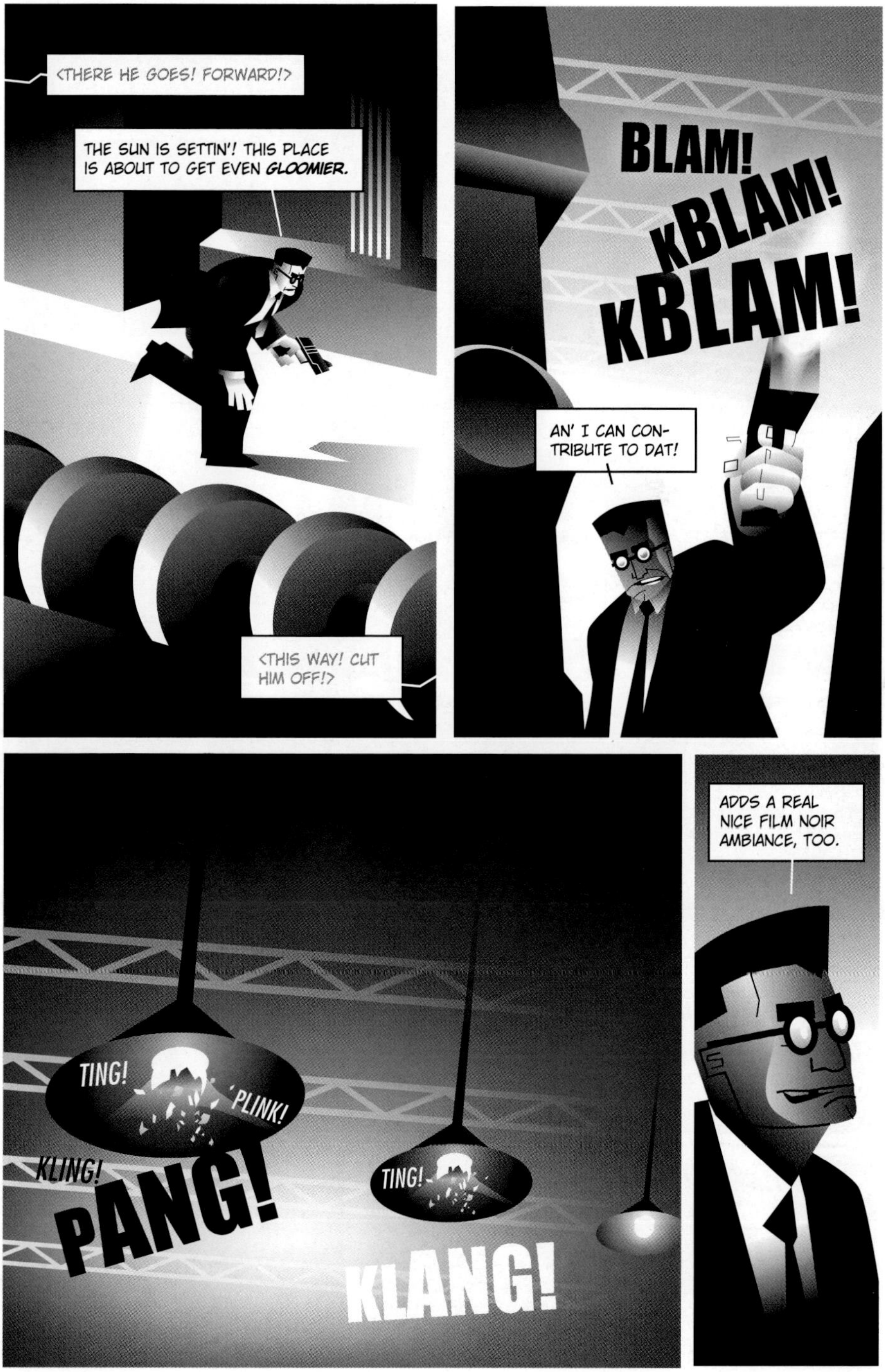
<THERE HE GOES! FORWARD!>
THE SUN IS SETTIN'! THIS PLACE IS ABOUT TO GET EVEN *GLOOMIER.*
<THIS WAY! CUT HIM OFF!>
BLAM!
kBLAM!
kBLAM!
AN' I CAN CON-TRIBUTE TO DAT!
TING!
PLINK!
KLING!
PANG!
TING!
KLANG!
ADDS A REAL NICE FILM NOIR AMBIANCE, TOO.

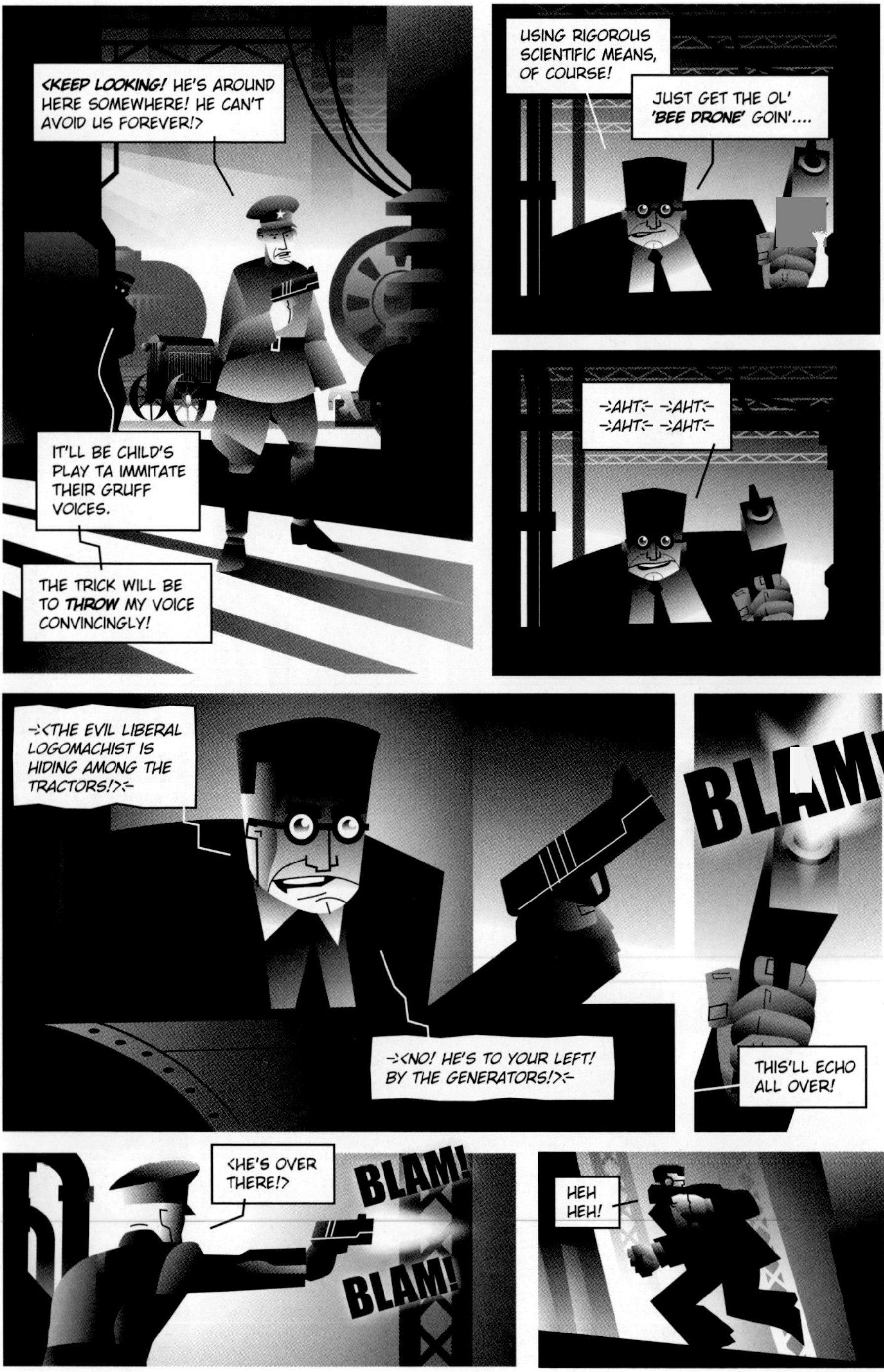
<KEEP LOOKING! HE'S AROUND HERE SOMEWHERE! HE CAN'T AVOID US FOREVER!>
IT'LL BE CHILD'S PLAY TA IMMITATE THEIR GRUFF VOICES.
THE TRICK WILL BE TO THROW MY VOICE CONVINCINGLY!
USING RIGOROUS SCIENTIFIC MEANS, OF COURSE!
JUST GET THE OL' 'BEE DRONE' GOIN'....
-AHT- -AHT- -AHT- -AHT-
-<THE EVIL LIBERAL LOGOMACHIST IS HIDING AMONG THE TRACTORS!>-
-<NO! HE'S TO YOUR LEFT! BY THE GENERATORS!>-
BLAM!
THIS'LL ECHO ALL OVER!
<HE'S OVER THERE!>
BLAM!
BLAM!
HEH HEH!

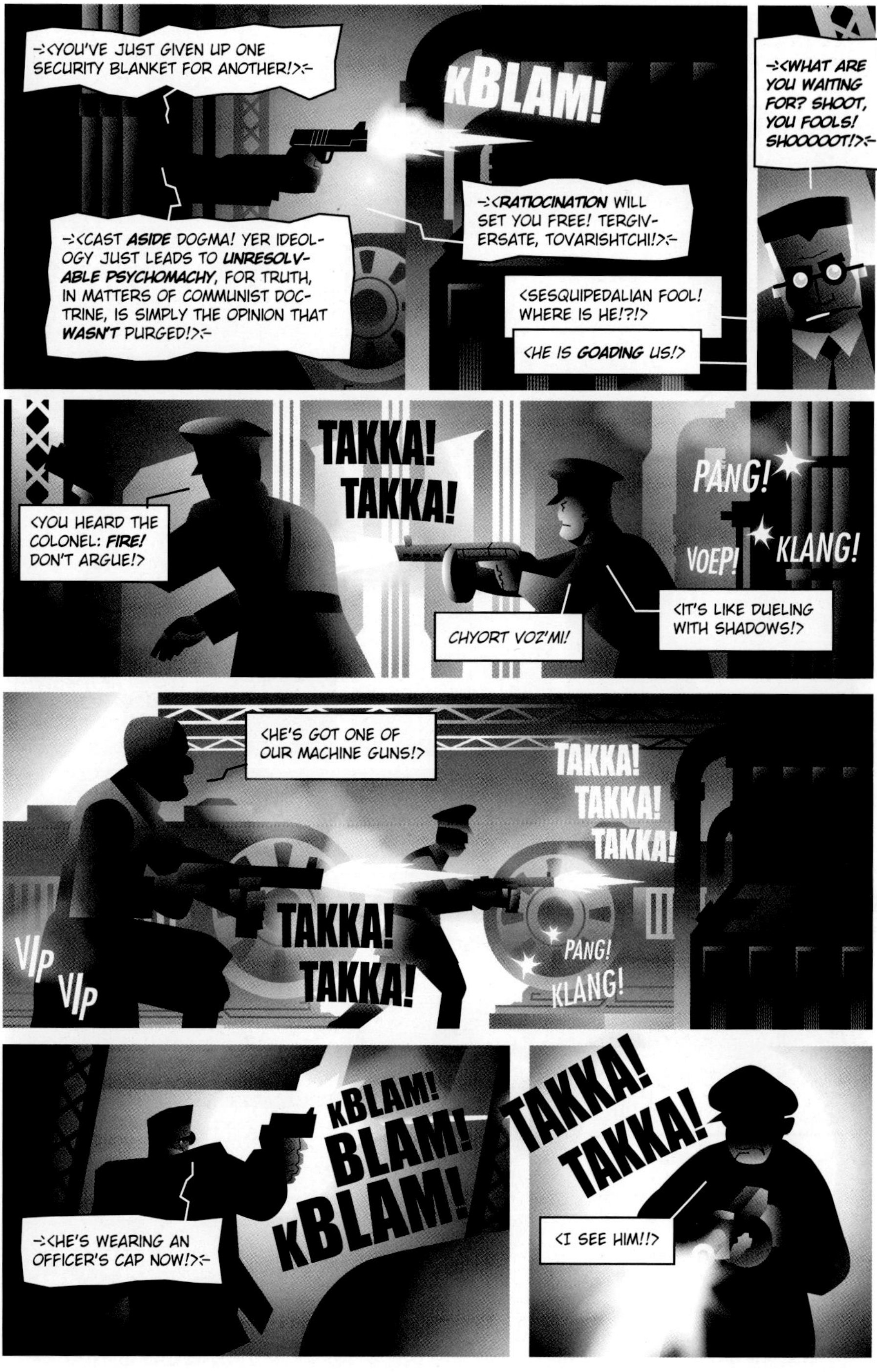

-:<YOU'VE JUST GIVEN UP ONE SECURITY BLANKET FOR ANOTHER!>:-
kBLAM!
-:<CAST ASIDE DOGMA! YER IDEOLOGY JUST LEADS TO UNRESOLVABLE PSYCHOMACHY, FOR TRUTH, IN MATTERS OF COMMUNIST DOCTRINE, IS SIMPLY THE OPINION THAT WASN'T PURGED!>:-
-:<RATIOCINATION WILL SET YOU FREE! TERGIVERSATE, TOVARISHTCHI!>:-
<SESQUIPEDALIAN FOOL! WHERE IS HE!?!>
<HE IS GOADING US!>
-:<WHAT ARE YOU WAITING FOR? SHOOT, YOU FOOLS! SHOOOOOT!>:-
TAKKA! TAKKA!
<YOU HEARD THE COLONEL: FIRE! DON'T ARGUE!>
PANG!
VOEP!
KLANG!
CHYORT VOZ'MI!
<IT'S LIKE DUELING WITH SHADOWS!>
<HE'S GOT ONE OF OUR MACHINE GUNS!>
TAKKA! TAKKA! TAKKA!
TAKKA! TAKKA!
VIP VIP
PANG!
KLANG!
kBLAM! BLAM! kBLAM!
-:<HE'S WEARING AN OFFICER'S CAP NOW!>:-
TAKKA! TAKKA!
<I SEE HIM!!>

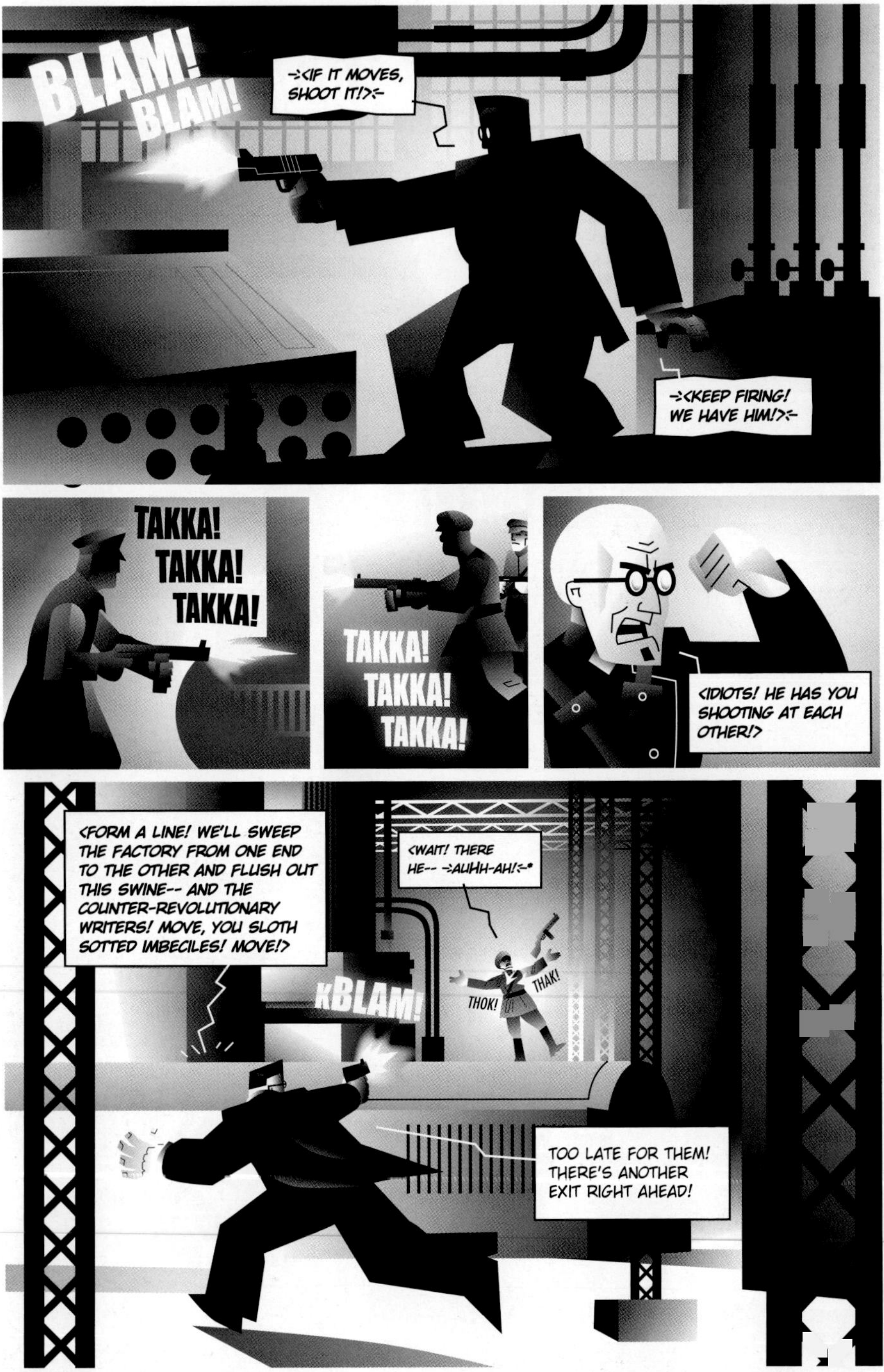
BLAM! BLAM!
-><IF IT MOVES, SHOOT IT!><-
-><KEEP FIRING! WE HAVE HIM!><-
TAKKA! TAKKA! TAKKA!
TAKKA! TAKKA! TAKKA!
<IDIOTS! HE HAS YOU SHOOTING AT EACH OTHER!>
<FORM A LINE! WE'LL SWEEP THE FACTORY FROM ONE END TO THE OTHER AND FLUSH OUT THIS SWINE-- AND THE COUNTER-REVOLUTIONARY WRITERS! MOVE, YOU SLOTH SOTTED IMBECILES! MOVE!>
<WAIT! THERE HE-- ->AUHH-AH!<-*
kBLAM!
THOK!
THAK!
TOO LATE FOR THEM! THERE'S ANOTHER EXIT RIGHT AHEAD!

*THE DISTINCTIVE 'WILHELM SCREAM'. THE FIRST IN COMIC BOOK HISTORY! ANOTHER INNOVATION BROUGHT TO YOU BY THE DEDICATED TEAM AT THE ***HORST COMIC BOOK RESEARCH AND DEVELOPMENT LABORATORY!*** -- BARRY

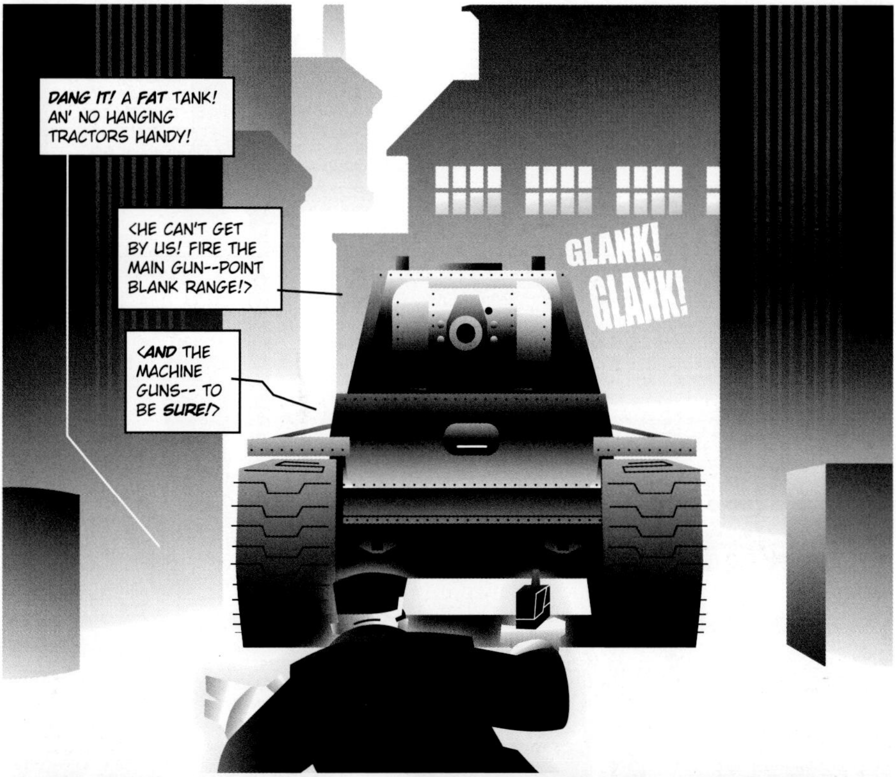
DANG IT! A FAT TANK! AN' NO HANGING TRACTORS HANDY!
<HE CAN'T GET BY US! FIRE THE MAIN GUN--POINT BLANK RANGE!>
GLANK! GLANK!
<AND THE MACHINE GUNS-- TO BE SURE!>

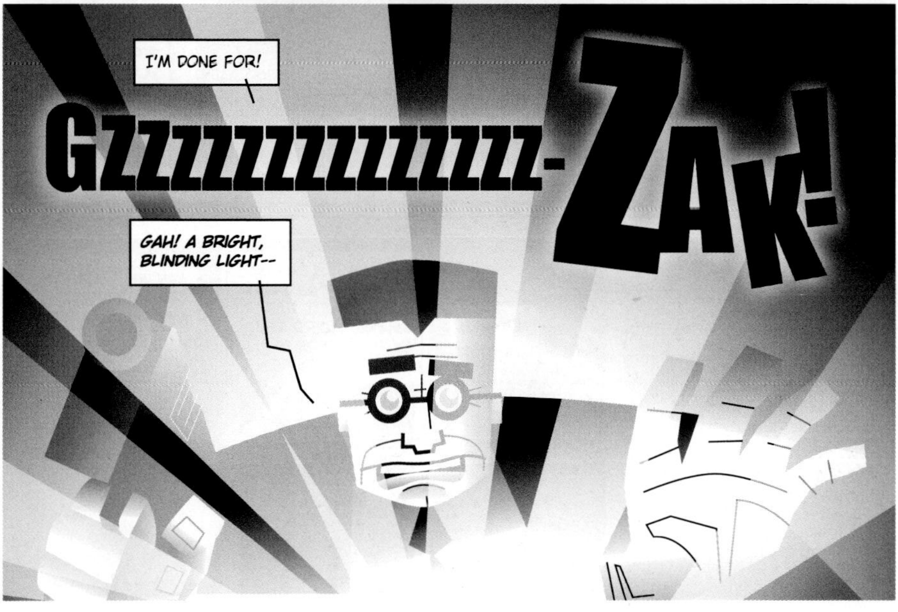
I'M DONE FOR!
GZZZZZZZZZZZZZZ-ZAK!
GAH! A BRIGHT, BLINDING LIGHT--

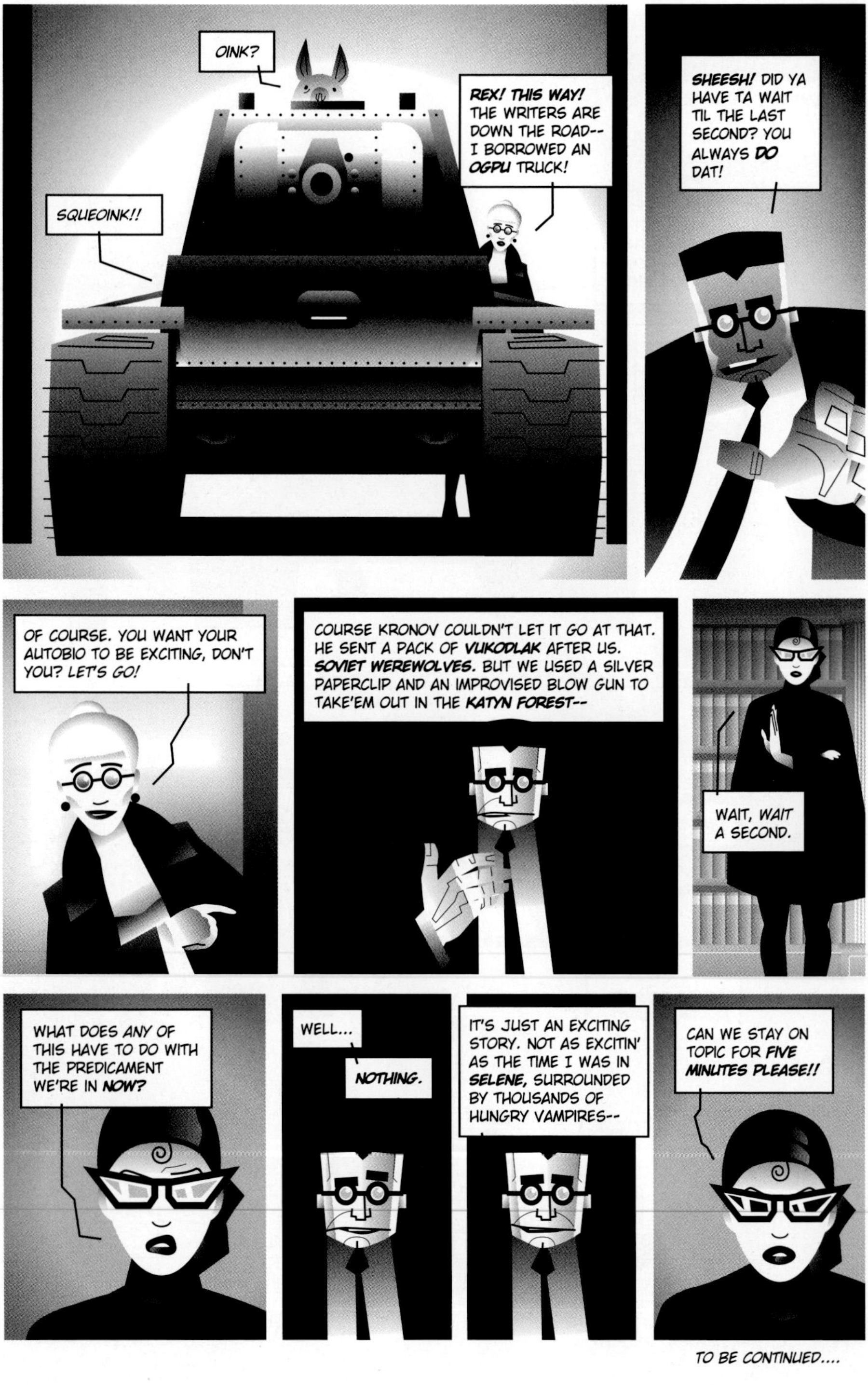

OINK?
SQUEOINK!!
REX! THIS WAY! THE WRITERS ARE DOWN THE ROAD-- I BORROWED AN OGPU TRUCK!
SHEESH! DID YA HAVE TA WAIT TIL THE LAST SECOND? YOU ALWAYS DO DAT!
OF COURSE. YOU WANT YOUR AUTOBIO TO BE EXCITING, DON'T YOU? LET'S GO!
COURSE KRONOV COULDN'T LET IT GO AT THAT. HE SENT A PACK OF VUKODLAK AFTER US. SOVIET WEREWOLVES. BUT WE USED A SILVER PAPERCLIP AND AN IMPROVISED BLOW GUN TO TAKE'EM OUT IN THE KATYN FOREST--
WAIT, WAIT A SECOND.
WHAT DOES ANY OF THIS HAVE TO DO WITH THE PREDICAMENT WE'RE IN NOW?
WELL...
NOTHING.
IT'S JUST AN EXCITING STORY. NOT AS EXCITIN' AS THE TIME I WAS IN SELENE, SURROUNDED BY THOUSANDS OF HUNGRY VAMPIRES--
CAN WE STAY ON TOPIC FOR FIVE MINUTES PLEASE!!

TO BE CONTINUED....

CHAPTER TEN

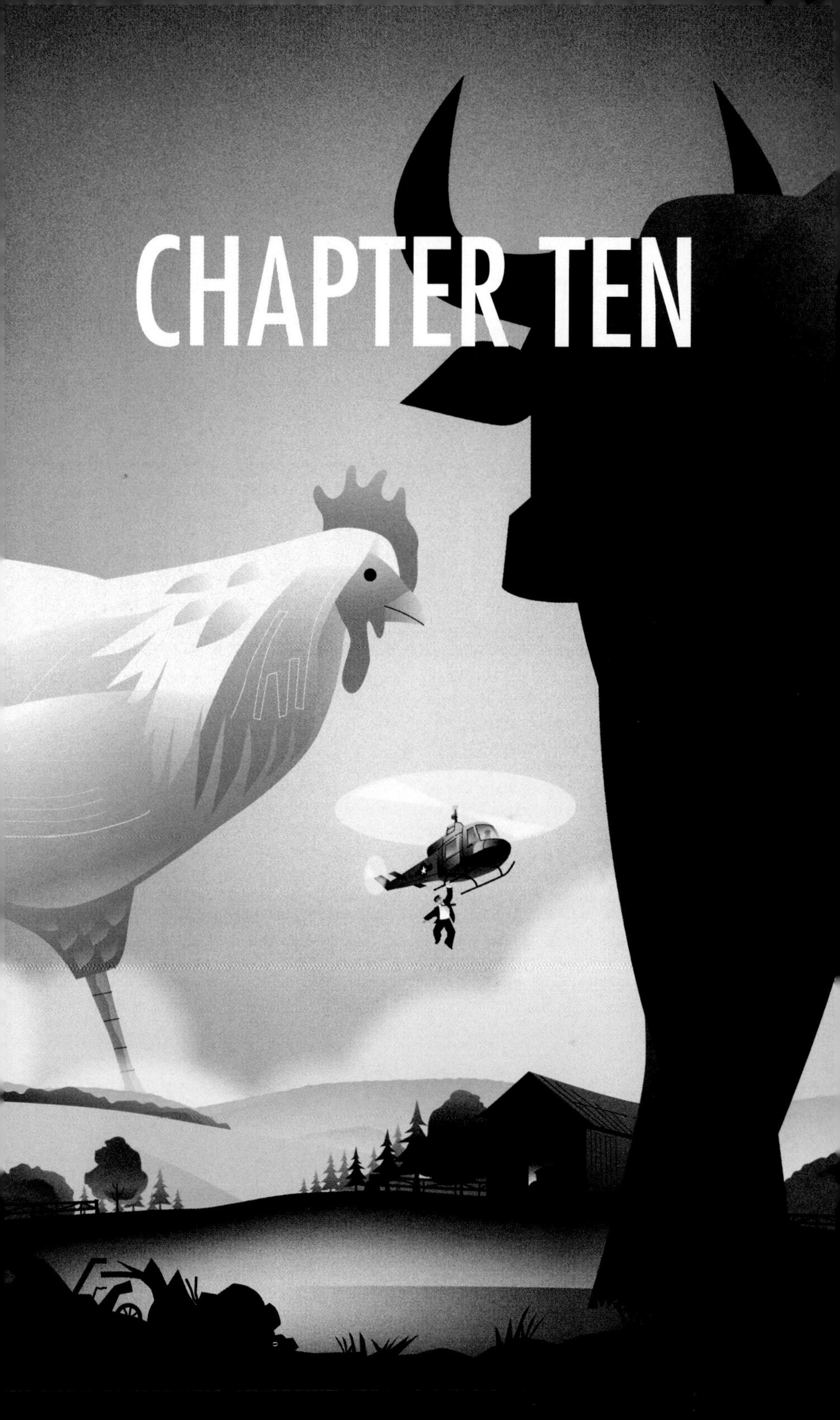

BARRY'S BRAIN

Long have I been receiving letters from readers asking for more Barry in Hermeneutic publications. Well, you, dear reader, spoke—or wrote, as the case may be—and I listened! The needs of my audience are of the utmost importance to me. So here it is: an issue of Rex Libris that is suffused with the illuminating and benevolent goodness of B. Barry Horst's thought! Indeed, my *being* permeates the very fabric of this issue like never before, from staple to fringe, from cover to cover. Bask in the beauty of Barry's percolating brain, my friends, for it is not often that such an opportunity as this arises. Well. Unless you buy my book *Fubar: Heironymous Snogg and the Sex Vixen Factory of the Post-Apocalypse.* Or *Barry's Guide to Blockbuster Publishing.*

I know what you're thinking: that's not enough. Of course it isn't! It never will be for the *true* aficionado. All the more reason to savour this issues' illimitable effervescent elucidation by the big double B. You never know how long the wait may be before you get more Barry.

Now I want to take a moment to mention our upcoming spin-off series: *Hypatia Phoenix.* That's right! Hypatia is getting her very own comic! The Ordo Bibliotheca has bestowed upon her the title 'Phoenix' in honour of her heroism in issue 8. Apparently, this naming procedure is done for every librarian the first time they save the planet. You learn a new thing every day! It makes for a catchy comic book title, too. We'll be following her adventures as she journeys from a wet-behind-the-ears novice to grisled veteran. There will be action, romance, and villains beyond sanity! For example, in the first issue she'll be taking on the despicable Bernardus Guidonis, the Immortal Inquisitor, and his crack team of torturers. But it will not be easy, for no one knows when or where the Inquisitors will strike next! Expect the unexpected! Only with the help of a talking book bearing the spirit of a long dead philosopher can she bring these obscenely puritanical ideologues and their free thought assassins to heel.

Now on to the rumour mill: some of you might have heard about financial troubles here at Hermeneutic. Fret not, friends, it's all been settled. My nephew Todd from Vancouver has come to the rescue! True, I must admit to some surprise, as all he ever seemed to do is laze around in a drug induced stupor—but he's proven me wrong! He got into the horticulture business last year and started up his own nursery. Now he's making money hand over fist! Incredible! I had no idea these little grow-ops could be so profitable. If I had, I'd have gone into horticulture too. At any rate, he's eager to invest in Heremeneutic Press! He says the arrangement is mutually beneficial, and who am I to argue? He's even offered to handle *all* the accounting! I hate accounting! What a nephew! Thanks to him, Heremeneutic will be around for the indefinite and undefinable future!

Exfoliate!

B. Barry Horst
Publisher

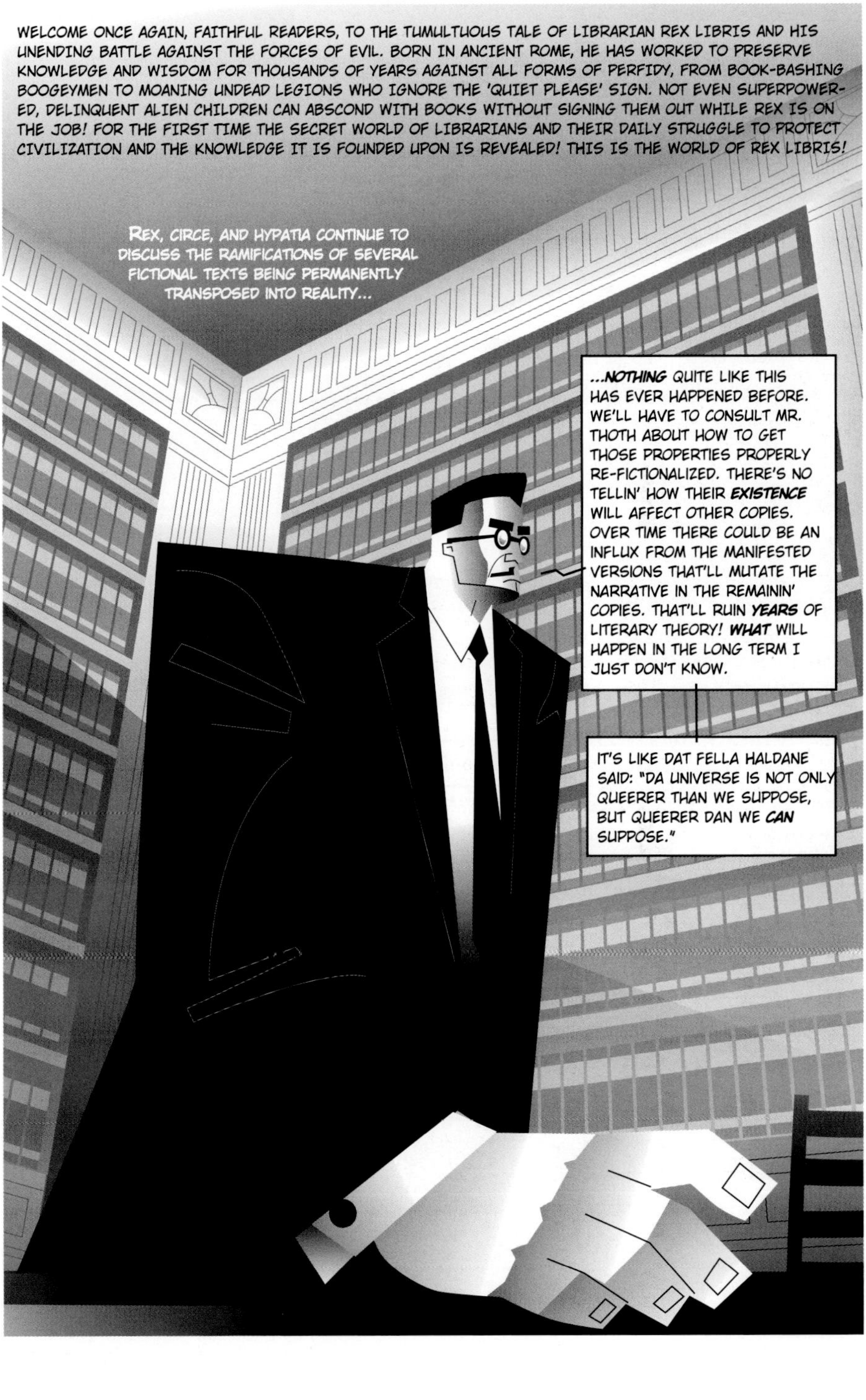
WELCOME ONCE AGAIN, FAITHFUL READERS, TO THE TUMULTUOUS TALE OF LIBRARIAN REX LIBRIS AND HIS UNENDING BATTLE AGAINST THE FORCES OF EVIL. BORN IN ANCIENT ROME, HE HAS WORKED TO PRESERVE KNOWLEDGE AND WISDOM FOR THOUSANDS OF YEARS AGAINST ALL FORMS OF PERFIDY, FROM BOOK-BASHING BOOGEYMEN TO MOANING UNDEAD LEGIONS WHO IGNORE THE 'QUIET PLEASE' SIGN. NOT EVEN SUPERPOWERED, DELINQUENT ALIEN CHILDREN CAN ABSCOND WITH BOOKS WITHOUT SIGNING THEM OUT WHILE REX IS ON THE JOB! FOR THE FIRST TIME THE SECRET WORLD OF LIBRARIANS AND THEIR DAILY STRUGGLE TO PROTECT CIVILIZATION AND THE KNOWLEDGE IT IS FOUNDED UPON IS REVEALED! THIS IS THE WORLD OF REX LIBRIS!
REX, CIRCE, AND HYPATIA CONTINUE TO DISCUSS THE RAMIFICATIONS OF SEVERAL FICTIONAL TEXTS BEING PERMANENTLY TRANSPOSED INTO REALITY...
...***NOTHING*** QUITE LIKE THIS HAS EVER HAPPENED BEFORE. WE'LL HAVE TO CONSULT MR. THOTH ABOUT HOW TO GET THOSE PROPERTIES PROPERLY RE-FICTIONALIZED. THERE'S NO TELLIN' HOW THEIR ***EXISTENCE*** WILL AFFECT OTHER COPIES. OVER TIME THERE COULD BE AN INFLUX FROM THE MANIFESTED VERSIONS THAT'LL MUTATE THE NARRATIVE IN THE REMAININ' COPIES. THAT'LL RUIN ***YEARS*** OF LITERARY THEORY! ***WHAT*** WILL HAPPEN IN THE LONG TERM I JUST DON'T KNOW.
IT'S LIKE DAT FELLA HALDANE SAID: "DA UNIVERSE IS NOT ONLY QUEERER THAN WE SUPPOSE, BUT QUEERER DAN WE ***CAN*** SUPPOSE."

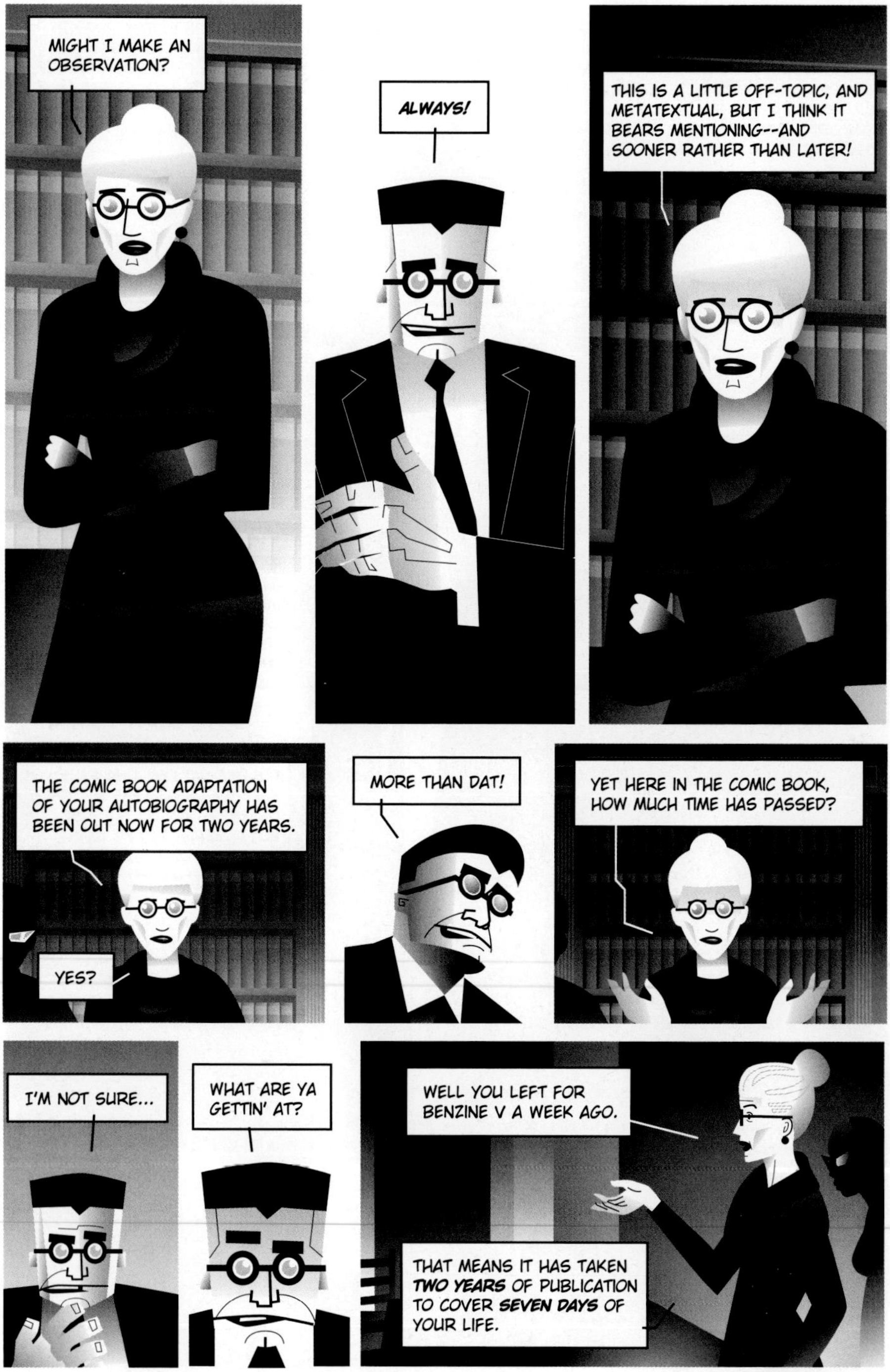
MIGHT I MAKE AN OBSERVATION?
ALWAYS!
THIS IS A LITTLE OFF-TOPIC, AND METATEXTUAL, BUT I THINK IT BEARS MENTIONING--AND SOONER RATHER THAN LATER!
THE COMIC BOOK ADAPTATION OF YOUR AUTOBIOGRAPHY HAS BEEN OUT NOW FOR TWO YEARS.
YES?
MORE THAN DAT!
YET HERE IN THE COMIC BOOK, HOW MUCH TIME HAS PASSED?
I'M NOT SURE...
WHAT ARE YA GETTIN' AT?
WELL YOU LEFT FOR BENZINE V A WEEK AGO.
THAT MEANS IT HAS TAKEN **TWO YEARS** OF PUBLICATION TO COVER **SEVEN DAYS** OF YOUR LIFE.

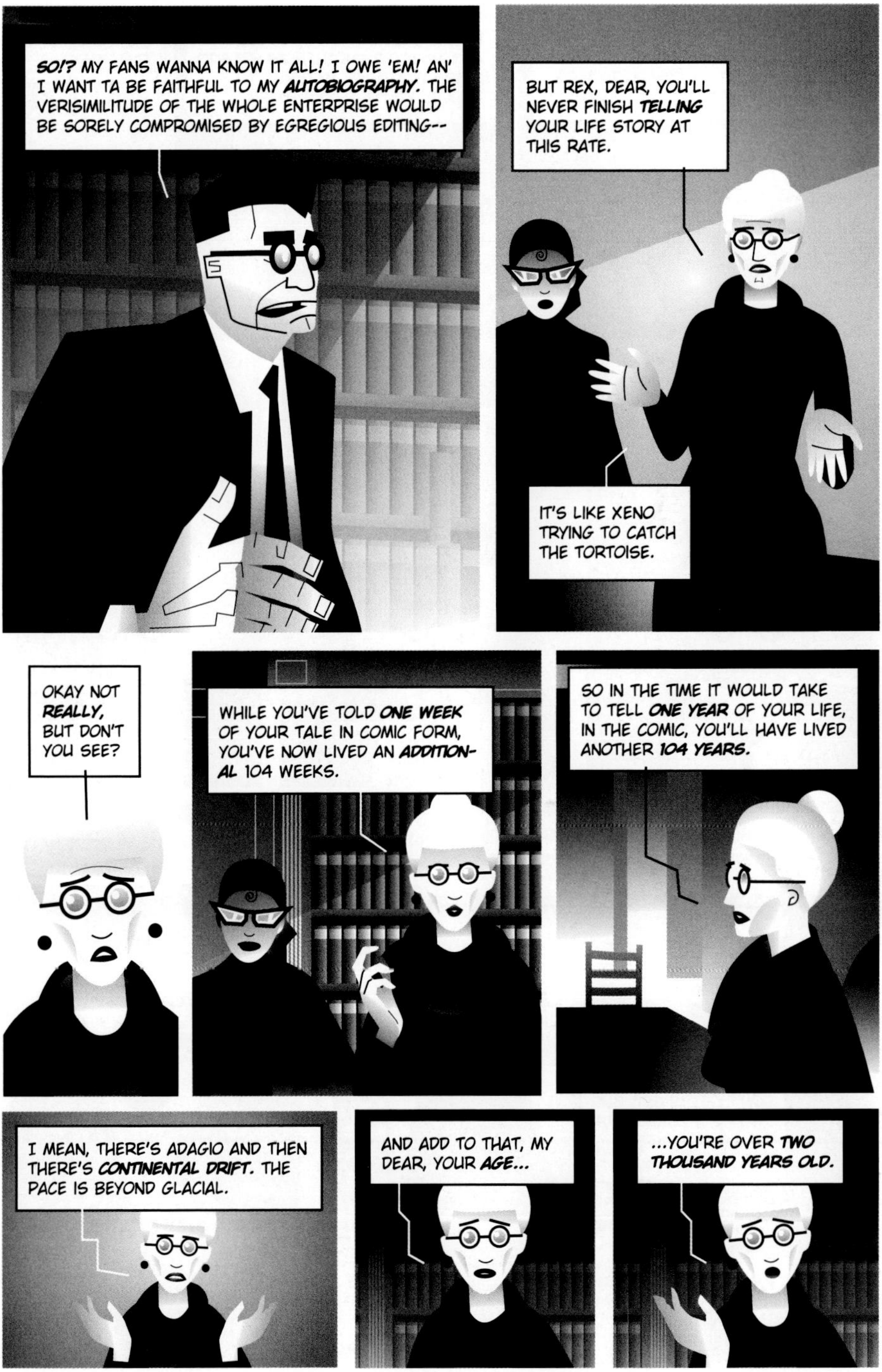

SO!? MY FANS WANNA KNOW IT ALL! I OWE 'EM! AN' I WANT TA BE FAITHFUL TO MY AUTOBIOGRAPHY. THE VERISIMILITUDE OF THE WHOLE ENTERPRISE WOULD BE SORELY COMPROMISED BY EGREGIOUS EDITING--
BUT REX, DEAR, YOU'LL NEVER FINISH TELLING YOUR LIFE STORY AT THIS RATE.
IT'S LIKE XENO TRYING TO CATCH THE TORTOISE.
OKAY NOT REALLY, BUT DON'T YOU SEE?
WHILE YOU'VE TOLD ONE WEEK OF YOUR TALE IN COMIC FORM, YOU'VE NOW LIVED AN ADDITION-AL 104 WEEKS.
SO IN THE TIME IT WOULD TAKE TO TELL ONE YEAR OF YOUR LIFE, IN THE COMIC, YOU'LL HAVE LIVED ANOTHER 104 YEARS.
I MEAN, THERE'S ADAGIO AND THEN THERE'S CONTINENTAL DRIFT. THE PACE IS BEYOND GLACIAL.
AND ADD TO THAT, MY DEAR, YOUR AGE...
...YOU'RE OVER TWO THOUSAND YEARS OLD.

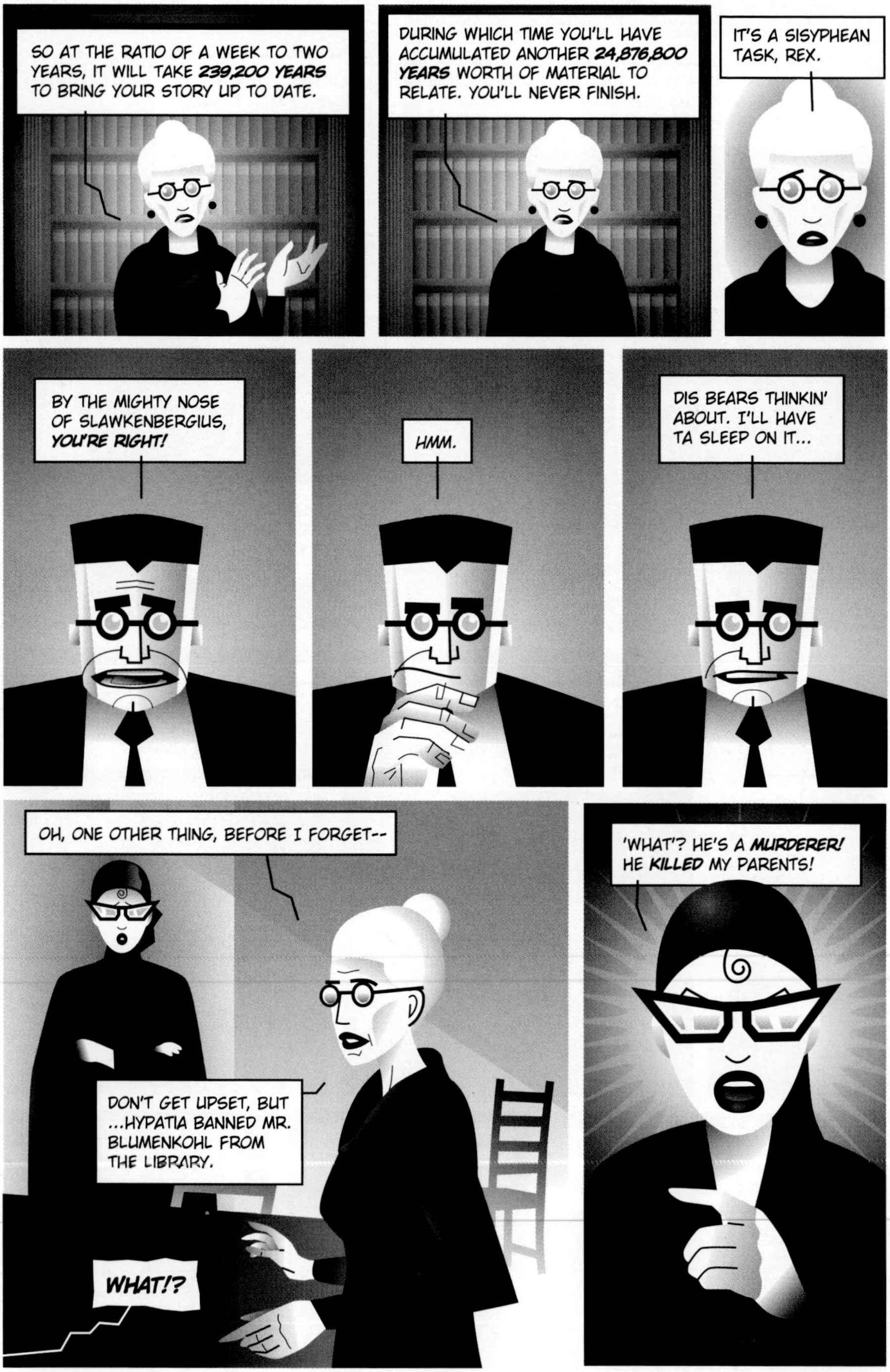
SO AT THE RATIO OF A WEEK TO TWO YEARS, IT WILL TAKE **239,200 YEARS** TO BRING YOUR STORY UP TO DATE.
DURING WHICH TIME YOU'LL HAVE ACCUMULATED ANOTHER **24,876,800 YEARS** WORTH OF MATERIAL TO RELATE. YOU'LL NEVER FINISH.
IT'S A SISYPHEAN TASK, REX.
BY THE MIGHTY NOSE OF SLAWKENBERGIUS, ***YOU'RE RIGHT!***
HMM.
DIS BEARS THINKIN' ABOUT. I'LL HAVE TA SLEEP ON IT...
OH, ONE OTHER THING, BEFORE I FORGET--
DON'T GET UPSET, BUT ...HYPATIA BANNED MR. BLUMENKOHL FROM THE LIBRARY.
WHAT!?
'WHAT'? HE'S A ***MURDERER!*** HE ***KILLED*** MY PARENTS!

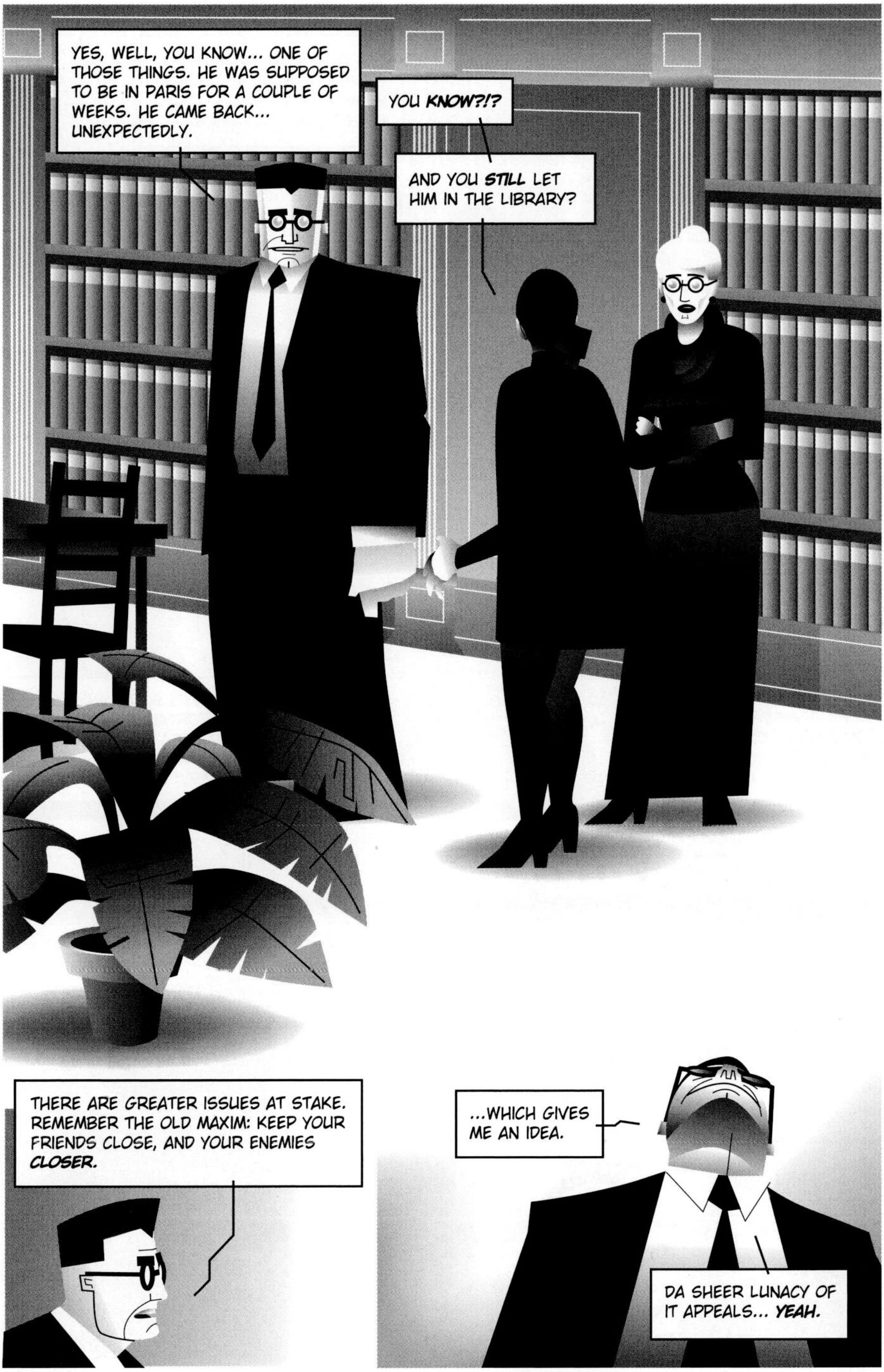
YES, WELL, YOU KNOW... ONE OF THOSE THINGS. HE WAS SUPPOSED TO BE IN PARIS FOR A COUPLE OF WEEKS. HE CAME BACK... UNEXPECTEDLY.
YOU **KNOW?!?**
AND YOU **STILL** LET HIM IN THE LIBRARY?
THERE ARE GREATER ISSUES AT STAKE. REMEMBER THE OLD MAXIM: KEEP YOUR FRIENDS CLOSE, AND YOUR ENEMIES ***CLOSER.***
...WHICH GIVES ME AN IDEA.
DA SHEER LUNACY OF IT APPEALS... ***YEAH.***

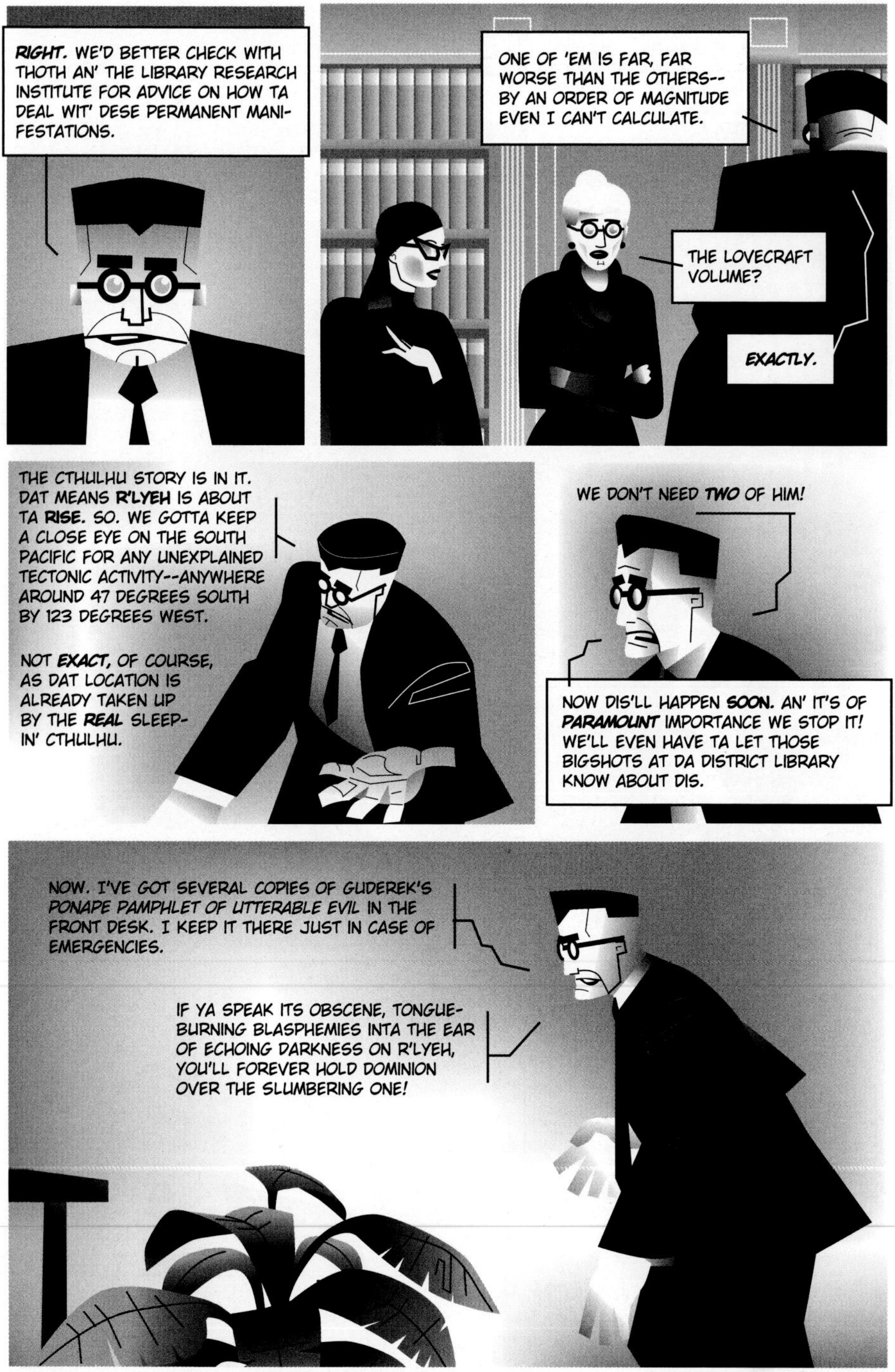
RIGHT. WE'D BETTER CHECK WITH THOTH AN' THE LIBRARY RESEARCH INSTITUTE FOR ADVICE ON HOW TA DEAL WIT' DESE PERMANENT MANIFESTATIONS.
ONE OF 'EM IS FAR, FAR WORSE THAN THE OTHERS-- BY AN ORDER OF MAGNITUDE EVEN I CAN'T CALCULATE.
THE LOVECRAFT VOLUME?
EXACTLY.
THE CTHULHU STORY IS IN IT. DAT MEANS R'LYEH IS ABOUT TA RISE. SO. WE GOTTA KEEP A CLOSE EYE ON THE SOUTH PACIFIC FOR ANY UNEXPLAINED TECTONIC ACTIVITY--ANYWHERE AROUND 47 DEGREES SOUTH BY 123 DEGREES WEST.
NOT EXACT, OF COURSE, AS DAT LOCATION IS ALREADY TAKEN UP BY THE REAL SLEEPIN' CTHULHU.
WE DON'T NEED TWO OF HIM!
NOW DIS'LL HAPPEN SOON. AN' IT'S OF PARAMOUNT IMPORTANCE WE STOP IT! WE'LL EVEN HAVE TA LET THOSE BIGSHOTS AT DA DISTRICT LIBRARY KNOW ABOUT DIS.
NOW. I'VE GOT SEVERAL COPIES OF GUDEREK'S PONAPE PAMPHLET OF UTTERABLE EVIL IN THE FRONT DESK. I KEEP IT THERE JUST IN CASE OF EMERGENCIES.
IF YA SPEAK ITS OBSCENE, TONGUE-BURNING BLASPHEMIES INTA THE EAR OF ECHOING DARKNESS ON R'LYEH, YOU'LL FOREVER HOLD DOMINION OVER THE SLUMBERING ONE!

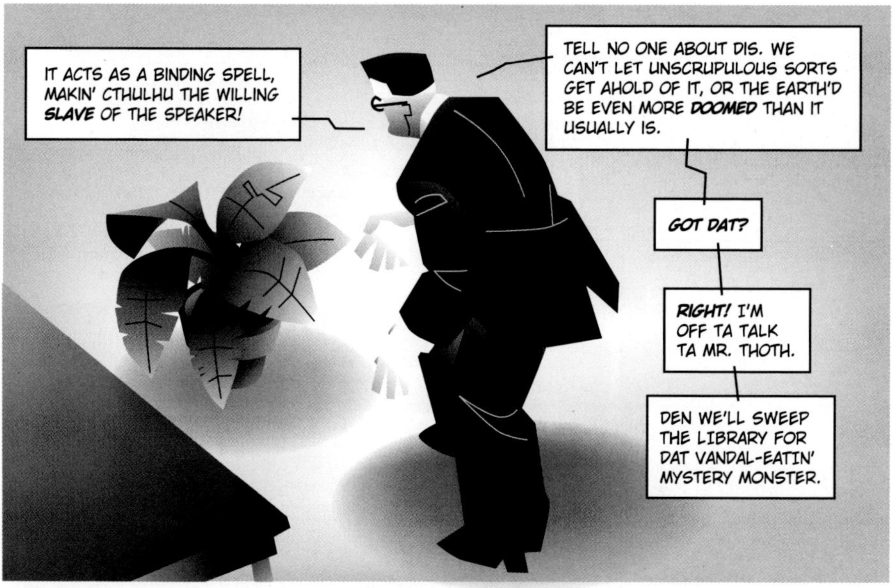
IT ACTS AS A BINDING SPELL, MAKIN' CTHULHU THE WILLING SLAVE OF THE SPEAKER!
TELL NO ONE ABOUT DIS. WE CAN'T LET UNSCRUPULOUS SORTS GET AHOLD OF IT, OR THE EARTH'D BE EVEN MORE DOOMED THAN IT USUALLY IS.
GOT DAT?
RIGHT! I'M OFF TA TALK TA MR. THOTH.
DEN WE'LL SWEEP THE LIBRARY FOR DAT VANDAL-EATIN' MYSTERY MONSTER.

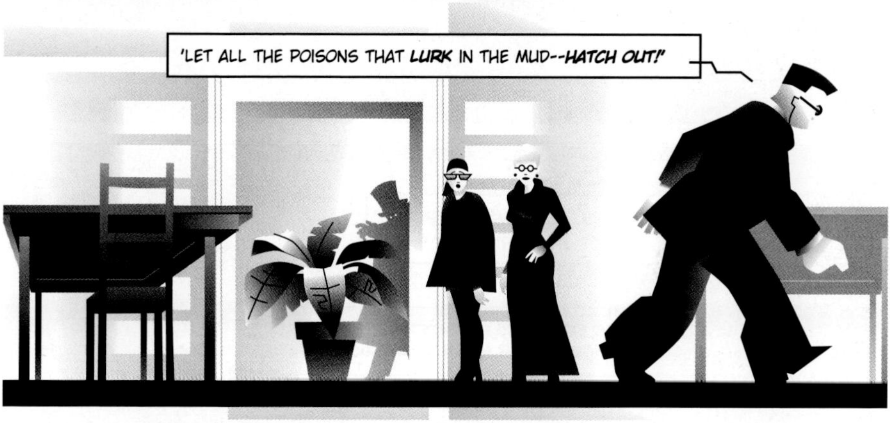
'LET ALL THE POISONS THAT LURK IN THE MUD--HATCH OUT!'

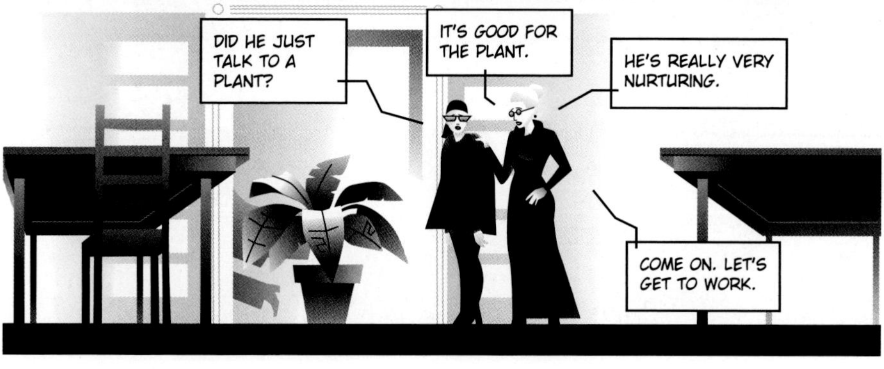
DID HE JUST TALK TO A PLANT?
IT'S GOOD FOR THE PLANT.
HE'S REALLY VERY NURTURING.
COME ON. LET'S GET TO WORK.

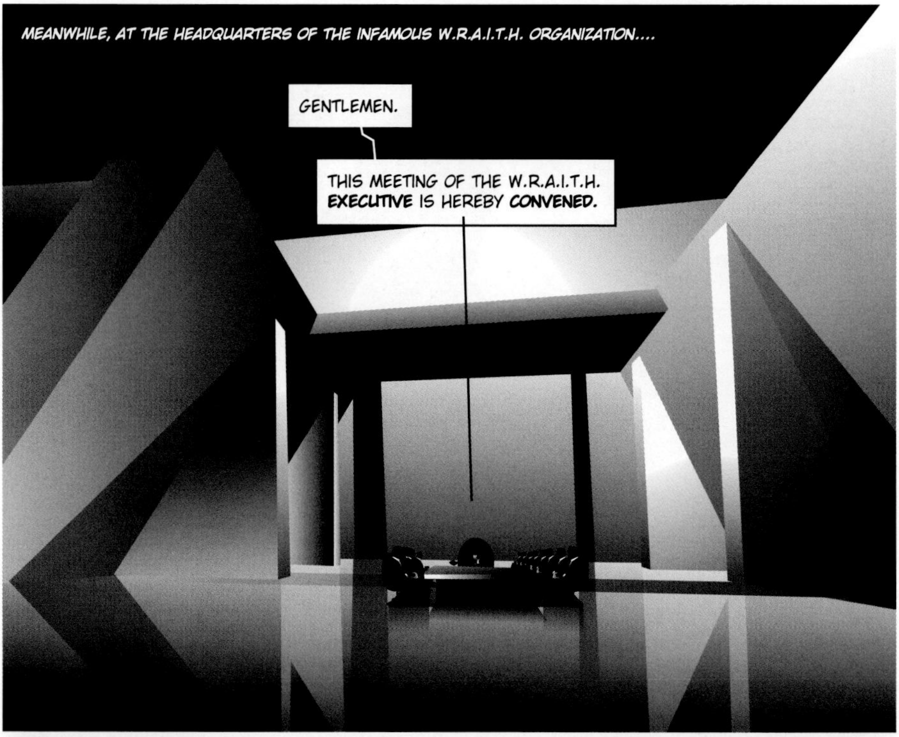
MEANWHILE, AT THE HEADQUARTERS OF THE INFAMOUS W.R.A.I.T.H. ORGANIZATION....
GENTLEMEN.
THIS MEETING OF THE W.R.A.I.T.H. EXECUTIVE IS HEREBY CONVENED.

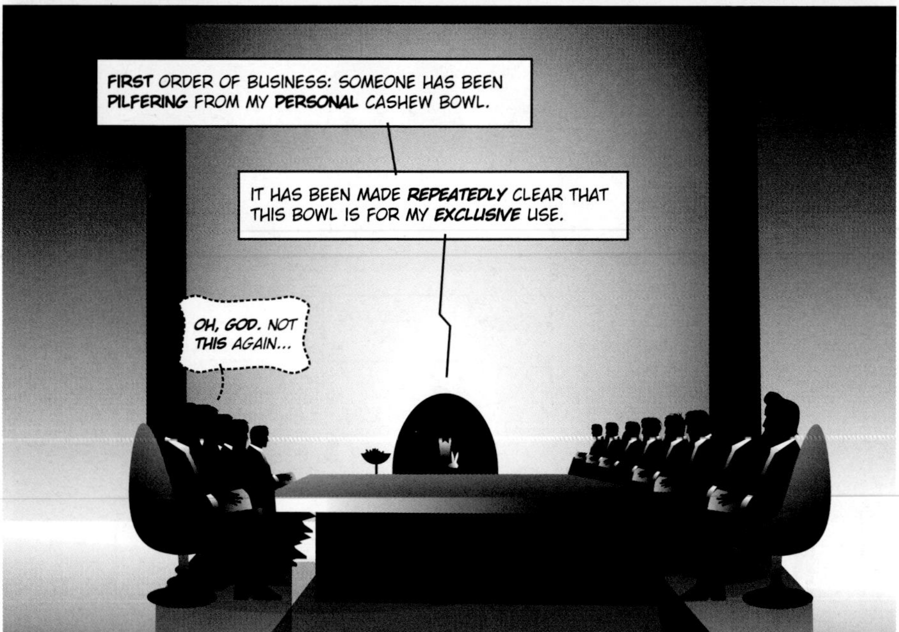
FIRST ORDER OF BUSINESS: SOMEONE HAS BEEN PILFERING FROM MY PERSONAL CASHEW BOWL.
IT HAS BEEN MADE REPEATEDLY CLEAR THAT THIS BOWL IS FOR MY EXCLUSIVE USE.
OH, GOD. NOT THIS AGAIN...

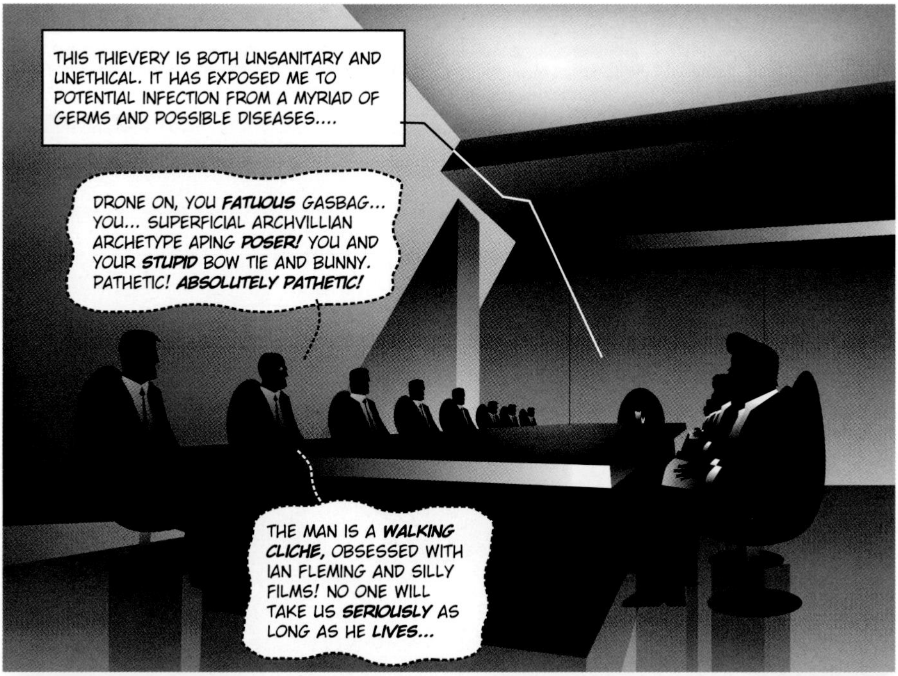
THIS THIEVERY IS BOTH UNSANITARY AND UNETHICAL. IT HAS EXPOSED ME TO POTENTIAL INFECTION FROM A MYRIAD OF GERMS AND POSSIBLE DISEASES....
DRONE ON, YOU FATUOUS GASBAG... YOU... SUPERFICIAL ARCHVILLIAN ARCHETYPE APING POSER! YOU AND YOUR STUPID BOW TIE AND BUNNY. PATHETIC! ABSOLUTELY PATHETIC!
THE MAN IS A WALKING CLICHE, OBSESSED WITH IAN FLEMING AND SILLY FILMS! NO ONE WILL TAKE US SERIOUSLY AS LONG AS HE LIVES...

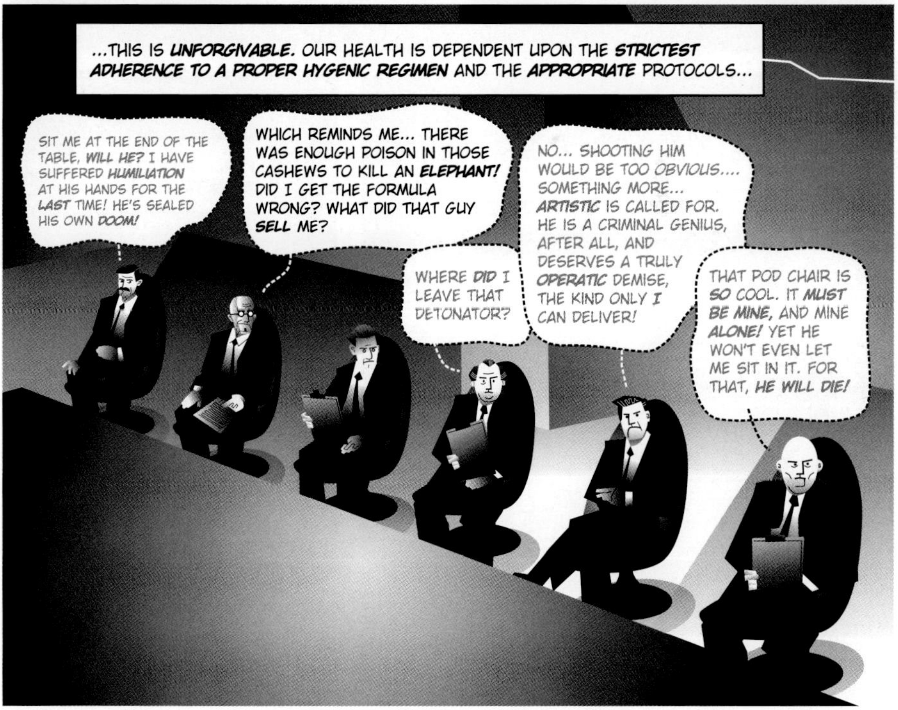
...THIS IS UNFORGIVABLE. OUR HEALTH IS DEPENDENT UPON THE STRICTEST ADHERENCE TO A PROPER HYGENIC REGIMEN AND THE APPROPRIATE PROTOCOLS...
SIT ME AT THE END OF THE TABLE, WILL HE? I HAVE SUFFERED HUMILIATION AT HIS HANDS FOR THE LAST TIME! HE'S SEALED HIS OWN DOOM!
WHICH REMINDS ME... THERE WAS ENOUGH POISON IN THOSE CASHEWS TO KILL AN ELEPHANT! DID I GET THE FORMULA WRONG? WHAT DID THAT GUY SELL ME?
WHERE DID I LEAVE THAT DETONATOR?
NO... SHOOTING HIM WOULD BE TOO OBVIOUS.... SOMETHING MORE... ARTISTIC IS CALLED FOR. HE IS A CRIMINAL GENIUS, AFTER ALL, AND DESERVES A TRULY OPERATIC DEMISE, THE KIND ONLY I CAN DELIVER!
THAT POD CHAIR IS SO COOL. IT MUST BE MINE, AND MINE ALONE! YET HE WON'T EVEN LET ME SIT IN IT. FOR THAT, HE WILL DIE!

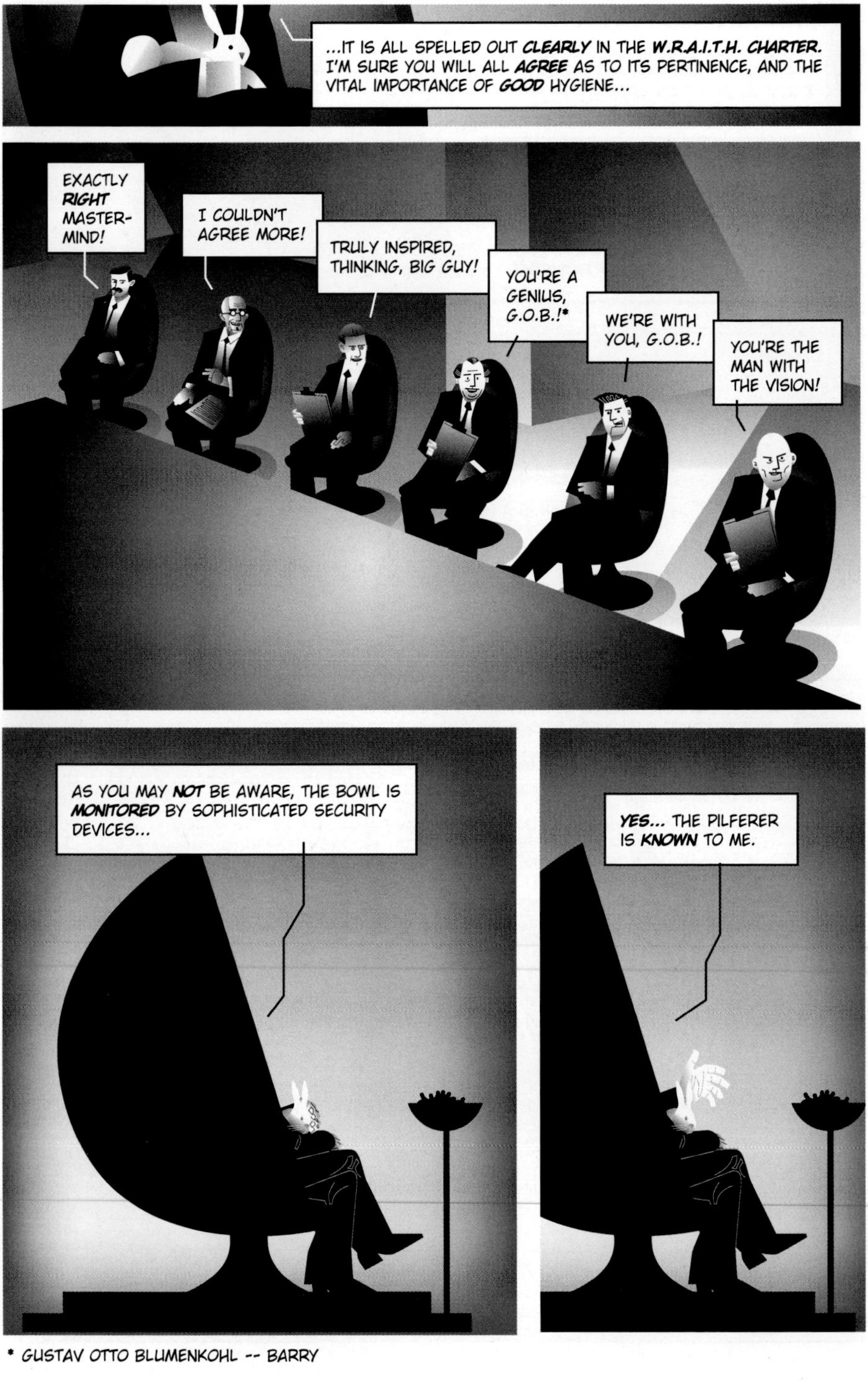
...IT IS ALL SPELLED OUT **CLEARLY** IN THE **W.R.A.I.T.H. CHARTER.** I'M SURE YOU WILL ALL **AGREE** AS TO ITS PERTINENCE, AND THE VITAL IMPORTANCE OF **GOOD** HYGIENE...
EXACTLY **RIGHT** MASTER-MIND!
I COULDN'T AGREE MORE!
TRULY INSPIRED, THINKING, BIG GUY!
YOU'RE A GENIUS, G.O.B.!*
WE'RE WITH YOU, G.O.B.!
YOU'RE THE MAN WITH THE VISION!
AS YOU MAY **NOT** BE AWARE, THE BOWL IS **MONITORED** BY SOPHISTICATED SECURITY DEVICES...
YES... THE PILFERER IS **KNOWN** TO ME.

* GUSTAV OTTO BLUMENKOHL -- BARRY

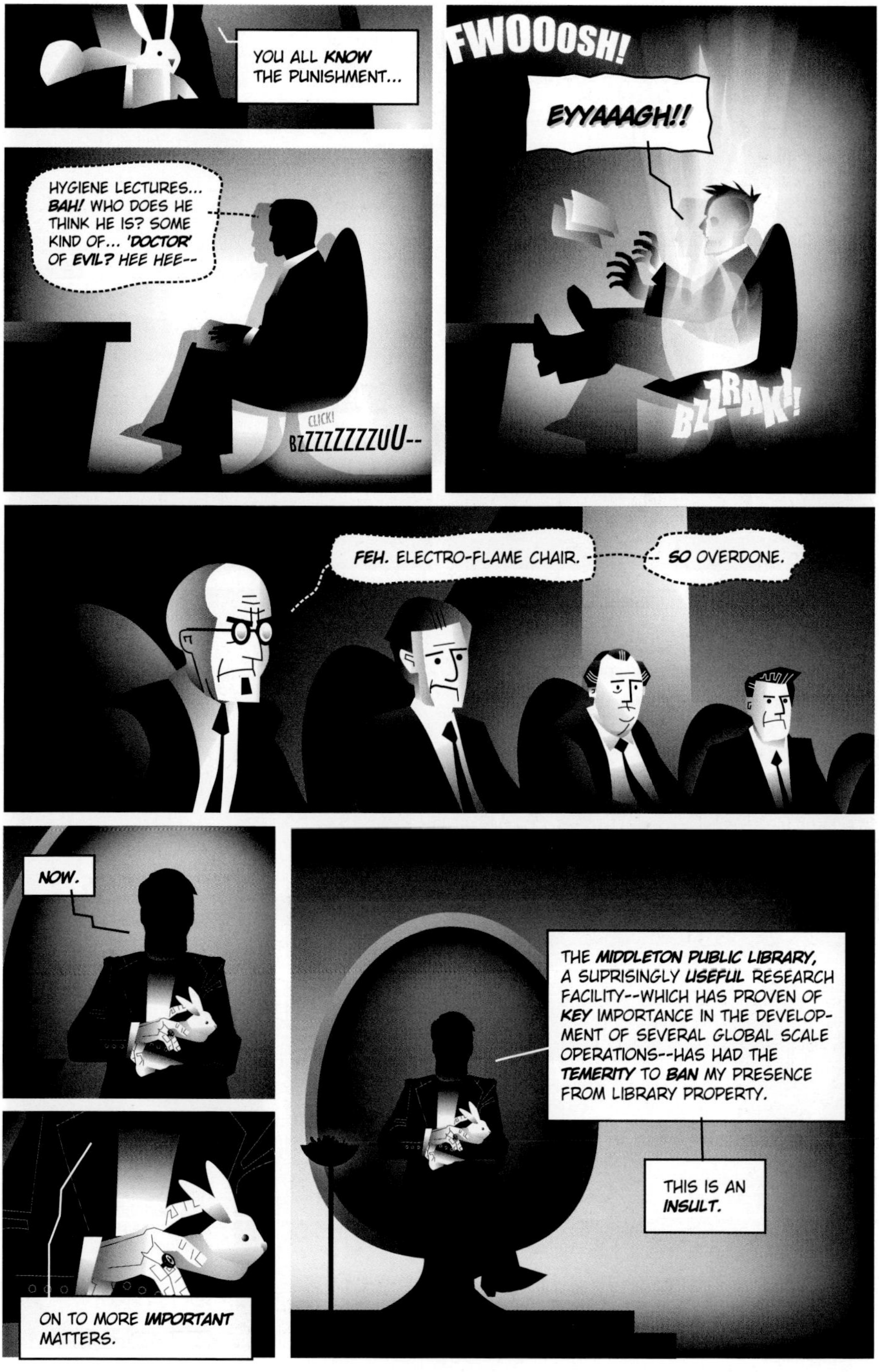
YOU ALL KNOW THE PUNISHMENT...
FWOOOSH!
EYYAAAGH!!
HYGIENE LECTURES... BAH! WHO DOES HE THINK HE IS? SOME KIND OF... 'DOCTOR' OF EVIL? HEE HEE--
CLICK!
BZZZZZZZZUU--
BZZRAK!!
FEH. ELECTRO-FLAME CHAIR.
SO OVERDONE.
NOW.
ON TO MORE IMPORTANT MATTERS.
THE MIDDLETON PUBLIC LIBRARY, A SUPRISINGLY USEFUL RESEARCH FACILITY--WHICH HAS PROVEN OF KEY IMPORTANCE IN THE DEVELOPMENT OF SEVERAL GLOBAL SCALE OPERATIONS--HAS HAD THE TEMERITY TO BAN MY PRESENCE FROM LIBRARY PROPERTY.
THIS IS AN INSULT.

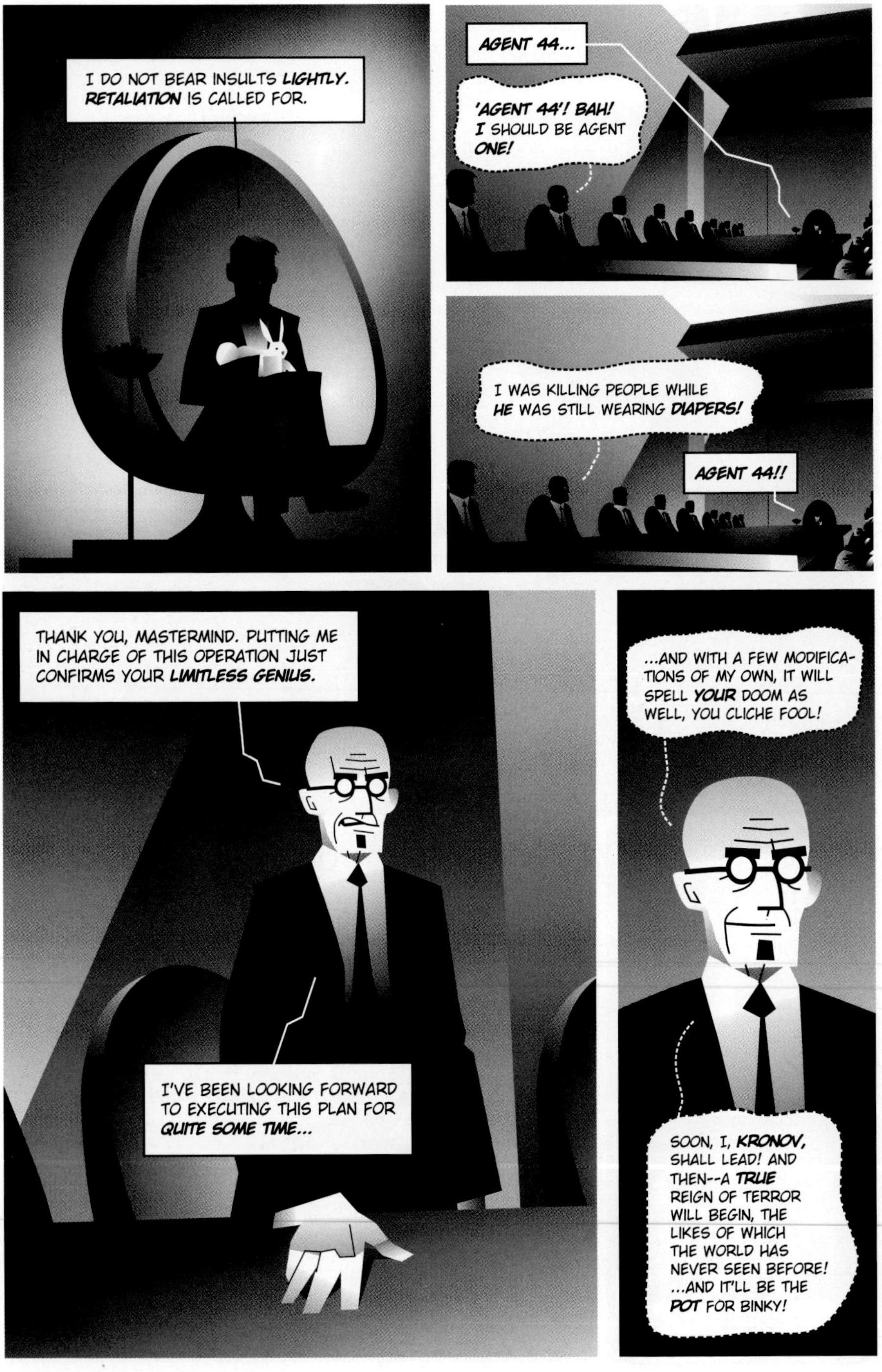
I DO NOT BEAR INSULTS LIGHTLY. RETALIATION IS CALLED FOR.
AGENT 44...
'AGENT 44'! BAH! I SHOULD BE AGENT ONE!
I WAS KILLING PEOPLE WHILE HE WAS STILL WEARING DIAPERS!
AGENT 44!!
THANK YOU, MASTERMIND. PUTTING ME IN CHARGE OF THIS OPERATION JUST CONFIRMS YOUR LIMITLESS GENIUS.
I'VE BEEN LOOKING FORWARD TO EXECUTING THIS PLAN FOR QUITE SOME TIME...
...AND WITH A FEW MODIFICATIONS OF MY OWN, IT WILL SPELL YOUR DOOM AS WELL, YOU CLICHE FOOL!
SOON, I, KRONOV, SHALL LEAD! AND THEN--A TRUE REIGN OF TERROR WILL BEGIN, THE LIKES OF WHICH THE WORLD HAS NEVER SEEN BEFORE! ...AND IT'LL BE THE POT FOR BINKY!

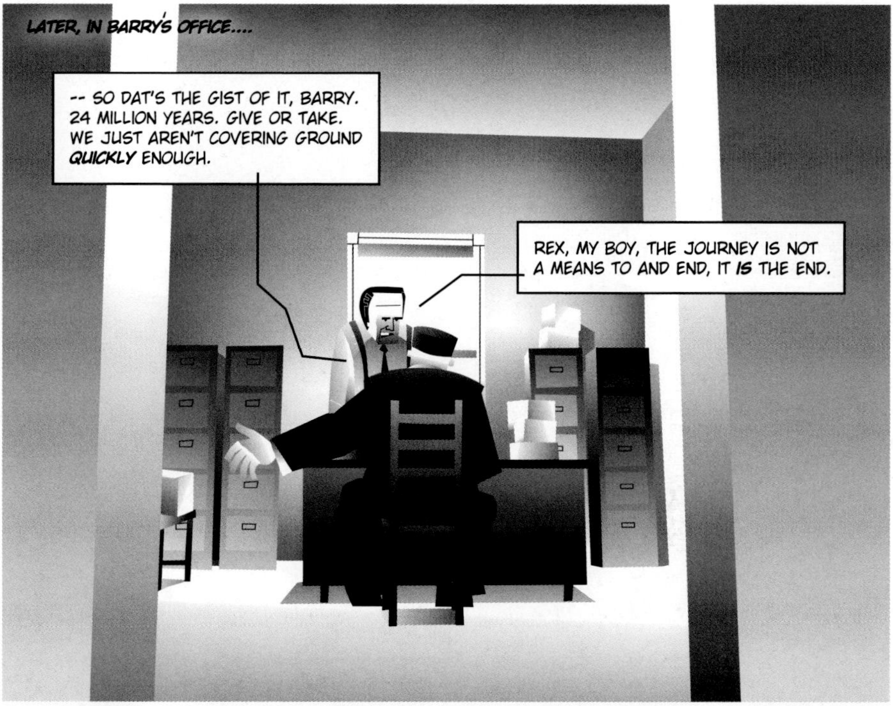
LATER, IN BARRY'S OFFICE....
-- SO DAT'S THE GIST OF IT, BARRY. 24 MILLION YEARS. GIVE OR TAKE. WE JUST AREN'T COVERING GROUND QUICKLY ENOUGH.
REX, MY BOY, THE JOURNEY IS NOT A MEANS TO AND END, IT IS THE END.

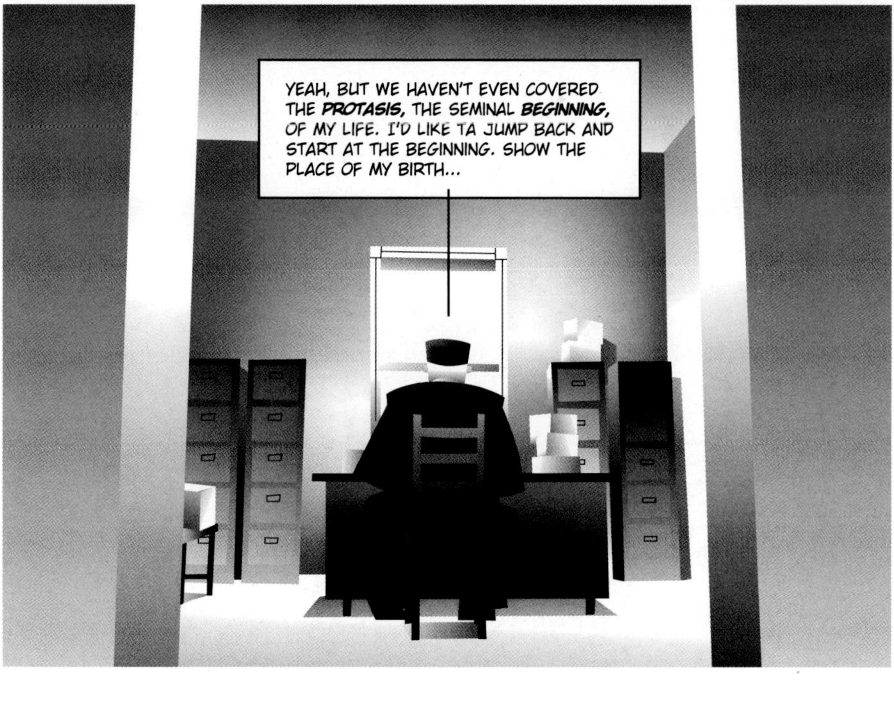
YEAH, BUT WE HAVEN'T EVEN COVERED THE PROTASIS, THE SEMINAL BEGINNING, OF MY LIFE. I'D LIKE TA JUMP BACK AND START AT THE BEGINNING. SHOW THE PLACE OF MY BIRTH...

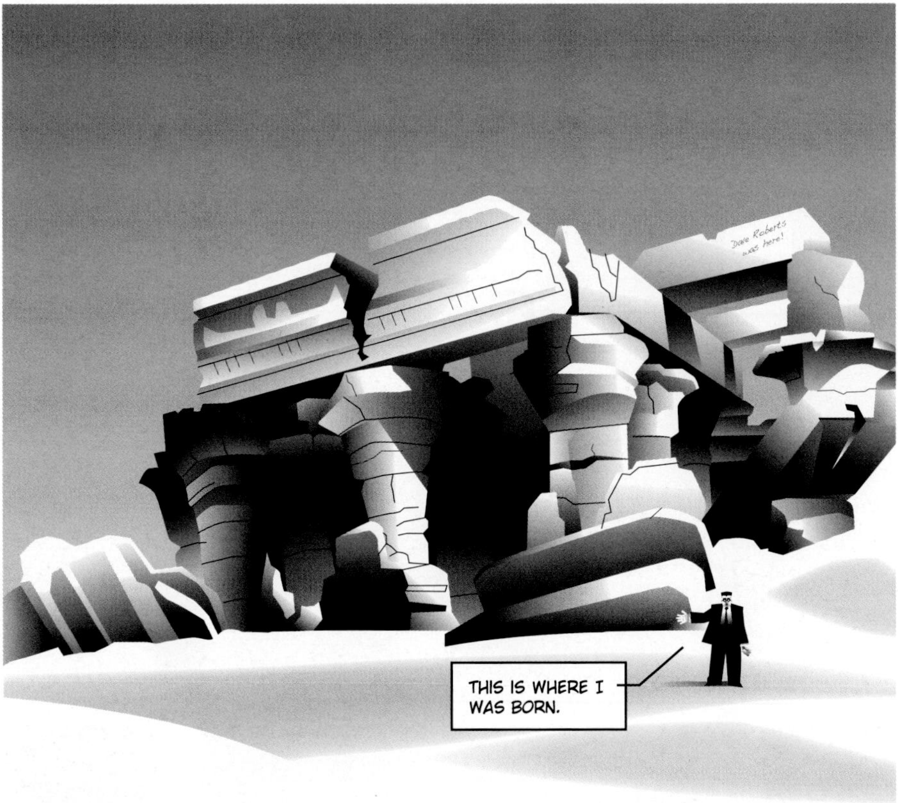
Dave Roberts was here!
THIS IS WHERE I WAS BORN.

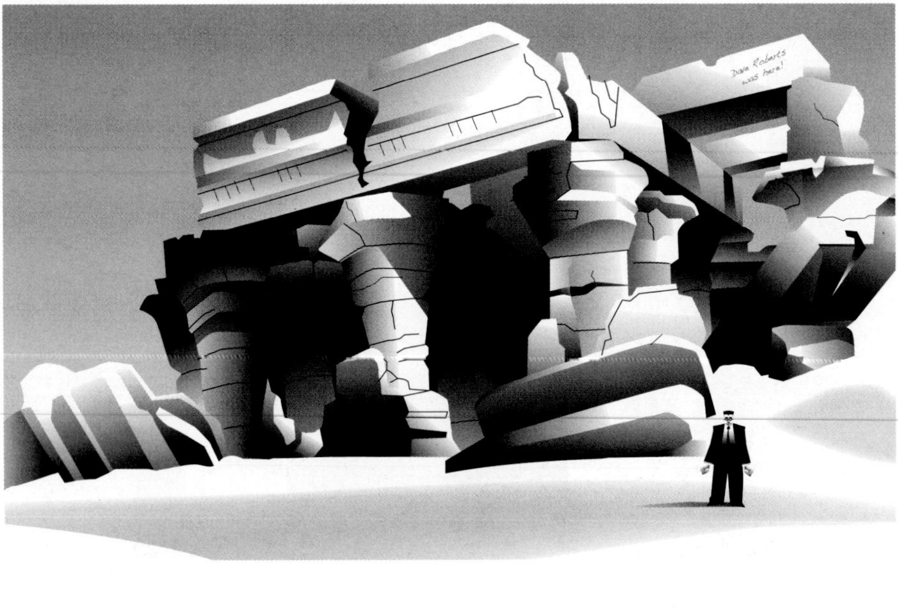
Dave Roberts was here!

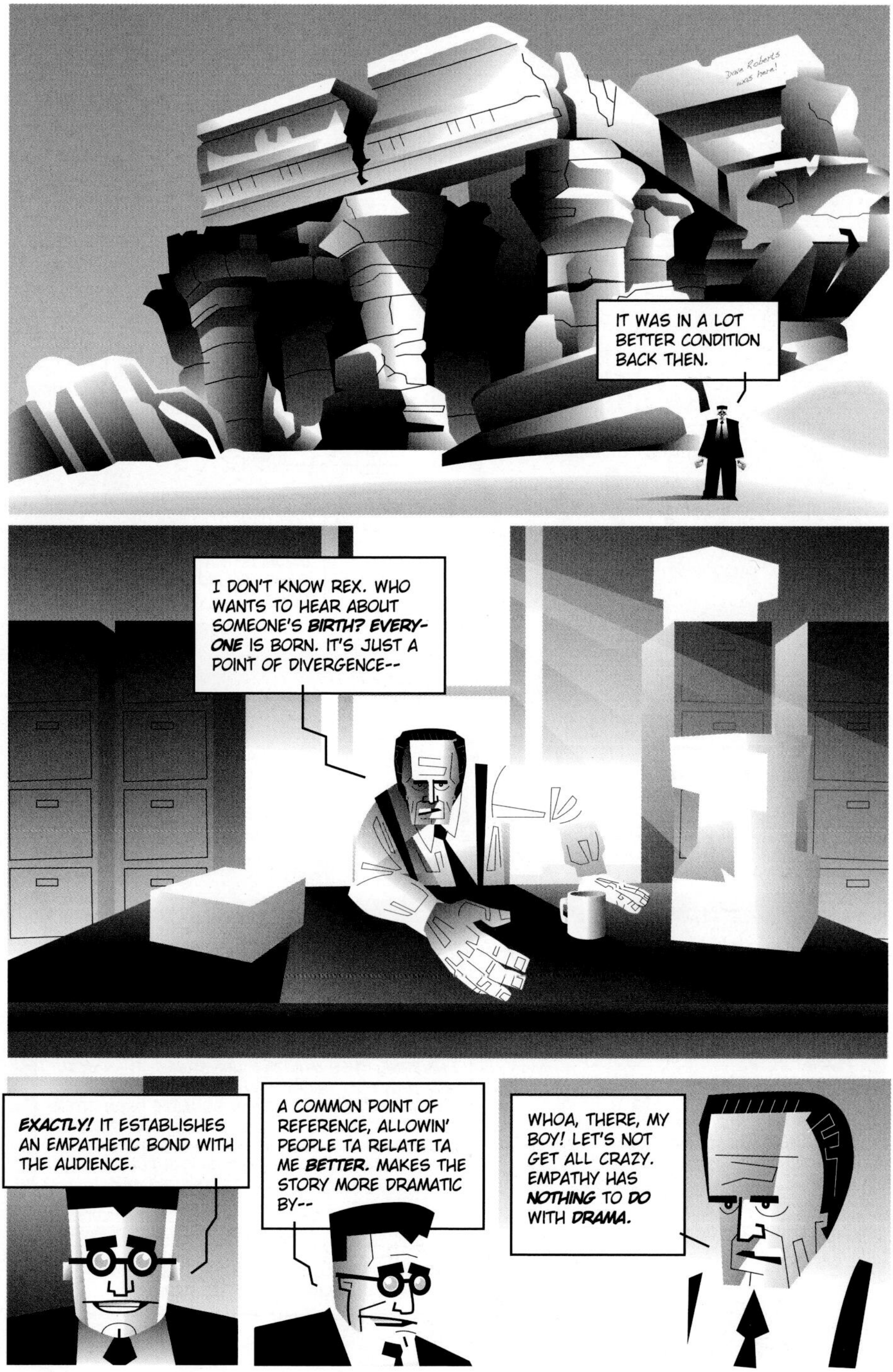
Dave Roberts was here!
IT WAS IN A LOT BETTER CONDITION BACK THEN.
I DON'T KNOW REX. WHO WANTS TO HEAR ABOUT SOMEONE'S **BIRTH? EVERYONE** IS BORN. IT'S JUST A POINT OF DIVERGENCE--
EXACTLY! IT ESTABLISHES AN EMPATHETIC BOND WITH THE AUDIENCE.
A COMMON POINT OF REFERENCE, ALLOWIN' PEOPLE TA RELATE TA ME **BETTER.** MAKES THE STORY MORE DRAMATIC BY--
WHOA, THERE, MY BOY! LET'S NOT GET ALL CRAZY. EMPATHY HAS **NOTHING** TO **DO** WITH **DRAMA.**

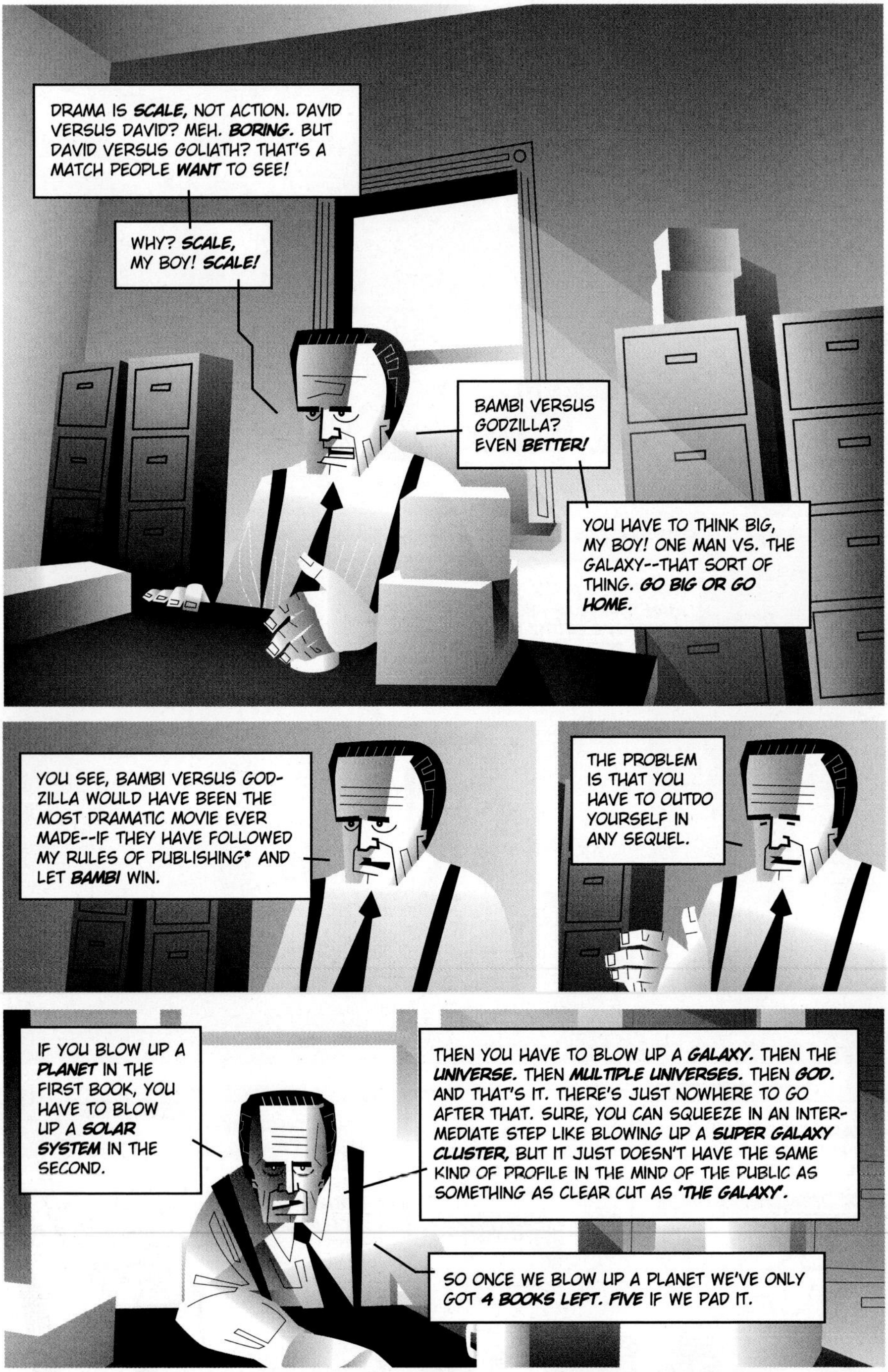
DRAMA IS SCALE, NOT ACTION. DAVID VERSUS DAVID? MEH. BORING. BUT DAVID VERSUS GOLIATH? THAT'S A MATCH PEOPLE WANT TO SEE!
WHY? SCALE, MY BOY! SCALE!
BAMBI VERSUS GODZILLA? EVEN BETTER!
YOU HAVE TO THINK BIG, MY BOY! ONE MAN VS. THE GALAXY--THAT SORT OF THING. GO BIG OR GO HOME.
YOU SEE, BAMBI VERSUS GODZILLA WOULD HAVE BEEN THE MOST DRAMATIC MOVIE EVER MADE--IF THEY HAVE FOLLOWED MY RULES OF PUBLISHING* AND LET BAMBI WIN.
THE PROBLEM IS THAT YOU HAVE TO OUTDO YOURSELF IN ANY SEQUEL.
IF YOU BLOW UP A PLANET IN THE FIRST BOOK, YOU HAVE TO BLOW UP A SOLAR SYSTEM IN THE SECOND.
THEN YOU HAVE TO BLOW UP A GALAXY. THEN THE UNIVERSE. THEN MULTIPLE UNIVERSES. THEN GOD. AND THAT'S IT. THERE'S JUST NOWHERE TO GO AFTER THAT. SURE, YOU CAN SQUEEZE IN AN INTERMEDIATE STEP LIKE BLOWING UP A SUPER GALAXY CLUSTER, BUT IT JUST DOESN'T HAVE THE SAME KIND OF PROFILE IN THE MIND OF THE PUBLIC AS SOMETHING AS CLEAR CUT AS 'THE GALAXY'.
SO ONCE WE BLOW UP A PLANET WE'VE ONLY GOT 4 BOOKS LEFT. FIVE IF WE PAD IT.

*SEE MY NEW BOOK *HOW TO PUBLISH THE B. BARRY HORST WAY*. THE PRINCIPLES ARE EASILY APPLIED TO FILM, TELEVISION, BOOKS, AND COMICS. I USE THEM IN ALL MY WORKS! IN STORES NOW!-- BARRY

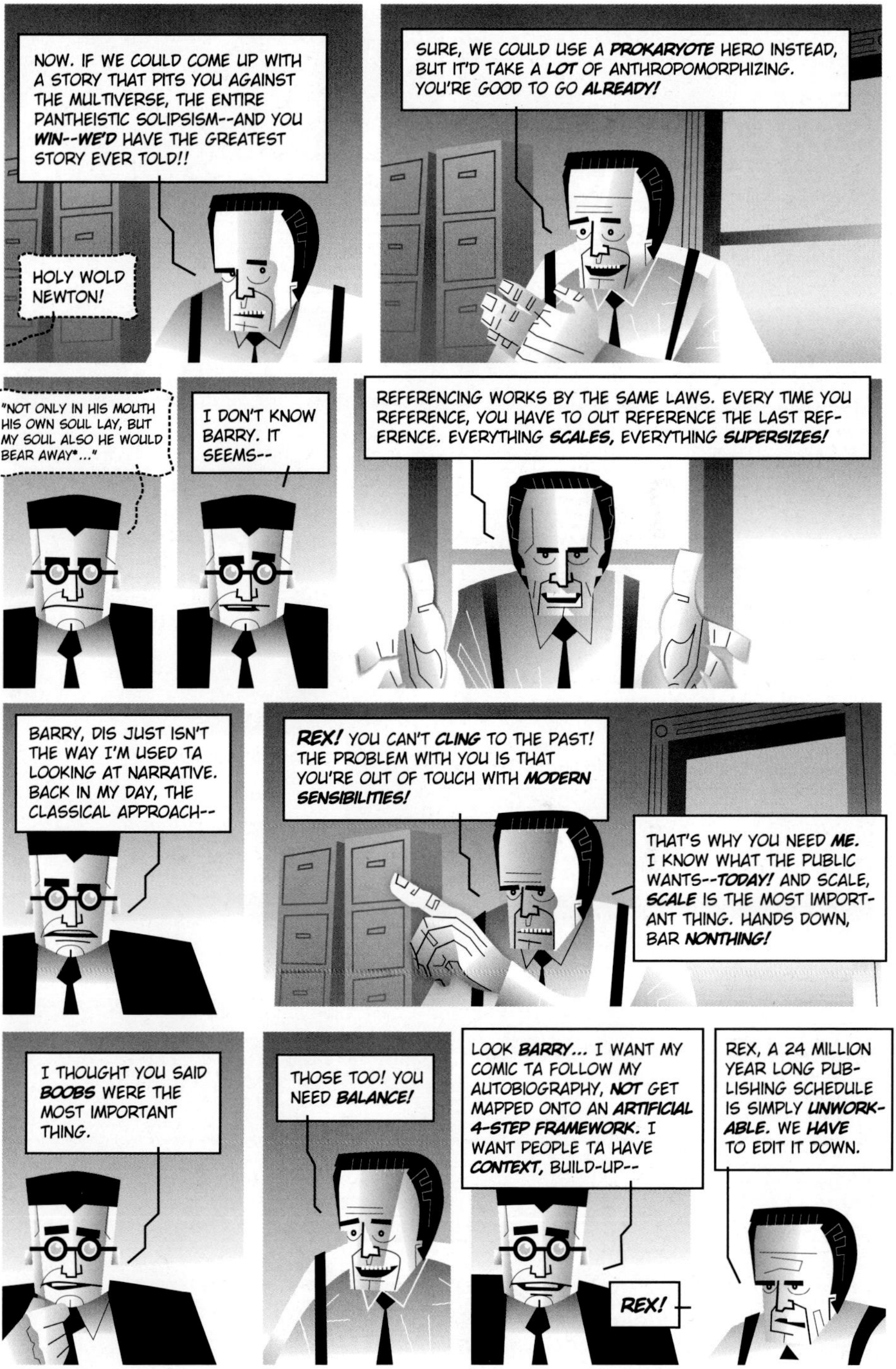
NOW. IF WE COULD COME UP WITH A STORY THAT PITS YOU AGAINST THE MULTIVERSE, THE ENTIRE PANTHEISTIC SOLIPSISM--AND YOU WIN--WE'D HAVE THE GREATEST STORY EVER TOLD!!
HOLY WOLD NEWTON!
SURE, WE COULD USE A PROKARYOTE HERO INSTEAD, BUT IT'D TAKE A LOT OF ANTHROPOMORPHIZING. YOU'RE GOOD TO GO ALREADY!
"NOT ONLY IN HIS MOUTH HIS OWN SOUL LAY, BUT MY SOUL ALSO HE WOULD BEAR AWAY*..."
I DON'T KNOW BARRY. IT SEEMS--
REFERENCING WORKS BY THE SAME LAWS. EVERY TIME YOU REFERENCE, YOU HAVE TO OUT REFERENCE THE LAST REFERENCE. EVERYTHING SCALES, EVERYTHING SUPERSIZES!
BARRY, DIS JUST ISN'T THE WAY I'M USED TA LOOKING AT NARRATIVE. BACK IN MY DAY, THE CLASSICAL APPROACH--
REX! YOU CAN'T CLING TO THE PAST! THE PROBLEM WITH YOU IS THAT YOU'RE OUT OF TOUCH WITH MODERN SENSIBILITIES!
THAT'S WHY YOU NEED ME. I KNOW WHAT THE PUBLIC WANTS--TODAY! AND SCALE, SCALE IS THE MOST IMPORTANT THING. HANDS DOWN, BAR NONTHING!
I THOUGHT YOU SAID BOOBS WERE THE MOST IMPORTANT THING.
THOSE TOO! YOU NEED BALANCE!
LOOK BARRY... I WANT MY COMIC TA FOLLOW MY AUTOBIOGRAPHY, NOT GET MAPPED ONTO AN ARTIFICIAL 4-STEP FRAMEWORK. I WANT PEOPLE TA HAVE CONTEXT, BUILD-UP--
REX!
REX, A 24 MILLION YEAR LONG PUBLISHING SCHEDULE IS SIMPLY UNWORKABLE. WE HAVE TO EDIT IT DOWN.

*WILLIAM BLAKE

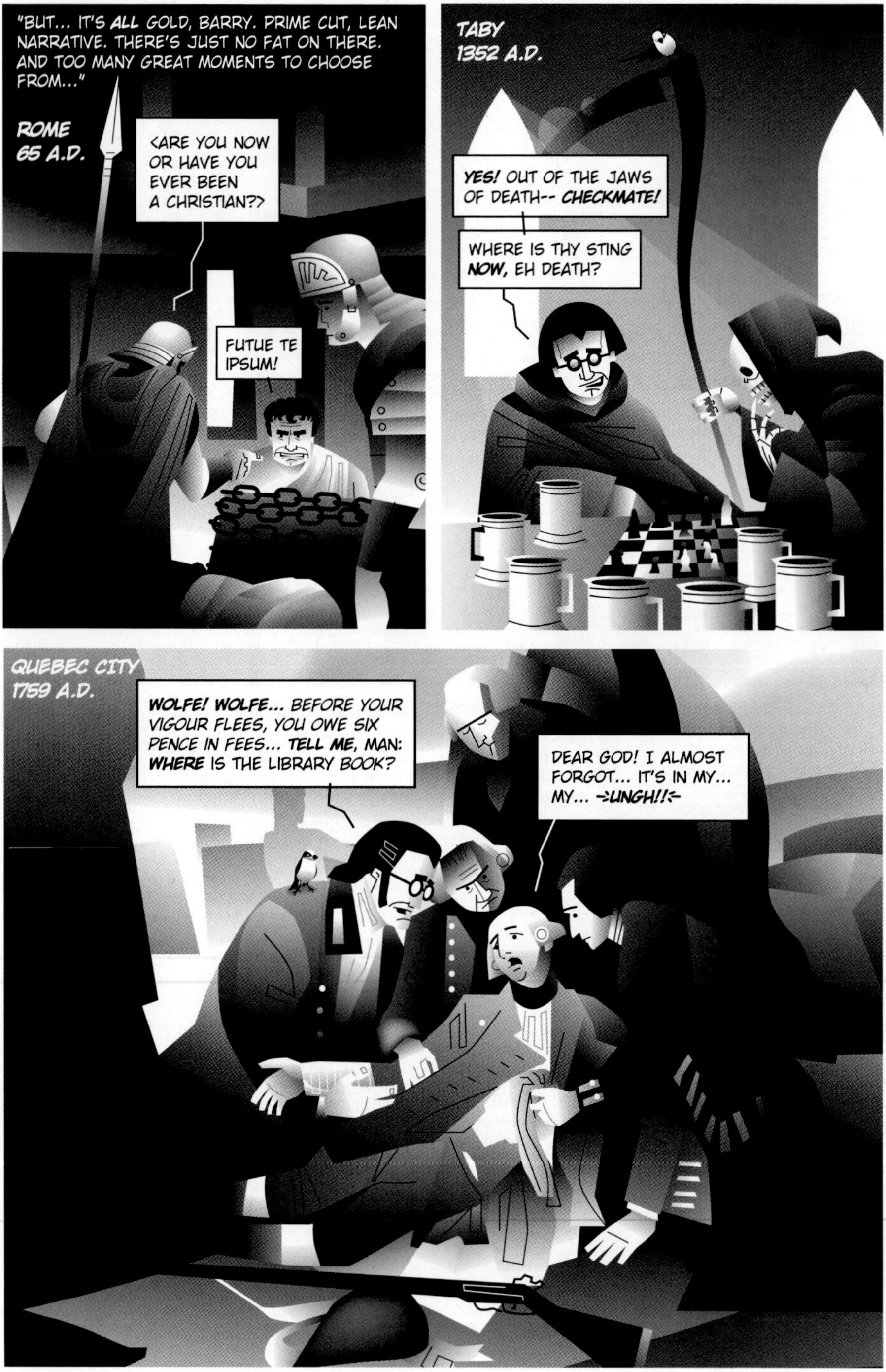
"BUT... IT'S ALL GOLD, BARRY. PRIME CUT, LEAN NARRATIVE. THERE'S JUST NO FAT ON THERE. AND TOO MANY GREAT MOMENTS TO CHOOSE FROM..."
ROME 65 A.D.
<ARE YOU NOW OR HAVE YOU EVER BEEN A CHRISTIAN?>
FUTUE TE IPSUM!
TABY 1352 A.D.
YES! OUT OF THE JAWS OF DEATH-- CHECKMATE!
WHERE IS THY STING NOW, EH DEATH?
QUEBEC CITY 1759 A.D.
WOLFE! WOLFE... BEFORE YOUR VIGOUR FLEES, YOU OWE SIX PENCE IN FEES... TELL ME, MAN: WHERE IS THE LIBRARY BOOK?
DEAR GOD! I ALMOST FORGOT... IT'S IN MY... MY... -UNGH!!-

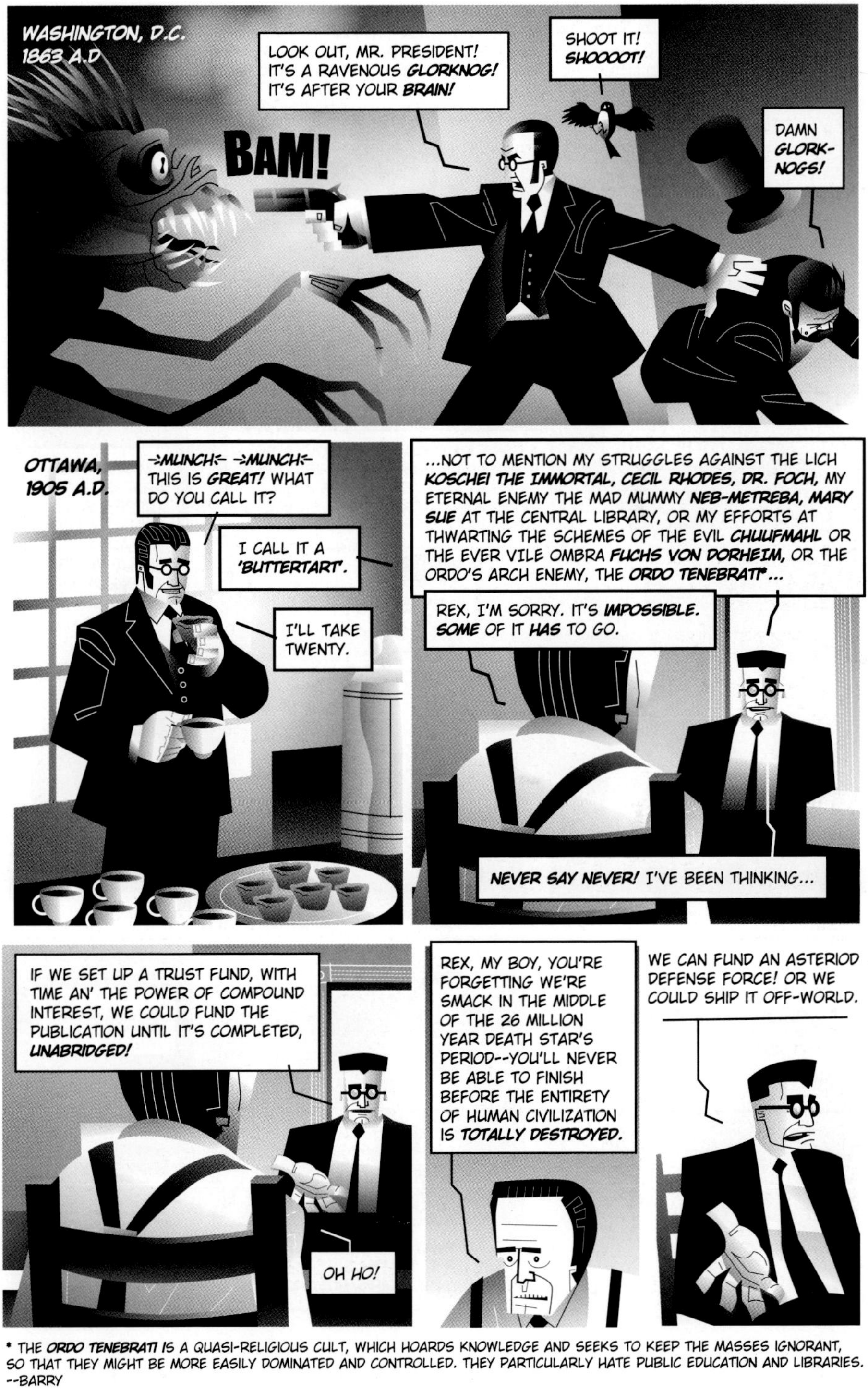
WASHINGTON, D.C. 1863 A.D
LOOK OUT, MR. PRESIDENT! IT'S A RAVENOUS GLORKNOG! IT'S AFTER YOUR BRAIN!
SHOOT IT! SHOOOOT!
BAM!
DAMN GLORK-NOGS!
OTTAWA, 1905 A.D.
-MUNCH- -MUNCH- THIS IS GREAT! WHAT DO YOU CALL IT?
I CALL IT A 'BUTTERTART'.
I'LL TAKE TWENTY.
...NOT TO MENTION MY STRUGGLES AGAINST THE LICH KOSCHEI THE IMMORTAL, CECIL RHODES, DR. FOCH, MY ETERNAL ENEMY THE MAD MUMMY NEB-METREBA, MARY SUE AT THE CENTRAL LIBRARY, OR MY EFFORTS AT THWARTING THE SCHEMES OF THE EVIL CHUUFMAHL OR THE EVER VILE OMBRA FUCHS VON DORHEIM, OR THE ORDO'S ARCH ENEMY, THE ORDO TENEBRATI*...
REX, I'M SORRY. IT'S IMPOSSIBLE. SOME OF IT HAS TO GO.
NEVER SAY NEVER! I'VE BEEN THINKING...
IF WE SET UP A TRUST FUND, WITH TIME AN' THE POWER OF COMPOUND INTEREST, WE COULD FUND THE PUBLICATION UNTIL IT'S COMPLETED, UNABRIDGED!
OH HO!
REX, MY BOY, YOU'RE FORGETTING WE'RE SMACK IN THE MIDDLE OF THE 26 MILLION YEAR DEATH STAR'S PERIOD--YOU'LL NEVER BE ABLE TO FINISH BEFORE THE ENTIRETY OF HUMAN CIVILIZATION IS TOTALLY DESTROYED.
WE CAN FUND AN ASTERIOD DEFENSE FORCE! OR WE COULD SHIP IT OFF-WORLD.

* THE *ORDO TENEBRATI* IS A QUASI-RELIGIOUS CULT, WHICH HOARDS KNOWLEDGE AND SEEKS TO KEEP THE MASSES IGNORANT, SO THAT THEY MIGHT BE MORE EASILY DOMINATED AND CONTROLLED. THEY PARTICULARLY HATE PUBLIC EDUCATION AND LIBRARIES. --BARRY

THERE ARE ECONOMIC BACKWATER PLANETS OF HIGHLY TALENTED ARTISTIC BEINGS THAT WOULD BE--

REX! I'M NOT SHIPPING HERMENEUTIC PRESS CONTRACTS TO OTHER PLANETS! SHIPPING COSTS ARE BAD ENOUGH FROM *QUEBEC!*

BE *REASONABLE,* MAN. REMEMBER YOU'RE A *LIBRARIAN!*

YES... *YES...* YOU'RE *RIGHT.*

I DON'T KNOW WHAT CAME OVER ME. IT *WOULD* BE HUBRISTIC EXHIBITIONISM TA INSIST ON EVERY LAST MOMENT BEING PUBLISHED... WHATEVER WAS I THINKIN'?

NOT TO WORRY, MY BOY!

I'M GLAD YOU DROPPED BY. THERE'S SOMETHING I WANTED TO TALK TO YOU ABOUT: WE'RE TAKING ON *ANOTHER* AUTOBIOGRAPHICAL COMIC!

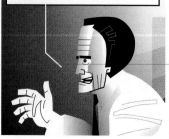

IT'S *FANTASTIC* STUFF! A REAL *WILD* RIDE OF A LIFE. AND BEST OF ALL, HE'S A *MORALLY AMBIGUOUS* LEAD. THAT'S HOT, HOT *HOT* RIGHT NOW REX. *HOT,* I SAY!

NOBODY WANTS MORAL INTEGRITY THESE DAYS. THAT'S JUST *BORING.* PEOPLE WANT *CHARISMATIC ROGUES!*

OR CHARMING PSYCHOPATHS?

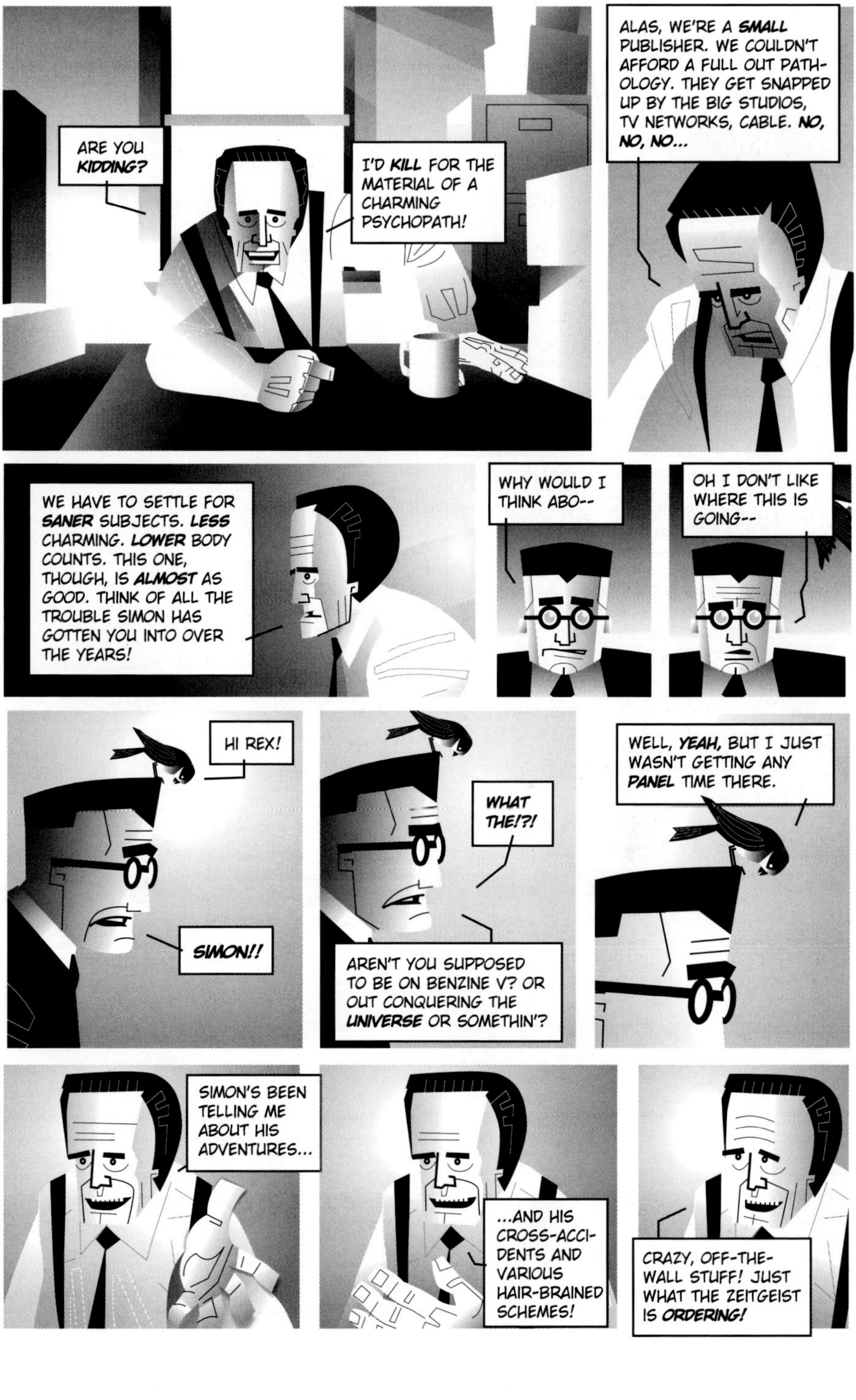
ARE YOU KIDDING?
I'D KILL FOR THE MATERIAL OF A CHARMING PSYCHOPATH!
ALAS, WE'RE A SMALL PUBLISHER. WE COULDN'T AFFORD A FULL OUT PATHOLOGY. THEY GET SNAPPED UP BY THE BIG STUDIOS, TV NETWORKS, CABLE. NO, NO, NO...
WE HAVE TO SETTLE FOR SANER SUBJECTS. LESS CHARMING. LOWER BODY COUNTS. THIS ONE, THOUGH, IS ALMOST AS GOOD. THINK OF ALL THE TROUBLE SIMON HAS GOTTEN YOU INTO OVER THE YEARS!
WHY WOULD I THINK ABO--
OH I DON'T LIKE WHERE THIS IS GOING--
HI REX!
SIMON!!
WHAT THE!?!
AREN'T YOU SUPPOSED TO BE ON BENZINE V? OR OUT CONQUERING THE UNIVERSE OR SOMETHIN'?
WELL, YEAH, BUT I JUST WASN'T GETTING ANY PANEL TIME THERE.
SIMON'S BEEN TELLING ME ABOUT HIS ADVENTURES...
...AND HIS CROSS-ACCIDENTS AND VARIOUS HAIR-BRAINED SCHEMES!
CRAZY, OFF-THE-WALL STUFF! JUST WHAT THE ZEITGEIST IS ORDERING!

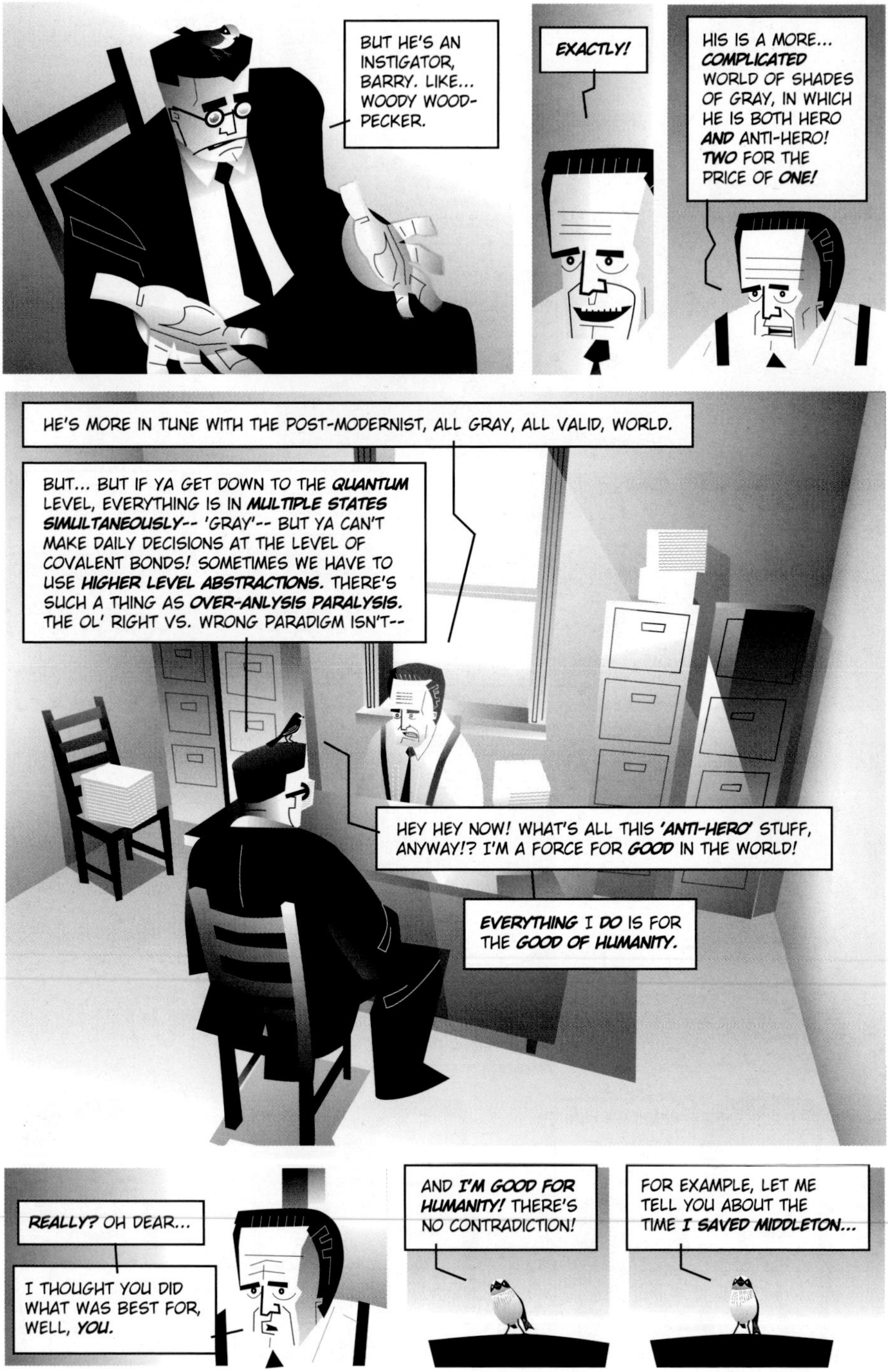
BUT HE'S AN INSTIGATOR, BARRY. LIKE... WOODY WOOD-PECKER.
EXACTLY!
HIS IS A MORE... COMPLICATED WORLD OF SHADES OF GRAY, IN WHICH HE IS BOTH HERO AND ANTI-HERO! TWO FOR THE PRICE OF ONE!
HE'S MORE IN TUNE WITH THE POST-MODERNIST, ALL GRAY, ALL VALID, WORLD.
BUT... BUT IF YA GET DOWN TO THE QUANTUM LEVEL, EVERYTHING IS IN MULTIPLE STATES SIMULTANEOUSLY-- 'GRAY'-- BUT YA CAN'T MAKE DAILY DECISIONS AT THE LEVEL OF COVALENT BONDS! SOMETIMES WE HAVE TO USE HIGHER LEVEL ABSTRACTIONS. THERE'S SUCH A THING AS OVER-ANLYSIS PARALYSIS. THE OL' RIGHT VS. WRONG PARADIGM ISN'T--
HEY HEY NOW! WHAT'S ALL THIS 'ANTI-HERO' STUFF, ANYWAY!? I'M A FORCE FOR GOOD IN THE WORLD!
EVERYTHING I DO IS FOR THE GOOD OF HUMANITY.
REALLY? OH DEAR...
I THOUGHT YOU DID WHAT WAS BEST FOR, WELL, YOU.
AND I'M GOOD FOR HUMANITY! THERE'S NO CONTRADICTION!
FOR EXAMPLE, LET ME TELL YOU ABOUT THE TIME I SAVED MIDDLETON...

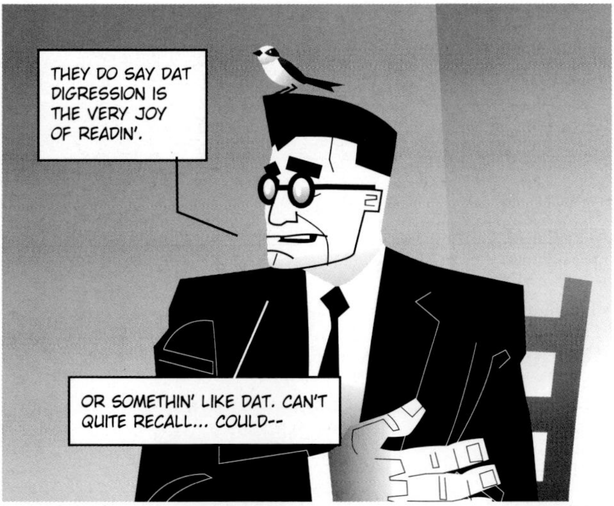
THEY DO SAY DAT DIGRESSION IS THE VERY JOY OF READIN'.
OR SOMETHIN' LIKE DAT. CAN'T QUITE RECALL... COULD--

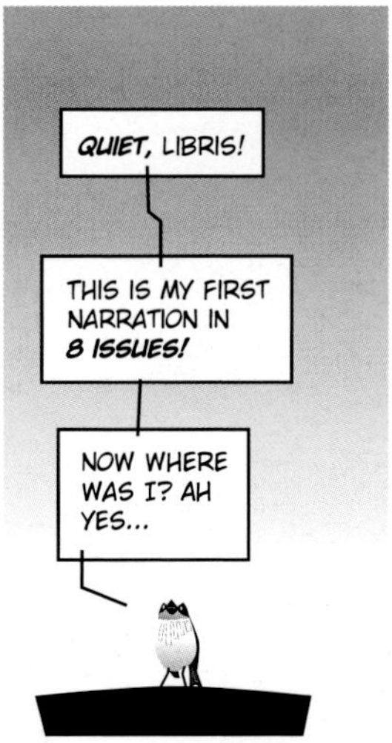
QUIET, LIBRIS!
THIS IS MY FIRST NARRATION IN 8 ISSUES!
NOW WHERE WAS I? AH YES...

"IT ALL STARTED A FEW YEARS BACK, WHEN AN AIR FORCE TRANSPORT CARRYING **FOOD OF THE GODS** TO **AREA 53** GOT INTO TROUBLE NOT FAR FROM MIDDLETON."

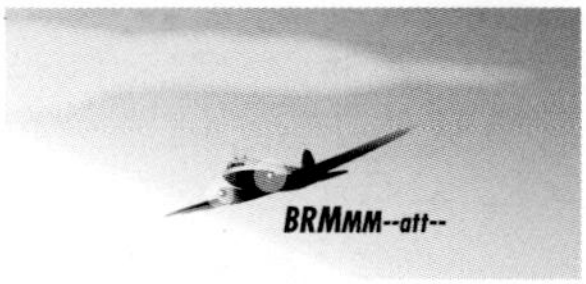
BRMMM--att--

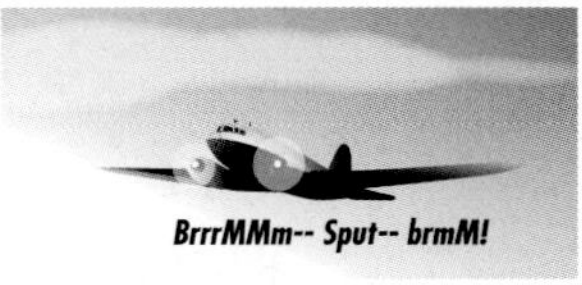
BrrrMMm-- Sput-- brmM!

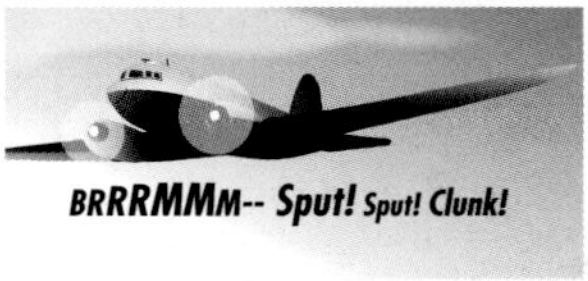
BRRRMMm-- Sput! Sput! Clunk!

"A SERIES OF **MECHANICAL MALFUNCTIONS** COMBINED TO CAUSE THE PREMATURE DROPPING OF A BOX FILLED WITH THE **FOOD OF THE GODS** ONTO OL' LARRY STERNE'S FARM."

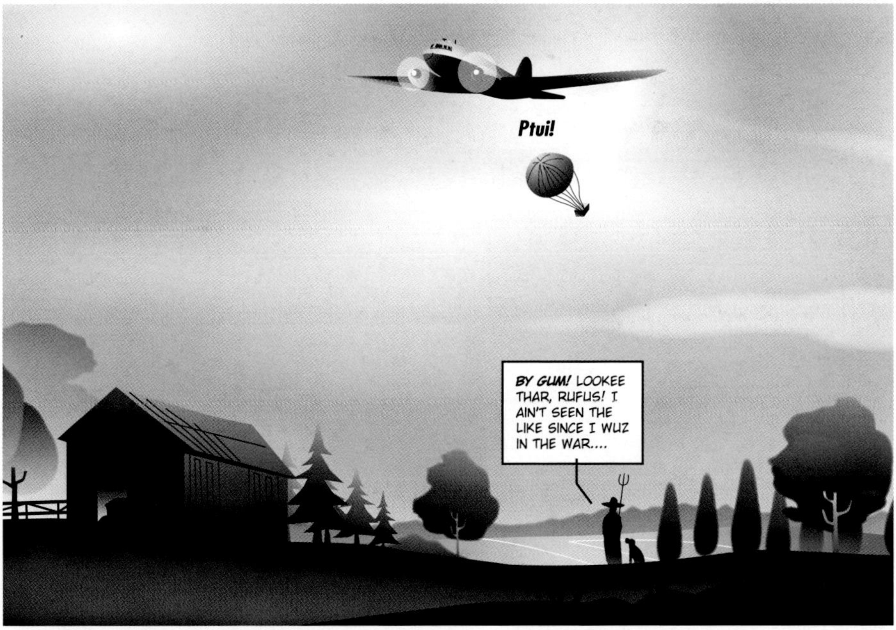
Ptui!
BY GUM! LOOKEE THAR, RUFUS! I AIN'T SEEN THE LIKE SINCE I WUZ IN THE WAR....

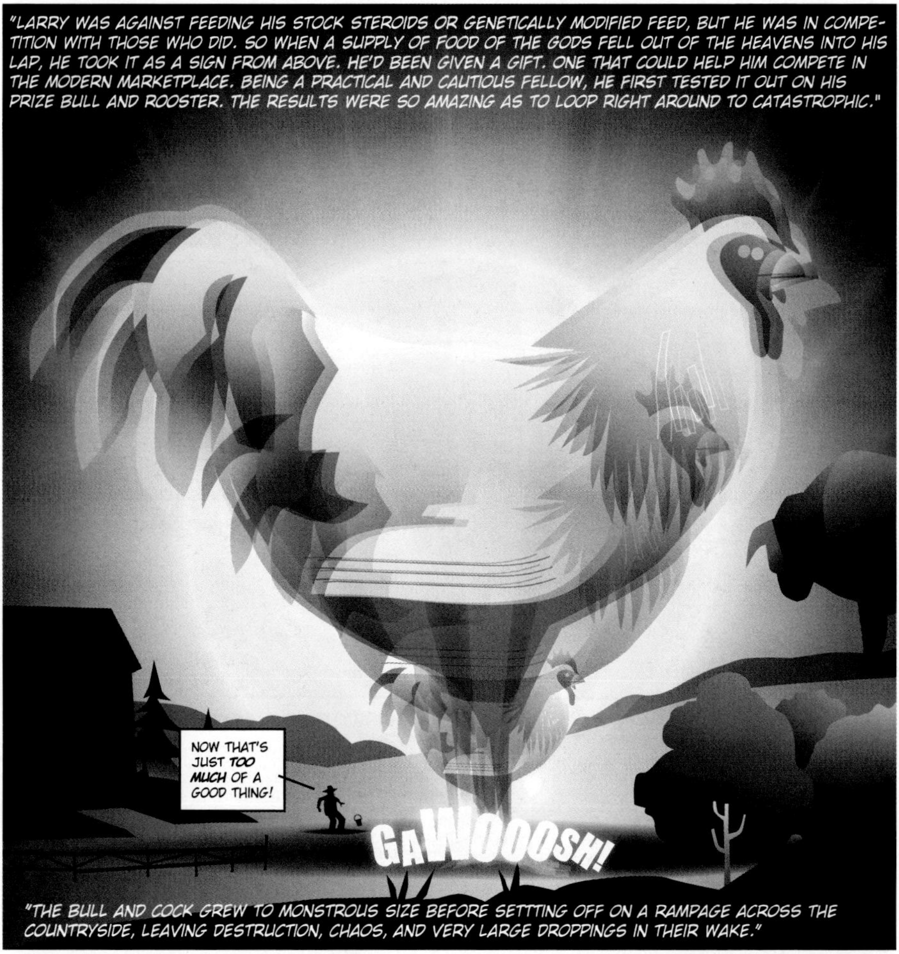
"LARRY WAS AGAINST FEEDING HIS STOCK STEROIDS OR GENETICALLY MODIFIED FEED, BUT HE WAS IN COMPETITION WITH THOSE WHO DID. SO WHEN A SUPPLY OF FOOD OF THE GODS FELL OUT OF THE HEAVENS INTO HIS LAP, HE TOOK IT AS A SIGN FROM ABOVE. HE'D BEEN GIVEN A GIFT. ONE THAT COULD HELP HIM COMPETE IN THE MODERN MARKETPLACE. BEING A PRACTICAL AND CAUTIOUS FELLOW, HE FIRST TESTED IT OUT ON HIS PRIZE BULL AND ROOSTER. THE RESULTS WERE SO AMAZING AS TO LOOP RIGHT AROUND TO CATASTROPHIC."
NOW THAT'S JUST **TOO MUCH** OF A GOOD THING!
GAWOOOOSH!
"THE BULL AND COCK GREW TO MONSTROUS SIZE BEFORE SETTTING OFF ON A RAMPAGE ACROSS THE COUNTRYSIDE, LEAVING DESTRUCTION, CHAOS, AND VERY LARGE DROPPINGS IN THEIR WAKE."

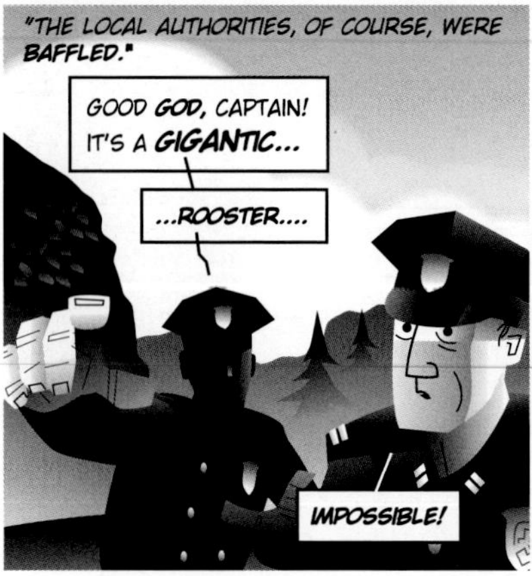
"THE LOCAL AUTHORITIES, OF COURSE, WERE **BAFFLED.**"
GOOD **GOD,** CAPTAIN! IT'S A **GIGANTIC...**
...ROOSTER....
IMPOSSIBLE!

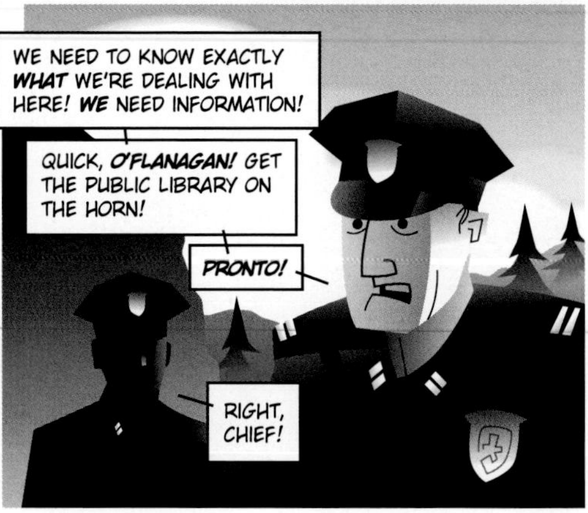
WE NEED TO KNOW EXACTLY **WHAT** WE'RE DEALING WITH HERE! **WE** NEED INFORMATION!
QUICK, **O'FLANAGAN!** GET THE PUBLIC LIBRARY ON THE HORN!
PRONTO!
RIGHT, CHIEF!

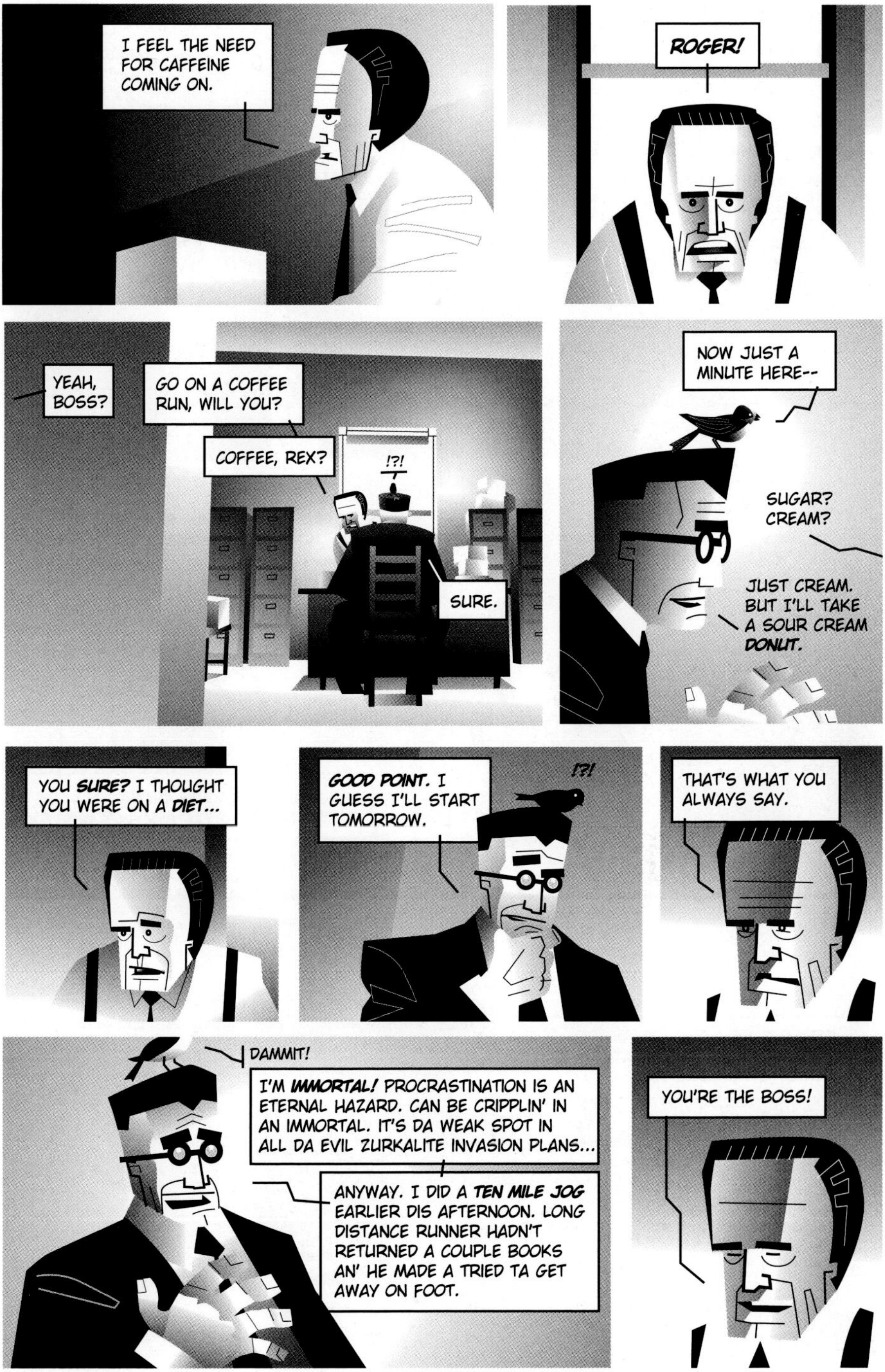
I FEEL THE NEED FOR CAFFEINE COMING ON.
ROGER!
YEAH, BOSS?
GO ON A COFFEE RUN, WILL YOU?
COFFEE, REX?
!?!
SURE.
NOW JUST A MINUTE HERE--
SUGAR? CREAM?
JUST CREAM. BUT I'LL TAKE A SOUR CREAM DONUT.
YOU SURE? I THOUGHT YOU WERE ON A DIET...
GOOD POINT. I GUESS I'LL START TOMORROW.
!?!
THAT'S WHAT YOU ALWAYS SAY.
DAMMIT!
I'M IMMORTAL! PROCRASTINATION IS AN ETERNAL HAZARD. CAN BE CRIPPLIN' IN AN IMMORTAL. IT'S DA WEAK SPOT IN ALL DA EVIL ZURKALITE INVASION PLANS...
ANYWAY. I DID A TEN MILE JOG EARLIER DIS AFTERNOON. LONG DISTANCE RUNNER HADN'T RETURNED A COUPLE BOOKS AN' HE MADE A TRIED TA GET AWAY ON FOOT.
YOU'RE THE BOSS!

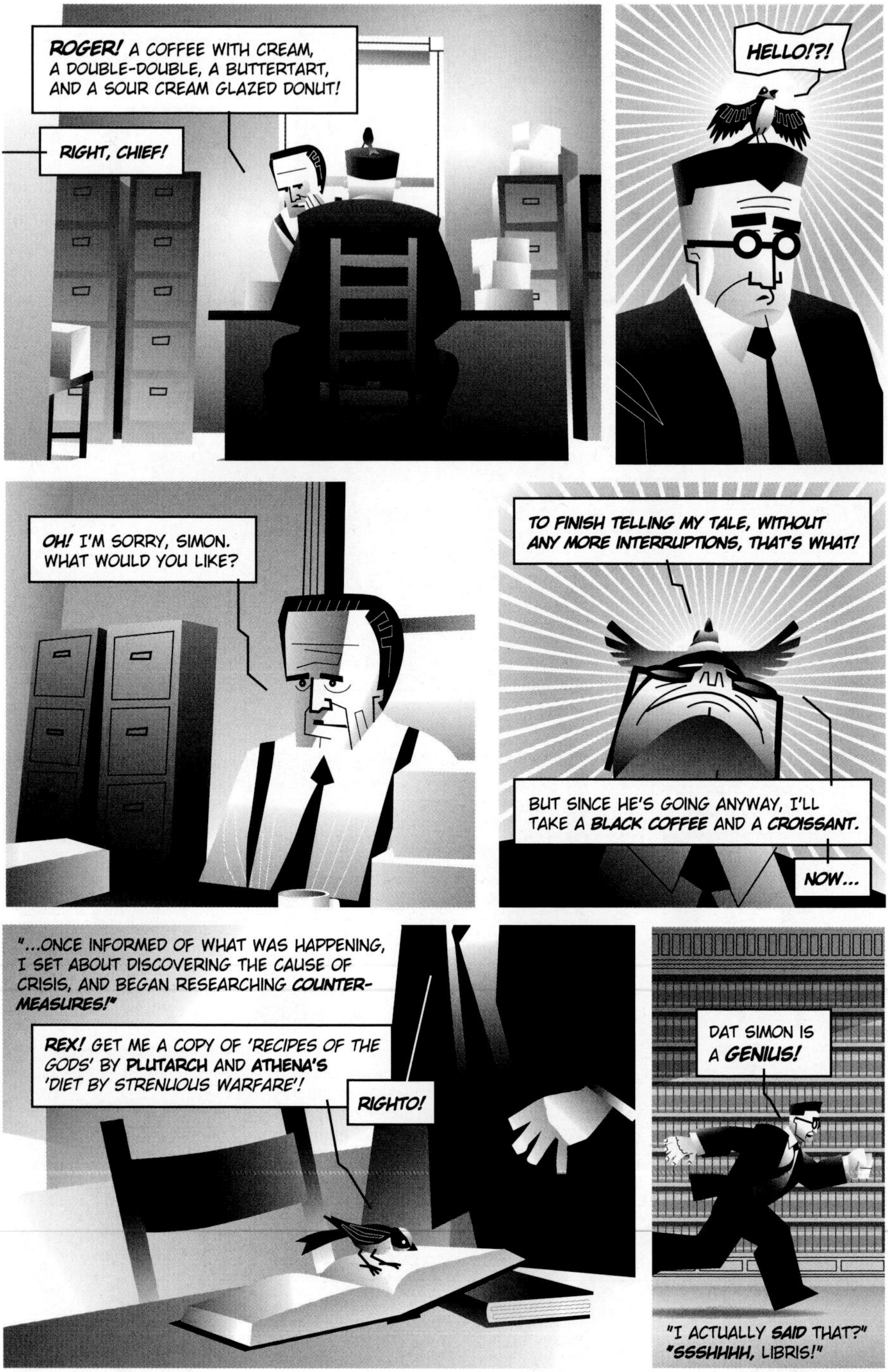
ROGER! A COFFEE WITH CREAM, A DOUBLE-DOUBLE, A BUTTERTART, AND A SOUR CREAM GLAZED DONUT!
RIGHT, CHIEF!
HELLO!?!
OH! I'M SORRY, SIMON. WHAT WOULD YOU LIKE?
TO FINISH TELLING MY TALE, WITHOUT ANY MORE INTERRUPTIONS, THAT'S WHAT!
BUT SINCE HE'S GOING ANYWAY, I'LL TAKE A BLACK COFFEE AND A CROISSANT.
NOW...
"...ONCE INFORMED OF WHAT WAS HAPPENING, I SET ABOUT DISCOVERING THE CAUSE OF CRISIS, AND BEGAN RESEARCHING COUNTER-MEASURES!"
REX! GET ME A COPY OF 'RECIPES OF THE GODS' BY PLUTARCH AND ATHENA'S 'DIET BY STRENUOUS WARFARE'!
RIGHTO!
DAT SIMON IS A GENIUS!
"I ACTUALLY SAID THAT?"
"SSSHHHH, LIBRIS!"

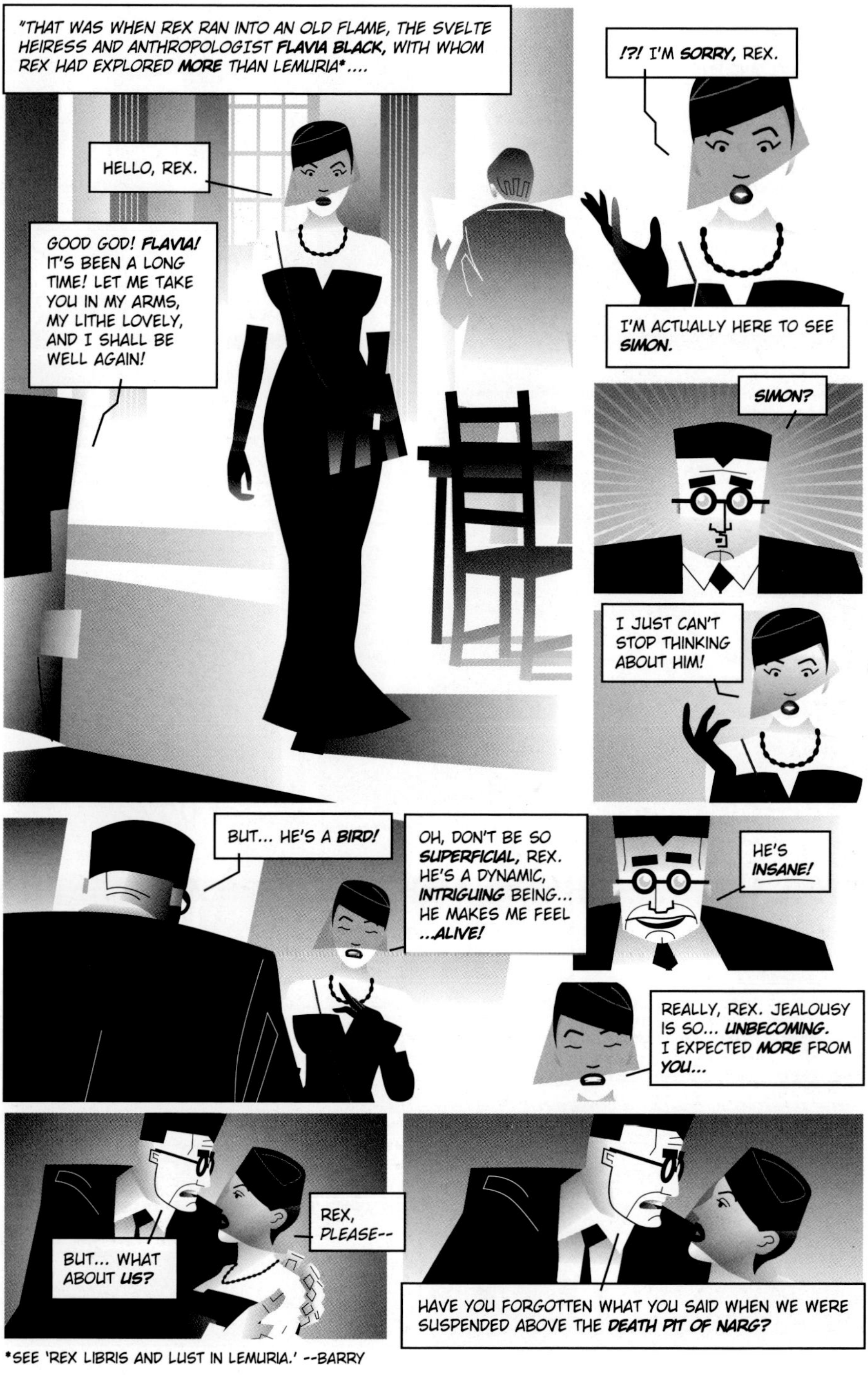

"THAT WAS WHEN REX RAN INTO AN OLD FLAME, THE SVELTE HEIRESS AND ANTHROPOLOGIST FLAVIA BLACK, WITH WHOM REX HAD EXPLORED MORE THAN LEMURIA*....
HELLO, REX.
GOOD GOD! FLAVIA! IT'S BEEN A LONG TIME! LET ME TAKE YOU IN MY ARMS, MY LITHE LOVELY, AND I SHALL BE WELL AGAIN!
!?! I'M SORRY, REX.
I'M ACTUALLY HERE TO SEE SIMON.
SIMON?
I JUST CAN'T STOP THINKING ABOUT HIM!
BUT... HE'S A BIRD!
OH, DON'T BE SO SUPERFICIAL, REX. HE'S A DYNAMIC, INTRIGUING BEING... HE MAKES ME FEEL ...ALIVE!
HE'S INSANE!
REALLY, REX. JEALOUSY IS SO... UNBECOMING. I EXPECTED MORE FROM YOU...
BUT... WHAT ABOUT US?
REX, PLEASE--
HAVE YOU FORGOTTEN WHAT YOU SAID WHEN WE WERE SUSPENDED ABOVE THE DEATH PIT OF NARG?

*SEE 'REX LIBRIS AND LUST IN LEMURIA.' --BARRY

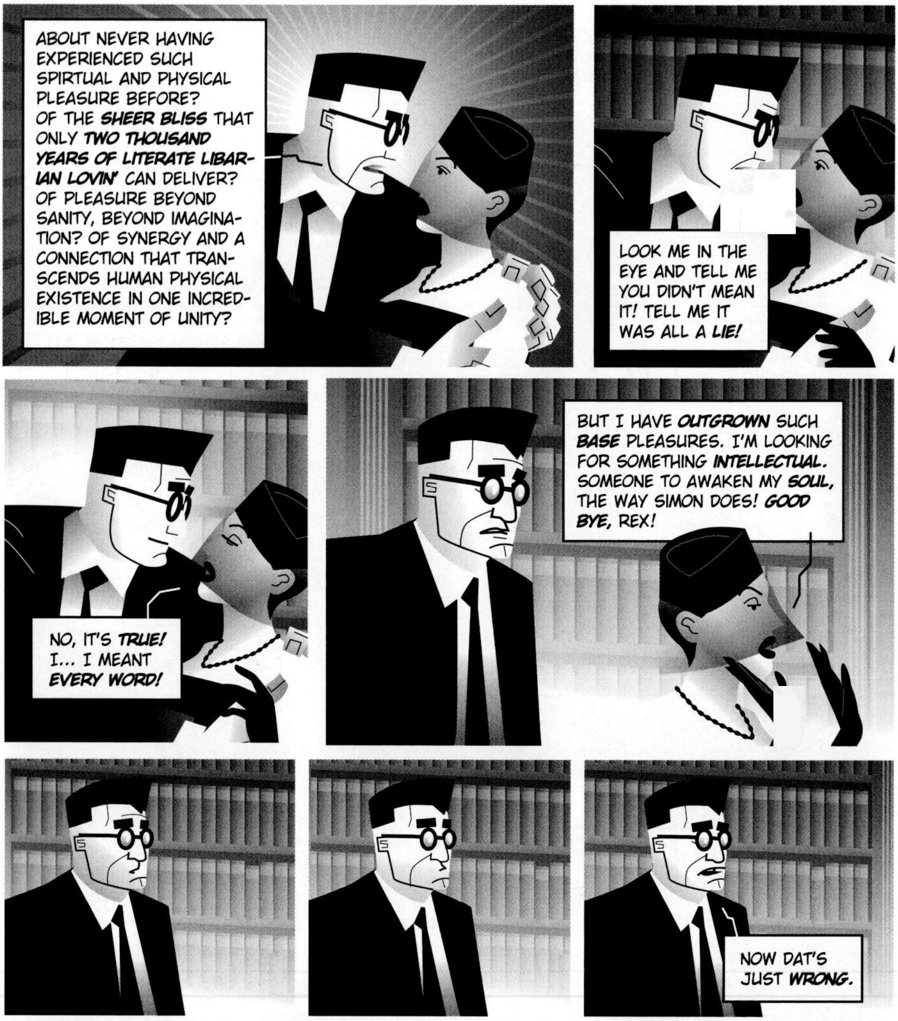
ABOUT NEVER HAVING EXPERIENCED SUCH SPIRTUAL AND PHYSICAL PLEASURE BEFORE? OF THE **SHEER BLISS** THAT ONLY **TWO THOUSAND YEARS OF LITERATE LIBAR-IAN LOVIN'** CAN DELIVER? OF PLEASURE BEYOND SANITY, BEYOND IMAGINA-TION? OF SYNERGY AND A CONNECTION THAT TRAN-SCENDS HUMAN PHYSICAL EXISTENCE IN ONE INCRED-IBLE MOMENT OF UNITY?
LOOK ME IN THE EYE AND TELL ME YOU DIDN'T MEAN IT! TELL ME IT WAS ALL A **LIE!**
NO, IT'S **TRUE!** I... I MEANT **EVERY WORD!**
BUT I HAVE **OUTGROWN** SUCH **BASE** PLEASURES. I'M LOOKING FOR SOMETHING **INTELLECTUAL.** SOMEONE TO AWAKEN MY **SOUL,** THE WAY SIMON DOES! **GOOD BYE,** REX!
NOW DAT'S JUST **WRONG.**

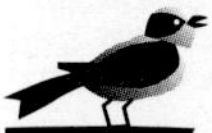

"USING MY INTUITIVE GENIUS, IT DID NOT TAKE ME LONG TO DETERMINE WHAT HAD HAPPENED TO THE COCK AND BULL. I RADIOED THE AUTHORITIES, AND WE WERE PICKED UP BY A NATIONAL GUARD HELICOPTER. WE STOPPED OFF AT STERNE'S FARM SO REX COULD PICK UP SOME FOOD OF THE GOD WAFERS FOR STUDY. THEN WE TRACKED DOWN THE BEHEMOTHS. THE AUTHORITIES WERE ***DESPERATE*** *FOR GUIDANCE. IT IS IN SUCH CRISES THAT WE PHILOSOPHER-KINGS* ***SHINE."***

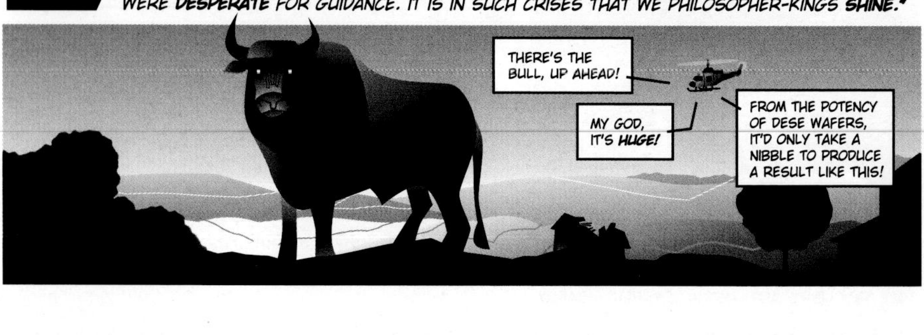
THERE'S THE BULL, UP AHEAD!
MY GOD, IT'S **HUGE!**
FROM THE POTENCY OF DESE WAFERS, IT'D ONLY TAKE A NIBBLE TO PRODUCE A RESULT LIKE THIS!

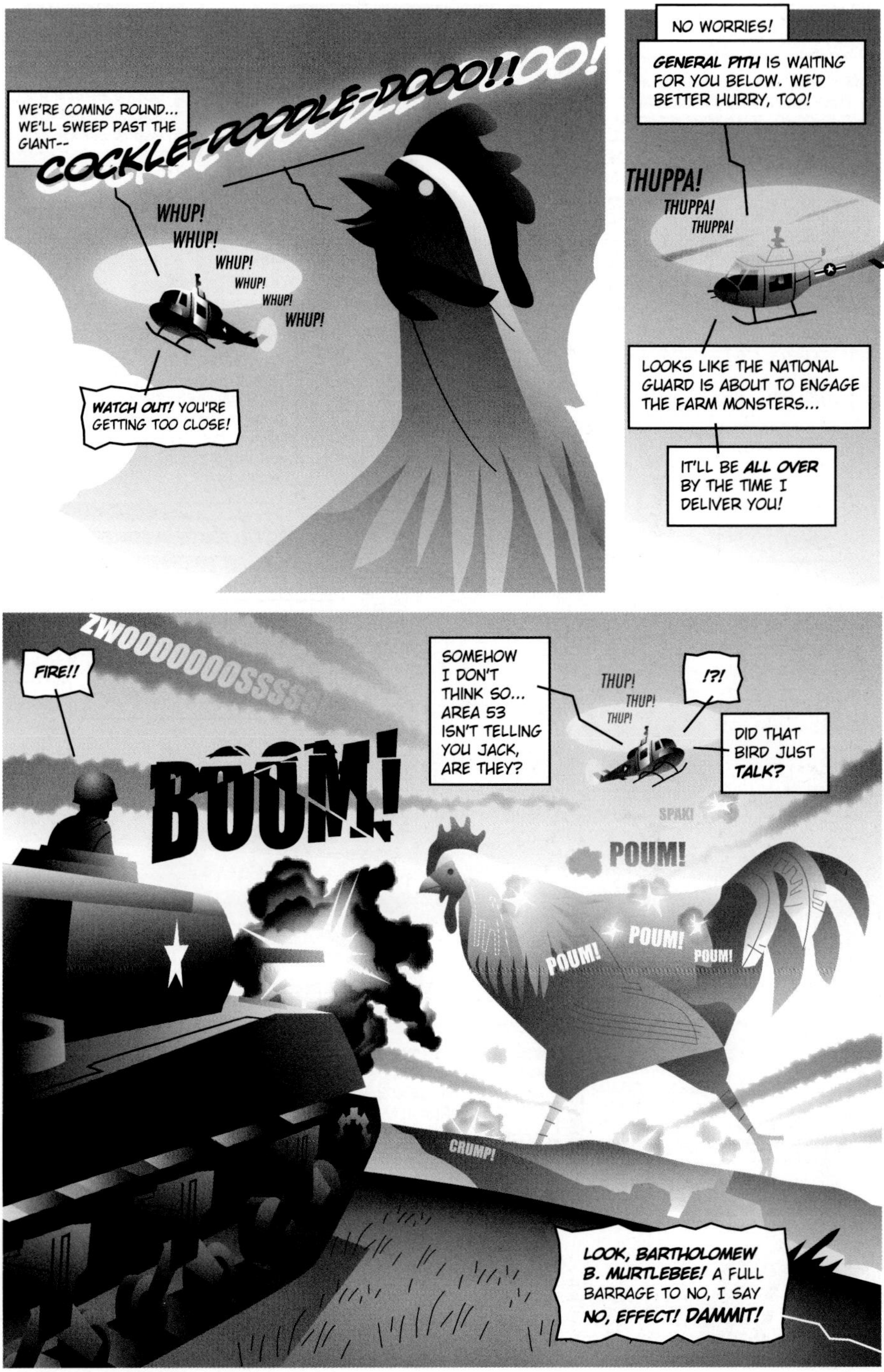
WE'RE COMING ROUND... WE'LL SWEEP PAST THE GIANT--
COCKLE-DOODLE-DOOO!!
WHUP! WHUP! WHUP! WHUP! WHUP! WHUP!
WATCH OUT! YOU'RE GETTING TOO CLOSE!
NO WORRIES!
GENERAL PITH IS WAITING FOR YOU BELOW. WE'D BETTER HURRY, TOO!
THUPPA! THUPPA! THUPPA!
LOOKS LIKE THE NATIONAL GUARD IS ABOUT TO ENGAGE THE FARM MONSTERS...
IT'LL BE ALL OVER BY THE TIME I DELIVER YOU!
ZWOOOOOOOOSSSS
FIRE!!
BOOM!
SOMEHOW I DON'T THINK SO... AREA 53 ISN'T TELLING YOU JACK, ARE THEY?
THUP! THUP! THUP!
!?!
DID THAT BIRD JUST TALK?
SPAK!
POUM!
POUM! POUM! POUM!
CRUMP!
LOOK, BARTHOLOMEW B. MURTLEBEE! A FULL BARRAGE TO NO, I SAY NO, EFFECT! DAMMIT!

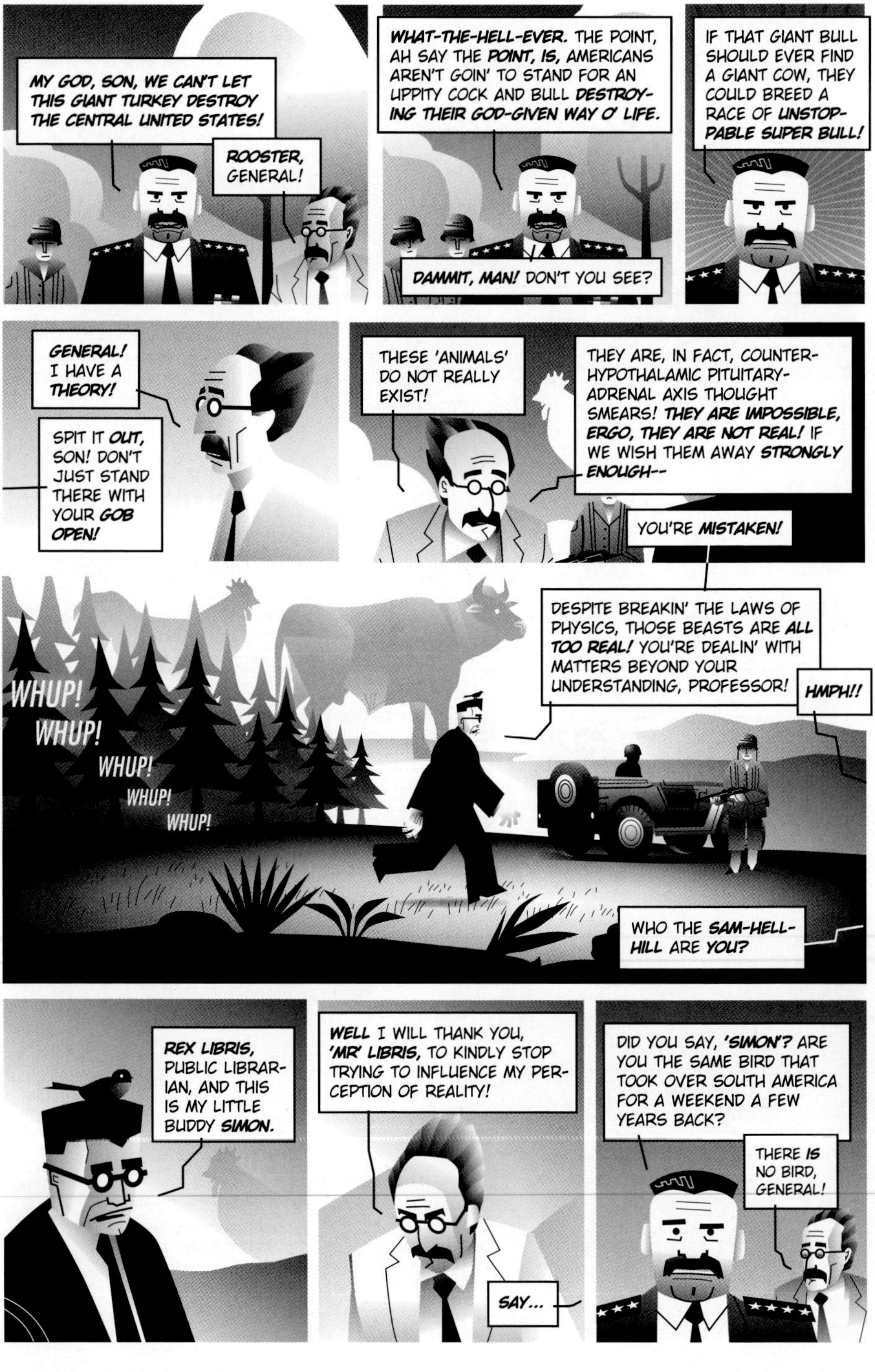
MY GOD, SON, WE CAN'T LET THIS GIANT TURKEY DESTROY THE CENTRAL UNITED STATES!
ROOSTER, GENERAL!
WHAT-THE-HELL-EVER. THE POINT, AH SAY THE POINT, IS, AMERICANS AREN'T GOIN' TO STAND FOR AN UPPITY COCK AND BULL DESTROYING THEIR GOD-GIVEN WAY O' LIFE.
DAMMIT, MAN! DON'T YOU SEE?
IF THAT GIANT BULL SHOULD EVER FIND A GIANT COW, THEY COULD BREED A RACE OF UNSTOPPABLE SUPER BULL!
GENERAL! I HAVE A THEORY!
SPIT IT OUT, SON! DON'T JUST STAND THERE WITH YOUR GOB OPEN!
THESE 'ANIMALS' DO NOT REALLY EXIST!
THEY ARE, IN FACT, COUNTER-HYPOTHALAMIC PITUITARY-ADRENAL AXIS THOUGHT SMEARS! THEY ARE IMPOSSIBLE, ERGO, THEY ARE NOT REAL! IF WE WISH THEM AWAY STRONGLY ENOUGH--
YOU'RE MISTAKEN!
DESPITE BREAKIN' THE LAWS OF PHYSICS, THOSE BEASTS ARE ALL TOO REAL! YOU'RE DEALIN' WITH MATTERS BEYOND YOUR UNDERSTANDING, PROFESSOR!
HMPH!!
WHUP! WHUP! WHUP! WHUP! WHUP!
WHO THE SAM-HELL-HILL ARE YOU?
REX LIBRIS, PUBLIC LIBRARIAN, AND THIS IS MY LITTLE BUDDY SIMON.
WELL I WILL THANK YOU, 'MR' LIBRIS, TO KINDLY STOP TRYING TO INFLUENCE MY PERCEPTION OF REALITY!
SAY...
DID YOU SAY, 'SIMON'? ARE YOU THE SAME BIRD THAT TOOK OVER SOUTH AMERICA FOR A WEEKEND A FEW YEARS BACK?
THERE IS NO BIRD, GENERAL!

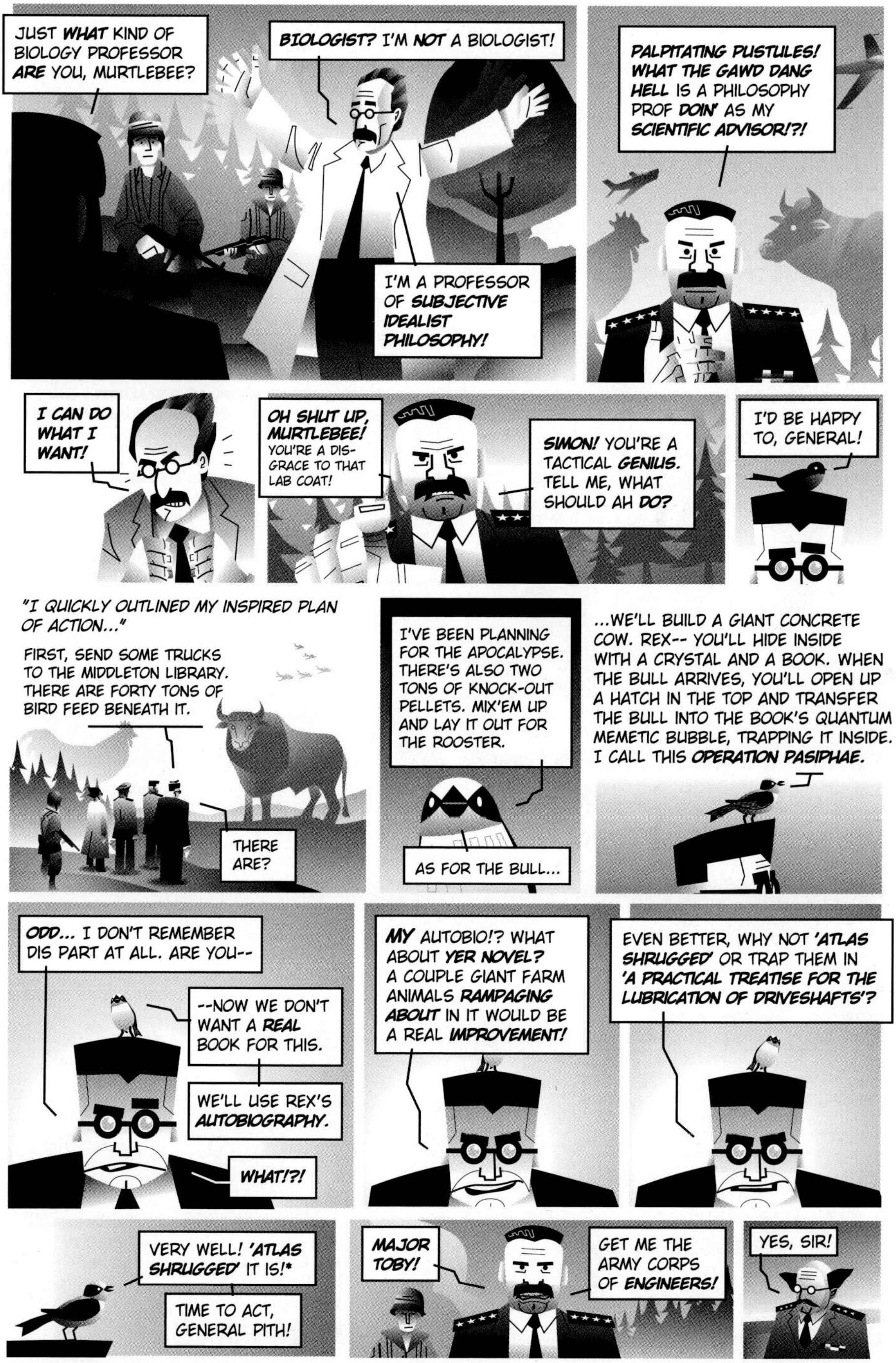
JUST WHAT KIND OF BIOLOGY PROFESSOR ARE YOU, MURTLEBEE?
BIOLOGIST? I'M NOT A BIOLOGIST!
I'M A PROFESSOR OF SUBJECTIVE IDEALIST PHILOSOPHY!
PALPITATING PUSTULES! WHAT THE GAWD DANG HELL IS A PHILOSOPHY PROF DOIN' AS MY SCIENTIFIC ADVISOR!?!
I CAN DO WHAT I WANT!
OH SHUT UP, MURTLEBEE! YOU'RE A DISGRACE TO THAT LAB COAT!
SIMON! YOU'RE A TACTICAL GENIUS. TELL ME, WHAT SHOULD AH DO?
I'D BE HAPPY TO, GENERAL!
"I QUICKLY OUTLINED MY INSPIRED PLAN OF ACTION..."
FIRST, SEND SOME TRUCKS TO THE MIDDLETON LIBRARY. THERE ARE FORTY TONS OF BIRD FEED BENEATH IT.
THERE ARE?
I'VE BEEN PLANNING FOR THE APOCALYPSE. THERE'S ALSO TWO TONS OF KNOCK-OUT PELLETS. MIX'EM UP AND LAY IT OUT FOR THE ROOSTER.
AS FOR THE BULL...
...WE'LL BUILD A GIANT CONCRETE COW. REX-- YOU'LL HIDE INSIDE WITH A CRYSTAL AND A BOOK. WHEN THE BULL ARRIVES, YOU'LL OPEN UP A HATCH IN THE TOP AND TRANSFER THE BULL INTO THE BOOK'S QUANTUM MEMETIC BUBBLE, TRAPPING IT INSIDE. I CALL THIS OPERATION PASIPHAE.
ODD... I DON'T REMEMBER DIS PART AT ALL. ARE YOU--
--NOW WE DON'T WANT A REAL BOOK FOR THIS.
WE'LL USE REX'S AUTOBIOGRAPHY.
WHAT!?!
MY AUTOBIO!? WHAT ABOUT YER NOVEL? A COUPLE GIANT FARM ANIMALS RAMPAGING ABOUT IN IT WOULD BE A REAL IMPROVEMENT!
EVEN BETTER, WHY NOT 'ATLAS SHRUGGED' OR TRAP THEM IN 'A PRACTICAL TREATISE FOR THE LUBRICATION OF DRIVESHAFTS'?
VERY WELL! 'ATLAS SHRUGGED' IT IS!*
TIME TO ACT, GENERAL PITH!
MAJOR TOBY!
GET ME THE ARMY CORPS OF ENGINEERS!
YES, SIR!

*THIS IS WHY CERTAIN COPIES OF 'ATLAS SHRUGGED' INEXPICABLY HAVE A GIANT BULL AND COCK STOMPING ABOUT, CRUSHING ATLASES AND DEMOLISHING RAILROAD CARS, SEEMINGLY WITHOUT MOTIVATION. THEIR PRESENCE HAS CAUSED A GREAT DEAL OF SPECULATION IN ACADEMIA. SOME HAVE THEORIZED THAT THESE BEASTS MIGHT BE THE REAL REASON FOR THE DEVELOPMENT OF PROJECT X. WE ARE GLAD TO HAVE FINALLY EXPLAINED THIS INTRIGUING MYSTERY.-- BARRY

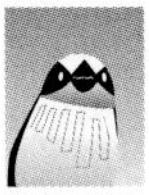

"IN AN ASTONISHINGLY SHORT TIME, THE ARMY CORPS OF ENGINEERS CONSTRUCTED THE CONCRETE COW. MEANWHILE THE MILITIA DEPLOYED THE BIRD SEED. WHEN EVERYTHING WAS READY, THEY WERE REVEALED SIMULTANEOUSLY. THE TWO GREAT BEASTS WERE IMMEDIATELY INTRIGUED, AND IT LED TO THE MOST BIZARRE, INSANE, AND MAGNIFICENT SCENE I HAVE EVER WITNESSED..."

*

* THIS SCENE IS SIMPLY SO FANTASTIC THAT IT COULD ONLY BE RENDERED USING ***VISICOMBOIC IMAGINAVISION!*** THIS ASTONISHING INNOVATION ALLOWS EACH INDIVIDUAL READER TO CREATE CUSTOMIZED IMAGERY AND DIALOGUE PERFECTLY ATUNED TO THEIR PERSONAL AESTHETIC SENSIBILITES. ARTISTS ARE MERELY FLAWED PEOPLE, AFTER ALL. IMAGINAVISION ALLOWS US TO TRANSCEND THEIR LIMITATIONS, AND ACHIEVE THE ***TRULY*** DIVINE, FOR NOTHING CAN COMPARE TO THE INCREDIBLE POWER OF ***CUSTOMIZED HUMAN IMAGINATION!*** THE ***SECRET*** OF IMAGINAVISION IS CLOSELY GUARDED, BUT YOU CAN EXPERIENCE IT BY CLOSING YOUR EYES AND IMAGINING THE MOST AWESOME SCENE POSSIBLE (ONLY DO THIS WITH ***OFFICIAL IMAGINAVISION*** MATERIALS). AT LAST, A TRULY INTERACTIVE, PARTICIPATORY COMIC!

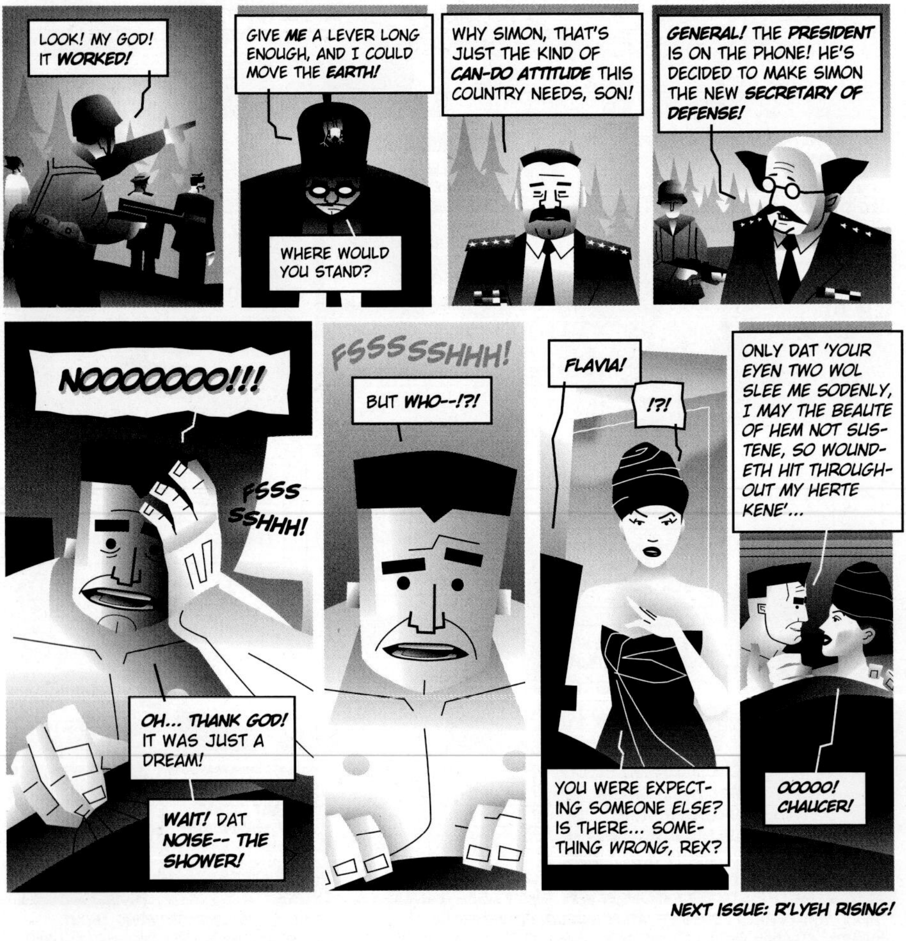

LOOK! MY GOD! IT WORKED!
GIVE ME A LEVER LONG ENOUGH, AND I COULD MOVE THE EARTH!
WHERE WOULD YOU STAND?
WHY SIMON, THAT'S JUST THE KIND OF CAN-DO ATTITUDE THIS COUNTRY NEEDS, SON!
GENERAL! THE PRESIDENT IS ON THE PHONE! HE'S DECIDED TO MAKE SIMON THE NEW SECRETARY OF DEFENSE!
NOOOOOOOO!!!
FSSS SSHHH!
OH... THANK GOD! IT WAS JUST A DREAM!
WAIT! DAT NOISE-- THE SHOWER!
FSSSSSHHH!
BUT WHO--!?!
FLAVIA!
!?!
YOU WERE EXPECT-ING SOMEONE ELSE? IS THERE... SOME-THING WRONG, REX?
ONLY DAT 'YOUR EYEN TWO WOL SLEE ME SODENLY, I MAY THE BEAUTE OF HEM NOT SUS-TENE, SO WOUND-ETH HIT THROUGH-OUT MY HERTE KENE'...
OOOOO! CHAUCER!

NEXT ISSUE: R'LYEH RISING!

CHAPTER ELEVEN

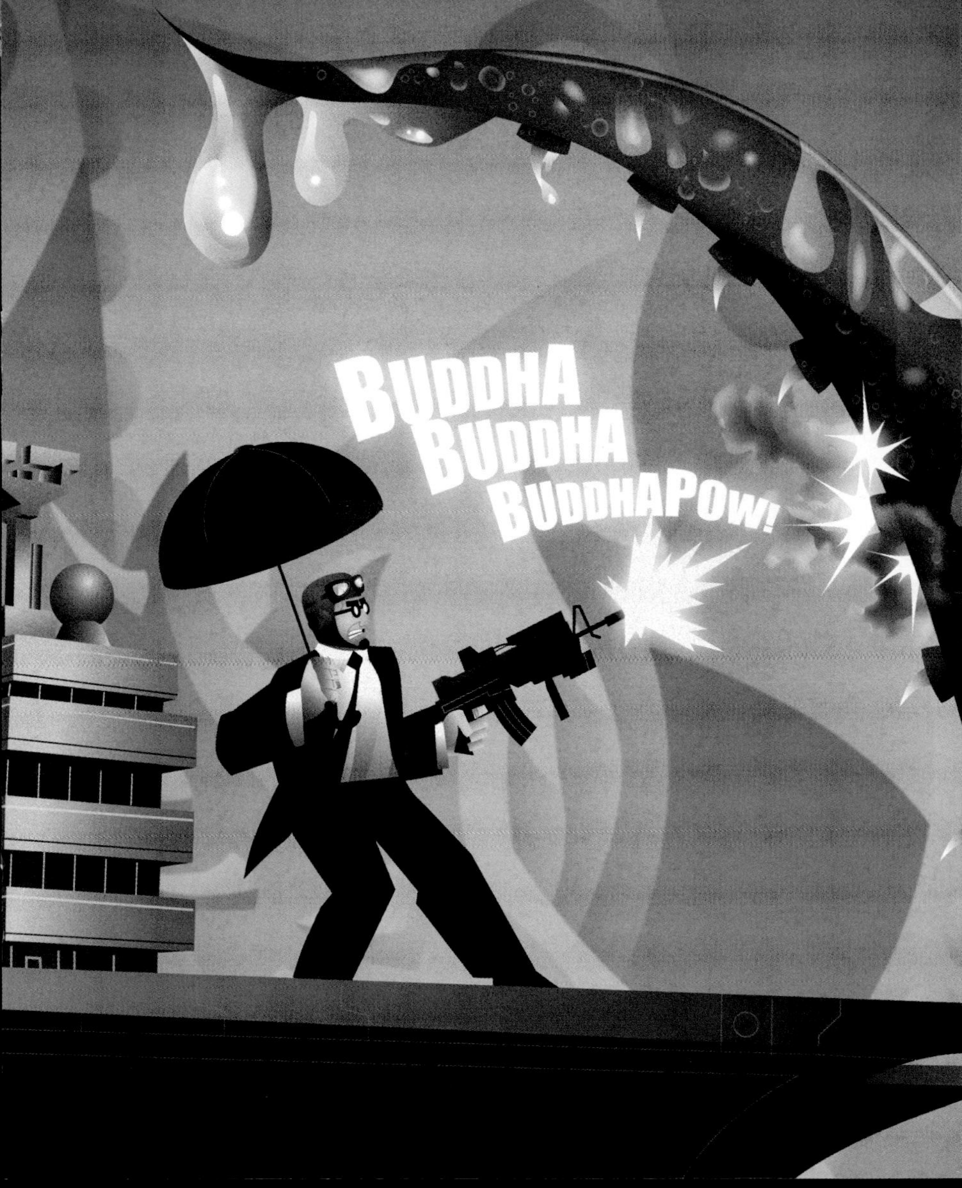
BUDDHA
BUDDHA
BUDDHAPOW!

BARRY'S BRAIN

Cthulhu! His very name strikes fear into the sane and prudent. Yet our team of crack librarians cannot turn away from this unspeakable horror, for it is their duty to see that he is returned to the short story from which he emerged. No challenge is too great, no beast to baffling for the elite of the Ordo Bibliotheca! Only they can deal with the deadliest threat of logos condensate that mankind has faced in all of recorded history!

Except, of course, for the meance of Oo-Ootepthet the Loathesome. The other day Rex related to me the cataclysmic battle that erupted when Oo-oo came too earth in '75. The battle with this fell beast, unfortunately, is a tale too terrible to tell, for it is saturated with soul-petrifying terror, and overflowing with gruesome vistas, ghastly charnels of unbelievable immensity and cyclopean aspect, abhorrent unnamable antechambers, evil and malignant netherfoyers, and the most dread of all shrieking vestibules of vaporous, gnawing demise.

No, that is a tale we can never tell, for there would be far too many lawsuits by the bereaved relatives of the poor multitude exposed to the unspeakable horror that is the very idea of Oo-oo. All who read of the roiling madness that curdles within Oo-oo are driven inexorably to a horrible death or lifelong madnesss. While we respect the public's right to know, we also believe it is our duty as a responsible publisher not to drive our audience stark raving mad, turn them into drooling Mogwops with fish features and fins, or send them screaming blasphemies to a hideous, lunacy-drenched death—only to rise again as a flesh devouring ghoul and awful servant of the unspeakable, unschematizable, unnamable... (blank) that lies beyond the veil of reality, and is truly real real (ie. horrific).

My nephew Todd is now vice-president of Hermeneutic Press! That's right! Thanks to him, and his hefty infusion of cash, Hemeneutic will be inundating you, dear readers, with quality products and ever more entertaining comic book confections for the indefinite future! Bankruptcy will be held in abeyance! Todd knows a good financial investment when he sees one, and there is none better than the comic book money making miracle machine! He's even doing the accounting now, and I *hate* accounting! What a nephew!

Yesterday I met his business partners, Guido and Tony, who also run a construction company in Vancouver. They don't look like people who'd be interested in gardening, or comic books, but Guido pitched me a comic book series about a mob enforcer that was pitch perfect! He described it in such vivid, exquisite detail it was almost like he'd lived that life himself! It just goes to show you can't judge a book by it's cover, and that comic book and gardening fans are indeed everywhere.

Exfoliate!

B. Barry Horst
Publisher

WELCOME ONCE AGAIN, FAITHFUL READERS, TO THE TUMULTUOUS TALE OF LIBRARIAN REX LIBRIS AND HIS UNENDING BATTLE AGAINST THE FORCES OF EVIL. BORN IN ANCIENT ROME, HE HAS WORKED TO PRESERVE KNOWLEDGE AND WISDOM FOR THOUSANDS OF YEARS AGAINST ALL FORMS OF PERFIDY, FROM BOOK-BASHING BOOGEYMEN TO MOANING UNDEAD LEGIONS WHO IGNORE THE 'QUIET PLEASE' SIGN. NOT EVEN SUPERPOWERED, DELINQUENT ALIEN CHILDREN CAN ABSCOND WITH BOOKS WITHOUT SIGNING THEM OUT WHILE REX IS ON THE JOB! FOR THE FIRST TIME THE SECRET WORLD OF LIBRARIANS AND THEIR DAILY STRUGGLE TO PROTECT CIVILIZATION AND THE KNOWLEDGE IT IS FOUNDED UPON IS REVEALED!

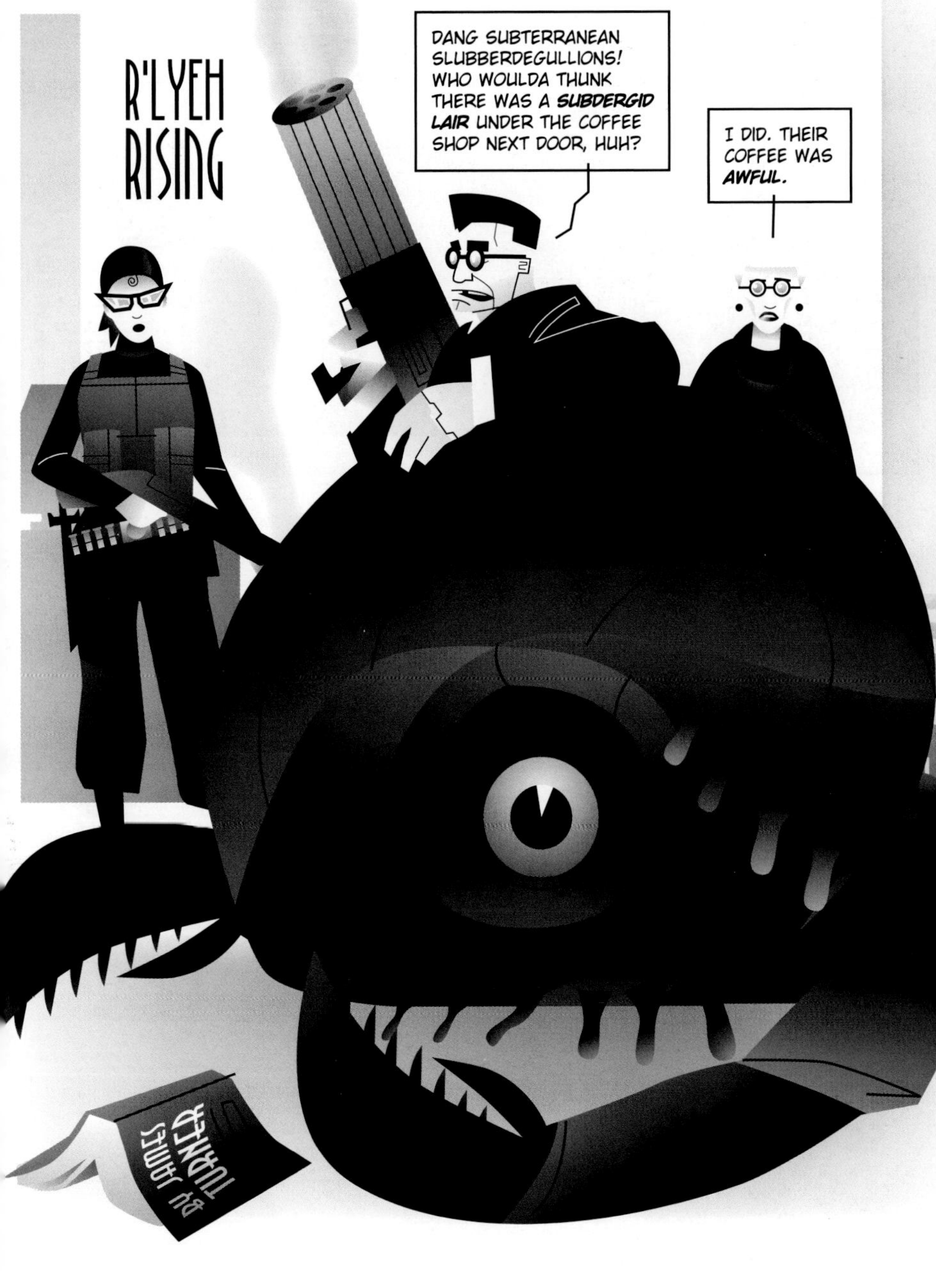
R'LYEH RISING
DANG SUBTERRANEAN SLUBBERDEGULLIONS! WHO WOULDA THUNK THERE WAS A SUBDERGID LAIR UNDER THE COFFEE SHOP NEXT DOOR, HUH?
I DID. THEIR COFFEE WAS AWFUL.
BY JAMES TURNER

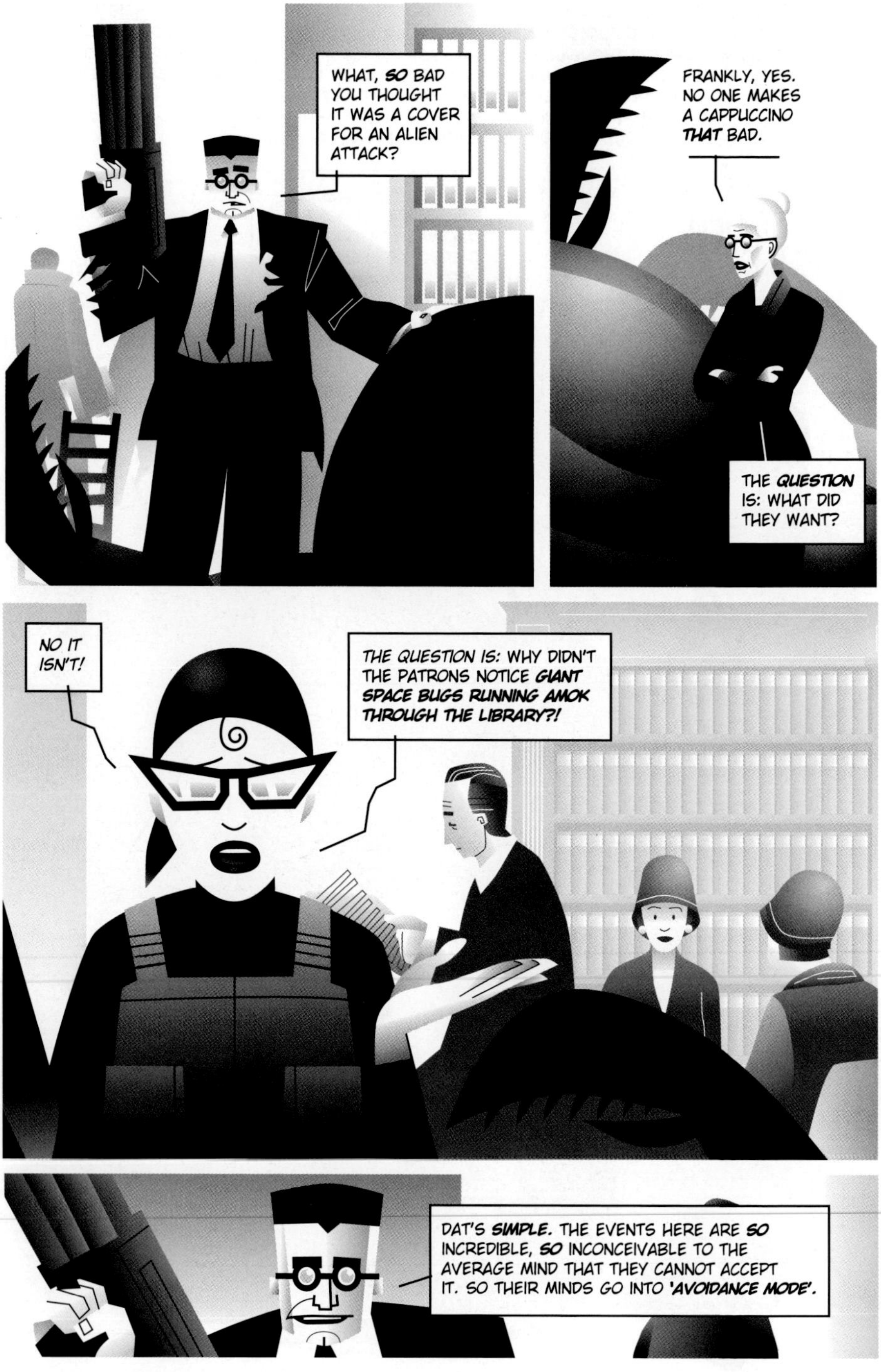
WHAT, SO BAD YOU THOUGHT IT WAS A COVER FOR AN ALIEN ATTACK?
FRANKLY, YES. NO ONE MAKES A CAPPUCCINO THAT BAD.
THE QUESTION IS: WHAT DID THEY WANT?
NO IT ISN'T!
THE QUESTION IS: WHY DIDN'T THE PATRONS NOTICE GIANT SPACE BUGS RUNNING AMOK THROUGH THE LIBRARY?!
DAT'S SIMPLE. THE EVENTS HERE ARE SO INCREDIBLE, SO INCONCEIVABLE TO THE AVERAGE MIND THAT THEY CANNOT ACCEPT IT. SO THEIR MINDS GO INTO 'AVOIDANCE MODE'.

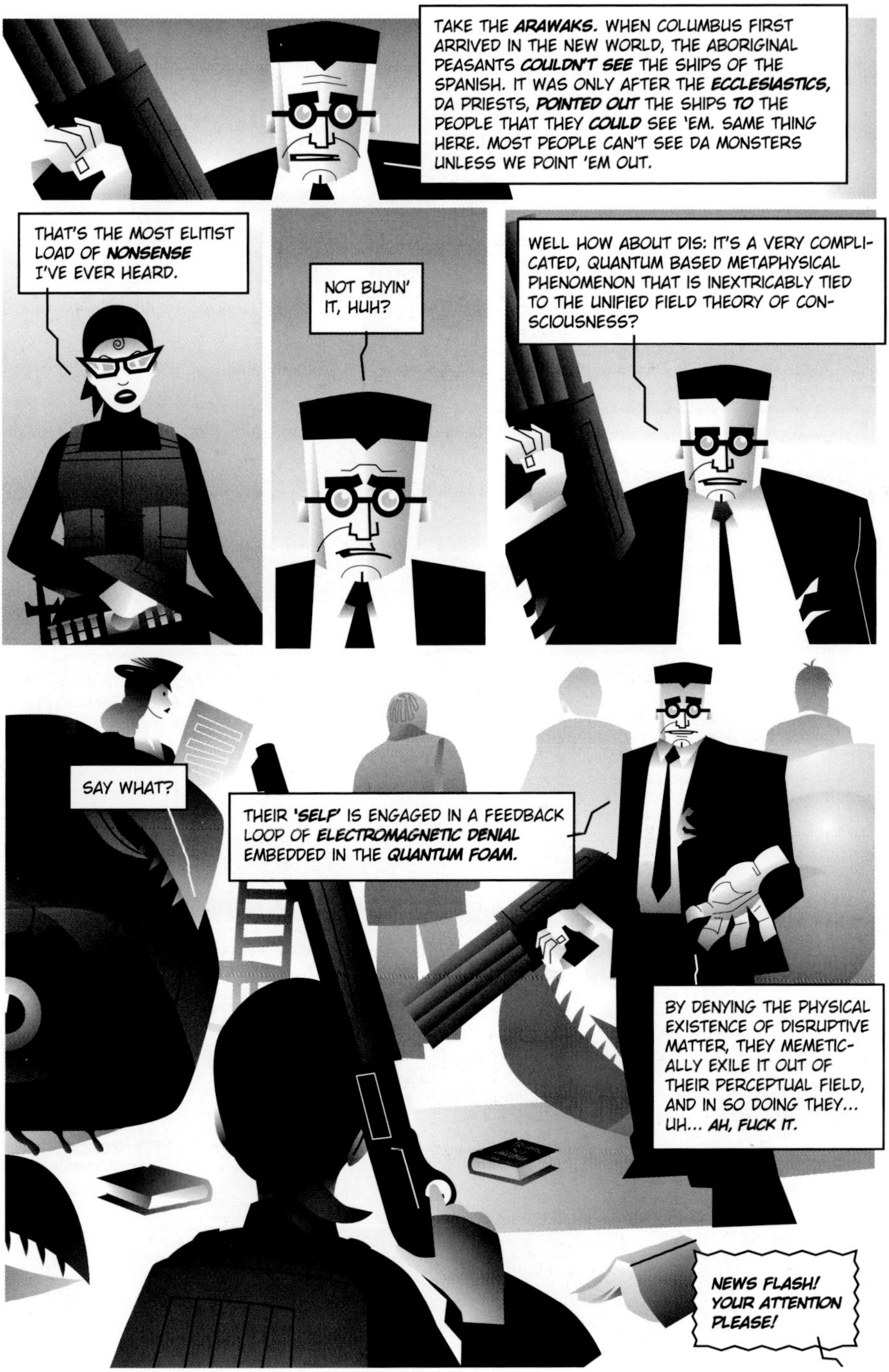
TAKE THE ARAWAKS. WHEN COLUMBUS FIRST ARRIVED IN THE NEW WORLD, THE ABORIGINAL PEASANTS COULDN'T SEE THE SHIPS OF THE SPANISH. IT WAS ONLY AFTER THE ECCLESIASTICS, DA PRIESTS, POINTED OUT THE SHIPS TO THE PEOPLE THAT THEY COULD SEE 'EM. SAME THING HERE. MOST PEOPLE CAN'T SEE DA MONSTERS UNLESS WE POINT 'EM OUT.
THAT'S THE MOST ELITIST LOAD OF NONSENSE I'VE EVER HEARD.
NOT BUYIN' IT, HUH?
WELL HOW ABOUT DIS: IT'S A VERY COMPLICATED, QUANTUM BASED METAPHYSICAL PHENOMENON THAT IS INEXTRICABLY TIED TO THE UNIFIED FIELD THEORY OF CONSCIOUSNESS?
SAY WHAT?
THEIR 'SELF' IS ENGAGED IN A FEEDBACK LOOP OF ELECTROMAGNETIC DENIAL EMBEDDED IN THE QUANTUM FOAM.
BY DENYING THE PHYSICAL EXISTENCE OF DISRUPTIVE MATTER, THEY MEMETICALLY EXILE IT OUT OF THEIR PERCEPTUAL FIELD, AND IN SO DOING THEY... UH... AH, FUCK IT.
NEWS FLASH! YOUR ATTENTION PLEASE!

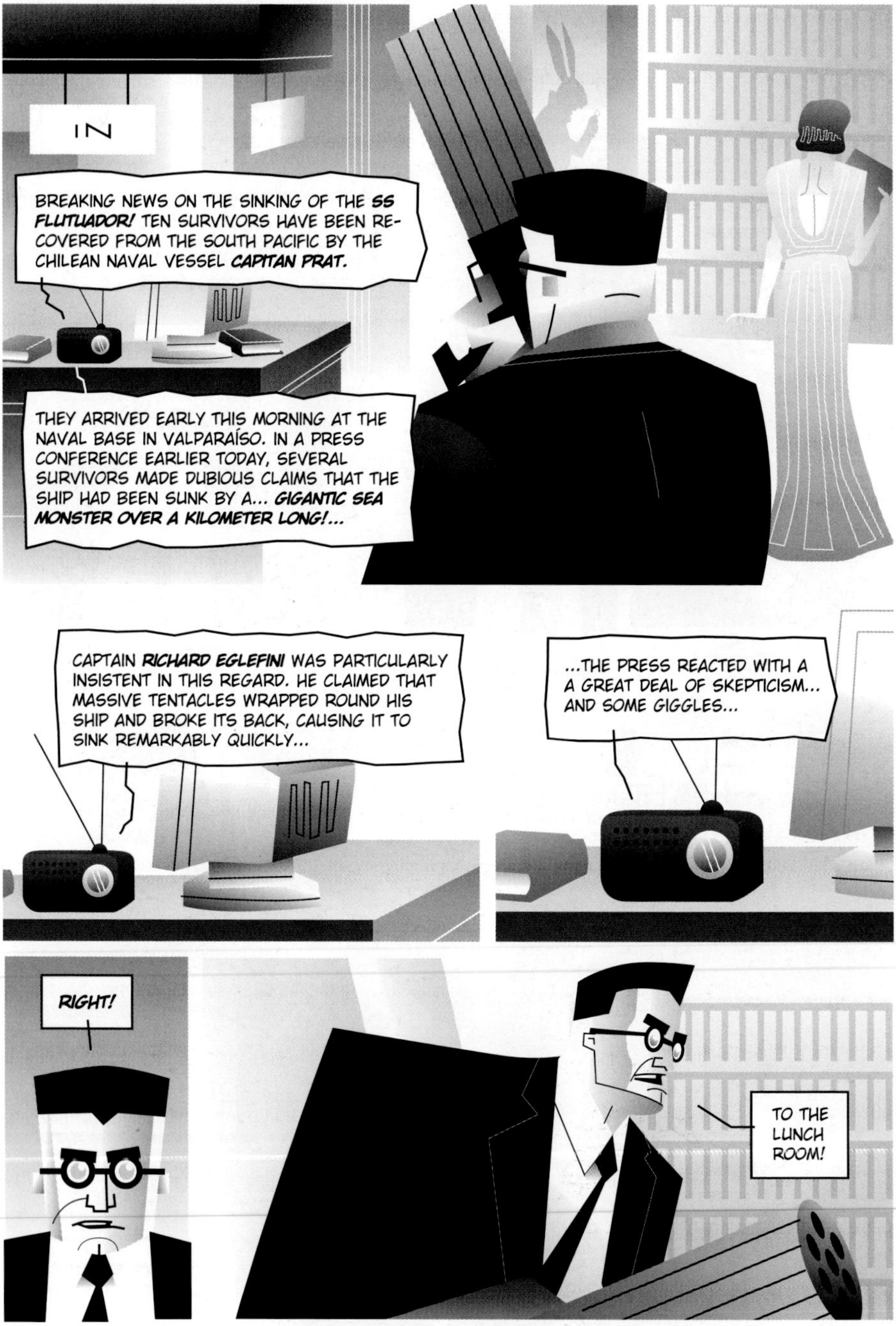
IN
BREAKING NEWS ON THE SINKING OF THE SS FLUTUADOR! TEN SURVIVORS HAVE BEEN RE-COVERED FROM THE SOUTH PACIFIC BY THE CHILEAN NAVAL VESSEL CAPITAN PRAT.
THEY ARRIVED EARLY THIS MORNING AT THE NAVAL BASE IN VALPARAÍSO. IN A PRESS CONFERENCE EARLIER TODAY, SEVERAL SURVIVORS MADE DUBIOUS CLAIMS THAT THE SHIP HAD BEEN SUNK BY A... GIGANTIC SEA MONSTER OVER A KILOMETER LONG!...
CAPTAIN RICHARD EGLEFINI WAS PARTICULARLY INSISTENT IN THIS REGARD. HE CLAIMED THAT MASSIVE TENTACLES WRAPPED ROUND HIS SHIP AND BROKE ITS BACK, CAUSING IT TO SINK REMARKABLY QUICKLY...
...THE PRESS REACTED WITH A A GREAT DEAL OF SKEPTICISM... AND SOME GIGGLES...
RIGHT!
TO THE LUNCH ROOM!

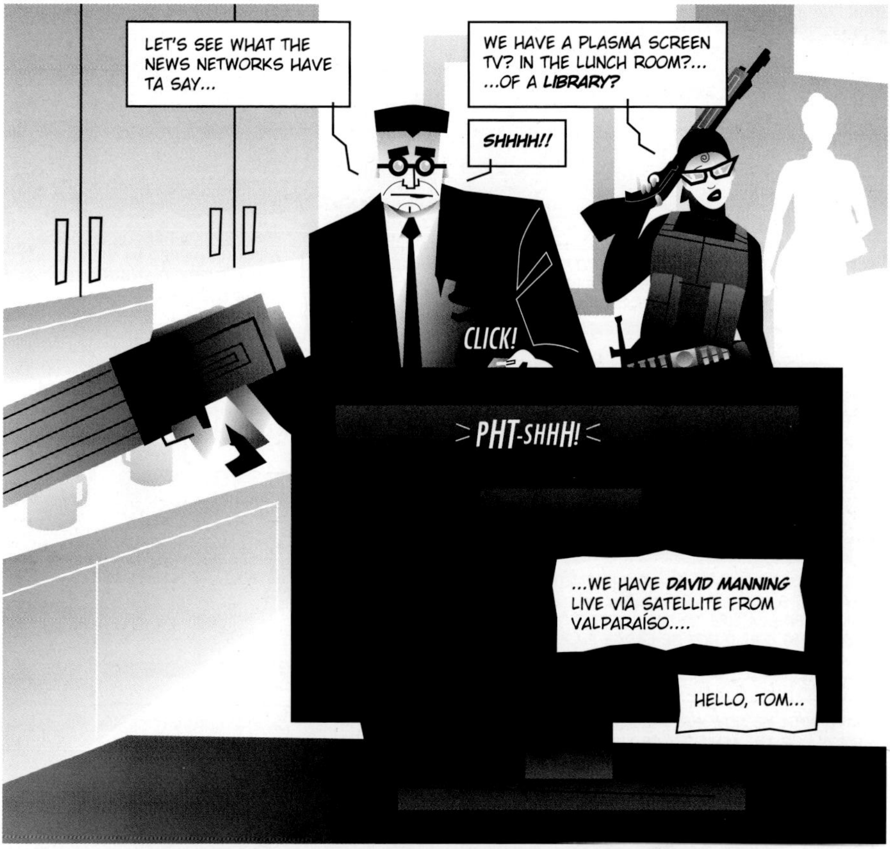
LET'S SEE WHAT THE NEWS NETWORKS HAVE TA SAY...
WE HAVE A PLASMA SCREEN TV? IN THE LUNCH ROOM?... ...OF A LIBRARY?
SHHHH!!
CLICK!
PHT-SHHH!
...WE HAVE DAVID MANNING LIVE VIA SATELLITE FROM VALPARAÍSO....
HELLO, TOM...

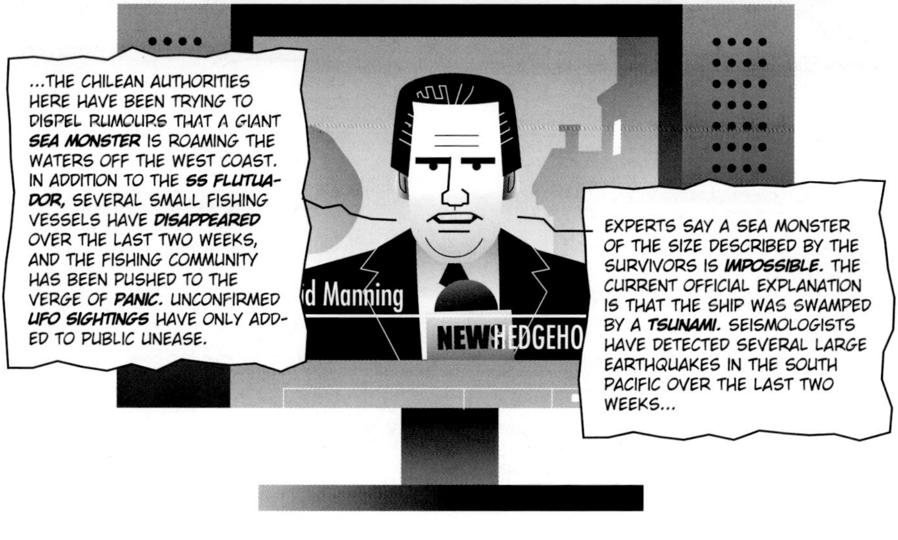
...THE CHILEAN AUTHORITIES HERE HAVE BEEN TRYING TO DISPEL RUMOURS THAT A GIANT SEA MONSTER IS ROAMING THE WATERS OFF THE WEST COAST. IN ADDITION TO THE SS FLUTUADOR, SEVERAL SMALL FISHING VESSELS HAVE DISAPPEARED OVER THE LAST TWO WEEKS, AND THE FISHING COMMUNITY HAS BEEN PUSHED TO THE VERGE OF PANIC. UNCONFIRMED UFO SIGHTINGS HAVE ONLY ADDED TO PUBLIC UNEASE.
id Manning
NEWSHEDGEHO
EXPERTS SAY A SEA MONSTER OF THE SIZE DESCRIBED BY THE SURVIVORS IS IMPOSSIBLE. THE CURRENT OFFICIAL EXPLANATION IS THAT THE SHIP WAS SWAMPED BY A TSUNAMI. SEISMOLOGISTS HAVE DETECTED SEVERAL LARGE EARTHQUAKES IN THE SOUTH PACIFIC OVER THE LAST TWO WEEKS...

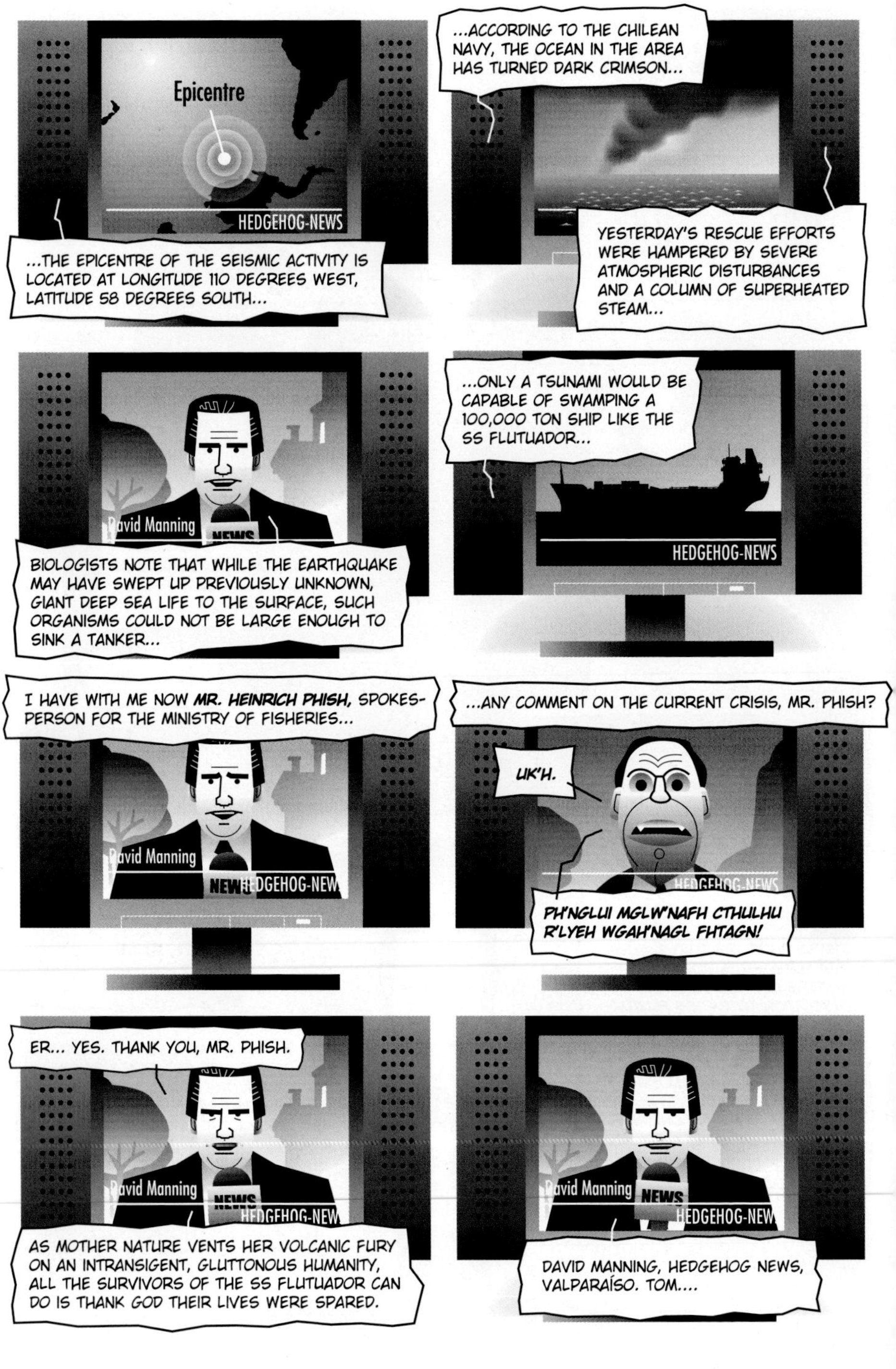
Epicentre
HEDGEHOG-NEWS
...THE EPICENTRE OF THE SEISMIC ACTIVITY IS LOCATED AT LONGITUDE 110 DEGREES WEST, LATITUDE 58 DEGREES SOUTH...
...ACCORDING TO THE CHILEAN NAVY, THE OCEAN IN THE AREA HAS TURNED DARK CRIMSON...
YESTERDAY'S RESCUE EFFORTS WERE HAMPERED BY SEVERE ATMOSPHERIC DISTURBANCES AND A COLUMN OF SUPERHEATED STEAM...
David Manning
BIOLOGISTS NOTE THAT WHILE THE EARTHQUAKE MAY HAVE SWEPT UP PREVIOUSLY UNKNOWN, GIANT DEEP SEA LIFE TO THE SURFACE, SUCH ORGANISMS COULD NOT BE LARGE ENOUGH TO SINK A TANKER...
...ONLY A TSUNAMI WOULD BE CAPABLE OF SWAMPING A 100,000 TON SHIP LIKE THE SS FLUTUADOR...
HEDGEHOG-NEWS
I HAVE WITH ME NOW ***MR. HEINRICH PHISH,*** SPOKESPERSON FOR THE MINISTRY OF FISHERIES...
David Manning
NEWS
...ANY COMMENT ON THE CURRENT CRISIS, MR. PHISH?
UK'H.
PH'NGLUI MGLW'NAFH CTHULHU R'LYEH WGAH'NAGL FHTAGN!
ER... YES. THANK YOU, MR. PHISH.
David Manning
NEWS
AS MOTHER NATURE VENTS HER VOLCANIC FURY ON AN INTRANSIGENT, GLUTTONOUS HUMANITY, ALL THE SURVIVORS OF THE SS FLUTUADOR CAN DO IS THANK GOD THEIR LIVES WERE SPARED.
David Manning
NEWS
DAVID MANNING, HEDGEHOG NEWS, VALPARAÍSO. TOM....

DAMN! THE ROGUE SUBDERGIDS... NOW I KNOW WHAT THEY WERE AFTER! WE... WE DIDN'T NEED TA FIGHT THEM!

!?! WHAT?

IT IS AS I FEARED.

HELL IS EMERGIN' OUTTA THE BELLINGHAUSEN ABYSSAL PLAIN! R'LYEH IS RISING ONCE AGAIN!

THE FORCES OF EVIL ARE MARSHALIN'! A BILEOUS CLOUD OF ROILING AND PERVERSE DARKNESS, IMMENSE AND IMPENETRABLE, IS SEEPIN' OUT ONTO THE SURFACE OF THE WORLD AS I SPEAK!*

METAPHORICAL TENDRILS OF CREEPIN' CHAOS ARE LEECHIN' INTO THE BIOSPHERE, GNAWIN' AND ABHORRENT, BURBLIN' WITH UNINTELLIGIBLE EVIL! WE GOTTA PROTECT THE FLICKERIN' CANDLE OF HOPE AN' KNOWLEDGE FROM DIS RAGIN' TSUNAMI OF MADNESS! IF SANITY AND SOOTH ARE TO PREVAIL WE MUST TAKE TO THE BATTLEMENTS!*

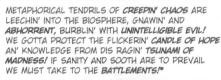

THE TIME HAS COME! SEND WORD AROUN' THE WORLD, TO EVERY LIBRARY BRANCH: TODAY... WE MOBILIZE!

EVERY BRANCH? EVEN THE CENTRAL LIBRARY?

*A PATENTED 'VISICOMBOIC EXPLICATION EXPLOSION'! YET ANOTHER INNOVATIVE FEATURE FOUND ONLY IN VISICOMBOICS! --BARRY

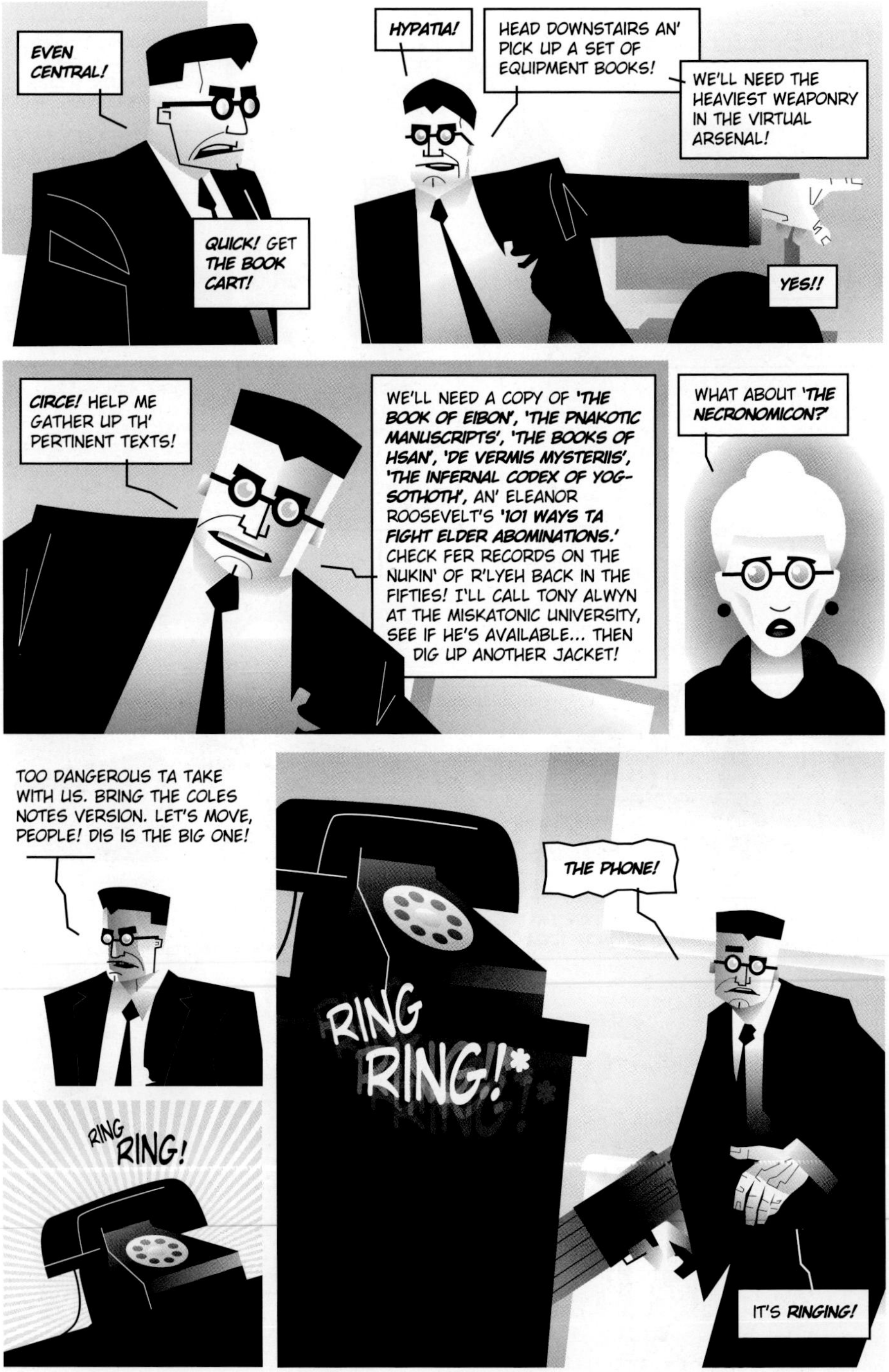
EVEN CENTRAL!
QUICK! GET THE BOOK CART!
HYPATIA!
HEAD DOWNSTAIRS AN' PICK UP A SET OF EQUIPMENT BOOKS!
WE'LL NEED THE HEAVIEST WEAPONRY IN THE VIRTUAL ARSENAL!
YES!!
CIRCE! HELP ME GATHER UP TH' PERTINENT TEXTS!
WE'LL NEED A COPY OF 'THE BOOK OF EIBON', 'THE PNAKOTIC MANUSCRIPTS', 'THE BOOKS OF HSAN', 'DE VERMIS MYSTERIIS', 'THE INFERNAL CODEX OF YOG-SOTHOTH', AN' ELEANOR ROOSEVELT'S '101 WAYS TA FIGHT ELDER ABOMINATIONS.' CHECK FER RECORDS ON THE NUKIN' OF R'LYEH BACK IN THE FIFTIES! I'LL CALL TONY ALWYN AT THE MISKATONIC UNIVERSITY, SEE IF HE'S AVAILABLE... THEN DIG UP ANOTHER JACKET!
WHAT ABOUT 'THE NECRONOMICON?'
TOO DANGEROUS TA TAKE WITH US. BRING THE COLES NOTES VERSION. LET'S MOVE, PEOPLE! DIS IS THE BIG ONE!
RING RING!
RING RING!*
THE PHONE!
IT'S RINGING!

* NOTICE HOW, WITH THE USE OF STRIKING ANGLES AND DRAMATIC POSES, ADVANCED VISICOMBOICS CAN TURN ORDINARY SITUATIONS INTO MOMENTS OF ***THRILLING HIGH DRAMA!*** ONLY WITH VISICOMBOICS, FOLKS! --BARRY

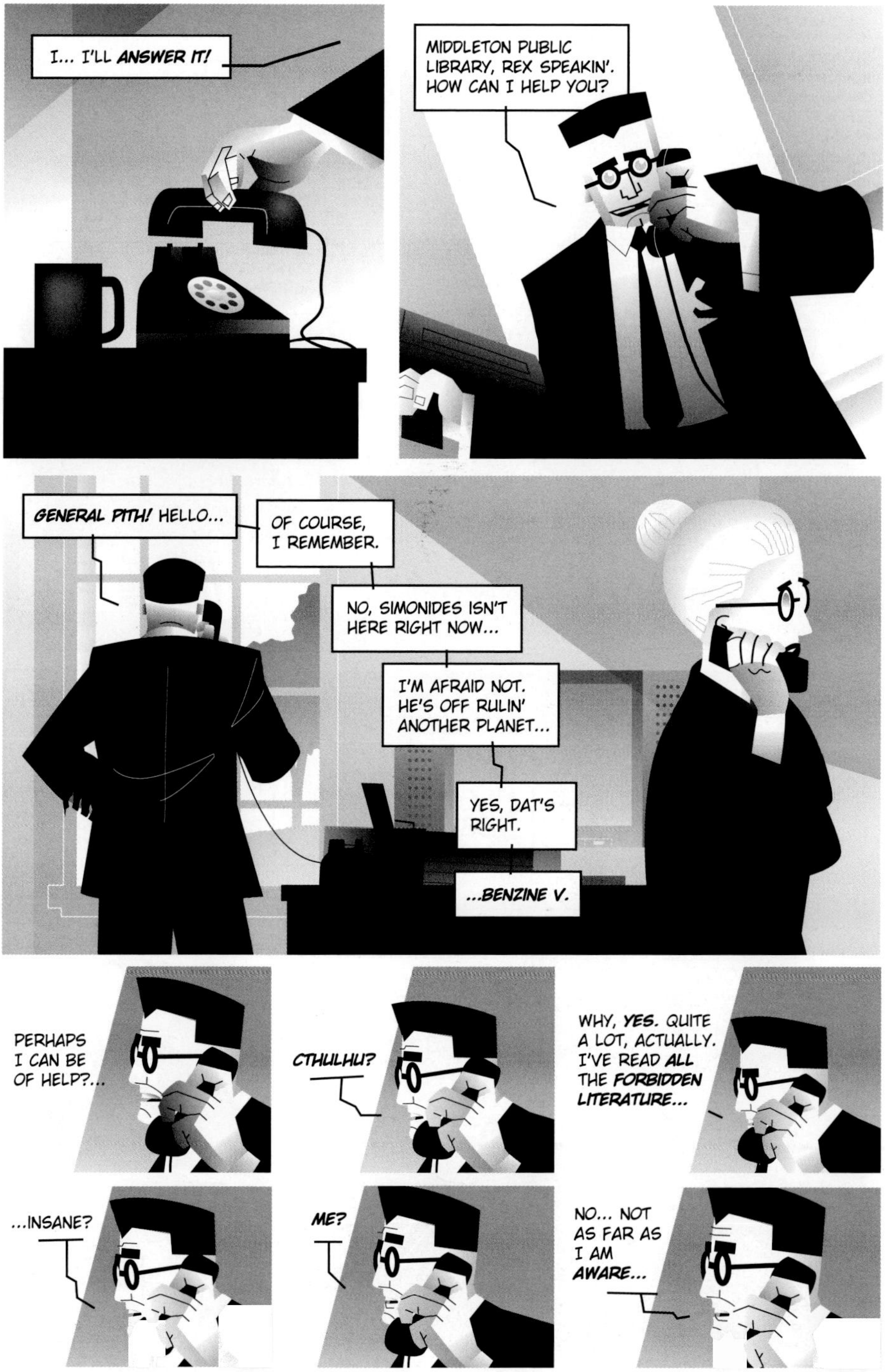
I... I'LL **ANSWER IT!**
MIDDLETON PUBLIC LIBRARY, REX SPEAKIN'. HOW CAN I HELP YOU?
GENERAL PITH! HELLO...
OF COURSE, I REMEMBER.
NO, SIMONIDES ISN'T HERE RIGHT NOW...
I'M AFRAID NOT. HE'S OFF RULIN' ANOTHER PLANET...
YES, DAT'S RIGHT.
...BENZINE V.
PERHAPS I CAN BE OF HELP?...
CTHULHU?
WHY, **YES.** QUITE A LOT, ACTUALLY. I'VE READ **ALL** THE **FORBIDDEN LITERATURE...**
...INSANE?
ME?
NO... NOT AS FAR AS I AM **AWARE...**

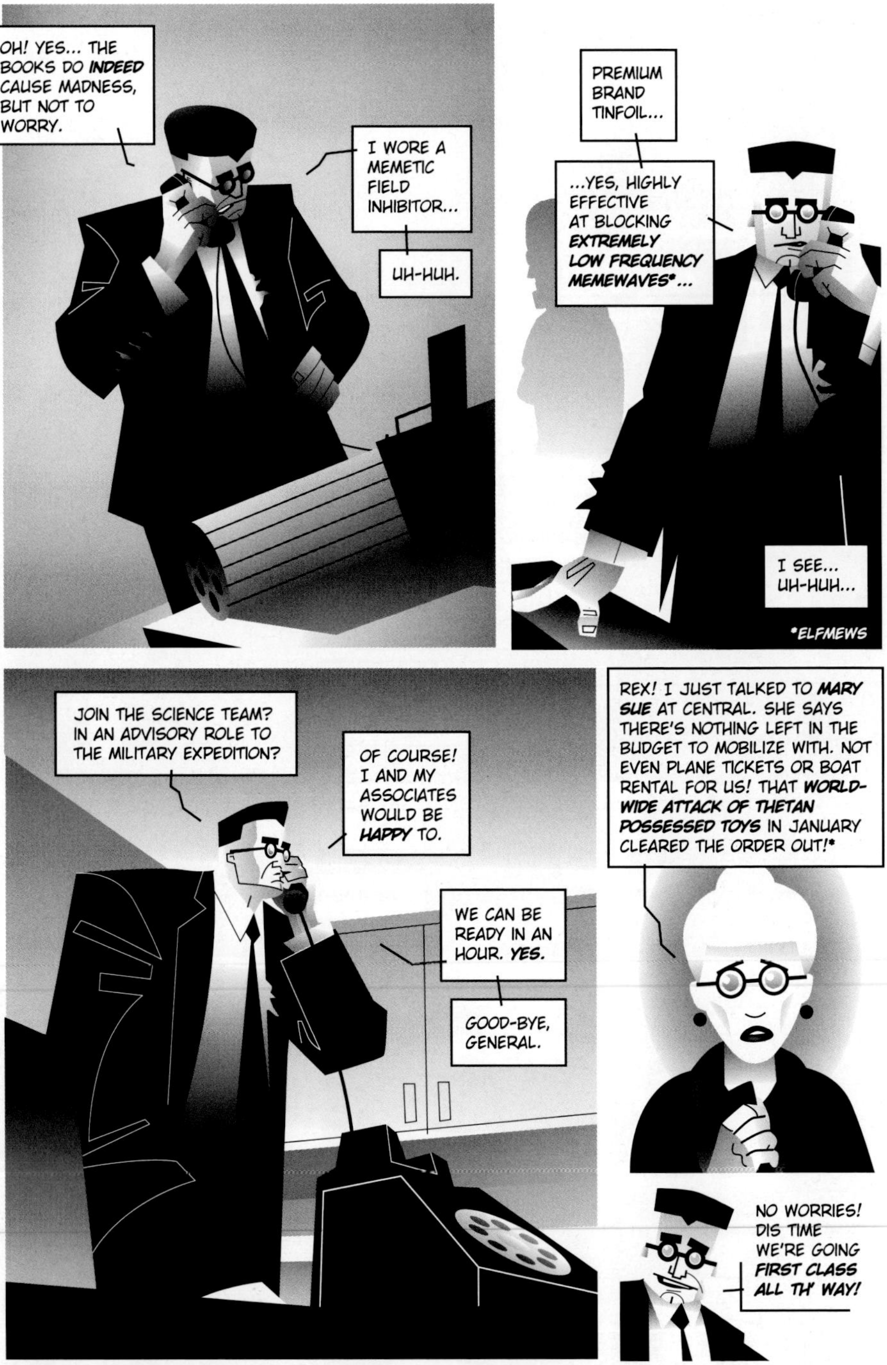
OH! YES... THE BOOKS DO INDEED CAUSE MADNESS, BUT NOT TO WORRY.
I WORE A MEMETIC FIELD INHIBITOR...
UH-HUH.
PREMIUM BRAND TINFOIL...
...YES, HIGHLY EFFECTIVE AT BLOCKING EXTREMELY LOW FREQUENCY MEMEWAVES*...
I SEE... UH-HUH...
*ELFMEWS
JOIN THE SCIENCE TEAM? IN AN ADVISORY ROLE TO THE MILITARY EXPEDITION?
OF COURSE! I AND MY ASSOCIATES WOULD BE HAPPY TO.
WE CAN BE READY IN AN HOUR. YES.
GOOD-BYE, GENERAL.
REX! I JUST TALKED TO MARY SUE AT CENTRAL. SHE SAYS THERE'S NOTHING LEFT IN THE BUDGET TO MOBILIZE WITH. NOT EVEN PLANE TICKETS OR BOAT RENTAL FOR US! THAT WORLD-WIDE ATTACK OF THETAN POSSESSED TOYS IN JANUARY CLEARED THE ORDER OUT!*
NO WORRIES! DIS TIME WE'RE GOING FIRST CLASS ALL TH' WAY!

* SEE *'REX LIBRIS AND THE TOYS OF DEATH'* FOR MORE INCREDIBLE DETAILS ON THE INSIDIOUS DISEMBODIED THETAN ATTACK FROM OUT OF THE WASTESPACE OF THE ***NTH*** DIMENSION. --BARRY

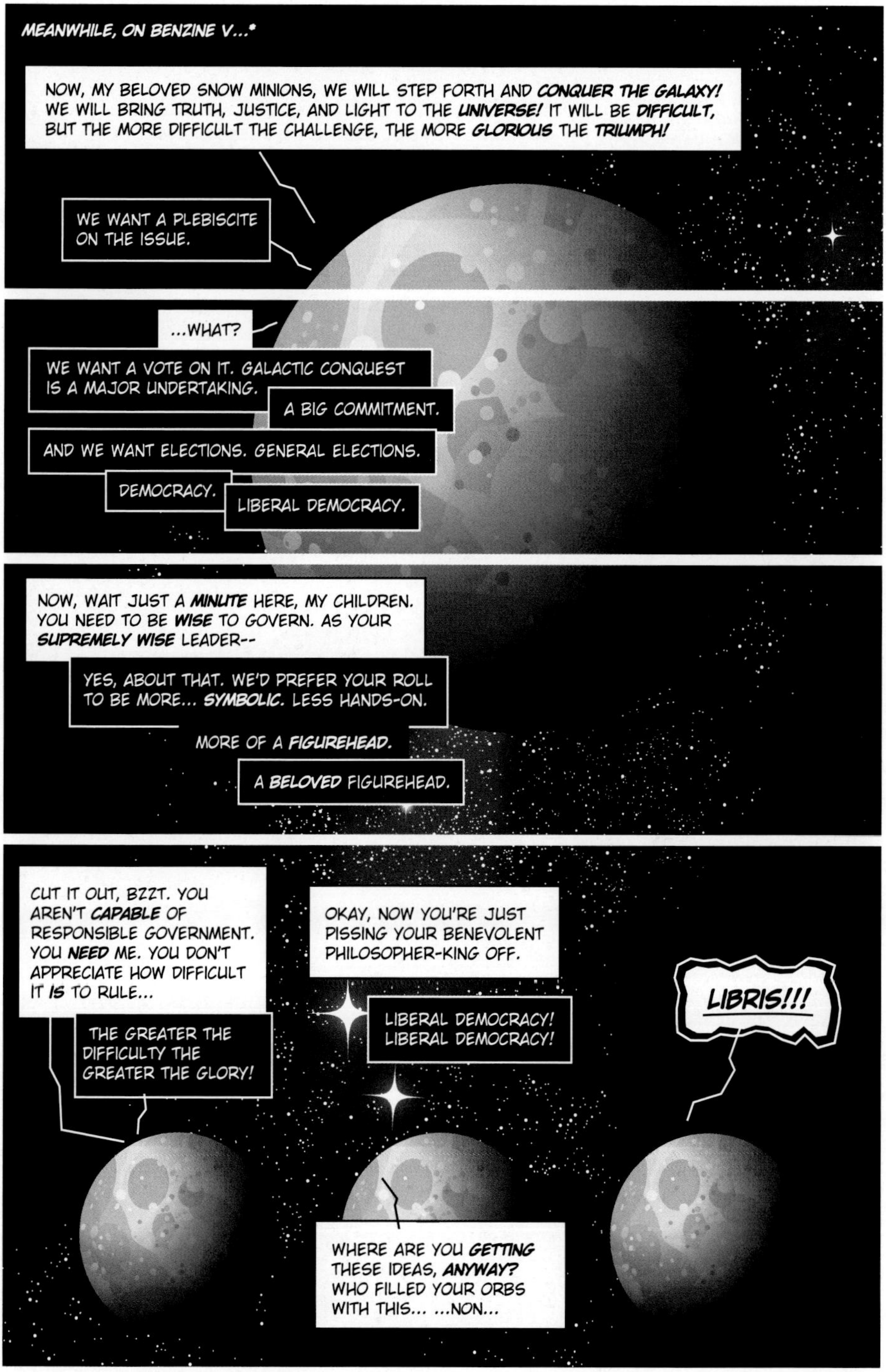
MEANWHILE, ON BENZINE V...*
NOW, MY BELOVED SNOW MINIONS, WE WILL STEP FORTH AND CONQUER THE GALAXY! WE WILL BRING TRUTH, JUSTICE, AND LIGHT TO THE UNIVERSE! IT WILL BE DIFFICULT, BUT THE MORE DIFFICULT THE CHALLENGE, THE MORE GLORIOUS THE TRIUMPH!
WE WANT A PLEBISCITE ON THE ISSUE.
...WHAT?
WE WANT A VOTE ON IT. GALACTIC CONQUEST IS A MAJOR UNDERTAKING.
A BIG COMMITMENT.
AND WE WANT ELECTIONS. GENERAL ELECTIONS.
DEMOCRACY.
LIBERAL DEMOCRACY.
NOW, WAIT JUST A MINUTE HERE, MY CHILDREN. YOU NEED TO BE WISE TO GOVERN. AS YOUR SUPREMELY WISE LEADER--
YES, ABOUT THAT. WE'D PREFER YOUR ROLL TO BE MORE... SYMBOLIC. LESS HANDS-ON.
MORE OF A FIGUREHEAD.
A BELOVED FIGUREHEAD.
CUT IT OUT, BZZT. YOU AREN'T CAPABLE OF RESPONSIBLE GOVERNMENT. YOU NEED ME. YOU DON'T APPRECIATE HOW DIFFICULT IT IS TO RULE...
THE GREATER THE DIFFICULTY THE GREATER THE GLORY!
OKAY, NOW YOU'RE JUST PISSING YOUR BENEVOLENT PHILOSOPHER-KING OFF.
LIBERAL DEMOCRACY! LIBERAL DEMOCRACY!
LIBRIS!!!
WHERE ARE YOU GETTING THESE IDEAS, ANYWAY? WHO FILLED YOUR ORBS WITH THIS... ...NON...

* SEE ISSUES 3 THROUGH 5 FOR MORE DETAILS ON SIMON AND THE STRANGE, SNOWY INHABITANTS OF BENZINE V.

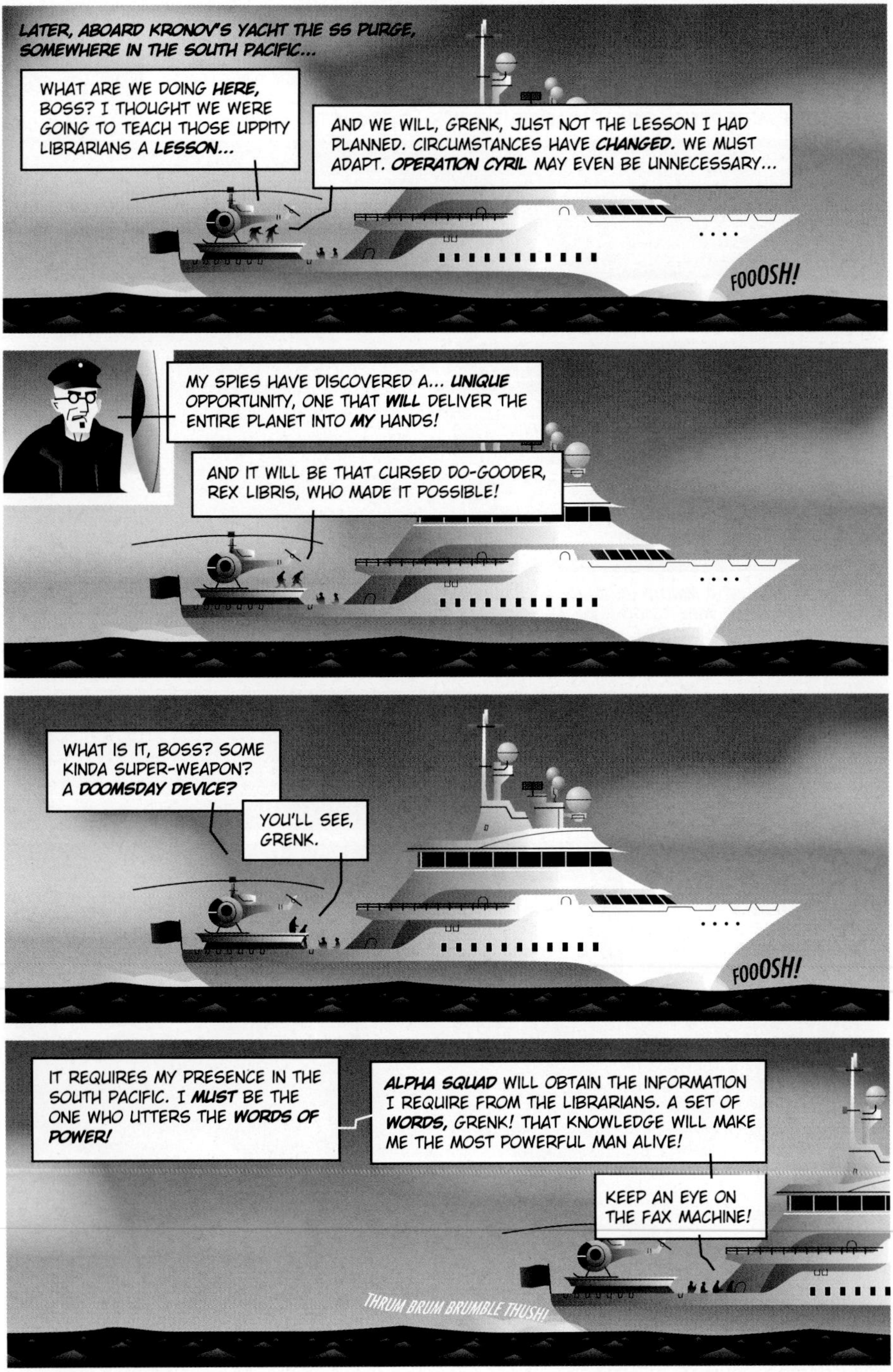
LATER, ABOARD KRONOV'S YACHT THE SS PURGE, SOMEWHERE IN THE SOUTH PACIFIC...
WHAT ARE WE DOING HERE, BOSS? I THOUGHT WE WERE GOING TO TEACH THOSE UPPITY LIBRARIANS A LESSON...
AND WE WILL, GRENK, JUST NOT THE LESSON I HAD PLANNED. CIRCUMSTANCES HAVE CHANGED. WE MUST ADAPT. OPERATION CYRIL MAY EVEN BE UNNECESSARY...
FOOOSH!
MY SPIES HAVE DISCOVERED A... UNIQUE OPPORTUNITY, ONE THAT WILL DELIVER THE ENTIRE PLANET INTO MY HANDS!
AND IT WILL BE THAT CURSED DO-GOODER, REX LIBRIS, WHO MADE IT POSSIBLE!
WHAT IS IT, BOSS? SOME KINDA SUPER-WEAPON? A DOOMSDAY DEVICE?
YOU'LL SEE, GRENK.
FOOOSH!
IT REQUIRES MY PRESENCE IN THE SOUTH PACIFIC. I MUST BE THE ONE WHO UTTERS THE WORDS OF POWER!
ALPHA SQUAD WILL OBTAIN THE INFORMATION I REQUIRE FROM THE LIBRARIANS. A SET OF WORDS, GRENK! THAT KNOWLEDGE WILL MAKE ME THE MOST POWERFUL MAN ALIVE!
KEEP AN EYE ON THE FAX MACHINE!
THRUM BRUM BRUMBLE THUSH!

MEANWHILE, FURTHER NORTH...

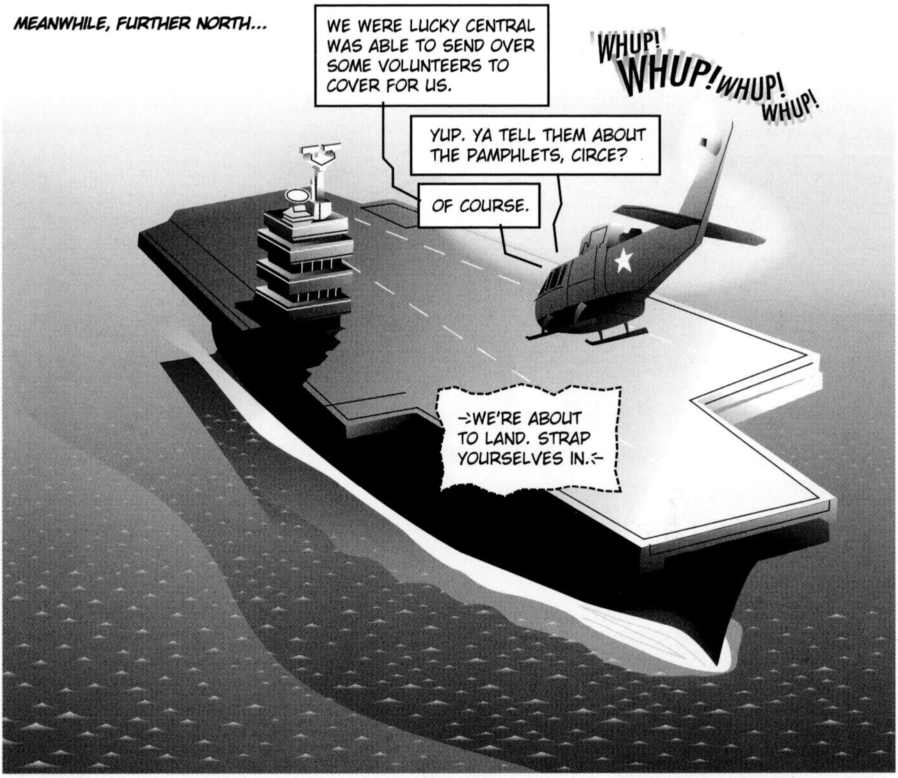
WE WERE LUCKY CENTRAL WAS ABLE TO SEND OVER SOME VOLUNTEERS TO COVER FOR US.
WHUP! WHUP! WHUP! WHUP!
YUP. YA TELL THEM ABOUT THE PAMPHLETS, CIRCE?
OF COURSE.
WE'RE ABOUT TO LAND. STRAP YOURSELVES IN.

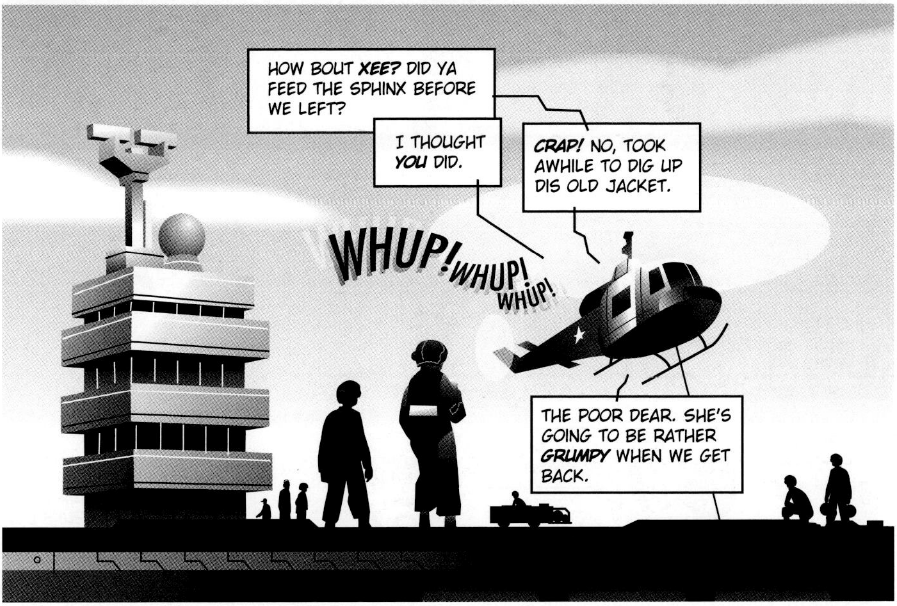
HOW BOUT ***XEE?*** DID YA FEED THE SPHINX BEFORE WE LEFT?
I THOUGHT ***YOU*** DID.
CRAP! NO, TOOK AWHILE TO DIG UP DIS OLD JACKET.
WHUP! WHUP! WHUP!
THE POOR DEAR. SHE'S GOING TO BE RATHER ***GRUMPY*** WHEN WE GET BACK.

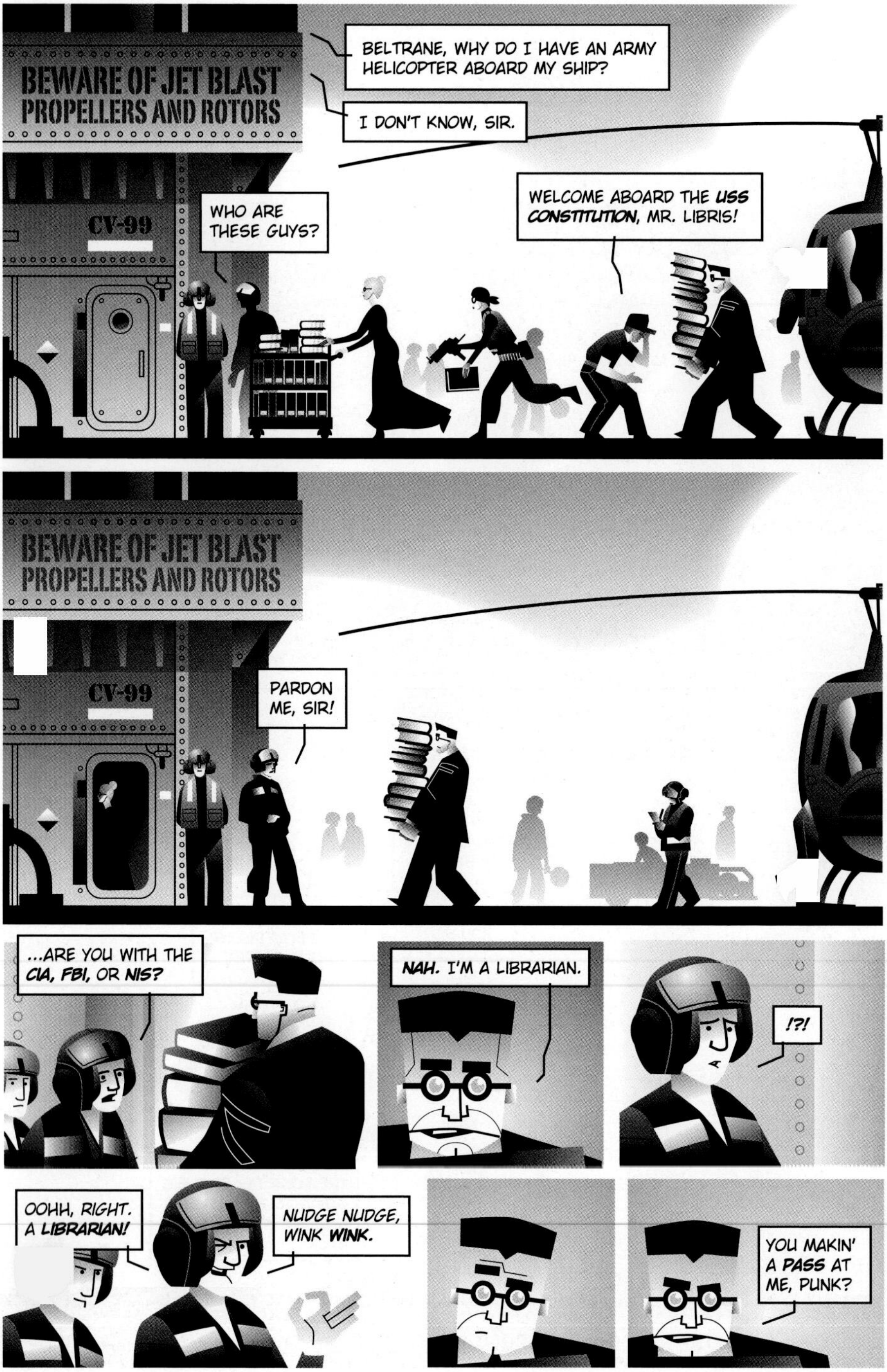
BEWARE OF JET BLAST
PROPELLERS AND ROTORS
BELTRANE, WHY DO I HAVE AN ARMY HELICOPTER ABOARD MY SHIP?
I DON'T KNOW, SIR.
CV-99
WHO ARE THESE GUYS?
WELCOME ABOARD THE USS CONSTITUTION, MR. LIBRIS!
BEWARE OF JET BLAST
PROPELLERS AND ROTORS
CV-99
PARDON ME, SIR!
...ARE YOU WITH THE CIA, FBI, OR NIS?
NAH. I'M A LIBRARIAN.
!?!
OOHH, RIGHT. A LIBRARIAN!
NUDGE NUDGE, WINK WINK.
YOU MAKIN' A PASS AT ME, PUNK?

AH, CAPTAIN QUIGGLY!

THIS WAY, MR. LIBRIS.

ADMIRAL STURGEON IS WAITIN'!

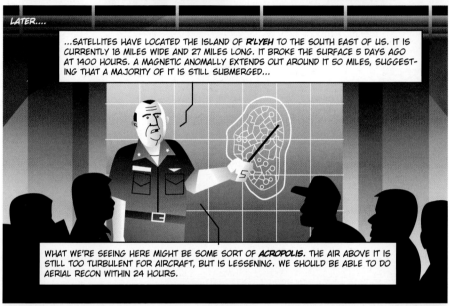

LATER....

...SATELLITES HAVE LOCATED THE ISLAND OF **R'LYEH** TO THE SOUTH EAST OF US. IT IS CURRENTLY 18 MILES WIDE AND 27 MILES LONG. IT BROKE THE SURFACE 5 DAYS AGO AT 1400 HOURS. A MAGNETIC ANOMALY EXTENDS OUT AROUND IT 50 MILES, SUGGESTING THAT A MAJORITY OF IT IS STILL SUBMERGED...

WHAT WE'RE SEEING HERE MIGHT BE SOME SORT OF **ACROPOLIS**. THE AIR ABOVE IT IS STILL TOO TURBULENT FOR AIRCRAFT, BUT IS LESSENING. WE SHOULD BE ABLE TO DO AERIAL RECON WITHIN 24 HOURS.

...THIS MORNING AT 0500 OUR SUBMARINE ESCORT **USS BARACUDA** WAS RAMMED BY AN UNIDENITIFIED OBJECT. OUR HELICOPTER **ASW** PATROLS TRACKED IT AND IDENTIFIED IT AS A 900 YARD LONG, NEON MAUVE **MESONYCHOTEUTHIS HAMILTONI.**

A COLOSSAL ANTARCTIC SQUID. AT 0530 IT DESCENDED BELOW THE THERMOCLINE AND CONTACT WAS **LOST.** THAT SUMS THINGS UP SO FAR, ADMIRAL.

ARE YOU TELLING ME THAT MY BATTLEGROUP IS BEING THREATENED BY A GIGANTIC, **GLOW-IN-THE-DARK** PEOPLE-EATING PURPLE SQUID?

NO, SIR. **MAUVE.**

WE'VE ALSO ANALYZED THE LOW FREQUENCY SOUNDS IT WAS GENERATING. CRYPTOLOGY HAS IDENTIFIED IT AS SLURRED AND HEAVILY ACCENTED SWEDISH. IT'S SAYING SOMETHING ABOUT ENDLESS EATING AND... PLASTER.

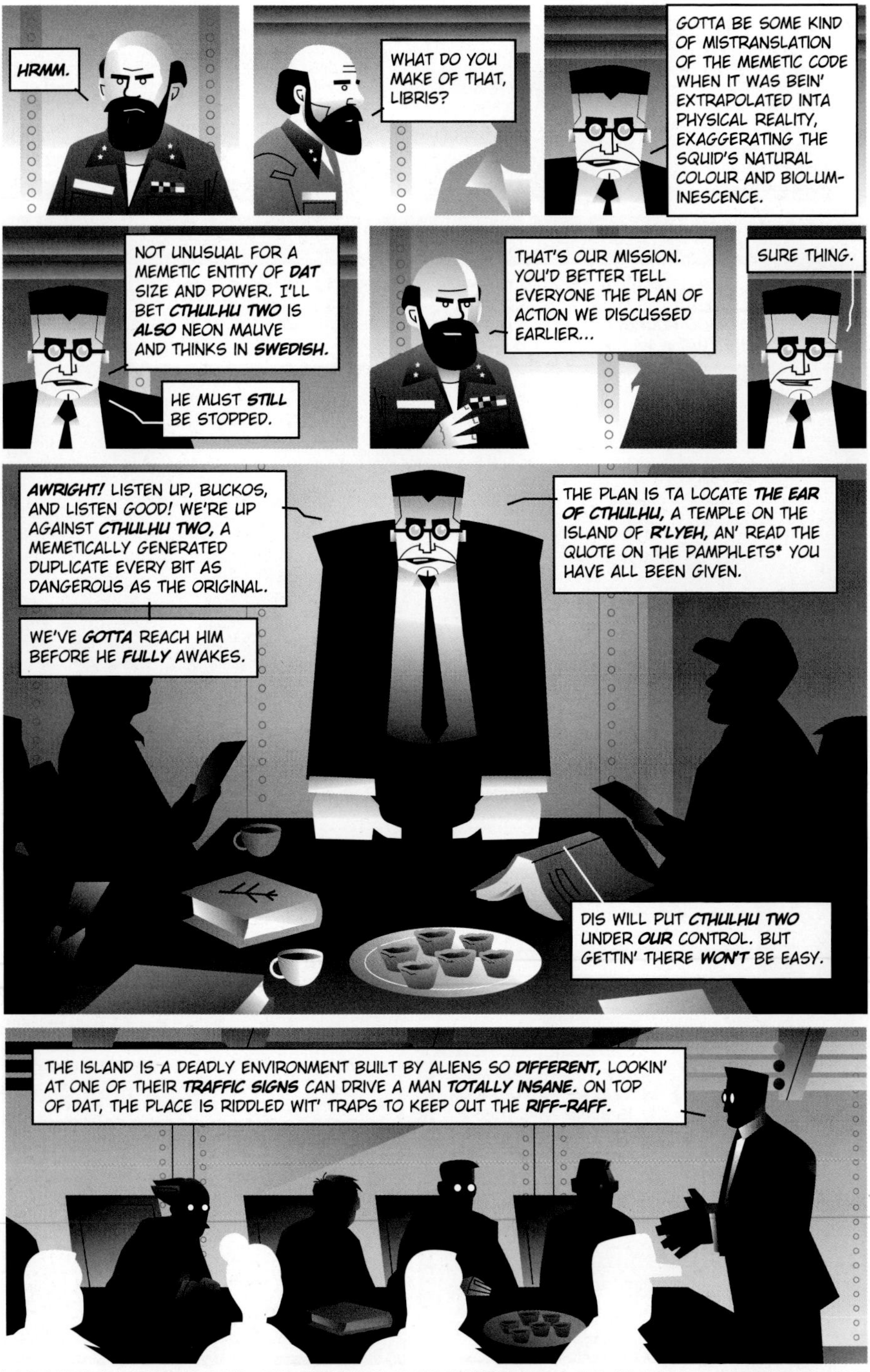
HRMM.
WHAT DO YOU MAKE OF THAT, LIBRIS?
GOTTA BE SOME KIND OF MISTRANSLATION OF THE MEMETIC CODE WHEN IT WAS BEIN' EXTRAPOLATED INTA PHYSICAL REALITY, EXAGGERATING THE SQUID'S NATURAL COLOUR AND BIOLUMINESCENCE.
NOT UNUSUAL FOR A MEMETIC ENTITY OF DAT SIZE AND POWER. I'LL BET CTHULHU TWO IS ALSO NEON MAUVE AND THINKS IN SWEDISH.
HE MUST STILL BE STOPPED.
THAT'S OUR MISSION. YOU'D BETTER TELL EVERYONE THE PLAN OF ACTION WE DISCUSSED EARLIER...
SURE THING.
AWRIGHT! LISTEN UP, BUCKOS, AND LISTEN GOOD! WE'RE UP AGAINST CTHULHU TWO, A MEMETICALLY GENERATED DUPLICATE EVERY BIT AS DANGEROUS AS THE ORIGINAL.
WE'VE GOTTA REACH HIM BEFORE HE FULLY AWAKES.
THE PLAN IS TA LOCATE THE EAR OF CTHULHU, A TEMPLE ON THE ISLAND OF R'LYEH, AN' READ THE QUOTE ON THE PAMPHLETS* YOU HAVE ALL BEEN GIVEN.
DIS WILL PUT CTHULHU TWO UNDER OUR CONTROL. BUT GETTIN' THERE WON'T BE EASY.
THE ISLAND IS A DEADLY ENVIRONMENT BUILT BY ALIENS SO DIFFERENT, LOOKIN' AT ONE OF THEIR TRAFFIC SIGNS CAN DRIVE A MAN TOTALLY INSANE. ON TOP OF DAT, THE PLACE IS RIDDLED WIT' TRAPS TO KEEP OUT THE RIFF-RAFF.

* THE PAMPHLET OF UTTERABLE EVIL, OTHERWISE KNOWN AS THE ***OFTA'WUP'UF-OOK-CHAL,*** ALLEGEDLY THE GREATEST AND MOST INTENSE WORK OF THE LUNATIC ONTARIAN ***LOTHAR VON DURGELSMEED,*** WHO WAS A DISCIPLE OF CTHULHU IN THE LATE 1930S, UNTIL HE BECAME AN IAGIST IN 1941, AND FINALLY AN ART DIRECTOR IN 1952. HE DIED PENNILESS SURROUNDED BY HORDES OF ANGRY PICAS, WHO STRIPPED THE FLESH FROM HIS BODY BEFORE THE CORONER COULD ARRIVE. --BARE FACTS BARRY

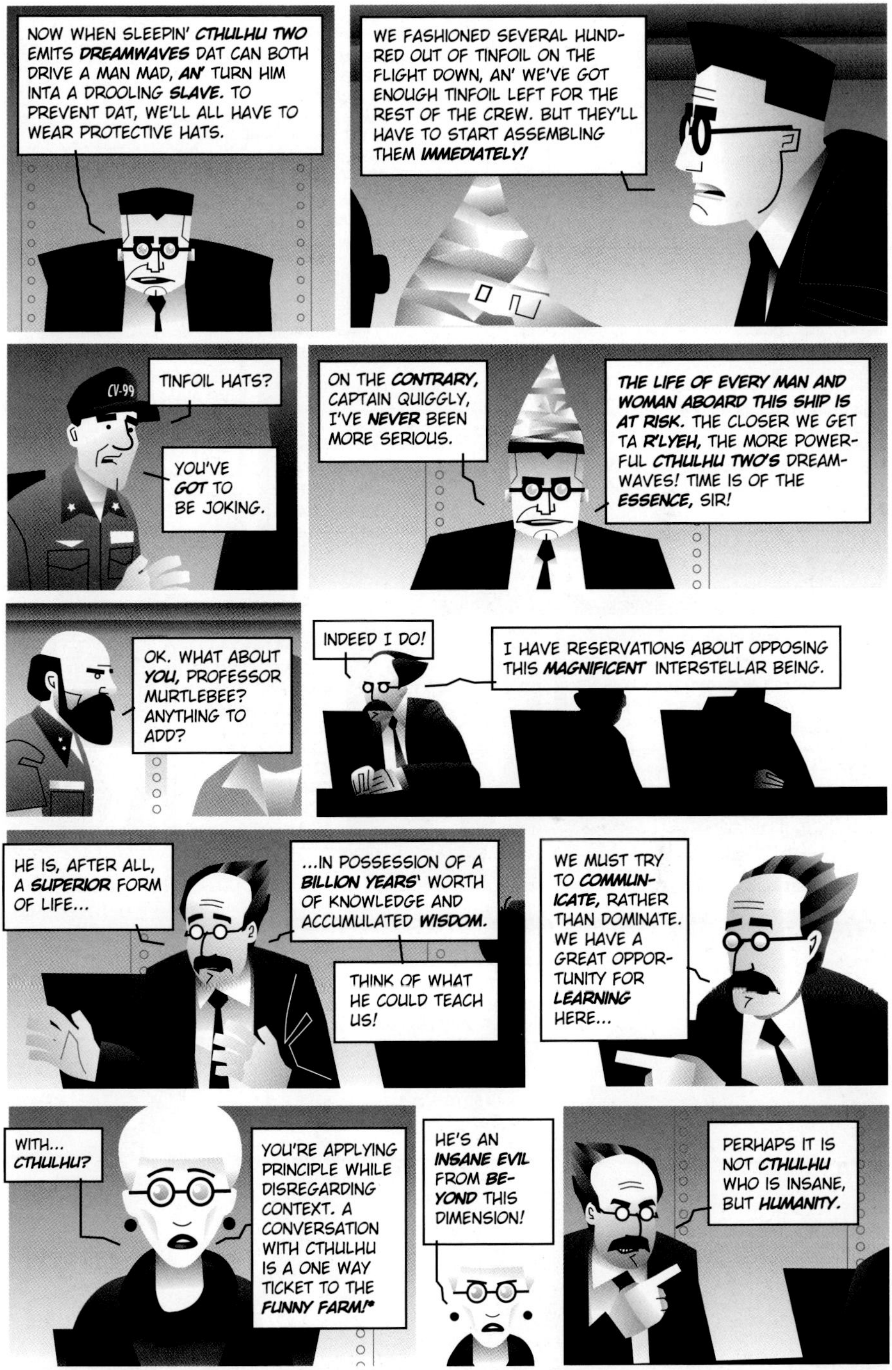
NOW WHEN SLEEPIN' CTHULHU TWO EMITS DREAMWAVES DAT CAN BOTH DRIVE A MAN MAD, AN' TURN HIM INTA A DROOLING SLAVE. TO PREVENT DAT, WE'LL ALL HAVE TO WEAR PROTECTIVE HATS.
WE FASHIONED SEVERAL HUNDRED OUT OF TINFOIL ON THE FLIGHT DOWN, AN' WE'VE GOT ENOUGH TINFOIL LEFT FOR THE REST OF THE CREW. BUT THEY'LL HAVE TO START ASSEMBLING THEM IMMEDIATELY!
CV-99
TINFOIL HATS?
YOU'VE GOT TO BE JOKING.
ON THE CONTRARY, CAPTAIN QUIGGLY, I'VE NEVER BEEN MORE SERIOUS.
THE LIFE OF EVERY MAN AND WOMAN ABOARD THIS SHIP IS AT RISK. THE CLOSER WE GET TA R'LYEH, THE MORE POWERFUL CTHULHU TWO'S DREAMWAVES! TIME IS OF THE ESSENCE, SIR!
OK. WHAT ABOUT YOU, PROFESSOR MURTLEBEE? ANYTHING TO ADD?
INDEED I DO!
I HAVE RESERVATIONS ABOUT OPPOSING THIS MAGNIFICENT INTERSTELLAR BEING.
HE IS, AFTER ALL, A SUPERIOR FORM OF LIFE...
...IN POSSESSION OF A BILLION YEARS' WORTH OF KNOWLEDGE AND ACCUMULATED WISDOM.
THINK OF WHAT HE COULD TEACH US!
WE MUST TRY TO COMMUNICATE, RATHER THAN DOMINATE. WE HAVE A GREAT OPPORTUNITY FOR LEARNING HERE...
WITH... CTHULHU?
YOU'RE APPLYING PRINCIPLE WHILE DISREGARDING CONTEXT. A CONVERSATION WITH CTHULHU IS A ONE WAY TICKET TO THE FUNNY FARM!*
HE'S AN INSANE EVIL FROM BEYOND THIS DIMENSION!
PERHAPS IT IS NOT CTHULHU WHO IS INSANE, BUT HUMANITY.

*SEE *'MY DINNER WITH CTHULHU, THE MIND DEVOURING HORROR FROM BEYOND SPACE'* BY STROZZI THE MAD. -- BARRY

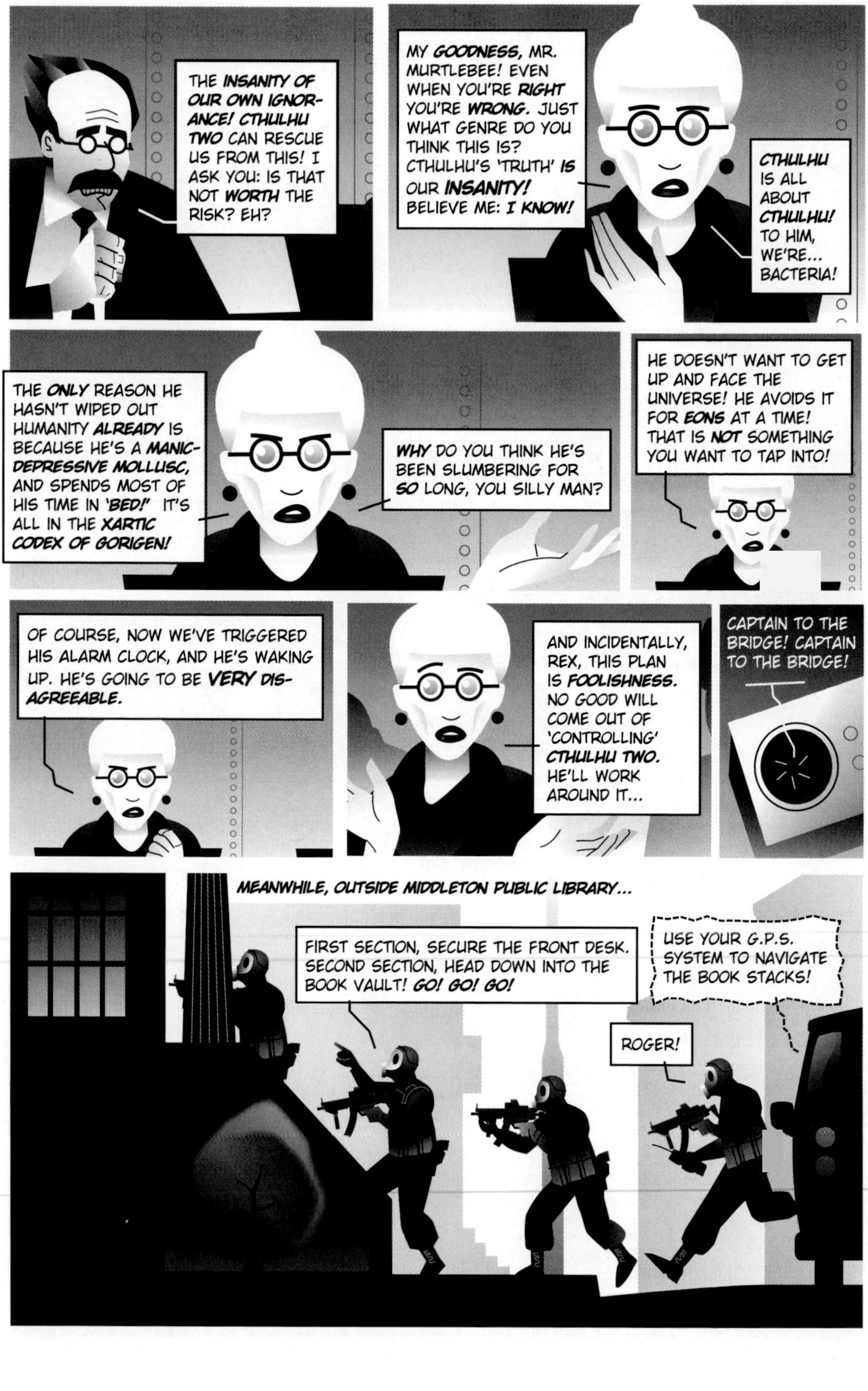
THE INSANITY OF OUR OWN IGNORANCE! CTHULHU TWO CAN RESCUE US FROM THIS! I ASK YOU: IS THAT NOT WORTH THE RISK? EH?
MY GOODNESS, MR. MURTLEBEE! EVEN WHEN YOU'RE RIGHT YOU'RE WRONG. JUST WHAT GENRE DO YOU THINK THIS IS? CTHULHU'S 'TRUTH' IS OUR INSANITY! BELIEVE ME: I KNOW!
CTHULHU IS ALL ABOUT CTHULHU! TO HIM, WE'RE... BACTERIA!
THE ONLY REASON HE HASN'T WIPED OUT HUMANITY ALREADY IS BECAUSE HE'S A MANIC-DEPRESSIVE MOLLUSC, AND SPENDS MOST OF HIS TIME IN 'BED!' IT'S ALL IN THE XARTIC CODEX OF GORIGEN!
WHY DO YOU THINK HE'S BEEN SLUMBERING FOR SO LONG, YOU SILLY MAN?
HE DOESN'T WANT TO GET UP AND FACE THE UNIVERSE! HE AVOIDS IT FOR EONS AT A TIME! THAT IS NOT SOMETHING YOU WANT TO TAP INTO!
OF COURSE, NOW WE'VE TRIGGERED HIS ALARM CLOCK, AND HE'S WAKING UP. HE'S GOING TO BE VERY DISAGREEABLE.
AND INCIDENTALLY, REX, THIS PLAN IS FOOLISHNESS. NO GOOD WILL COME OUT OF 'CONTROLLING' CTHULHU TWO. HE'LL WORK AROUND IT...
CAPTAIN TO THE BRIDGE! CAPTAIN TO THE BRIDGE!
MEANWHILE, OUTSIDE MIDDLETON PUBLIC LIBRARY...
FIRST SECTION, SECURE THE FRONT DESK. SECOND SECTION, HEAD DOWN INTO THE BOOK VAULT! GO! GO! GO!
USE YOUR G.P.S. SYSTEM TO NAVIGATE THE BOOK STACKS!
ROGER!

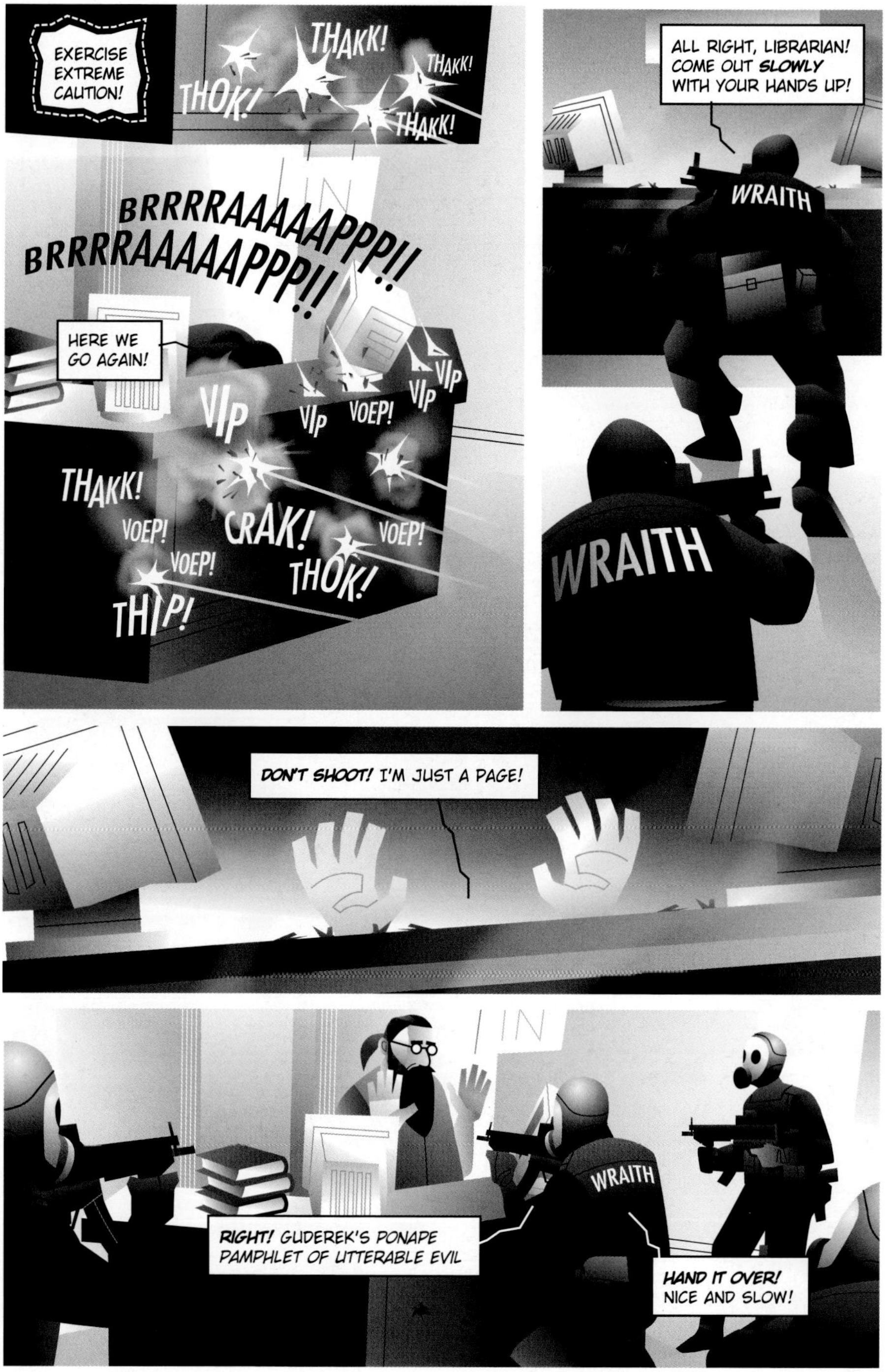
EXERCISE EXTREME CAUTION!
THAKK!
THAKK!
THOK!
THAKK!
BRRRRAAAAAAPPP!!
BRRRRAAAAAAPPP!!
HERE WE GO AGAIN!
VIP
VIP
VOEP!
VIP
VIP
THAKK!
VOEP!
CRAK!
VOEP!
VOEP!
THOK!
THIP!
ALL RIGHT, LIBRARIAN! COME OUT SLOWLY WITH YOUR HANDS UP!
WRAITH
WRAITH
DON'T SHOOT! I'M JUST A PAGE!
WRAITH
RIGHT! GUDEREK'S PONAPE PAMPHLET OF UTTERABLE EVIL
HAND IT OVER! NICE AND SLOW!

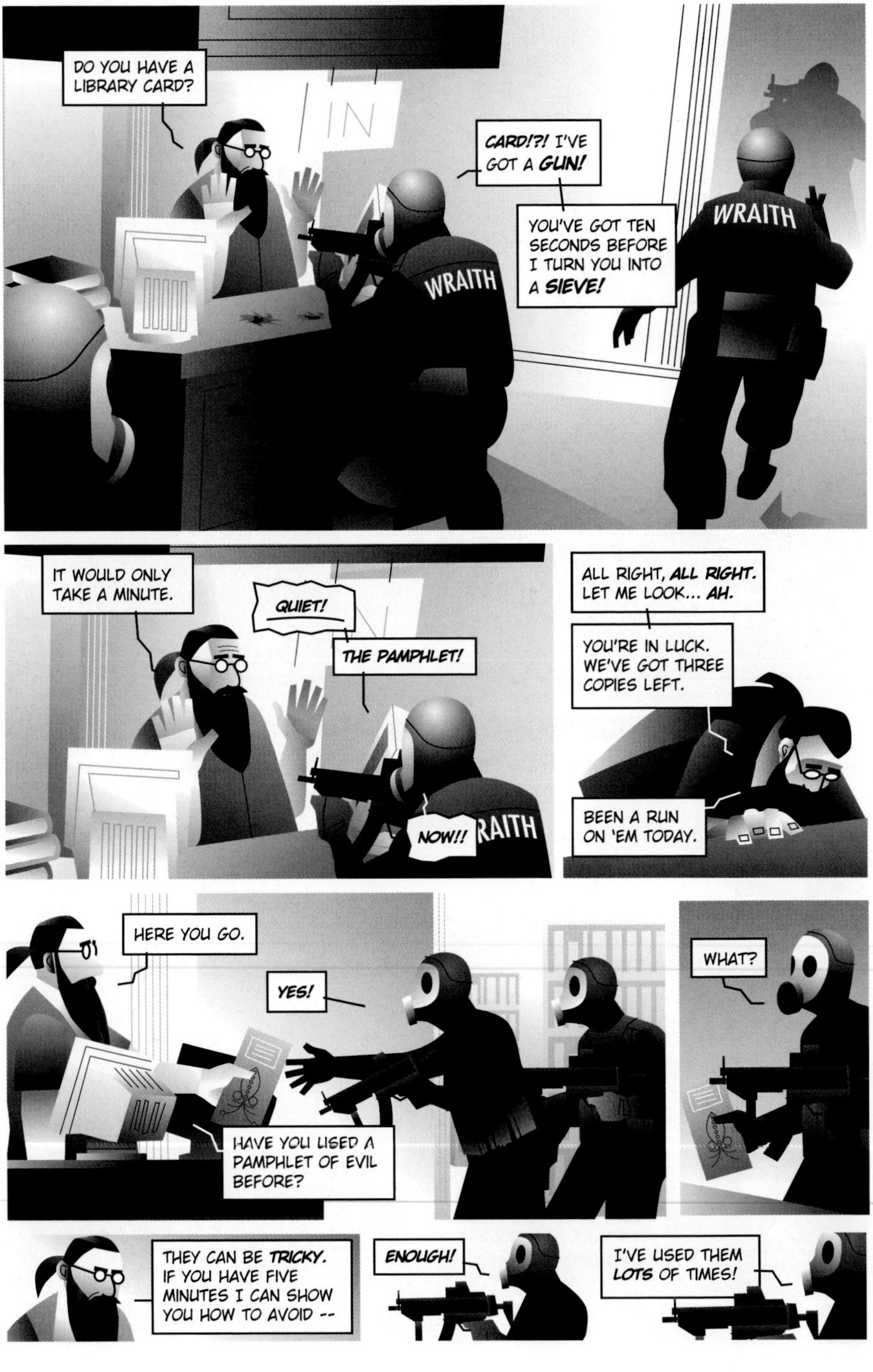

DO YOU HAVE A LIBRARY CARD?
IN
CARD!?! I'VE GOT A GUN!
YOU'VE GOT TEN SECONDS BEFORE I TURN YOU INTO A SIEVE!
WRAITH
WRAITH
IT WOULD ONLY TAKE A MINUTE.
QUIET!
THE PAMPHLET!
NOW!!
RAITH
ALL RIGHT, ALL RIGHT. LET ME LOOK... AH.
YOU'RE IN LUCK. WE'VE GOT THREE COPIES LEFT.
BEEN A RUN ON 'EM TODAY.
HERE YOU GO.
YES!
HAVE YOU USED A PAMPHLET OF EVIL BEFORE?
WHAT?
THEY CAN BE TRICKY. IF YOU HAVE FIVE MINUTES I CAN SHOW YOU HOW TO AVOID --
ENOUGH!
I'VE USED THEM LOTS OF TIMES!

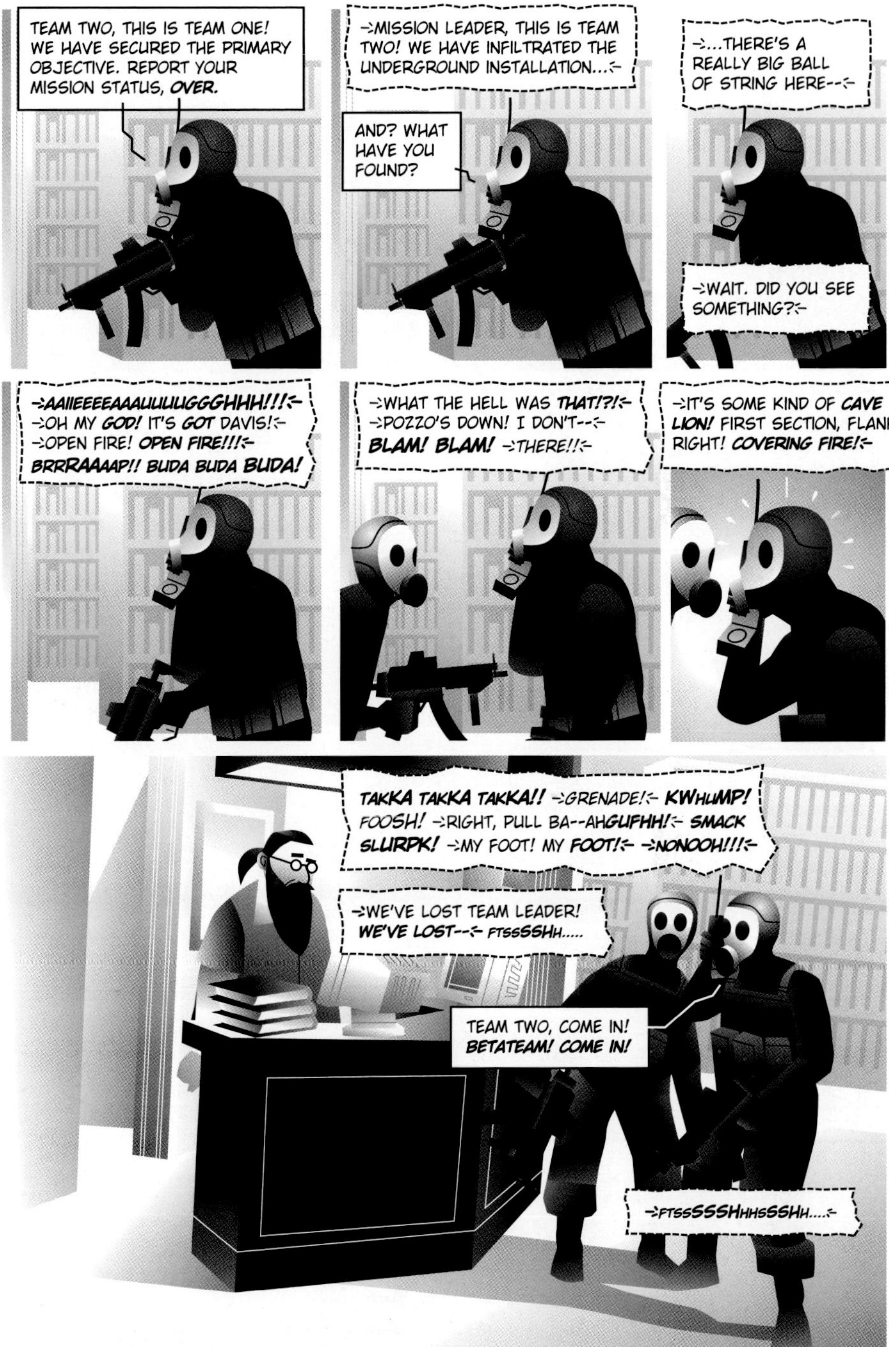
TEAM TWO, THIS IS TEAM ONE! WE HAVE SECURED THE PRIMARY OBJECTIVE. REPORT YOUR MISSION STATUS, *OVER.*
MISSION LEADER, THIS IS TEAM TWO! WE HAVE INFILTRATED THE UNDERGROUND INSTALLATION...
AND? WHAT HAVE YOU FOUND?
...THERE'S A REALLY BIG BALL OF STRING HERE--
WAIT. DID YOU SEE SOMETHING?
AAIIEEEEAAAUUUUUGGGHHH!!! OH MY *GOD!* IT'S *GOT* DAVIS! OPEN FIRE! *OPEN FIRE!!!* *BRRRAAAAP!! BUDA BUDA BUDA!*
WHAT THE HELL WAS *THAT!?!* POZZO'S DOWN! I DON'T-- *BLAM! BLAM!* THERE!!
IT'S SOME KIND OF *CAVE LION!* FIRST SECTION, FLANK RIGHT! *COVERING FIRE!*
TAKKA TAKKA TAKKA!! GRENADE! *KWHUMP!* *FOOSH!* RIGHT, PULL BA--AH*GUFHH!* *SMACK SLURPK!* MY FOOT! MY *FOOT!* *NONOOH!!!*
WE'VE LOST TEAM LEADER! *WE'VE LOST--* FTSSSSHH.....
TEAM TWO, COME IN! *BETATEAM! COME IN!*
FTSSSSSHHHSSSHH....

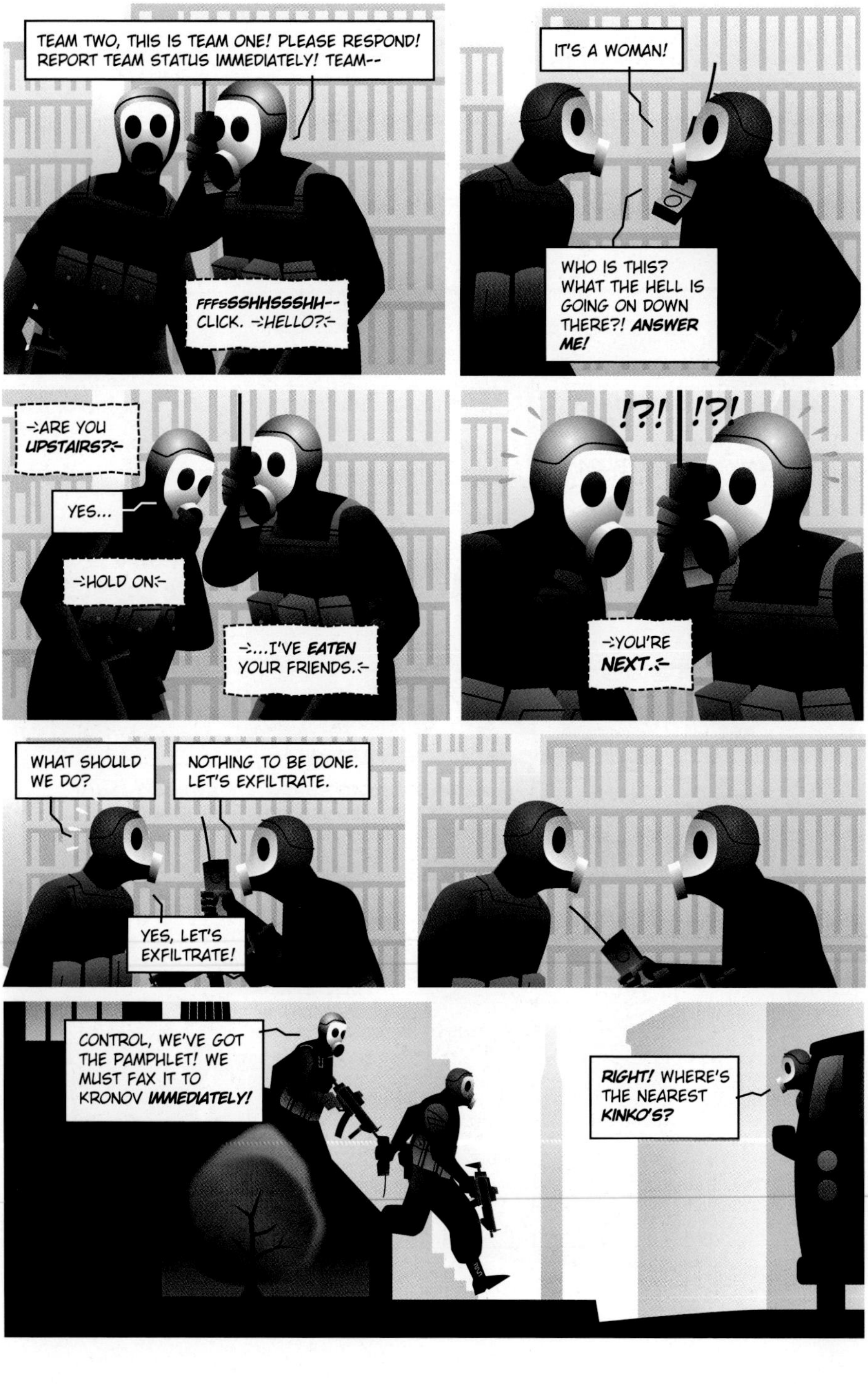
TEAM TWO, THIS IS TEAM ONE! PLEASE RESPOND! REPORT TEAM STATUS IMMEDIATELY! TEAM--
FFFSSSHHSSSHH-- CLICK. HELLO?
IT'S A WOMAN!
WHO IS THIS? WHAT THE HELL IS GOING ON DOWN THERE?! ANSWER ME!
ARE YOU UPSTAIRS?
YES...
HOLD ON
...I'VE EATEN YOUR FRIENDS.
!?! !?!
YOU'RE NEXT.
WHAT SHOULD WE DO?
NOTHING TO BE DONE. LET'S EXFILTRATE.
YES, LET'S EXFILTRATE!
CONTROL, WE'VE GOT THE PAMPHLET! WE MUST FAX IT TO KRONOV IMMEDIATELY!
RIGHT! WHERE'S THE NEAREST KINKO'S?

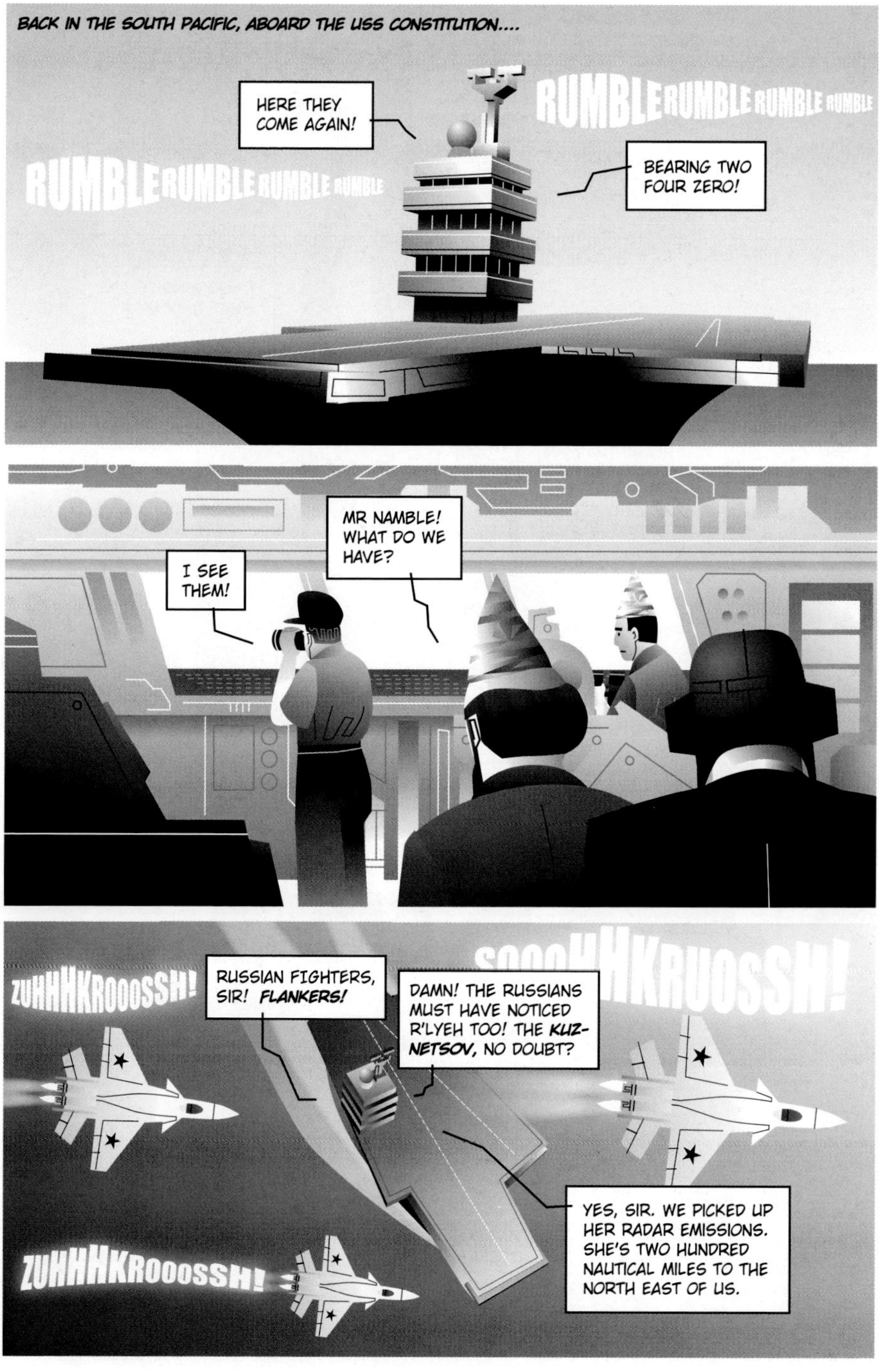
BACK IN THE SOUTH PACIFIC, ABOARD THE USS CONSTITUTION....
HERE THEY COME AGAIN!
RUMBLE RUMBLE RUMBLE RUMBLE
RUMBLE RUMBLE RUMBLE RUMBLE
BEARING TWO FOUR ZERO!
MR NAMBLE! WHAT DO WE HAVE?
I SEE THEM!
ZUHHHKROOOSSH!
RUSSIAN FIGHTERS, SIR! FLANKERS!
DAMN! THE RUSSIANS MUST HAVE NOTICED R'LYEH TOO! THE KUZNETSOV, NO DOUBT?
SOOOHHKRUOSSH!
YES, SIR. WE PICKED UP HER RADAR EMISSIONS. SHE'S TWO HUNDRED NAUTICAL MILES TO THE NORTH EAST OF US.
ZUHHHKROOOSSH!

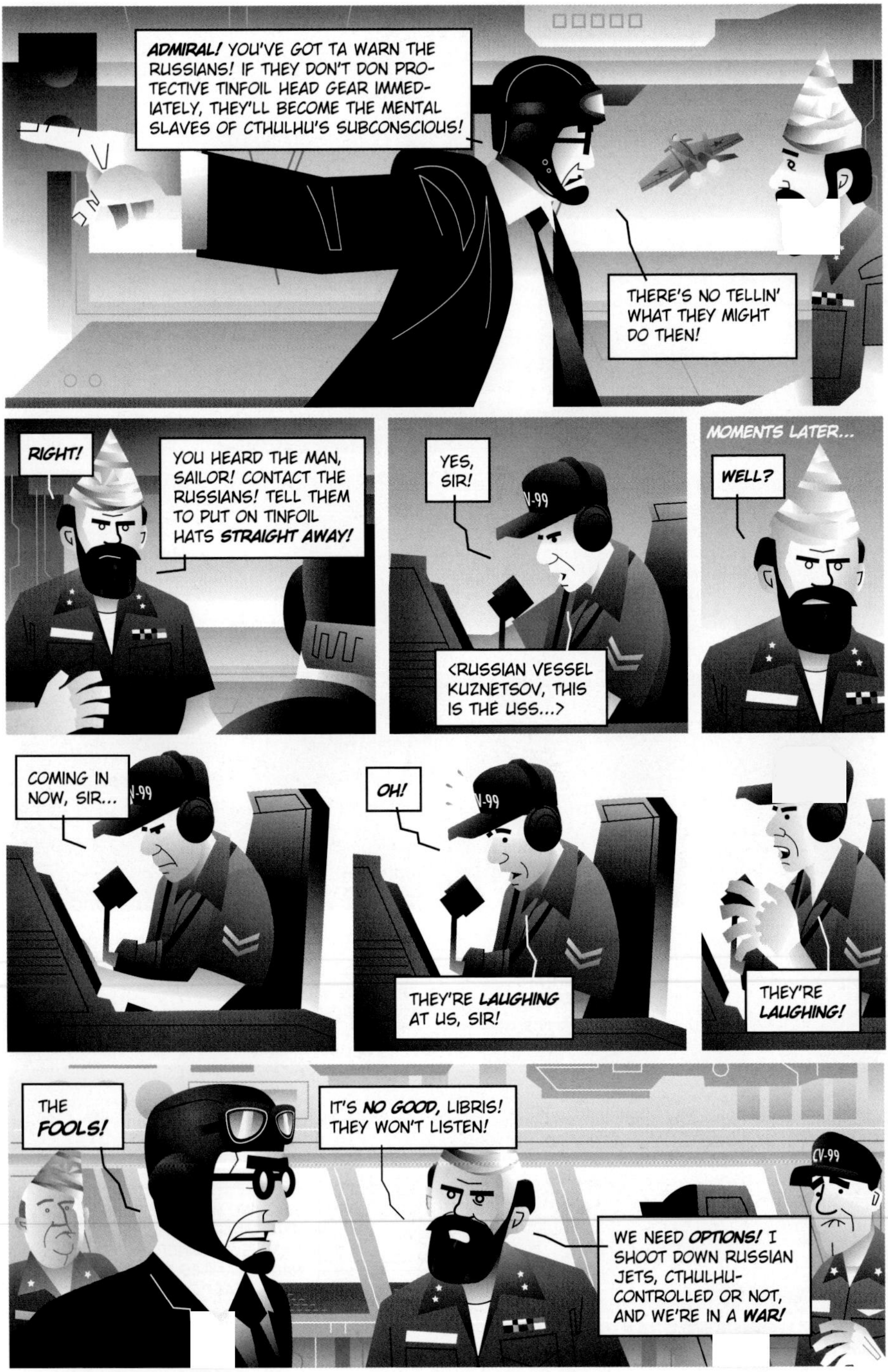
ADMIRAL! YOU'VE GOT TA WARN THE RUSSIANS! IF THEY DON'T DON PROTECTIVE TINFOIL HEAD GEAR IMMEDIATELY, THEY'LL BECOME THE MENTAL SLAVES OF CTHULHU'S SUBCONSCIOUS!
THERE'S NO TELLIN' WHAT THEY MIGHT DO THEN!
RIGHT!
YOU HEARD THE MAN, SAILOR! CONTACT THE RUSSIANS! TELL THEM TO PUT ON TINFOIL HATS STRAIGHT AWAY!
YES, SIR!
<RUSSIAN VESSEL KUZNETSOV, THIS IS THE USS...>
MOMENTS LATER...
WELL?
COMING IN NOW, SIR...
OH!
THEY'RE LAUGHING AT US, SIR!
THEY'RE LAUGHING!
THE FOOLS!
IT'S NO GOOD, LIBRIS! THEY WON'T LISTEN!
WE NEED OPTIONS! I SHOOT DOWN RUSSIAN JETS, CTHULHU-CONTROLLED OR NOT, AND WE'RE IN A WAR!
CV-99

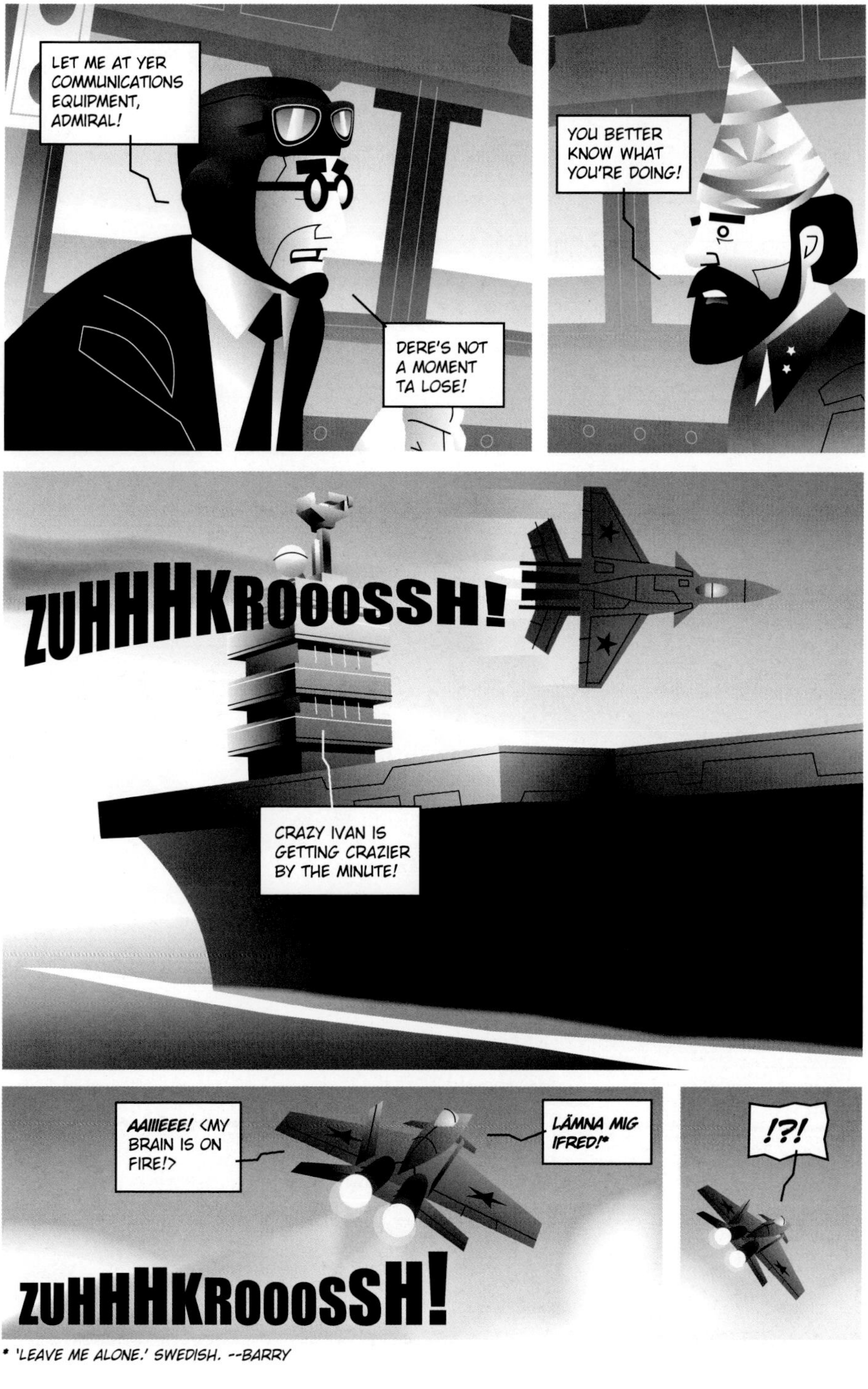
LET ME AT YER COMMUNICATIONS EQUIPMENT, ADMIRAL!
DERE'S NOT A MOMENT TA LOSE!
YOU BETTER KNOW WHAT YOU'RE DOING!
ZUHHHKROOOSSH!
CRAZY IVAN IS GETTING CRAZIER BY THE MINUTE!
AAIIIEEE! <MY BRAIN IS ON FIRE!>
LÄMNA MIG IFRED!*
ZUHHHKROOOSSH!
!?!

* 'LEAVE ME ALONE.' SWEDISH. --BARRY

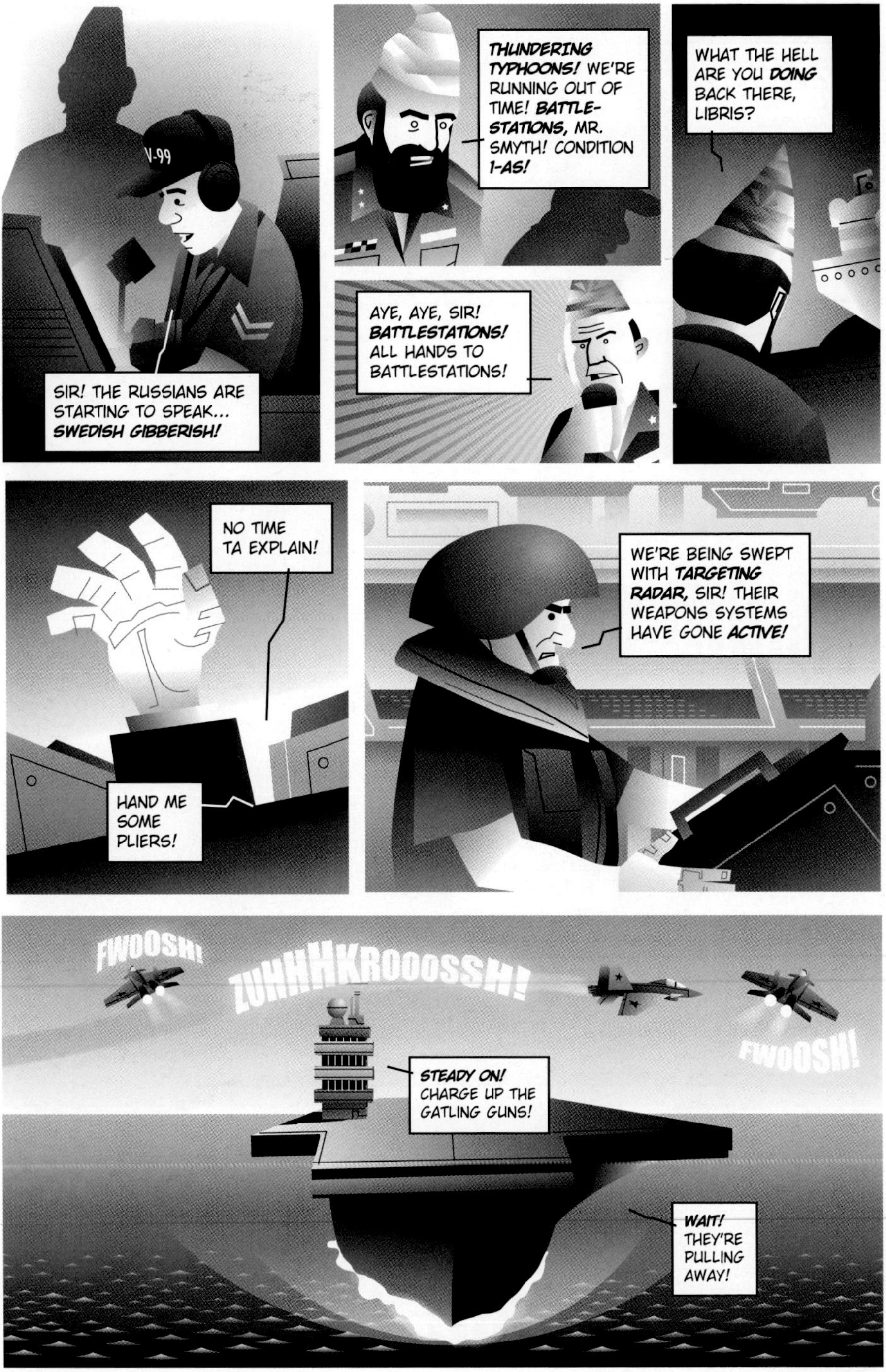
V-99
SIR! THE RUSSIANS ARE STARTING TO SPEAK... SWEDISH GIBBERISH!
THUNDERING TYPHOONS! WE'RE RUNNING OUT OF TIME! BATTLE-STATIONS, MR. SMYTH! CONDITION 1-AS!
AYE, AYE, SIR! BATTLESTATIONS! ALL HANDS TO BATTLESTATIONS!
WHAT THE HELL ARE YOU DOING BACK THERE, LIBRIS?
NO TIME TA EXPLAIN!
HAND ME SOME PLIERS!
WE'RE BEING SWEPT WITH TARGETING RADAR, SIR! THEIR WEAPONS SYSTEMS HAVE GONE ACTIVE!
FWOOSH!
ZUHHHKROOOOSSH!
FWOOSH!
STEADY ON! CHARGE UP THE GATLING GUNS!
WAIT! THEY'RE PULLING AWAY!

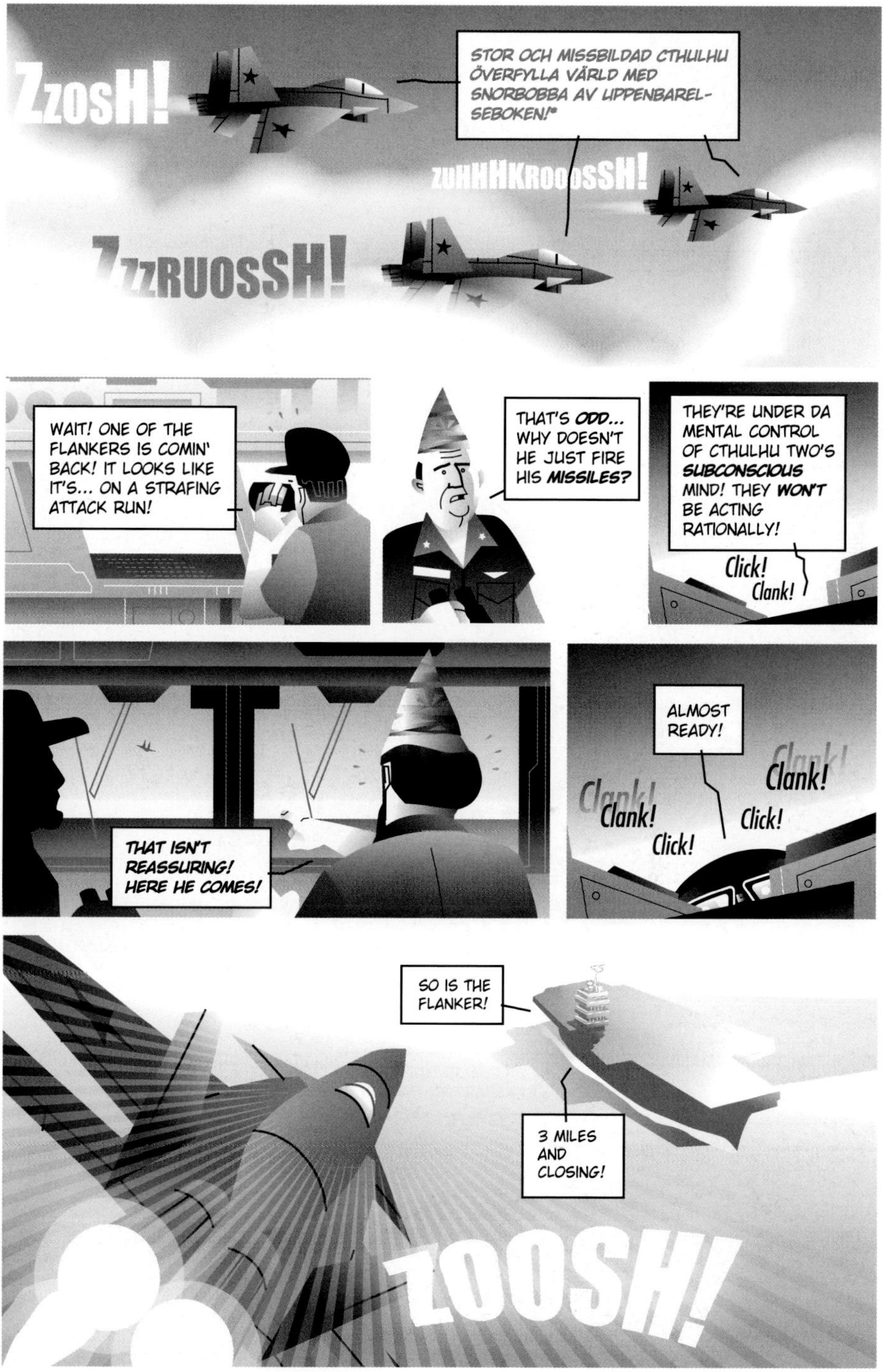
ZzosH!
STOR OCH MISSBILDAD CTHULHU ÖVERFYLLA VÄRLD MED SNORBOBBA AV UPPENBAREL-SEBOKEN!*
ZUHHHKROOOSSH!
ZzzRUOSSH!
WAIT! ONE OF THE FLANKERS IS COMIN' BACK! IT LOOKS LIKE IT'S... ON A STRAFING ATTACK RUN!
THAT'S ODD... WHY DOESN'T HE JUST FIRE HIS MISSILES?
THEY'RE UNDER DA MENTAL CONTROL OF CTHULHU TWO'S SUBCONSCIOUS MIND! THEY WON'T BE ACTING RATIONALLY!
Click!
Clank!
THAT ISN'T REASSURING! HERE HE COMES!
ALMOST READY!
Clank!
Clank!
Click!
Clank!
Click!
Clank!
SO IS THE FLANKER!
3 MILES AND CLOSING!
ZOOSH!

* NONSENSE IN MASSACRED SWEDISH. -- BARRY

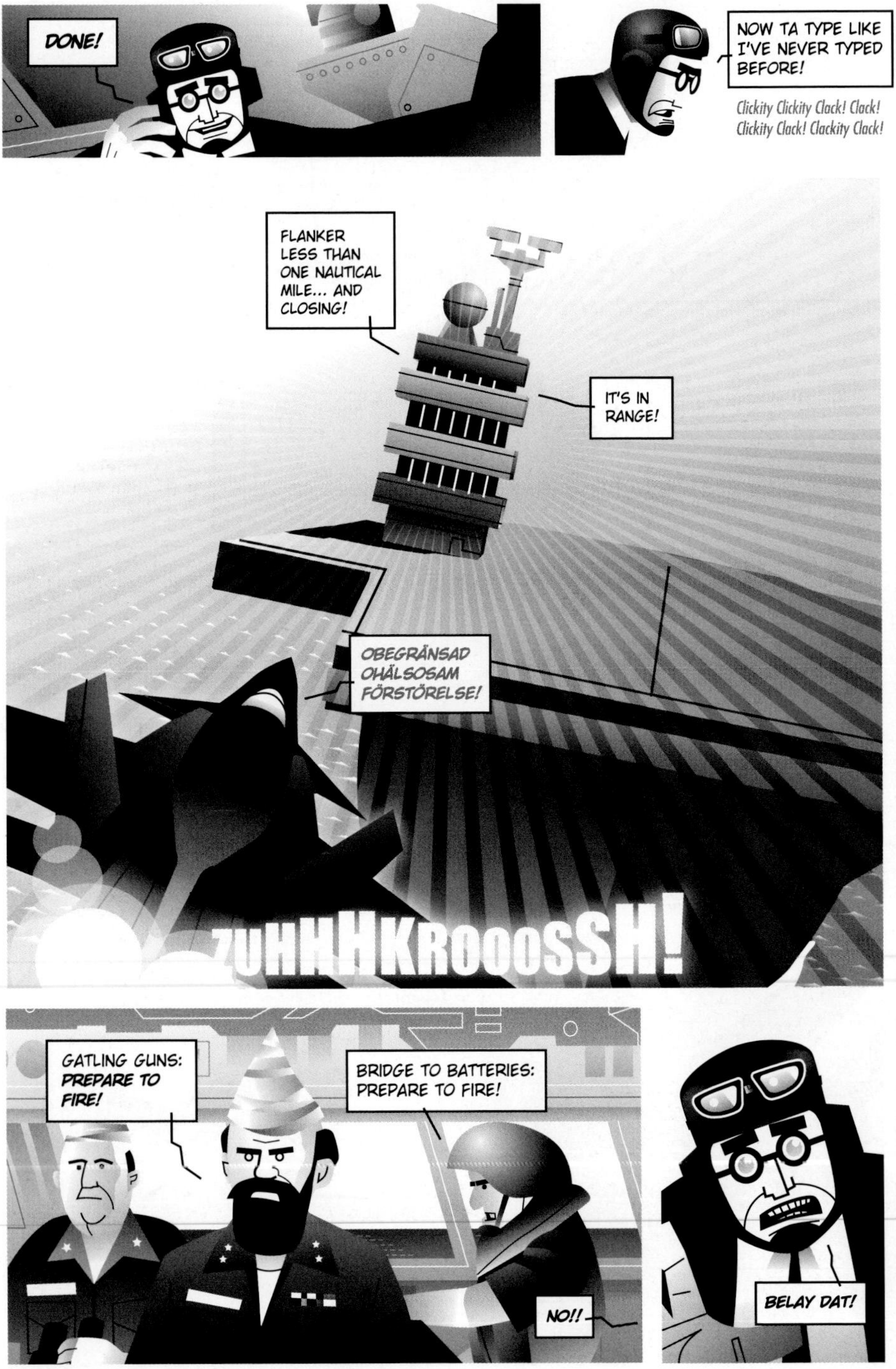
DONE!
NOW TA TYPE LIKE I'VE NEVER TYPED BEFORE!
Clickity Clickity Clack! Clack! Clickity Clack! Clackity Clack!
FLANKER LESS THAN ONE NAUTICAL MILE... AND CLOSING!
IT'S IN RANGE!
OBEGRÄNSAD OHÄLSOSAM FÖRSTÖRELSE!
ZUHHHKROOOSSH!
GATLING GUNS: PREPARE TO FIRE!
BRIDGE TO BATTERIES: PREPARE TO FIRE!
NO!!
BELAY DAT!

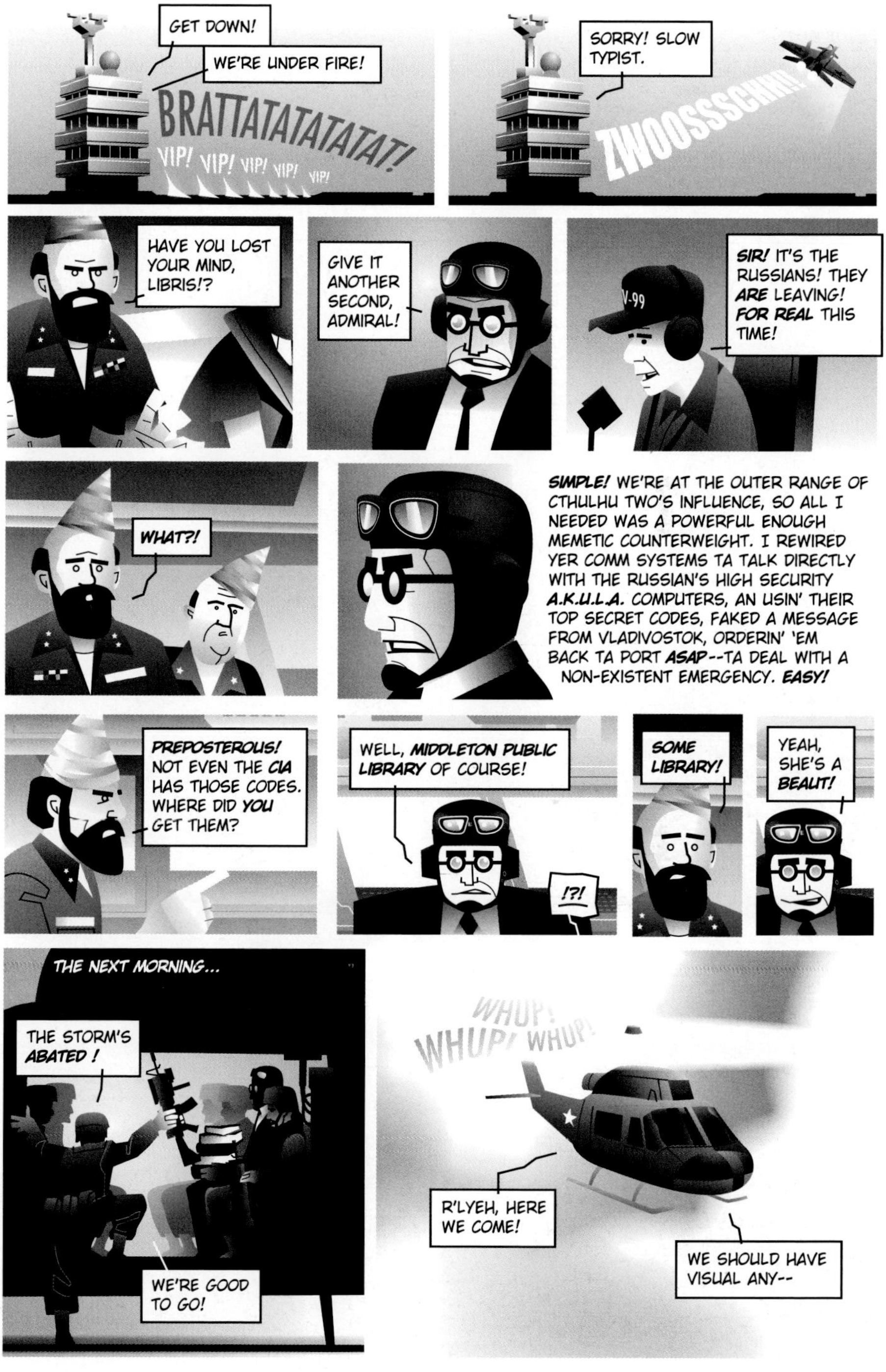
GET DOWN!
WE'RE UNDER FIRE!
BRATTATATATATAT!
VIP! VIP! VIP! VIP! VIP!
SORRY! SLOW TYPIST.
ZWOOSSSCHH!!
HAVE YOU LOST YOUR MIND, LIBRIS!?
GIVE IT ANOTHER SECOND, ADMIRAL!
V-99
SIR! IT'S THE RUSSIANS! THEY ARE LEAVING! FOR REAL THIS TIME!
WHAT?!
SIMPLE! WE'RE AT THE OUTER RANGE OF CTHULHU TWO'S INFLUENCE, SO ALL I NEEDED WAS A POWERFUL ENOUGH MEMETIC COUNTERWEIGHT. I REWIRED YER COMM SYSTEMS TA TALK DIRECTLY WITH THE RUSSIAN'S HIGH SECURITY A.K.U.L.A. COMPUTERS, AN USIN' THEIR TOP SECRET CODES, FAKED A MESSAGE FROM VLADIVOSTOK, ORDERIN' 'EM BACK TA PORT ASAP--TA DEAL WITH A NON-EXISTENT EMERGENCY. EASY!
PREPOSTEROUS! NOT EVEN THE CIA HAS THOSE CODES. WHERE DID YOU GET THEM?
WELL, MIDDLETON PUBLIC LIBRARY OF COURSE!
!?!
SOME LIBRARY!
YEAH, SHE'S A BEAUT!
THE NEXT MORNING...
THE STORM'S ABATED !
WE'RE GOOD TO GO!
WHUP! WHUP! WHUP!
R'LYEH, HERE WE COME!
WE SHOULD HAVE VISUAL ANY--

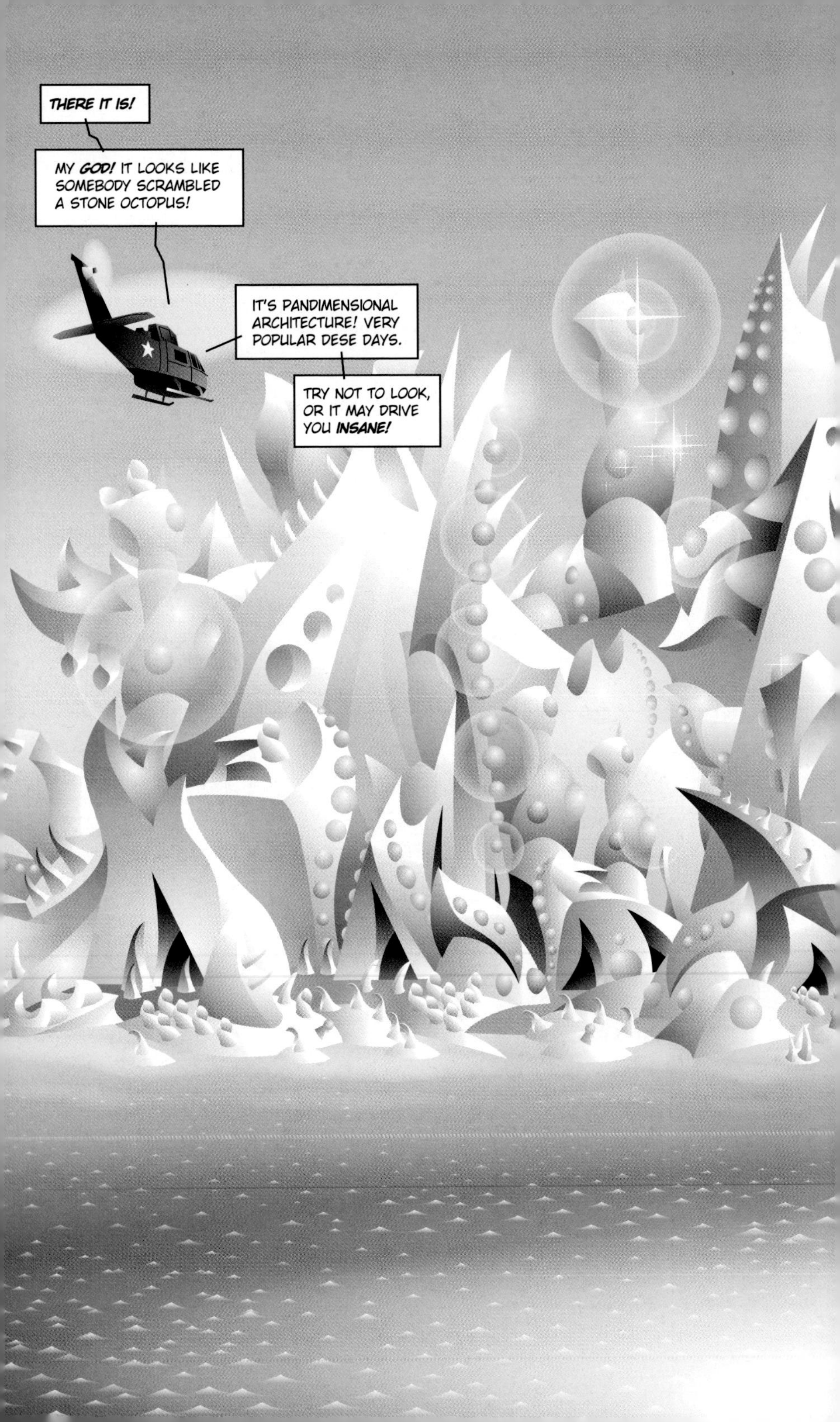
THERE IT IS!
MY GOD! IT LOOKS LIKE SOMEBODY SCRAMBLED A STONE OCTOPUS!
IT'S PANDIMENSIONAL ARCHITECTURE! VERY POPULAR DESE DAYS.
TRY NOT TO LOOK, OR IT MAY DRIVE YOU INSANE!

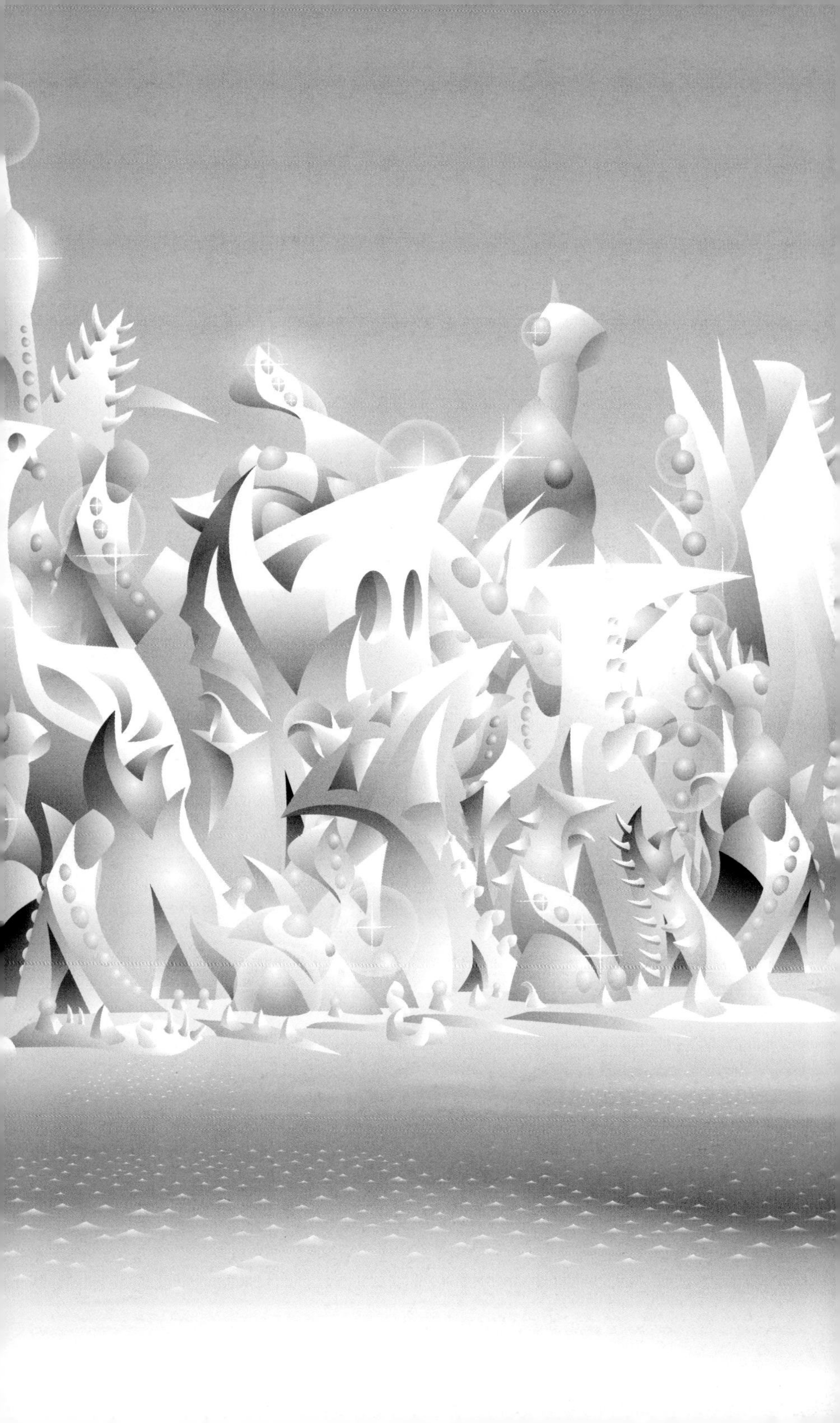

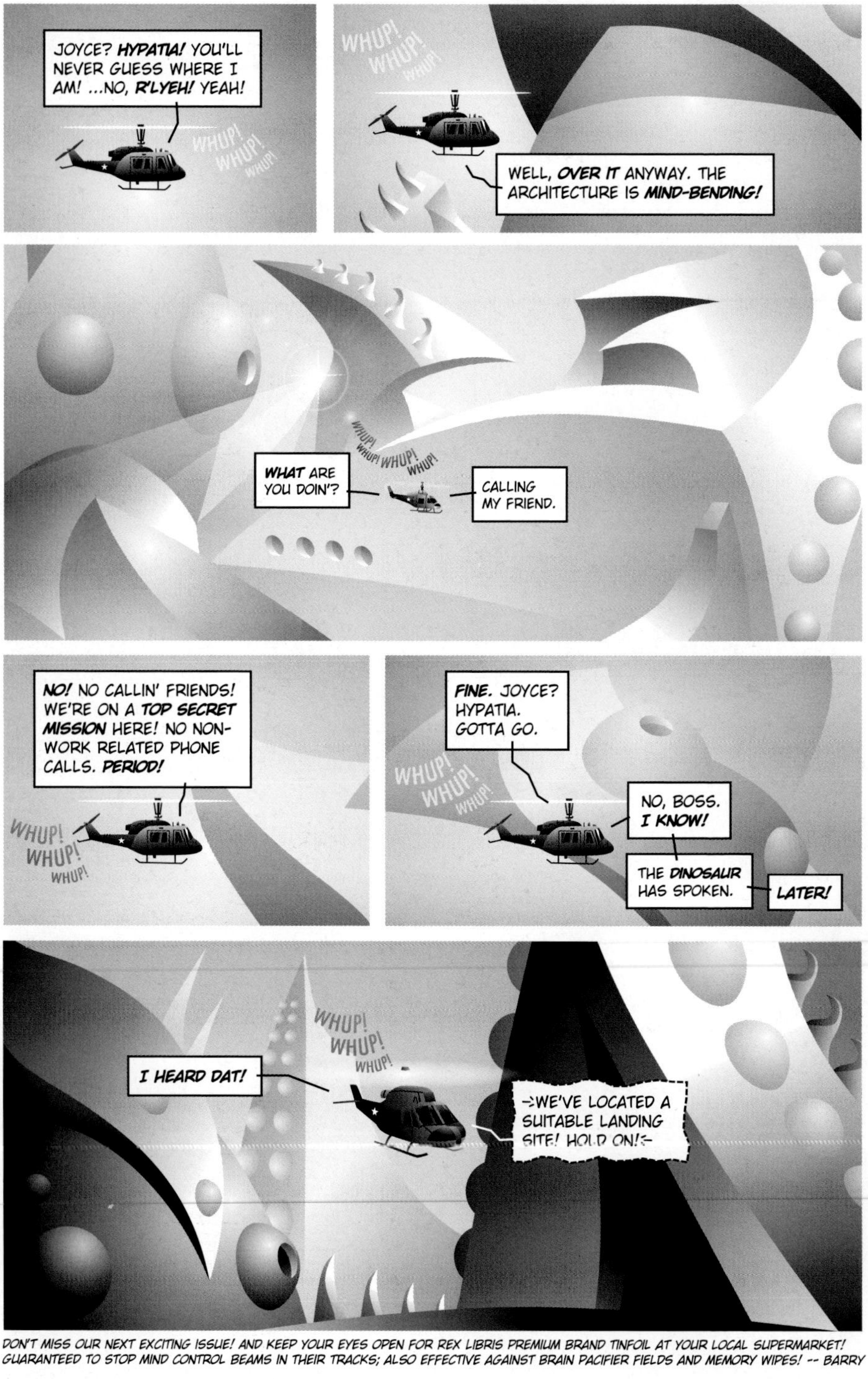
JOYCE? HYPATIA! YOU'LL NEVER GUESS WHERE I AM! ...NO, R'LYEH! YEAH!
WHUP! WHUP! WHUP!
WHUP! WHUP! WHUP!
WELL, OVER IT ANYWAY. THE ARCHITECTURE IS MIND-BENDING!
WHUP! WHUP! WHUP! WHUP!
WHAT ARE YOU DOIN'?
CALLING MY FRIEND.
NO! NO CALLIN' FRIENDS! WE'RE ON A TOP SECRET MISSION HERE! NO NON-WORK RELATED PHONE CALLS. PERIOD!
WHUP! WHUP! WHUP!
FINE. JOYCE? HYPATIA. GOTTA GO.
WHUP! WHUP! WHUP!
NO, BOSS. I KNOW!
THE DINOSAUR HAS SPOKEN.
LATER!
WHUP! WHUP! WHUP!
I HEARD DAT!
WE'VE LOCATED A SUITABLE LANDING SITE! HOLD ON!

DON'T MISS OUR NEXT EXCITING ISSUE! AND KEEP YOUR EYES OPEN FOR REX LIBRIS PREMIUM BRAND TINFOIL AT YOUR LOCAL SUPERMARKET! GUARANTEED TO STOP MIND CONTROL BEAMS IN THEIR TRACKS; ALSO EFFECTIVE AGAINST BRAIN PACIFIER FIELDS AND MEMORY WIPES! -- BARRY

CHAPTER TWELVE

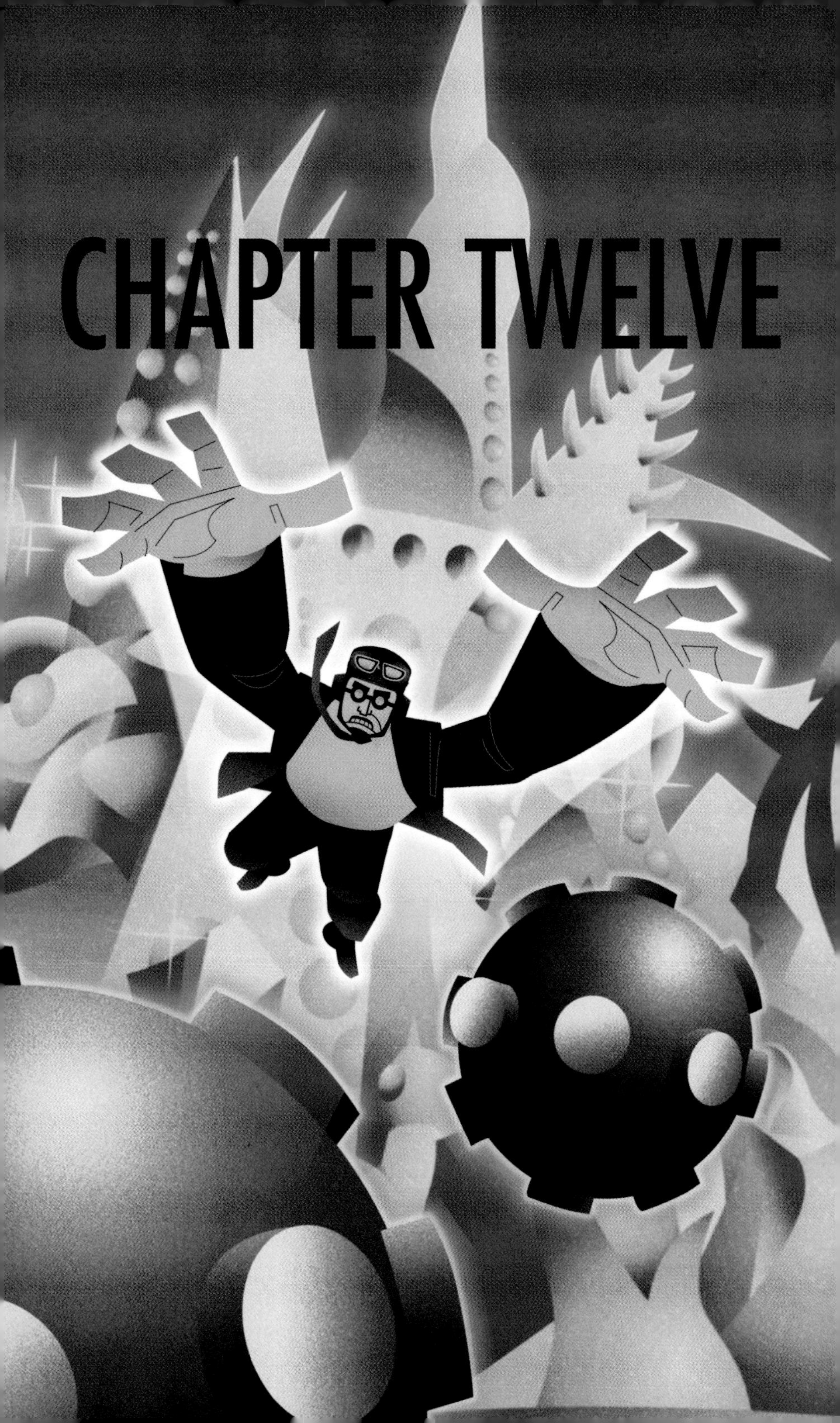

BARRY'S BRAIN

Once more Hermeneutic Press is on a roll! Thanks to the efforts of my nephew Todd, the new Vice-President of International Operations here at Hermeneutic Press, we've expanded our operations to Lichtenstein, Durdenois, Pentixore, Qualding, Vespugia, Camelerd, Plutusia, Fingiswold, Kazakhstan, Azerbaijan, Oceania, Opar, Archenland, Syldavia, Borduria, Jurgolia, and Upper Voltage. That's right! We've now got comcs coming out in all these under-exploited markets. Todd has hand picked dozens of local talents in each and given them the opportunity of a lifetime—to participate in the Hermeneutic Miracle, and join the Hermeneutiverse!

I haven't seen any of the new comics myself, just a few mock-ups that look like they were done by ten-year-olds, but hey, you never know what's going to sell in a foreign market. They have crazy tastes, those foreigners! And by the sales figures Todd has shown me, and the hefty profits flowing into our coffers, they're willing to pay for them! We're selling in volumes the likes of which I've never seen before. I'm talking AC (Awesome Comics) type figures! At this rate, we'll dominate the industry in no time.

Oddly enough half the countries we're now doing business with I'd never heard of before. I mean, a country called 'Azerbaijan'? Or 'Kazakhstan'? I mean really. They sound made up. And 'Lichtenstein'? Seems to me like Liechtenstein has good grounds to file charges for copyright infringement. Some of the others sound vaguely familiar, true, but Todd always was the geography whiz! And he knows where profitable economies are. Turns out that's what this industry needed: someone to seek out markets that were sadly neglected by the mainstream publishers, such as Bordurians and women. Those customers have been forfeited by the blundering and the bloated big two! Nimble, quick-witted Hermeneutic Press has scooped

the prize away from them, and we'll never relinquish it. Never! Not with titles like *Bzaj the Sheep Herding Philosopher Assassin*, *Galactic Godfathers*, *The Velvet Executioner*, or *Szplug!* coming out!

This is a coup that I will be drinking to most frequently. In fact, I now have the money to indulge my penchant for celebratory toasts as much as I like! With Todd and his friends Guido and Tony now running day to day operations, I can spend more time making toasts and dreaming up innovative new ways to expand the envelope of the comic book creativity. What might the next great innovation be? Smellorama! 3-D visuals! Electroshock stimulation! And I just came up with those right now! There's no telling what I'll come up with when I've really got my noggin well marinated. Watch out world, B. Barry Horst is about to unleash his genius. Nothing can stop me now! And be sure to visit our brand new website at : http://www.jtillustration.com/hermeneutic

Adumbrate!

B. Barry Horst
Publisher

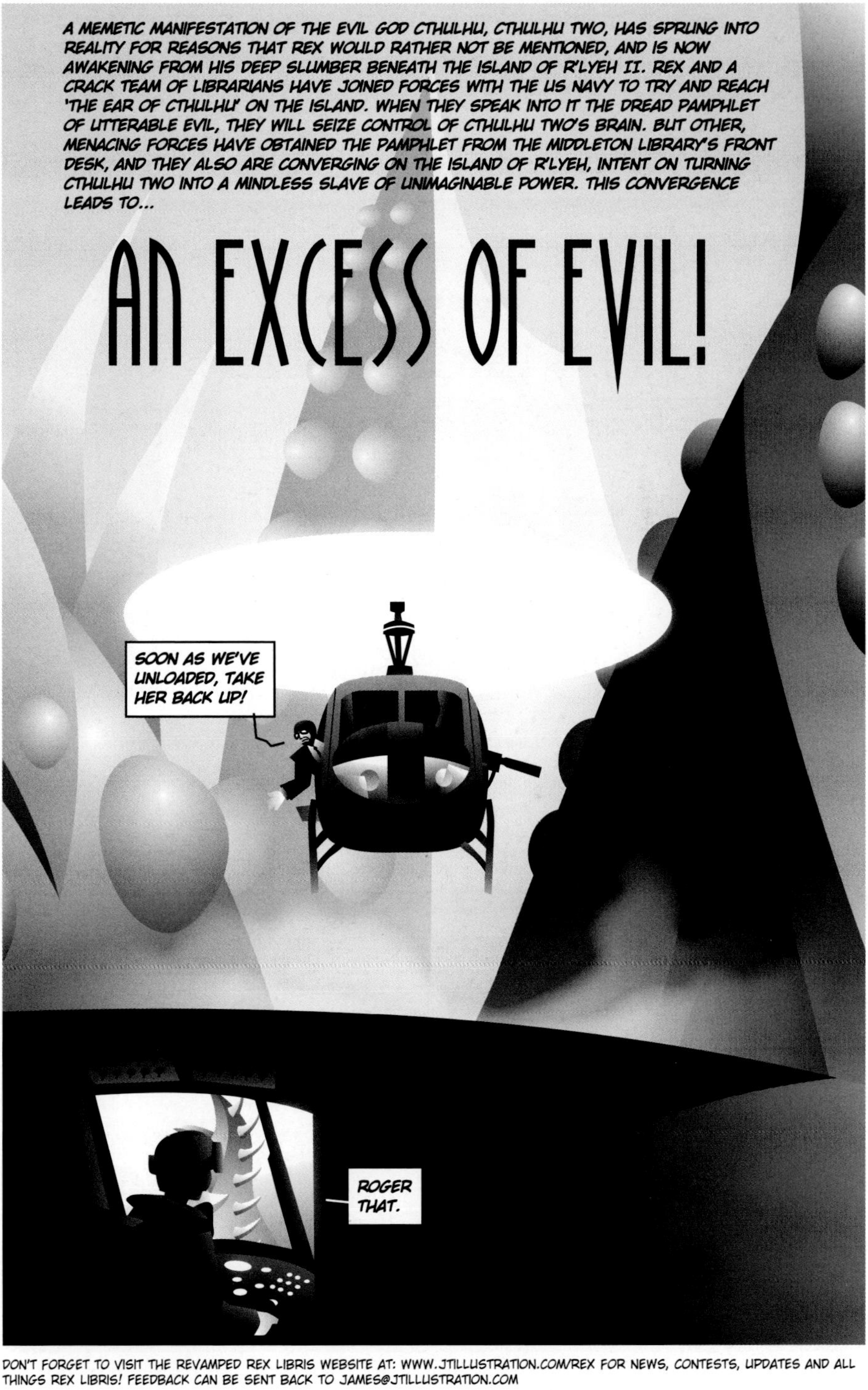
A MEMETIC MANIFESTATION OF THE EVIL GOD CTHULHU, CTHULHU TWO, HAS SPRUNG INTO REALITY FOR REASONS THAT REX WOULD RATHER NOT BE MENTIONED, AND IS NOW AWAKENING FROM HIS DEEP SLUMBER BENEATH THE ISLAND OF R'LYEH II. REX AND A CRACK TEAM OF LIBRARIANS HAVE JOINED FORCES WITH THE US NAVY TO TRY AND REACH 'THE EAR OF CTHULHU' ON THE ISLAND. WHEN THEY SPEAK INTO IT THE DREAD PAMPHLET OF UTTERABLE EVIL, THEY WILL SEIZE CONTROL OF CTHULHU TWO'S BRAIN. BUT OTHER, MENACING FORCES HAVE OBTAINED THE PAMPHLET FROM THE MIDDLETON LIBRARY'S FRONT DESK, AND THEY ALSO ARE CONVERGING ON THE ISLAND OF R'LYEH, INTENT ON TURNING CTHULHU TWO INTO A MINDLESS SLAVE OF UNIMAGINABLE POWER. THIS CONVERGENCE LEADS TO...
AN EXCESS OF EVIL!
SOON AS WE'VE UNLOADED, TAKE HER BACK UP!
ROGER THAT.

DON'T FORGET TO VISIT THE REVAMPED REX LIBRIS WEBSITE AT: WWW.JTILLUSTRATION.COM/REX FOR NEWS, CONTESTS, UPDATES AND ALL THINGS REX LIBRIS! FEEDBACK CAN BE SENT BACK TO JAMES@JTILLUSTRATION.COM

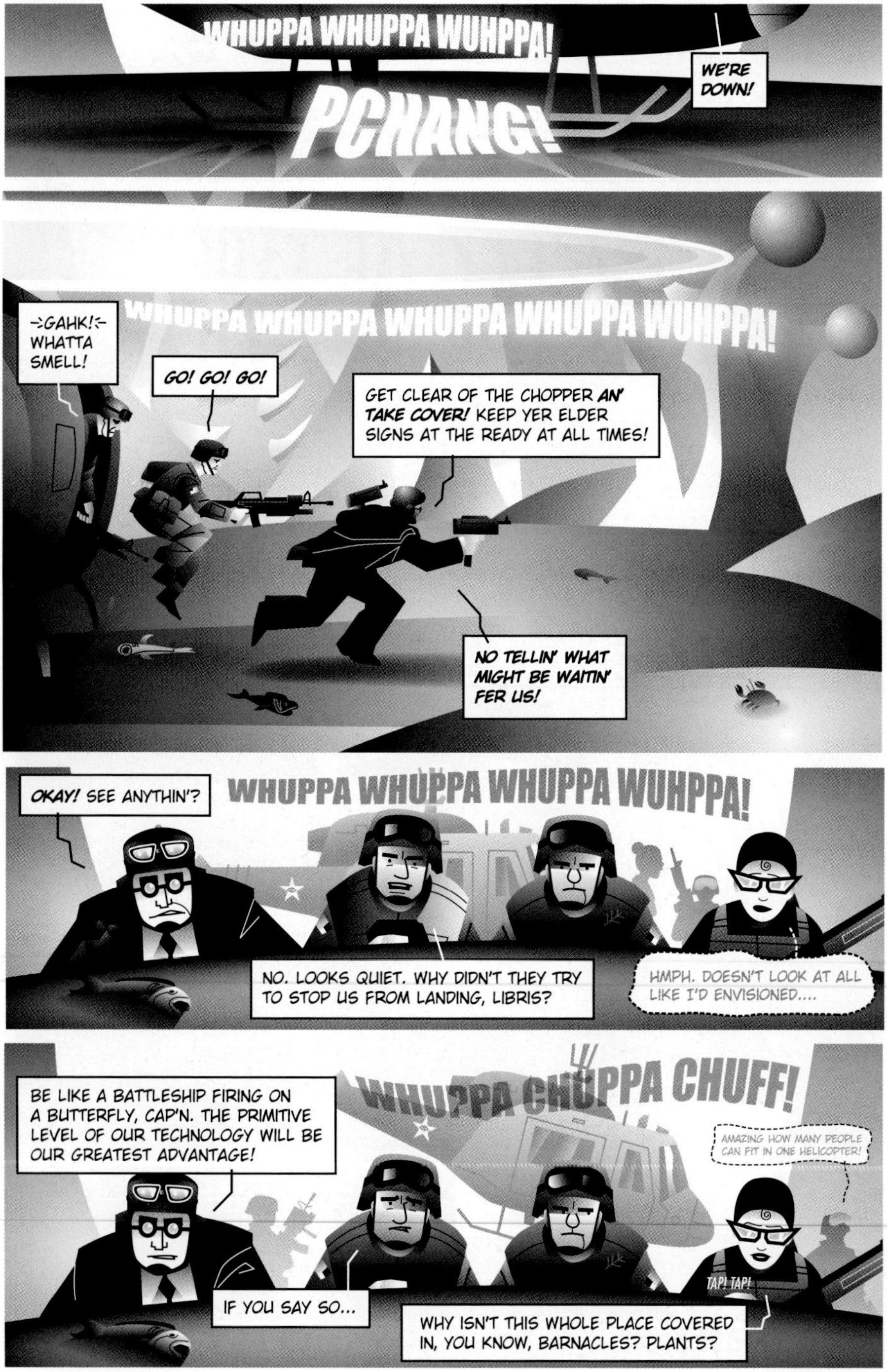
WHUPPA WHUPPA WUHPPA!
PCHANG!
WE'RE DOWN!
WHUPPA WHUPPA WHUPPA WHUPPA WUHPPA!
-GAHK!- WHATTA SMELL!
GO! GO! GO!
GET CLEAR OF THE CHOPPER AN' TAKE COVER! KEEP YER ELDER SIGNS AT THE READY AT ALL TIMES!
NO TELLIN' WHAT MIGHT BE WAITIN' FER US!
WHUPPA WHUPPA WHUPPA WUHPPA!
OKAY! SEE ANYTHIN'?
NO. LOOKS QUIET. WHY DIDN'T THEY TRY TO STOP US FROM LANDING, LIBRIS?
HMPH. DOESN'T LOOK AT ALL LIKE I'D ENVISIONED....
WHUPPA CHUPPA CHUFF!
BE LIKE A BATTLESHIP FIRING ON A BUTTERFLY, CAP'N. THE PRIMITIVE LEVEL OF OUR TECHNOLOGY WILL BE OUR GREATEST ADVANTAGE!
AMAZING HOW MANY PEOPLE CAN FIT IN ONE HELICOPTER!
IF YOU SAY SO...
TAP! TAP!
WHY ISN'T THIS WHOLE PLACE COVERED IN, YOU KNOW, BARNACLES? PLANTS?

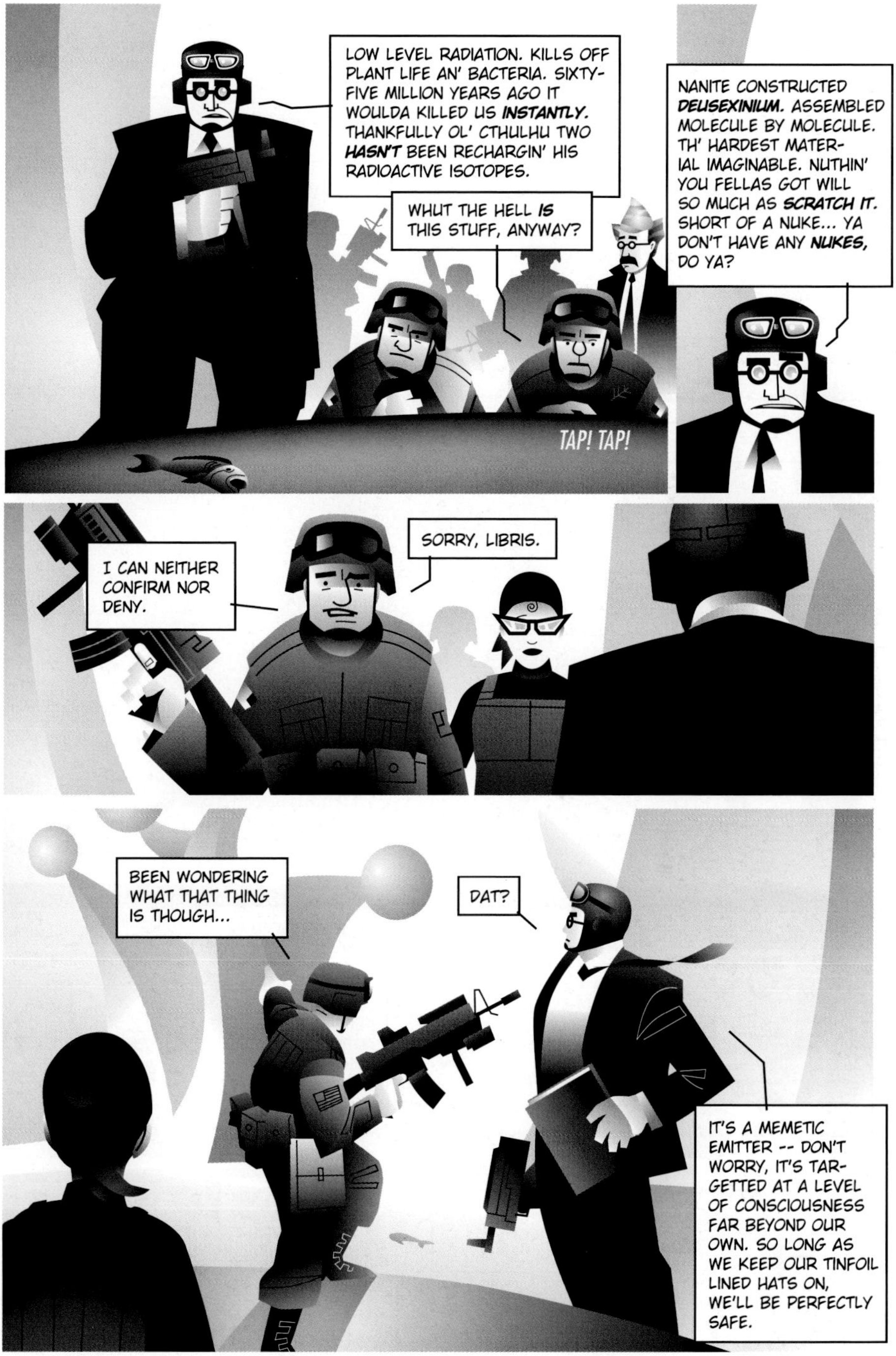
LOW LEVEL RADIATION. KILLS OFF PLANT LIFE AN' BACTERIA. SIXTY-FIVE MILLION YEARS AGO IT WOULDA KILLED US INSTANTLY. THANKFULLY OL' CTHULHU TWO HASN'T BEEN RECHARGIN' HIS RADIOACTIVE ISOTOPES.
WHUT THE HELL IS THIS STUFF, ANYWAY?
TAP! TAP!
NANITE CONSTRUCTED DEUSEXINIUM. ASSEMBLED MOLECULE BY MOLECULE. TH' HARDEST MATERIAL IMAGINABLE. NUTHIN' YOU FELLAS GOT WILL SO MUCH AS SCRATCH IT. SHORT OF A NUKE... YA DON'T HAVE ANY NUKES, DO YA?
I CAN NEITHER CONFIRM NOR DENY.
SORRY, LIBRIS.
BEEN WONDERING WHAT THAT THING IS THOUGH...
DAT?
IT'S A MEMETIC EMITTER -- DON'T WORRY, IT'S TARGETTED AT A LEVEL OF CONSCIOUSNESS FAR BEYOND OUR OWN. SO LONG AS WE KEEP OUR TINFOIL LINED HATS ON, WE'LL BE PERFECTLY SAFE.

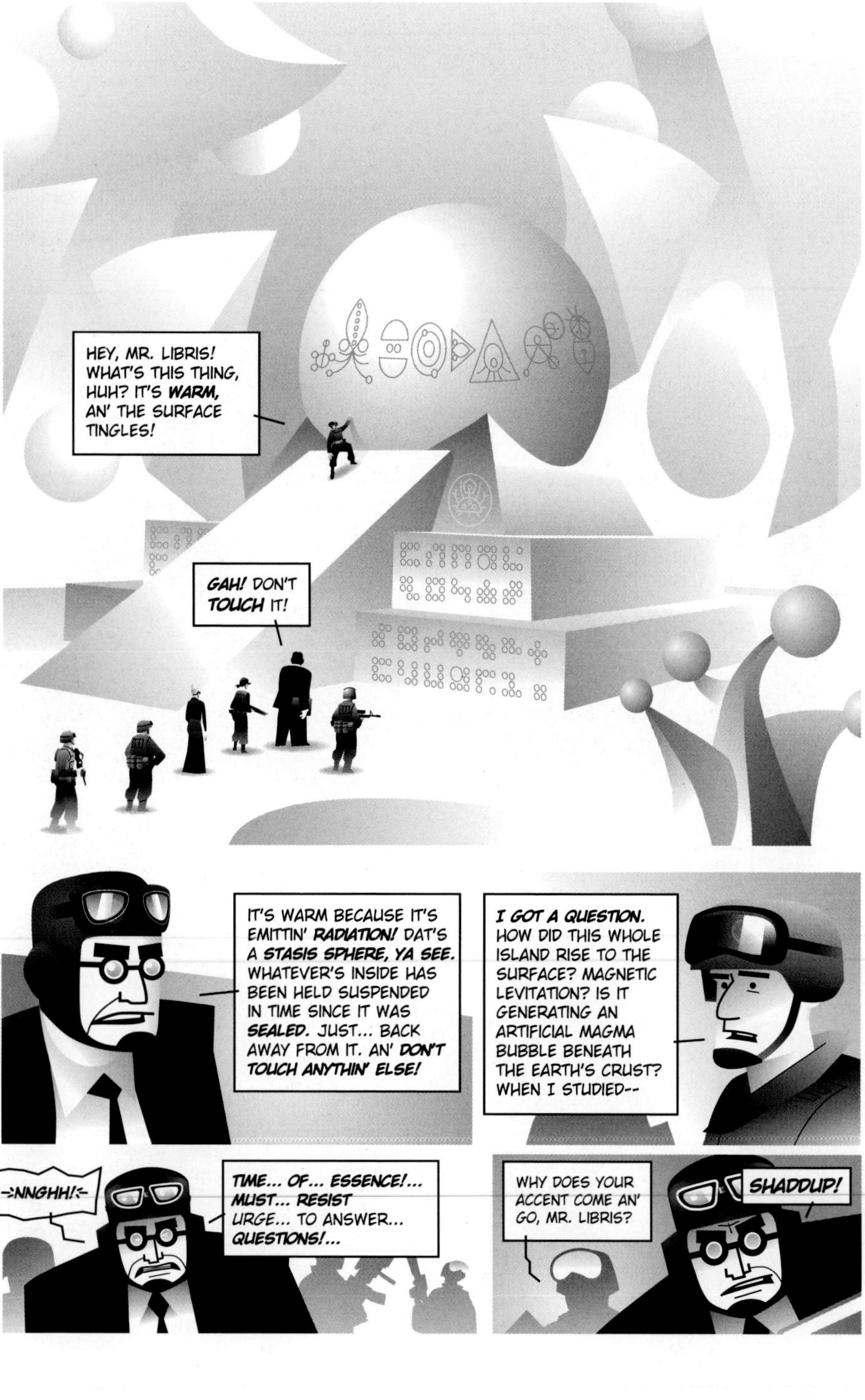
HEY, MR. LIBRIS! WHAT'S THIS THING, HUH? IT'S **WARM,** AN' THE SURFACE TINGLES!
GAH! DON'T ***TOUCH*** IT!
IT'S WARM BECAUSE IT'S EMITTIN' ***RADIATION!*** DAT'S A ***STASIS SPHERE, YA SEE.*** WHATEVER'S INSIDE HAS BEEN HELD SUSPENDED IN TIME SINCE IT WAS ***SEALED.*** JUST... BACK AWAY FROM IT. AN' ***DON'T TOUCH ANYTHIN' ELSE!***
I GOT A QUESTION. HOW DID THIS WHOLE ISLAND RISE TO THE SURFACE? MAGNETIC LEVITATION? IS IT GENERATING AN ARTIFICIAL MAGMA BUBBLE BENEATH THE EARTH'S CRUST? WHEN I STUDIED--
-NNGHH!-
TIME... OF... ESSENCE!... MUST... RESIST URGE... TO ANSWER... ***QUESTIONS!...***
WHY DOES YOUR ACCENT COME AN' GO, MR. LIBRIS?
SHADDUP!

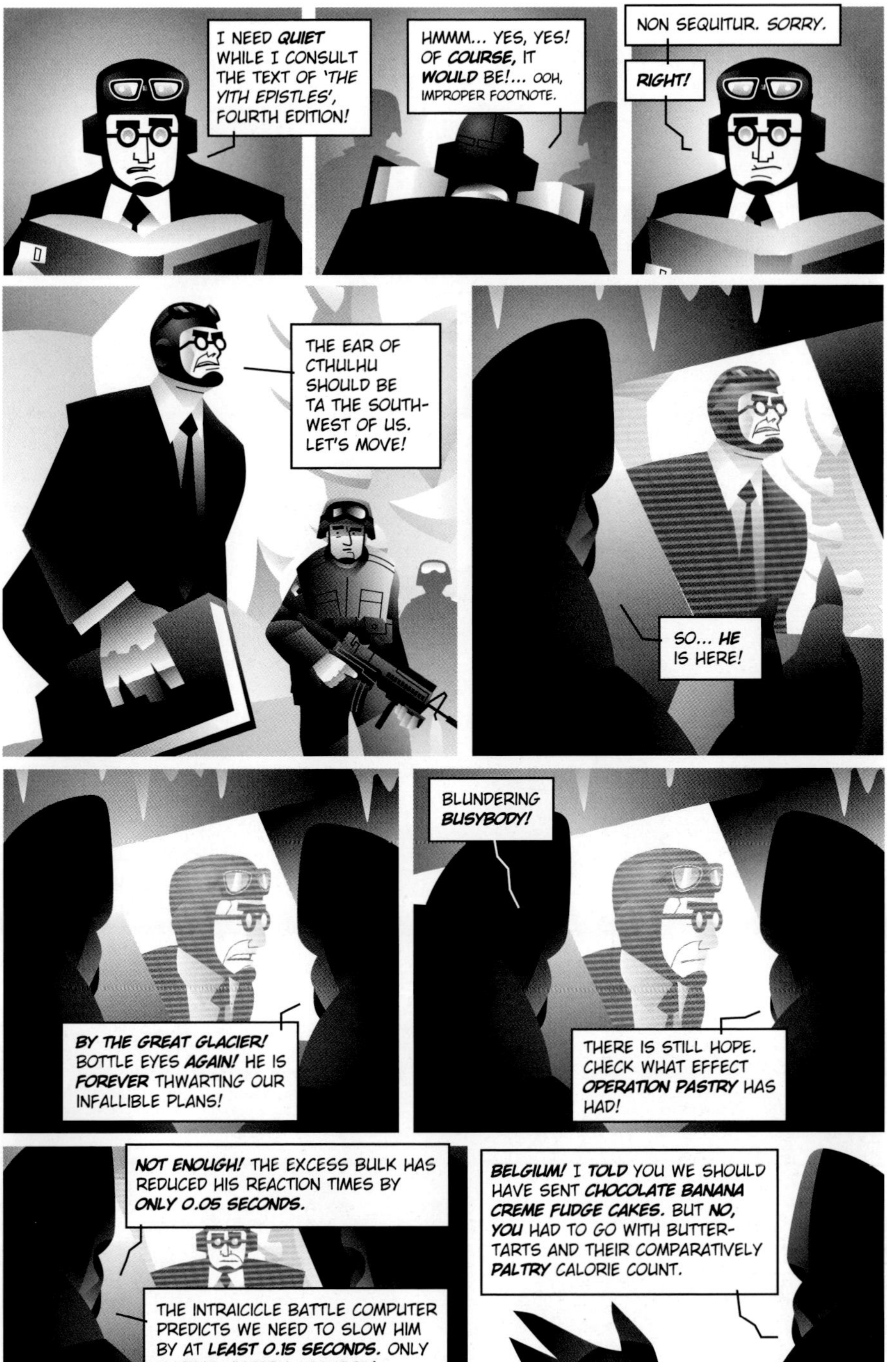
I NEED **QUIET** WHILE I CONSULT THE TEXT OF 'THE YITH EPISTLES', FOURTH EDITION!
HMMM... YES, YES! OF **COURSE,** IT **WOULD** BE!... OOH, IMPROPER FOOTNOTE.
NON SEQUITUR. *SORRY.*
RIGHT!
THE EAR OF CTHULHU SHOULD BE TA THE SOUTH-WEST OF US. LET'S MOVE!
SO... **HE** IS HERE!
BY THE GREAT GLACIER! BOTTLE EYES **AGAIN!** HE IS **FOREVER** THWARTING OUR INFALLIBLE PLANS!
BLUNDERING **BUSYBODY!**
THERE IS STILL HOPE. CHECK WHAT EFFECT **OPERATION PASTRY** HAS HAD!
NOT ENOUGH! THE EXCESS BULK HAS REDUCED HIS REACTION TIMES BY **ONLY 0.05 SECONDS.**
THE INTRAICICLE BATTLE COMPUTER PREDICTS WE NEED TO SLOW HIM BY AT **LEAST 0.15 SECONDS.** ONLY **THEN** IS VICTORY ASSURED!
BELGIUM! I **TOLD** YOU WE SHOULD HAVE SENT **CHOCOLATE BANANA CREME FUDGE CAKES.** BUT **NO, YOU** HAD TO GO WITH BUTTER-TARTS AND THEIR COMPARATIVELY **PALTRY** CALORIE COUNT.

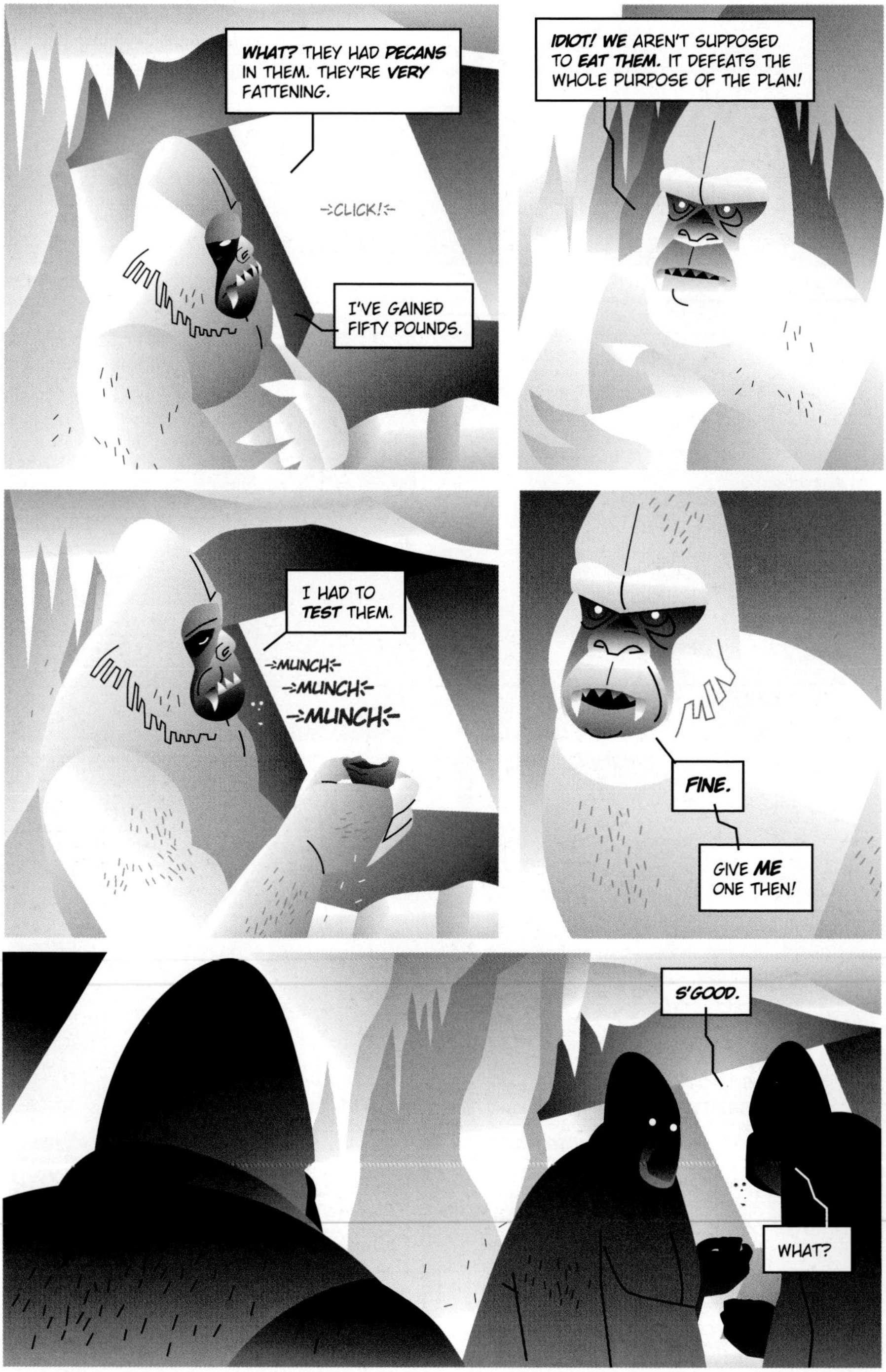
WHAT? THEY HAD PECANS IN THEM. THEY'RE VERY FATTENING.
CLICK!
I'VE GAINED FIFTY POUNDS.
IDIOT! WE AREN'T SUPPOSED TO EAT THEM. IT DEFEATS THE WHOLE PURPOSE OF THE PLAN!
I HAD TO TEST THEM.
MUNCH
MUNCH
MUNCH
FINE.
GIVE ME ONE THEN!
S'GOOD.
WHAT?

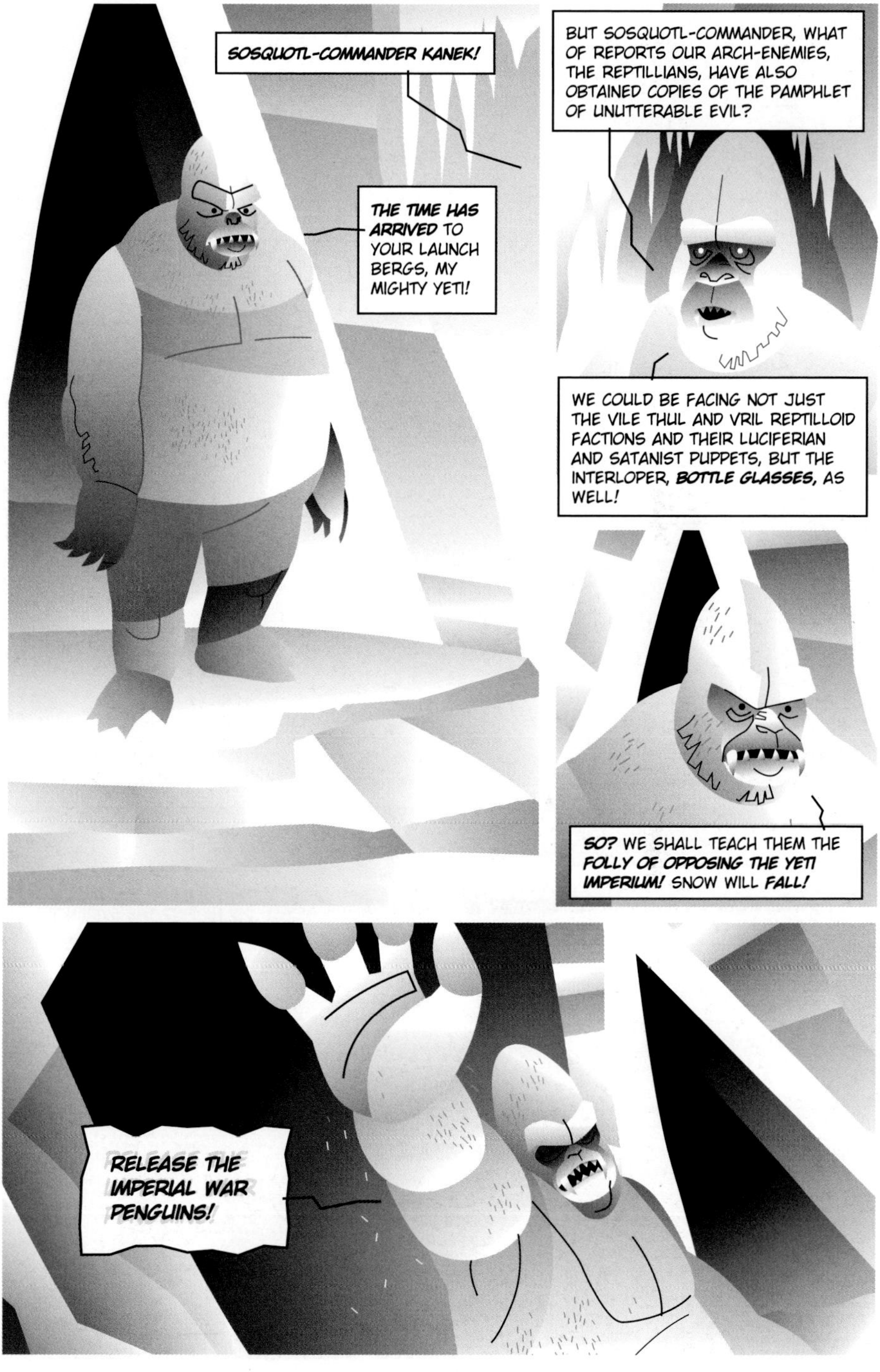
SOSQUOTL-COMMANDER KANEK!
THE TIME HAS ARRIVED TO YOUR LAUNCH BERGS, MY MIGHTY YETI!
BUT SOSQUOTL-COMMANDER, WHAT OF REPORTS OUR ARCH-ENEMIES, THE REPTILLIANS, HAVE ALSO OBTAINED COPIES OF THE PAMPHLET OF UNUTTERABLE EVIL?
WE COULD BE FACING NOT JUST THE VILE THUL AND VRIL REPTILLOID FACTIONS AND THEIR LUCIFERIAN AND SATANIST PUPPETS, BUT THE INTERLOPER, BOTTLE GLASSES, AS WELL!
SO? WE SHALL TEACH THEM THE FOLLY OF OPPOSING THE YETI IMPERIUM! SNOW WILL FALL!
RELEASE THE IMPERIAL WAR PENGUINS!

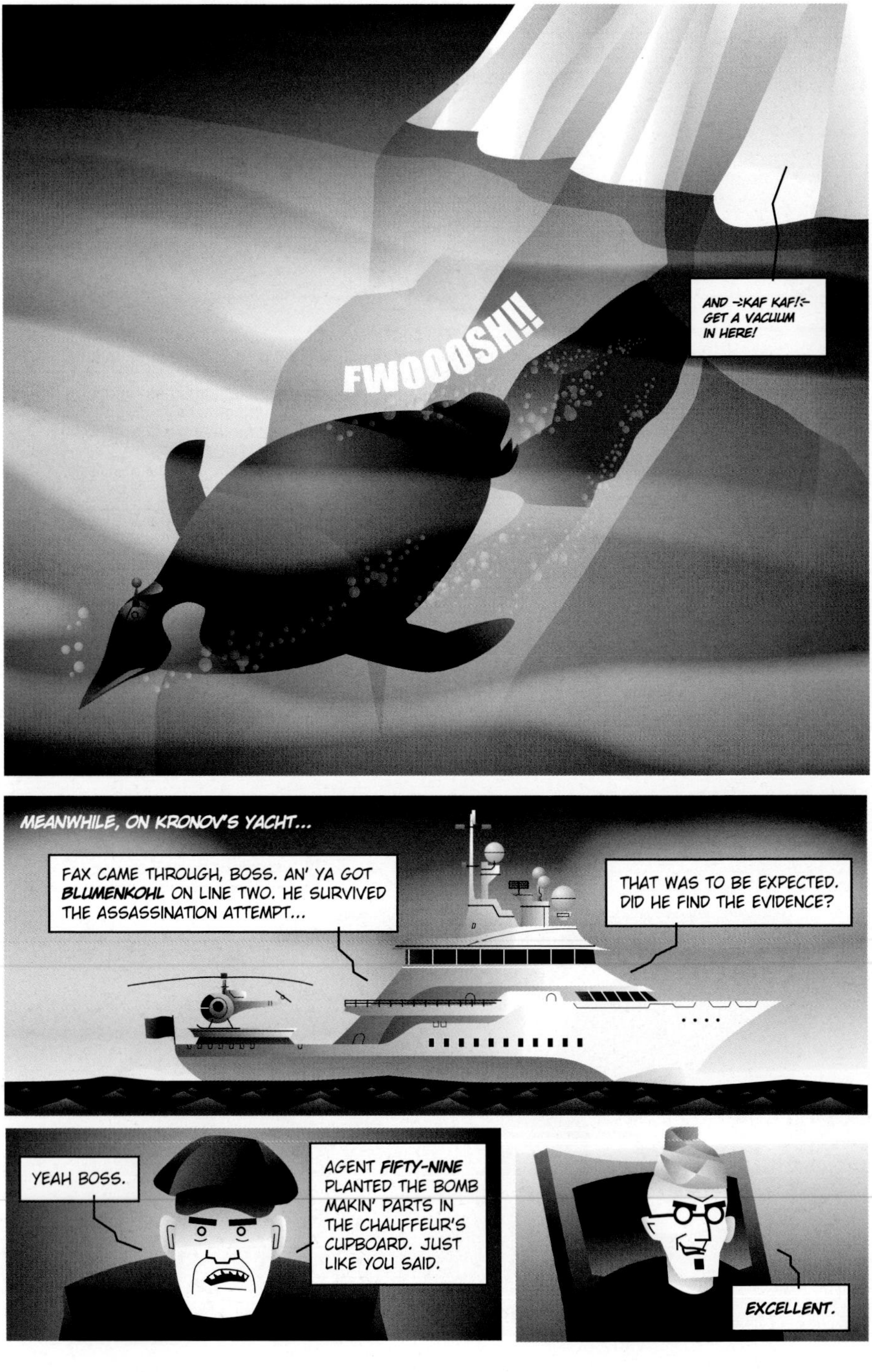
FWOOOSH!!
AND ->KAF KAF!<- GET A VACUUM IN HERE!
MEANWHILE, ON KRONOV'S YACHT...
FAX CAME THROUGH, BOSS. AN' YA GOT BLUMENKOHL ON LINE TWO. HE SURVIVED THE ASSASSINATION ATTEMPT...
THAT WAS TO BE EXPECTED. DID HE FIND THE EVIDENCE?
YEAH BOSS.
AGENT FIFTY-NINE PLANTED THE BOMB MAKIN' PARTS IN THE CHAUFFEUR'S CUPBOARD. JUST LIKE YOU SAID.
EXCELLENT.

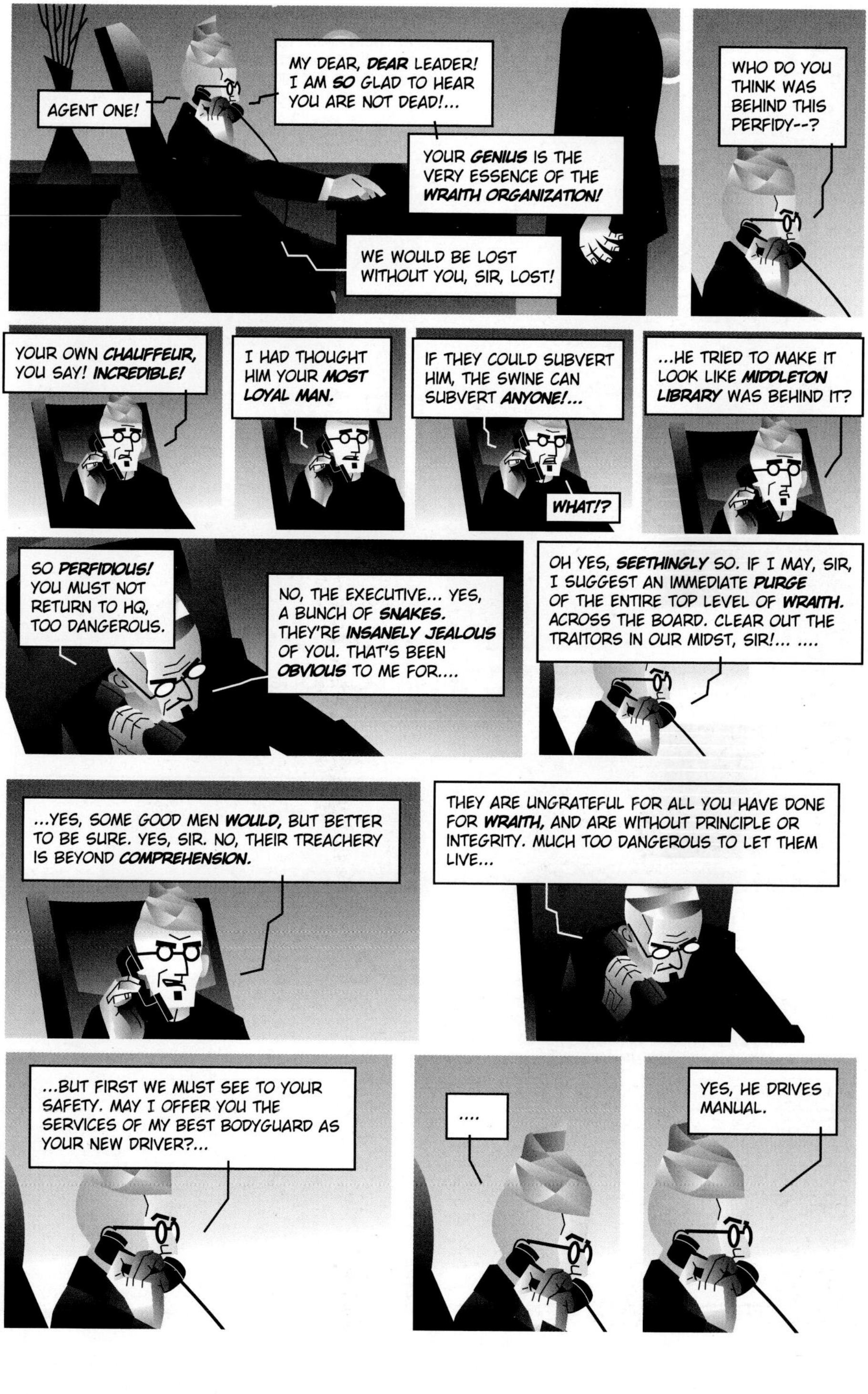
AGENT ONE!
MY DEAR, DEAR LEADER! I AM SO GLAD TO HEAR YOU ARE NOT DEAD!...
YOUR GENIUS IS THE VERY ESSENCE OF THE WRAITH ORGANIZATION!
WE WOULD BE LOST WITHOUT YOU, SIR, LOST!
WHO DO YOU THINK WAS BEHIND THIS PERFIDY--?
YOUR OWN CHAUFFEUR, YOU SAY! INCREDIBLE!
I HAD THOUGHT HIM YOUR MOST LOYAL MAN.
IF THEY COULD SUBVERT HIM, THE SWINE CAN SUBVERT ANYONE!...
WHAT!?
...HE TRIED TO MAKE IT LOOK LIKE MIDDLETON LIBRARY WAS BEHIND IT?
SO PERFIDIOUS! YOU MUST NOT RETURN TO HQ, TOO DANGEROUS.
NO, THE EXECUTIVE... YES, A BUNCH OF SNAKES. THEY'RE INSANELY JEALOUS OF YOU. THAT'S BEEN OBVIOUS TO ME FOR....
OH YES, SEETHINGLY SO. IF I MAY, SIR, I SUGGEST AN IMMEDIATE PURGE OF THE ENTIRE TOP LEVEL OF WRAITH. ACROSS THE BOARD. CLEAR OUT THE TRAITORS IN OUR MIDST, SIR!... ....
...YES, SOME GOOD MEN WOULD, BUT BETTER TO BE SURE. YES, SIR. NO, THEIR TREACHERY IS BEYOND COMPREHENSION.
THEY ARE UNGRATEFUL FOR ALL YOU HAVE DONE FOR WRAITH, AND ARE WITHOUT PRINCIPLE OR INTEGRITY. MUCH TOO DANGEROUS TO LET THEM LIVE...
...BUT FIRST WE MUST SEE TO YOUR SAFETY. MAY I OFFER YOU THE SERVICES OF MY BEST BODYGUARD AS YOUR NEW DRIVER?...
....
YES, HE DRIVES MANUAL.

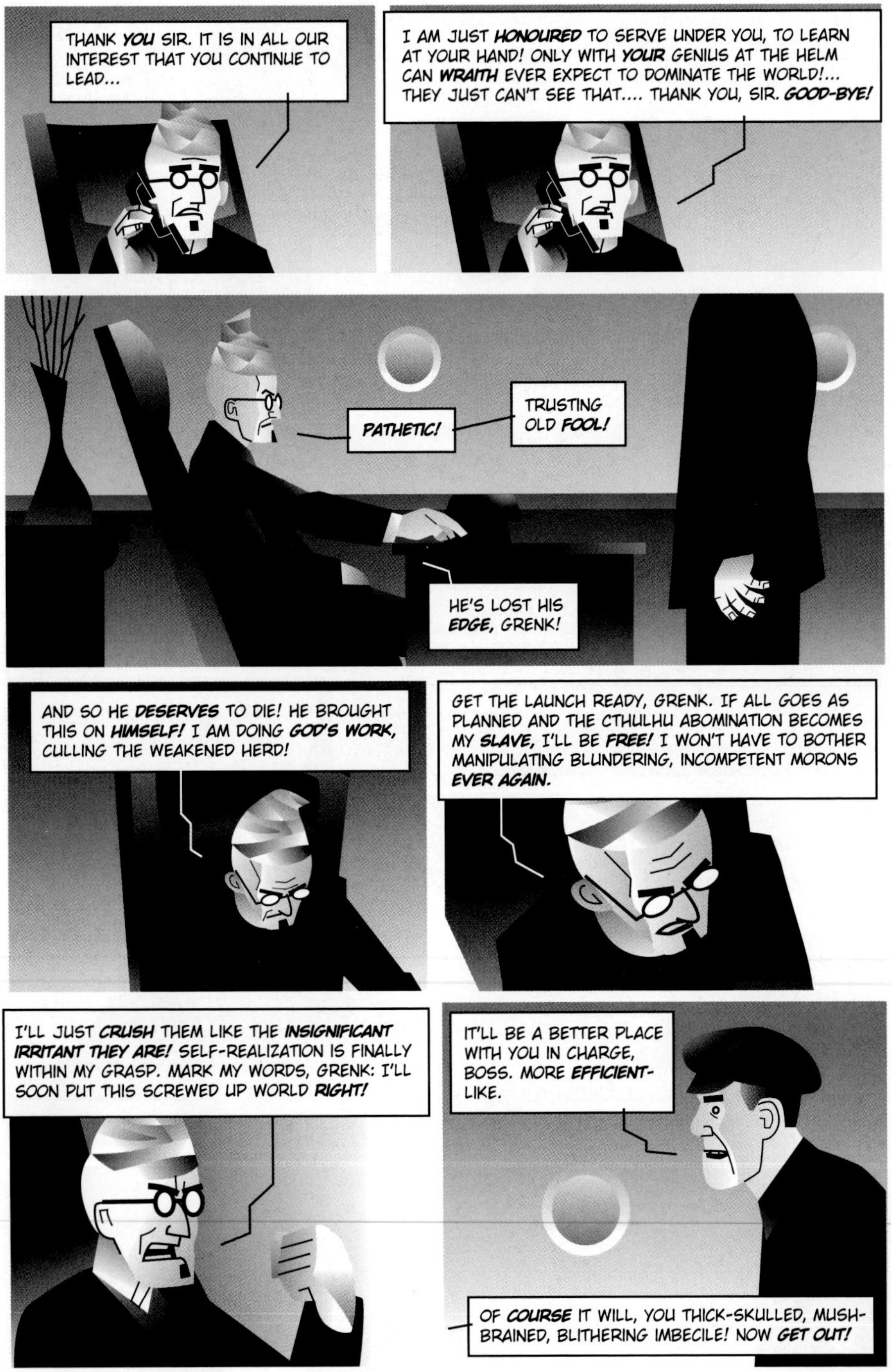

THANK YOU SIR. IT IS IN ALL OUR INTEREST THAT YOU CONTINUE TO LEAD...
I AM JUST HONOURED TO SERVE UNDER YOU, TO LEARN AT YOUR HAND! ONLY WITH YOUR GENIUS AT THE HELM CAN WRAITH EVER EXPECT TO DOMINATE THE WORLD!... THEY JUST CAN'T SEE THAT.... THANK YOU, SIR. GOOD-BYE!
PATHETIC!
TRUSTING OLD FOOL!
HE'S LOST HIS EDGE, GRENK!
AND SO HE DESERVES TO DIE! HE BROUGHT THIS ON HIMSELF! I AM DOING GOD'S WORK, CULLING THE WEAKENED HERD!
GET THE LAUNCH READY, GRENK. IF ALL GOES AS PLANNED AND THE CTHULHU ABOMINATION BECOMES MY SLAVE, I'LL BE FREE! I WON'T HAVE TO BOTHER MANIPULATING BLUNDERING, INCOMPETENT MORONS EVER AGAIN.
I'LL JUST CRUSH THEM LIKE THE INSIGNIFICANT IRRITANT THEY ARE! SELF-REALIZATION IS FINALLY WITHIN MY GRASP. MARK MY WORDS, GRENK: I'LL SOON PUT THIS SCREWED UP WORLD RIGHT!
IT'LL BE A BETTER PLACE WITH YOU IN CHARGE, BOSS. MORE EFFICIENT-LIKE.
OF COURSE IT WILL, YOU THICK-SKULLED, MUSH-BRAINED, BLITHERING IMBECILE! NOW GET OUT!

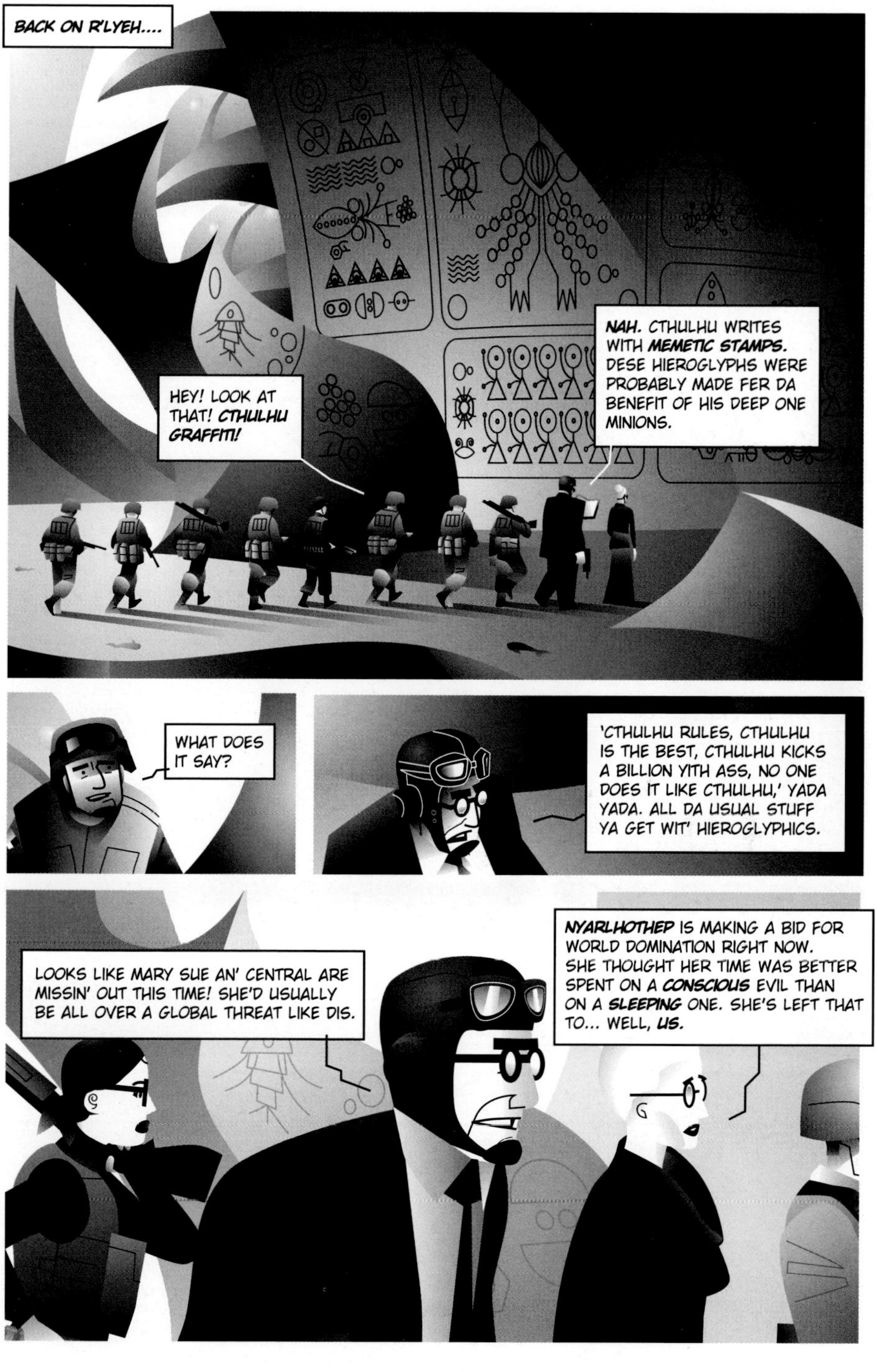
BACK ON R'LYEH....
HEY! LOOK AT THAT! CTHULHU GRAFFITI!
NAH. CTHULHU WRITES WITH MEMETIC STAMPS. DESE HIEROGLYPHS WERE PROBABLY MADE FER DA BENEFIT OF HIS DEEP ONE MINIONS.
WHAT DOES IT SAY?
'CTHULHU RULES, CTHULHU IS THE BEST, CTHULHU KICKS A BILLION YITH ASS, NO ONE DOES IT LIKE CTHULHU,' YADA YADA. ALL DA USUAL STUFF YA GET WIT' HIEROGLYPHICS.
LOOKS LIKE MARY SUE AN' CENTRAL ARE MISSIN' OUT THIS TIME! SHE'D USUALLY BE ALL OVER A GLOBAL THREAT LIKE DIS.
NYARLHOTHEP IS MAKING A BID FOR WORLD DOMINATION RIGHT NOW. SHE THOUGHT HER TIME WAS BETTER SPENT ON A CONSCIOUS EVIL THAN ON A SLEEPING ONE. SHE'S LEFT THAT TO... WELL, US.

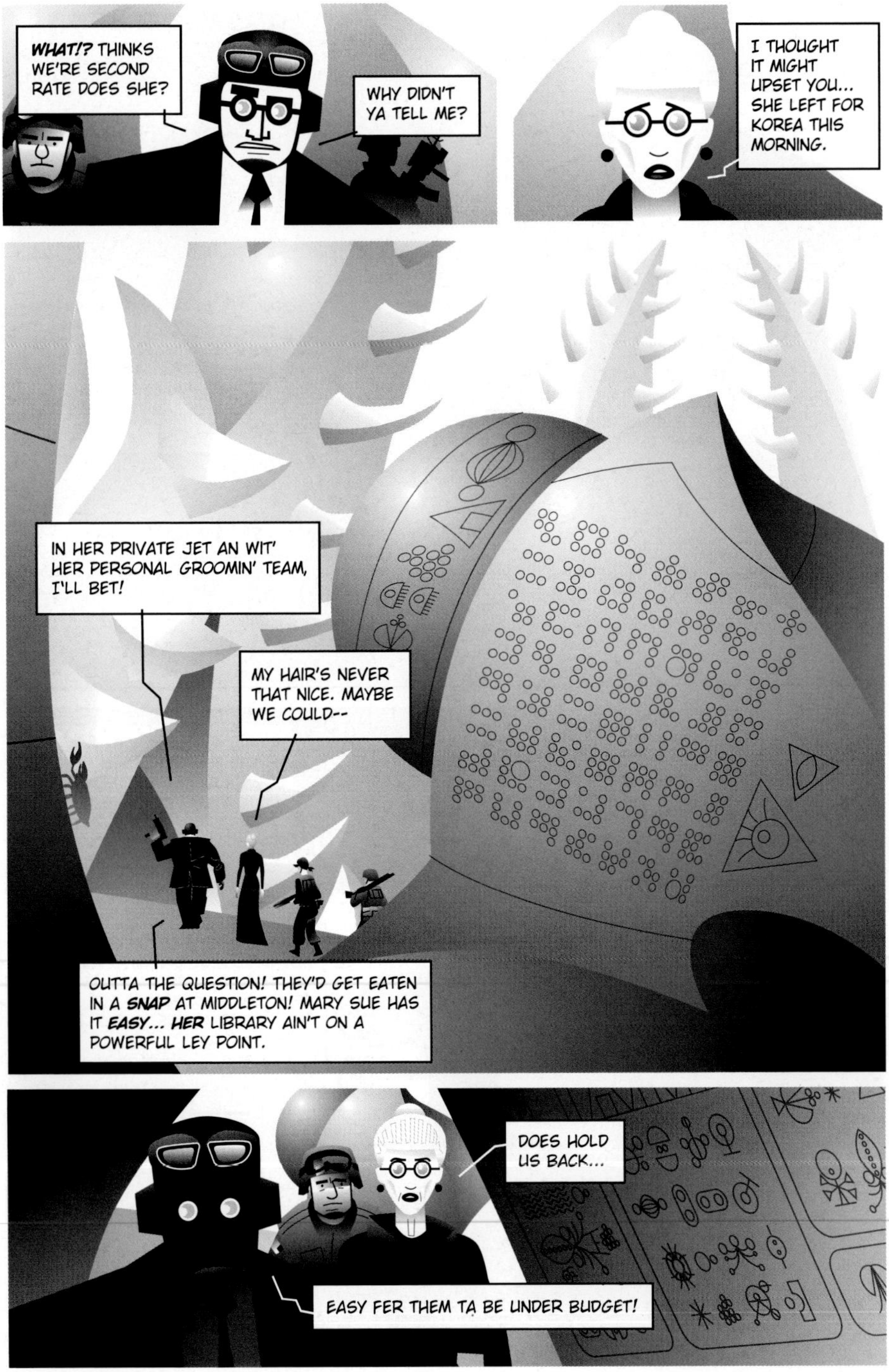

WHAT!? THINKS WE'RE SECOND RATE DOES SHE?
WHY DIDN'T YA TELL ME?
I THOUGHT IT MIGHT UPSET YOU... SHE LEFT FOR KOREA THIS MORNING.
IN HER PRIVATE JET AN WIT' HER PERSONAL GROOMIN' TEAM, I'LL BET!
MY HAIR'S NEVER THAT NICE. MAYBE WE COULD--
OUTTA THE QUESTION! THEY'D GET EATEN IN A *SNAP* AT MIDDLETON! MARY SUE HAS IT *EASY... HER* LIBRARY AIN'T ON A POWERFUL LEY POINT.
DOES HOLD US BACK...
EASY FER THEM TA BE UNDER BUDGET!

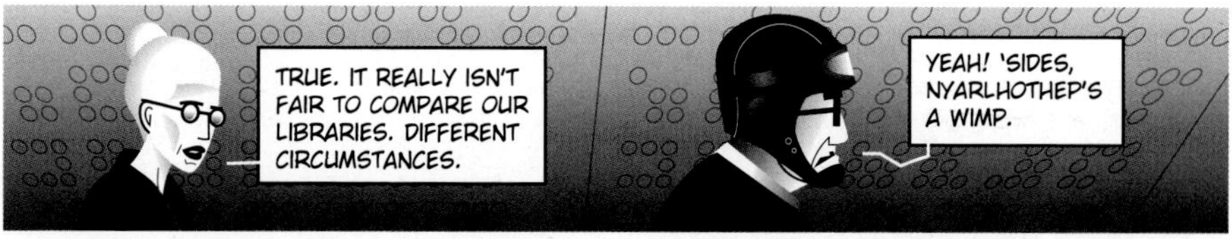
TRUE. IT REALLY ISN'T FAIR TO COMPARE OUR LIBRARIES. DIFFERENT CIRCUMSTANCES.
YEAH! 'SIDES, NYARLHOTHEP'S A WIMP.

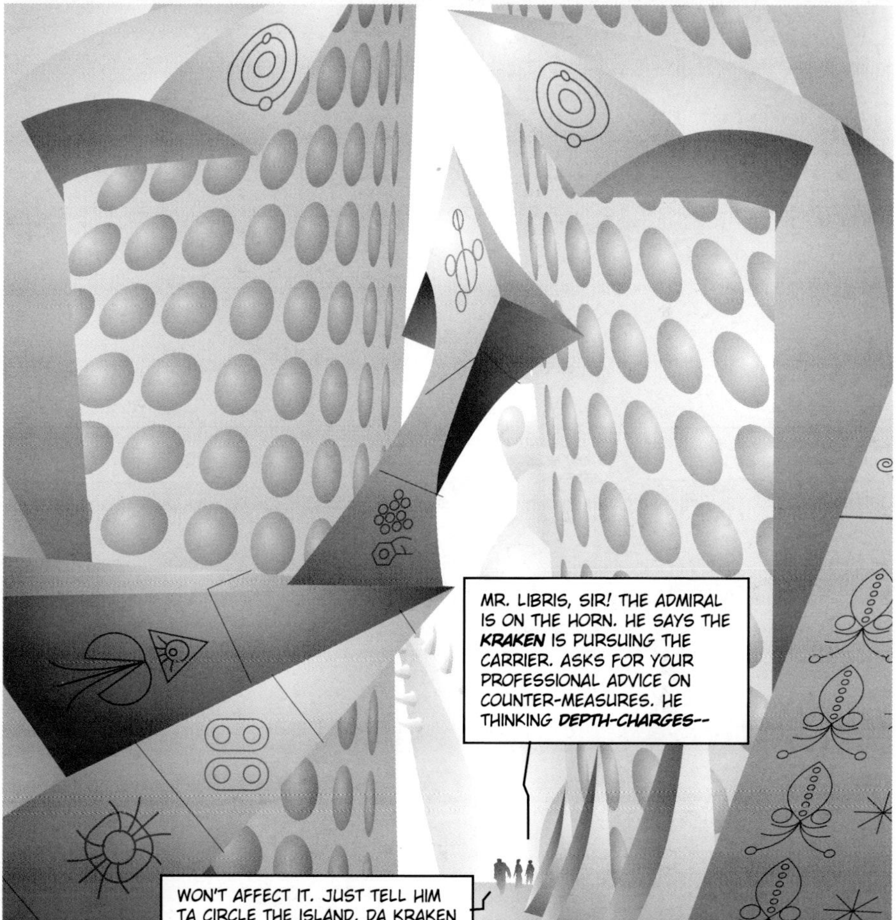
MR. LIBRIS, SIR! THE ADMIRAL IS ON THE HORN. HE SAYS THE **KRAKEN** IS PURSUING THE CARRIER. ASKS FOR YOUR PROFESSIONAL ADVICE ON COUNTER-MEASURES. HE THINKING **DEPTH-CHARGES--**
WON'T AFFECT IT. JUST TELL HIM TA CIRCLE THE ISLAND. DA KRAKEN CAN CRUSH THE CARRIER LIKE A TIN CAN, BUT IT'S SLOW AN' NONE TOO BRIGHT, IT'LL JUST FOLLOW THEM AROUND ENDLESSLY...

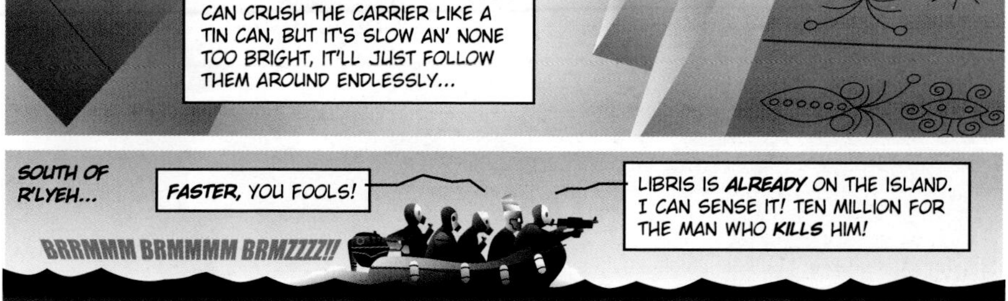
SOUTH OF R'LYEH...
FASTER, YOU FOOLS!
LIBRIS IS **ALREADY** ON THE ISLAND. I CAN SENSE IT! TEN MILLION FOR THE MAN WHO **KILLS** HIM!
BRRMMM BRMMMM BRMZZZZ!!

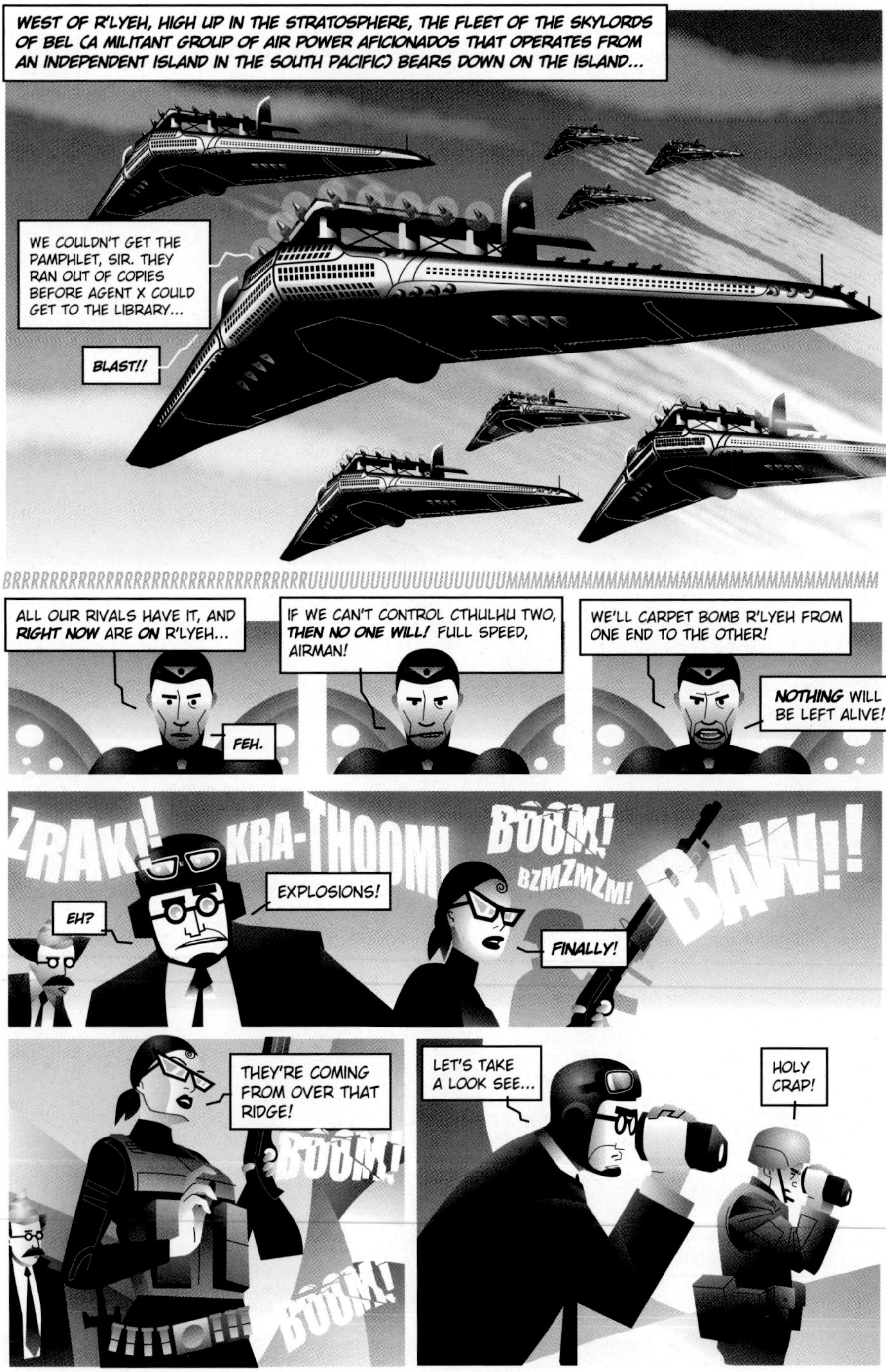
WEST OF R'LYEH, HIGH UP IN THE STRATOSPHERE, THE FLEET OF THE SKYLORDS OF BEL (A MILITANT GROUP OF AIR POWER AFICIONADOS THAT OPERATES FROM AN INDEPENDENT ISLAND IN THE SOUTH PACIFIC) BEARS DOWN ON THE ISLAND...
WE COULDN'T GET THE PAMPHLET, SIR. THEY RAN OUT OF COPIES BEFORE AGENT X COULD GET TO THE LIBRARY...
BLAST!!
BRRRRRRRRRRRRRRRRRRRRRRRRRRRRRRRRRUUUUUUUUUUUUUUUUUUUUMMMMMMMMMMMMMMMMMMMMMMMMMMMMMMMM
ALL OUR RIVALS HAVE IT, AND RIGHT NOW ARE ON R'LYEH...
FEH.
IF WE CAN'T CONTROL CTHULHU TWO, THEN NO ONE WILL! FULL SPEED, AIRMAN!
WE'LL CARPET BOMB R'LYEH FROM ONE END TO THE OTHER!
NOTHING WILL BE LEFT ALIVE!
ZRAK!!
KRA-THOOM!
BOOM!
BZMZMZM!
BAW!!
EH?
EXPLOSIONS!
FINALLY!
THEY'RE COMING FROM OVER THAT RIDGE!
BOOM!
BOOM!
LET'S TAKE A LOOK SEE...
HOLY CRAP!

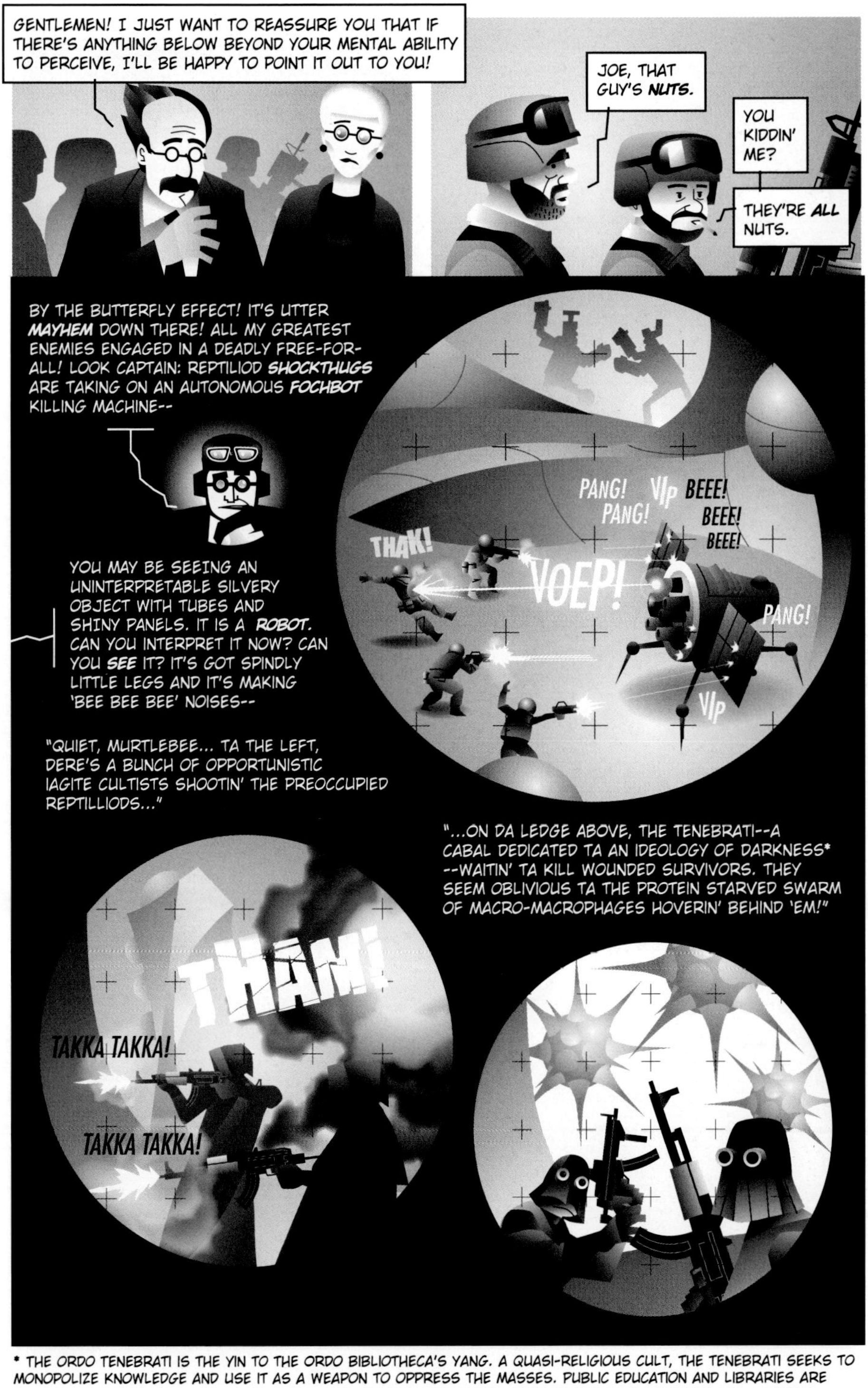
GENTLEMEN! I JUST WANT TO REASSURE YOU THAT IF THERE'S ANYTHING BELOW BEYOND YOUR MENTAL ABILITY TO PERCEIVE, I'LL BE HAPPY TO POINT IT OUT TO YOU!
JOE, THAT GUY'S NUTS.
YOU KIDDIN' ME?
THEY'RE ALL NUTS.
BY THE BUTTERFLY EFFECT! IT'S UTTER MAYHEM DOWN THERE! ALL MY GREATEST ENEMIES ENGAGED IN A DEADLY FREE-FOR-ALL! LOOK CAPTAIN: REPTILIOD SHOCKTHUGS ARE TAKING ON AN AUTONOMOUS FOCHBOT KILLING MACHINE--
PANG! PANG!
VIP
BEEE! BEEE! BEEE!
THAK!
VOEP!
PANG!
VIP
YOU MAY BE SEEING AN UNINTERPRETABLE SILVERY OBJECT WITH TUBES AND SHINY PANELS. IT IS A ROBOT. CAN YOU INTERPRET IT NOW? CAN YOU SEE IT? IT'S GOT SPINDLY LITTLE LEGS AND IT'S MAKING 'BEE BEE BEE' NOISES--
"QUIET, MURTLEBEE... TA THE LEFT, DERE'S A BUNCH OF OPPORTUNISTIC IAGITE CULTISTS SHOOTIN' THE PREOCCUPIED REPTILLIODS..."
"...ON DA LEDGE ABOVE, THE TENEBRATI--A CABAL DEDICATED TA AN IDEOLOGY OF DARKNESS* --WAITIN' TA KILL WOUNDED SURVIVORS. THEY SEEM OBLIVIOUS TA THE PROTEIN STARVED SWARM OF MACRO-MACROPHAGES HOVERIN' BEHIND 'EM!"
THAM!
TAKKA TAKKA!
TAKKA TAKKA!

* THE ORDO TENEBRATI IS THE YIN TO THE ORDO BIBLIOTHECA'S YANG. A QUASI-RELIGIOUS CULT, THE TENEBRATI SEEKS TO MONOPOLIZE KNOWLEDGE AND USE IT AS A WEAPON TO OPPRESS THE MASSES. PUBLIC EDUCATION AND LIBRARIES ARE ANATHEMA TO THEIR GOAL OF AN EDUCATED ELITE GUIDING UNEDUCATED MASSES OF ILLITERATE PEASANTS. --BARRY

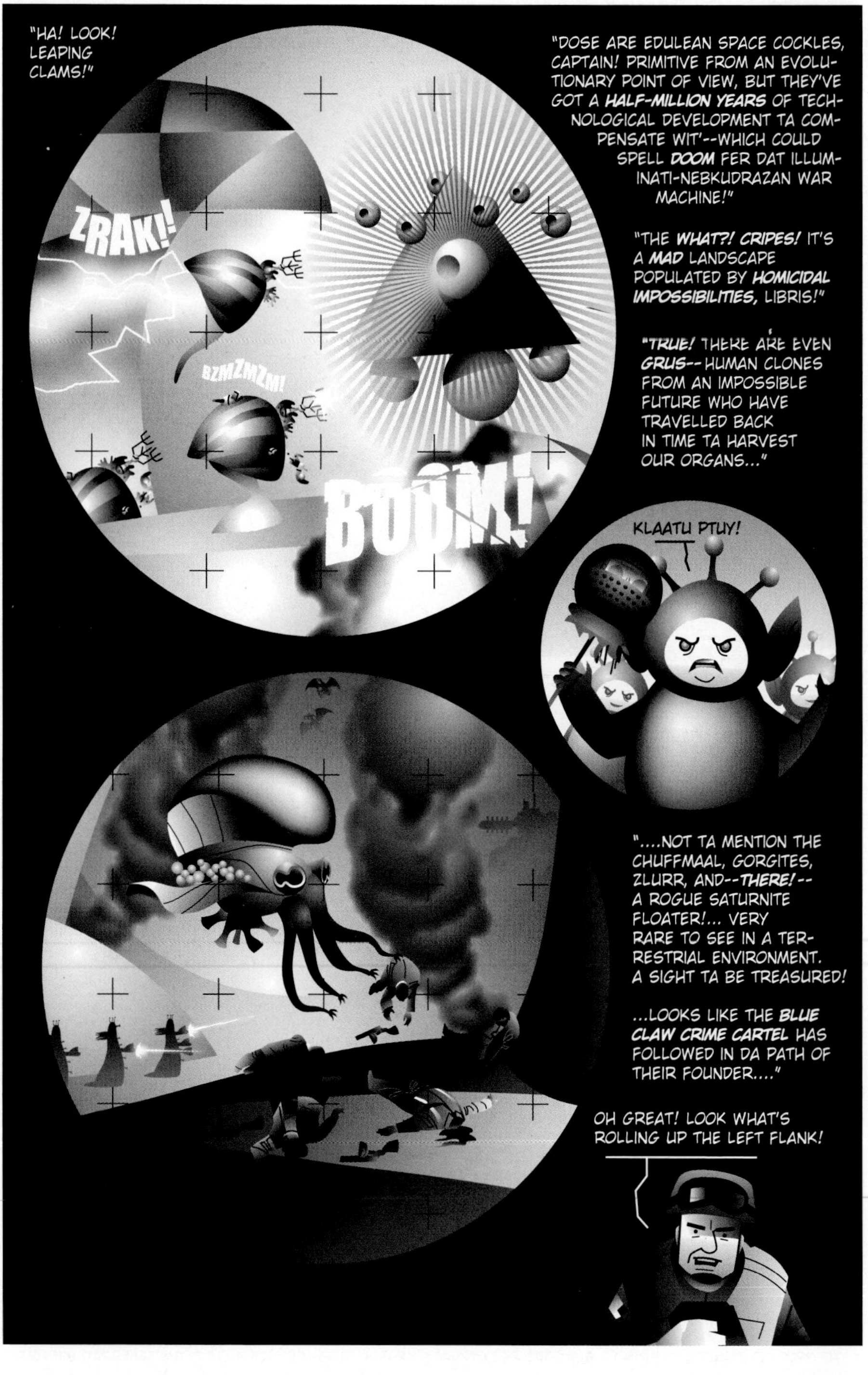
"HA! LOOK! LEAPING CLAMS!"
"DOSE ARE EDULEAN SPACE COCKLES, CAPTAIN! PRIMITIVE FROM AN EVOLUTIONARY POINT OF VIEW, BUT THEY'VE GOT A HALF-MILLION YEARS OF TECHNOLOGICAL DEVELOPMENT TA COMPENSATE WIT'--WHICH COULD SPELL DOOM FER DAT ILLUMINATI-NEBKUDRAZAN WAR MACHINE!"
ZRAK!!
BZMZMZM!
BOOM!
"THE WHAT?! CRIPES! IT'S A MAD LANDSCAPE POPULATED BY HOMICIDAL IMPOSSIBILITIES, LIBRIS!"
"TRUE! THERE ARE EVEN GRUS-- HUMAN CLONES FROM AN IMPOSSIBLE FUTURE WHO HAVE TRAVELLED BACK IN TIME TA HARVEST OUR ORGANS..."
KLAATU PTUY!
"....NOT TA MENTION THE CHUFFMAAL, GORGITES, ZLURR, AND--THERE!-- A ROGUE SATURNITE FLOATER!... VERY RARE TO SEE IN A TERRESTRIAL ENVIRONMENT. A SIGHT TA BE TREASURED!
...LOOKS LIKE THE BLUE CLAW CRIME CARTEL HAS FOLLOWED IN DA PATH OF THEIR FOUNDER...."
OH GREAT! LOOK WHAT'S ROLLING UP THE LEFT FLANK!

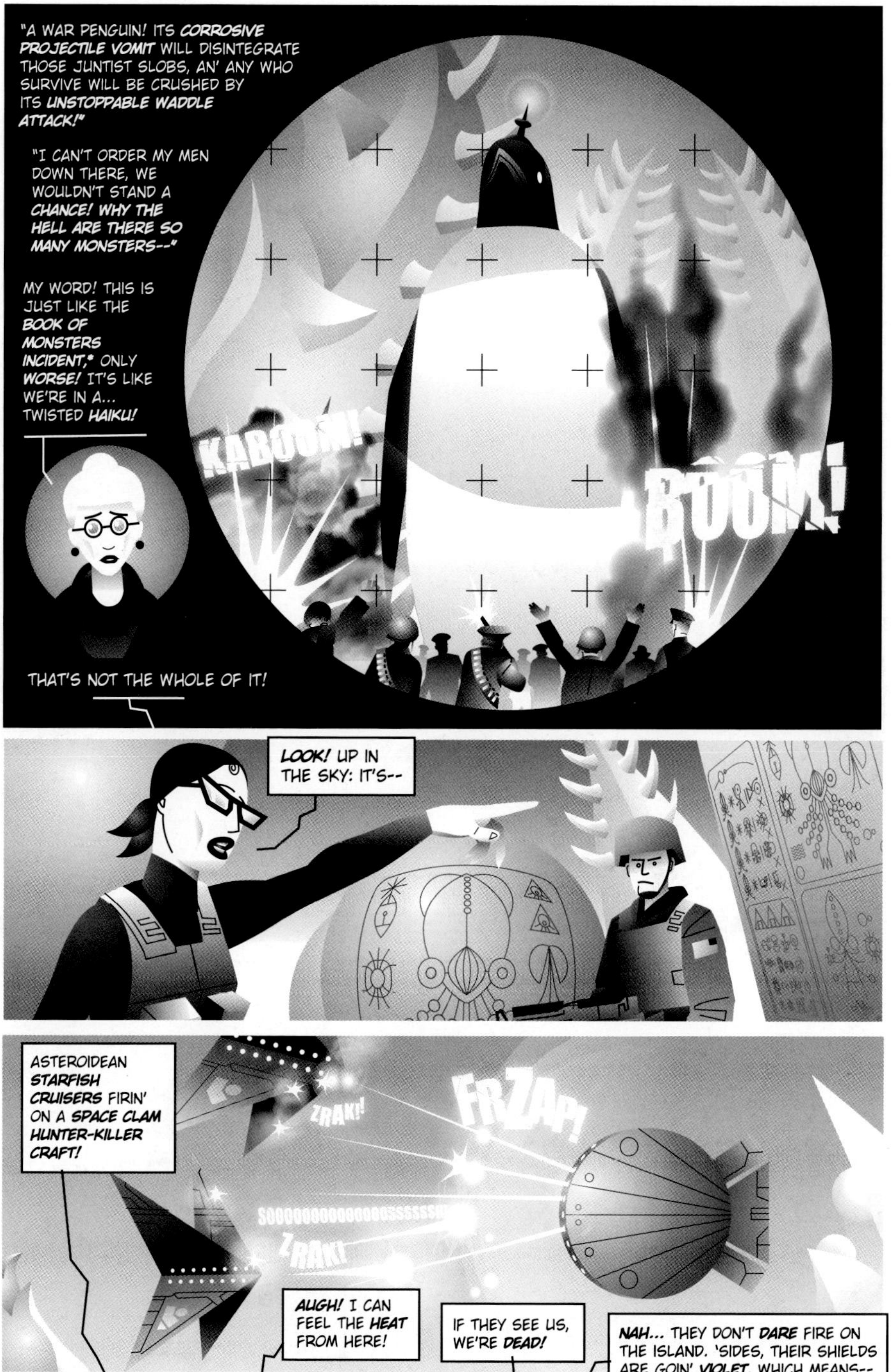
"A WAR PENGUIN! ITS CORROSIVE PROJECTILE VOMIT WILL DISINTEGRATE THOSE JUNTIST SLOBS, AN' ANY WHO SURVIVE WILL BE CRUSHED BY ITS UNSTOPPABLE WADDLE ATTACK!"
"I CAN'T ORDER MY MEN DOWN THERE, WE WOULDN'T STAND A CHANCE! WHY THE HELL ARE THERE SO MANY MONSTERS--"
MY WORD! THIS IS JUST LIKE THE BOOK OF MONSTERS INCIDENT,* ONLY WORSE! IT'S LIKE WE'RE IN A... TWISTED HAIKU!
KABOOM!
BOOM!
THAT'S NOT THE WHOLE OF IT!
LOOK! UP IN THE SKY: IT'S--
ASTEROIDEAN STARFISH CRUISERS FIRIN' ON A SPACE CLAM HUNTER-KILLER CRAFT!
ZRAK!
FRZAP!
ZRAK!
AUGH! I CAN FEEL THE HEAT FROM HERE!
IF THEY SEE US, WE'RE DEAD!
NAH... THEY DON'T DARE FIRE ON THE ISLAND. 'SIDES, THEIR SHIELDS ARE GOIN' VIOLET, WHICH MEANS--

* *SEE REX LIBRIS AND THE BOOK OF MONSTERS (ISSUES 6, 7, AND 8) FOR ALL THE DETAILS! --BARRY*

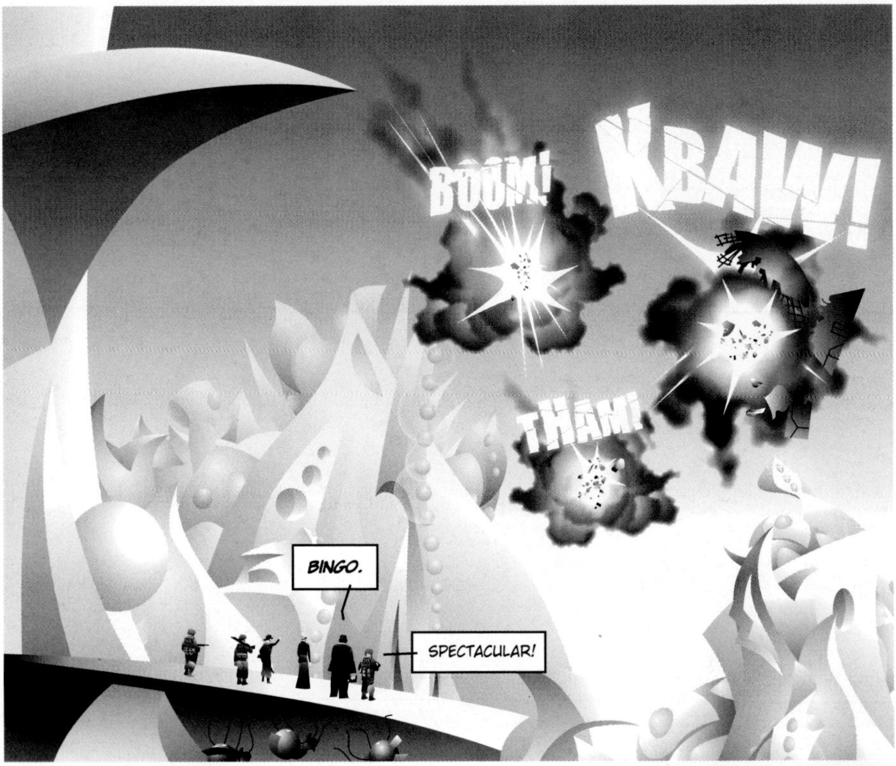
BOOM!
KBAW!
THAM!
BINGO.
SPECTACULAR!

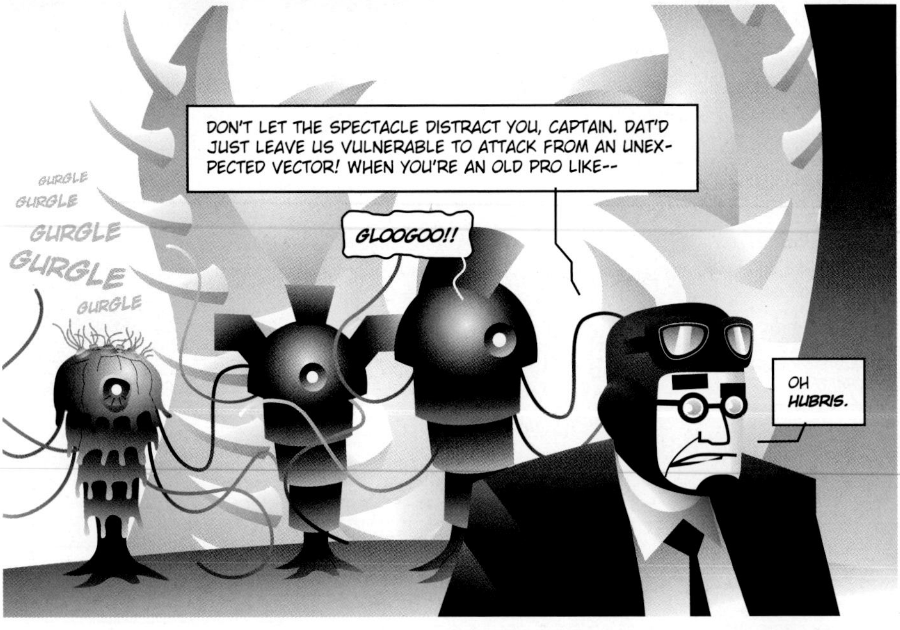
DON'T LET THE SPECTACLE DISTRACT YOU, CAPTAIN. DAT'D JUST LEAVE US VULNERABLE TO ATTACK FROM AN UNEXPECTED VECTOR! WHEN YOU'RE AN OLD PRO LIKE--
GURGLE
GURGLE
GURGLE
GURGLE
GURGLE
GLOOGOO!!
OH HUBRIS.

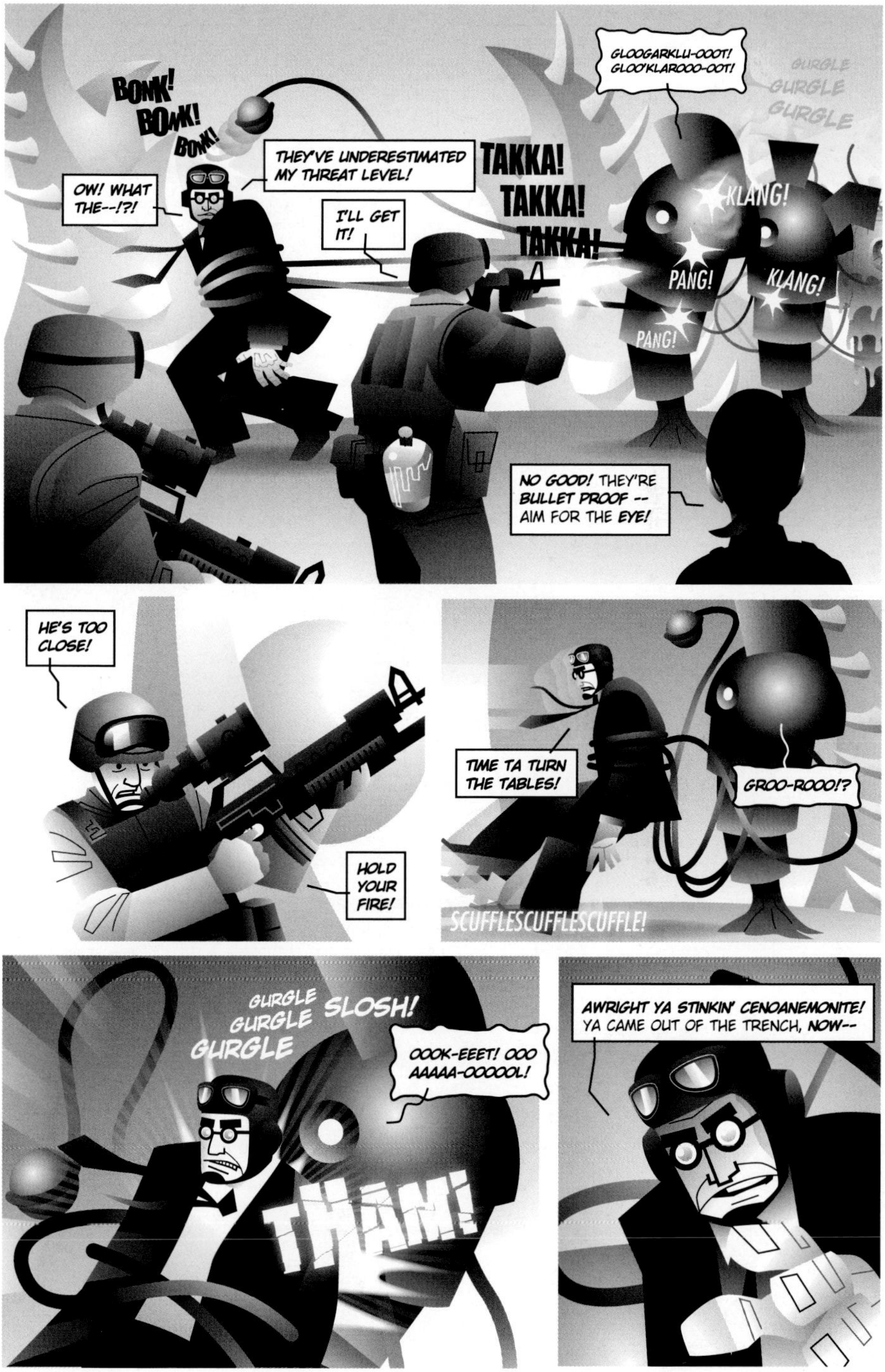
BONK!
BONK!
BONK!
GLOOGARKLU-OOOT! GLOO'KLAROOO-OOT!
GURGLE
GURGLE
GURGLE
OW! WHAT THE--!?!
THEY'VE UNDERESTIMATED MY THREAT LEVEL!
TAKKA!
TAKKA!
TAKKA!
I'LL GET IT!
KLANG!
PANG!
KLANG!
PANG!
NO GOOD! THEY'RE BULLET PROOF -- AIM FOR THE EYE!
HE'S TOO CLOSE!
HOLD YOUR FIRE!
TIME TA TURN THE TABLES!
GROO-ROOO!?
SCUFFLESCUFFLESCUFFLE!
GURGLE
GURGLE
GURGLE
SLOSH!
OOOK-EEET! OOO AAAAA-OOOOOL!
THAM!
AWRIGHT YA STINKIN' CENOANEMONITE!
YA CAME OUT OF THE TRENCH, NOW--

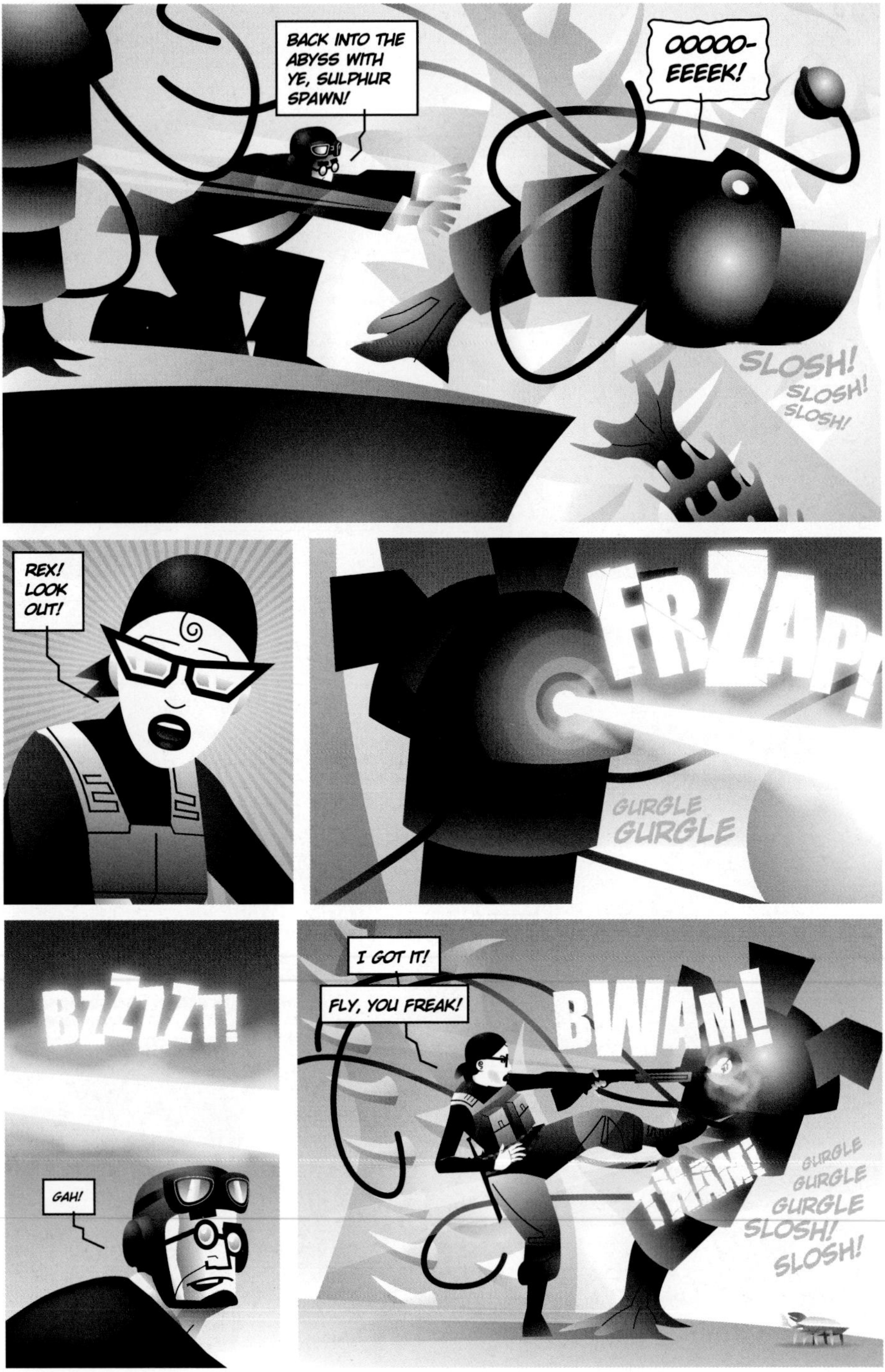
BACK INTO THE ABYSS WITH YE, SULPHUR SPAWN!
OOOOO-EEEEK!
SLOSH! SLOSH! SLOSH!
REX! LOOK OUT!
FRZAP!
GURGLE GURGLE
BZZZZT!
GAH!
I GOT IT!
FLY, YOU FREAK!
BWAM!
THAM!
GURGLE GURGLE GURGLE
SLOSH! SLOSH!

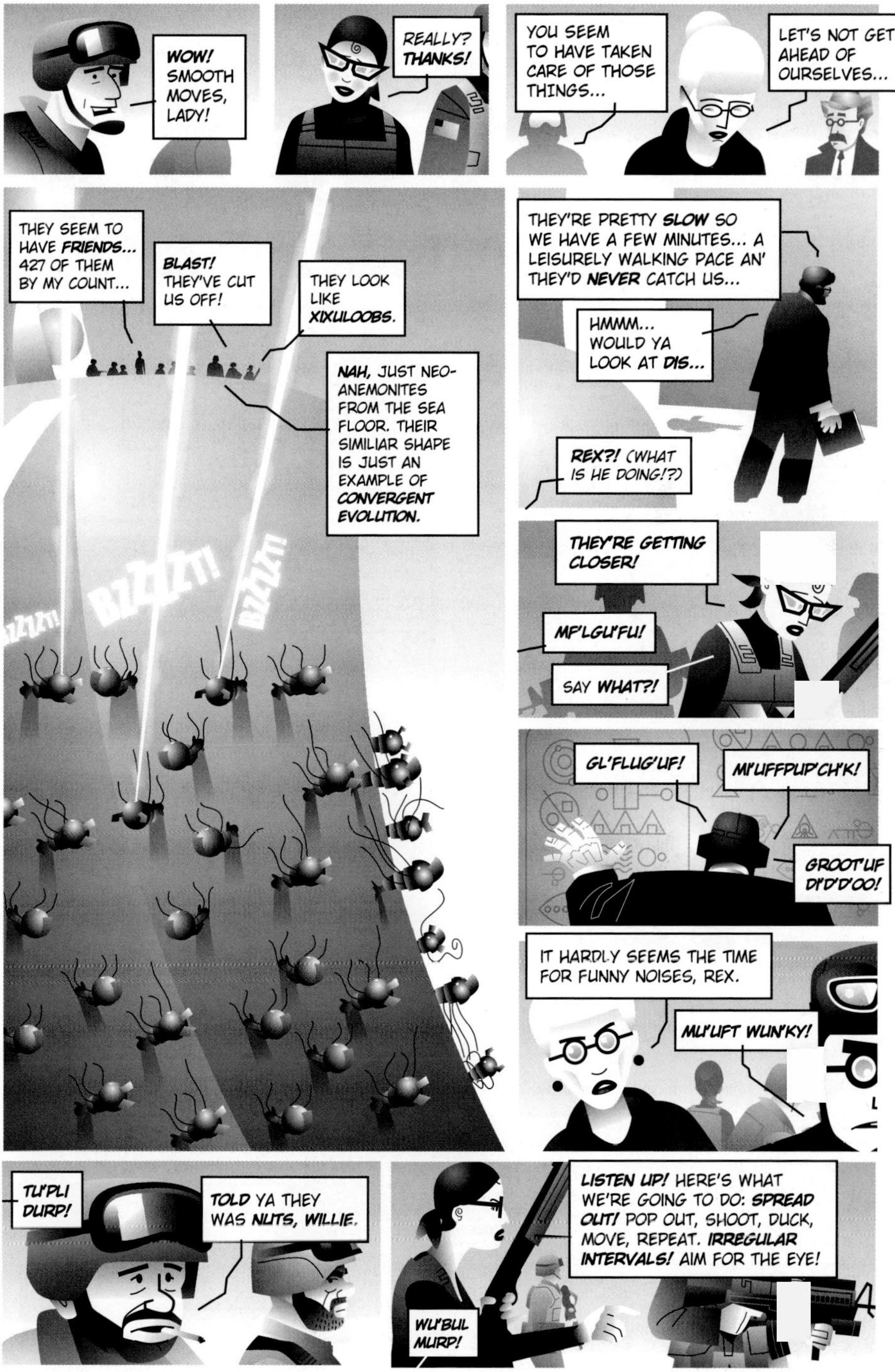
WOW! SMOOTH MOVES, LADY!
REALLY? THANKS!
YOU SEEM TO HAVE TAKEN CARE OF THOSE THINGS...
LET'S NOT GET AHEAD OF OURSELVES...
THEY SEEM TO HAVE FRIENDS... 427 OF THEM BY MY COUNT...
BLAST! THEY'VE CUT US OFF!
THEY LOOK LIKE XIXULOOBS.
NAH, JUST NEO-ANEMONITES FROM THE SEA FLOOR. THEIR SIMILIAR SHAPE IS JUST AN EXAMPLE OF CONVERGENT EVOLUTION.
BZZZZT!
BZZZZT!
BZZZZT!
THEY'RE PRETTY SLOW SO WE HAVE A FEW MINUTES... A LEISURELY WALKING PACE AN' THEY'D NEVER CATCH US...
HMMM... WOULD YA LOOK AT DIS...
REX?! (WHAT IS HE DOING!?)
THEY'RE GETTING CLOSER!
MF'LGU'FU!
SAY WHAT?!
GL'FLUG'UF!
MI'UFFPUP'CH'K!
GROOT'UF DI'D'D'OO!
IT HARDLY SEEMS THE TIME FOR FUNNY NOISES, REX.
MU'UFT WUN'KY!
TU'PLI DURP!
TOLD YA THEY WAS NUTS, WILLIE.
LISTEN UP! HERE'S WHAT WE'RE GOING TO DO: SPREAD OUT! POP OUT, SHOOT, DUCK, MOVE, REPEAT. IRREGULAR INTERVALS! AIM FOR THE EYE!
WU'BUL MURP!

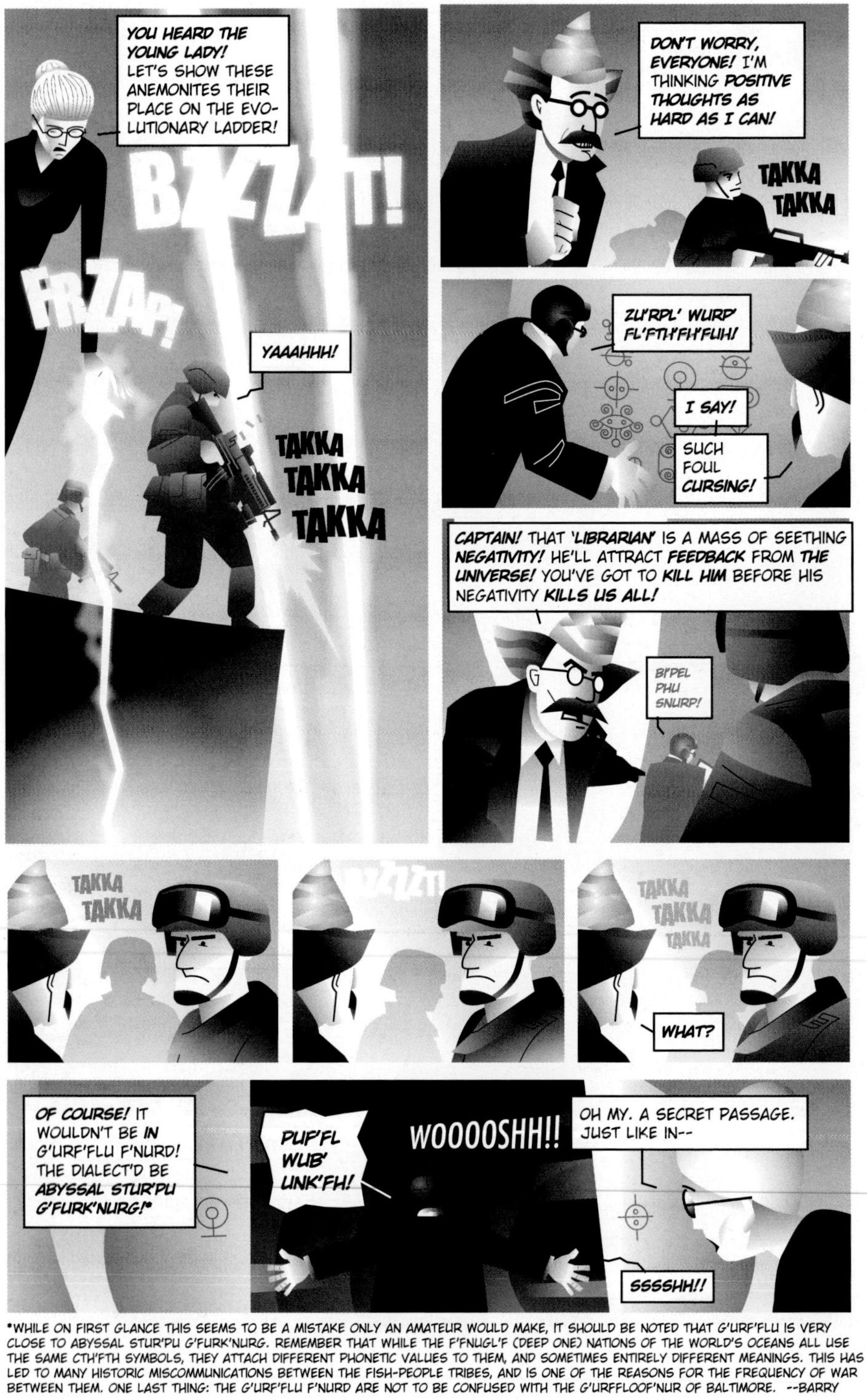
YOU HEARD THE YOUNG LADY! LET'S SHOW THESE ANEMONITES THEIR PLACE ON THE EVOLUTIONARY LADDER!
BZZZZAT!
FRZAP!
YAAAHHH!
TAKKA TAKKA TAKKA
DON'T WORRY, EVERYONE! I'M THINKING POSITIVE THOUGHTS AS HARD AS I CAN!
TAKKA TAKKA
ZU'RPL' WURP' FL'FTH'FH'FUH!
I SAY!
SUCH FOUL CURSING!
CAPTAIN! THAT 'LIBRARIAN' IS A MASS OF SEETHING NEGATIVITY! HE'LL ATTRACT FEEDBACK FROM THE UNIVERSE! YOU'VE GOT TO KILL HIM BEFORE HIS NEGATIVITY KILLS US ALL!
BI'PEL PHU SNURP!
TAKKA TAKKA
ZZZZT!
TAKKA TAKKA TAKKA
WHAT?
OF COURSE! IT WOULDN'T BE IN G'URF'FLU F'NURD! THE DIALECT'D BE ABYSSAL STUR'PU G'FURK'NURG!*
PUP'FL WUB' UNK'FH!
WOOOOSHH!!
OH MY. A SECRET PASSAGE. JUST LIKE IN--
SSSSHH!!

*WHILE ON FIRST GLANCE THIS SEEMS TO BE A MISTAKE ONLY AN AMATEUR WOULD MAKE, IT SHOULD BE NOTED THAT G'URF'FLU IS VERY CLOSE TO ABYSSAL STUR'PU G'FURK'NURG. REMEMBER THAT WHILE THE F'FNUGL'F (DEEP ONE) NATIONS OF THE WORLD'S OCEANS ALL USE THE SAME CTH'FTH SYMBOLS, THEY ATTACH DIFFERENT PHONETIC VALUES TO THEM, AND SOMETIMES ENTIRELY DIFFERENT MEANINGS. THIS HAS LED TO MANY HISTORIC MISCOMMUNICATIONS BETWEEN THE FISH-PEOPLE TRIBES, AND IS ONE OF THE REASONS FOR THE FREQUENCY OF WAR BETWEEN THEM. ONE LAST THING: THE G'URF'FLU F'NURD ARE NOT TO BE CONFUSED WITH THE G'URFFLOOF'NUR OF BALTIMORE. --BARRY

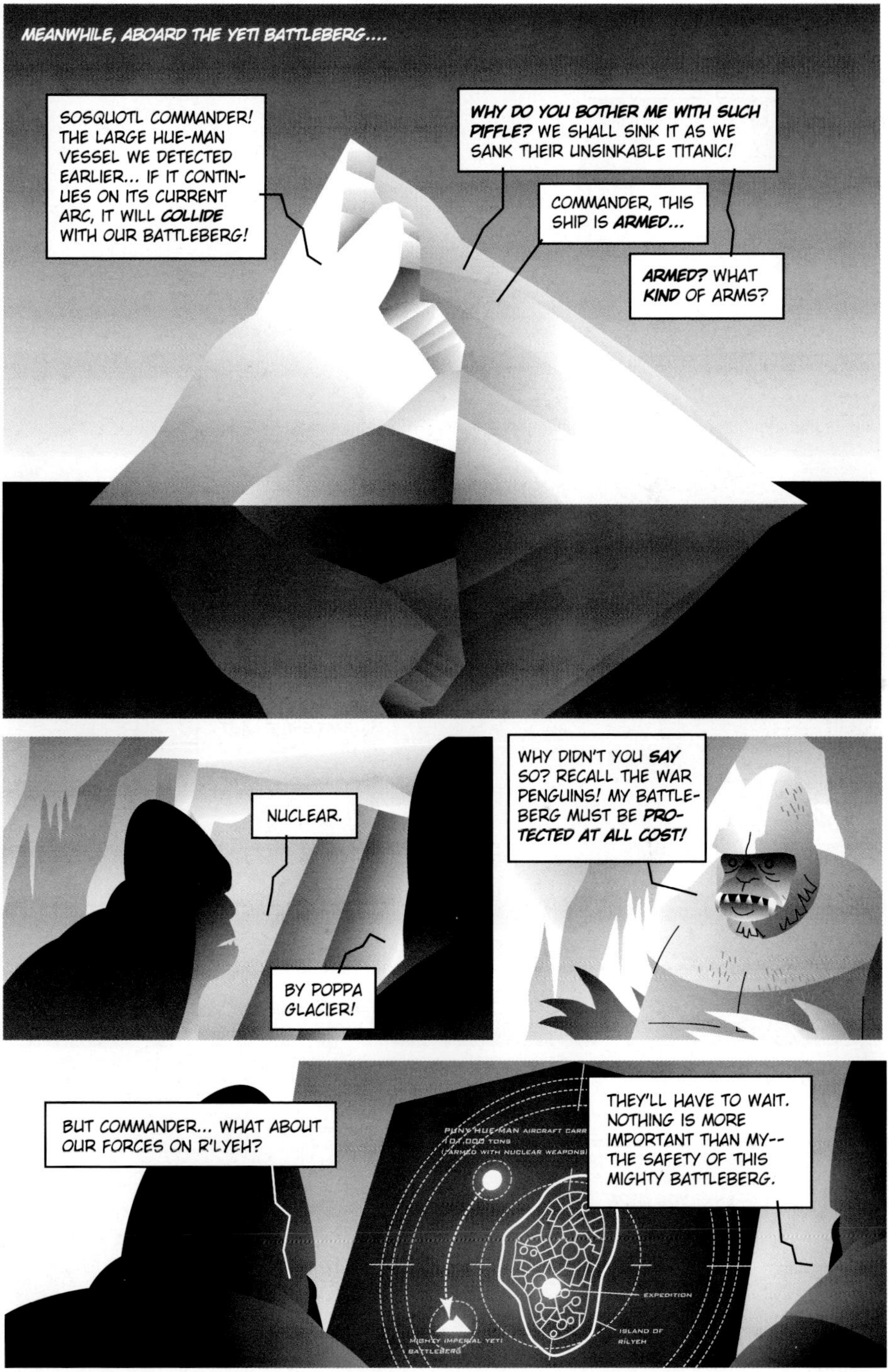
MEANWHILE, ABOARD THE YETI BATTLEBERG....
SOSQUOTL COMMANDER! THE LARGE HUE-MAN VESSEL WE DETECTED EARLIER... IF IT CONTINUES ON ITS CURRENT ARC, IT WILL COLLIDE WITH OUR BATTLEBERG!
WHY DO YOU BOTHER ME WITH SUCH PIFFLE? WE SHALL SINK IT AS WE SANK THEIR UNSINKABLE TITANIC!
COMMANDER, THIS SHIP IS ARMED...
ARMED? WHAT KIND OF ARMS?
NUCLEAR.
BY POPPA GLACIER!
WHY DIDN'T YOU SAY SO? RECALL THE WAR PENGUINS! MY BATTLEBERG MUST BE PROTECTED AT ALL COST!
BUT COMMANDER... WHAT ABOUT OUR FORCES ON R'LYEH?
THEY'LL HAVE TO WAIT. NOTHING IS MORE IMPORTANT THAN MY-- THE SAFETY OF THIS MIGHTY BATTLEBERG.
PUNY HUE-MAN AIRCRAFT CARR
(ARMED WITH NUCLEAR WEAPONS)
EXPEDITION
ISLAND OF R'LYEH
MIGHTY IMPERIAL YETI BATTLEBERG

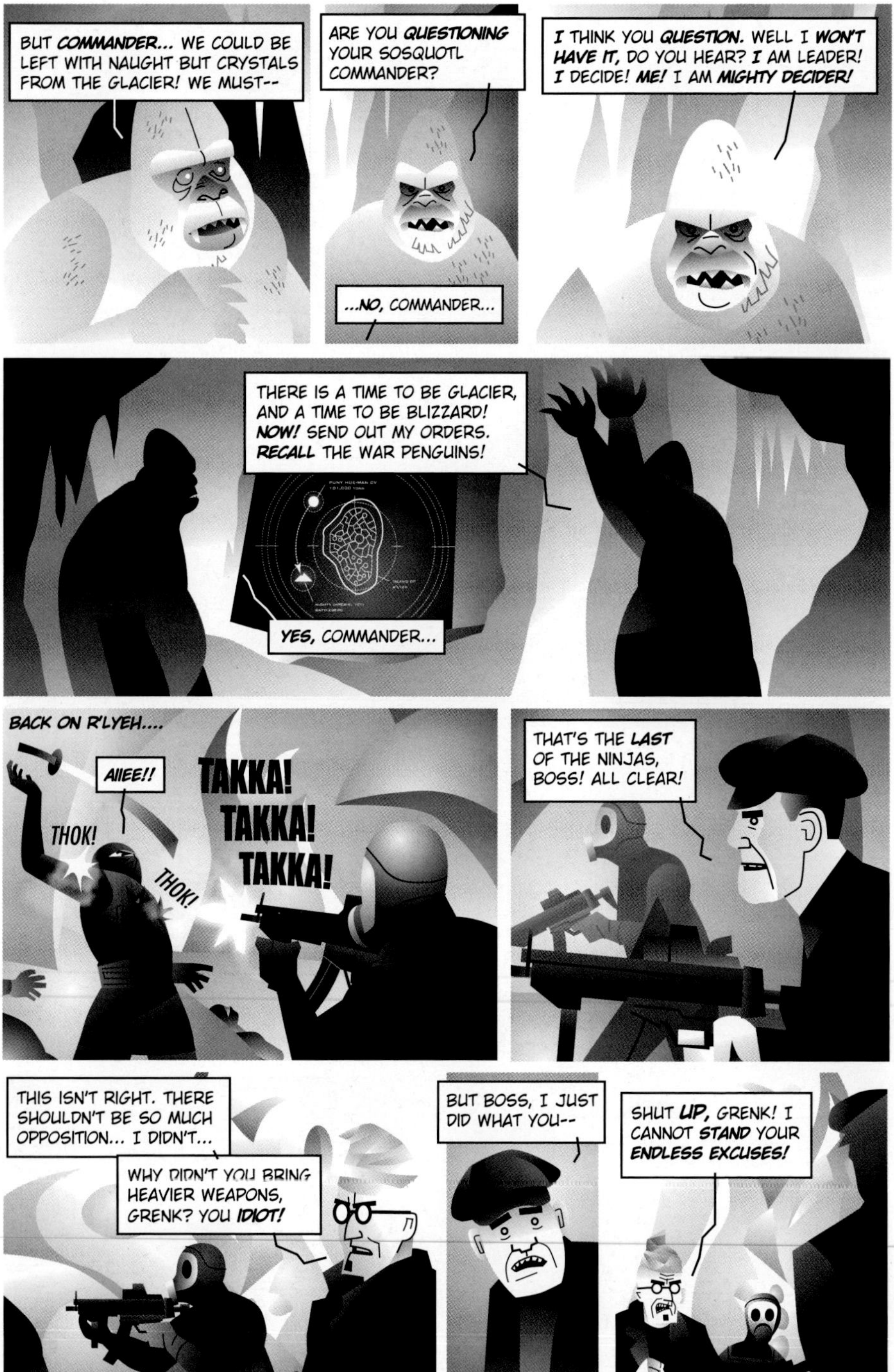
BUT COMMANDER... WE COULD BE LEFT WITH NAUGHT BUT CRYSTALS FROM THE GLACIER! WE MUST--
ARE YOU QUESTIONING YOUR SOSQUOTL COMMANDER?
...NO, COMMANDER...
I THINK YOU QUESTION. WELL I WON'T HAVE IT, DO YOU HEAR? I AM LEADER! I DECIDE! ME! I AM MIGHTY DECIDER!
THERE IS A TIME TO BE GLACIER, AND A TIME TO BE BLIZZARD! NOW! SEND OUT MY ORDERS. RECALL THE WAR PENGUINS!
YES, COMMANDER...
BACK ON R'LYEH....
AIIEE!!
THOK!
THOK!
TAKKA! TAKKA! TAKKA!
THAT'S THE LAST OF THE NINJAS, BOSS! ALL CLEAR!
THIS ISN'T RIGHT. THERE SHOULDN'T BE SO MUCH OPPOSITION... I DIDN'T...
WHY DIDN'T YOU BRING HEAVIER WEAPONS, GRENK? YOU IDIOT!
BUT BOSS, I JUST DID WHAT YOU--
SHUT UP, GRENK! I CANNOT STAND YOUR ENDLESS EXCUSES!

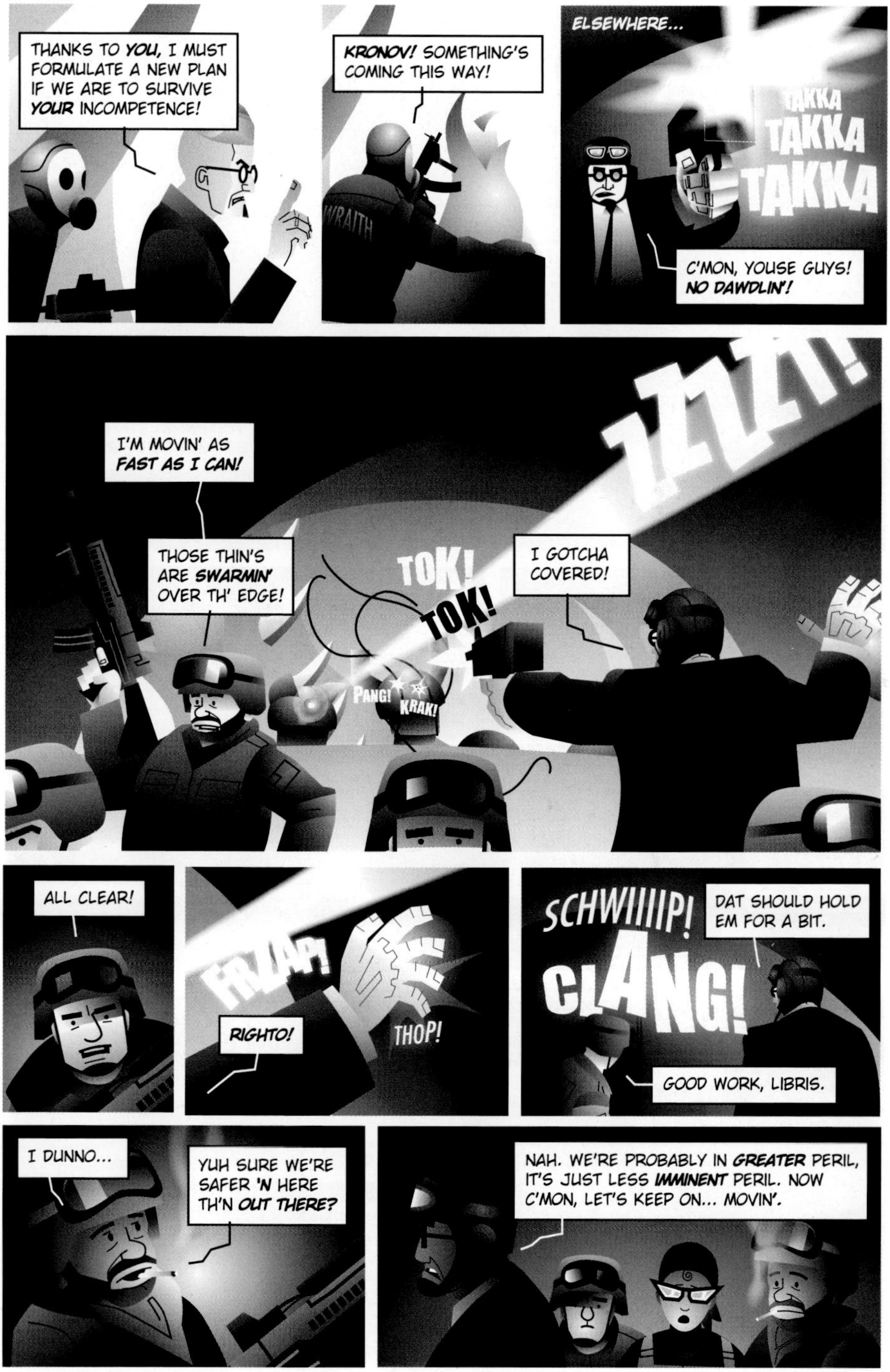
THANKS TO **YOU,** I MUST FORMULATE A NEW PLAN IF WE ARE TO SURVIVE **YOUR** INCOMPETENCE!
KRONOV! SOMETHING'S COMING THIS WAY!
WRAITH
ELSEWHERE...
TAKKA TAKKA TAKKA
C'MON, YOUSE GUYS! **NO DAWDLIN'!**
ZZZZT!
I'M MOVIN' AS **FAST AS I CAN!**
THOSE THIN'S ARE **SWARMIN'** OVER TH' EDGE!
TOK! TOK!
I GOTCHA COVERED!
PANG! KRAK!
ALL CLEAR!
FRZAP!
THOP!
RIGHTO!
SCHWIIIIP! CLANG!
DAT SHOULD HOLD EM FOR A BIT.
GOOD WORK, LIBRIS.
I DUNNO...
YUH SURE WE'RE SAFER **'N** HERE TH'N **OUT THERE?**
NAH. WE'RE PROBABLY IN **GREATER** PERIL, IT'S JUST LESS **IMMINENT** PERIL. NOW C'MON, LET'S KEEP ON... MOVIN'.

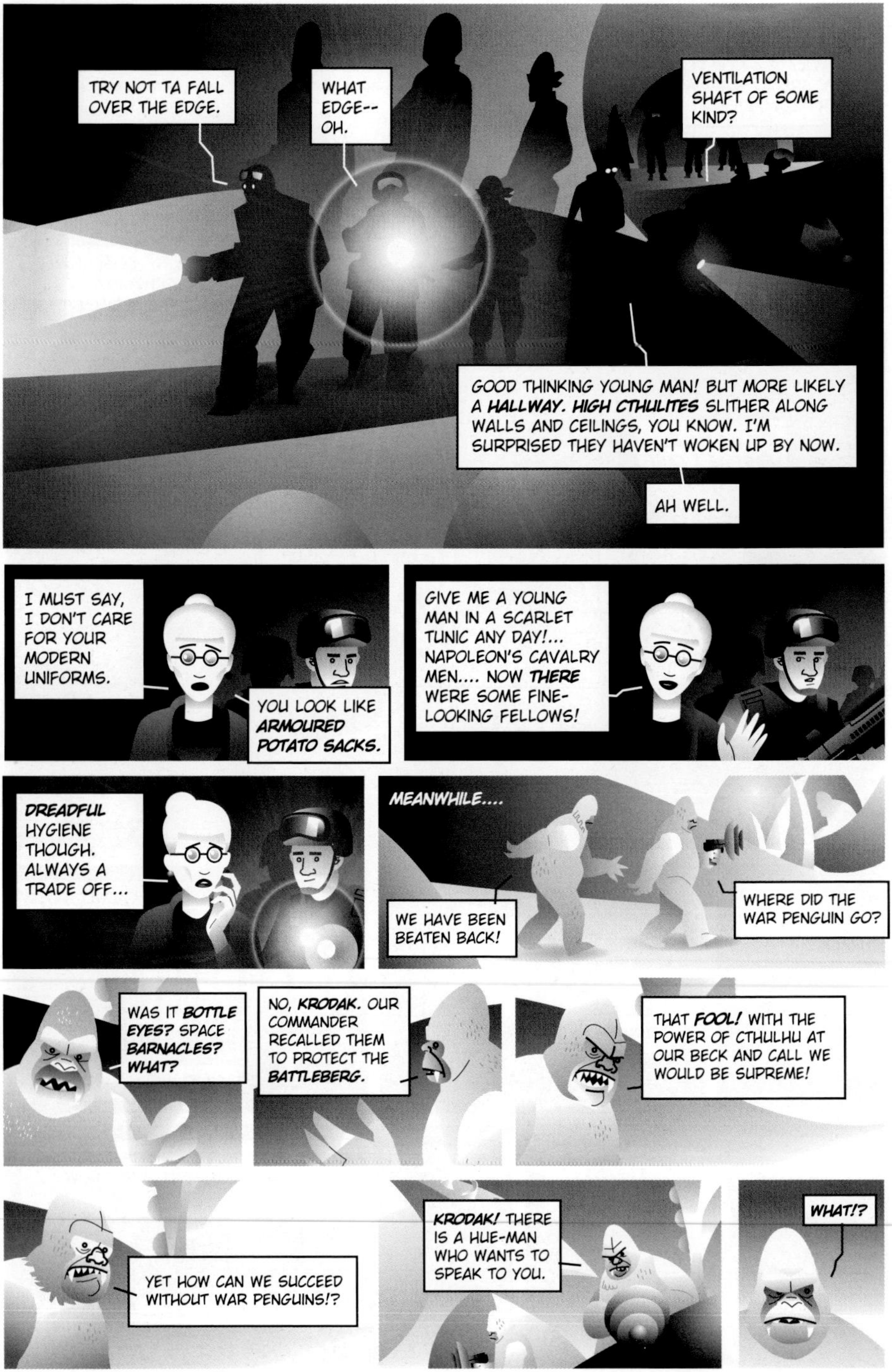

TRY NOT TA FALL OVER THE EDGE.
WHAT EDGE-- OH.
VENTILATION SHAFT OF SOME KIND?
GOOD THINKING YOUNG MAN! BUT MORE LIKELY A ***HALLWAY. HIGH CTHULITES*** SLITHER ALONG WALLS AND CEILINGS, YOU KNOW. I'M SURPRISED THEY HAVEN'T WOKEN UP BY NOW.
AH WELL.
I MUST SAY, I DON'T CARE FOR YOUR MODERN UNIFORMS.
YOU LOOK LIKE ***ARMOURED POTATO SACKS.***
GIVE ME A YOUNG MAN IN A SCARLET TUNIC ANY DAY!... NAPOLEON'S CAVALRY MEN.... NOW ***THERE*** WERE SOME FINE-LOOKING FELLOWS!
DREADFUL HYGIENE THOUGH. ALWAYS A TRADE OFF...
MEANWHILE....
WE HAVE BEEN BEATEN BACK!
WHERE DID THE WAR PENGUIN GO?
WAS IT ***BOTTLE EYES?*** SPACE ***BARNACLES? WHAT?***
NO, ***KRODAK.*** OUR COMMANDER RECALLED THEM TO PROTECT THE ***BATTLEBERG.***
THAT ***FOOL!*** WITH THE POWER OF CTHULHU AT OUR BECK AND CALL WE WOULD BE SUPREME!
YET HOW CAN WE SUCCEED WITHOUT WAR PENGUINS!?
KRODAK! THERE IS A HUE-MAN WHO WANTS TO SPEAK TO YOU.
WHAT!?

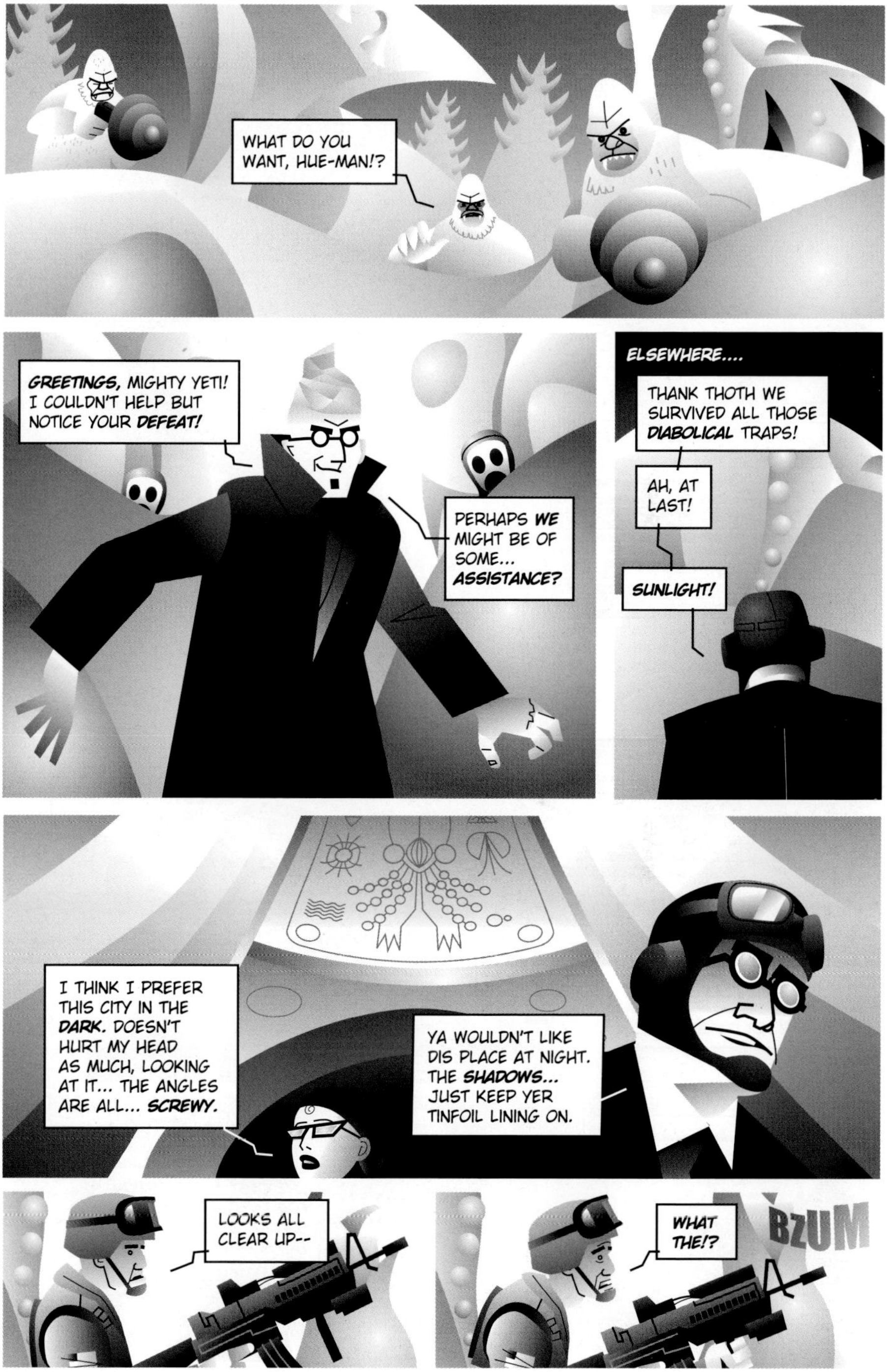
WHAT DO YOU WANT, HUE-MAN!?
GREETINGS, MIGHTY YETI! I COULDN'T HELP BUT NOTICE YOUR DEFEAT!
PERHAPS WE MIGHT BE OF SOME... ASSISTANCE?
ELSEWHERE....
THANK THOTH WE SURVIVED ALL THOSE DIABOLICAL TRAPS!
AH, AT LAST!
SUNLIGHT!
I THINK I PREFER THIS CITY IN THE DARK. DOESN'T HURT MY HEAD AS MUCH, LOOKING AT IT... THE ANGLES ARE ALL... SCREWY.
YA WOULDN'T LIKE DIS PLACE AT NIGHT. THE SHADOWS... JUST KEEP YER TINFOIL LINING ON.
LOOKS ALL CLEAR UP--
WHAT THE!?
BZUM

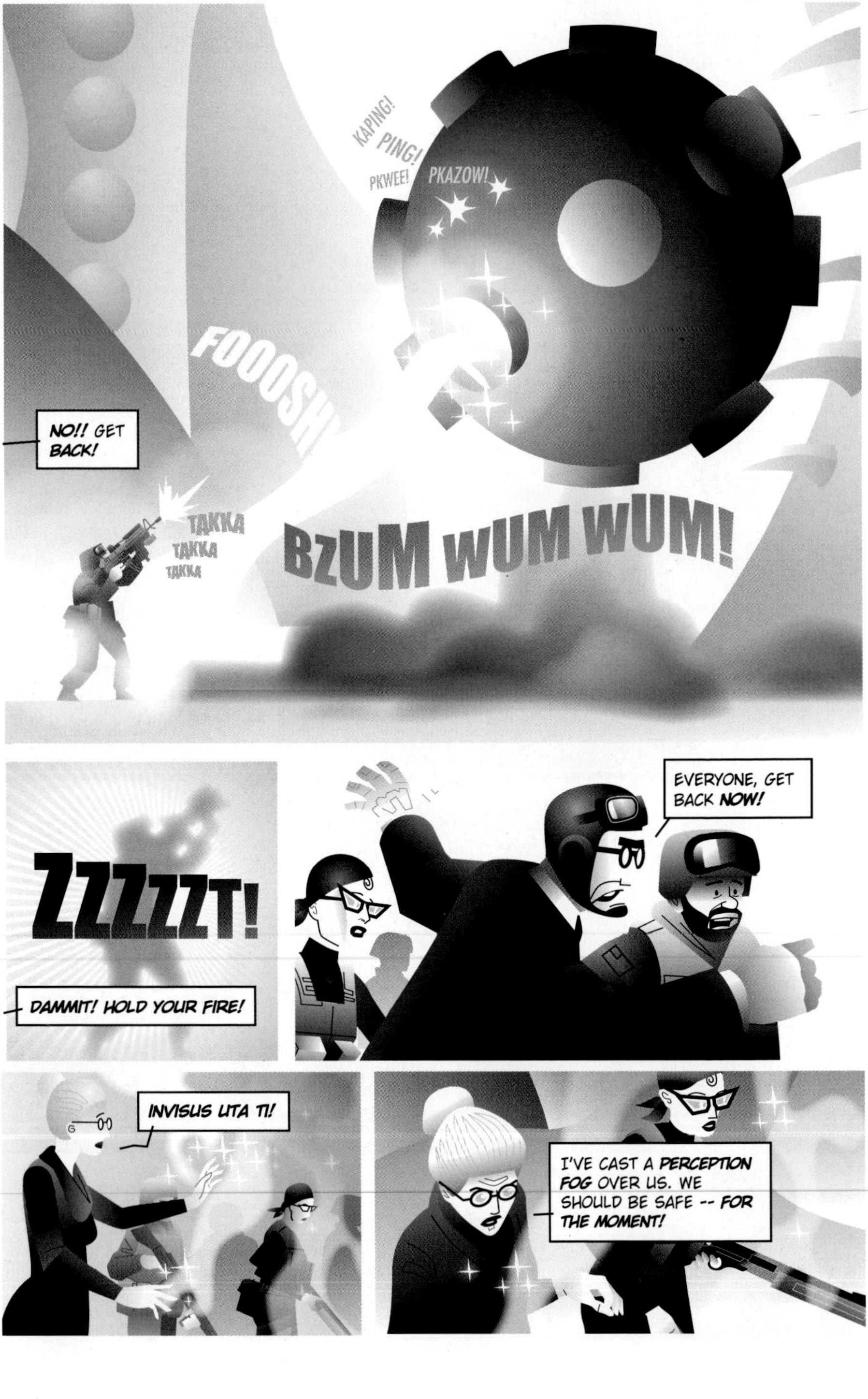
KAPING!
PING!
PKWEE!
PKAZOW!
FOOOSH!
NO!! GET BACK!
TAKKA
TAKKA
TAKKA
BZUM WUM WUM!
ZZZZZT!
DAMMIT! HOLD YOUR FIRE!
EVERYONE, GET BACK NOW!
INVISUS UTA TI!
I'VE CAST A PERCEPTION FOG OVER US. WE SHOULD BE SAFE -- FOR THE MOMENT!

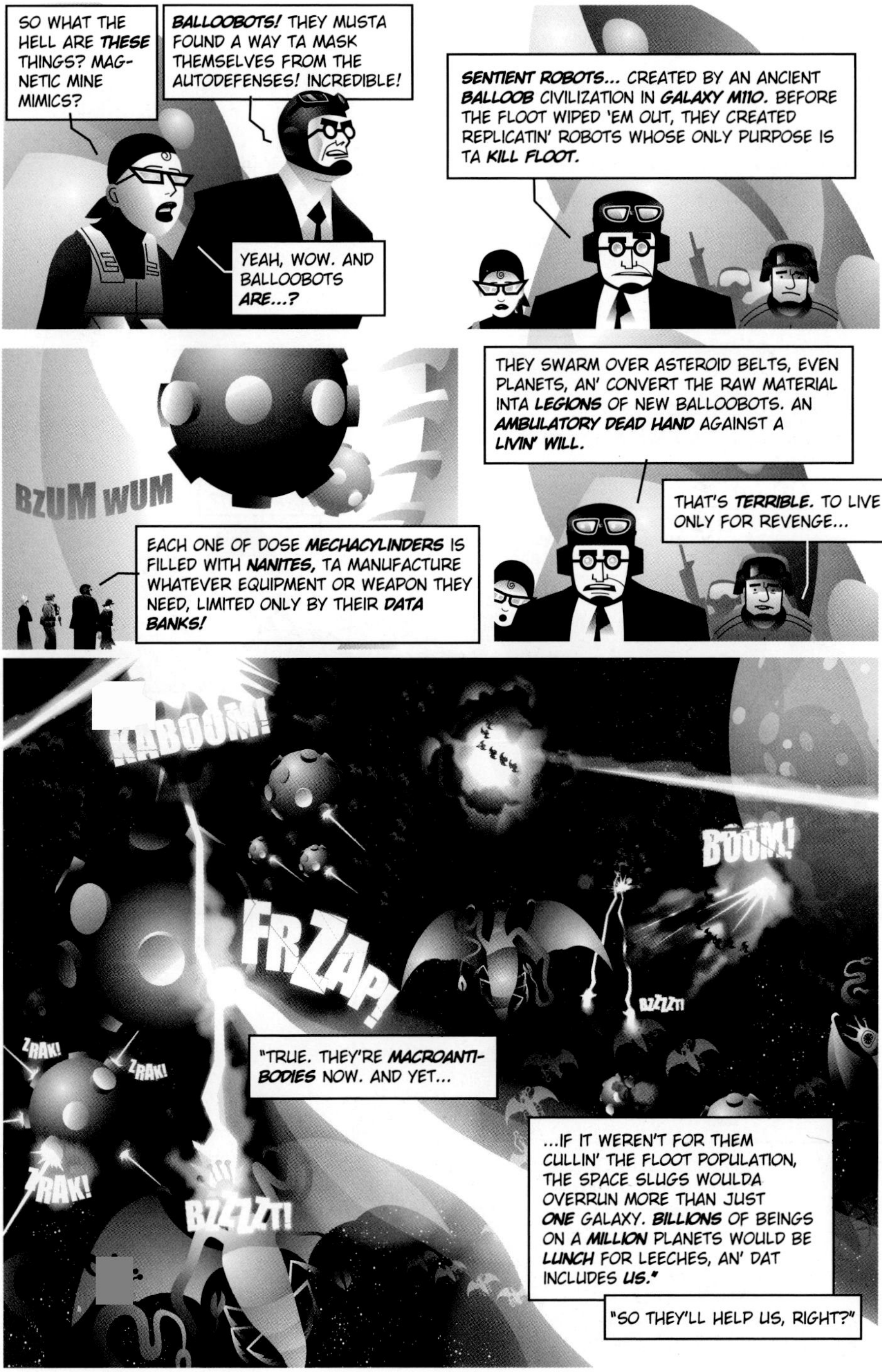
SO WHAT THE HELL ARE *THESE* THINGS? MAG-NETIC MINE MIMICS?
BALLOOBOTS! THEY MUSTA FOUND A WAY TA MASK THEMSELVES FROM THE AUTODEFENSES! INCREDIBLE!
YEAH, WOW. AND BALLOOBOTS *ARE...?*
SENTIENT ROBOTS... CREATED BY AN ANCIENT *BALLOOB* CIVILIZATION IN *GALAXY M110.* BEFORE THE FLOOT WIPED 'EM OUT, THEY CREATED REPLICATIN' ROBOTS WHOSE ONLY PURPOSE IS TA *KILL FLOOT.*
BZUM WUM
EACH ONE OF DOSE *MECHACYLINDERS* IS FILLED WITH *NANITES,* TA MANUFACTURE WHATEVER EQUIPMENT OR WEAPON THEY NEED, LIMITED ONLY BY THEIR *DATA BANKS!*
THEY SWARM OVER ASTEROID BELTS, EVEN PLANETS, AN' CONVERT THE RAW MATERIAL INTA *LEGIONS* OF NEW BALLOOBOTS. AN *AMBULATORY DEAD HAND* AGAINST A *LIVIN' WILL.*
THAT'S *TERRIBLE.* TO LIVE ONLY FOR REVENGE...
KABOOM!
BOOM!
FRZAP!
BZZZZT!
ZRAK!
ZRAK!
"TRUE. THEY'RE *MACROANTI-BODIES* NOW. AND YET...
ZRAK!
BZZZZZT!
...IF IT WEREN'T FOR THEM CULLIN' THE FLOOT POPULATION, THE SPACE SLUGS WOULDA OVERRUN MORE THAN JUST *ONE* GALAXY. *BILLIONS* OF BEINGS ON A *MILLION* PLANETS WOULD BE *LUNCH* FOR LEECHES, AN' DAT INCLUDES *US.*"
"SO THEY'LL HELP US, RIGHT?"

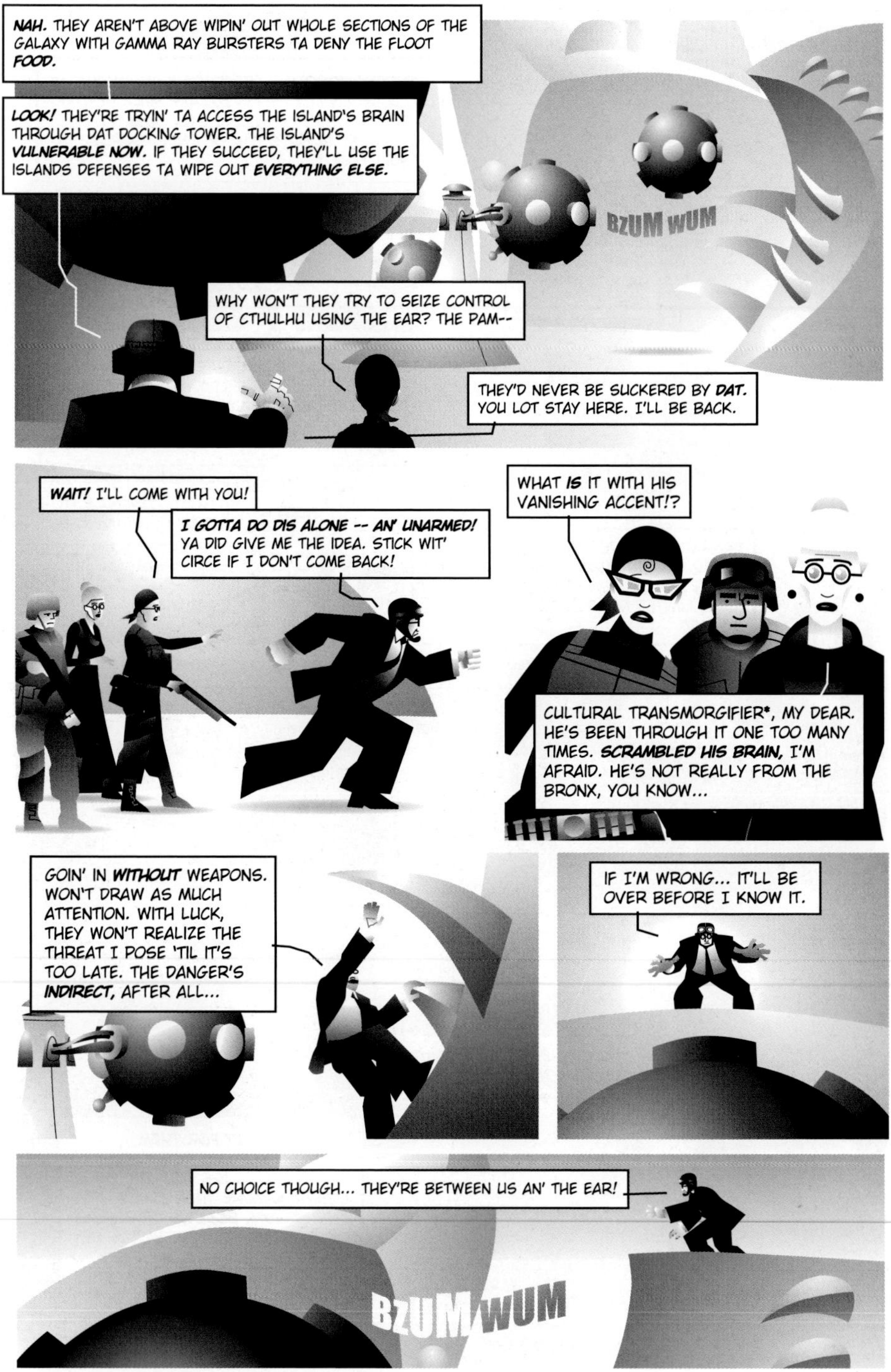
NAH. THEY AREN'T ABOVE WIPIN' OUT WHOLE SECTIONS OF THE GALAXY WITH GAMMA RAY BURSTERS TA DENY THE FLOOT FOOD.
LOOK! THEY'RE TRYIN' TA ACCESS THE ISLAND'S BRAIN THROUGH DAT DOCKING TOWER. THE ISLAND'S VULNERABLE NOW. IF THEY SUCCEED, THEY'LL USE THE ISLANDS DEFENSES TA WIPE OUT EVERYTHING ELSE.
BZUM WUM
WHY WON'T THEY TRY TO SEIZE CONTROL OF CTHULHU USING THE EAR? THE PAM--
THEY'D NEVER BE SUCKERED BY DAT. YOU LOT STAY HERE. I'LL BE BACK.
WAIT! I'LL COME WITH YOU!
I GOTTA DO DIS ALONE -- AN' UNARMED! YA DID GIVE ME THE IDEA. STICK WIT' CIRCE IF I DON'T COME BACK!
WHAT IS IT WITH HIS VANISHING ACCENT!?
CULTURAL TRANSMORGIFIER*, MY DEAR. HE'S BEEN THROUGH IT ONE TOO MANY TIMES. SCRAMBLED HIS BRAIN, I'M AFRAID. HE'S NOT REALLY FROM THE BRONX, YOU KNOW...
GOIN' IN WITHOUT WEAPONS. WON'T DRAW AS MUCH ATTENTION. WITH LUCK, THEY WON'T REALIZE THE THREAT I POSE 'TIL IT'S TOO LATE. THE DANGER'S INDIRECT, AFTER ALL...
IF I'M WRONG... IT'LL BE OVER BEFORE I KNOW IT.
NO CHOICE THOUGH... THEY'RE BETWEEN US AN' THE EAR!
BZUM WUM

* SEE ISSUE 1 FOR MORE INFORMATION ON THIS INCREDIBLE DEVICE! -- BARRY

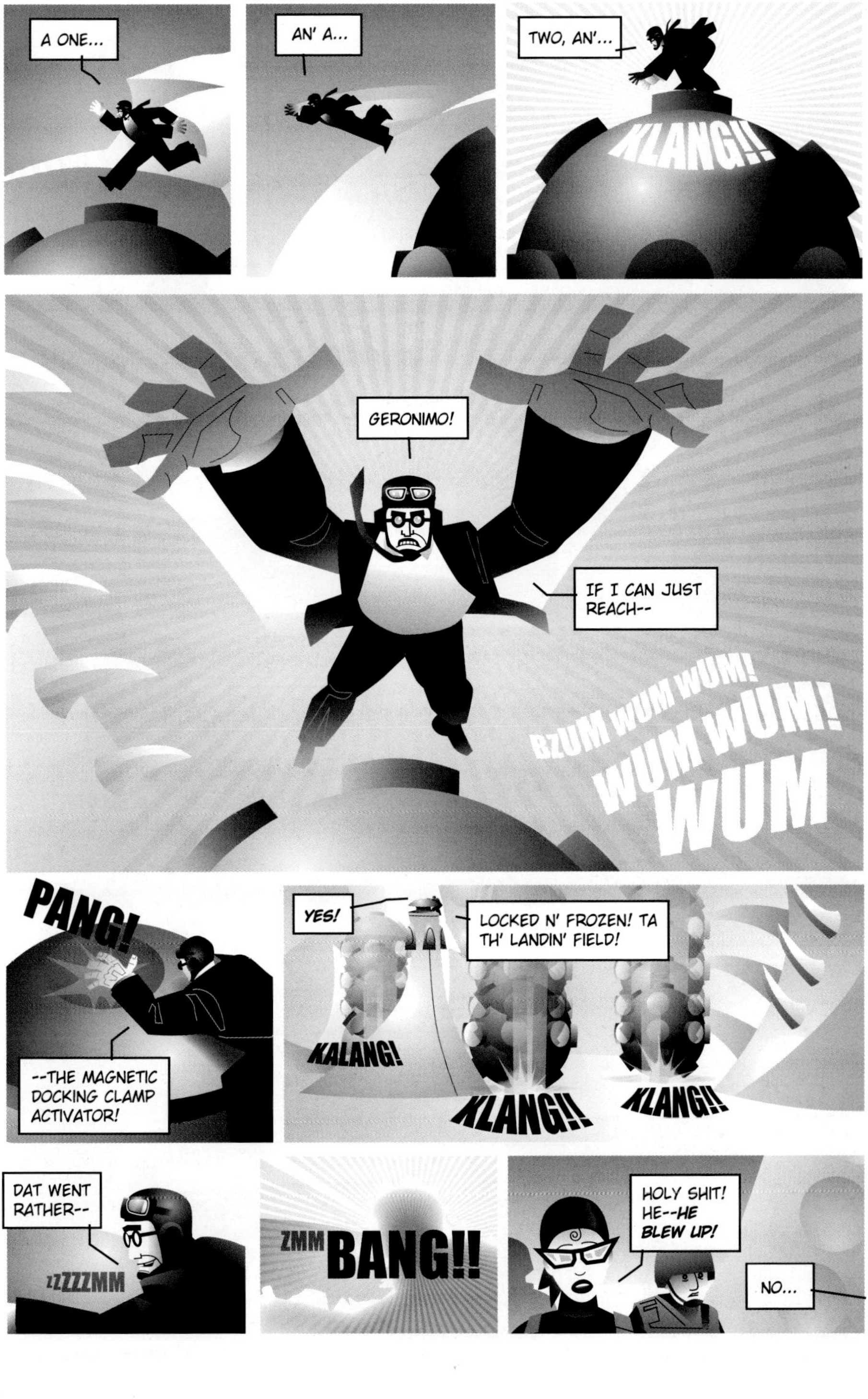
A ONE...
AN' A...
TWO, AN'...
KLANG!!
GERONIMO!
IF I CAN JUST REACH--
BZUM WUM WUM! WUM WUM! WUM
PANG!
--THE MAGNETIC DOCKING CLAMP ACTIVATOR!
YES!
LOCKED N' FROZEN! TA TH' LANDIN' FIELD!
KALANG!
KLANG!!
KLANG!!
DAT WENT RATHER--
zZZZZMM
ZMM BANG!!
HOLY SHIT! HE--HE BLEW UP!
NO...

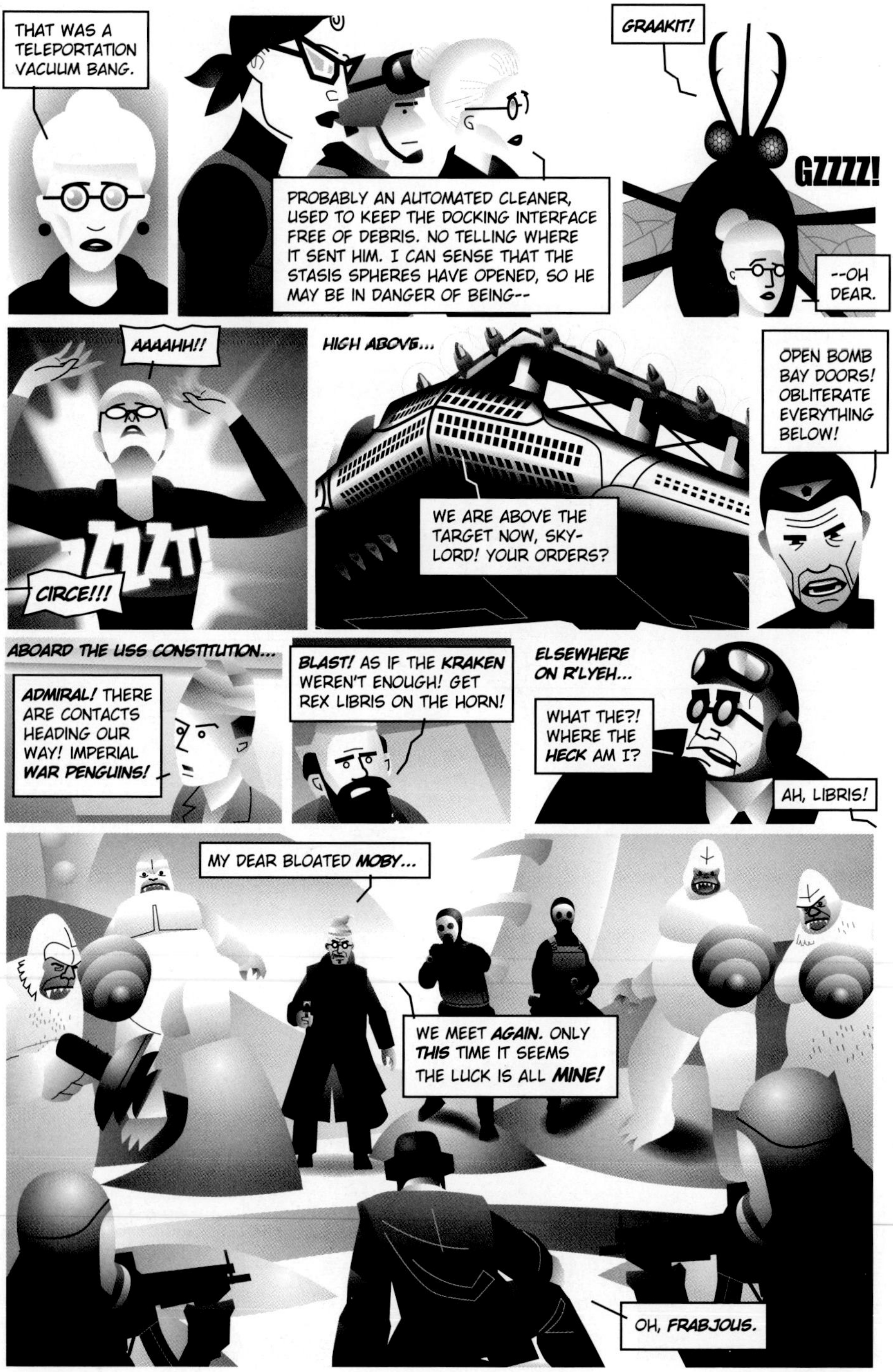
THAT WAS A TELEPORTATION VACUUM BANG.
PROBABLY AN AUTOMATED CLEANER, USED TO KEEP THE DOCKING INTERFACE FREE OF DEBRIS. NO TELLING WHERE IT SENT HIM. I CAN SENSE THAT THE STASIS SPHERES HAVE OPENED, SO HE MAY BE IN DANGER OF BEING--
GRAAKIT!
GZZZZ!
--OH DEAR.
AAAAHH!!
ZZZT!
CIRCE!!!
HIGH ABOVE...
WE ARE ABOVE THE TARGET NOW, SKY-LORD! YOUR ORDERS?
OPEN BOMB BAY DOORS! OBLITERATE EVERYTHING BELOW!
ABOARD THE USS CONSTITUTION...
ADMIRAL! THERE ARE CONTACTS HEADING OUR WAY! IMPERIAL WAR PENGUINS!
BLAST! AS IF THE KRAKEN WEREN'T ENOUGH! GET REX LIBRIS ON THE HORN!
ELSEWHERE ON R'LYEH...
WHAT THE?! WHERE THE HECK AM I?
AH, LIBRIS!
MY DEAR BLOATED MOBY...
WE MEET AGAIN. ONLY THIS TIME IT SEEMS THE LUCK IS ALL MINE!
OH, FRABJOUS.

TO BE CONTINUED....

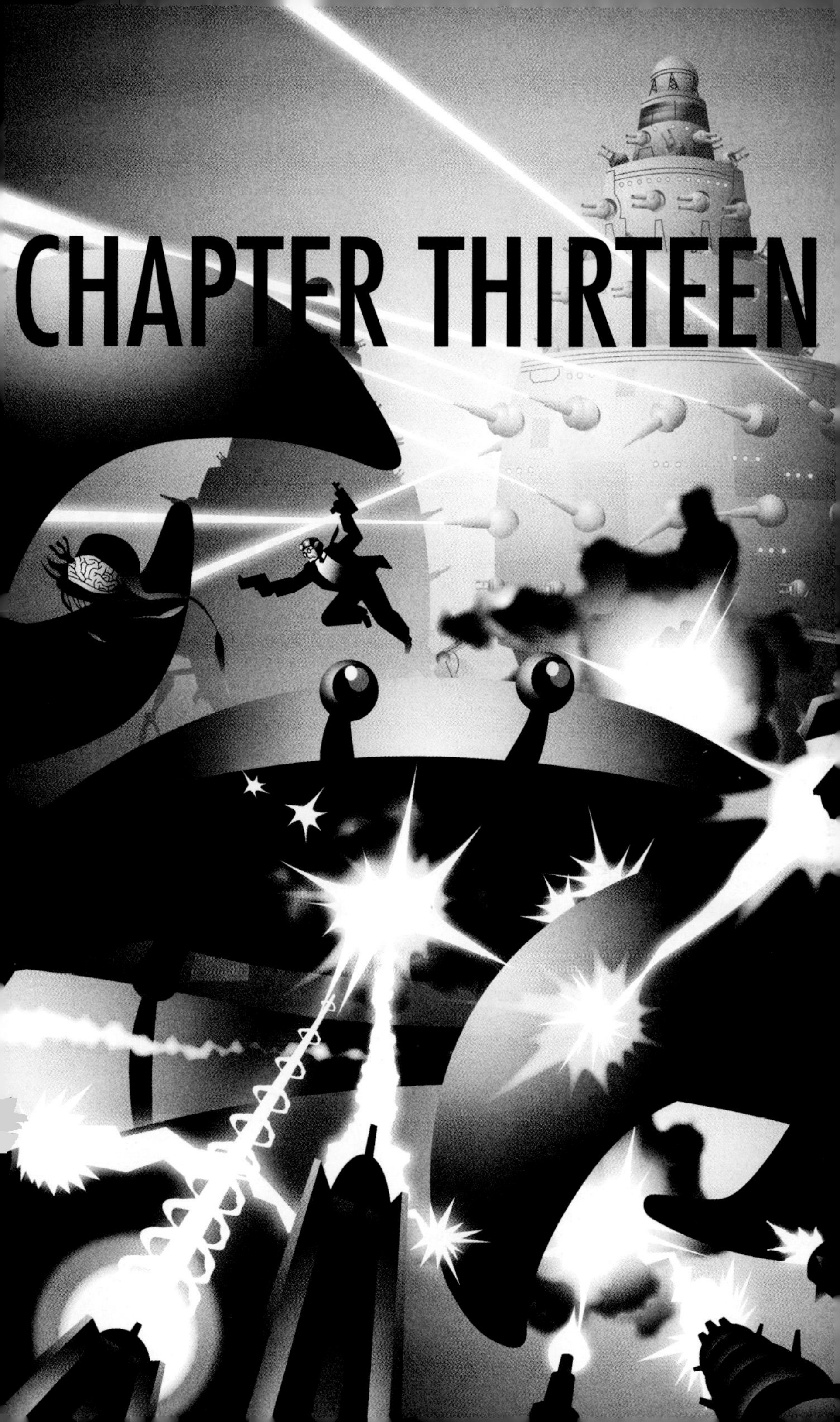
CHAPTER THIRTEEN

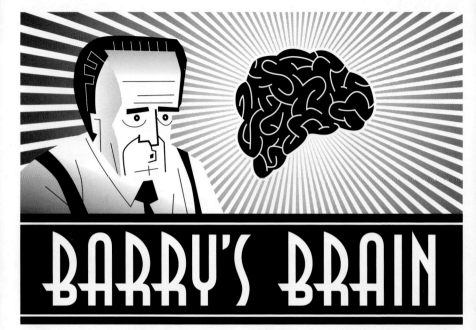

BARRY'S BRAIN

This will be a rather short and rushed column, with somewhat less of the renowned thought filtering that usually goes into my amazing musings. I have a planet to catch and little time to spare. But don't worry: I'm employing the homeopathic principles of infinitesimals, so if it does lacks considered thought, it is infinitely considered.

You know what I mean.

This column is being written, incredibly, at my local public library. True! I'm on the run. Impossible? I would have thought so—until today! Believe it! The police have cordoned off the office of Hermeneutic Press and impounded all our equipment. Madness, no question. But wily ol' B. Barry is infinitesimally paranoid, and thus monumentally so, and I have a dozen social insurance numbers, half-a-dozen identities, and four addresses. I've evaded the flat-footed police, and fortunately the files for this issue are already at the printer. This issue will get into your hands, I assure you, and not even the combined powers of a dozen agencies of the Federal Government will be able to stop it!

Why should they want to do so? Other than being driven mad with an all-consuming jealousy generated by the astonishing success of Hermeneutic Press, that is? Apparently my nephew has been running a massive marijuana grow-op out on the West Coast, and he's been laundering his ill-gotten gains through my comic book company. More specifically, he's been laundering mob money—they muscled in on his highly lucrative operation a year ago. It seems that most of the overseas comics I was so enthusiastic about do not actually exist. Which is a pity, as we had some great 'noh-comics' for you.

Events are trasnpiring very quickly today: Guido went down in a blaze of gunfire this morning. Tony got nabbed after a forty minute high-speed car chase across the city involving 20 police cars, 12 accidents, and a helicopter. My nephew, Todd, got nabbed at a bus stop with a suitcase full of cash and a Fabergé egg less than an hour ago.

This has taught me a valuable lesson, Hermeneutifans. Forget publishing! The smart thing to do is start your own religion. So I'm off to Tlon to do just that. I'm going to combine Autology with homeopathic principles and create a for-export religious business enterprise. No content means infinite content! Think of how much I'll save on material! I'm going to sell possiblity foam, otherwise known as vacuum! Scientists have noted how everything that is possible is constantly emerging and disappearing in vacuum. It's time someone harnessed this for the good of consumers around the world!

Exfiltrate!

B. Barry Horst
Publisher

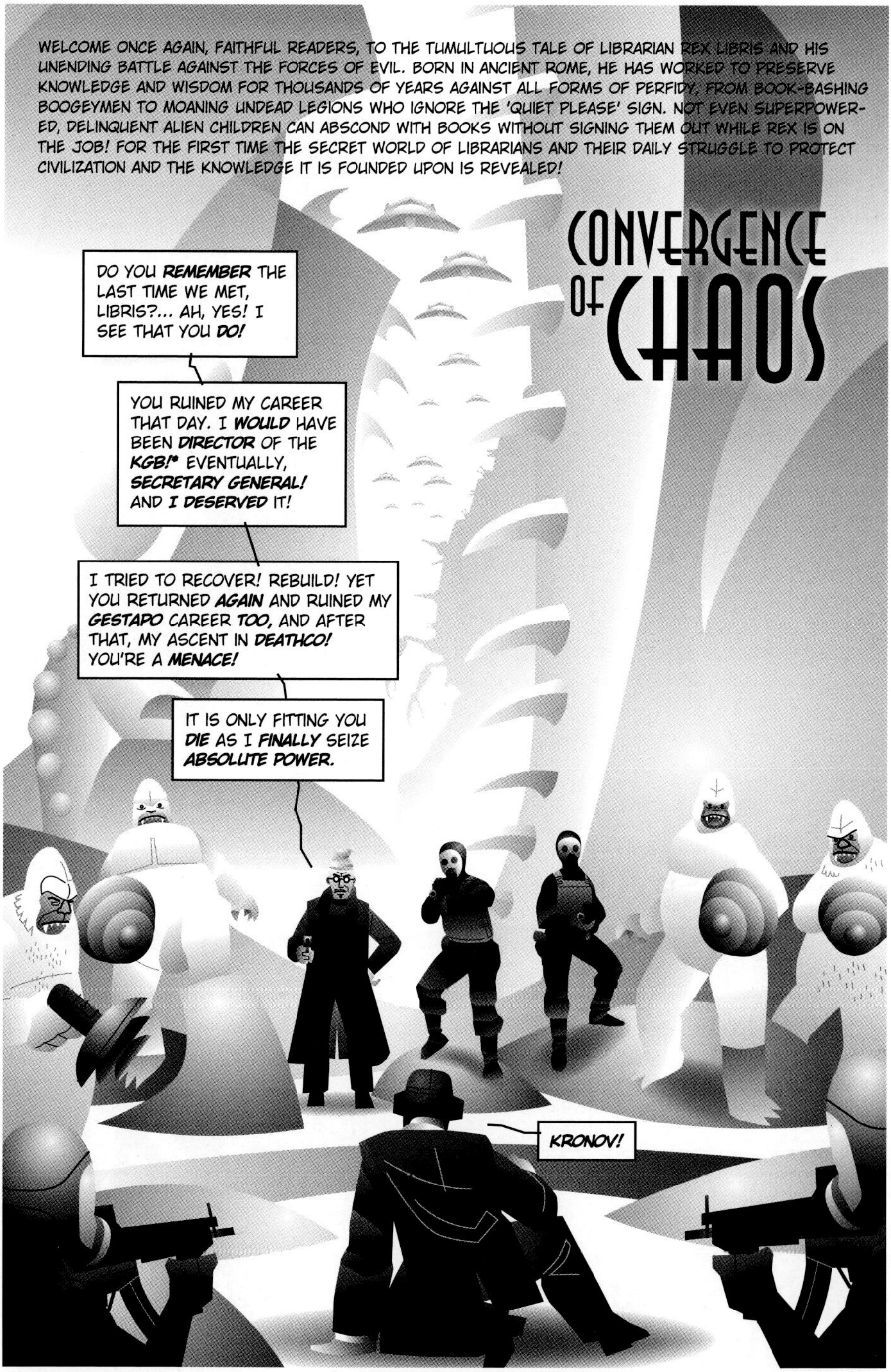
WELCOME ONCE AGAIN, FAITHFUL READERS, TO THE TUMULTUOUS TALE OF LIBRARIAN REX LIBRIS AND HIS UNENDING BATTLE AGAINST THE FORCES OF EVIL. BORN IN ANCIENT ROME, HE HAS WORKED TO PRESERVE KNOWLEDGE AND WISDOM FOR THOUSANDS OF YEARS AGAINST ALL FORMS OF PERFIDY, FROM BOOK-BASHING BOOGEYMEN TO MOANING UNDEAD LEGIONS WHO IGNORE THE 'QUIET PLEASE' SIGN. NOT EVEN SUPERPOWERED, DELINQUENT ALIEN CHILDREN CAN ABSCOND WITH BOOKS WITHOUT SIGNING THEM OUT WHILE REX IS ON THE JOB! FOR THE FIRST TIME THE SECRET WORLD OF LIBRARIANS AND THEIR DAILY STRUGGLE TO PROTECT CIVILIZATION AND THE KNOWLEDGE IT IS FOUNDED UPON IS REVEALED!
CONVERGENCE OF CHAOS
DO YOU REMEMBER THE LAST TIME WE MET, LIBRIS?... AH, YES! I SEE THAT YOU DO!
YOU RUINED MY CAREER THAT DAY. I WOULD HAVE BEEN DIRECTOR OF THE KGB!* EVENTUALLY, SECRETARY GENERAL! AND I DESERVED IT!
I TRIED TO RECOVER! REBUILD! YET YOU RETURNED AGAIN AND RUINED MY GESTAPO CAREER TOO, AND AFTER THAT, MY ASCENT IN DEATHCO! YOU'RE A MENACE!
IT IS ONLY FITTING YOU DIE AS I FINALLY SEIZE ABSOLUTE POWER.
KRONOV!

* KRONOV WAS ORIGINALLY A MEMBER OF THE SOVIET SECURITY SERVICES AND ON TRACK FOR THE DIRECTOR'S CHAIR WHEN HE FLUBBED A MAJOR OPERATION IN 1933. IT LEFT HIS CAREER IN LIMBO. HE FELL INTO THE SOVIET SORCEROR CIRCLE IN 1938. DURING THE SECOND WORLD WAR HE DEFECTED TO THE NAZIS WHEN HE THOUGHT THE SOVIETS WERE LOSING, TAKING HIS SPELLS WITH HIM. IN 1943 HE LED THE NAZI INVASION OF HELL WHICH ENDED IN DISASTER, LEADING HIM TO DEFECT BACK TO THE SOVIETS. AFTER AMERICA DETONATED THE ATOMIC BOMB, HE DEFECTED TO THE UNITED STATES, THEN BACK TO THE USSR IN 1949 AFTER THE DETONATION OF JOE-1. HE RECEIVED A SURLY RECEPTION AND GREW DISCONTENT. IN 1952 HE BECAME A COG IN THE W.R.A.I.TH. ORGANIZATION OF WAR CRIMINALS. --BBH

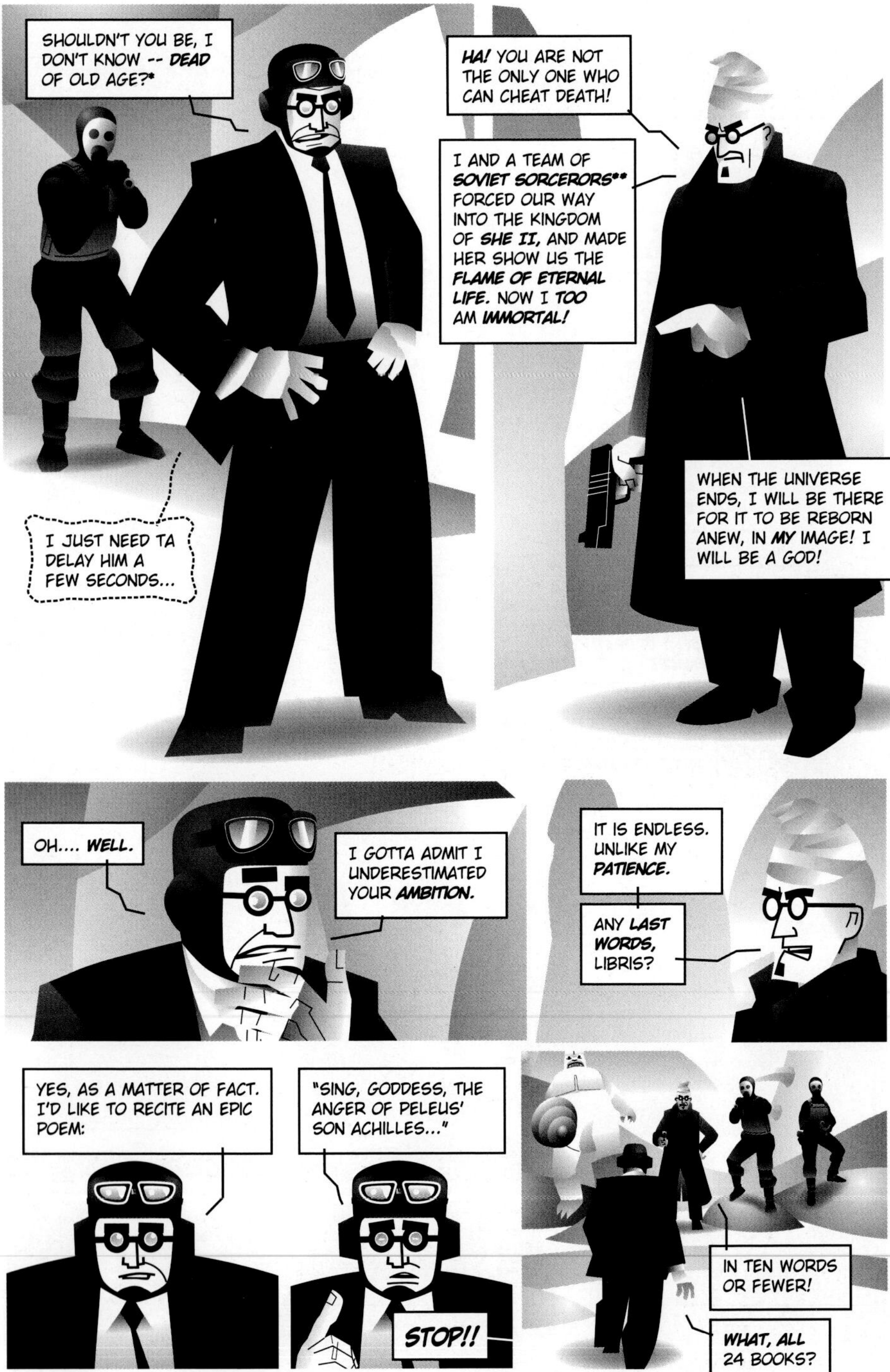
SHOULDN'T YOU BE, I DON'T KNOW -- DEAD OF OLD AGE?*
I JUST NEED TA DELAY HIM A FEW SECONDS...
HA! YOU ARE NOT THE ONLY ONE WHO CAN CHEAT DEATH!
I AND A TEAM OF SOVIET SORCERORS** FORCED OUR WAY INTO THE KINGDOM OF SHE II, AND MADE HER SHOW US THE FLAME OF ETERNAL LIFE. NOW I TOO AM IMMORTAL!
WHEN THE UNIVERSE ENDS, I WILL BE THERE FOR IT TO BE REBORN ANEW, IN MY IMAGE! I WILL BE A GOD!
OH.... WELL.
I GOTTA ADMIT I UNDERESTIMATED YOUR AMBITION.
IT IS ENDLESS. UNLIKE MY PATIENCE.
ANY LAST WORDS, LIBRIS?
YES, AS A MATTER OF FACT. I'D LIKE TO RECITE AN EPIC POEM:
"SING, GODDESS, THE ANGER OF PELEUS' SON ACHILLES..."
STOP!!
IN TEN WORDS OR FEWER!
WHAT, ALL 24 BOOKS?

* SEE ISSUE 9 FOR REX'S FIRST FOOT-IN-THE-FACE ALTERCATION WITH KRONOV. --BARRY

** REX CONFRONTED THE SOVIET SORCERORS IN 1953, WHEN THEIR ARMY OF TAMERLANE CLONES, CONCEIVED IN 1941 UNDER GERASIMOV AND INITIALLY INTENDED TO FIGHT AGAINST THE FASCISTS, CAME OF AGE AND WERE UNLEASHED ON AMERICA. REX TRICKED THEM INTO ENTERING ANOTHER DIMENSION. THE DEBACLE BROKE THE BACK OF THE SOVIET COMISSAR/SORCEROR PROGRAM, AND THEY FLED TO TLÖN, WHERE THEY ESTABLISHED A SORCEROR SOVIET. --BARRY

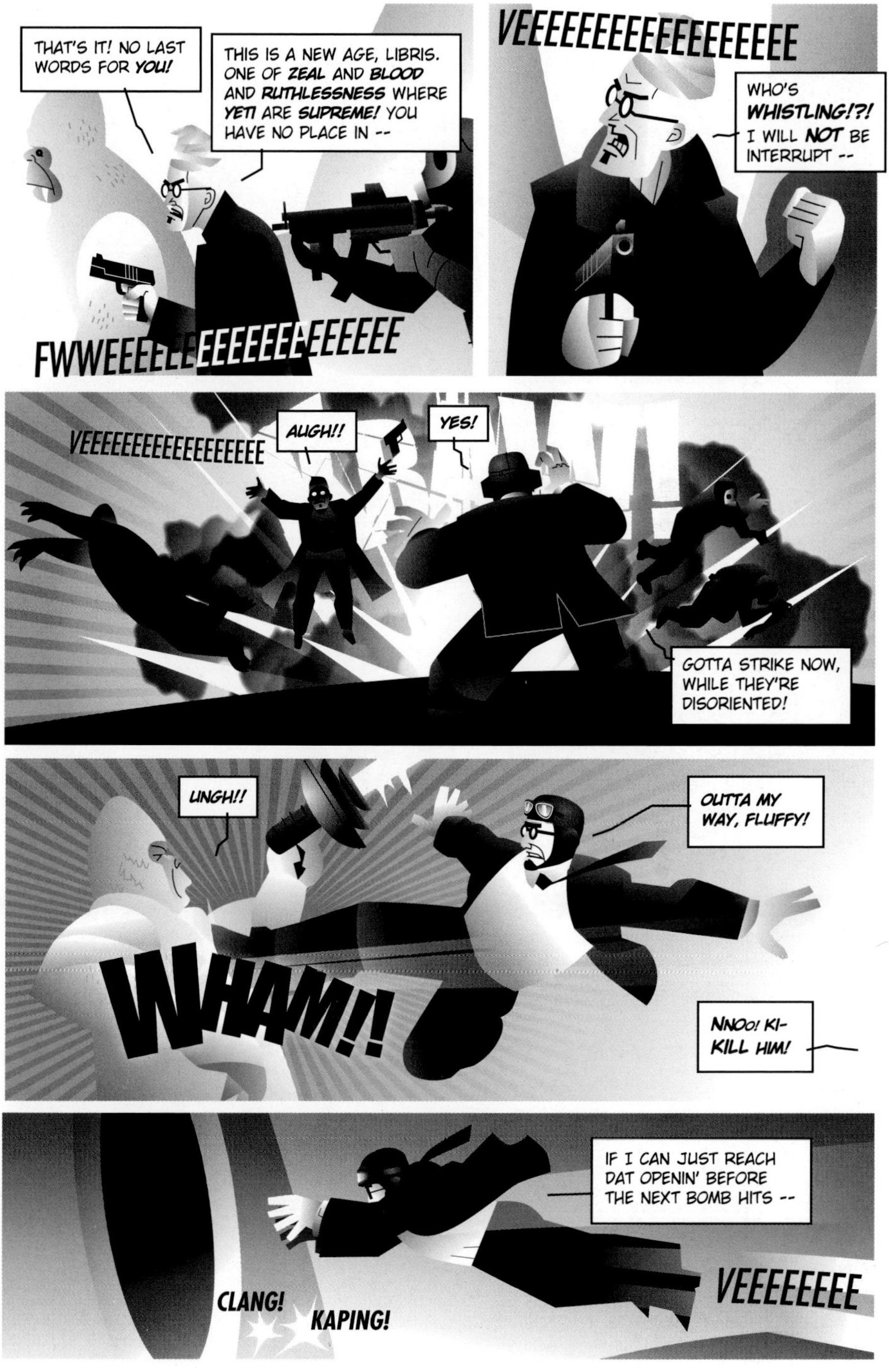
THAT'S IT! NO LAST WORDS FOR YOU!
THIS IS A NEW AGE, LIBRIS. ONE OF ZEAL AND BLOOD AND RUTHLESSNESS WHERE YETI ARE SUPREME! YOU HAVE NO PLACE IN --
FWWEEEEEEEEEEEEEEEEEE
VEEEEEEEEEEEEEEEEEE
WHO'S WHISTLING!?! I WILL NOT BE INTERRUPT --
VEEEEEEEEEEEEEEEEEE
AUGH!!
YES!
GOTTA STRIKE NOW, WHILE THEY'RE DISORIENTED!
UNGH!!
OUTTA MY WAY, FLUFFY!
WHAM!!
NNOo! KI-KILL HIM!
IF I CAN JUST REACH DAT OPENIN' BEFORE THE NEXT BOMB HITS --
VEEEEEEE
CLANG!
KAPING!

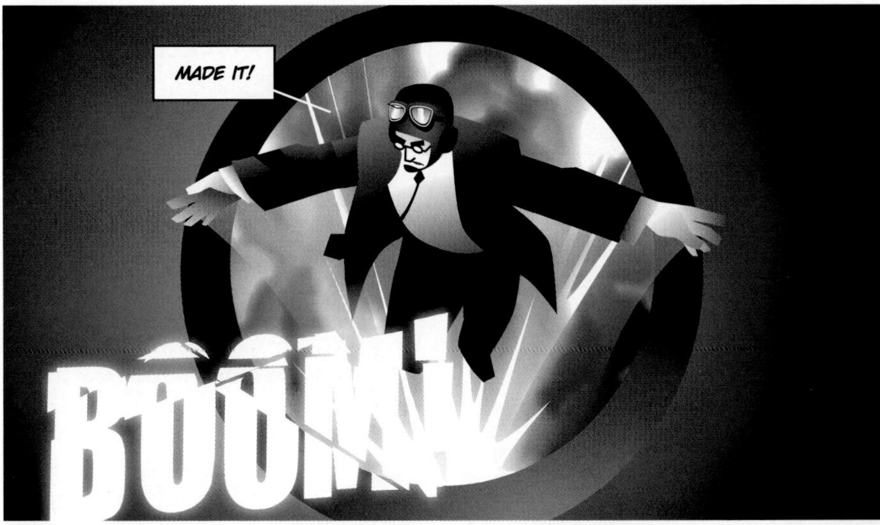
MADE IT!
BOOM!

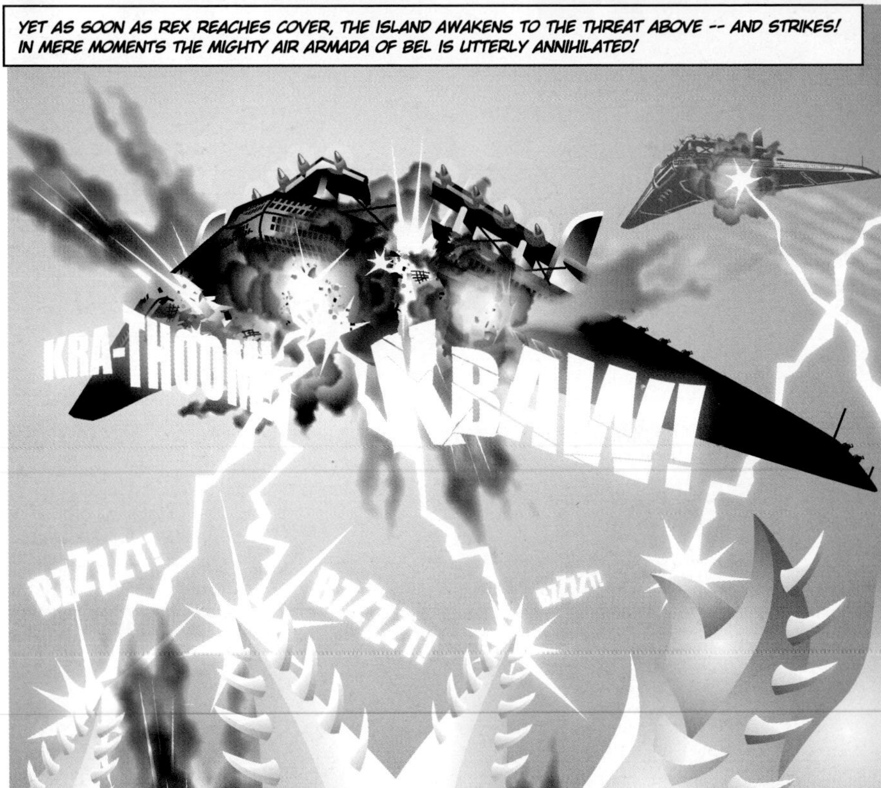
YET AS SOON AS REX REACHES COVER, THE ISLAND AWAKENS TO THE THREAT ABOVE -- AND STRIKES! IN MERE MOMENTS THE MIGHTY AIR ARMADA OF BEL IS UTTERLY ANNIHILATED!
KRA-THOOM!
KBAW!
BZZZZT!
BZZZZT!
BZZZZT!

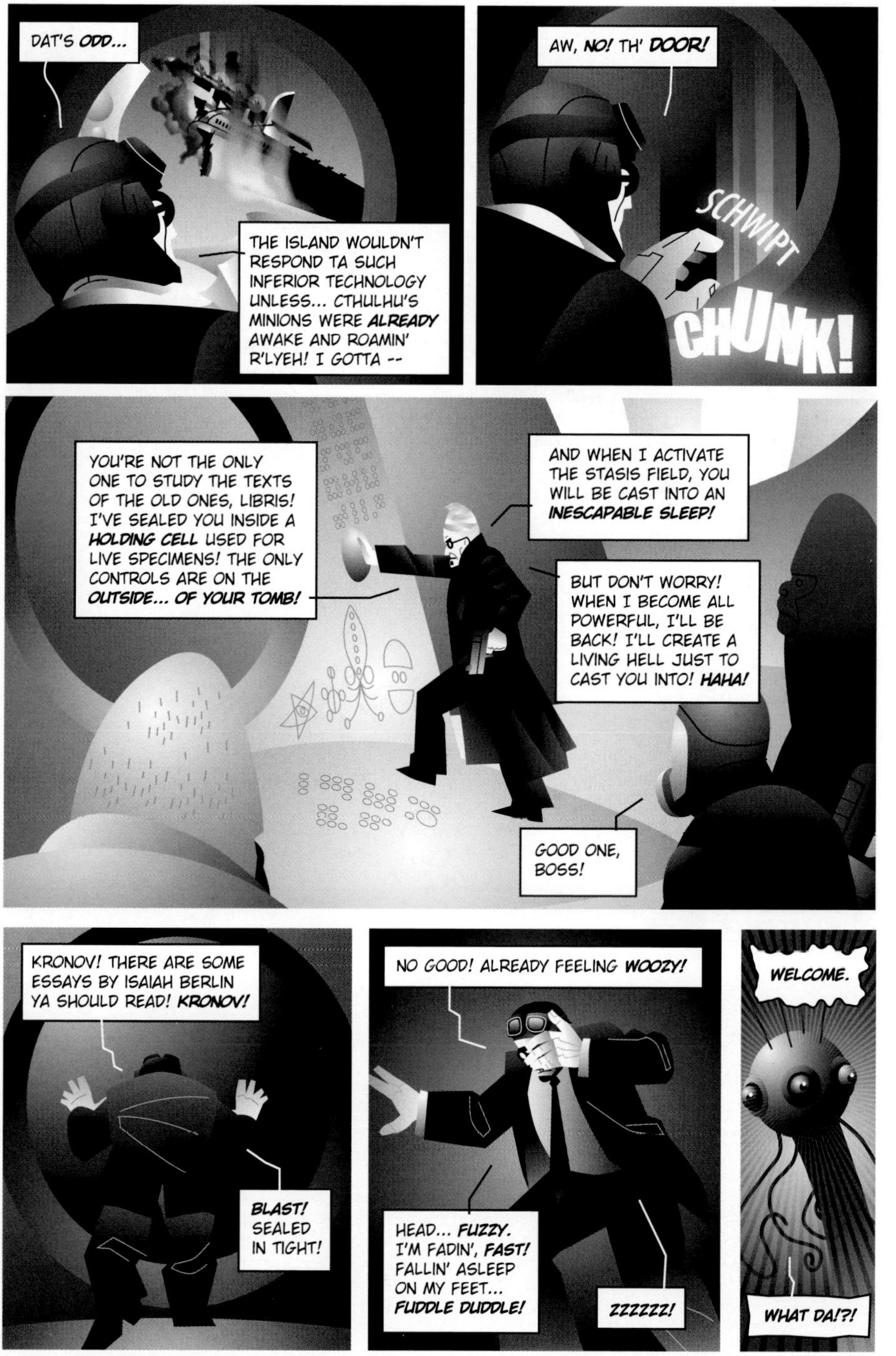
DAT'S ODD...
THE ISLAND WOULDN'T RESPOND TA SUCH INFERIOR TECHNOLOGY UNLESS... CTHULHU'S MINIONS WERE ALREADY AWAKE AND ROAMIN' R'LYEH! I GOTTA --
AW, NO! TH' DOOR!
SCHWIPT
CHUNK!
YOU'RE NOT THE ONLY ONE TO STUDY THE TEXTS OF THE OLD ONES, LIBRIS! I'VE SEALED YOU INSIDE A HOLDING CELL USED FOR LIVE SPECIMENS! THE ONLY CONTROLS ARE ON THE OUTSIDE... OF YOUR TOMB!
AND WHEN I ACTIVATE THE STASIS FIELD, YOU WILL BE CAST INTO AN INESCAPABLE SLEEP!
BUT DON'T WORRY! WHEN I BECOME ALL POWERFUL, I'LL BE BACK! I'LL CREATE A LIVING HELL JUST TO CAST YOU INTO! HAHA!
GOOD ONE, BOSS!
KRONOV! THERE ARE SOME ESSAYS BY ISAIAH BERLIN YA SHOULD READ! KRONOV!
BLAST! SEALED IN TIGHT!
NO GOOD! ALREADY FEELING WOOZY!
HEAD... FUZZY. I'M FADIN', FAST! FALLIN' ASLEEP ON MY FEET... FUDDLE DUDDLE!
ZZZZZZ!
WELCOME.
WHAT DA!?!

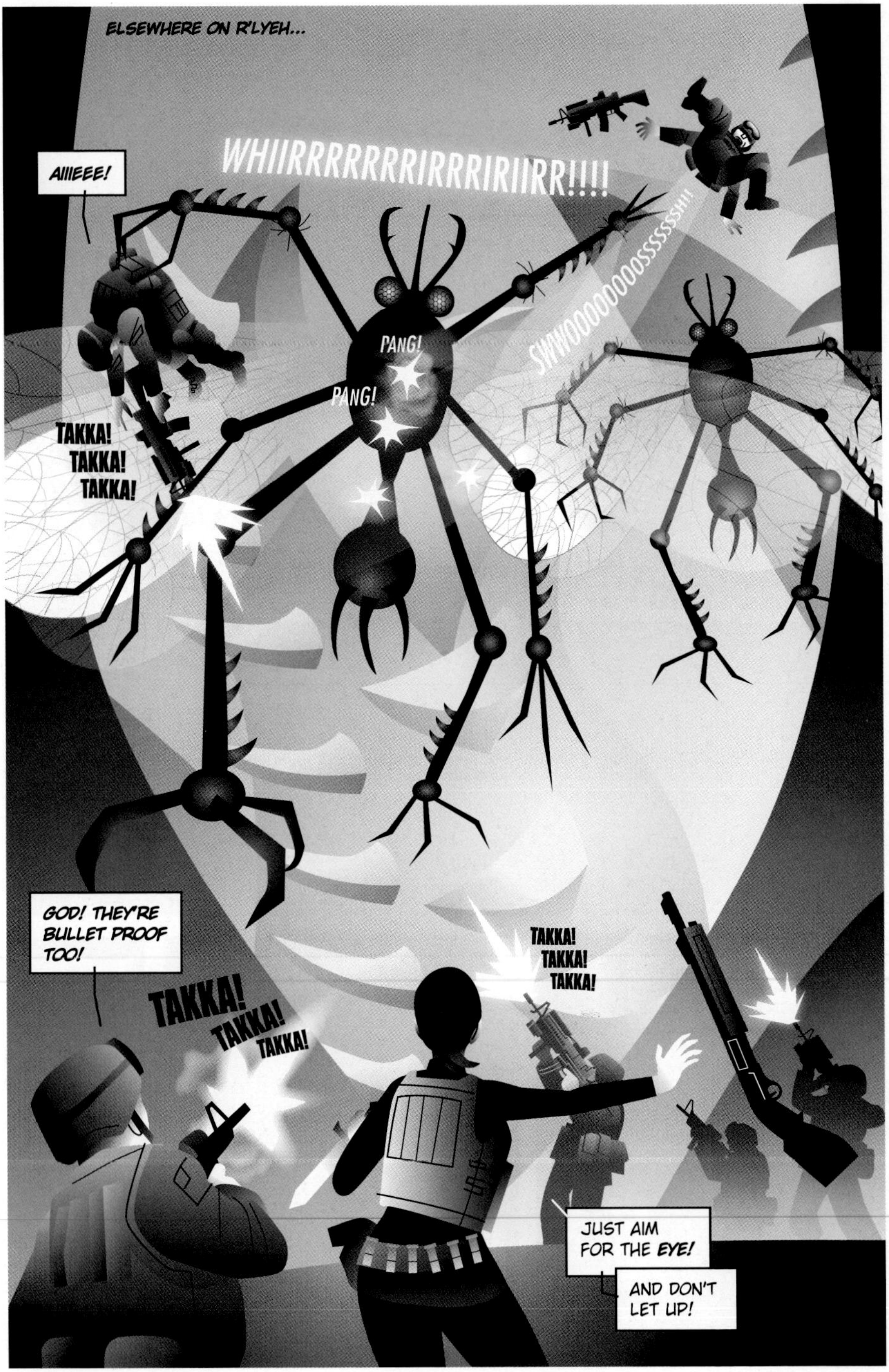
ELSEWHERE ON R'LYEH...
AIIIEEE!
WHIIRRRRRRRIRRRIRIIRR!!!!
SWWOOOOOOOOOSSSSSSH!!
PANG!
PANG!
TAKKA! TAKKA! TAKKA!
GOD! THEY'RE BULLET PROOF TOO!
TAKKA! TAKKA! TAKKA!
TAKKA! TAKKA! TAKKA!
JUST AIM FOR THE EYE!
AND DON'T LET UP!

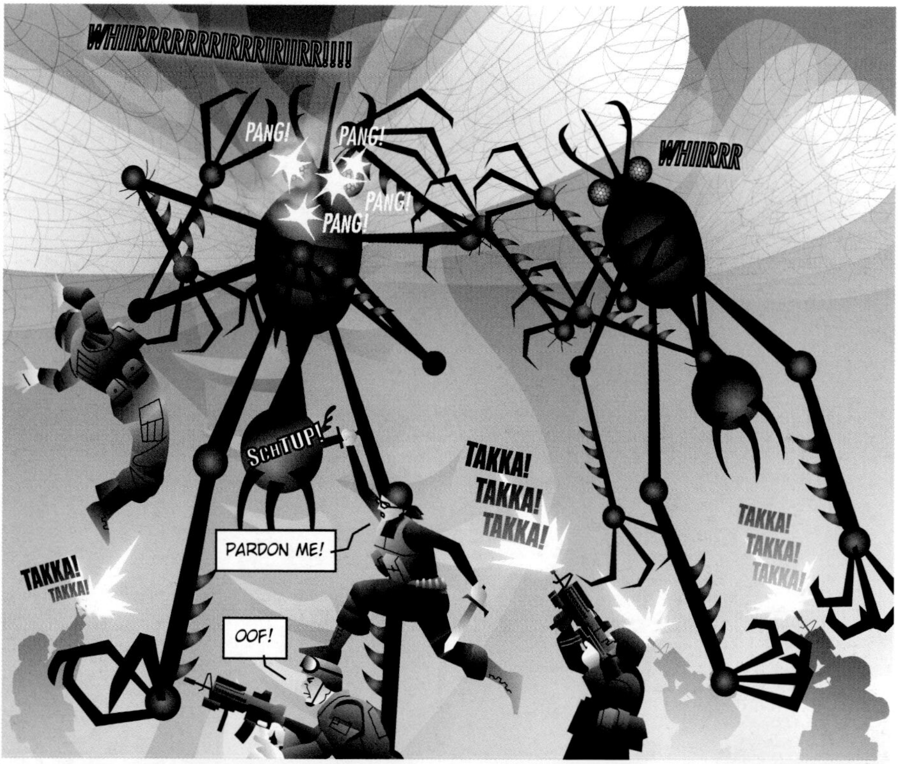
WHIIRRRRRRRIRRRIRIIRR!!!!
PANG!
PANG!
PANG!
PANG!
WHIIRRR
SCHTUP!
PARDON ME!
TAKKA! TAKKA! TAKKA!
TAKKA! TAKKA! TAKKA!
TAKKA! TAKKA!
OOF!

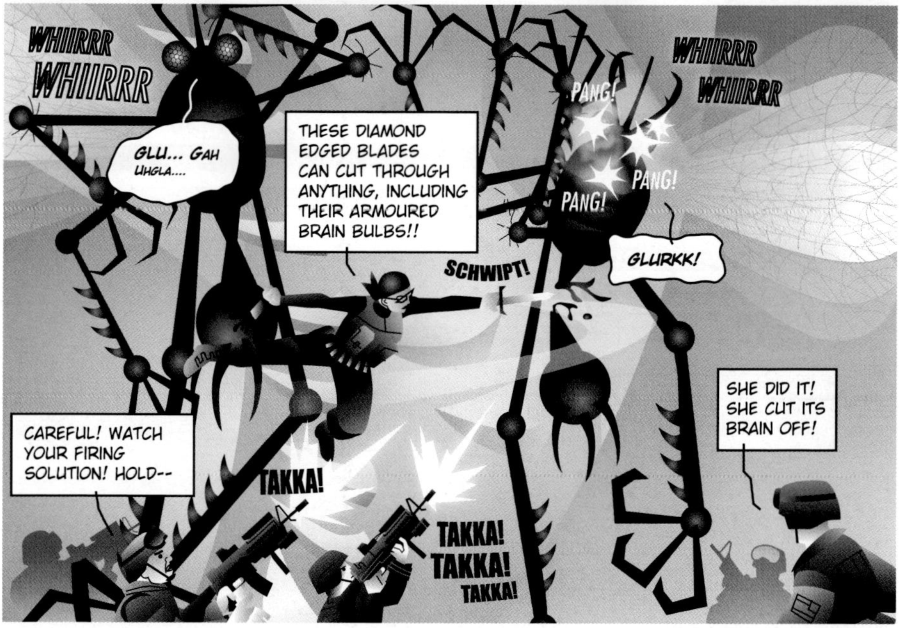
WHIIRRR
WHIIRRR
GLU... GAH UHGLA....
THESE DIAMOND EDGED BLADES CAN CUT THROUGH ANYTHING, INCLUDING THEIR ARMOURED BRAIN BULBS!!
WHIIRRR
WHIIRRR
PANG!
PANG!
PANG!
SCHWIPT!
GLURKK!
CAREFUL! WATCH YOUR FIRING SOLUTION! HOLD--
TAKKA!
TAKKA! TAKKA! TAKKA!
SHE DID IT! SHE CUT ITS BRAIN OFF!

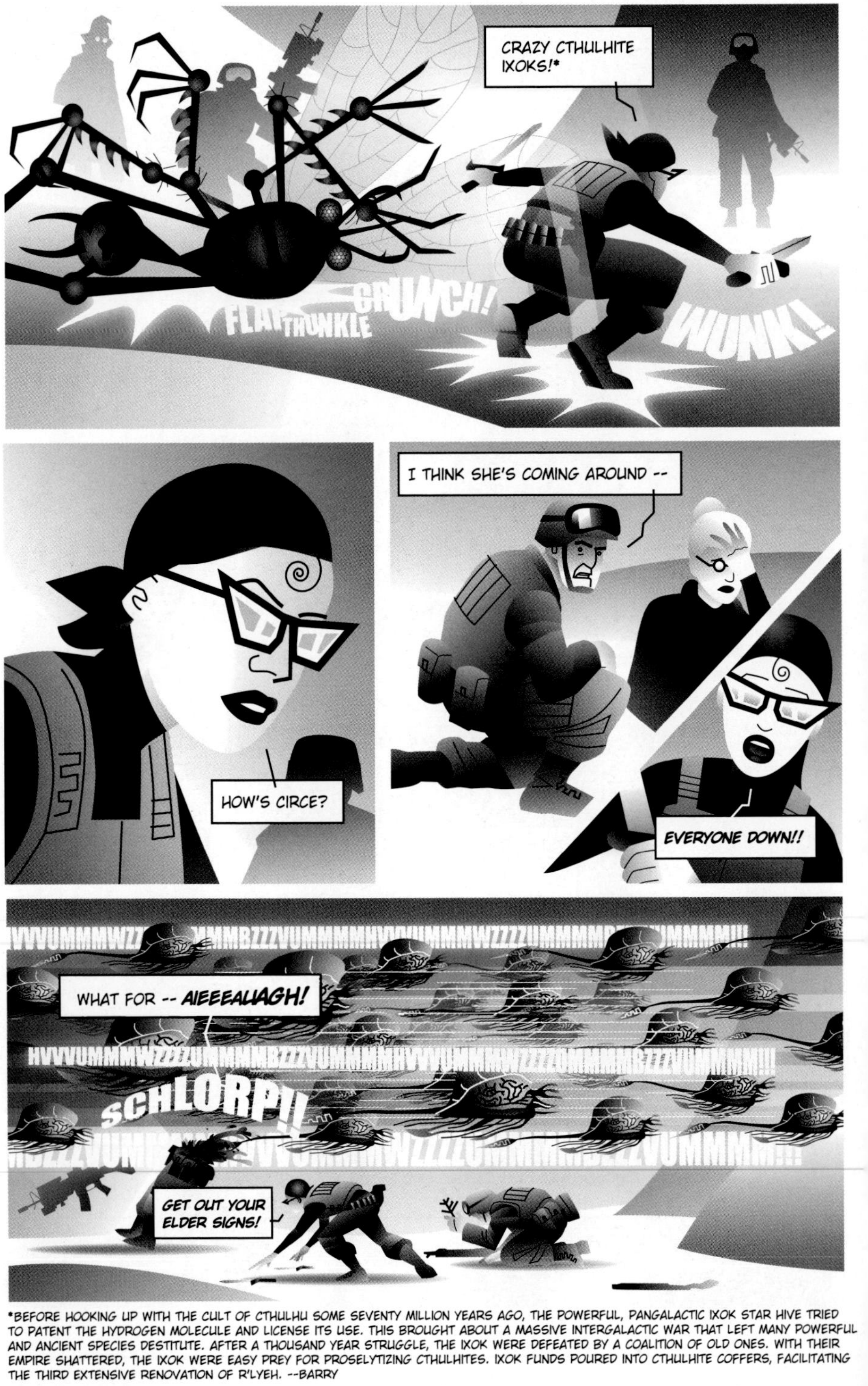

CRAZY CTHULHITE IXOKS!*
FLAP
THUNKLE
CRUNCH!
WUNK!
HOW'S CIRCE?
I THINK SHE'S COMING AROUND --
EVERYONE DOWN!!
WHAT FOR -- AIEEEAUAGH!
SCHLORP!!
GET OUT YOUR ELDER SIGNS!

*BEFORE HOOKING UP WITH THE CULT OF CTHULHU SOME SEVENTY MILLION YEARS AGO, THE POWERFUL, PANGALACTIC IXOK STAR HIVE TRIED TO PATENT THE HYDROGEN MOLECULE AND LICENSE ITS USE. THIS BROUGHT ABOUT A MASSIVE INTERGALACTIC WAR THAT LEFT MANY POWERFUL AND ANCIENT SPECIES DESTITUTE. AFTER A THOUSAND YEAR STRUGGLE, THE IXOK WERE DEFEATED BY A COALITION OF OLD ONES. WITH THEIR EMPIRE SHATTERED, THE IXOK WERE EASY PREY FOR PROSELYTIZING CTHULHITES. IXOK FUNDS POURED INTO CTHULHITE COFFERS, FACILITATING THE THIRD EXTENSIVE RENOVATION OF R'LYEH. --BARRY

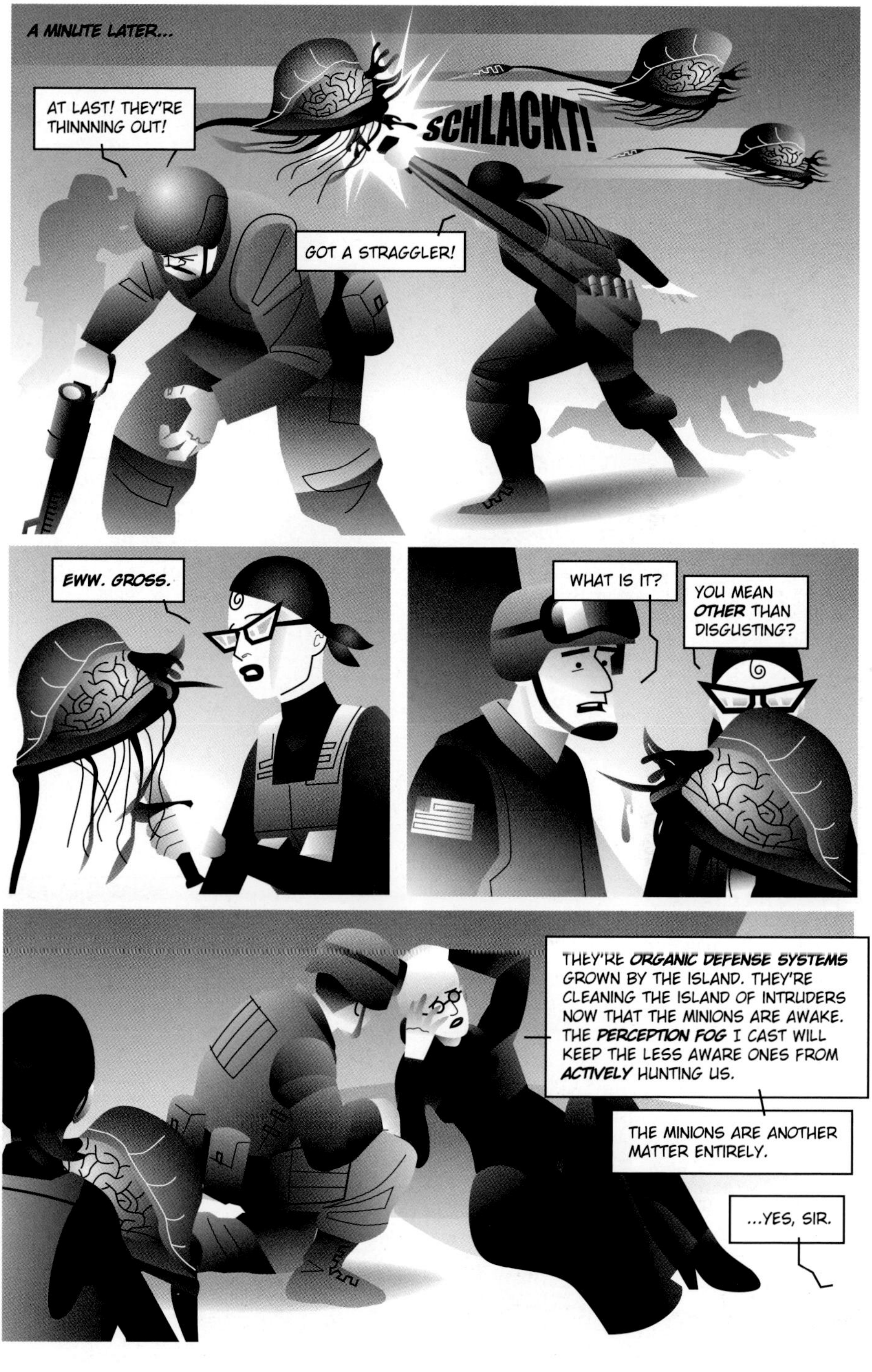
A MINUTE LATER...
AT LAST! THEY'RE THINNNING OUT!
SCHLACKT!
GOT A STRAGGLER!
EWW. GROSS.
WHAT IS IT?
YOU MEAN OTHER THAN DISGUSTING?
THEY'RE ORGANIC DEFENSE SYSTEMS GROWN BY THE ISLAND. THEY'RE CLEANING THE ISLAND OF INTRUDERS NOW THAT THE MINIONS ARE AWAKE. THE PERCEPTION FOG I CAST WILL KEEP THE LESS AWARE ONES FROM ACTIVELY HUNTING US.
THE MINIONS ARE ANOTHER MATTER ENTIRELY.
...YES, SIR.

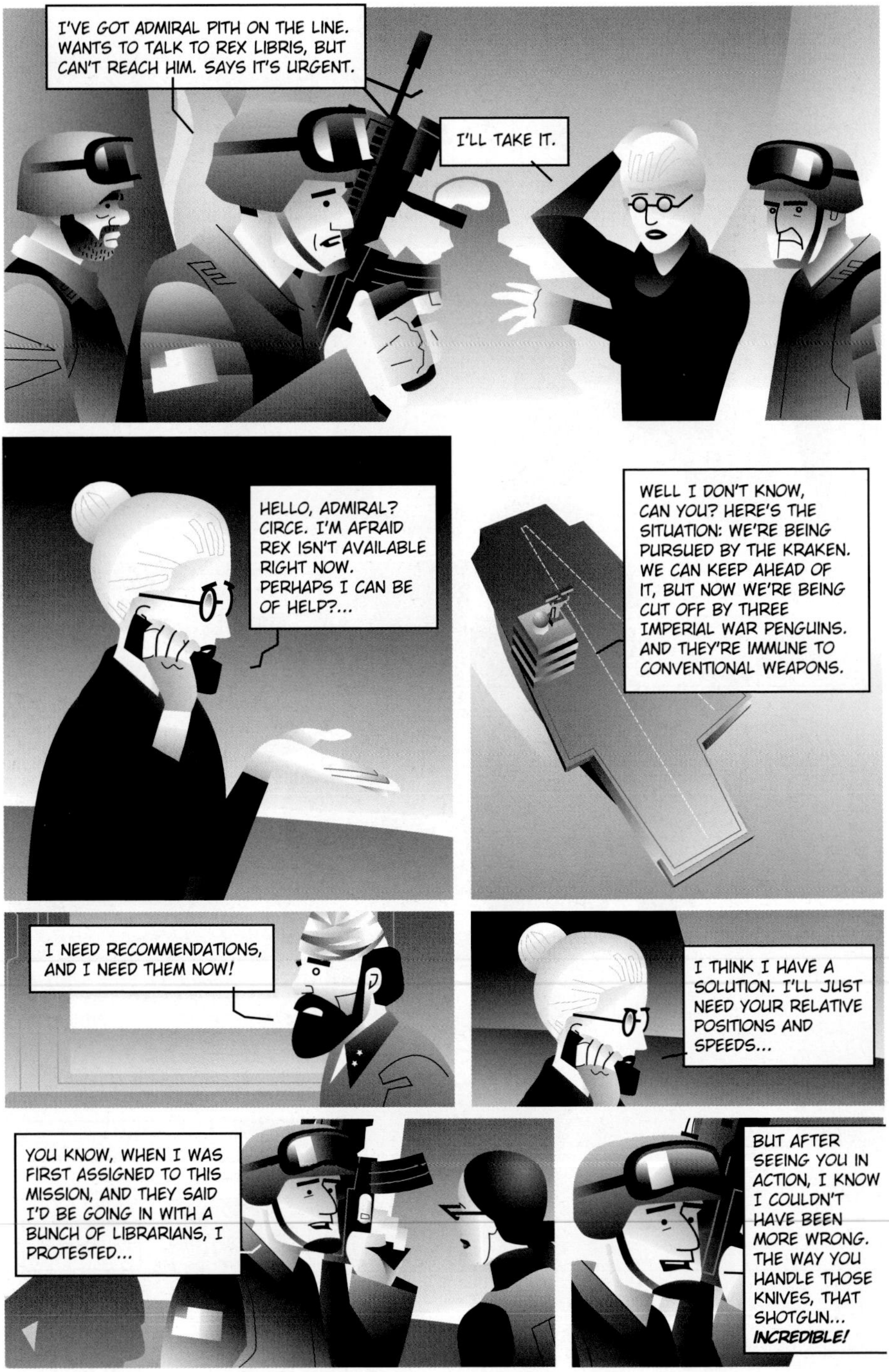
I'VE GOT ADMIRAL PITH ON THE LINE. WANTS TO TALK TO REX LIBRIS, BUT CAN'T REACH HIM. SAYS IT'S URGENT.
I'LL TAKE IT.
HELLO, ADMIRAL? CIRCE. I'M AFRAID REX ISN'T AVAILABLE RIGHT NOW. PERHAPS I CAN BE OF HELP?...
WELL I DON'T KNOW, CAN YOU? HERE'S THE SITUATION: WE'RE BEING PURSUED BY THE KRAKEN. WE CAN KEEP AHEAD OF IT, BUT NOW WE'RE BEING CUT OFF BY THREE IMPERIAL WAR PENGUINS. AND THEY'RE IMMUNE TO CONVENTIONAL WEAPONS.
I NEED RECOMMENDATIONS, AND I NEED THEM NOW!
I THINK I HAVE A SOLUTION. I'LL JUST NEED YOUR RELATIVE POSITIONS AND SPEEDS...
YOU KNOW, WHEN I WAS FIRST ASSIGNED TO THIS MISSION, AND THEY SAID I'D BE GOING IN WITH A BUNCH OF LIBRARIANS, I PROTESTED...
BUT AFTER SEEING YOU IN ACTION, I KNOW I COULDN'T HAVE BEEN MORE WRONG. THE WAY YOU HANDLE THOSE KNIVES, THAT SHOTGUN... ***INCREDIBLE!***

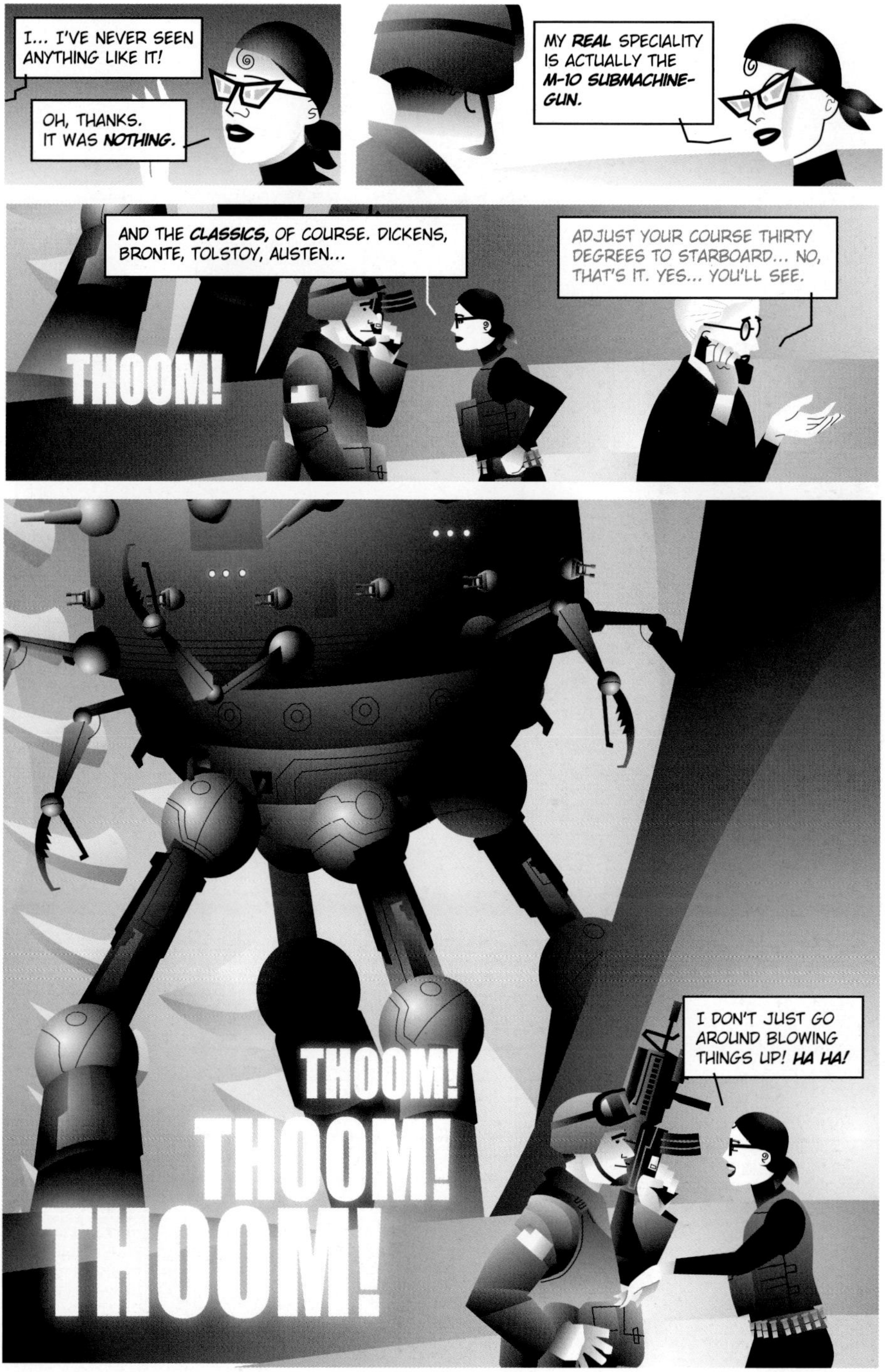
I... I'VE NEVER SEEN ANYTHING LIKE IT!
OH, THANKS. IT WAS NOTHING.
MY REAL SPECIALITY IS ACTUALLY THE M-10 SUBMACHINE-GUN.
AND THE CLASSICS, OF COURSE. DICKENS, BRONTE, TOLSTOY, AUSTEN...
ADJUST YOUR COURSE THIRTY DEGREES TO STARBOARD... NO, THAT'S IT. YES... YOU'LL SEE.
THOOM!
I DON'T JUST GO AROUND BLOWING THINGS UP! HA HA!
THOOM!
THOOM!
THOOM!

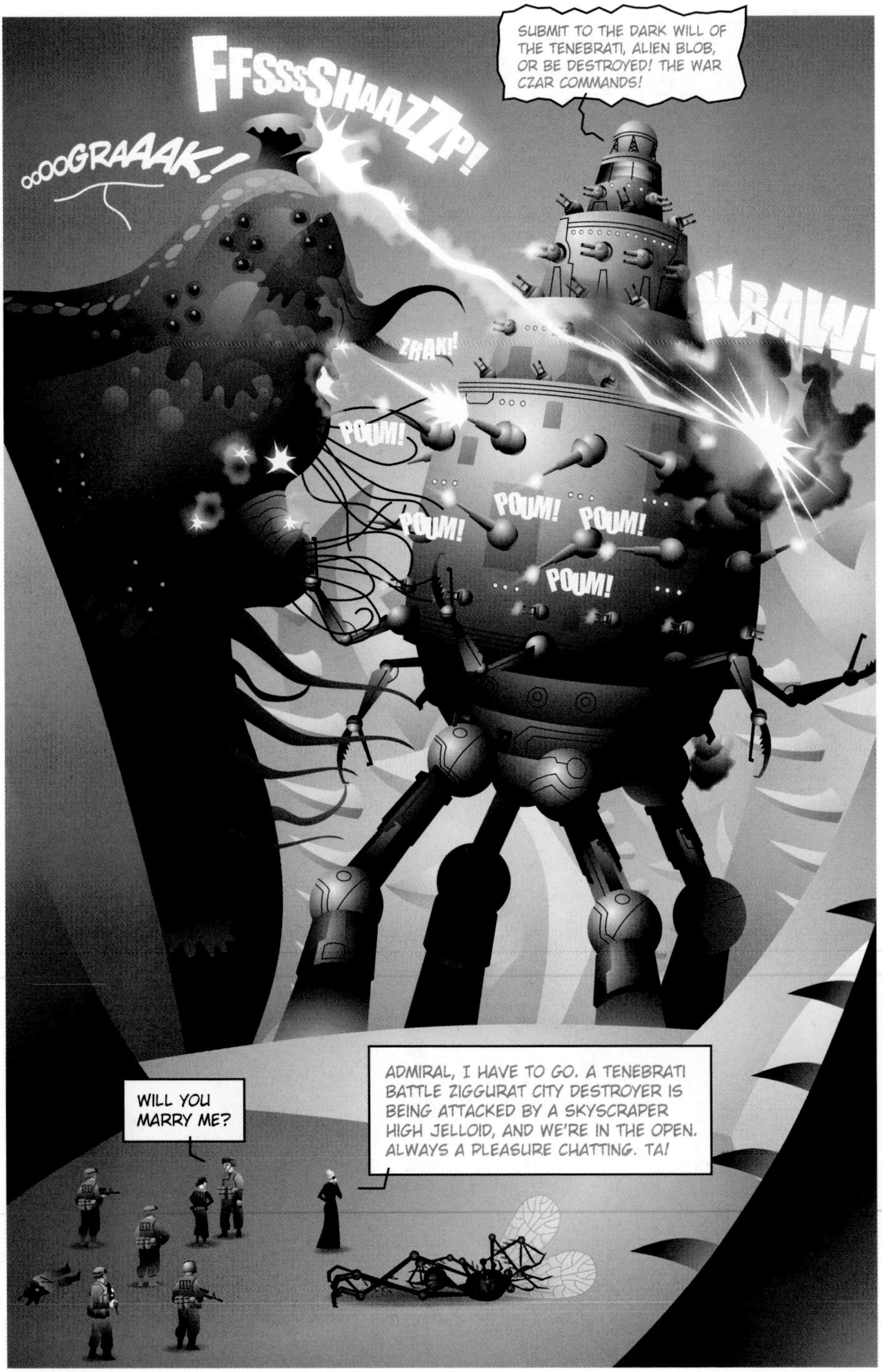
FFSSSSHAAZZZP!
SUBMIT TO THE DARK WILL OF THE TENEBRATI, ALIEN BLOB, OR BE DESTROYED! THE WAR CZAR COMMANDS!
oOOGRAAAK!
KBAW!
ZRAK!
POUM!
POUM!
POUM!
POUM!
POUM!
WILL YOU MARRY ME?
ADMIRAL, I HAVE TO GO. A TENEBRATI BATTLE ZIGGURAT CITY DESTROYER IS BEING ATTACKED BY A SKYSCRAPER HIGH JELLOID, AND WE'RE IN THE OPEN. ALWAYS A PLEASURE CHATTING. TA!

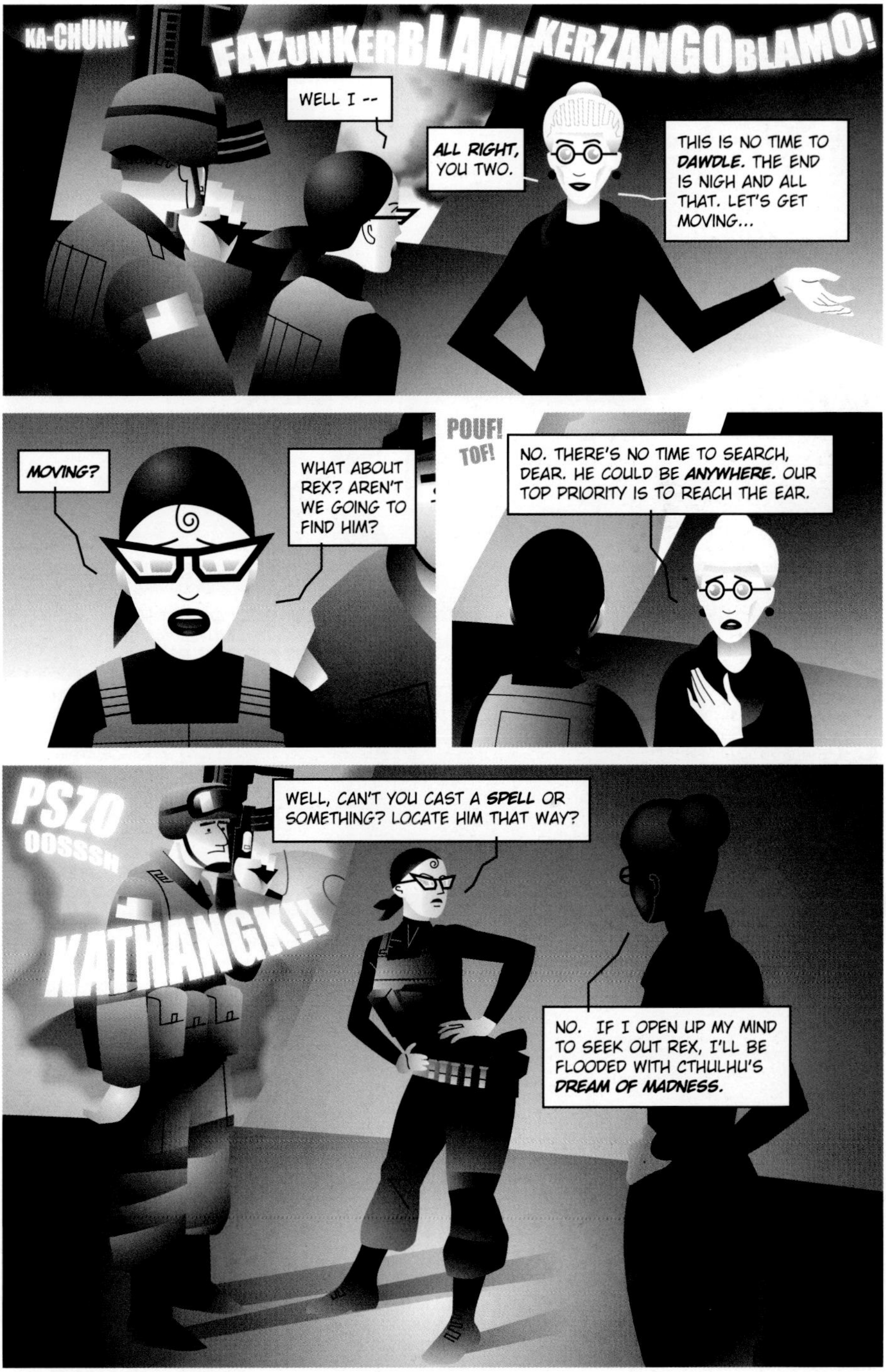
KA-CHUNK-
FAZUNKERBLAM!
KERZANGOBLAMO!
WELL I --
ALL RIGHT, YOU TWO.
THIS IS NO TIME TO DAWDLE. THE END IS NIGH AND ALL THAT. LET'S GET MOVING...
MOVING?
WHAT ABOUT REX? AREN'T WE GOING TO FIND HIM?
POUF! TOF!
NO. THERE'S NO TIME TO SEARCH, DEAR. HE COULD BE ANYWHERE. OUR TOP PRIORITY IS TO REACH THE EAR.
PSZO OOSSSH
KATHANGK!!
WELL, CAN'T YOU CAST A SPELL OR SOMETHING? LOCATE HIM THAT WAY?
NO. IF I OPEN UP MY MIND TO SEEK OUT REX, I'LL BE FLOODED WITH CTHULHU'S DREAM OF MADNESS.

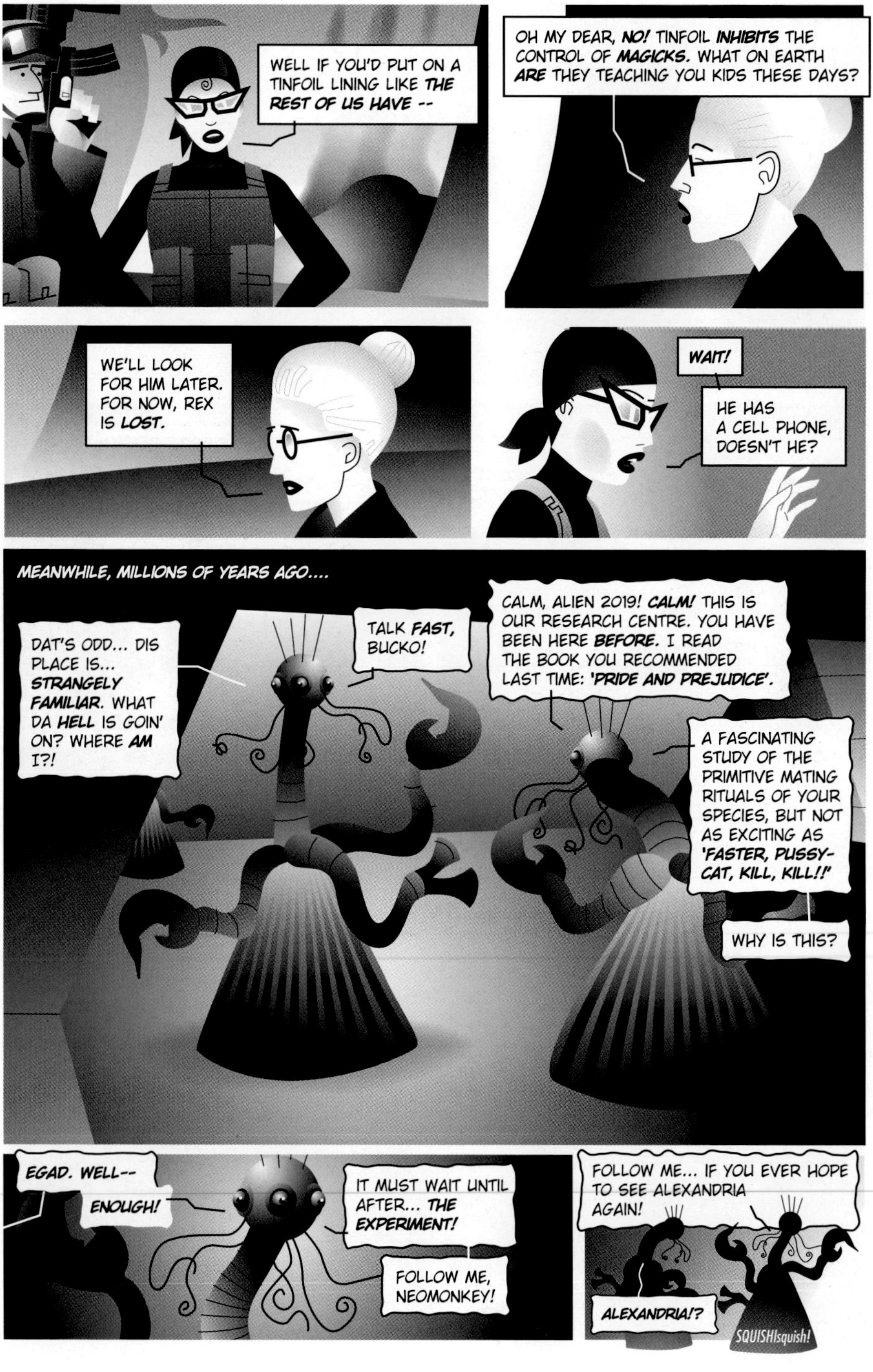

WELL IF YOU'D PUT ON A TINFOIL LINING LIKE THE REST OF US HAVE --
OH MY DEAR, NO! TINFOIL INHIBITS THE CONTROL OF MAGICKS. WHAT ON EARTH ARE THEY TEACHING YOU KIDS THESE DAYS?
WE'LL LOOK FOR HIM LATER. FOR NOW, REX IS LOST.
WAIT!
HE HAS A CELL PHONE, DOESN'T HE?
MEANWHILE, MILLIONS OF YEARS AGO....
DAT'S ODD... DIS PLACE IS... STRANGELY FAMILIAR. WHAT DA HELL IS GOIN' ON? WHERE AM I?!
TALK FAST, BUCKO!
CALM, ALIEN 2019! CALM! THIS IS OUR RESEARCH CENTRE. YOU HAVE BEEN HERE BEFORE. I READ THE BOOK YOU RECOMMENDED LAST TIME: 'PRIDE AND PREJUDICE'.
A FASCINATING STUDY OF THE PRIMITIVE MATING RITUALS OF YOUR SPECIES, BUT NOT AS EXCITING AS 'FASTER, PUSSY-CAT, KILL, KILL!!'
WHY IS THIS?
EGAD. WELL--
ENOUGH!
IT MUST WAIT UNTIL AFTER... THE EXPERIMENT!
FOLLOW ME, NEOMONKEY!
FOLLOW ME... IF YOU EVER HOPE TO SEE ALEXANDRIA AGAIN!
ALEXANDRIA!?
SQUISHIsquish!

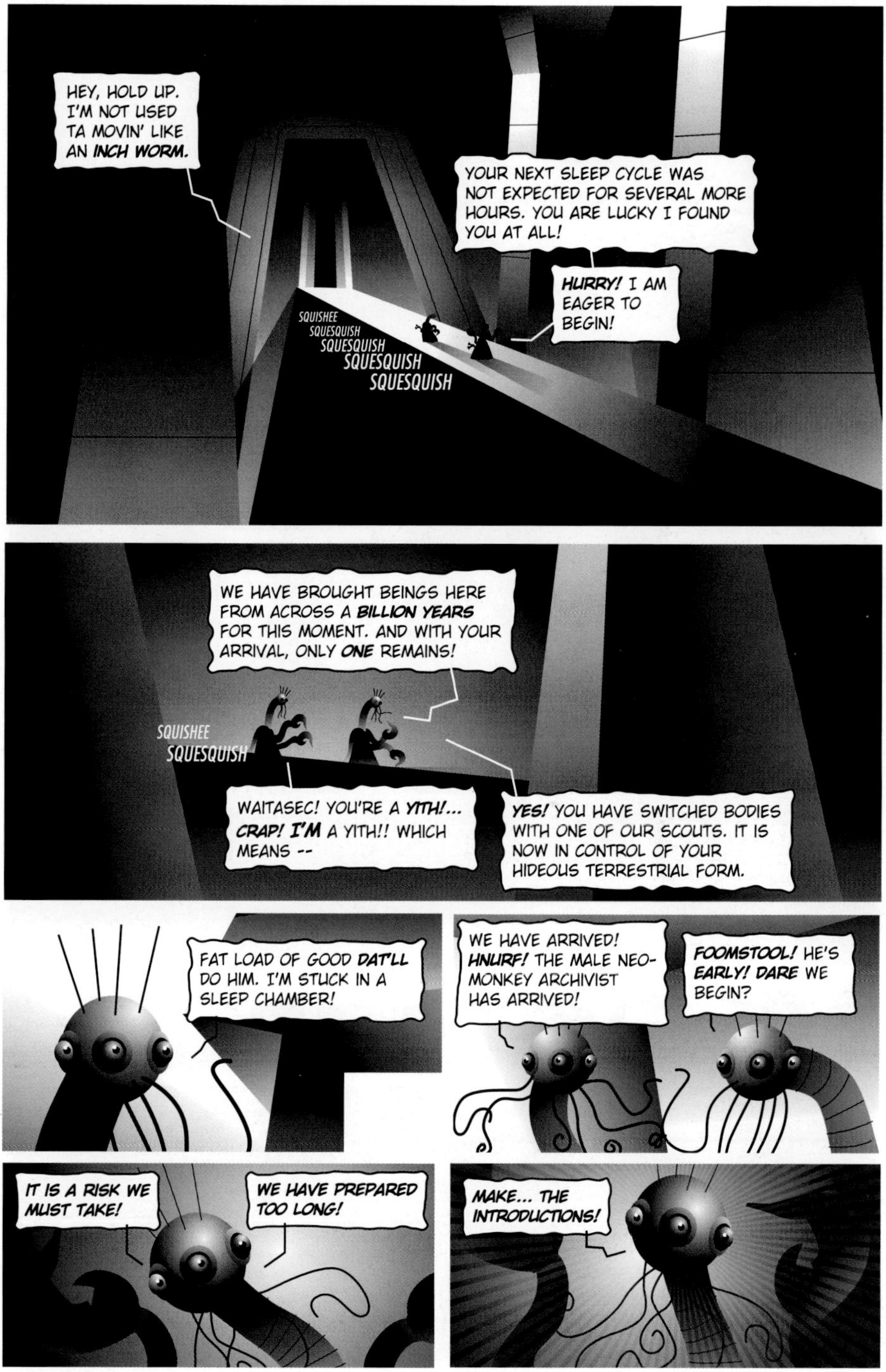
HEY, HOLD UP. I'M NOT USED TA MOVIN' LIKE AN INCH WORM.
YOUR NEXT SLEEP CYCLE WAS NOT EXPECTED FOR SEVERAL MORE HOURS. YOU ARE LUCKY I FOUND YOU AT ALL!
HURRY! I AM EAGER TO BEGIN!
SQUISHEE SQUESQUISH SQUESQUISH SQUESQUISH SQUESQUISH
WE HAVE BROUGHT BEINGS HERE FROM ACROSS A BILLION YEARS FOR THIS MOMENT. AND WITH YOUR ARRIVAL, ONLY ONE REMAINS!
SQUISHEE SQUESQUISH
WAITASEC! YOU'RE A YITH!... CRAP! I'M A YITH!! WHICH MEANS --
YES! YOU HAVE SWITCHED BODIES WITH ONE OF OUR SCOUTS. IT IS NOW IN CONTROL OF YOUR HIDEOUS TERRESTRIAL FORM.
FAT LOAD OF GOOD DAT'LL DO HIM. I'M STUCK IN A SLEEP CHAMBER!
WE HAVE ARRIVED! HNURF! THE MALE NEO-MONKEY ARCHIVIST HAS ARRIVED!
FOOMSTOOL! HE'S EARLY! DARE WE BEGIN?
IT IS A RISK WE MUST TAKE!
WE HAVE PREPARED TOO LONG!
MAKE... THE INTRODUCTIONS!

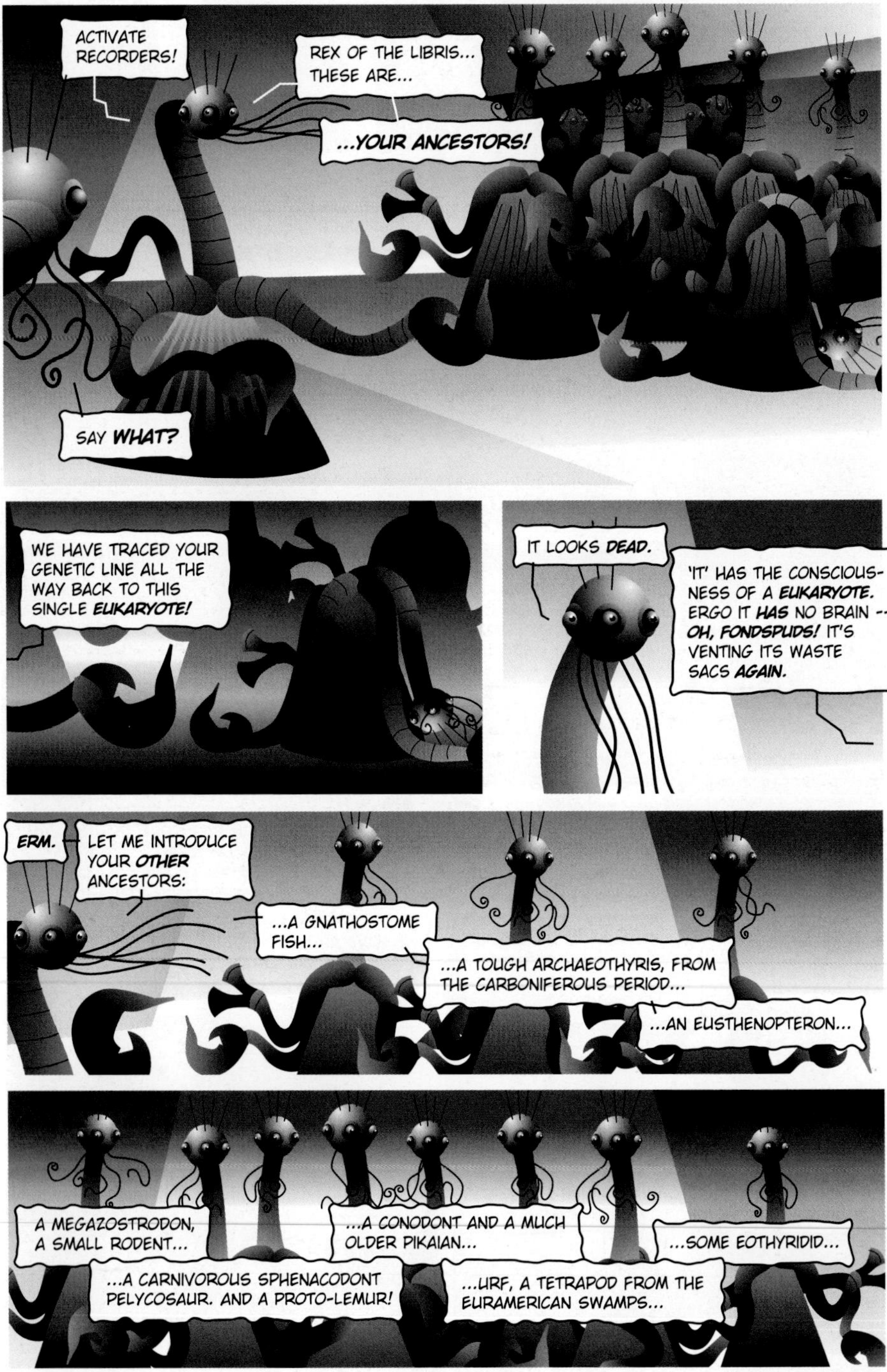
ACTIVATE RECORDERS!
REX OF THE LIBRIS... THESE ARE...
...YOUR ANCESTORS!
SAY WHAT?
WE HAVE TRACED YOUR GENETIC LINE ALL THE WAY BACK TO THIS SINGLE EUKARYOTE!
IT LOOKS DEAD.
'IT' HAS THE CONSCIOUSNESS OF A EUKARYOTE. ERGO IT HAS NO BRAIN -- OH, FONDSPUDS! IT'S VENTING ITS WASTE SACS AGAIN.
ERM.
LET ME INTRODUCE YOUR OTHER ANCESTORS:
...A GNATHOSTOME FISH...
...A TOUGH ARCHAEOTHYRIS, FROM THE CARBONIFEROUS PERIOD...
...AN EUSTHENOPTERON...
A MEGAZOSTRODON, A SMALL RODENT...
...A CARNIVOROUS SPHENACODONT PELYCOSAUR. AND A PROTO-LEMUR!
...A CONODONT AND A MUCH OLDER PIKAIAN...
...URF, A TETRAPOD FROM THE EURAMERICAN SWAMPS...
...SOME EOTHYRIDID...

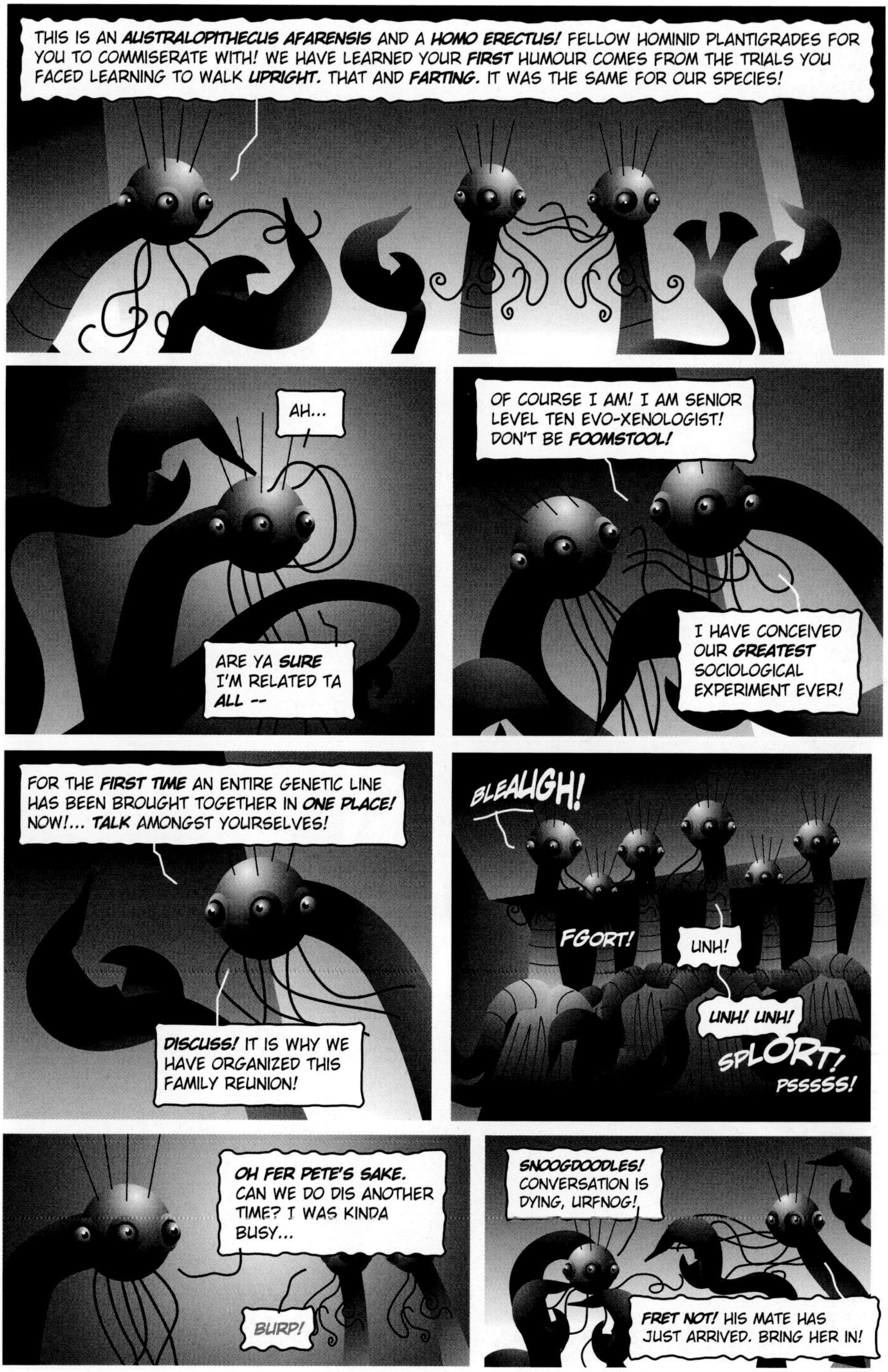
THIS IS AN AUSTRALOPITHECUS AFARENSIS AND A HOMO ERECTUS! FELLOW HOMINID PLANTIGRADES FOR YOU TO COMMISERATE WITH! WE HAVE LEARNED YOUR FIRST HUMOUR COMES FROM THE TRIALS YOU FACED LEARNING TO WALK UPRIGHT. THAT AND FARTING. IT WAS THE SAME FOR OUR SPECIES!
AH...
ARE YA SURE I'M RELATED TA ALL --
OF COURSE I AM! I AM SENIOR LEVEL TEN EVO-XENOLOGIST! DON'T BE FOOMSTOOL!
I HAVE CONCEIVED OUR GREATEST SOCIOLOGICAL EXPERIMENT EVER!
FOR THE FIRST TIME AN ENTIRE GENETIC LINE HAS BEEN BROUGHT TOGETHER IN ONE PLACE! NOW!... TALK AMONGST YOURSELVES!
DISCUSS! IT IS WHY WE HAVE ORGANIZED THIS FAMILY REUNION!
BLEAUGH!
FGORT!
UNH!
UNH! UNH!
SPLORT!
PSSSSS!
OH FER PETE'S SAKE. CAN WE DO DIS ANOTHER TIME? I WAS KINDA BUSY...
BURP!
SNOOGDOODLES! CONVERSATION IS DYING, URFNOG!
FRET NOT! HIS MATE HAS JUST ARRIVED. BRING HER IN!

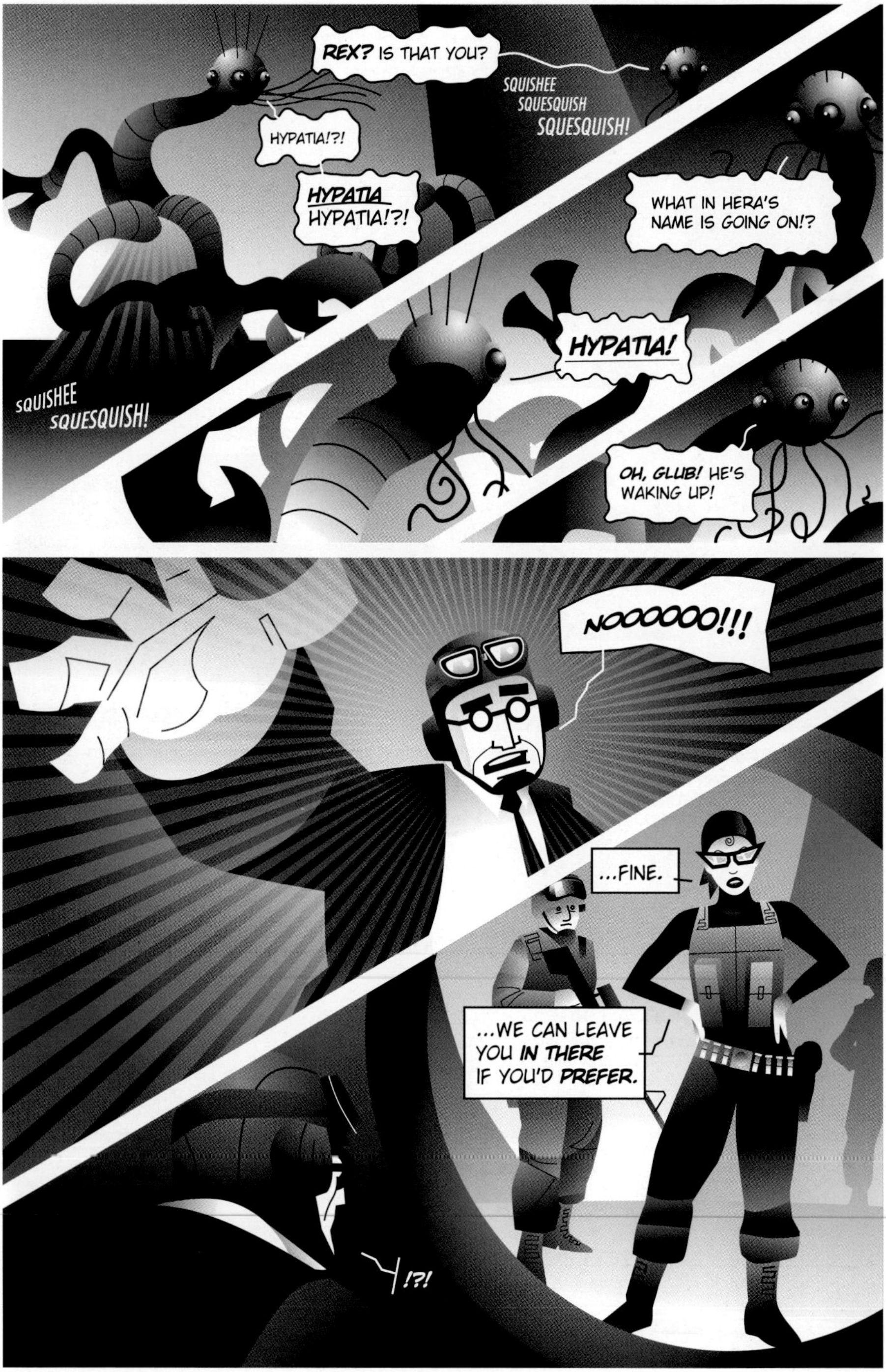
REX? IS THAT YOU?
HYPATIA!?!
HYPATIA HYPATIA!?!
SQUISHEE SQUESQUISH SQUESQUISH!
SQUISHEE SQUESQUISH!
WHAT IN HERA'S NAME IS GOING ON!?
HYPATIA!
OH, GLUB! HE'S WAKING UP!
NOOOOOO!!!
...FINE.
...WE CAN LEAVE YOU IN THERE IF YOU'D PREFER.
!?!

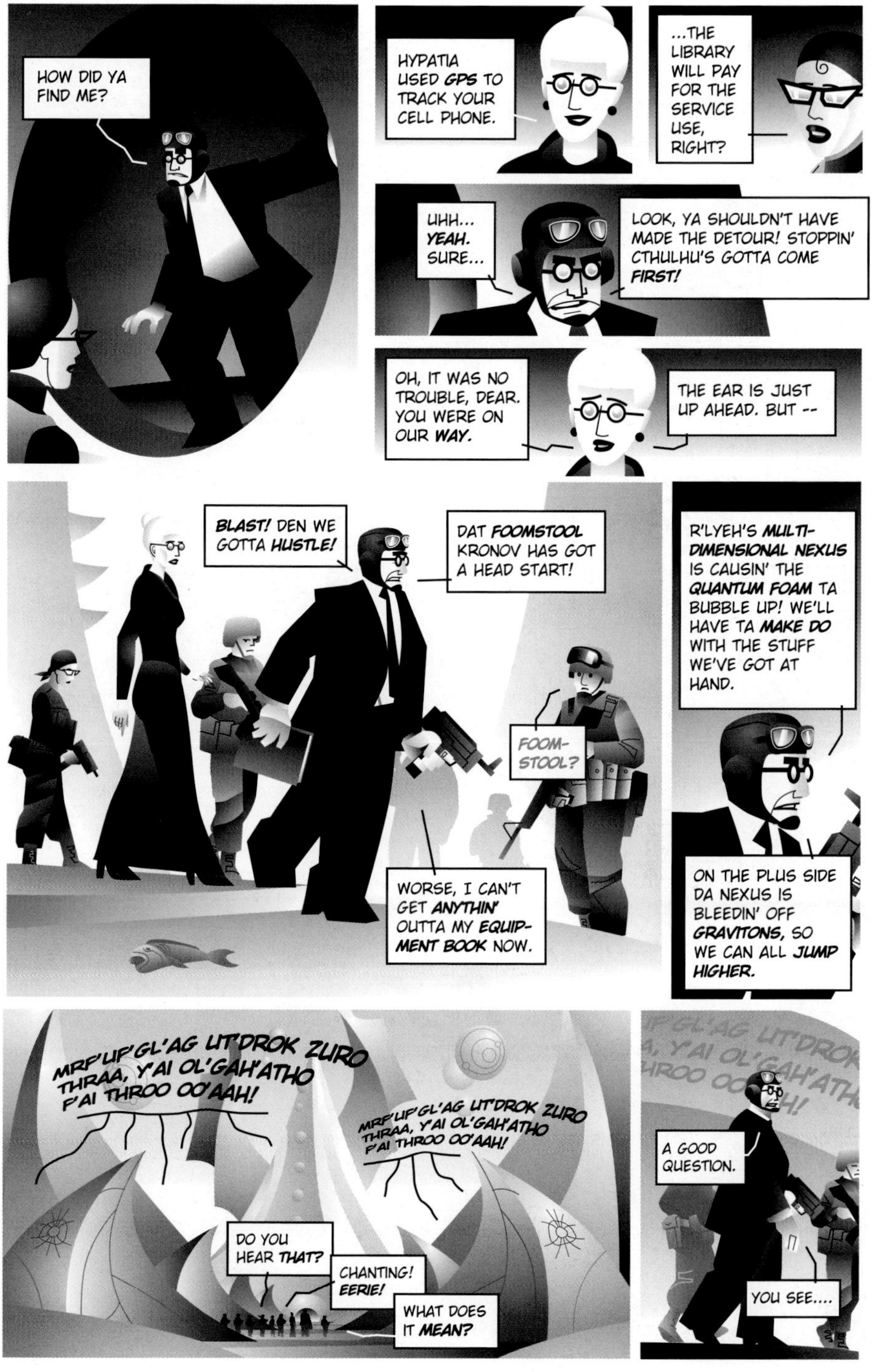
HOW DID YA FIND ME?
HYPATIA USED GPS TO TRACK YOUR CELL PHONE.
...THE LIBRARY WILL PAY FOR THE SERVICE USE, RIGHT?
UHH... YEAH. SURE...
LOOK, YA SHOULDN'T HAVE MADE THE DETOUR! STOPPIN' CTHULHU'S GOTTA COME FIRST!
OH, IT WAS NO TROUBLE, DEAR. YOU WERE ON OUR WAY.
THE EAR IS JUST UP AHEAD. BUT --
BLAST! DEN WE GOTTA HUSTLE!
DAT FOOMSTOOL KRONOV HAS GOT A HEAD START!
FOOM-STOOL?
WORSE, I CAN'T GET ANYTHIN' OUTTA MY EQUIP-MENT BOOK NOW.
R'LYEH'S MULTI-DIMENSIONAL NEXUS IS CAUSIN' THE QUANTUM FOAM TA BUBBLE UP! WE'LL HAVE TA MAKE DO WITH THE STUFF WE'VE GOT AT HAND.
ON THE PLUS SIDE DA NEXUS IS BLEEDIN' OFF GRAVITONS, SO WE CAN ALL JUMP HIGHER.
MRF'UF'GL'AG UT'DROK ZURO THRAA, Y'AI OL'GAH'ATHO F'AI THROO OO'AAH!
MRF'UF'GL'AG UT'DROK ZURO THRAA, Y'AI OL'GAH'ATHO F'AI THROO OO'AAH!
DO YOU HEAR THAT?
CHANTING! EERIE!
WHAT DOES IT MEAN?
A GOOD QUESTION.
YOU SEE....

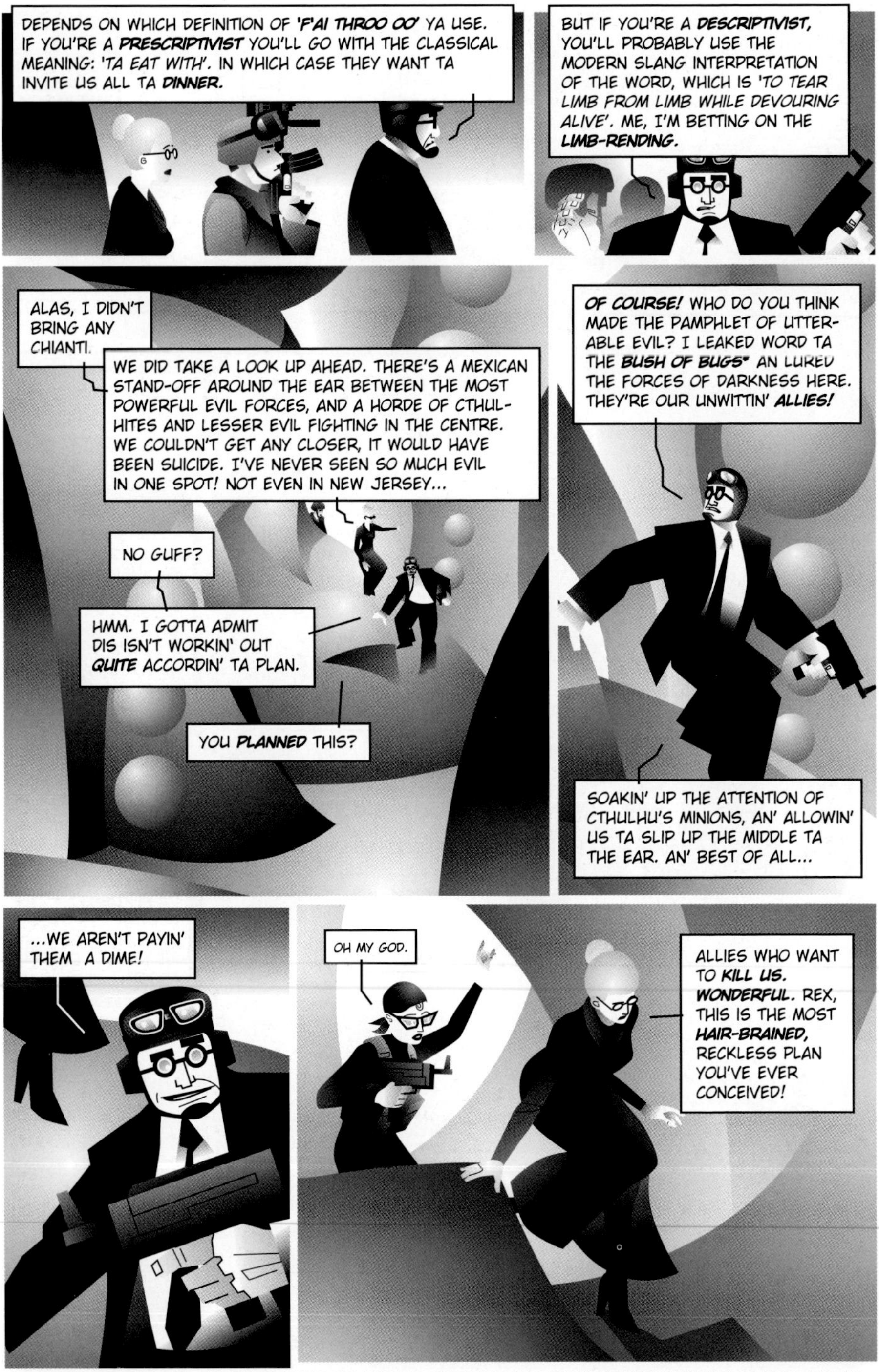
DEPENDS ON WHICH DEFINITION OF 'F'AI THROO OO' YA USE. IF YOU'RE A PRESCRIPTIVIST YOU'LL GO WITH THE CLASSICAL MEANING: 'TA EAT WITH'. IN WHICH CASE THEY WANT TA INVITE US ALL TA DINNER.
BUT IF YOU'RE A DESCRIPTIVIST, YOU'LL PROBABLY USE THE MODERN SLANG INTERPRETATION OF THE WORD, WHICH IS 'TO TEAR LIMB FROM LIMB WHILE DEVOURING ALIVE'. ME, I'M BETTING ON THE LIMB-RENDING.
ALAS, I DIDN'T BRING ANY CHIANTI.
WE DID TAKE A LOOK UP AHEAD. THERE'S A MEXICAN STAND-OFF AROUND THE EAR BETWEEN THE MOST POWERFUL EVIL FORCES, AND A HORDE OF CTHULHITES AND LESSER EVIL FIGHTING IN THE CENTRE. WE COULDN'T GET ANY CLOSER, IT WOULD HAVE BEEN SUICIDE. I'VE NEVER SEEN SO MUCH EVIL IN ONE SPOT! NOT EVEN IN NEW JERSEY...
NO GUFF?
HMM. I GOTTA ADMIT DIS ISN'T WORKIN' OUT QUITE ACCORDIN' TA PLAN.
YOU PLANNED THIS?
OF COURSE! WHO DO YOU THINK MADE THE PAMPHLET OF UTTERABLE EVIL? I LEAKED WORD TA THE BUSH OF BUGS* AN LURED THE FORCES OF DARKNESS HERE. THEY'RE OUR UNWITTIN' ALLIES!
SOAKIN' UP THE ATTENTION OF CTHULHU'S MINIONS, AN' ALLOWIN' US TA SLIP UP THE MIDDLE TA THE EAR. AN' BEST OF ALL...
...WE AREN'T PAYIN' THEM A DIME!
OH MY GOD.
ALLIES WHO WANT TO KILL US. WONDERFUL. REX, THIS IS THE MOST HAIR-BRAINED, RECKLESS PLAN YOU'VE EVER CONCEIVED!

* THE BUSH OF BUGS IS THE ONE PLACE IN THE LIBRARY THAT REX DOESN'T SWEEP FOR LISTENING DEVICES, AND SO, OVER THE YEARS, THEY HAVE ALL ACCUMULATED HERE. THIS GIVES REX A HOTLINE TO THE FORCES OF EVIL! -- BARRY

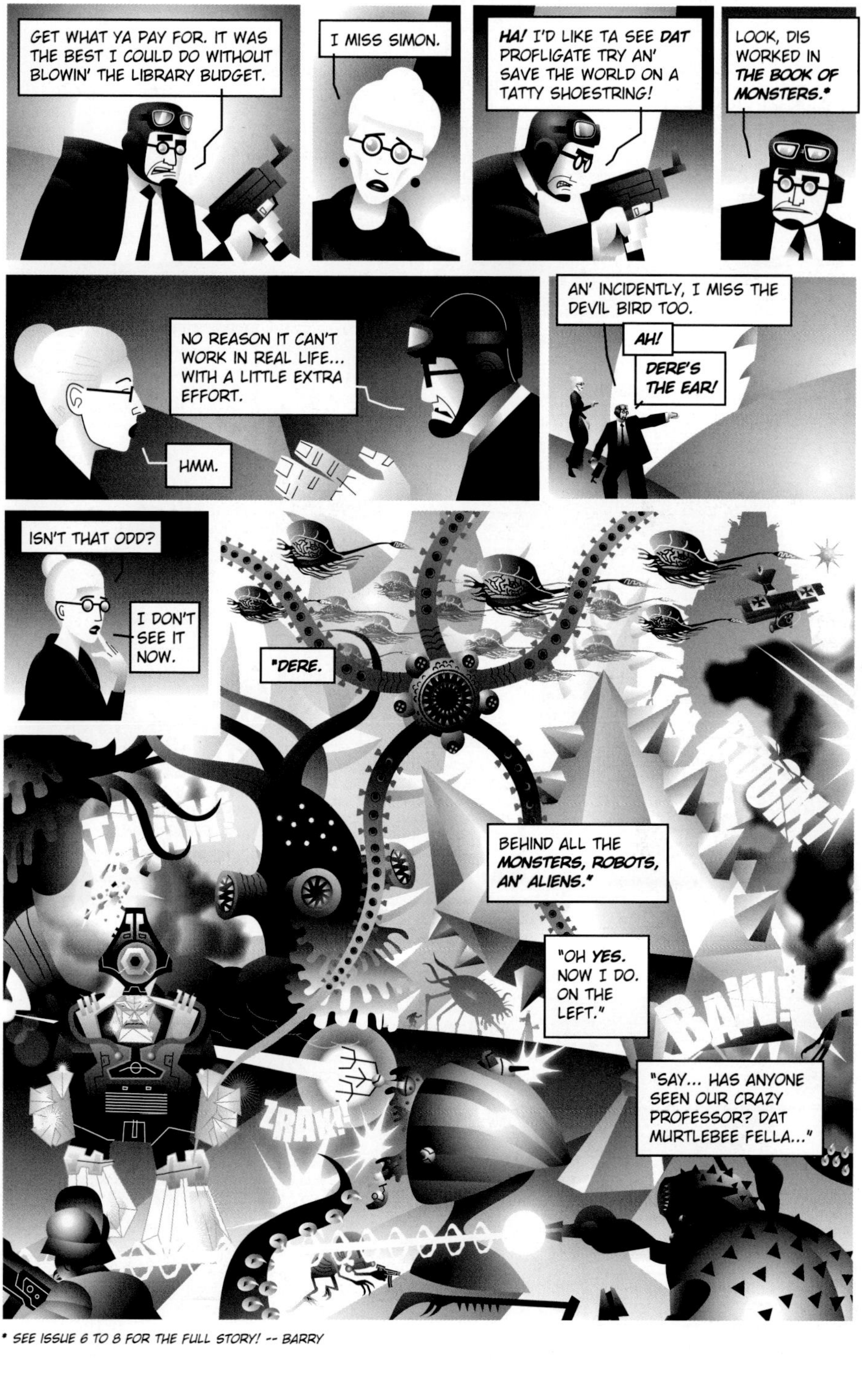
GET WHAT YA PAY FOR. IT WAS THE BEST I COULD DO WITHOUT BLOWIN' THE LIBRARY BUDGET.
I MISS SIMON.
HA! I'D LIKE TA SEE DAT PROFLIGATE TRY AN' SAVE THE WORLD ON A TATTY SHOESTRING!
LOOK, DIS WORKED IN THE BOOK OF MONSTERS.*
NO REASON IT CAN'T WORK IN REAL LIFE... WITH A LITTLE EXTRA EFFORT.
HMM.
AN' INCIDENTLY, I MISS THE DEVIL BIRD TOO.
AH!
DERE'S THE EAR!
ISN'T THAT ODD?
I DON'T SEE IT NOW.
"DERE.
BEHIND ALL THE MONSTERS, ROBOTS, AN' ALIENS."
THOOM!
TOOM!
"OH YES. NOW I DO. ON THE LEFT."
BAM!
"SAY... HAS ANYONE SEEN OUR CRAZY PROFESSOR? DAT MURTLEBEE FELLA..."
ZRAK!

* SEE ISSUE 6 TO 8 FOR THE FULL STORY! -- BARRY

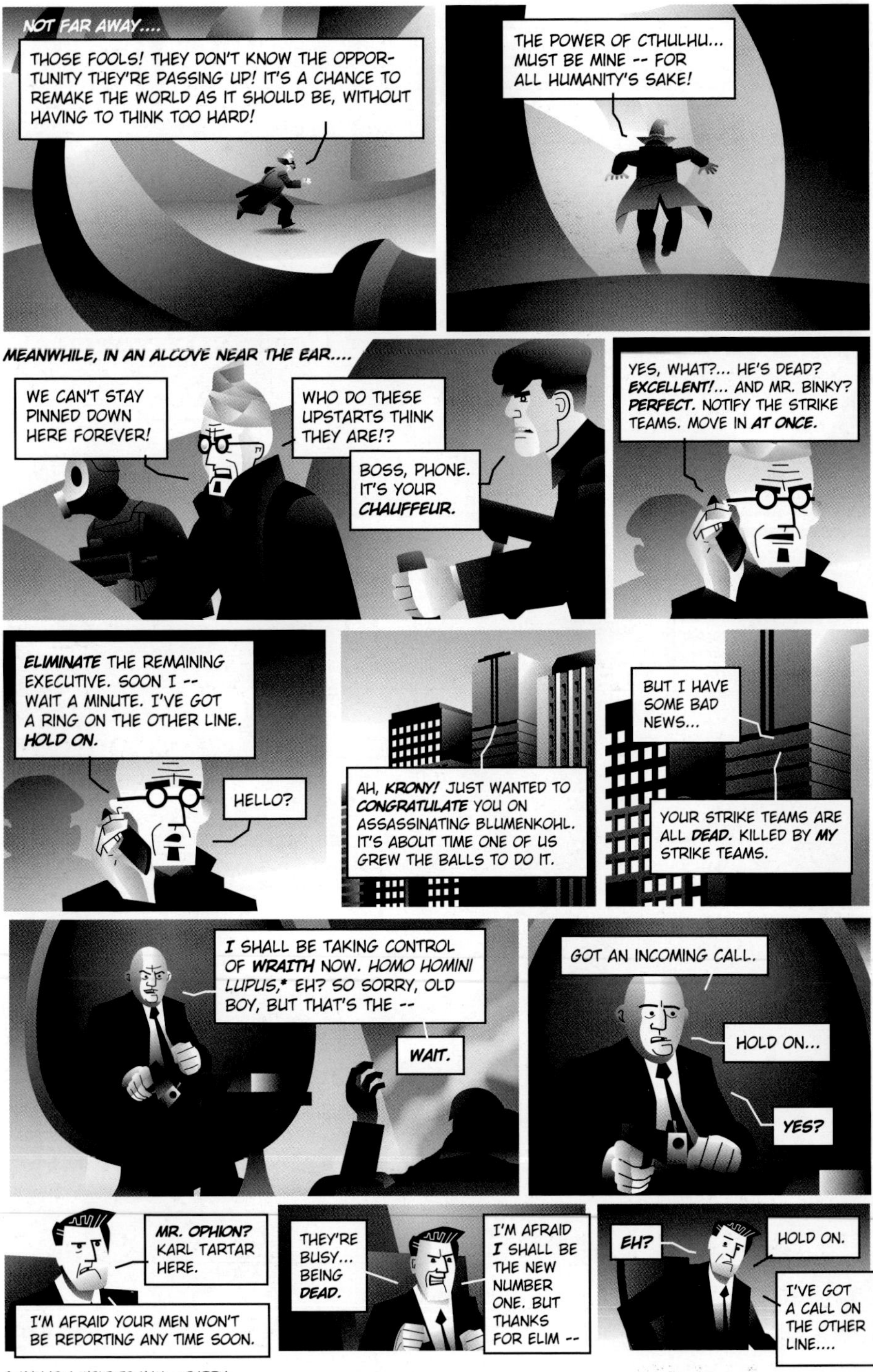
NOT FAR AWAY....
THOSE FOOLS! THEY DON'T KNOW THE OPPORTUNITY THEY'RE PASSING UP! IT'S A CHANCE TO REMAKE THE WORLD AS IT SHOULD BE, WITHOUT HAVING TO THINK TOO HARD!
THE POWER OF CTHULHU... MUST BE MINE -- FOR ALL HUMANITY'S SAKE!
MEANWHILE, IN AN ALCOVE NEAR THE EAR....
WE CAN'T STAY PINNED DOWN HERE FOREVER!
WHO DO THESE UPSTARTS THINK THEY ARE!?
BOSS, PHONE. IT'S YOUR CHAUFFEUR.
YES, WHAT?... HE'S DEAD? EXCELLENT!... AND MR. BINKY? PERFECT. NOTIFY THE STRIKE TEAMS. MOVE IN AT ONCE.
ELIMINATE THE REMAINING EXECUTIVE. SOON I -- WAIT A MINUTE. I'VE GOT A RING ON THE OTHER LINE. HOLD ON.
HELLO?
AH, KRONY! JUST WANTED TO CONGRATULATE YOU ON ASSASSINATING BLUMENKOHL. IT'S ABOUT TIME ONE OF US GREW THE BALLS TO DO IT.
BUT I HAVE SOME BAD NEWS...
YOUR STRIKE TEAMS ARE ALL DEAD. KILLED BY MY STRIKE TEAMS.
I SHALL BE TAKING CONTROL OF WRAITH NOW. HOMO HOMINI LUPUS,* EH? SO SORRY, OLD BOY, BUT THAT'S THE --
WAIT.
GOT AN INCOMING CALL.
HOLD ON...
YES?
MR. OPHION? KARL TARTAR HERE.
I'M AFRAID YOUR MEN WON'T BE REPORTING ANY TIME SOON.
THEY'RE BUSY... BEING DEAD.
I'M AFRAID I SHALL BE THE NEW NUMBER ONE. BUT THANKS FOR ELIM --
EH?
HOLD ON.
I'VE GOT A CALL ON THE OTHER LINE....

* MAN IS A WOLF TO MAN. --BARRY

BACK AT THE EAR....
YOU WANT US TO GO OUT THERE?
FWOOSH!
OKAY, THAT'S JUST CRAZY!
EVEN TO ME!
WE'RE LIBRARIANS! OUR JOB IS ALL ABOUT THE IMPOSSIBLE!
!?!
WHAT HAVE I GOT IN MY POCKETS?
I DON'T KNOW. MOTHBALLS? THAT JACKET HAS BEEN IN THE CLOSET FOR FIFTY YEARS.*
NOT MOTHBALLS -- THE ONG ZWARBA GEM!** SO DAT'S WHERE IT'S BEEN!
AN IN THE OTHER POCKET, -- WHAT LUCK! -- WAFERS OF THE GODS FROM STERNE'S FARM!***
OH FOR GOODNESS' SAKE, REX! I'VE BEEN LOOKING FOR THE ONG ZWARBA GEM FOR DECADES!
YES WELL-- HOLD ON A MINUTE!
CIRCE, CAN YOU ESTABLISH MAGICAL CONTROL OVER THESE CRABS?
WITH A TOUCH. THEY'RE DEFENSELESS.
THEN I GOT US A PLAN...

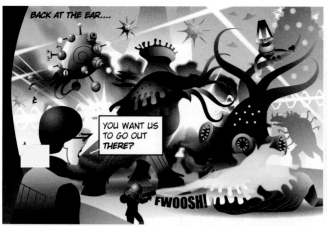

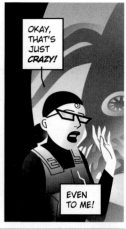

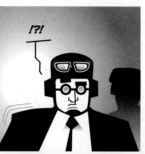

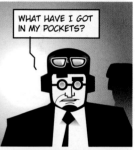

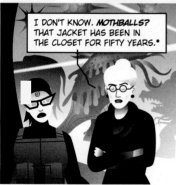

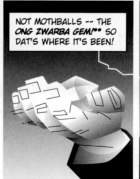

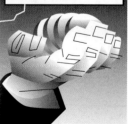

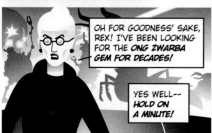

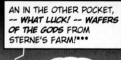

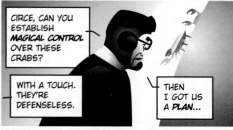

* REX GOT OUT THE OLD JACKET AFTER HIS CURRENT ONE WAS RIPPED DURING A SUBDERGID ATTACK. SEE ISSUE 11 FOR MORE ON THIS WARDROBE MALFUNCTION!! ** SEE ISSUE 9 FOR MORE ON THE INCREDIBLE, LUCK GENERATING GEMSTONE!
*** SEE ISSUE 10 FOR THE LOW DOWN THE ASTONISHING, GROWTH INDUCING **FOOD OF THE GOD WAFERS** AND HOW THEY WOUND UP ON LARRY STERNE'S FARM! --BARRY

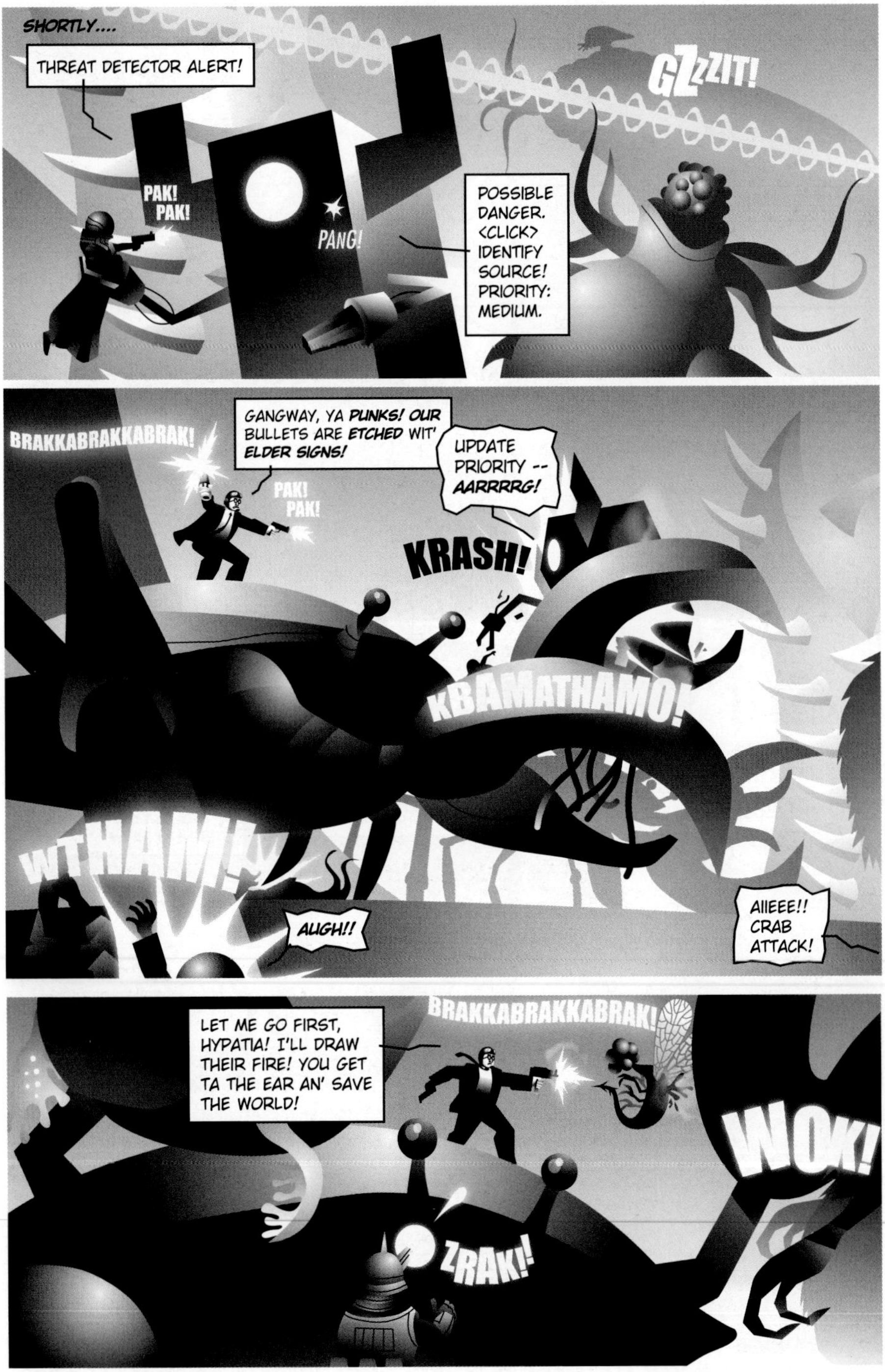
SHORTLY....
THREAT DETECTOR ALERT!
PAK! PAK!
PANG!
GZZZIT!
POSSIBLE DANGER. <CLICK> IDENTIFY SOURCE! PRIORITY: MEDIUM.
BRAKKABRAKKABRAK!
GANGWAY, YA PUNKS! OUR BULLETS ARE ETCHED WIT' ELDER SIGNS!
PAK! PAK!
UPDATE PRIORITY -- AARRRRG!
KRASH!
KBAMATHAMO!
WTHAM!
AUGH!!
AIIEEE!! CRAB ATTACK!
LET ME GO FIRST, HYPATIA! I'LL DRAW THEIR FIRE! YOU GET TA THE EAR AN' SAVE THE WORLD!
BRAKKABRAKKABRAK!
WOK!
ZRAK!!

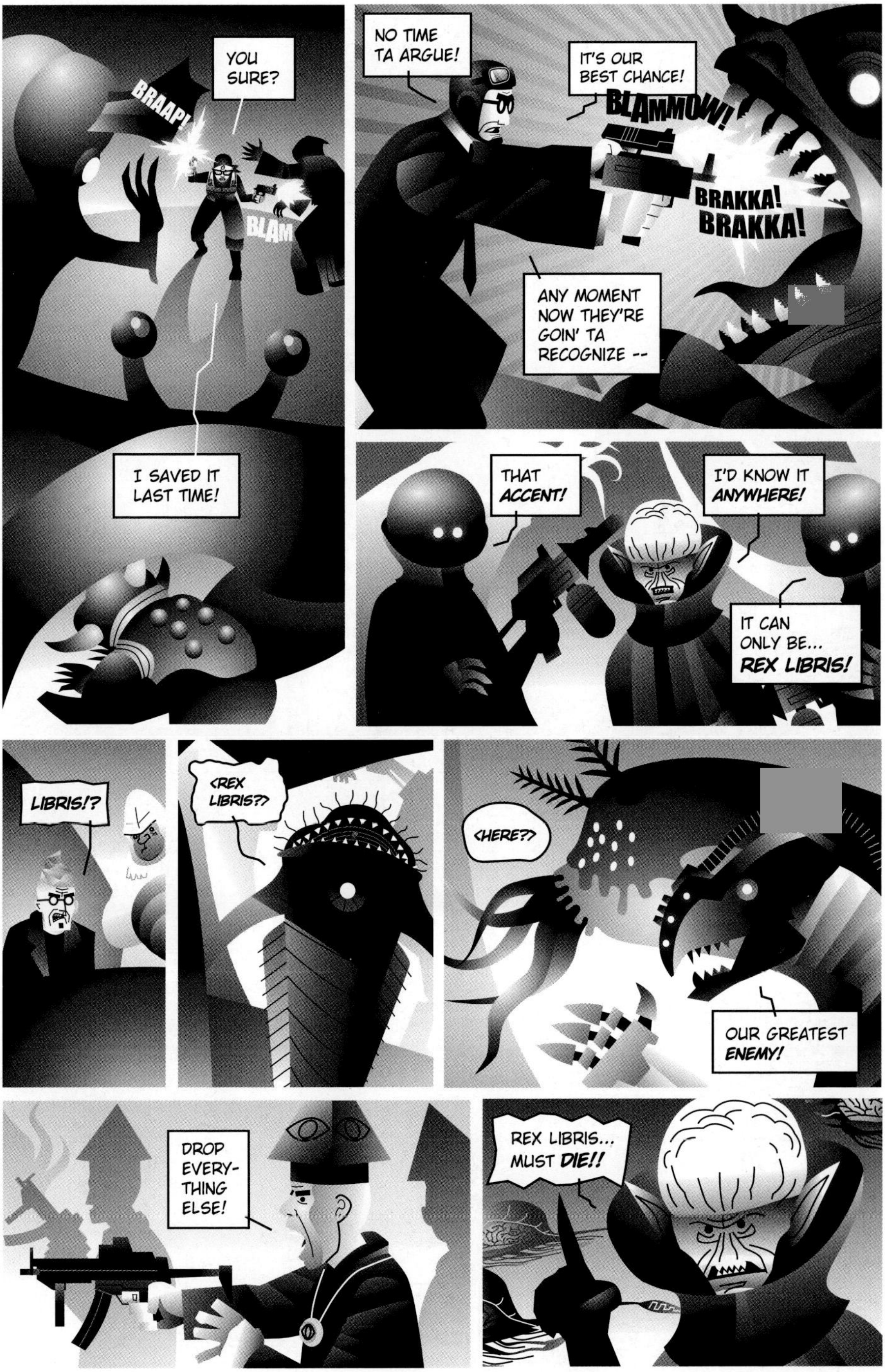

YOU SURE?
BRAAP!
BLAM
I SAVED IT LAST TIME!
NO TIME TA ARGUE!
IT'S OUR BEST CHANCE!
BLAMMOW!
BRAKKA! BRAKKA!
ANY MOMENT NOW THEY'RE GOIN' TA RECOGNIZE --
THAT *ACCENT!*
I'D KNOW IT *ANYWHERE!*
IT CAN ONLY BE... **REX LIBRIS!**
LIBRIS!?
<REX LIBRIS?>
<HERE?>
OUR GREATEST *ENEMY!*
DROP EVERY-THING ELSE!
REX LIBRIS... MUST *DIE!!*

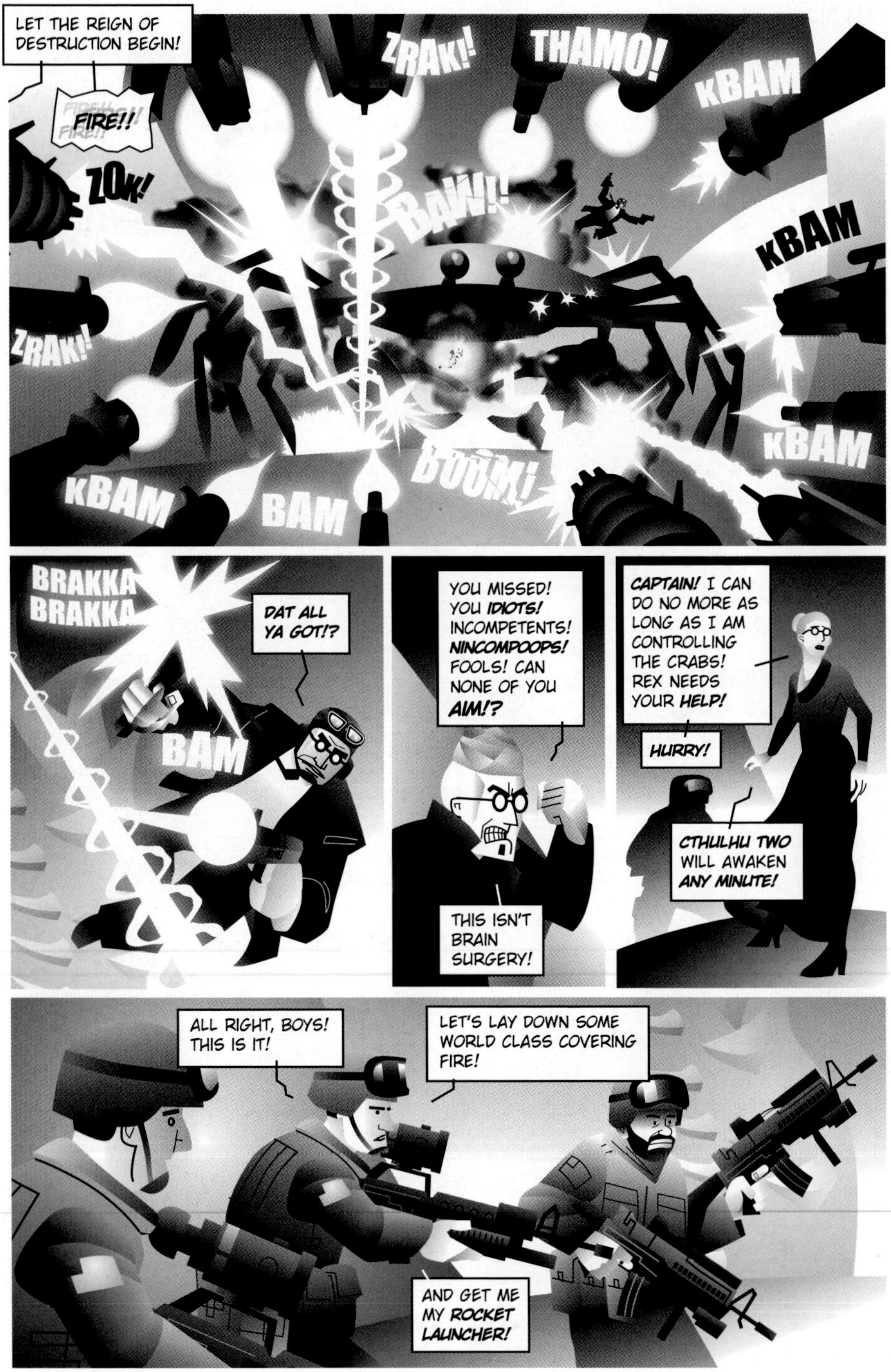

LET THE REIGN OF DESTRUCTION BEGIN!
FIRE!!
ZRAK!!
THAMO!
KBAM
ZOK!
BAW!!
KBAM
ZRAK!!
KBAM
BOOM!
KBAM
BAM
BRAKKA BRAKKA
DAT ALL YA GOT!?
BAM
YOU MISSED! YOU IDIOTS! INCOMPETENTS! NINCOMPOOPS! FOOLS! CAN NONE OF YOU AIM!?
THIS ISN'T BRAIN SURGERY!
CAPTAIN! I CAN DO NO MORE AS LONG AS I AM CONTROLLING THE CRABS! REX NEEDS YOUR HELP!
HURRY!
CTHULHU TWO WILL AWAKEN ANY MINUTE!
ALL RIGHT, BOYS! THIS IS IT!
LET'S LAY DOWN SOME WORLD CLASS COVERING FIRE!
AND GET ME MY ROCKET LAUNCHER!

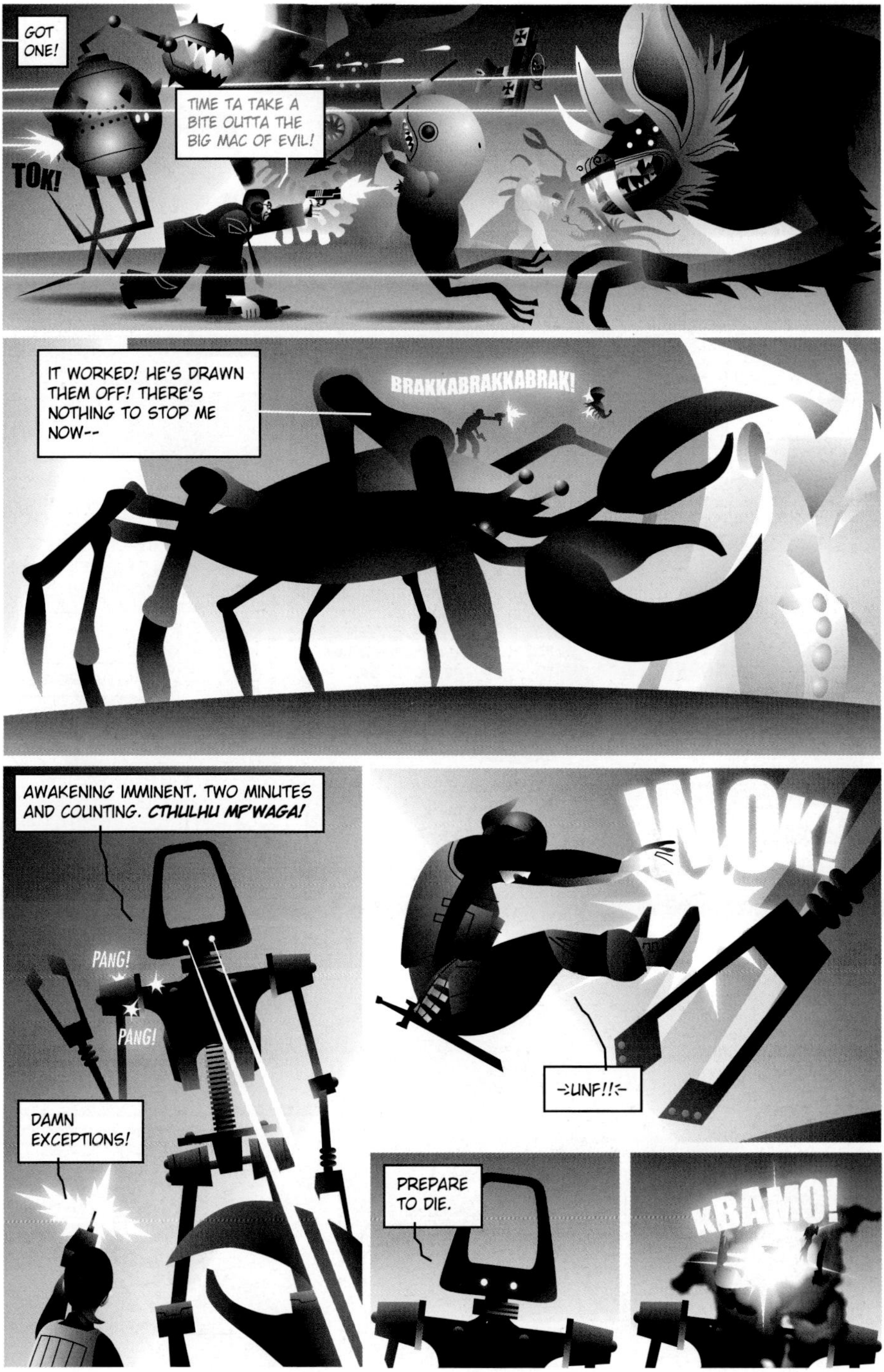
GOT ONE!
TIME TA TAKE A BITE OUTTA THE BIG MAC OF EVIL!
TOK!
IT WORKED! HE'S DRAWN THEM OFF! THERE'S NOTHING TO STOP ME NOW--
BRAKKABRAKKABRAK!
AWAKENING IMMINENT. TWO MINUTES AND COUNTING. CTHULHU MP'WAGA!
PANG!
PANG!
DAMN EXCEPTIONS!
WOK!
UNF!!
PREPARE TO DIE.
KBAMO!

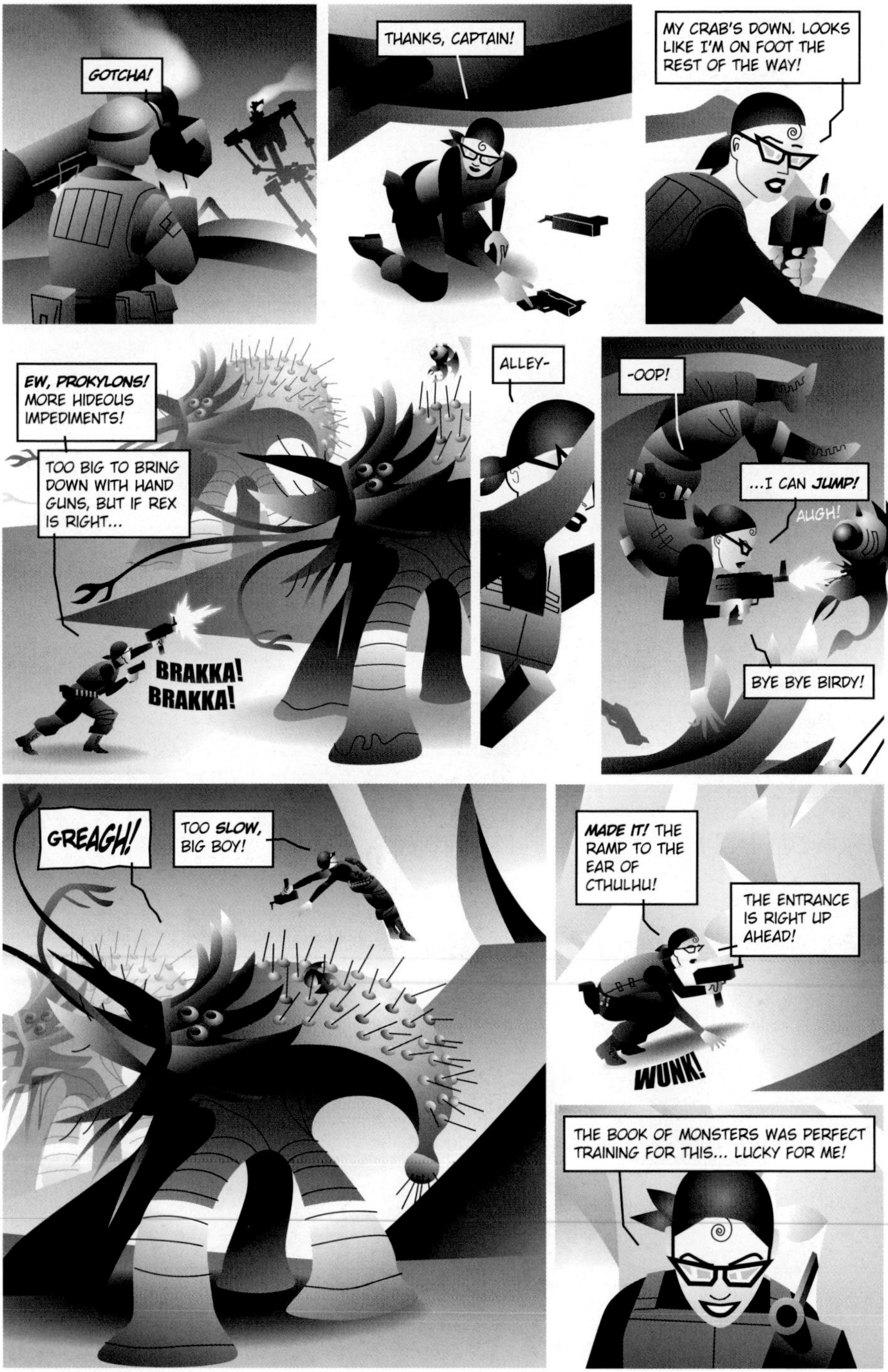
GOTCHA!
THANKS, CAPTAIN!
MY CRAB'S DOWN. LOOKS LIKE I'M ON FOOT THE REST OF THE WAY!
EW, PROKYLONS! MORE HIDEOUS IMPEDIMENTS!
TOO BIG TO BRING DOWN WITH HAND GUNS, BUT IF REX IS RIGHT...
BRAKKA! BRAKKA!
ALLEY-
-OOP!
...I CAN JUMP!
AUGH!
BYE BYE BIRDY!
GREAGH!
TOO SLOW, BIG BOY!
MADE IT! THE RAMP TO THE EAR OF CTHULHU!
THE ENTRANCE IS RIGHT UP AHEAD!
WUNK!
THE BOOK OF MONSTERS WAS PERFECT TRAINING FOR THIS... LUCKY FOR ME!

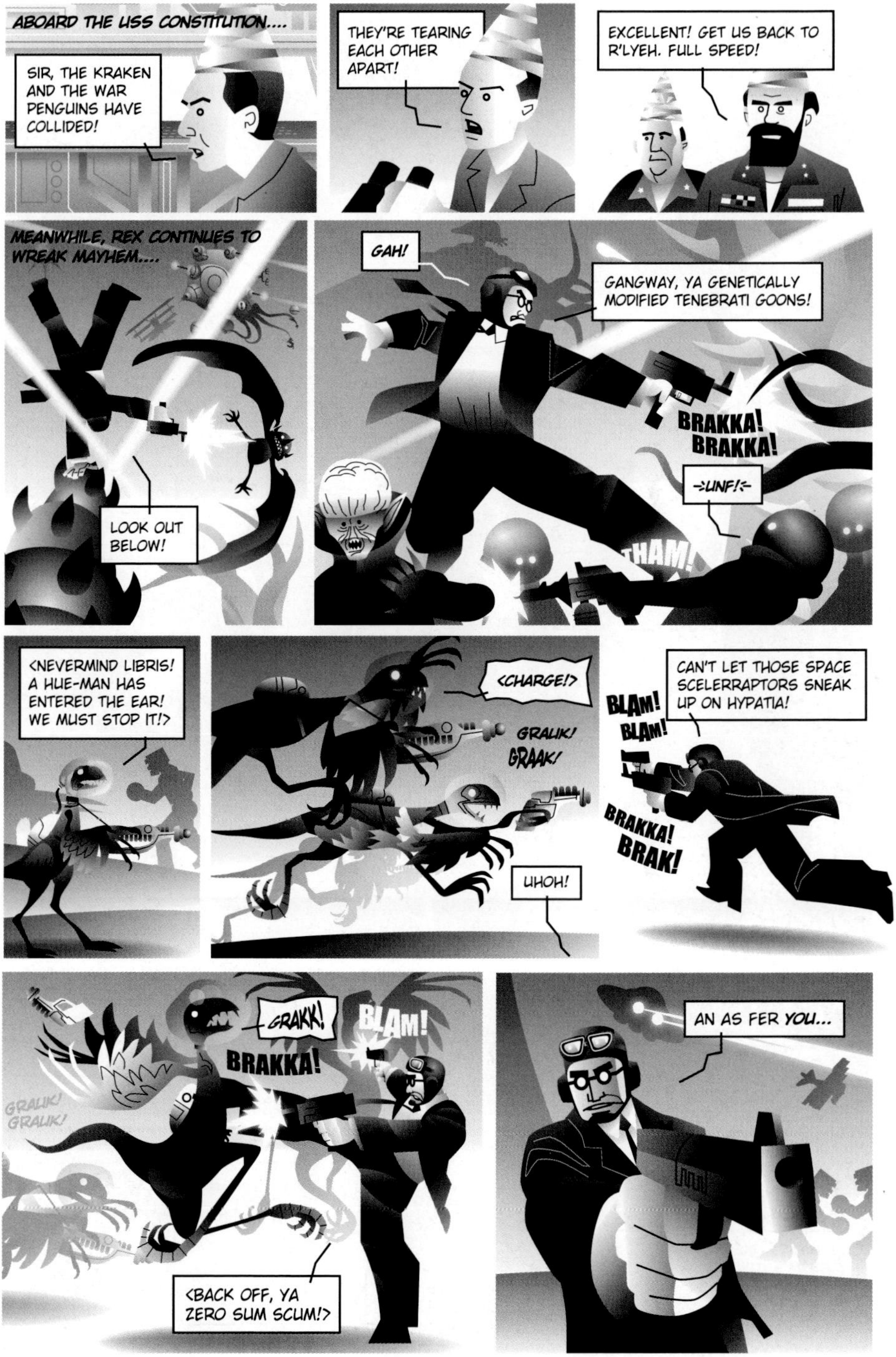

ABOARD THE USS CONSTITUTION....
SIR, THE KRAKEN AND THE WAR PENGUINS HAVE COLLIDED!
THEY'RE TEARING EACH OTHER APART!
EXCELLENT! GET US BACK TO R'LYEH. FULL SPEED!
MEANWHILE, REX CONTINUES TO WREAK MAYHEM....
LOOK OUT BELOW!
GAH!
GANGWAY, YA GENETICALLY MODIFIED TENEBRATI GOONS!
BRAKKA! BRAKKA!
UNF!
THAM!
<NEVERMIND LIBRIS! A HUE-MAN HAS ENTERED THE EAR! WE MUST STOP IT!>
<CHARGE!>
GRAUK! GRAAK!
UHOH!
CAN'T LET THOSE SPACE SCELERRAPTORS SNEAK UP ON HYPATIA!
BLAM! BLAM!
BRAKKA! BRAK!
GRAKK!
BLAM!
BRAKKA!
GRAUK! GRAUK!
<BACK OFF, YA ZERO SUM SCUM!>
AN AS FER *YOU*...

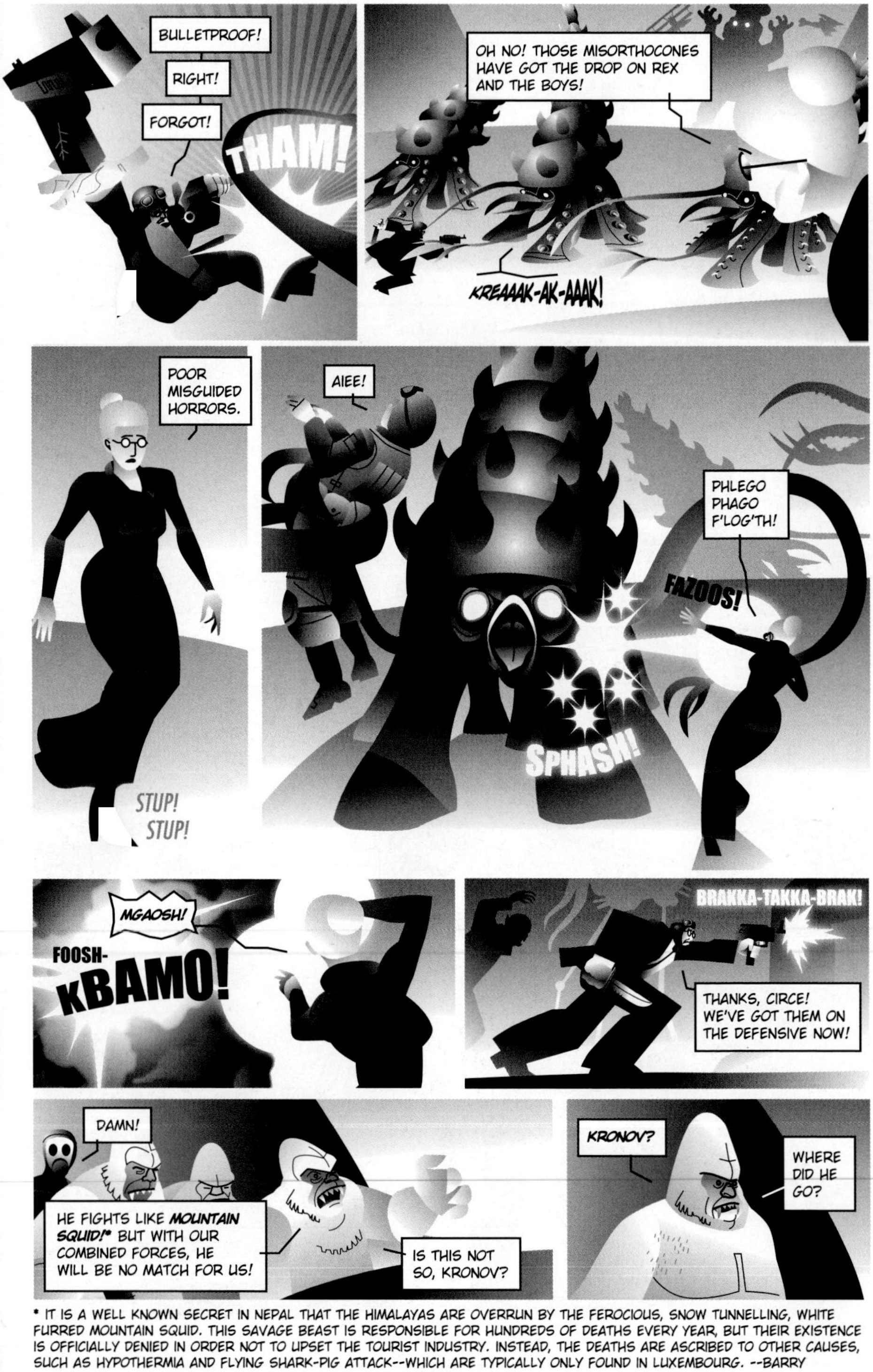
BULLETPROOF!
RIGHT!
FORGOT!
THAM!
OH NO! THOSE MISORTHOCONES HAVE GOT THE DROP ON REX AND THE BOYS!
KREAAAK-AK-AAAK!
POOR MISGUIDED HORRORS.
STUP! STUP!
AIEE!
PHLEGO PHAGO F'LOG'TH!
FAZOOS!
SPHASH!
MGAOSH!
FOOSH-kBAMO!
BRAKKA-TAKKA-BRAK!
THANKS, CIRCE! WE'VE GOT THEM ON THE DEFENSIVE NOW!
DAMN!
HE FIGHTS LIKE MOUNTAIN SQUID!* BUT WITH OUR COMBINED FORCES, HE WILL BE NO MATCH FOR US!
IS THIS NOT SO, KRONOV?
KRONOV?
WHERE DID HE GO?

* IT IS A WELL KNOWN SECRET IN NEPAL THAT THE HIMALAYAS ARE OVERRUN BY THE FEROCIOUS, SNOW TUNNELLING, WHITE FURRED MOUNTAIN SQUID. THIS SAVAGE BEAST IS RESPONSIBLE FOR HUNDREDS OF DEATHS EVERY YEAR, BUT THEIR EXISTENCE IS OFFICIALLY DENIED IN ORDER NOT TO UPSET THE TOURIST INDUSTRY. INSTEAD, THE DEATHS ARE ASCRIBED TO OTHER CAUSES, SUCH AS HYPOTHERMIA AND FLYING SHARK-PIG ATTACK--WHICH ARE TYPICALLY ONLY FOUND IN LUXEMBOURG. --BARRY

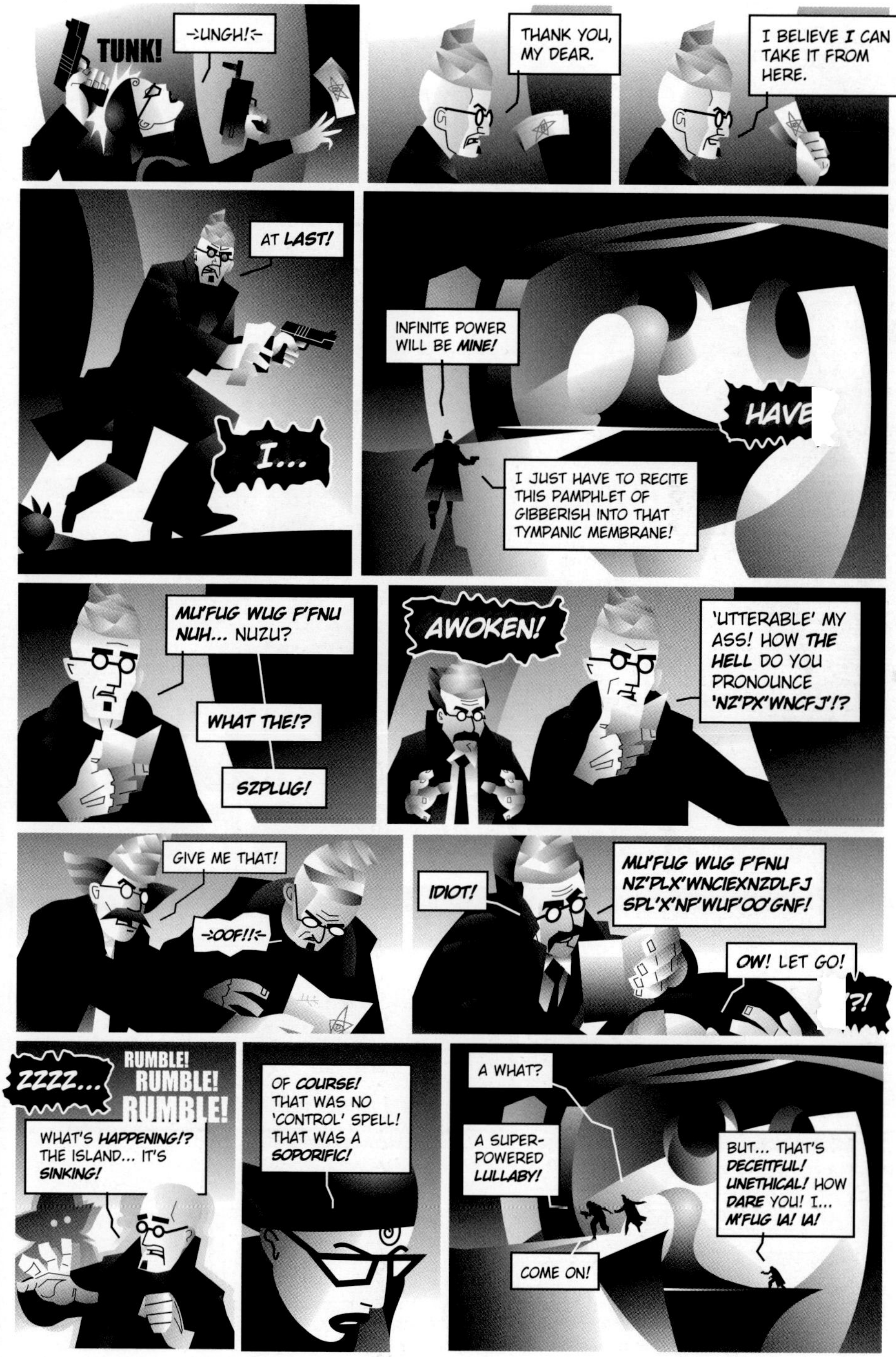
TUNK!
-UNGH!-
THANK YOU, MY DEAR.
I BELIEVE I CAN TAKE IT FROM HERE.
AT LAST!
I...
INFINITE POWER WILL BE MINE!
HAVE
I JUST HAVE TO RECITE THIS PAMPHLET OF GIBBERISH INTO THAT TYMPANIC MEMBRANE!
MU'FUG WUG F'FNU NUH... NUZU?
WHAT THE!?
SZPLUG!
AWOKEN!
'UTTERABLE' MY ASS! HOW THE HELL DO YOU PRONOUNCE 'NZ'PX'WNCFJ'!?
GIVE ME THAT!
-OOF!!-
IDIOT!
MU'FUG WUG F'FNU NZ'PLX'WNCIEXNZDLFJ SPL'X'NF'WUF'OO'GNF!
OW! LET GO!
?!
ZZZZ...
RUMBLE! RUMBLE! RUMBLE!
WHAT'S HAPPENING!? THE ISLAND... IT'S SINKING!
OF COURSE! THAT WAS NO 'CONTROL' SPELL! THAT WAS A SOPORIFIC!
A WHAT?
A SUPER-POWERED LULLABY!
BUT... THAT'S DECEITFUL! UNETHICAL! HOW DARE YOU! I... M'FUG IA! IA!
COME ON!

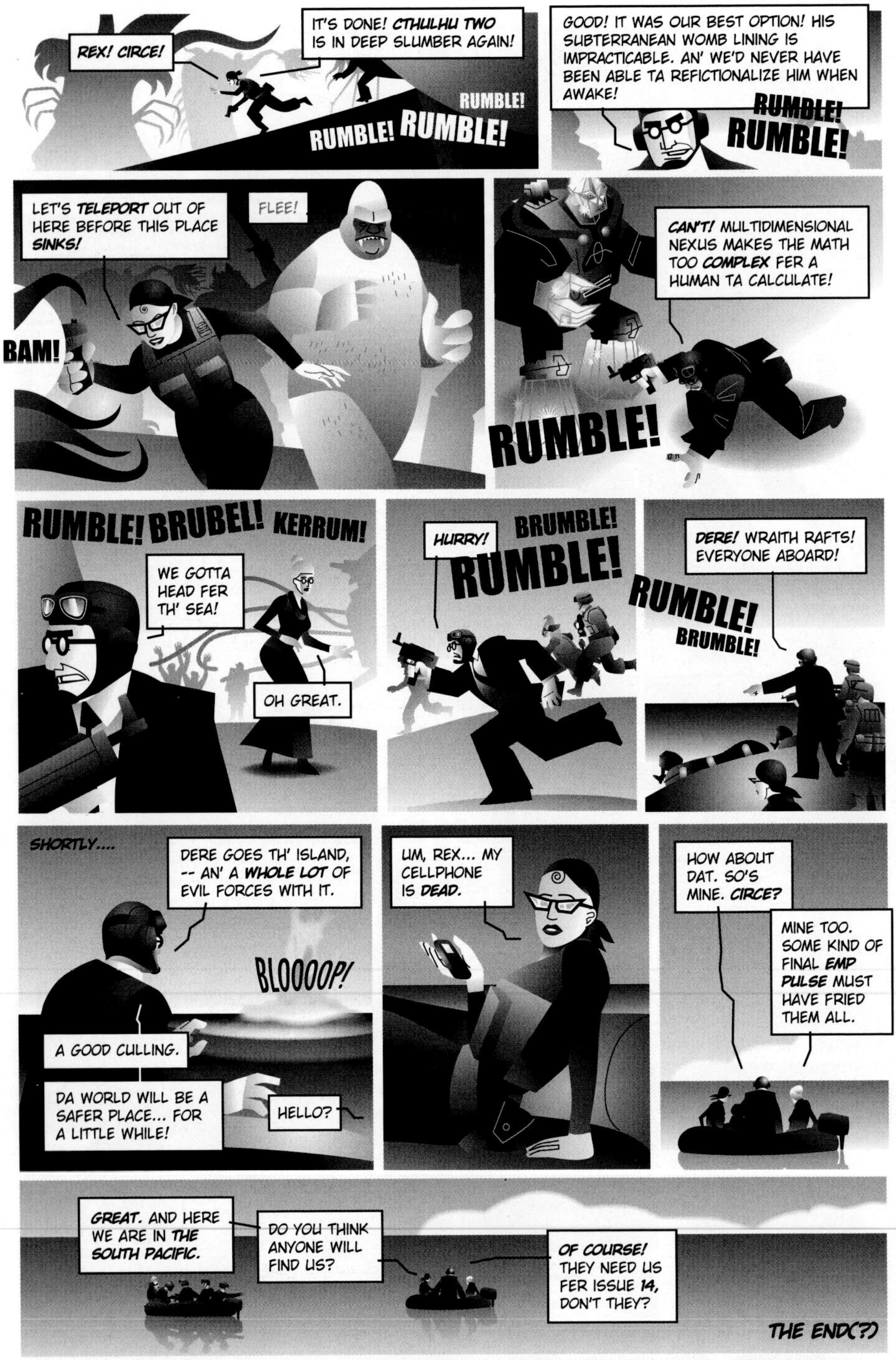
REX! CIRCE!
IT'S DONE! CTHULHU TWO IS IN DEEP SLUMBER AGAIN!
RUMBLE!
RUMBLE! RUMBLE!
GOOD! IT WAS OUR BEST OPTION! HIS SUBTERRANEAN WOMB LINING IS IMPRACTICABLE. AN' WE'D NEVER HAVE BEEN ABLE TA REFICTIONALIZE HIM WHEN AWAKE!
RUMBLE!
RUMBLE!
LET'S TELEPORT OUT OF HERE BEFORE THIS PLACE SINKS!
FLEE!
BAM!
CAN'T! MULTIDIMENSIONAL NEXUS MAKES THE MATH TOO COMPLEX FER A HUMAN TA CALCULATE!
RUMBLE!
RUMBLE! BRUBEL! KERRUM!
WE GOTTA HEAD FER TH' SEA!
OH GREAT.
HURRY!
BRUMBLE!
RUMBLE!
RUMBLE!
BRUMBLE!
DERE! WRAITH RAFTS! EVERYONE ABOARD!
SHORTLY....
DERE GOES TH' ISLAND, -- AN' A WHOLE LOT OF EVIL FORCES WITH IT.
BLOOOOP!
A GOOD CULLING.
DA WORLD WILL BE A SAFER PLACE... FOR A LITTLE WHILE!
HELLO?
UM, REX... MY CELLPHONE IS DEAD.
HOW ABOUT DAT. SO'S MINE. CIRCE?
MINE TOO. SOME KIND OF FINAL EMP PULSE MUST HAVE FRIED THEM ALL.
GREAT. AND HERE WE ARE IN THE SOUTH PACIFIC.
DO YOU THINK ANYONE WILL FIND US?
OF COURSE! THEY NEED US FER ISSUE 14, DON'T THEY?
THE END(?)

I'D LIKE TO OFFER MY SINCEREST THANKS TO ALL THE READERS WHO GAVE REX LIBRIS A WHIRL, AND ALSO TO DAN AND JENNIFER AT SLG FOR TAKING A CHANCE ON MY ECCENTRIC NONSENSE. I HOPE YOU ALL ENJOYED THE ADVENTURE AS MUCH AS I DID. MAY YOUR TRIPS TO THE LIBRARY ALWAYS BE REWARDING!

CHEERS, JAMES TURNER
MARCH 15TH, 2008

CHAPTER 3: BIOTA OF THE SOL SYSTEM

by Juan E. Strozzi

The first self-organizing chemical systems to appear in the universe were crystalline silicates. Within two billion years, carbon-based life-forms would supplant these slow and relatively inefficient organisms (and their clay relatives) throughout the galaxy. Today, few silicate biospheres still exist, and then only in niche environments too hostile for carbonites. Silicate fossils, on the other hand, are relatively common.

Most modern space biota absorb energy from protons and ions in the solar wind; billions of years ago, the high levels of ultraviolet radiation in the comet fields spurred evolution on at a much faster rate than on planets. Life abounds in our solar system. The discovery of lithified remains of space-based stromatolites in meteorites in the 1890s by Martin-Cosgrove and the recent discovery of thousands of photosynthetic plastid swarms living in the hydrogen-laden solar disc around the Sun have done much to increase the credibility of the study of space organisms, and our knowledge of these unusual and elusive lifeforms is increasing by leaps and bounds. Cyclic photosynthesis is now known to be the dominant means of energy processing in stellar flora, and it should be noted that oxygen-based photosynthesis is an entirely terrestrial-based phenomenon. Some seventy per cent of stellar void biota find oxygen both poisonous and corrosive, although the remainder are able to function in both environments, to their considerable advantage. Space biota are in general rather sluggish, due to their

Fig 3.1 Meteorite with fossilized silicate lifeform. From Utah crater, 1842.

anaerobic metabolism, but when able to function in atmosphere, their capabilities and activity levels increase greatly. Such versatile extraterrestrial species pose a grave threat to the future of humanity, as man's capabilities are considerably more limited. For the most part these potentially hostile aliens are kept away from the Earth by the large numbers of energy liches that live in the magnetosphere. High intensity conflict among the advanced spacefaring extelligences has also been of benefit, and kept the number of functional alien communities in the solar system to a minimum. Save for some extreme and notable exceptions, humanity has advanced relatively unhindered.

Fig 3.2 Space based organisms from the Sol system (Clockwise from left): stromatolite, starplankton, solarbacteria, comet nematode, asteroid flitter, cosmic prion, Kuiperarchaean, asteroid algae, spacefungus, protoplankton, deep space metaprokaryote colony.

This Pelarological study has been assembled from a wide array of sources, both direct and indirect. Written records have been supplemented by psychic castings by sensitives tuned in to the background microwave radiation of the universe. The subconscious thought patterns of the Nebkudrazar entity itself were surfed and recorded, until, that is, the psychics' heads exploded. Several dozen other researchers went insane in the process of accumulating this text. Their dedication is an example to all academia.

3.1 THE ARCHAEANS: GODS OF THE HADEAN ERA

Banderson theory posits that they were originally a form of sluggish, comet-based coelentrate that metabolized by anaerobic fermentation, but this is all speculation. The Archaean extelligence harnessed the power of hox trigger genes more than three billion years ago, enabling individuals to consciously stimulate their genetic code. This liberated the species from having a single physical form, allowing them to adapt to new environments at will. Haskett-Banderson believe this phylomorphic process could be accomplished over a period of several days, accompanied by a great ingestion of food. Archaeans were capable of interpreting and adapting genes by eating them and were said to use this ability to infiltrate alien societies. Banderson speculates that lycanthropes such as the beast of Gevaudon were in actuality Archaeans, but this is considered highly unlikely by respected pelarologists. Separating myth from fact when it

Fig 3.3 Beast of Gevaudon devouring hapless villager

comes to this intensely feared and vilified cryptid is all but impossible. Some claim that they stimulated the growth and development of life throughout the universe with the intent of harvesting the genetic code for their own use.

Unfortunately, everything we know of the Archaeans has been assembled from second- or third-hand accounts, all of which display a degree of bias. To this date, no direct evidence of the existence of Archaeans has been found, and there are those who regard them as being entirely mythical. Archaean society was, supposedly, intensely hierarchial in nature. The species cooperated in order to compete more effectively, and over the aeons formed into two diametrically opposed factions. Banderson claims they reached the level of a class III civilization, capable of harnessing the power of an entire galaxy, before wiping themselves out over two and a half billion years ago. The survivors were hunted down and extirpated by jealous younger species in a series of artificially induced supernovas that sterilized large sections of numerous galaxies.

The extent of Archaean colonization is unknown. During their height, the universe was substantially smaller and intergalactic distances more easily breached. Banderson believes the Archaeans in some form may still exist in other galaxies. Spoken of with reverence today by species of almost godlike power, Archaeans are not to be underestimated, and arguing with them, should one be encountered, is not recommended.

3.2 DENIZENS OF THE OORT CLOUD

The Oort Cloud extends from the orbit of Pluto out to 100,000 astronomical units from the sun. It is rich in hydrogen, ice, and carbon and is teeming with exotic forms of life. The low temperatures (below 20 K) mean that life here is lived out at a leisurely, contemplative pace. Among the grazing filter-feeders can be found numerous species of highly intelligent anerobic cephalopods and coelentrates, most of which nest in the asteroids. They move in towards the Sun to mate and spawn. Space jellies like the Grooplooks seed their spores in the methane thick upper atmosphere of Uranus, while the grazing Bondlefronds prefer to lay their egg clutches in the ice slush of Europa.

Many of these species, particularly the larger space jellies, possess great mental powers. Initially these abilities were developed to facilitate communication over long distances in the cold, black

Fig 3.4 A Grooplook scout uses mentalism to freeze two foolish human worshippers who have stumbled upon its terrestrial base in North Africa.

void of space. Today their memetic manipulation of the universe is not limited to mere telepathy; there are recorded instances of Grooplook invaders using both teleporation and telekinesis.

The Kroppen Space Puffer

An odd mixture of bilateral and radial symmetry, the Kroppen grows up to twenty feet long from stinger-lined ostium to ventral suckerpods. Highly intelligent, Kroppen divide their time between terrestrial and extraterrestrial environments. They are omnivorous and alters their diet according to environment. In space, they live on solarplankton, while in an aquatic environment they are piscivorous. Their metabolic rate is much lower when they are outside of a planetary environment, and they aestivate for years at a time when travelling between solar systems. Kroppen use an anti-graviton generating organelle that allows them to enter and leave gravity wells without mechanical assistance. While they do not have any obvious sensory organs, all evidence indicates that they are highly aware of their surroundings. Some pelarologists suspect that their scales are tipped with electrosensory receptors.

Their large, ovoid body can tumefy, causing the posion spikes that cover it to rise into defensive position. Two solar wind sails augment the propulsive fins when in liquid; directly below each solar sail are a pair of prehensile tentacles.

The ventral, graviportal suckerpods are capable of bearing a Kroppen's weight vertically through the use of a hydrostatic skeletal system. By flapping their solar sails, and fore and rear stabilizer fins to maintain balance, Kroppen can manage a slow gait in terrestrial environments. In water they can swim quickly and withstand enormous pressures, but their lack of a large anal fin results in yawing and rolling when maneuvering.

The purplescent, telescoping mouth is surrounded by stingers containing nematocysts. Their powerful tentacles are capable of snatching up space-born biota, and their throat is lined with macrocilia which tear the prey into digestible chunks. Kroppen lay polyps on the sea floor, which in turn produce Kroppenpuffs. During mating season, photophores on the surface of their bulbous torso light up, and they flash elaborate patterns at each other in the asteroid belts.

They communicate using directed electromagnetic bursts from the central spinal rod and are widely believed to have powerful telepathic abilities.

Kroppen arrived in our solar system at the start of the Phanerozoic period, some 570 million years ago, a time of intense competition between dozens of other newly arrived space-born species for food and resources. This instense struggle led to five solar system wide mass extinctions.

Today the few surviving Kroppen clutches live primarily in the Oort Cloud. They dislike travelling close to the

Fig 3.5 An adult Kroppen

Sun and only visit the Earth at the South Pole. During the Proterozoic ice age they are said to have operated several of their distinctive, pyramidal bases as far as 25 degrees North of the pole. Kroppen live around type M-dwarf stars and build their cities in the condrite rock of asteroids at a range of approximately 1 AU. Like Susslook, they use hydrocarbons to pass nutrients to cells instead of water. Like most space biota, they generally do not acknowledged human attempts at communication, unless accompanied by memetic rituals, sacrific, and a good spot of grovelling.

Plasmaphagous Star Worms (The Floot)

Fig 3.5 A plasmaphagous space worm trying to untangle its tentacles

Often improperly referred to as space slugs, these malevolent, hideous creatures are highly aggressive and tend to gravitate towards extreme memes. They have two long tentacles which extend forward from their semi-amorphous body and end in sharp claws. The tentacles have a tendency to become tangled; to untangle them required the development of intelligence in the creature, resulting in the addition of several more brains (It currently has 58). As it became more intelligent, the tentacles became more and more prone to becoming intricately entangled, which, in turn, required further brain additions and development. Thus sentience was reached ahead of most other species; this has led the Floot to view the universe as their buffet, and they are unwilling to share the table with latecomers.

These segmented worms have a pair of wings for flying, which double as solar sails for moving between planetary bodies. They absorb food through the membrane of their gelatinous torso. When attacking, they wrap their tentacles around their prey and squeeze while their torso excretes digestive enzymes.

Four sensor pods on stalks extend from the top of their bulbous head. When threatened, the star worm emits a noxious, acidic odour that causes itching and sneezing. Contact with salt causes them to combust, so it is always wise to carry sodium if Floot are in the area. Aeons ago Floot science-priests discovered the secrets of phase space, which enabled their brethren to pass through physical matter at will. Note that they must alter the vibration of their molecular structure to do so, which takes several minutes. In this transitional state, Floot are immobile and highly vulnerable to salt.

Fig 3.6 A Jovian Balloob, archenemy of the Floot.

Floot are unpleasant and constantly at war with all other sentient lifeforms. Some speculate they were behind the destruction of the archosaur genetic experiment. Their latest act of aggression was to propel a comet, known to us as Shoemaker-Levy, into Jupiter, at the capital cloudcluster nest of the Jovian Balloobs. The larger fragments impacted with the force of over 100 trillion tons of TNT, and the mushroom clouds were visible from Earth. Floot communes worship Iagu, the black hole at the centre of the Milky Way galaxy, and Flootean communes spend much of their time listening to his microwave emissions. They hate the Kanamit, Vril, and Phthireans, as they compete for the same bioresources.

3.3 THE SPACE MOLLUSCS

There are several hundred species of space molluscs in the Sol system. Of these, the most notable are the Susslook, the Sl'uklu'uhk, the G'sok (the exotic Neptonian ammonia ammonites); and the great Megalocephalopods, the Ooslooloo.

Fig 3.7 In 1872 a hideous Kameraceras orthocone invader crashed into the sea off of Denmark. As it emerged from the ocean it was mistakenly attacked by a boat of whalers. They soon regretted this decision. One man, Gunther Krier, survived the incident.

All these species all preternaturally intelligent (the Sl'uklu'uhk have a cephalization quotient of 15), and exude a quantum memetic field from their large brains. In space, where thought flows without resistance, they form a kind of

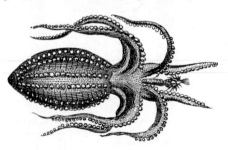

Fig 3.8 The giant Sl'uklu'uhk can weigh up to thirty tons and grow over 20 metres long

communal brain when in close proximity to each other. On Earth, the effect of this is known to cause confusion and headaches in nearby mammals. Gravol easily negates the effect. The telepathic abilities, and the QMF (quantum memetic field) of the Ooslooloo and Sl'uklu'uhk are particularly powerful. The space molluscs are genereally aloof and indifferent towards other phylum; only the Sl'uklu'uhk are demonstrably malevolent in both purpose and policy. All space molluscs are fond of liquid water environments (and the higher metabolic rate they can achieve when in it); psychics have claimed that the nearest analogous human emotion that the molluscs associate with oxygen is euphoria. This has led to repeated efforts to colonize the earth; mollusc domination of this planet, however, would tip the delicate balance of power between the surviving ancient extelligent societies in the solar system, so rival phylum work to oppose any mollusc return. The Susslook cities on the ocean floor of the Pacific, which have been abandoned since the Mesozoic Era, extend over an area of several thousand square kilometres. An extensive underground cavern system is said to run between their former civic centres, and during the Cold War these were repaired by the Soviets and used by their nuclear submarines. The most significant mollusc invasion efforts during the Holocene Epoch have occurred relatively recently: the Mesopotamian Bridgehead circa 1100 BC (which ran afoul of a pre-existing, and populated, subterranean Subdergid refuge in the Sinai), and the Great Magnetosphere Fiasco of 1967, in which the Sl'uklu'uhk invasion swarm was destroyed by magnetosphere leeches under the guidance of an unknown public librarian.

Susslook

The Susslookeans are an unusual species that exhibit characteristics of both crustaceans and cephalopod orthocones, and yet are distantly related to the unipadae phylum. Some believe they are the product of genetic engineering or that they appropriated the genes from other phylum to improve themselves. Known to have conducted genetic experiments in phase space, and they breed many forms of large cephalopods, such as the hundred-armed, hundred-eyed Huecasquid and the terrestrial-bound Kraken monstrosity.

Two powerful grasping chelicerae and two prehensile tentacles lined with manipulative feelers flank the beak-like mouth which projects out from the bottom of their conical shell. A Susslook's bite injects concentrated cyclic diketones. The thick shell is tougher than twaron armour and protects all of the Susslooks vital organs, and their arms and tentacles can be withdrawn inside it when threatened.

Susslook communicate by emitting amplitude modulated radio waves and have an organelle along their notochord which is dense with iron. It is used to orient the creature in magnetic fields. The top interior of the shell contains an anti-graviton-generating organelle, which allows them to operate independent of the effects of gravity. The chlorophyll-lined solar fan can be extended from their abdomen when in space, allowing Susslook to achieve great speeds. Two short hyponome jet tubes, one on either side of the mouth are used as propulsion in

Fig 4.0 A Susslook with claws and tentacles deployed, but solar fin retracted

both space and atmosphere. During interstellar trips they store energy in phosphate bonds, and like the Kroppen they aestivate when travelling between solar systems, during which time their migration swarms are often preyed upon by Beroid Clouds and Deep Space Ipsidic Filaments. Susslook enjoy good relations with the benevolent, filter-feeding space

Fig 4.1 Saturnian Gilyuk, coelenterate floaters, shown here finishing construction of a pyramidal stone cocoon around their moulting orthocone leader Nooglok in Ancient Egypt. Their ascension cocoons were incorporated into Egyptian architecture.

Grakalaks that swim between solar systems, singing ancient star songs and devouring interstellarblastula.

Exiled from the Chronosynclastic Infundibulum millions of years ago, Susslook spread throughout the galaxy, living in the comet and debris fields that surround solar systems. Later they invaded terrestrial environments, and today lay their jellied eggs in oxyhydride slush in the freezing seas of Enceladus and Europa rather than upon comets. Some of the more adventuresome lay their eggs in the Antarctic. They have built large protective stone pyramids over their ancestral hatcheries, and are known to inhabit enormous underwater colonies for extended periods of time. There are several Susslook cities on Europa, but none on earth that are currently inhabited. Susslook are known to have hostile relations

relations with the aquatic Xixuloobs, and also war with the globular Kroppenpuffs. They are friendly with the slug like Ukk and the Necroborg.

An especially unusual feature of Susslookean biology, and possibly the result of genetic engineering at the quantum level, is that they are able to excrete quantum foam from glands along the base of their beak; this microscopic foam is subsequently carried across the surface of their body by bacteria, giving the Susslook an iridescent sheen; it takes approximately an hour for the foam to completely cover the surface, but once it has, they are capable of teleporting between distant points.

As self-appointed guardians of Nebkudrazar, the parent infinite singularity, they view followers of Iagu as heretics who must be annihilated for the good of the universal body. Every hundred years Susslook enter a dream state in which their bodies are given over to the background radiation of the universe, which is believed to be the realm of Nebkudrazar's thoughts.

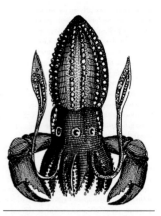

Fig 3.7 An Ooslooloo megalocephalopod monstrosity: a ferocious deep space predator

3.4 THE CRUSTACEAN EXILES OF VENUS

While many terrestrial extelligences have built extensive underground facilities for protection, only certain space-faring crustaceans, insectoids, boring molluscs, and segmented worms prefer subterranean lairs on Earth. Of these, the Subdergids and their less common cousins, the Cephalocrabs, are the most significant. The affinity of all of these space-based species for underground living is no doubt due to the similairity of subterranean caves to asteroid nests. Organs and instruments adapted for boring asteroid rock can be easily adapted to terrestrial environments, and the visual continuity maintained by the transposition of designs is no doubt helpful in creating a sense of security. Certain areas of Mesopotamia, Central America, and Asia are riddled with ancient tunnel systems, many constructed eons ago (primarily in the Ordovician, Devonian, and Jurassic). Many of these are partially collapsed, but others are intact and can be reached and explored even today. Such exploratory missions can be exceedingly dangerous for novices and are not recommended for the faint of heart. Even more extensive ruins are to be found on Venus and Mars.

Fig 3.7 Adult Subdergid male. Note the enlarged brain casing. Subdergids have a CQ of 28

Subdergid

A species of fossorial arthropod, these burrowing insectoids exhibit an extremely high degree of cephalization. They arrived in the solar system before the Kroppenpuffs, and originally colonized Venus. Unfortunately, their intense industrialization heated the planet. As water evaporated, it was broken up in the atmosphere by ultraviolet radiation and lost to space. Once the surface temperature hit 340 Kelvin, the greenhouse effect became an unstoppable positive feedback loop and the planet had to be abandoned. Escape by space at the time was impossible due to the presence of hostile Susslooks, Zorgids, Blugogic Slimewhorls and Kroppenpuff comet colonies.

The Subdergids understand M-theory and the survivors used it to escape into interstitial space and quantum dimensions, where they live today. Occasionally small underground lairs can be found on Earth, although why they are there, and what their purpose might be, is unknown. As only a small population survived the Venusian catastrophy, they have little genetic diversity and live in great fear

of disease.

They are ametabolous, and their chitin exterior is extremely tough and the only vulnerable location on their body is their large central eye. Four nasal pits and short barbels flank their small mouth. Preternaturally strong, their four digging claws can cut through solid rock.

They hate and fear amphisbaenians and react negatively to all forms of music, although it is not understood why this should be so. Subdergids built

Fig 3.7 Mandelugs excrete a rock dissolving enzyme that makes them useful servants for the Subdergids

unspeakably massive basalt stone cities on Venus, and many of what we believe to be natural formations, such as the Ovda Regio and Maxwell Montes, are actually early, cyclopean Subdergid temple complexes, formed out of the excavated earth from the mining tunnels that honeycomb the planet. An unidentified species of silicate lifeforms now lives amidst the crumbling Subdergid ruins, shrouded and protected from prying eyes by the boiling atmospheric soup that envelopes the planet.

Relations between Subdergids and other asteroid field and Kuiper belt crustaceans are generally congenial, and the species is known to provide assistance and technology to their less developed brethren. This is done as quietly and surreptitiously as possible, so as not to arouse the ire of their blood enemies and bring about another campaign of extermination against their now

Fig 3.7 *Cephalocrabs also exhibit an excessive degree of cephalization, and have adapted a chitin armour brain casing that moults, allowing their brain to gradually expand*

rare species. It is unknown whether there are other interstellar colonies of Subdergids. Records recovered from the Subdergid ruins in Egypt were vandalized by the French during Napoleon's expedition in 1795, and the few undamaged ones have yet to be deciphered.

Banaxeans

Also known as banana beasts, this volant animal evolved in tandem with the banana tree (which is not, in fact, indigineous to earth at all, but a plant from the Crab Nebula) and preyed on the albino Zargonomes of that star cluster for thousands of years. Relatives of the globular Kroppen, they have armoured torsos and bat-like solar sails that can be used in atmosphere as wings. The mouth is surrounded by velar tentacles, each laden with thousands of nematocysts.

The susurration of the Banaxean filigree feelers is unnerving to the human ear and causes most who hear it to flee in unreasoning terror. Natural hunters, Banaxean ancestors hid in banana trees and dangled their pseudo-banana laden tail for unsuspecting fauna. When prey moved to take the bait, the Banaxean stung it with the 'flower tip' stinger, snatched it up in its four thoracic claws, and flew away to its nest, where it devoured the immobilized prey at leisure. Today, the banana lure is largely vestigal. Instead, these hunters use highly

Fig 3.7 *Banaxean with banana lure deployed. Contrary to popular belief, Banaxeans do not eat bananas*

advanced atomic powered weaponry to bring down prey at great distances. Nevertheless, they enjoy nothing more than laying in ambush for their enemies while perched in a banana tree. Even now they can sometimes be found hiding in fields of banana trees; it is said that this is where they are most at ease (Always think twice about picking from a buzzing banana tree).

The Banaxeans, also known as the Bwof'ook'clugbug in ancient Sumerian texts, had developed a type II civilization by the early Mesozoic Era, but as they are frequently being bombed back to lower states of sophistication, no one really knows what state they are in today.

Fig 3.7 *Massive asteroid crabs, under Subdergid control, attack the temple of Karnak during the Mesopotamian Incursion*

3.5 *CREATURES OF THE THERMAL VENTS*

Found most frequently on aquatic planets with a frozen surface of ice several kilometres thick, sulfothermophiles do not depend on the sun for energy, unlike almost all other forms of life. Instead, they depend upon heat from the molten core of the planet they dwell upon. There are several different species in the solar system, but the most dominant of these are the hideous Xixuloob.

Xixuloob

It is suspected that these inscrutable sulfothermophiles live in large numbers in cities around volcanic vents on Europa. Xixuloob tend to build their cyclopean, labyrinthine cities in areas of high tectonic activity; unfortunately, this tendency means that all their ancient cities on earth have long since been subducted, so little evidence of their presence remains today. Most were driven from the planet hundreds of millions of years ago, around the same time that the atmosphere of Mars was dissipated by unknown forces.

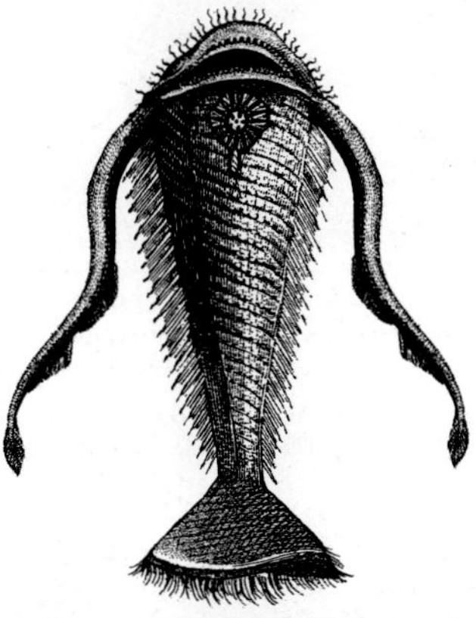

Fig 3.7 An obscene Xixuloob, as oriented when on land, stands some eleven feet tall

Chemisynthesitic poikilotherms, these cylindrical creatures have flexible hydrostatic skeletons and are up to eleven feet long. In water they propel themselves like a jet, expelling water out their caudal cone. They have a polyphyodont lined megachasma fringed by oral papillae, and a prehensile glossus almost six feet long, dotted with barbs and sucker pods coated with adhesive ooze. Like all unipedae, the Xixuloob are capable of regeneration: cells around wounds revert to blastema, and reactivate embryogenesitic programming, allowing lost limbs to be regrown. Their thick skin is covered with small, hollow silicon fibres containing toxins, which break off when rubbed against, embedding themselves in flesh and causing excruciating pain. They are omnivorous, and will eat everything from 'marine snow' to plankton and amphipods.

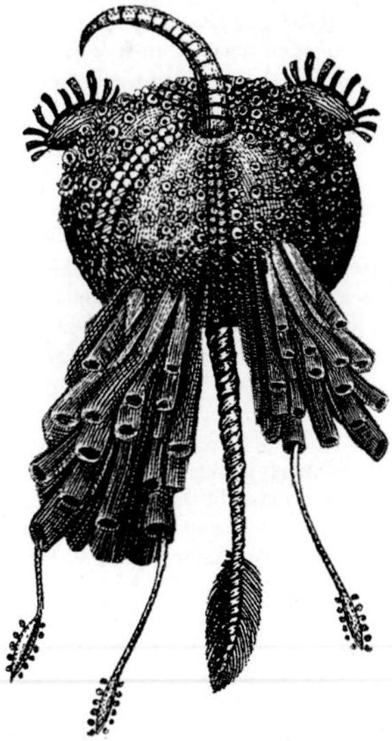

Fig 3.7 The asteroid eating Urcho is one of the few species the Xixuloob will deal with

Two prehensile tentacles, tipped with manipulative stingers that secrete a potent neurotoxin, flank the megachasma. Ansible spines run along their flanges, and vibrate in harmony with the prime frequency of the universe, which allows faster than light communication between Xixuloobs. When active, a nimbus of amethystine light forms around the spines, giving them a spectral appearance. Their large, bioluminescent holochroal eye can see beyond the visible spectrum of light, and emits biophotons when in complete darkness. This beam of light can penetrate even the murky dark of the deepest ocean trenches. The caudal cone doubles as a pseudopod for walking, although they can only manage slow speeds on land.

Their stone structures are tightly packed and cramped, as Xixuloobs crave body contact; they congregate in groups for warmth and protection, and prefer to stay near deep sea vents. Unlike most deep sea biota, they are capable of surviving at sea level without exploding. They do, however, burst spectacularly in vaccuum.

The only known alien species to suffer from catolepsy, they have banned humour, and are highly vulnerable to it.

They travel the galaxy in water-filled ships made of impregnable transuranic metals and armed with weapons of inconceivable power. Xixuloob civilization is between type I and type II in terms of its capabilities. They believe in orthogenesis, and as such resent younger species, such as the Yogah of Yag. Xix have mild telekinetic manipulative powers.

Stromoblobs (aka Immanissimum ac foedissimum monstrum)

These jet black, amorphous aquatic horrors are believed to be massive polyp colonies that consist of dozens of specialized organs interspersed between pseudopods and muscle polyps. They interchange position as necessary, and roll, slide, and pull themselves along the bottom of the ocean, swallowing up food with their specialized polyp mouths, after their stinger polyps have subdued it with massive doses of neurotoxin. Colonies can grow to be up to a football field across, and no one

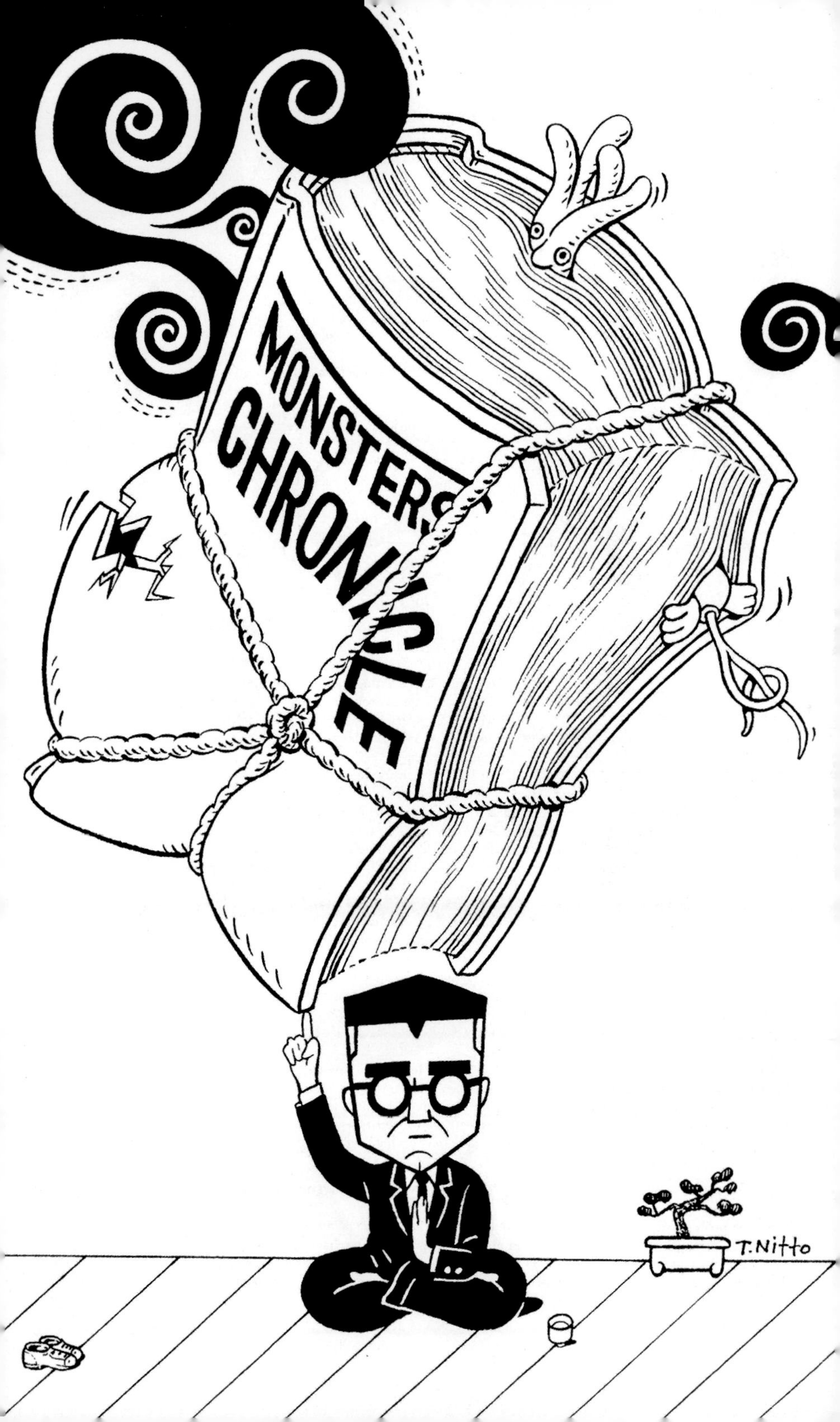
MONSTERS' CHRONICLE
T.Nitto

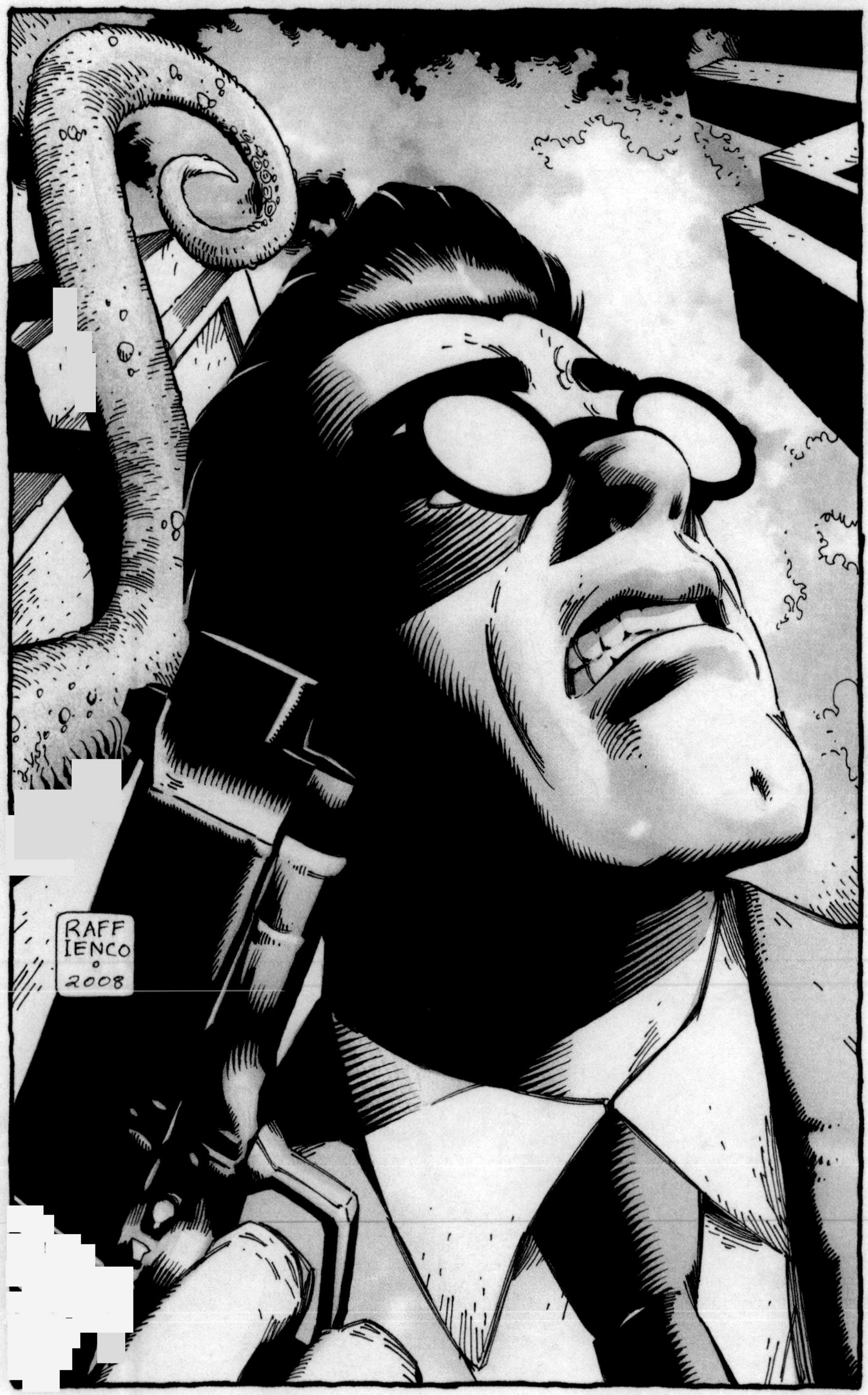
RAFF IENCO 2008

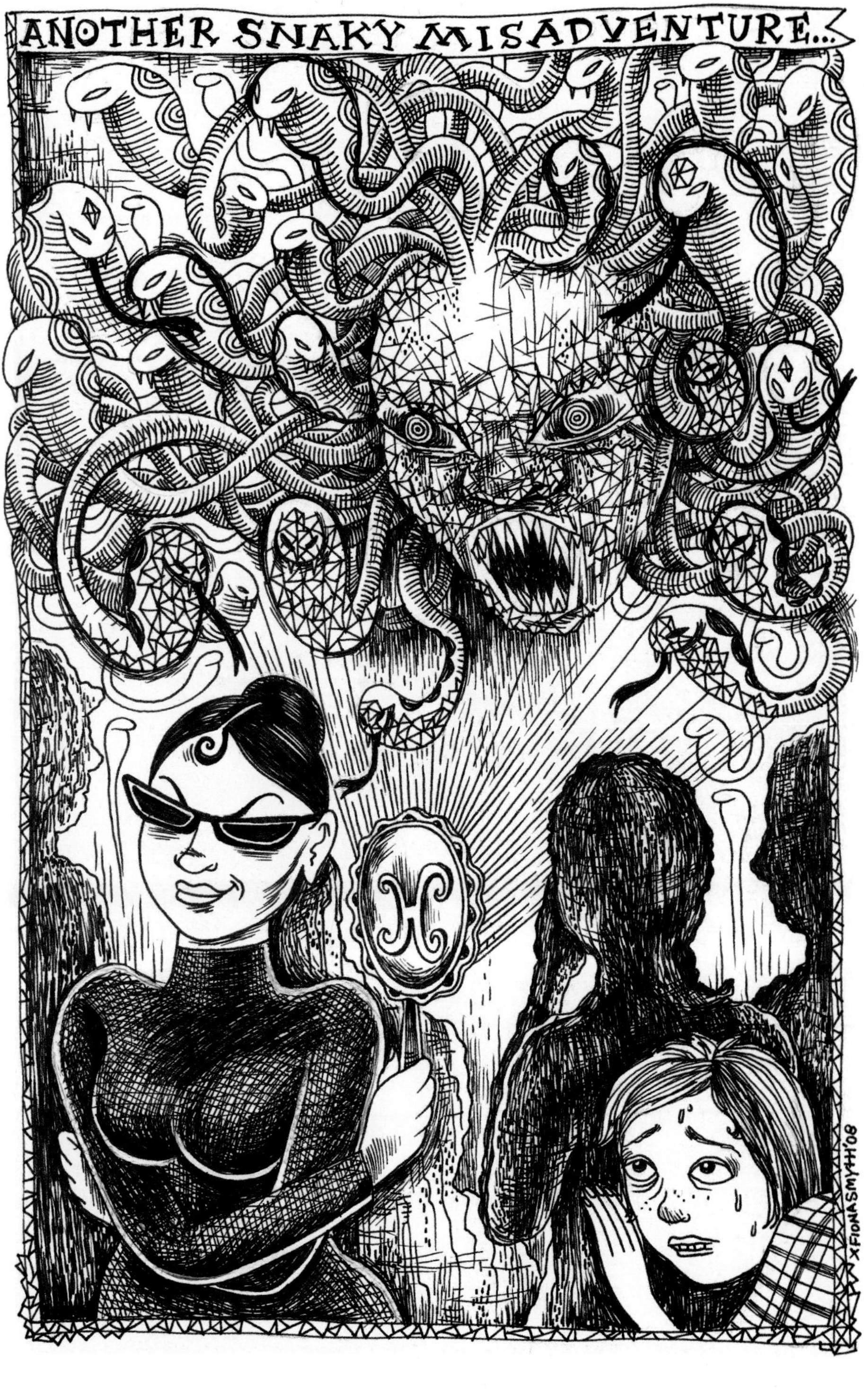
ANOTHER SNAKY MISADVENTURE...
X.FIONASMYTH'08

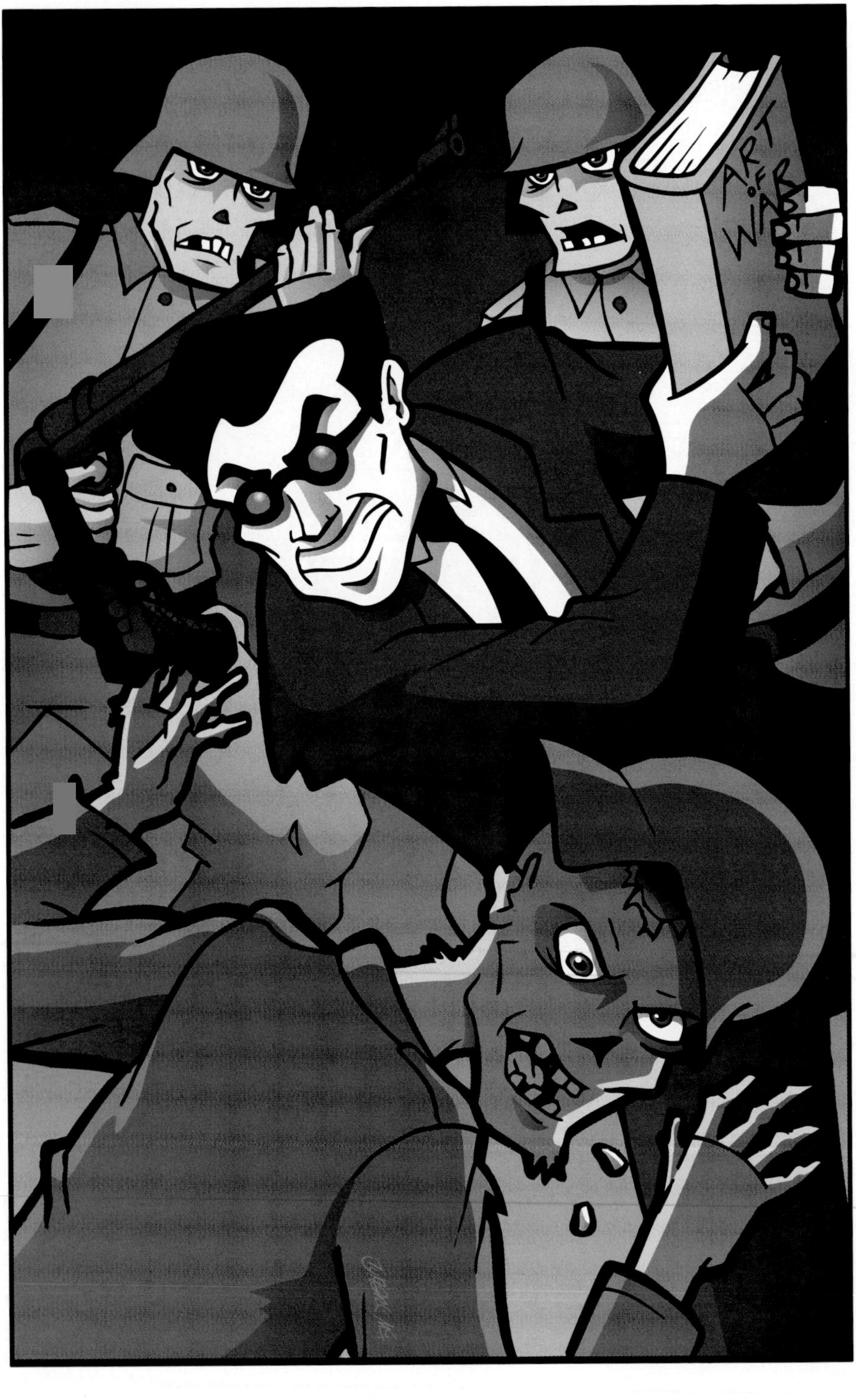
ART OF WAR

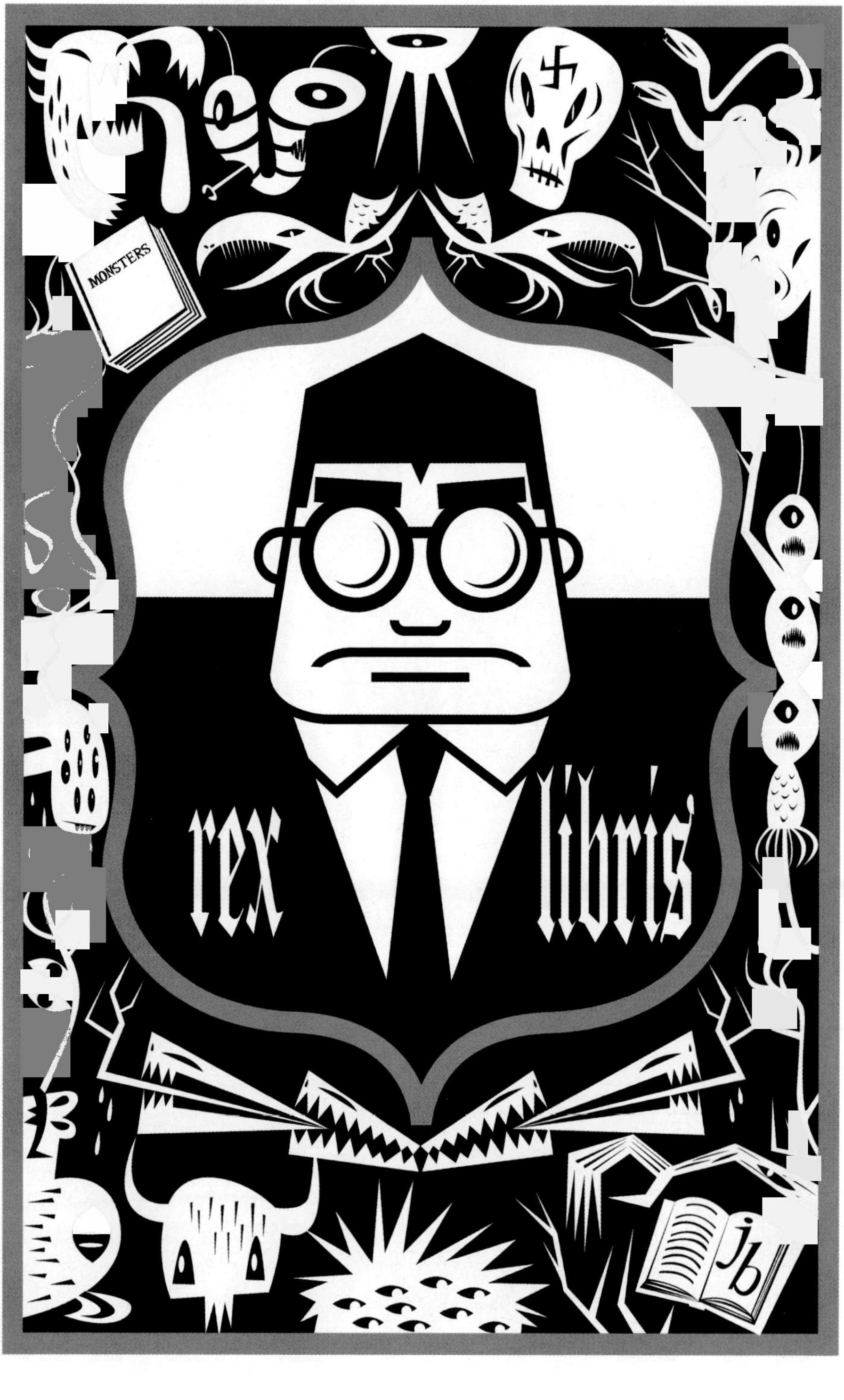
MONSTERS
rex
libris
jb

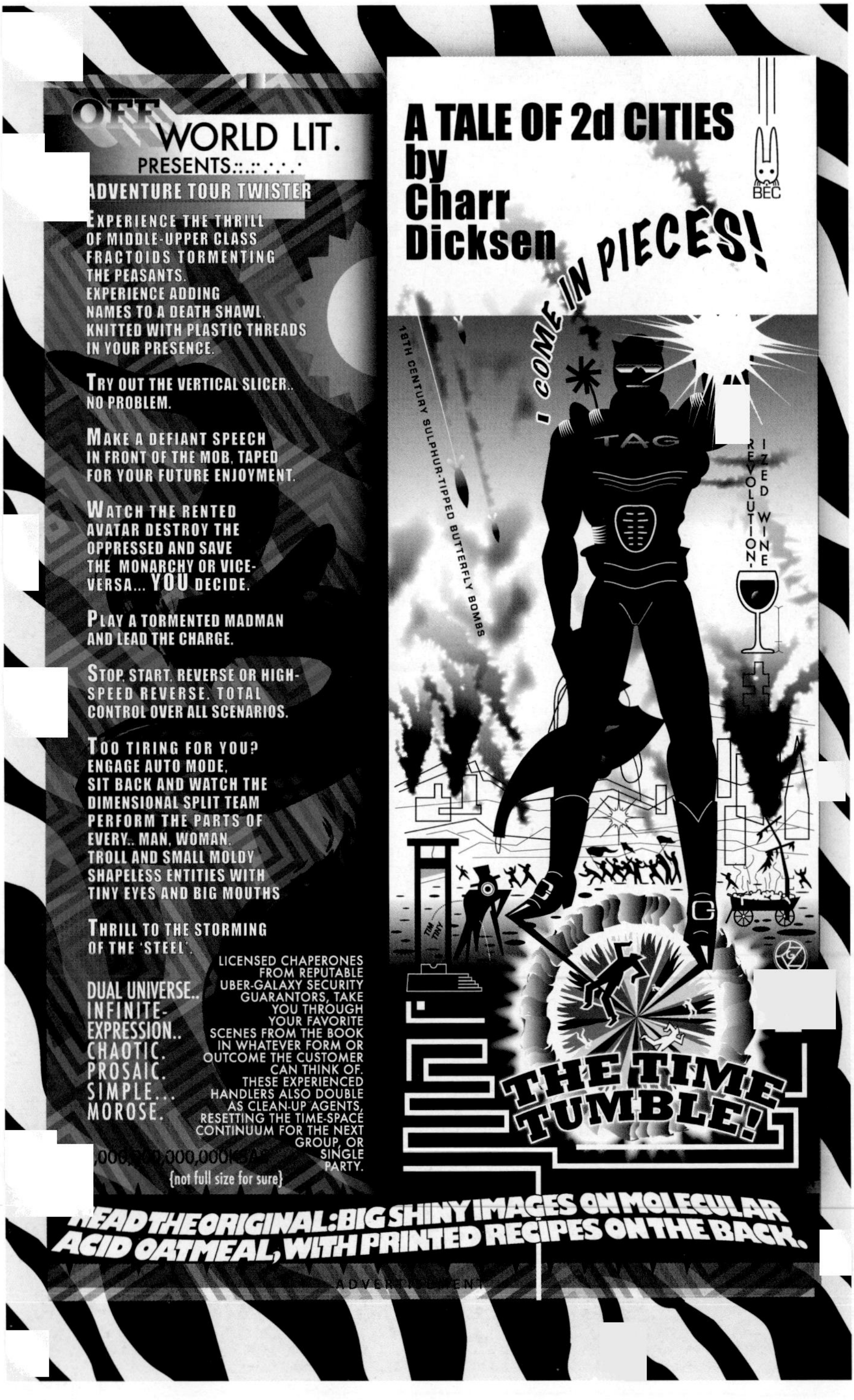
OFF WORLD LIT.
PRESENTS
ADVENTURE TOUR TWISTER
EXPERIENCE THE THRILL OF MIDDLE-UPPER CLASS FRACTOIDS TORMENTING THE PEASANTS.
EXPERIENCE ADDING NAMES TO A DEATH SHAWL, KNITTED WITH PLASTIC THREADS IN YOUR PRESENCE.
TRY OUT THE VERTICAL SLICER.. NO PROBLEM.
MAKE A DEFIANT SPEECH IN FRONT OF THE MOB, TAPED FOR YOUR FUTURE ENJOYMENT.
WATCH THE RENTED AVATAR DESTROY THE OPPRESSED AND SAVE THE MONARCHY OR VICE-VERSA... YOU DECIDE.
PLAY A TORMENTED MADMAN AND LEAD THE CHARGE.
STOP, START, REVERSE OR HIGH-SPEED REVERSE. TOTAL CONTROL OVER ALL SCENARIOS.
TOO TIRING FOR YOU? ENGAGE AUTO MODE, SIT BACK AND WATCH THE DIMENSIONAL SPLIT TEAM PERFORM THE PARTS OF EVERY.. MAN, WOMAN, TROLL AND SMALL MOLDY SHAPELESS ENTITIES WITH TINY EYES AND BIG MOUTHS
THRILL TO THE STORMING OF THE 'STEEL'.
DUAL UNIVERSE.. INFINITE-EXPRESSION.. CHAOTIC. PROSAIC. SIMPLE... MOROSE.
LICENSED CHAPERONES FROM REPUTABLE UBER-GALAXY SECURITY GUARANTORS, TAKE YOU THROUGH YOUR FAVORITE SCENES FROM THE BOOK IN WHATEVER FORM OR OUTCOME THE CUSTOMER CAN THINK OF. THESE EXPERIENCED HANDLERS ALSO DOUBLE AS CLEAN-UP AGENTS, RESETTING THE TIME-SPACE CONTINUUM FOR THE NEXT GROUP, OR SINGLE PARTY.
{not full size for sure}
A TALE OF 2d CITIES by Charr Dicksen
BEC
I COME IN PIECES!
18TH CENTURY SULPHUR-TIPPED BUTTERFLY BOMBS
TAG
REVOLUTION-IZED WINE
THE TIME TUMBLE!
READ THE ORIGINAL: BIG SHINY IMAGES ON MOLECULAR ACID OATMEAL, WITH PRINTED RECIPES ON THE BACK.